An Exposition on Prayer

Igniting the Fuel to Flame Our Communication with God

Old Testament
Volume 1
{Genesis thru 2 Chronicles}

An Exposition on Prayer

Igniting the Fuel to Flame Our Communication with God

Dr. Jim Rosscup

AMG Publishers

Exposition on Prayer: Igniting the Flame to Fuel Our Communication with God
Old Testament Volume 1 (Genesis thru 2 Chronicles)

PUBLISHED BY AMG PUBLISHERS
6815 SHALLOWFORD ROAD
CHATTANOOGA, TN 37421

ISBN 13: 978-1-61715-491-1

FIRST PRINTING: FEBRUARY 2011

PRINTED IN UNITED STATES OF AMERICA
POD

It is deeply fulfilling to dedicate these writings
to my precious wife Mildred,
one of the greatest testimonies of godly living I have ever known. God called her home in April of 2008 to celestial worship in His rest and joy. This daughter of God was in all fruitfulness a shining example for our Savior's sake. She taught me to use a computer, and sweetly gave countless loving assists that selflessly set me free me for all my ministries in prayer, study, teaching, counseling, witnessing, and writing.

I also dedicate this work
to our family whom He has bonded in love—
our elder daughter Dianne with her husband Caleb, and younger daughter Carolyn with her husband Randall, as well as their sons, Zachary and Benjamin, both teenagers.

Foreword

Prayer is the simplest, most basic of all the spiritual disciplines. It is perhaps the least demanding of all Christian duties. It can be done anywhere at any time under any circumstances by any believer. Even the youngest, least experienced Christian is fully equipped to pray. In fact, prayer has often been compared to breathing. It is the first, most natural, most essential, and most beneficial exercise resulting from the new birth.

Furthermore, prayer is one of the most non-controversial of all biblical topics. Everyone agrees that prayer is vital for Christian growth and spiritual health. Every true believer senses the need to pray. That's why our first instinct in times of trouble or moments of alarm is to pray—then to seek the prayers of others.

And yet I have never met a Christian who is fully satisfied with his or her prayer life. We don't pray as often, as well, or as faithfully as we should. We stifle our own spiritual vitality and stint our own usefulness by failing to pray as we ought.

Dr. James Rosscup knows more about prayer than anyone I know. He has devoted himself for many years to an intensive study of the prayers of Scripture. These volumes are the fruit of that labor, and it is a rich treasure-trove of insight into the subject.

Dr. Rosscup carefully examines every prayer in Scripture, analyzing more than a thousand passages, providing outlines, highlighting cross-references, and clarifying contexts. He writes in a clear and lively way, and his enthusiasm for prayer is infectious.

An Exposition on Prayer is as practical and informative as it is encyclopedic. This may be the most comprehensive study of biblical prayers ever written. But don't be intimidated by the volume of material; this is an amazing tool that will deepen your understanding of what Scripture teaches about prayer while increasing your hunger for constant communion with God.

John MacArthur
Pastor of Grace Community Church
President of The Master's College and Seminary

Introducing the Legacy of Prayer

The writings before the reader are the result of countless hours in the Scriptures since around 1992. And these were outgrowths from former years of meditations in studies and special devotional times.

One ready admission is that no work by a fallible writer is without errors, oversights, omissions, or putting too light a touch on some matters. I have labored diligently to refine this effort, yet continue to find flaws, and to be humbled.

Several features have been very important in the gradual forming of the work.

Here are the main ones.

(1) I sought to include every prayer and all references to prayer in all sixty-six books of the Bible, Genesis through Revelation. Two exceptions qualify this. One is that only sixty-one of the books refer to prayer, as it does not occur in Esther, Song of Solomon, Obadiah, Haggai, and 2 John. Another is that since the Psalms are so many, 150, I deliberately chose to write expositions for only 21 key, or representative psalms. In these, an attempt is made to follow the flow of each psalm and also, where pertinent, to integrate references to prayer from psalms on which I do not devote express exposition. In this way, at least much of the flavor even of the other psalms can be incorporated

(2) The chosen format is to give an introduction to each Bible book. This offers the authorship, date, purpose, outline, theme, and a brief synopsis about prayer. After this the study takes up each successive reference to prayer, and offers both an outline of it in the flow of its own context, and an exposition of what it contributes on prayer. In this way a reader can see the true context in which, in the Bible itself, each statement about prayer fits.

(3) Since prayer is often so frequent, the user can benefit not only from the prayer itself but from a veritable exposition that surveys Scripture, at least to a substantial degree. One sees each passage's

background and attendant features firsthand. A reader can even gain insight helping to explain problems as these occur in the passages, even if the exposition must be kept fairly brief.

(4) On prophecy, a premillennial understanding of Israel's future appears most reasonable and natural to this writer. And so his expositions of passages flows in accord with this, consistently (cf. Gen. 12, Isa., Jer., Ezek., Dan., pertinent Minor Prophets, Matt. 13, 14–25, the Thessalonian Epistles, the Revelation, etc.). Time and time again one encounters wording that seems most feasibly to expect a literal fulfillment in Israel's own, ancient land, with specific details realized there, and so the writer has taken these according to their most natural, apparent intent. At the same time, those who do not share this interpretive orientation can still gather much benefit from what is said about prayer.

(5) Principles to impact the personal life appear at the end of each passage in the expository effort. One can see the maxims to inculcate and make relevant applications to his own life and to those with whom he shares God's Word.

(6) Since prayer is to be "in everything" (Phil. 4:6) and permeates every aspect of life, the exposition of passages naturally gathers in various facets of the entire spiritual life. One sees different elements of godliness coming into a harmony, being interrelated, rather than looking only at prayer in a disconnected study just by itself.

(7) Early on in the study it appeared necessary to assume certain conclusions about prayer.

a. One is that passages on men's words to God's visiting holy angels refer to talking to the One (God) who sent the angels. These instances are in essence prayer to God.

b. Passages that have no outright reference to prayer but involve acts of worship in which prayer has its rightful, vital part are understood as bearing on prayer. For example, this study takes the offerings of Leviticus 1–7 as related to prayer that attended them (cf. on the Peace Offering 7:12–13).

c. Words people spoke to Jesus, God in the flesh, receive comment as essentially talking with the Lord, that is, prayer. They were speaking to Him when He was on earth just as really as people speak to Him from earth to heaven.

d. References to angels speaking to God are understood as in essence prayer, whether spoken in the earth scene (praise, Luke 2) or in heaven (Rev. 4:8–11; 5:11–14).

e. Prayer is basically involved in passages where men in the after life speak with God (Luke 16, Lazarus; Rev. 6:9–11, saints in heaven).

f. Men sometimes pray in the secondhand sense that they inquire of God through some other person they are convinced is close to Him.

g. God hears prayer cries of the unsaved, for example the pagan sailors in Jonah 1 and the Ninevites of Jonah 3. He allowed the pagan Abimelech to speak with Him in a dream (Gen. 20:3–7).

h. God also spoke at times to believers in their dreams, for He is able to cause communication to be real even in that venue (Gen. 31:11; 46:2; 1 Kgs. 3:4–14).

(8) The work develops in its various passages the recurring parts/aspects that can comprise prayer. For example it looks at the main aspects in which prayer appears—praise/thanks, confession, petition, intercession, affirmation, oath, vow, blessing, availability ("Here I am"), question. It also points out the attitudes or keys to effective prayer which ought to be permeating realities invested in the aspects, such as faith, listening, watching, meditating on God's Word, and the result in being saturated, shaped, and led by that Word. Countless other attitudes also appear: love, joy, peace, longsuffering, gentleness, goodness, faithfulness, meekness, self-control (cf. Gal. 5:22–23), humility, unity, and so forth.

It is understood that petitions can be for personal concerns and even for benefits to bless others. More particularly for the latter, however, it seems good to use the specific, distinctive word intercession.

An assumption is that intercession can come in various ways of phrasing concerns, that is, "do this for this person," "may grace be with you," "bless these," "may the Lord make His face shine on you," and others.

(9) The words "praise" and "thanksgiving" are shown by various definitive biblical factors, as in the Psalms, to be virtually interchangeable expressions. We praise God for who He is in His majestic and glorious Person, and also praise Him for what He does that is a consistent extension and expression of this. We thank God for who He is and also for His acts which are beautiful gestures flowing out of what He dependably is. Psalms often use both "praise" and "thanks" interchangeably for the same things in their contexts. By praise/thanks, this study refers to such expressions to God as exalting Him, admiring, extolling, magnifying, glorifying, appreciating, paying tribute to Him, giving Him plaudits or accolades, lifting up His name on high, and so on.

(10) What God does in answer to prayer in one case does not bind Him to do the same in some other instance. He has liberty to answer in the way His wisdom and will incline Him. He has unerring perception and sees all the factors in any case, whereas we do not. He may give good health to one person, and entrust another such as Job with a great trial of ill health to accomplish some good purpose. He may work safety to keep one person alive, but take another into the life after death (cf. John the Baptist, Matt. 14; James taken in death yet Peter spared, Acts 12). He may permit a special trial as he did for Paul with his "thorn" to teach: "My grace is sufficient for you" (2 Cor. 12:7–9), or allow another believer an easier life. He may heal one, or allow another such as Timothy to have a stomach ailment (1 Tim. 5:23).

(11) In relation to feature 10 above, to say to God in true sincerity, "Your will be done," may be a weak acceptance of things that need not be, an evasion of faith. Or it may be said in no sense of hedging, hindering, or sidestepping great things He is able to do, or it can be voiced in sensitively honoring Him as all-wise and responsibly in control. It can be saying "You know better than I do; You make no mistakes; You have the right of way to give what Your sovereignty and grace deem best in my case; should it be different from the fixation I have on what should be done, I trust You, for You can do anything (cf. Jer. 32:17, 27), and I rest in Your faithfulness that

works for me. So, screen what I ask, and give what You see as the most wise, in the final analysis. Nevertheless, here is what I ask, as I have complete confidence in You."

Here, then, from God's Word and my heart to yours are blessed legacies of prayer. Savor what blesses. Forgive what in the length of such a product has come up short. May the Lord be pleased to help each of us go forward in prayer to Him and in all the godliness of which prayer is a permeating part.

"In everything by prayer" (Phil. 4:6)
James E. Rosscup

Prayer in Genesis

Introduction

The Relevance of Prayer

Genesis is a book of creation, flood, Tower of Babel, a multiplying human race, covenant, faith, crises for individual and family life, and sovereign deliverance. It also is provocative in its prayers and even has episodes that do not mention prayer but are the kinds of cases where prayer could be very fitting. This is true in a great variety of situations.

Prayer is obviously before us often and is otherwise relevant for a plethora of reasons in this first of the Bible's sixty-six books. Other parts of the Bible speak of prayer in the kinds of venues Genesis brings into view and show how it is relevant, even when a writer does not refer to it. But other vital subjects also may or may not always be brought into an account, even where they were vital to people or can be to those later who read the biblical record.

Specific prayer passages soon will be taken up in sequence. Where verses are silent about prayer, it often is in situations where the Bible eventually shows prayer is very appropriate. Examples occur quite naturally as one reads Genesis. Consider instances even in a list very far from exhaustive.

The almighty God is able to do anything that is true to His purposes. He can create heaven and earth, a matter often cogent in praise, as in the Psalms and the Book of Revelation. If He can do the miracle that the very first verse, Genesis 1:1, reviews, He can do other miracles in the rest of Scripture, or in any case where this pleases Him. His ability is a challenge for faith that comes to Him in prayer expecting great answers (cf. Jer. 32:17; Eph. 3:20).

Prayer can be suitable to One whose power could also bring about a great flood (Gen. 6–8), and cause its waters to subside in due time. It draws near Him who could summon Abram from his ancestral home in Ur and lead him to a far away land, give it to him, and bless him in it (12:1–3, etc.). Prayer can be encouraged by a God who can give a mighty victory in battle over incredible odds (Chap. 14), or promise a son and give him (Chap. 15, 21). It finds courage from the Lord who has such command of nations that He can work among them to accomplish blessing for H is people, for example in bringing them out from subjugation to others (Chaps. 15, 37–50; Ex. 1–15).

The Lord's might and wisdom to carry out His purposes is an encouragement to prayer when the He promises to bless not only Abram, but the people in His lineage and even people of all nations who will trust Him (12:1–3). He pledges in covenant here and often reaffirms His good purpose to follow through with this covenant, even to later generations in Abram's line (46:1–4, etc.). God has the power and sensitive intention to answer prayer for children (Chaps. 26, 30), prosper those of His covenant even in difficult cases, as Jacob (28:11–Chap. 35), or his people, and most notably his son Joseph, whom He kept safe through great trial (Chaps. 37–50).

This God of power and wisdom is relevant to prayer as He desires fellowship with people (Chaps. 2–3, etc.), made male and female and cares for their needs, works in orderly acts as in the six days of creation, tests men for their obedience (Chaps. 2–3; cf. Deut. 8; 1 Cor. 10:13; James 1:2), provides a way out of sinful failure (Chap. 3), and distinguishes between those who choose sinful resolutions, or act in genuine worship to Him as in Cain and Abel. A bright prospect in which prayer can gain God's blessing is laid in His provision of bounty (Gen. 1–2), as the Bible later says He gives all things richly to enjoy (1 Tim. 6:17).

This God hears when men speak to Him (Chaps. 3, 4), in contrast to false gods which cannot hear, and can provide no help. This contrast is developed later in Isaiah 41–48, and often in the Psalms, for example. Yet He sees the difference between the humbly sincere in Genesis 3–4 and the insincere who merely mouth words about Him in a nominal sense of what is to their advantage, as Laban (Chap. 31).

This God who hears prayer can provide a way out of any situation if it is His will—a flood, barrenness of the womb, the devices of a deceptive partner such as Laban, danger of surrounding peoples, separation by distance as Joseph's case, seeming loss of a beloved son (Chap. 22), or famine, to name a few cases in the drama. Prayer can prosper with a God who cares, and is able (cf. Ps. 55:22; 1 Pet. 5:7). The power and wisdom that enhance prayer can even speak and keep prophetical promises, even through what we now know are mind-boggling centuries (Gen. 3:15; 12:1–3, 7).

Prayer will have good environment with a God who can keep track of all the multiplying descendants of Adam and Eve and later, Noah and his sons in the entire Table of Nations (Chaps. 10–11). And He is exact and on the spot in care even for a lonely woman, Hagar, in a desert trek at a remote spring (Chap. 16), or a troubled man, Jacob, fleeing from a brother intending murder (Chap. 28), or Joseph as a youth bartered away and carried into a distant country (Chap. 37), or women within a home who cry to Him for help in child-bearing (Chap. 30). Prayer can gain impetus from an account about God bringing a man, Abram, far from the country he left to a face-to-face meeting with another man, Melchizedek, who worships the same God (Chap. 14).

Respect and praise in prayer can leap in hearts that read of God's ability to bring massive judgment on a world via a flood (Chaps. 6–8), or destruction on cities wallowing in sinful filth (Chaps. 18–19). And prayer can find new onrush in a heart encouraged when it has failed as Abram did, yet gains merciful help to rebound and be usable to God again (Chaps. 12, 20). Prayer, too, can be very real in the heart of a man who travels on a mission to find a bride for his master's son and finds that God is faithful to guide and to provide in sure success (Chap. 24).

The God who enhances prayer does this without being remiss to bring judgment back on a man, Judah, who has sinned (Chap. 38).

Still, God can use this man as he stands tall later in self-sacrificial commitment of love (Chap. 43:8–10; 44:18–34).

We can return to prayer shortly, but it is good now to set the stage in pertinent ways of introduction for Genesis.

The Authorship

Before about the middle of the eighteenth century of our era, the traditional view that a single writer authored the first five books of the Old Testament remained almost unchallenged. Since then, higher critics of the Bible have hammered away at the view that Moses wrote the "Pentateuch." However, Mosaic authorship seems natural from many statements within these five books, is suggested by Old Testament statements, was the view of the ancient Jewish synagogue, the inspired New Testament writers, and the early Christian church, even by almost all biblical scholars before this time.

Who wrote Genesis is actually settled for the conservative student once the authorship of the Pentateuch as a larger unit is decided by reasonable evidence. Most of the critics are beyond a point of being convinced by fair lines of argument. Fine surveys of the evidence for Moses producing these books are given by Merrill F. Unger (Introductory Guide to the Old Testament), and other writers in their Old Testament introductions, scholars such as R. K. Harrison, Edward J. Young, and Gleason Archer.

Authorship of Genesis by Moses can go hand in hand with a use of source materials that were preserved until his day, oral or written. These could be selectively chosen under the inspiration of the Holy Spirit, who superintended the writing. The events of Genesis began long before Moses, and so he could have relied on records kept by the patriarchs. Divine inspiration was given Moses by a God of miracles (cf. Gen. 1:1) for the creation account, or he used records from a pure source to whom God gave this truth. Noah could have kept a log of details about the building of the ark, animals being drawn by the God who made them, the flood, and the landing after the flood.

The Date

Moses wrote the book sometime between his return to Egypt (cf. Ex. 3–4) and his death. This would put the date when the writing was being brought along to completion between ca. 1445 B.C. to 1400 B.C.

The Title

Genesis, as a name, is derived from the title that the LXX version attributes to the book. In reality, the title springs quite naturally from the book itself. It is used as a heading for ten key portions to designate various "beginnings." These ten sections, each introduced by the phrase ***he biblos geneseos*** to denote material that follows them (except in the first case), can be listed:

1:1–2:6 Generations [histories] of the heavens and the earth

2:7–6:8 Generations of Adam

6:9–9:29 Generations of Noah

10:1–11:9 Generations of the Sons of Noah

11:10–26 Generations of the Sons of Shem [rest of Gen. focuses mainly here]

11:27–25:11 Generations of Terah [Abram's family]

25:12–18 Generations of Ishmael

25:19–35:29 Generations of Isaac

36:1–37:1 Generations of Esau

37:2–50:26 Generations of Jacob

The book, then, is the book of beginnings, origins, or histories. As what some have called "the seed plot of the Bible," it also describes various other beginnings. We see the first animals, trees and other plants and vegetables and fruits, woman (wife) as a helpmate for man (husband), the Sabbath, responsibility to God's testing, the home, sin, sacrifice, a way of righteousness before God (cf. Gen. 15:6), covenants, kings, priests, setting up worship altars, trade, industry, agriculture, city life, the races and nations, languages, and God's chosen covenant nation.

So, looked at historically, Genesis is the book of beginnings. But if considered doctrinally, it deals with God's election (choosing): He chose Shem from the three sons of Noah to be the channel through which would come, eventually, the Savior (Gen. 3:15; later in 49:8–12 in the line of Judah) and ultimate King (cf. 17; 36; 49:8–12). He also selected Abram, later named Abraham, to be the father of the chosen nation within the covenant of 12:1–3. He passed by Ishmael and chose Isaac as the one through whom the seed line to covenant fulfillment would run (21:12). He rejected Esau and picked Jacob; and He appointed Joseph from all of Jacob's twelve sons to be His honored instrument for preserving His people from famine.

The Relation to the Rest of Scripture

Genesis is indeed "the seed plot of the Bible." On prayer and any other biblical theme, the various lines of truth in Scripture relate back to this initial, foundational book. The great concepts of the other sixty-five books in the Bible are like branches that rely on their ultimate roots back in Genesis. As the book of origins and beginnings, Genesis introduces and prepares for what is to follow in the progressive drama of the ages that God reveals.

The two paramount themes which begin in Genesis are the redemptive and the royal emphases. These are intimately bound together, intertwined, and inseparably dependent on one another. The redemptive aspect is the one that speaks of a redeemer from sin, and the royal focus refers to God's ultimate king. Those the Lord redeems from their sin will be in a kingdom, serving their King; and the King can have kingdom subjects from among sinners only by a gracious redemptive provision the Lord gives.

The roots of the redemptive theme are seen primarily in the promise of Genesis 3:15 and the need for coverings due to sin in 3:21. In Chapter 22, God Himself provides a ram for Abraham to sacrifice, and in later books of the Old Testament, He develops the idea of sacrifices as an atonement for sin. In the New Testament Christ fulfills the sacrificial lamb idea (John 1:29; 1 Cor. 5:7), providing redemption through His blood (Eph. 1:7).

God's regal line, relating to His kingdom program, is spotlighted in Genesis 1:26 where the idea of man's delegated authority is introduced as from a king to his sub-ruler. Man governs the earth, and later the ideal man, the King/Messiah, will do this perfectly. The royal purpose is seen also in the covenant God made with Abram. It includes the promise to Abram (Abraham), "kings shall come of you" (17:6). After making the covenant with Abraham, the Lord reaffirms it in several phases later in Genesis, to Abraham himself (Chaps. 15, 17), Isaac (Chap. 26), and Jacob (Chap. 46) and continues it in Exodus 6–7, for example.

Both of the themes run the entire length of Scripture. They gather a monumental structure of details. Without the book of Genesis, the remainder of the canon would be a baffling mystery without an intelligible beginning.

The Theme

It is true that Genesis is the book of beginnings and is historically prior to the other biblical books (possibly Job overlaps it). But beginnings does not constitute the actual theme of the fifty chapters. Genesis seems to introduce God's sovereign program which He will develop through His redemptive and royal lines of emphasis. Beginnings of the book simply furnish a framework within which the central theme fits. For example, the creation of the heavens and the earth provides a stage upon which the divine-human drama can be enacted. The beginning of man is only a brief introduction to the theme, which soon involves sin due to the Fall, and a redemptive line through God's promise of seed (3:15).

Likewise, the origination of nations is a backdrop for the introduction of Abraham, the father of the chosen nation to come and also the person through whose lineage kings will come (12:1–3; 17:1–8; cf. Isa. 51:1–2). And so the Book of Genesis prepares the way for the redemptive and royal content that later Bible books develop, all the way to the end of the Book of Revelation, where Christ is Redeemer (1:5; 5:6, 9; 7:14) and final King (17:14; 19:16; 21:24–26).

The Outline

Prayer in Genesis occurs at its various points within this broad structure.

I. The Introduction of God's Plan With the Human Race (1:1–11:9)
   A. The Creation (1:1–2:4a)
   B. The Fall (2:4b–5:32)
   C. The Flood (6:1–10:32)
   D. The Confusion of Tongues (11:1–9)
II. The Introduction of God's Plan with the Chosen Nation (11:10–50:26)
   A. Abram/Abraham (11:10–25:18)
   B. Isaac (25:19–27:46)
   C. Jacob (28:1–37:2a)
   D. Joseph (37:2b–50:26)

Prayer is a sub-theme intimately related with faith, obedience, godliness, and various other currents of life. Now it is time to look at the specific passages in the book where prayer shows its relevancy.

Genesis

Man's first prayer in the Bible is a kind of confession; the last, a petitionary passion: "Even so, come, Lord Jesus." The first is in the situation of the fall into sin; the last, an appeal for the Christ who has provided a way back from sin into righteousness.

Genesis 3:10, 12, 13

When Adam and Eve commit sin, they feel convicted of their unstrung relationship with God, and He confronts them about the sin. He talks with them, and they talk with Him. This is in essence a kind of prayer in that they react to His words and respond in conversation with Him.

The Commitment of Sin (3:1–6)

The tempter entices, then the woman bites at his bait and swallows his line. She tells Adam, and he too falls as they both eat of the forbidden fruit. The decision and act constitute disobedience to God's word calling them not to eat of the "tree of the knowledge of good and evil" (2:18). Their prayer after this pivots around their departure from obeying His will. God placed this tree amidst other trees of the garden as a test for Adam and Eve. Created by God in purity and innocence of misconduct, they will confirm a living out of obedience as their choice. Or they will deviate from His expressly revealed will and be in a state of sin, estranged from fellowship with Him. Suppose that they continued with sterling fulfillment of His mandate. In such a case they apparently would have, at His point of timing, received His gift in eating from "the tree of life." Then, without sin they would have been given the gift, eternal life, that the tree symbolized, blessing in His presence (cf. Rev. 2:17; 22:2). But should they, while fallen and still in a state of sin, partake of this tree's fruit, they would be sealed in a perpetual condition of sin. God would provide a better solution in the redeeming Christ, whowould pay the penalty for man's sin and also free him finally from the sin and give him passage into the gift of eternal life in that freedom (cf. John 5:24; 8:32, 36).

The Conviction of Sin (7–8)

Adam and Eve immediately sensed an empty, undone quality toning their existence. They felt distant from the God who had seemed so near before. This was so unsettling that they sensed their alienation from God even in regard to their bodies He had made. Their feet had carried them to the "off limits" tree; their eyes been dazzled in disobedient desire; their hands had picked, fondled, and lifted the fruit to their mouths; their mouths had been filled with the forbidden; their stomachs had begun to digest the fruit; indeed, they were aware of guilt affecting them within and without. Their outward members were in coordination, but the implements to secure and partake of what their inward faculties chose (cf. Rom. 6:13; 12:1). And so the conviction of sin tainting their entire existence made them feel the consciousness of the wrong even in their entire outward beings.

Stung by conviction, they sought a remedy by which they might try to "cover up" the sin from God. They gathered leaves near at hand to fashion into apparel, and also sought to draw back into seclusion, trying to hide from the scrutiny of the God to whom they must answer. Genesis 3 is distinctly clear about their *awareness* (v. 7a). Their eyes, which had danced in gazing at the fruit, now saw everything in an unpleasant light. And the grinding consciousness of their stripped condition ran rampant in their conviction. They covered themselves with *apparel* from the most likely items at hand (v. 7b). Then followed their *attempt* to avoid a reckoning with God. When they heard the sound of the Lord God walking not far away, they no longer felt it delightful to be before Him, but distasteful. They retreated in their estrangement, foolishly supposing that they could conceal themselves (v. 8a, b).

The Confrontation of Sin (9–13)

What is in its essence prayer is apparent here. They talk to God about their sin, an element of prayer often in God's Word.

God enters into a counseling session with the two. He probes their lives with three questions.

Where are you (v. 9)? God already knows, for He is the God who knows all things, as displayed in His carrying out the work of creation. He acts to stir them to accountability, and provoke response to Him. Their reply is prayer in the aspect of confession (v. 10). Since they are talking with God, this in essence is prayer. Adam voices the confession as his own acknowledgment, and surely it is fitting also for Eve. He *heard* God's approach, felt smitten with *fear* due to his vulnerability, *naked* as he sensed being laid bare before the Lord's scrutiny. So he retreated to stall from the inevitable, the showdown. What he confesses is, at its roots, what confession is in 1 John 1:9. It is agreeing with God, seeing eye to eye, so to speak, about sin. All that God draws from him is a frank, open admission of the stark truth. He is convinced that the Lord "has the goods" on him, and the counselor pulls it from his heart and lips. The second question from the Lord pierces the garden scene.

Have you disobeyed? This hits the nail on the head, in effect (v. 11). Again Adam answers. His reply fits the aspect of prayer we can call *affirmation*. He utters a direct declaration of how he sees things (v. 12). What he affirms is true. "The woman You gave me, gave me from the tree, and I ate." It is true, yet apparently framed in such a way as to hint at a complaint about God's gift to him. It also at first casts blame on Eve, which again is true, but Adam frames things to relieve himself of his direct culpability as long as he can. Finally, he is out with it about his own guilt, "and I ate."

Affirming things in talking with God can be in complete, candid statement of a point in His Word or from the field of human thought or action. It also can be put into words that seek to maneuver things to one's own advantage, colored even if true.

Adam does at last own up to his own sin.

The Lord moves to His third question, piercing now to Eve.

What have you done (v. 13a)? The query opens a door of reception to the woman's answer, which combines *confession* and *affirmation.* First, Eve declares the deception, "The serpent deceived me. . . ." That is "passing the buck," yet an aspect very true, even if not all of the picture. The serpent indeed hoodwinked her. The Spirit of God later leads the apostle Paul to the commentary in 1 Timothy 2:12 that uses a special, stronger word for the woman's being deceived. She was "really deceived," not just "deceived" (***apatao***) but "profoundly deceived" (***exapatao***). She was apparently deceived even beyond Adam's reason for sinning in going along with her, or his sort of deception in his full guilt for sin (Rom. 5:12).

Second, Eve enlarges on the picture, and *pours out her confession of guilt*, "and I ate." She comes clean about her own culpability in the deviation. She, too, had acted out of harmony with what she realizes, sadly, God's word had made clear as the way of obedience.

The Consequences of Sin (14–19)

Briefly, the Lord follows up His counseling interchange by stating His consequences for each of the guilty parties. The culprit He first deals with for the sin is finally the instigator who trip up the two, the serpent.

It appears right to conclude from Scripture later that the animal serpent is himself a tool through which the personal Serpent tempts "that old serpent the devil" (Rev. 12:9). The biblical commentary sees it this way. The animal is "cursed." God consigns him to slithering his ignoble way in the dust (Gen. 3:14).

Verse 15 transitions to the greater Serpent, as many have believed. Enmity between the serpent and the woman is God's verdict. The enmity would even be expressed by the serpent's seed—the unsaved whose father is the greater serpent, the devil (John 8:44)—in conflict with the seed eventuating from the woman—the person ("He"), the savior who eventually sets people free from sin (John 8:32, 36), and in union with Him the saved, the righteous. The ultimate seed coming from the woman, the redeemer from sin, will register a fatal blow that crushes the Serpent's head or puts him to his doom (Rev. 19:20; 20:10). On his part, while he still is freed to do so, the Serpent will bruise the woman's seed, the Savior, on his heel. This is in the death that people of the devil consigned this "Seed" to on the cross.

Third in the consequences of sin is that which applies to the woman, Eve and other women (cf. 3:20). This is discomfort in childbirth, apparently not her portion before her fall should she have conceived (1:28) when all was "good" (1:31a). Desire in submitting to her husband is also God's part for her, accepting his leadership over her in the marriage, and sexual intimacy even with painful difficulty that can be entailed in this (cf. 1 Tim. 2:11–15).

Finally, the fourth consequence is that of the man (3:17–19). God immediately faces him on his personal guilt in sinful irresponsibly, his part in the rebellion. The Lord makes it clear that what he violated was His word, His will (v. 17). The consequence includes the ground being cursed so that the man will experience toil facing obstacles in making a living. The ground God cursed would yield weeds heightening the difficulty of his work, and this would wring sweat out of him in his efforts to furnish food. Apparently had he not fallen, his God-assigned labor (1:28–30; 2:15) could have been carried out free of the toilsome difficulties found in the opposition he must face.

This, then, is the first biblical passage where the essence of prayer plays a part. A man and a woman talk with God. The Lord makes this possible by drawing close in some kind of fashion. His movement and voice in the garden suggests, reasonably, a visualization to Adam and Eve. This may or may not be in the concessionary form of a human, as God's angel appears to Hagar (Gen. 16) or as the Lord Himself visits along with two angels Abraham can see and hear (Gen. 18).

Summary

What amounts to prayer is evident here in people speaking with God. Prayer's aspects in this case, as often in later Scripture, are in confession and affirmation. What the man and woman affirm is true, in contrast to the line the serpent peddles as "a liar from the beginning" (John 8:44).

The passage readily suggests principles related to prayer. First, confessing sin is a step forward—to God and with God. It is best to go all the way in this closure of the heart with Him, deal with the guilt squarely and fully, and not shift the blame to someone else. Second, when we confess frankly to put sins behind us, we find the Lord more willing than we are that things be right between us. For as the revelation about God mounts in Scripture, we now gather that He has great mercy to forgive (Ex. 34; Ps. 103), and, through the sacrifice system and later the sacrifice of Christ, has made full provision to take away sins (cf. John 1:29; Heb. 9–10).

Genesis 4:1–15

The Prayer of Cain

What is again of the essence of prayer comes in Cain's lying words to the Lord, answering Him and assessing His sentence.

How Cain Fails (4:1–8)

First the passage is explicit about the setting, the *births* of Cain and Abel (1–2). Then it moves on to their *bringing* offerings to God (3–7), finally to Cain's *bloodshed* in murder (8).

Both of the two bring gifts to worship the Lord. Abel's receives God's approval; Cain's is rejected. Some see the reason in Abel's sacrifice being an animal whereas Cain's is a plant offering. This assumes that God had revealed this early the specific distinction of what He would accept and what He would not in these terms. Genesis 3 does not provide clear-cut proof. Another possibility is to see the contrast in this passage on its own right. Abel is specifically said to offer the choice parts of the animal, the fatty portions, a statement that goes beyond merely defining the gift as an animal. Cain, on the other hand, is stated only to bring of his produce, a generality. On this line of reasoning, Abel invested more devotion in his offering, showing a heart passion to give the best, while Cain is not viewed as going to such length. Should this be the point, the offerings contrast a heart devotion in worship (Abel) with a perfunctory performance, merely pacing oneself through the motions.

Whatever defines the difference, Abel was pleasing; Cain was not. Perhaps the Lord spoke in some way not brought into the detail, revealing how He regarded the gifts. He does speak later in the context, making that a natural probability.

Cain compounds his falsity in worship by pouting, plotting, and then murdering his brother. To hide his bloodshed, he conceals the body. His attitude and action expose the spuriousness of his worship to God. Later, a commentary in 1 John 3:12 is quite clear about his source (he was "of that wicked one") and the sin of hate within him that festered until it erupted in the slaying. His pride had been wounded in being disapproved and his brother's offering preferred. This rankled and galled him. God showed merciful long-suffering in according him opportunity for a turnabout in repenting. He could see everything changed and set right and his offerings pleasing. But rather than rectify, he retaliated. He could not strike out at God directly, but he could get at his brother and hit God through him. In this he revealed that he was against God and despised God's word, whereas a true attitude for prayer would be to delight in it, agree with God in confession, and find that God opened his way back. In such a case, God could testify of his gifts as He did Abel's (Heb. 11:4), assessing them as true sacrifice. Lashing away in bitter resentment, Cain dashed out Abel's life. In his hatred he was in heart attitude already a murderer (1 John 3:12–15). So all of the New Testament references to Cain condemn him (Heb. 11:4; 1 John 3:12; Jude 11), the final verse even warning against "the way of Cain." That is a terrible sign-post to alert other travelers on the road of life to take another path.

What the Lord Asks (9a)

"Where is Abel your brother?" As the Lord was aware of where Adam and Eve were, He knew where Abel was. Knowing all, He stepped in to confront Cain. He intended His question to stimulate Cain to reflection and repentance, if the man of hate would.

What Cain Answers (9b)

His surly response is first untruthful, then uncaring. Love finds no abode in him (1 John 3:12–15). The untruthful reply is his duplicity that shuns confession: "I do not know" (9b). What a lie! The uncaring answer is a dodge from any responsibility: "Am I my brother's keeper?" The truth is, yes, but he takes his stand against it.

The words to God are prayer, in essence, but of a very calloused nature. It is as cold as an Arctic iceberg.

What God Assigns (10–12)

First, God pins the sinner to the facts. True confession in prayer acknowledges God's truth, and one's own swerving away from it. It owns up. This Cain has not done, and God gives him opportunity to face up to reality. "What have you done?" Let him dwell on that, and realize the enormity of sin's ugliness. Let him acknowledge things as they are, tolerate no cover-ups. The guilt is obvious. "The voice of your brother's blood is crying to Me from the ground" (10). This is a figurative way of saying that the stark reality of what sin has done is blaring its truth before God. How apt is the time-worn statement, "Secret sin on earth is open scandal in heaven." Cain has had God's open door to do an about-face; he has let the opportunity slip away.

Second, God pronounces the consequences for Cain (11–12). A curse on the ground would be on his efforts to make a living from it. He would not prosper from blessing but would find but a sparse yield for all his effort. The low productivity of the soil would keep him on the move from place to place as a vagrant and wanderer, striving to gain an existence. A means to enhance this meager agricultural output, plus an impulse to violence, could explain some of his people branching out to another livelihood. They began forging implements of bronze and iron (v. 22).

In later reflection, a writer of proverbs would say with candid frankness, "the way of the treacherous is hard" (Prov. 13:15). God's sovereign will gives this hardness to some as to Cain, yet in other cases He may allow temporal prosperity, at least.

How Cain Assesses This (13–14)

Here now is Cain's anguished assessment of God's sentence. Two things sum it up: he recognizes the sentence (13), then rates its severity (13–14). His prayerful wail voicing the difficulty he must face from others trying to strike down the murderer meets with a merciful allowance from the Lord.

What God Allows (15)

First is the Lord's statement of punishment (15a), then His sign for Cain's protection (15b). In the "mark of Cain," the word for "mark" is later used to mean the sign of the rainbow (9:12). It is not a blemish on Cain's body to call attention to him, despite many wild conjectures of different disfigurements. Rather, it is some kind of sign God would manifest when Cain was in danger of being struck down, to enforce his safety in this life. The verse reads "a mark [sign] for Cain," not "a mark on Cain." We do not know what that sign was but should remember God's ability to make it work effectively.

The three New Testament passages that comment on Cain appear to place him among the unredeemed. In Hebrews 11, where faith is a great theme, Cain is the opposite of Abel in his sacrifice and apparently not a man of faith. The focus is on Abel, but the contrast seems clearly to be made. Likewise in 1 John 3:12–15, Cain as a man whose pattern was hate and his product murder illustrates John's point, "no murderer has eternal life abiding in him." Cain's whole characteristic trend was a dogged defiance and disobedience. Jude 11 relates Cain within a flow of statements that refer to the ungodly. In Jude 4 they are condemned, turning grace into license via sinful outlets and denying God. Cain is also in a line of men such as later Israelites who did not believe (v. 5), and comparable to evil angels who defected from God (6). He also is in a context of those in Sodom and Gomorrah who gratified their hearts with what God rejected as sin (7). God wrote across Cain's dark way an appraisal, "the way of Cain" and used it in company with the error in Balaam's greed for self-aggrandizement and the gainsaying that blackened Korah's name (11).

Guidelines relevant to prayer surface here. First, men should not be evasive about sin before God, but forthrightly acknowledge it and turn obediently to Him. Second, the way we deal with God about sin may expose a servant spirit, and even be one thing that gives proper confidence that we really are His people.

Genesis 4:26

Men Began to Call on the Lord

The Background of Connection with the Lord

Before men began to "call with the name of the Lord" (v. 26), the context depicts the setting of *creation*. God created men and all things, manifesting His power, wisdom, and goodness. He has been the great provider of all that men need—time, dust, a garden of trees producing beauty to behold and food to eat. Besides these, He has furnished the two special trees, rivers, gold and precious stones, roles of service, animals, a companion who is fitting for man, sleep, marriage, a test of obedience, such capacities as the ability to think, move, see, taste, speak, hear, and know a marriage partner in sexual intimacy. God has given man rule over His creation, woman the power to conceive and procreate, the privilege of approaching Him with gifts and receiving His blessing (4:3–4), counseling with wisdom from His word, opportunity to repent (4:6–7), punishment when it is due, and the instruction this bears (4:13–15). He has supplied a sign for Cain's protection from any who might plot to harm him, the skill to build a city and invent implements, the enjoyment of music, and the ability to parent a child and name him in honor of God's graciousness (4:25).

It is very natural for men to look to God as their ultimate source of supply and to speak to Him. For He created all, sustains all, knows all, cares about all, and is sufficient in all things.

That is not all. The context also lays a background of *commitment* to obedience in the Adam and Eve scene (Gen. 2, 3) and in the Cain and Abel drama (Chap. 4). In both, God has spoken to them, and they have conversed with Him about being accountable to Him.

One other thing, quite momentous, stands out in the background. It is the *civilization* that is beginning to develop in self-sufficiency apart from God (4:16–24). Due to distance and difficulty in knowing what was happening in far-flung places, it is not clear how much Adam, Eve, Seth, and Enosh would realize about the trend away from the Lord. But the fact that a specific record is supplied suggests the possibility of some mutual awareness between Cainite and Sethite people, so that some record could be kept. If not this, the Lord who knows all things could furnish the information then and not just at a later time of writing.

Cain's civilization built a city, tents, musical instruments, metal implements. But they also displayed the dark intrusion of sin in living self-sufficiently with God largely left out. This was the essence of worldliness. They named children after their own projects (4:17; cf. 25), entered into plural marriages (bigamy), and resorted to vengefulness and proud boasting.

The Sethite people, if aware of the Cainite slide from the Lord, could learn from it the way not to go (cf. Jude 11) and the way they should live as pleasing to the Lord.

The Beginning of Contact with the Lord (4:25–26)

Contact seems evident in associating with God (v. 25) and in addressing Him (v. 26).

In associating with God. When God gave another son to Adam and Eve after Cain had struck down Abel, they named that son in tribute to God's bounty. The name they chose was a celebration in thanksgiving, a memorial in recognizing God's provision. The passage tells us both that Eve named him (4:25) and Adam named him (5:3). In the name they discern Seth as "appointed," and as seed of the woman, the parents recognize him as God's act in going on with His plan of 3:15. By this new life God had triumphed over the death Cain had dealt, which casts its long shadow even here in Eve's sadness, "for Cain killed him."

The thanksgiving was a reality that the couple felt and which they would directly relate to the Lord. For He was the giver of life in the creation context and here.

It is in this spirit of gratitude relating life to God and His will that the passage notes the beginning of appeals to God.

In addressing God. Since the passage up to now is abundant with God's causing all blessings and committing Himself to His plan, it is fitting that people turn to Him, the source of life. His blessing of life is in contrast to sin that embitters it (cf. Gen. 3), dealing death.

Observe two emphases in 4:26.

(1) One is calling a *son* by a name. When the human lineage continued from Adam and Eve to Seth and from Seth to his son Enosh, the last name means "man" or "mankind." The passage does not say so, but this would naturally have been in commemorating the ongoing humanity God had shown in appointing Seth. This connection with God, and the very next focus that men began to call with the name of the Lord intimates that Seth intended the name "Enosh" to be a tribute to the One who gave this latest of mankind.

Closely tied with the calling of a son's name, both in Seth (v. 25) and in Enosh (26) is the next statement about calling on the Lord's name.

(2) So, second is the calling with the *Lord's* name. The calling is a communion that addresses the Lord in worship, devoting attention to Him. The nature of this has been subject to different explanations.

Some view "call" in verse 26 as not prayer but proclamation designating the Lord as worthy of worship and testimony associating with Him. That "call" often is used of naming or designating a person or a thing could point to this idea. It is a word used in calling a city by name (4:17) or a child such as Seth (v. 25) and Enosh (v. 26). Still, calling with the name of the Lord in prayer has much in its favor.

(1) In the context, calling, if seen as to God in prayer, quite naturally fits the situation. Eve has just voiced gratitude, crediting the Lord for His giving a new son, Seth. That He had supplied even after human weakness in Abel's vulnerability to death makes it reasonable that men call to Him in prayer. The creator and sustainer of life is sufficient to provide His bestowals. So was it also in the coming of Enosh.

(2) The particular phrase, "call with the name of" features the verb "call" and then the word "name" having a prefix letter attached to it, a preposition, ***beth.*** Literally we can translate the phrase "call *with* the name of," or "call invoking the name." Bietenhard writes that this "is a common phrase for to worship Yahweh cultically," that is in religious practice. It often appears in prayer when men call or

address God. It fits Abram's case of calling at an altar set up to God (Gen. 12:8), which we will see later. It is the phrase in 2 Kings 5:11 as well. Naaman the leper expected that when he met Elisha, the prophet would call on the name of the Lord to summon His powerful healing, wave his hand, and cure Naaman. A further example of prayer is Jeremiah 10:25 and its parallel verse, Psalm 79:6. In that instance, it refers to a specific appeal to the Lord to manifest His might. A very famous case is Elijah's challenge for a battle on Mount Carmel, his God vs. the false gods of the spurious prophets (1 Kgs. 18). Elijah proposed, "you call on the name of your god" (vv. 24, 25), "and I will call on the name of the Lord . . ." (v. 24). The same word for "call," the word for "name" and the letter ***beth*** affixed to "name" appear as in Genesis 4:26. This is true in all three instances in verses 24–25. After the false gods failed to respond, Elijah prayed directly to the Lord (vv. 36–37). He pled for a powerful act to demonstrate His Godhood and Elijah's authenticity as His servant. The Lord answered by fire that fell from heaven, consuming the offering, wood, stones, dust and water (v. 38).

Prayer is also the idea in Psalm 116:17. The psalmist calls on the name of the Lord in thanksgiving and praise as he offers a sacrifice. Zephaniah 3:9 can embrace prayer too. There, God in His future kingdom will grant purified lips to Gentiles. They then will call on His name. This fits in a sequence in which the next verse (10) says, "My worshipers, My dispersed ones, will bring My offerings" meaning tributes in worship to God.

(3) The verb "call" in Genesis 4:26 is used often when a person calls on or to another person. It may or may not appear as in 4:26 with a preposition, whether ***beth*** or some other construction. In Genesis 3:9, the Lord God called *to* Adam, and in Exodus 3:4 *to* Moses out of the burning bush. Psalm 66:17 speaks of men calling upon God in prayer (praise). "Call" also can occur without a preposition as the psalmist calls God for help (not "to," "with," or "upon," etc.).

Now it is time to return to Genesis 4:26. Granted that the phrase can be variously understood, evidence is plenteous for calling with the name of the Lord in prayer. And in a wider context where God speaks to man and man speaks to God in Chapters 1–4, response to Him in prayer would fit very naturally.

What would the content of prayer be at this early time? Given the background so far leading to 4:26, such calling reflects a commitment to Him as creator and giver of life, most recently in Seth and Enosh. Thanksgiving would be a natural aspect of prayer, and Genesis 1–4 shows many things men could thank Him for. The calling also is quite reasonably invested with God's right to allegiance. He demonstrated this in confronting Adam and Eve and later, Cain. The gifts of Cain and Abel acknowledged Him too, the one falsely and the other genuinely. Prayer in affirmation would be appropriate—affirming God's goodness, their dependence on Him who met human insufficiency with His sufficiency, and their yearnings in His will for the future.

The beginning of prayer in 4:26 is immediately related to the time of Seth and the arrival of Enosh. The word "at that time" or "then" can denote this later point only, or the entire statement may sum up a sweep of time that verses 25–26 deal with as a unit. If the former, the focus can be on men as a civilization overall, a trend characterizing the Sethite branch as contrasted with the Cainite just before it. That is, while Adam and Eve conversed with God (Gen. 3) or as Eve individually gave tribute to the Lord (4:1), or Cain spoke to God, now communion with Him becomes a greater experience in the stream of many calling on the Lord. If, however, 4:26 utilizes the words as a summary of the whole unit, men called on the Lord as Adam and Eve did earlier and as Eve gave tribute to Him in 4:1, 25, witnessing to His faithfulness at work. Eve's words about God's appointing Seth could be the essence of thankgiving that would be natural in communing with Him and not only to testify to Him before her family circle.

Which principles are cogent? First, it is a great privilege to call on God in prayer that engages heart with heart, so let us have much of this (cf. Phil. 4:6). Second, praying to the Lord is a natural spiritual impulse amid the blessing of His gifts, in this case a son. Third, to have recourse in the name of the Lord is to be in the best company where one finds the best answers.

Genesis 8:20

Noah's Prayer at an Altar

Here is how the worship fits its situation.

God's Release from the Ark (8:15–19)

The overwhelming flood and the long stay on the ark of safety (cf. 1 Pet. 3:20–21) is over. The Lord who summoned men, animals, and birds to this protection and closed the door permits Noah and other voyagers to disembark.

Noah's Response at an Altar (20)

No reference to prayer appears—only Noah's erection of an altar and his offering of sacrifices. Yet this is highly suggestive of a spirit responding in gratitude to God. For God had directed Noah to preserve people, animals, and birds, even extra animals that were clean for sacrifice (7:2). It is not easy to imagine prayer was nil in a context of such great deliverance. Also, God had just spoken to Noah again, and it would be very natural for this man who "walked with God" (6:9) to speak also to Him. However, among many silences in Genesis in very opportune prayer situations, we never read of Noah speaking at all, in prayer or not in prayer, until 9:25–27. In centuries from Adam and Eve to Noah, only Lamech's words are given (5:29), these in a prophetic vein which God orders to fulfillment.

Some of the passages on altar worship in Genesis also mention calling on the Lord (12:8; 13:4). Some do not, as in 12:7 and here. Still, God has spoken to men and men to God (Gen. 3, 4), and prayer accompanying Noah's sacrifices would be an appropriate gesture along with the spirit of worship he showed. In what aspects? Adoration in praise and thanks would suit the situation of being kept safe when so many lives perished. How could a man not be deeply touched? Prayer in the aspect of affirmation would fit well too. How apropos to affirm the great deliverance riding safely above waters so great in magnitude, and stepping forth to live again on the ground not seen for months. And how suited to the case to affirm the resolution to walk even more with a God of such power, goodness, and commission (cf. v. 17). At the same time, petition in prayer could accompany the offerings, asking for God-given success to please Him in this fresh new venture in contrast to all but eight perishing because of their corruption (6:11–13).

Whether Noah prayed here is impossible to say with certainty. That the circumstances are the most likely to draw prayer from the heart and lips of a man who walked with God (6:9) is true.

Principles for prayer fit well. First, God's deliverance is one of the apt prompts to come before Him with grateful heart and words. Second, when God at a certain time transplants us from one venue to another to a new beginning is prayer time. Third, fresh reminders of our God's power to do almighty things can give new motivations to lay hold of Him in prayer.

Genesis 9:24–27

Noah's Prophetic Prayer

This is an early case of prophecy as God prompts a man and enables him to say what will turn out to be true. God has already helped Lamech to predict what He will fulfill (5:29). That prayer can be interwoven with what is prophetic will be seen shortly. First, note the setting.

The Provocation

Ham's sin of disrespect for his father in gazing on his uncovered body while he slept is the background. He not only failed in this, by indecency, but was at fault in not covering his father as his two brothers later did. He made a spectacle of him to make him look bad by pointing out his exposure to the brothers.

The Prayer

Noah awoke and learned in some way, which the passage does not explain, that his son had made sport of him. Perhaps Ham brought it up to him in a fool's indiscretion. Or the two brothers may have been so incensed that they felt the responsibility to deal forthrightly with the matter, hard as that was.

Then Noah made his famous utterance, the only words specifically recorded from his life. The passage does not clarify when he gave the words, whether immediately or after long spiritual reflection before the Lord.

That the utterance expresses Noah's own wishes, albeit guided by the Lord, seems evident in his own direct involvement in the sin just committed. The sin had been against him. Not only that, but he says "Cursed be Canaan," using a participle invoking God's curse, then following this with prayer wishes "May he," and "Let" him be. God shows in other Scripture that His own action in bringing things into realization can be intertwined with the wishes He tutors within a person, His prophetic channel (Jer. 29:10–12; Dan. 9:4–19).

The Prophecy

Remarkably, what God enables Noah to speak finds fulfillment later in Canaanite peoples being brought into subservience to Shemite peoples (Josh. 9:22–27; Judg. 1:28). Descendants of Japheth are enlarged in growth and conquest, fulfilled largely in the Indo-European peoples. The God of Shem carries out His plan as the human race progresses, blessed at least often in His sufficiency and success. His people in the line of Shem and, by extension, others as related to Him receive blessing. For the God who made the prediction of a coming "seed" who would crush the serpent's head (3:15) also promises covenant blessing to all nations (12:1–3; 46:2–4). And He forecasts blessed rule in Judah's line of the Shemites (49:10). That Japheth would dwell in the tents of Shem refers, most probably, to blessing of these peoples who would submit to the God of Shem and participate in the international benefits of 12:1–3.

Noah bypasses Ham and speaks of Canaan, his youngest son. Though the reason is not explained here, the leap often is taken as a gracious gesture to Ham personally in the immediate picture. The same would be true of Canaan personally, as the prophecy jumps on to his descendants, assuming that corrupt traits in Ham and Canaan would also be in their line of people, calling for God's rejection. This would be in an overall sense, leaving opportunity for some individuals who would trust God and be saved. Rahab is an illustration of this (Josh. 2; Heb 11:31).

The God of Shem could carry out His plans fulfilling 9:25–27 just as in fulfilling 3:15, 5:29, 12:1–3 and similar covenant passages, Joseph's dreams, dreams God caused the Pharaoh to have, and Jacob's prophetic pronouncements on his sons (49:1ff.).

We have here an early example of a prayerful series of wishes from a man, God's instrument. These blend harmoniously with God's sure prophetical will. The main focus is on the word of God, marked to be realized, and then the commitment by the person who prays in accord with that will.

A guideline for talking with God is quite natural here. When it is His will for His Word, He can prompt a person who is His channel to pray in accord with what it is His heart's plan to accomplish.

Genesis 12:7, 8

Abram's Calling on the Lord

It was natural for Abram to speak to God. For God had spoken to him even to initiate his trek to the land he now beheld.

First, it is cogent to see Abram's background, then his building of altars.

The Background for Abram (11:26–12:6)

God's call to the land (11:26–12:1). We learn when we get to 12:1 that the Lord "had said" to Abram previously what we now read. The account takes time to supplement 11:26ff. In the earlier verses the movement of Abram's people is obvious, as from Ur of the Chaldees to Haran far to the southwest. But in 12:1 we are apprised of the motivation behind this movement. God had called Abram to pull up stakes and go about seven hundred miles to a land He pledged to show him. Further insight in Joshua 24:1 explains that the family worshipped other gods in Ur; the true God summoned Abram and his family to a new life lived with His promises.

God's covenant with Abram (12:2–3, 7). What the Lord put before this man He chose was a covenant pledge. It featured various aspects: blessing to the nation comprising Abram's descendants (v. 2a), blessing to him personally (2b-d, 3a, b), and finally blessing to all nations (3c). Later in verse 7, the originator of the pact makes it clear that His promises include possession of the land of Canaan.

The company with Abram (12:4–5). These verses show who finally came with Abram into the promised land.

The coming to the land (12:6). The long journey has brought the travelers "to the land which I will show you" (v. 1). This prepares the scene for the building of altars.

The Building of Altars (12:7, 8)

(1) First is his altar at Moreh, at an oak grove in the vicinity that would later be Shechem. Though Abram will move on to a mountain in verse 8 and construct a second altar, neither altar is said to be a place of prayer. As in the genealogy of Genesis 5, the narrative goes on without mention of men speaking—whether to men or to God—except that 5:29 finally has Lamech's prophecy. And as in the account of Noah, except for 9:25–27, the description procedes without reference to man speaking. God alone speaks in what is recorded.

But that Abram reasonably did pray at his altar of verse 7 seems to follow from the situation. One factor is the peril in which the newcomer to the land found himself and people in his care. The Canaanite then occupied the area! That danger would threaten a man who had human fears, as Jacob later did on a different trek (28:11ff.). Abram as yet had no pact of peace with these peoples, and they were ominous on every side, he an island within a sea of many unknowns. He would surely find God's promise of the land a test of faith now, for the land promised was in control of others! As he would be gripped by anxiety when he had no son (15:1–3), he probably felt its clutch now. It was a situation ready-made to arouse within him the impulse to pray for safety as well as surety about having the land.

A natural instigator of prayer to be factored in as Abram came to his altar was the Lord's proclamation that the land would belong to him and his descendants (v. 7; cf. 1). How timely God sometimes can be in His placement of His promise. He gave this reassurance when Abram sorely needed it, Canaanite or no Canaanite. Such cheering words to a possibly thumping heart would quite naturally evoke spontaneous *thanksgiving* in prayer, or a *request* for protection in the face of the enemy and of the encouragement. This would be as when Abram later faced the peril of a Mesopotamian invader's reprisal, and after that the fear of having no son. In the later episode, he responded to God's encouragement (15:1) with prayer (vv. 2–3).

(2) Next is his altar on a mountain. A new facet of the passage that might suggest prayer from the altar is Abram's action at his next altar (v. 8). He moved on to a mountain near the spot he later would name Bethel (28:11ff.), set up an altar there, and "called on the name of the Lord." The features of 4:26 reappear: the call, the name, the Lord, and a preposition ***beth*** affixed as the first letter before "name." He called with the name, or invoked the name. As has already been shown on 4:26, this combination in Scripture often occurs where men pray.

In Genesis 12:8, the context has said twice that the Lord "appeared" to Abram (v. 7). It is a matter of His action *to* the recipient of His promise of 12:1–3, 7. For Abram to respond in action from his altar *to* the Lord would be eminently cogent to the occasion. God's presence with him would impress on him the rightness of his own presence responding to the Lord, and as God spoke he too would appropriately speak.

This appears to be far more fitting than erecting altars simply in honor of the Lord, a silent tribute of his sentiment without ever voicing it.

What of maxims that can be pertinent in prayer? First, a life that is vital with God can find that a central place of prayer is very meaningful in pouring forth devotion to Him and seeking Him in times of need. Second, a believer's circumstances can often provoke relevant urgencies to utter in quest of God's action. Third, sure points to emphasize in prayer are things God has promised, and our needs and fears (cf. Ps. 34:6; Heb. 4:16).

Genesis 13:4

Abram's Return to the Altar

After a sojourn in Egypt and a return to Canaan, Abram seeks out his former altar near Bethel, set up in 12:8. That he prayed here is a real possibility for several reasons.

First, the emphasis is on what he did at the altar, not on the effect the altar would have on the Canaanites or on his profession of the Lord. Canaanites are not brought into the picture again until 13:7, and this in a later connection.

Second, Abram's predicament again is a prime one for seeking God in prayer to praise Him and elicit His help. God had just preserved him and Sarai in Egypt and delivered them out of high danger without a loss but with gain. This would set a situation in which prayer in praise would be quite apt. And back in a land which he did not yet possess, he would likewise sense his need for help.

Third, Abram's insistence on reaching this very campsite suggests a sense of God's special presence drawing him there for communion. His escape from a terrible end for his wife and for him in Egypt could easily convict him of the wisdom in drawing near to the Lord. Having been spared, he might ponder the goodness of God attending his new steps once back.

Principles fit the case. First, God's rescue from danger is a fitting catalyst to evoke prayer that celebrates and magnifies Him. Second, the sense that God is our only sure refuge can draw the heart powerfully to keep close communication with Him.

Genesis 13:18

Abram's New Altar to the Lord

The verse again mentions no specific action carried out from the altar to define it one way or another. As above, the context is rich with the relevancy of reciprocal contact with the God who is said to be in touch with him (vv. 14–17).

The Choices of the Men (13:5–12)

Grazing needs for Lot's livestock and Abram's leads the latter to a magnanimous offer that Lot take his choice of land.

The choice of Lot (vv. 5–11). The kinsman makes his advantageous pick of land that pleases the eye. Abram awaits his turn, having God's promises and being an object of His covenant generosity. Whether or not Abram's heart fluttered with the thought that he could be losing out we do not know. Sometimes nice guys finish last, but not always. God can see to it that those who trust Him do not.

The choice of Abram (v. 12). He gets his turn, and God will soon appear to confirm his future blessing. In the meantime, Sodom rises on the landscape like an ugly sore that defiles all it touches.

The conspicuousness of Sodom's opposition (v. 13). It is clear-cut that the Sodomites stand against God and would be against His people. So the situation is one across that this sinkhole of sin spews out its dark cloud of danger. Prayer could be a natural magnet to men in that ominous environment—for Abram if not for Lot.

The confirmation of the covenant (vv. 14–17). The Lord appears to Abram to pledge giving him possession of the promised land (14, 15, 17) and also promise giving him propagation to populate it (16). It is in this flow of circumstances that attention focuses again on an altar. And an altar is a natural focus.

The Commitment of One Man (13:18)

Abram's response would fit in well as erecting an altar of:

Thanksgiving to the Lord. God's reaffirmation of His covenant promise was a great encouragement against the threat that the Canaanites posed (v. 13). Words to bolster Abram would be very relevant. The Lord's sufficiency to pursue so big a promise and deliver on it would freshen a man's vision when he was, as yet, only an upstart in the land.

Petition. This could easily be the quest of a man needing protection from Canaanites as well as Sodomites who so intensely set themselves against the Lord and His interests.

As time passed, the man of the altar would also have provocation caused by the Mesopotamian invasion against nearby areas (14:1–13). For this, petition would be rather spontaneous to quell a man's anxieties. As it worked, a fugitive's report of the invaders' conquest, even snatching away of Lot, provoked Abram's bold strike in reprisal (vv. 14–16). The God of the altar gave him a victory rout and rescue of Lot and all the prisoners of war. The covenant God whom Abram honored at his altar was not just a God of renown in theory but in concrete situations that were natural to elicit human prayer for assistance. The possessions that the armies had seized (vv. 11–12, 16) they were not able to defend against the power of the God who possessed heaven and earth (v. 19; cf. 1:1). The God to whom the entire earth belonged (cf. Ps. 24:1) blessed the pursuing Abram with the triumph.

A principle here is this. A covenant of God and men that expresses their separation to Him and away from values of those who spurn Him is important. Of even higher importance is the God Himself who initiated the covenant and keeps the soul safely in the midst of its enemies.

Genesis 14:18–20

Melchizedek's Prayer of Praise

Abram's Rout (14:13–17)

Worship of God at the altar had prepared Abram to be a man of resolute action against great odds. He made a torrid march with his own small army of servants and a few fighters from the invaded area. Hitting the encamped soldiers out of the dead of night, he came away with a great victory.

On his way homeward, Abram was to receive God's intervention in a pause that refreshed him. The king of Sodom came out of hiding from the invaders with the intent to meet Abram. He would later offer him the loot regained in the battle, but before he could reach him, God caused another king to intercept the returning hero. Melchizedek got there first!

Abram's Reassurance (14:18–20)

A priest-king who worshiped the Lord also came into Abram's life at a strategic time.

The things he brought (v. 18). Melchizedek brought bread and wine, apparently not only for refreshing food but as reminding tokens in worship to God. As God's priest, he pointed Abram's attention to God, using these as symbols of giving glory to Him.

The ways he blessed (vv. 19–20). Melchizedek led in prayer in two ways. First, he pronounced blessing on Abram. He drew his worship focus to God's preeminence ("God Most High") and His possession ("heaven and earth"). He was blessing the victor by placing emphasis on the One from whom his triumph came. And so, ultimately, he was giving a grand tribute to God, the giver of the victory. Winning came from the God preeminent above all and, in this recent case, overwhelmingly sufficient to uphold Abram's interests and adequate for him in covenant faithfulness. And it came from the God who displayed control over all, even a great Mesopotamian army, possessor even of heaven and earth. That would fix Abram's heart on Him as the author of the triumph.

Second, Melchizedek uttered blessing toward God, again crediting Him as "God Most High," worthy of all praiseful blessing. That he is thinking of the exhibit of His worthiness for praise in the battle to the north is clear. God "has delivered your enemies into your hand."

In view of such reminders, it would be fitting for Abram's life to be caught up in worshipful adoration. And we see that it was, as evidenced by his response.

Abram's Response (14:20–24)

"And he gave him a tenth of all." Abram made sure he gave God a gift memorializing His help, a token acknowledging that all really belonged to such a Possessor. He gave this to God but placed it in the custody of God's priest, to be used in God's interests. His testimony in this was personal, and at the same time he acted on behalf of his entire force of men, a good model to them in showing who should be worshiped.

Further display of Abram's response shows in his refusing gifts of Sodom's king (vv. 21–24). He was zealous that all the glory go to God for victory and all the the spoils taken in battle. As victor, Abram had the Kuman control over these riches, and he proved to be a man who honored God. Yet in the fairness of a good leader, he permitted men who joined with him in going to battle to take shares, a gesture that could leave a good testimony among nearby peoples.

Abram's personal involvement in the praiseful prayer in which Melchizedek led is etched in verse 22. "I have sworn," he says, "to the Lord God Most High, possessor of heaven and earth. . . ." He had done this in solemn praise to God, acknowledging that all things belonged to Him (cf. 1 Tim. 6:7, 17–19).

Several principles cap this off. First, certain people who walk very closely with God refresh others to draw near to Him also. Second, it stimulates the spirit to dwell on tributes to God for the greatness of who He is, and it exalts God as worthy. Third, a heart filled with God longs to give to Him out of the bounties with which His grace has enriched the life. Psalmists later do this often, and lavishly (cf. Ps. 48:1). Fourth, when one is supplied with the greatest possession, God Himself, he can confidently loosen his clutch on riches that this world provides and still see security ahead.

Genesis 15:1–21

Abram's Question in Prayer

Several times in Scripture those who pray probe God's wisdom by questions about details that honestly disturb them. An example is in Habakkuk's dialogue with God (Hab. 1–2).

Here, Abram presses legitimate queries, and God answers fairly. We see, concerning Abram, three things.

His Resource in a Person (15:1)

God appeared to Abram in a vision. The man would see certain aspects of that in verse 17.

The exhortation—"fear not" (v. 1). God is fully aware of His servant's fears and wants to calm them as he later offers composure through Paul in Philippians 4:6, 7. He approaches Abram with the exhortation He uses most frequently in His Word: "Fear not." It is frequent because a man's heart is assaulted by so many fears. In this case, at least three matters could be eating at the heart of Abram, three things to fear. One could be a possible return of armies regrouped from Mesopotamia. As they had come, they could come again, this time with revenge in their eyes. Another fear could be in second thoughts about letting go of all the riches he could have taken from Sodom's king, riches he had declined, riches he might have used. Finally, he realizes what incites in him a very pressing uneasiness. He voices this in verses 2–3. He needs a son if the covenant promise is to be fulfilled.

The encouragement: "I am" (v. 1). God's own resource is so consistently the antidote to human fear in Scripture. So it is in Isaiah 41:10 and 40:29–31. These describe what God is, how near He is, and what He can do to relieve the anxiety men feel. God encourages Abram by two things He is to him. He is, first, "your shield" for protection. This would be relevant for either of his first two fears above, the showdown return of the enemy or the refusal to seize advantage of riches. God will protect him against all that could harm him; security in safety is his because God is his "I am." God is, second, "Your reward" which will be very great. This "reward" can be in children as the Scripture later shows (Ps. 127:3) and as is relevant here. Of course the "reward" can be various aspects of blessing, such as wages or supply to meet one's needs (Gen. 30:28, 32, 33), even a soldier's (Ezek. 29:18, 19) or a shepherd's (Zech. 11:12). Or the reward can consist of passage-money to get one where he is going (Jon. 1:3). God was Abram's supply, sufficient for any situation. Not only protection was his, but provision.

His Request in Prayer (15:2, 3)

Abram speaks to God in prayer, piercing right to the need that tries him the most. He asks what God will give him to remedy his situation so far, having no son to realize fulfillment of 12:1–3 and 13:14–17.

His Reassurance in a Promise (15:4–21)

The pledge of a son (v. 4). The Lord promises to provide an heir from Abram's own body. This He would fulfill in Chapter 21. The heir would not be the patriarch's steward, but a direct son. And so it was definite for faith to contemplate. Abram would fail (Gen. 16), God would not (Gen. 21).

The picture of the seed (v. 5). God used the innumerable stars in the sky, beyond human counting, as a graphic picture of the many descendants He would give. This is the second picture of a vast progeny in the covenant. The first one was "as the dust of the earth" (13:16). The two pictures are both combined after Abram's offering that went all the way (22:17).

The pursuit of the subject (vv. 6–21). Abram's response is one of faith (v. 6a; Ps. 56:3). He believes God will do what He promises. Then God's reckoning to him is righteousness (v. 6b). This is evidently in view of his faith ever since 12:1 (and in 11:26ff.), summarizing the reckoning God made. He could have been saved from the time of his earliest faith.

The passage goes on to give God's reminder of His identity. He is the God who brought Abram out of Ur to give him this land (v. 7). This precipitates Abram's request for a confirmation (v. 8), a prayer in essence. How will he have assurance that he will possess the land? To this God responds with His ratification (vv. 9–21). He enacts a formal covenant ceremony, using a custom of the time, to register the strongest kind of verification that He surely will make good on the promise. He directs Abram to lay out parts of sacrifices in two rows. Normally, two men formalizing a covenant agreement would join hands, walk together between the sacrifices, and both promise to fulfill their aspects in the covenant. They would say, in effect, "May my life be dismembered as these animal parts, may my very being be dissolved, should I fail to do all I pledge!"

How significant here that Abram falls asleep and is not able to not walk between the sacrifices with God. But coming to an awareness of the vision during the ratifying ceremony, he sees a brightness of God alone passing through. The same reminds Abram of a smoking oven and a flaming torch (v. 17). God is the only party who enacts the covenant in this case. He swears by the certainty of His own life, the continuance of His own being, that He will fulfill His promise. It is His unconditional, gracious covenant. He cannot fail.

The Lord predicts to Abram that his descendants would sojourn in another land, but He would bring them back to the covenant land promised (vv. 12–16). Abram apparently receives those words in a dream vision while asleep (v. 12). God follows up the enactment and the words with further promise that He will give the land, and even specifies its boundaries north and south (vv. 18–22).

The chapter combines God's promise, prayer (in questions), God's further promise, and God's ratification showing that Abram's prayer concerns are sure of answers with God's blessing. Illustration is evident here that some prayers can have answers fulfilled even centuries later. It is mind-boggling yet true.

Principles abound. First, when God enters into a promise, we can talk freely with Him about things that go with it as we ask and receive. Second, be specific in asking of a God who is specifically able. Third, God cares before we care about what matters in our godly hearts (cf. 1 Pet. 5:7), so we can face a big-hearted God with big asking. Fourth, in some prayers the answer of the almighty God is so much more than the one request we asked (cf. Eph. 3:20).

Genesis 16:8, 13

Hagar's Prayer on a Retreat

Sarai's servant woman deserted Abram and Sarai, talked with the Lord, and obeyed His counsel to return to her servant role.

The Reason for the Retreat (16:1–6)

Hagar's reason unfolds clearly in three things.

The proposal of Sarai (vv. 1–3). Abram's wife was disturbed over her inability to conceive a child to realize the covenant. So she succumbed to a method not of the Lord but of the flesh, not of faith but of human sinful worry. Aware of a custom in her day that the world relied on, she resorted to it to remedy the childlessness in the home. The custom was that a wife unable to bear a child could provide a servant woman to take her place in sexual relations with her husband and produce a child for her.

The device was not of God's will, but hers and Abram's. They should have trusted Him to fulfill His own promise in His own way and time. God clearly shows later that His will is Isaac, begotten by His power that enables Sarai (Gen. 17:20, 21; 18:10; 21:12). And His Spirit validates the son borne by His power, not just of the flesh (Gal. 4:24ff.). Believers do not need to gain their blessings by capitulating to worldly devices that run counter to God's will.

Abram, inclined to Sarai's proposal, went against God's design of marriage as a union of two people (Gen. 2:24) and engaged in sexual intimacy with Hagar.

The pride of Hagar (v. 4). Once the servant woman saw that she was pregnant, she felt superior to Sarai and held her in contempt. In her own pride, she fancied Abram's attention as promoting her to a higher place than Sarai and was haughty. This catapulted Sarai to decisive action.

The punishment by Sarai (vv. 5–6). The wife blamed Abram for Hagar's spite, for she felt that he should have set the record straight about his affections but had been lax. Abram responded by making it clear that Sarai was his wife and could exercise authority over the servant woman. She held the prerogative to deal with Hagar as she chose. So Sarai made life so miserable for Hagar that the maid retreated, running away from the home, rather than living in submission. She plodded her way toward Egypt, her former home (cf. v. 3).

The Rendezvous during the Retreat (16:7–14)

The coming of the angel (vv. 7, 8). Hagar had stopped at a spring to refresh herself from the weary trek. She suddenly became aware that an angel was there, and he confronted her about her flight from where she belonged.

The angel was in this case the Lord in verse 13, just as one of three angels who later visits Abraham (Gen. 18) turns out to be the Lord Himself.

Hagar's visitor at the spring asked her the lead question. "Where have you come from and where are you going?" Her words in reply to him are, in essence, prayer. She answered honestly, without hedging. She was fleeing from her mistress Sarai.

The counsel of the angel (vv. 9–12). He then forthrightly counsels Hagar along two lines. First, God's will for her is to go back and serve in submission to Sarai's authority (9). Then His promise to her is designed to reassure her. He will bless her with descendants through the child she bears (10). And He also will bless the child himself, a son. She is to name the boy Ishmael, meaning "God hears," in honor of the Lord for His hearing her in her need. Like his mother, however, the son will be flighty, following traits of antagonism to others.

The compliance of Hagar (vv. 13–16). The woman's submission at last shows itself in two ways. One is in her designation of the spot where God met her and turned her life around. Her name for it is "Beer-lahai-roi," signifying "a well of the Living One who sees me." He had seen her far out in the desert retreating from duty, as He would later see Jonah. As she thinks about the significance of God seeing and knowing her so particularly, she is baffled by His mercy when she had been so selfish and head-strong. She had removed herself from serving in her place of duty, and had even spitefully borne away the child for which Abram and Sarai waited. She is in tender wonderment that God has spared her in the confrontation. "Have I even remained alive here after seeing Him?"

Hagar's compliance with the Lord's counsel becomes clear in a second way as well. It is in her delivery of the son (vv. 15–16). She trudged back to her place of failure to try again and bore the son to Abram. Her time of hearing God's words and praying to Him registered a deep impression that resulted in its fruit.

What, now, of beacons for the prayer life? First, prayer to the God who hears can work even at the back side of a remote desert that seems to be at the end of nowhere. Second, God can give new, wise direction in an interchange of prayer overshadowed by His counseling Word. Third, even a lowly servant in a home turns out to have high value for a compassionate God to pursue in a venue of prayer. Fourth, God not only listens to prayer, but displays ability in the ways He can look after one who turns to do what He says.

Genesis 17:15–21

Abram's Doubt in Prayer

Sometimes in His mercy, God overcomes man's doubt as he talks with Him and gives him blessing despite his misgivings. This is the scenario here in the great chapter reaffirming covenant fulfillment and specifying the sign (circumcision) of that covenant. Prayer plays a vital role in this.

God's Design through Sarah (17:15–16)

God reaffirms His covenant that parents of males in Israel are to observe. In doing this, the Lord tells the patriarch that his name will no longer be Abram meaning "high father," but Abraham, denoting "father of a multitude" (v. 5). For him God will provide multitudes of descendants, agreeing with earlier pictures of their mind-boggling numbers, like dust (13:16), and like stars (15:5). This brings the focus to Sarai, and on to the prayer.

The meaning of her name (v. 15). As God reveals a new name for Abram, so He does for Sarai. She is henceforth to be Sarah. The first name means "my princess," the latter "princess." The difference may be that she was Abram's princess, involving her relationship to him, but now she is to be "princess related to many who will come in her lineage (v. 16). As Eve was mother of all living among humanity, Sarah is mother to her descendants. This is the next idea.

The multiplication of her seed (v. 16). God promised Abraham innumerable descendants earlier in the chapter, and kings in his line (v. 6). The kings will be Saul, David, many others on the throne, and finally the greatest Son of David (Matt. 1:1).

Abraham's Doubt (17:17, 18)

At first, the man reacts to this promise as a laughing matter. The impossibility of it all overwhelms him in two ways. He speaks to God, engaging in the essence of prayer, in this instance asking questions (cf. 15:2). The impossibility is in his being a hundred years old and Sarah ninety.

Rather immediately, Abraham engages in prayerful intercession. He wistfully exclaims, "Oh that Ishmael might live before thee." Humanly speaking, Ishmael, who already is living, seems to be the only hope of gaining descendants. Abraham longs that God would bless that tangible possibility. And in this he expresses doubt, unbelief. Yet God replies graciously, despite doubt such as is repeated in 18:11–15.

God's Definiteness through Sarah (18:19–21)

He answers Abraham's prayerful yearning with His real plan. He cites three details.

His provision of a child through the wife (v. 19a). Sarah herself is to bear a child. God is able to overcome seeming impossibilities.

His particularization of a covenant with her son (vv. 19c, 21). Sarah is to give birth to a son, to be named Isaac, through whom God will fulfill His covenant of 12:1–3, 7. God even specifies when the son is to be born (17:21), and gives a reminder of this in 18:14. When Sarah laughs in doubt in the later account, the Lord again specifies the name Isaac, and the interesting meaning of the name is "laughter." It will call to memory human collapse in not believing and God's power to do what man dimisses as impossible (cf. 18:14a).

His prospering of Ishmael (v. 20). Pursuing integrity to His promise to Hagar in chapter 16, the Lord will multiply Ishmael's descendants, too. Yet His covenant blessing will run through Isaac's descendants (v. 21). For this is an answer to petition, the son Abram prayed to receive in 15:2.

Now principles are apropos. First, even those who are best in faith have times of doubt, yet the giving God remains steadfast. Second, the Lord can get very specific in His method of answering prayer. After all, He was very specific in details of stars He put in space, people He created, the covenant He made with Abram, and many other things. So why not in prayer? Third, gaze not at the impossibility before God but at God before the things that seem impossible. Spies later scouting out the promised land, like Joshua and Caleb, would look at the challenge in light of God, and would see how small this was before Him who could assure it would be done.

Genesis 18

Abraham's Intercession for Sodom

Three angelic visitors pay a call on Abraham. One of the guests promises that Sarah will bear a son at this time next year (vv. 10, 14), and this one is defined to be the Lord. Sarah laughs behind the tent flap, but the Lord is aware of the doubt and calls her on it. She then speaks to the Lord in what is the essence of prayer, in this case denying her laugh due to fear of some reprisal. He affirms that she did laugh, and that settles the matter, yet He is gracious. Later, as Abraham walks with the three to see them off, the Lord renews His promise to make him a great nation and bless other nations through him. He also speaks of His concern against the terrible sin of Sodom and His resolve to bring judgment on those who wallow in the filth.

This flow of events brings the reader to Abraham's prayerful concern. He asks, "Will you indeed sweep away the righteous with the wicked?" (v. 23). Lot and his family lived there!

His Cases of Intercession (18:24ff.)

Abraham pleads for the sparing of the righteous in Sodom, moving in six steps of intercession. His prayers of advocacy mingle in dialogue with the Lord as Jeremiah's do (Chaps. 14–15) and Habakkuk's as well (Chaps. 1–2). They also are in three aspects of prayer that the Scripture often uses, *question*, *affirmation*, and of course *intercession.* A beginning of praise for God's worthiness is also vital for the six stages (v. 25).

When some criticize Abraham for stopping at six steps, short of seven for completeness, the fault-finding is artificial. Abraham displays selflessness in righteous advocacy for others, not sin. This is upheld by a number of reflections: (1) He voices concern (v. 23); (2) lauds God's righteousness (v. 25); (3) displays humility (v. 27); (4) draws God's commendation (v. 19); (5) receives no rebuke for a sin or failure (as in Gen. 3, 4, 6, 9, 12, 16, 19, 20, 25, 27, 34, 37, 38, etc.); (6) is in line with biblical examples where prayers are short of seven, as those of Jesus (Matt. 26:44; Mark 8:24, 25); and (7) the passage closes saying that the Lord had finished talking with him (Gen. 18:33). This is quite different from suggesting that his prayers had fallen short of completion.Still another point is that Abraham did not fail in faith by ceasing after narrowing the number to ten. It is reasonable that he stopped at ten due to a hope that more of Lot's family and contacts were righteous than he felt God knew to be the reality. Abraham starts with fifty, drops to forty-five, then forty, and prays from there on in tens—thirty, twenty, and ten. The next step would be none. He possibly felt that five would be too few to hope God would spare. It turns out that even five was above the true number, one (Lot) or three (Lot plus his two daughters).

The intercessor's questions in prayer posed in genuine concern for people's welfare can be as legitimate as questions in direct conversation with Jesus when He walked the earth. Also, affirmations in prayer (vv. 25, 27, 31a) spoken in respectful submission can be a part of true worship. Of course, intercessions pleading for others can be with sensitivity to God's own will as the intercessor is respectfully committed to His purposes.

Are there principles? Yes. First, we learn that Abraham had others on his heart in prayer, and so can we (cf. 1 Sam. 12:23). Second, it is no insult to God to reason sincerely with Him, as Abraham thought from fifty to ten. God looks at the heart and the motives. Third, when God has "finished talking with" a believer on one occasion as here, He will be there for the next prayer also (cf. 20:17).

He seems to be endless in His interest, resource, and the variety of situations He is up to.

Genesis 20

Prayers of Abimelech and Abraham

Prayer occurring in a dream is unusual, yet it does appear elsewhere, as in Solomon's prayer (1 Kgs. 3).

The Cause of the Dream (20:1–3)

Abraham has expressed faith at times (15:6; cf. 12:1; 18:23ff.) but also a lack of it (12:9ff.; 16:1ff.). Here he fails again, out of step with his action in better moments. Dwelling in Gerar, in Philistine territory, he spins a half-truth, amounting to a lie, that Sarah is his sister, not his wife. He falls into the same sin as in Chapter 12.

King Abimelech, who has no rightful relation with Sarah, exerts his royal authority and lust selfishly to command that the woman be taken. This step, which places Sarah in danger of being violated, causes God to throw up a roadblock to stop Abimelech's scheming designs.

The Concern of Abimelech (20:3–5)

God moves so quickly that the king has not yet carried out his intentions. The latter is shocked by God confronting him in a dream, stating the married status of Sarah and warning that the king is in mortal peril. Abimelech pleads for his life in the dream, in which God has power to make things vividly clear. As to particular awareness of Sarah's marriage, the leader has been previously uninformed, though this does not make him blameless of high-handedness. He is in panic for himself and others in his nation.

The Compassion to Abimelech (20:6–7)

God acknowledges the king's unawareness and stresses His own providence to prevent a wrong from distorting the oneness of Sarah and Abraham (Gen. 2:24). He will lift the pressure if Abimelech returns Sarah unmolested; otherwise, He will put to death all the king's people.

The Clearing of Abimelech (20:8–16)

Part of this is through the king's own zeal to correct the wrong (vv. 8–16). And part is through Abraham's prayer for him and his people (vv. 17–18). God had made a point with the king that Abraham would pray for him (v. 7), and Abraham does (v. 17). The answer God works is a healing of the wombs of the king's wife and maids, assuming some kind of distress they would have gone on suffering.

That God would hear the prayer of a man who had lied (cf. Ps. 66:18) is a difficulty. It can be resolved when one remembers that those who trust God do fluctuate between righteousness and sin, being imperfect and inconsistent. God also is forgiving, and Abraham could have dealt with Him about his sin and predicament. The passage does not supply details that could have transpired. If God waited for any believer to prove flawless at all times before He could honor his prayer, human failure would close the door to any blessed answer.

Let us finish this with principles. First, though God does not normally honor prayers of the unsaved, He can when it is His will or when a believer prays for an unsaved person. Second, it does not matter whether one person or many is involved in a possible answer from God, for He can work with few or with many. Third, one person who prays can, with God, form a majority, whatever the odds. Our prayers and His power can form a mighty combination.

Genesis 21:33

God's Preparation of His Man for Trial (21:33, 34)

The next scenes one sees of Abraham are his receiving and weaning of the promised son (cf. v. 12), sending away Hagar and Ishmael, agreeing peacefully with the Philistines, and continuing in a life of prayer.

His Planting of a Tree (21:33a)

He planted a tamarisk tree to provide shade and solitude in a special place where he could worship. His putting the foliage there seems to indicate that he expected God to sustain it and him. Even his Philistine neighbors testified, "God is with you in all that you do" (v. 22).

His Prayer to the Lord (21:33b-34)

The direction of it. He "called with the name of the Lord. . . ." As in 4:26, the words include the same verb "called," the "name" with the prefix letter (preposition) ***beth*** meaning "with" or "on," and "the Lord." Again, as in 4:26 and a number of other passages mentioned there, Abraham is not testifying to (proclaiming) the Lord as the One he worships. He is directing his worship to the Lord, calling with His name, invoking it in prayer. This is as, many centuries later, believers would be given the privilege to pray in Jesus' name (John 14–16). Possibly the freshening life of the tree reminded Abraham of the life of God, the sustainer, Himself "everlasting."

The duration of it. Since verse 34 immediately notes that Abraham sojourned in the Philistine area "many days," the intention may be to leave the impression that his prayer continued in a pattern. That God did bless him in all that he did (v. 22) favors his ongoing realization of His blessing and the naturalness of his seeking Him. To the same effect is 18:19. Then, when the Lord calls upon him to face the greatest trial of his life so far (22:1), his dwelling long before the Lord has prepared him to obey resolutely.

Principles enclose this passage. First, having an apt place to pray can be a great help. Some use a boulder, or a secluded nook in a garden, or a resort under a brush canopy, or an old car, or a tree crotch, or a forest path, even a quiet room—on and on. They come there to meet with God, the God who is there. Second, a place alone is not enough, for once there, it is engaging with God that counts. Third, if God gives "many days" in an area, let these be days marked by going apart to Him. Some fall apart, but others go apart and find the way to meet life head on, with God ahead.

Genesis 22

Prayer in Responding to a Trial

God's preparing Abraham has just been the focus above, and this appears to relate well in "after these things" (22:1).

God's Purpose in the Trial (22:1a, 14)

It is quickly clear that God's aim is to "test" Abraham (vv. 1a, 2, 12, 18) and to show that he can be trusted (v. 14). In his immediate response to do what God directs and his later actual offering of his son, he meets the test with God's approval. In verse 12, God testifies, "for now I know that you fear God," and in verse 18, God's angel says, "because you have obeyed My voice." The angel is apparently the Lord. Abraham showed that he could be trusted (v. 14) in that he has expected God to provide an offering and for Him to keep Isaac safe in the final analysis (vv. 6, 7). And God also shows His trustworthiness through His over-arching faithfulness. For He does provide (v. 14).

Abraham's Profile In the Trial

The true character God can build within a man surfaces in several traits in action, the fruit of the faith.

He is prayerful (v. 1). Having been available to the Lord's calling on Him in prayer (21:33), Abraham now continues to be available. He is sensitive, approachable, ready to do God's will. "Here I am." This is the shortest kind of prayer in the Bible, one Hebrew word, hanani. Abraham was listening to God's word, and his own tender words in a breath of prayer are a natural flow with this.

He is prompt (v. 3). Once God has called him to take his son and offer him, he is not a man to dilly-dally. He rises early and goes resolutely about the details of carrying out God's will.

He is worshipful (v. 5). Arriving near the mountain spot where he is to offer, he leaves his men at a camp site to await his return. He and his son would go and worship.

He is trustful (vv. 5, 8). He can tell the men he expects Isaac to be alive to return to the camp after the offering. Hebrews 11:19 supplies insight. He believed that if need be God was able to bring Isaac back from the dead to be with him when he rejoined the men. As a father, he could also answer his son's question about the sacrifice. God would provide one. Of course God did! We can summarize these verses by saying that the father of faith expected Isaac's return (v. 5) and God's resource to make this happen (v. 8).

He is resolute (vv. 9–10). The person Abraham takes up the mountain is his son, his only son (of the covenant, 21:12), whom he loves, Isaac (v. 2)! Yet the offerer is ever so resolute. Each act is a new focus on that. He goes to God's appointed place, builds the altar, arranges the wood, binds Isaac, arranges him on the altar atop the wood, stretches out his hand, and lifts up the knife.

As the knife is apparently poised, Abraham's God, even more resolute, and always on time, calls to him. Now it is not the patriarch calling to the Lord (21:33), but the Lord calling to His servant. "Abraham, Abraham," He shouts, doubling this intensity. Great drama is in that saving voice. And in prayer, his hand poised but not plunging, Abraham, as in verse 1, is available to God. "Here I am." God stills Abraham's hand to transfer it to another sacrifice. He knows that His servant fears Him, for in Abraham's heart, the obedience has gone all the way. God notes the purpose that is in the heart, whether David's desire to build a temple (1 Kgs. 8:18) or Abraham's decision to obey at so dear a cost.

A ram God has provided near at hand and again right on time is before Abraham's gaze. So this was God's plan when He put him to the test! The father releases his son and offers the ram, no doubt an Old Testament picture in advance of the greater offering God's own Son would become (cf. John 1:29).

He is thankful (v. 14). Not only does this verse reflect that Abraham could be trusted to expect God's provision, but it also shows his gratitude for the provision. Thanksgiving so pervades Abraham that he names the place "Jehovah-jireh," commemorating that "The Lord Will Provide."

The angel then freshly reaffirms the Abrahamic Covenant which the Lord has frequently emphasized (Gen. 12, 13, 15, 17, 18, 21). Verses 16–18 are a record of this. So Abraham, and with him Isaac (though not mentioned here), return as the father had promised to his men at camp. All is well as they journey home (v. 19).

Principles are meaningful. One is that some prayer can be ever so brief ("Here I am"), yet ever so much in touch with God. One might exult, "You are beautiful," or "Thank you," or "You are here!," or "I love You," or "You are so good," or "I need You." Many are the possibilities. Another principle is apropos: God may work "in the nick of time," but that is still on time. Third, prayer counts best when one means business with God and gets to the matter of obeying (cf. John 14:21–23). Fourth, God is ever testing us, as He did Abraham (cf. Deut. 8:2). Will we be prompt to pray and follow through sincerely? This is the servant path and the path of blessing in finding out the greatness of what God can do. Determine to live life on that basis, and go for it—all out.

Genesis 24

The Servant's Petition and Praise

Abraham's oldest servant, possibly Eliezer of 15:2, now in his advanced senior age, prays and praises God during his journey to bring home a bride for Isaac.

The Prelude to the Prayer (24:1–11)

Action has its catalyst in Abraham's concern to secure marriage for Isaac to carry on the covenant fulfillment in his own family. His urgency is to keep the line as pure as he can and true to faith in the God who initiated the covenant.

The commission (vv. 1–6). Summoning his trusted servant, Abraham commits to him the charge to travel several hundred miles and back. The reason for the trip to Padan-aram is to secure a wife for the son of the covenant (cf. 21:12), and the covenant leader wants the servant to utter an oath of promise as God is his witness that he will carry out the mission.

The comfort of God's help (vv. 7–8). First Abraham comforts the servant about success by the guarantee in the very Person of the covenant God. He is the Lord with whose name men have been calling in prayer since 4:26. He is the Lord in whom Abraham has put his faith (15:6). Not only that, He is the Lord of heaven, bringing His power of creation into the picture and possibly suggesting His control over the whole span of distance the trek entailed. For the servant, this would be relevant as the route to the east would stretch far off over the circle of the earth under heaven. All was under the power of the God of creation in Genesis 1. A third comfort was that this Lord and God had acted in His own authority to take Abraham from his home far away to lead him to Canaan. It was He who had initiated that and carried it out by unfailing support, and similarly He could support the servant on a trip back the other way! His own will acting in the first case would be a comforting force in the present one. Still further, this Lord and God had expressly spoken to Abraham and guaranteed by personal oath that He would give the land to his descendants. His own honor was at stake not to fail to make good on this, and the wife the servant was to bring to Isaac must relate to *this* land (cf. v. 5). Added to this encouragement, Abraham is confident of one other detail. God would send His angel to guide the servant and assure that he would accomplish his mission.The servant has uttered no doubt about the Lord, directly. Still, he entertains the possibility of man's failure to support him (v. 5). This points up a frequent human problem relating to prayer, an inconsistency in trusting God for all aspects. Or it might illustrate the factor that, while a person believes God is entirely faithful to do His will, he is not always certain from the human side that God's will is infallibly grasped. God may not choose to work the particular way a man holds Him to. At least the servant has this one hesitation (v. 5). Abraham is perceptive of his difficulty, and addresses it. In case he has not correctly understood how God will provide and the woman will not come back with the servant, "then you will be free from this my oath" (v. 8). Of course, whatever is God's will, the servant can expect Him to work even in the wills of men.

The commitment of the servant (v. 9). As Abraham has already proposed (v. 2), his servant displays his commitment by a sign that pledges his honor with his oath. Other acts could formalize and guarantee a promise, as when they walk hand in hand between sacrifices (15:9–10, 17). But in this case the oath to fulfill is sealed by the servant placing his hand under the second party's thigh. Both of the men pledged commitment (vv. 8, 9, 41). Since progeny to realize the covenant of 12:1–3, 7 was strategic, it was fitting to use the gesture near the area of human generation. It was, as well, a powerful part of the body and so could convey the voucher, "I most solemnly guarantee to do in my power, God enabling me, what you yourself would do. Consider it as good as done."

The caravan for the mission (vv. 10, 11). The servant soon sets out on his journey with ten camels, food and gifts, and men in his party (cf. vv. 32, 54).

So the prelude has set the stage for the servant's prayer.

The Petition in the Prayer (24:12–14)

Reaching his destination in Mesopotamia, the servant positions himself where women by custom come to secure water, and prays.

The summary of his prayer (v. 12). He simply petitions for success in securing the bride by the covenant mercy this would be to his master. He is quite specific in this and in the details that follow.

The specifics of his prayer (vv. 13–14). No "beating around the bush" characterizes this request. No wandering around the Milky Way in nebulous words is here. The servant cuts right to the point as to his place, women who fill their water pots here, the very woman, and further particulars to confirm that this is of God. Others like Gideon with his fleece would quell their human fears by spelling their needs right out to the Lord. The servant is passionate for God's guiding to help the bride who would help carry on the covenant. Let her be the woman who would take the time, lower her vessel to quench his thirst, and even go to the trouble of watering the caravan camels.

The Provisions for the Prayer (24:15ff.)

These are many. God is specific, too. Before the prayer is over, the answer is arriving (vv. 15–16)! Rebekah, of the right family, pops on the scene. She does the very thing the servant has requested; he drinks, as do his camels (17–22). God does even more than the man petitioning has mentioned in prayer (cf. Eph. 3:20). Lodging is waiting for him and all those in the caravan (vv. 25, 31, 33). The family and the woman are willing to say "yes" to his huge request (50–51, 57–61). And the comfort that God's answer gives is satisfying (67).

The Praise in the Prayer (24:26, 27)

Praise to God pours forth from the servant's heart and lips (26–27, 48; cf. 52). He bows in worship and utters praise that recognizes the blessedness of the Lord. His accolades enter into specific facets—display of covenant loyalty, truth, and guidance (27). He extols God in the presence of Rebekah and later her entire family (52).

The family's actions in the will of the God who inclines hearts are part of the scene. The servant had broached the very possibility of not securing the bride (5) and Abraham had comforted him about this (8). But where faith or human knowledge of the future come short, God sees the entire picture and arranges all things to work together for good (cf. Rom. 8:28). The family is positve, Rebekah's heart inclines (cf. Phil. 2:13), and the family unites in prayer (60). When, in saying goodbye, they bless Rebekah, this is essentially in intercessory prayer, wishing God's covenant blessing on her future and her descendants. Their sentiment for her posterity and their possession is in the will of God, true to His own word, and an instance of prayer in a prophetical wish. God can put His prompt in people so that they pray in the stream of His plan (Jer. 29:10–12; 33:3 with 33:4–26).

Consider principles. First, we, too, can pray while on the way in doing the will of God. God is approachable at the outset, in the midst, and at the end of things. Second, God may send us a long way and supply His answers with success at different stages of the journey.

Genesis 24:63

Isaac's Meditation in the Field

It is quite possible, and some believe, that Isaac's meditation included prayer. Certain factors enhance this as plausible.

First, forms of the word, whether noun or verb, are used in the Old Testament for meditation or rehearsing a matter in the mind silently (Ps. 77:8, Heb. 7; 119:53, 23, 27, 48, 78) or while speaking aloud to God. In the silent times, it appears for reflecting on God's works (Ps. 77:8) or word (119:15, etc.). In speaking in prayer, it is also for His acts (Ps. 105:2; 145:15), His word (119:97, 99), or voicing needs and seeking His help (Ps. 55:17; Heb. 18).

In view of this, the meditation can refer to a prayerful flow of thought or even issue in words in Isaac's case.

Second, Isaac's context supplies substantial relevancy for his prayer at such a stratetic time. His father Abraham has practiced prayer in the sweep of his life after God called him. His servant has felt moved to pray over the very concern of securing Isaac a wife. On the homeward side of the scene, it would be highly probable that the specific man to whom the bride was coming would be exercised in prayer. If so, the prayer would naturally be in thanksgiving for the covenant God's past faithfulness, such as in his own sparing in

Genesis 22. And it would relevantly entail petition for the safety of the party in the caravan along the way, approval by the family, and the bride's consent. With the latter cogent detail, on which so much depended, Isaac would be apt to petition for his own joyful approval once the woman arrived and her genuine pleasure with him, both so necessary for a happy union.

The covenant son's later prayer over his wife's *barrenness* (25:21) leaves the possibility of his prayer even earlier about *betrothal* itself. Both are strategic to the covenant.

A banner thought is evident here. For a truly godly believer, thoughts of meditation are often in direct communion with God. As the compass needle orientates to the north, the heart stayed on God (cf. Isa. 26:3) gravitates even to prayer and to the One who is Lord over prayer. Another principle emerges. The one who looks to God can often find that as he meditates in a life of need, God has some answer already on the way.

Genesis 25:21, 22

Isaac's and Rebekah's Prayers

Isaac spoke to God about his wife's inability to have a child, and during her pregnancy she was exercised in prayer about her disturbing feelings.

Isaac's Concern Arousing Prayer (25:21)

This is the situation of verse 21. He did not repeat a human device such as Abraham and Sarah had in Chapter 16. He took the matter to God. Of course, upon reflection, he would have encouragement to expect the Lord's help. The covenant promises showed this to be consistent. Children must come of this union to continue the covenant fulfillment, just as Isaac himself had come (21:12). The covenant God had acted in complete faithfulness to spare him at Mount Moriah, to give success to Abraham's mission for his servant and give him a woman who brought him comfort (24:67). He could intercede for his wife and for the sake of God's will with much to stir his faith.

Rebekah's Conception Answering the Prayer (25:21c)

God answered by granting her ability to conceive and gave her the anticipation of a child. This surely caused much joy for both partners. For Isaac, it was a confirmation replacing concern when humanly speaking no possibility was in sight (cf. 2 Cor. 5:7). For Rebekah, elation surged due to her God-given ability to please Isaac who counted on her, and the opening up of a way to see the fulfillment of all that Abraham had sought in sending his servant to her. Fulfillment was sweet to contemplate, replacing a frustration that she was letting Isaac down and being a barrier to family hopes on both sides.

God's Choice Answering the Prayer (25:22–26)

Rebekah's perplexity in prayer (v. 22). Though she did not realize it yet, "children" had been conceived. More than the child they expected was within. Her pregnancy was so turbulent and painful at times that the obvious movement inside her indicated something very disturbing. The struggling she had to bear brought her to the Lord in grief. "If You are indeed working fulfillment of Your covenant promise, which suggests only good, then why this which seems to suggest trouble?"

God's plan in answering prayer (vv. 23–26). The prayers of both Isaac and Rebekah have related to a child to further the covenant. God's reply, possibly in a vision (as 15:1), focuses here as well. He reveals the fact of twins that helps explain the jostling and also the dominance of the younger, in His own will. More is involved even than two individuals; two nations will result, one having ascendancy over the other. Verses 24–26 recount the births of Esau, the older, and Jacob, the younger, the latter gripping the heel of his brother and the names of the two given due to what the parents observe when they appear. The first is reddish, suggesting Esau and later his people, Edom, meaning red. The latter is Jacob, "heel-gripper."

Fresh principles crop up. First, God wants our prayers to be about "everything" (Phil. 4:6) and to relate in some way to doing His will. For to us as to Paul, "to live is Christ" (Phil. 1:21). Second, God is altogether able to bring about what is a part of His plan, and prayer can meet Him in a harmony of fellowship concerning this.

Genesis 26:25

Isaac's Altar of Prayer

The appearance of the Lord to Isaac seems immediately to excite him to erect the altar. What the Lord does is repeat to him His covenant with Abraham (12:1–3, 7, etc.). He introduces Himself as the God of Abraham, and of course of Abraham's covenant son to whom He now speaks. His presence and His blessing in Isaac's life personally and in multiplication are His emphases. Back in 26:2–5, He had also encouraged Isaac by covenant pledges, in that case to multiply him and his descendants as the stars, and bless all nations through them.

His altar would have vital relevance to his relationship with God, then. Not only would prayer in thanksgiving for the Lord's new words be appropriate. He might also voice gratitude for God protecting Rebekah and him in Philistine country when he had lied, saying she was his sister, and she might have been violated (vv. 6–11). Thanksgiving would be fitting as well for God blessing him one hundredfold (v. 12) and granting him peaceful possession of a well (v. 22). In addition to the prayers of appreciation, the altar might have been the scene of petitions for the Lord's continuing care to bring His promises to further fulfillment.

The Response of Isaac (v. 25)

His preparation of an altar. God's word to him is the catalyst.

His prayer to the Lord. Prayer is natural here as the words "called with (on) the name of the Lord" suggest. The wording as in 4:26

reappears. Along with thanksgiving and petition, as have just been suggested, Isaac may have prayed voicing affirmation. To affirm the Lord as His God as Jacob would do in 28:21 would be a corollary of putting up an altar devoted to His name.

His pitching of his tent. The act of planning to dwell in the area of Beersheba (v. 23) is a demonstration that Isaac is resting in faith's confidence. God's word in verse 24, and His words earlier in 26:2–5 assure him of the Lord's presence and blessing. The covenant son depends on the Lord to take care of him there.

His placing of a well. Philistine leaders visit Isaac, seeking a pledge of peace. This meeting in verses 26–31 includes the guests' observation that the Lord has been with Isaac (v. 28), and they respect his growing success. This is so real to them that they desire his pledge of friendliness to guarantee their own safety. The meeting is followed by the mention of the well (v. 32). Work to gain water there began in verse 25; now Isaac's men report back their success in having it ready. Finally, the meaning of the well is significant. Beersheba (v. 33) signifies "well of oath," memorializing the area of the oath Isaac has just entered into with the Philistine leaders. But an even more basic reason gives rise to the name, too. Isaac has been naming wells he brought into use by designations honoring Abraham's earlier names (v. 18). Abraham had called this well by his own oath with the Philistines (21:31), so a renewing of the same title is apt.

Blessing that the neighbors mention and blessing in peace with the neighbors are evidences that God is fulfilling His will (26:2–5; 24). It is possible that they also are fruit of His word impacting Isaac in his altar prayers, as God's word and prayer faithful to it can so vitally mingle (cf. John 15:7, 8).

The Problem Posed by Esau (vv. 34–35)

Esau acted in stark contrast to Abraham, who had been so careful that the covenant family tree branch through his own people (Gen. 24).

Abraham had specified that his son's wife not be from the Canaanite women. Now Esau marries Canaanite stock and even does it twice, Judith and Basemath. This will stand in distinction to Isaac's determination that Jacob marry within his own family to keep the line pure and protect against idolatry (28:1–4). Isaac's wife Rebekah, even earlier, is said to have voiced this deep concern (27:46)!

But back in 26:34–35, Esau's marriages pierced the hearts of Isaac and Rebekah. They felt painful grief. As this relates to the overall passage it leaves a very sobering reminder. A life may have its prayer but still have its problems. The serene mingles with the sorrowful, the pleasantness with the pain. Self-will in its sinful alienation from what God can bring about is a stubborn part of man's life since the fall into sin.

Guidelines based on this occur spontaneously. First, what one godly believer does, another believer can follow as a good example and do as well. Here, the habit of the altar to meet with the Lord can be "like father, like son," first Abraham (12:8) and later Isaac. Or it can be brother like brother, or sister like sister, or wife like husband, or any other relationship. Live a life of setting good examples. Second, an altar to God works well when faith is in God, but when it is not, one's view of the altar needs to be altered.

Genesis 27:28, 29

A Prayerful Wish of Blessing

God orders the affairs of life so that, despite men's willful devices, His will triumphs. Isaac confers the prayerful blessing on Jacob the younger, not Esau the elder.

The Situation for the Blessing (vv. 1–17)

Isaac's preference and plan (vv. 1–4). His heart is set on blessing Esau, whom he prefers for the way this son is skillful to gratify his appetite. Only human will flourishes here, and he goes on with his plan to pronounce the blessing on Esau when the son comes back from his hunt and packs on his shoulders venison to make tantalizing stew.

This thinking is contrary to God's will (25:23), which Rebekah surely had shared with her husband. "The elder shall serve the younger." That was what God laid down when he answered the mother's prayer.

Had Isaac really been submissive to God's will at this point, he could have reflected in harmony with His word and waited for Him to show the way. He could bless Jacob, in line with God's light to him, and trust Him as to Esau's reaction. Later Isaac would do things right, even though it took God's overruling of his impulse to do it, and then by faith, thinking straight, he would act (Heb. 11:20).

Rebekah's preference and plan (vv. 5–17). Concerned for Jacob to receive what God had indicated but resorting to using a trick, she also was wrong. Had she looked to God in faith and waited, God could have intervened to stop Isaac as He had done in 26:2. "Do not go down to Egypt: stay in the land. . . ." The message might have been, "Do not give the blessing to Esau; give it to Jacob." As Isaac failed, so did Rebekah the plotter and Jacob for going along with her masquerade. Zeal to do God's work is never right when it cuts away from harmony with God's will. God is resourceful to work around it to accomplish His own unerring purpose, so here.

The Scenario of the Blessing (vv. 18–29)

The deceit of Jacob (vv. 18–27b). He pretended before his father to be Esau, acting out a lie in his absent brother's garments, his smell of the field, his words, and the stew he carried. God does not bless a lie; He cannot lie (Titus 1:2). He did step into the scenario and turn Isaac's prayerful pronouncement *wish* into the *form* true to His own will. The essence of blessing that Isaac desired would be fulfilled, yet not in the form Isaac thought. God can just as surely work His own will in this as later in changing Paul's desire for sufficiency to be realized in a different form than Paul's limited understanding fancied to be best (2 Cor. 12:7–9).

The declaration of Isaac (vv. 27c-29). The blessing, a prophetical pronouncement that God enabled, would surely be fulfilled by His own will. This was as other pronouncements in Genesis are certain, whether from His own utterance (3:15; 12:1–3, 7; 26:2–5, 24) or His impulse through a human instrument (5:29; 9:25–27; 49:8–12). While it was of God's own inclining—not to bless Esau but Jacob who actually received it—it was also a wish voiced in prayer, "My God" give this and that. For even prayer in its proper inclination is to be in the Spirit, of God (cf. Eph. 6:20). The Spirit uses a man to speak God's word (2 Sam. 23:2).

The blessing for Jacob and his descendants is in three aspects. One is *prosperity* in God's blessed provision (v. 28); another is *preeminence* in the family and, as a nation developed from him, honor among nations (29); finally, *protection* upon those who cursed them (29).

All of the aspects have numerous illustrations in the Old Testament later. Finally, all will have their grandest fulfillment in the future Messianic Kingdom. God prepares for this in His covenant anticipation to include kings in His plan (17:6, 16; 35:11; 49:10).

Prayer in this case is integrated with the will of God, and is certain to receive the answer His will can work on His schedule.

Seeking for the Blessing (vv. 30–40)

Esau arrived with venison and came into his father's quarters seeking the blessing. In a sense he would discover himself to be the victim of a plot, a loser in the very scene where he expected victory. In another, as the narrative has carefully prepared readers to discern, he himself had already forfeited the way of blessing. He had bartered away his birthright to Jacob as if it was of less value than a helping of stew (25:29–34).

The deer slayer had also broken with precedent passionately guarded by Abraham to whom God had first committed covenant promises. For Esau had waved aside matters important to the covenant line, preferring a Canaanite woman in marriage (26:34–35).

That not only showed cheap regard for the God of the covenant, but callousness against his parents' heartbreak.

Esau found no place for repentance in Isaac's decision once the father had conferred the blessing, though the son sought it with tears (Heb. 12:17). The father only pronounced upon him a concession that was of less significance (Gen. 27:39, 40). He would find his way at a distance from the blessing, live by his sword in violence, be under his brother in power, and only on some occasions cast off the yoke.

What Esau had lost and the way he had lost it rankled the hunter. He nourished a deep vow to snuff out the life of Jacob (v. 41).

Chapter 27 says only a little about prayer, though what it says is of great importance to subsequent biblical history. While prayer is not frequent, it is natural to see how scenes here could urge prayer that a summary record does not include.

Take Rebekah for example. She would have momentous occasion for thanksgiving to God for His over-arching work in human affairs to prosper His will. This was highly relevant to her own joy, that the blessing be on Jacob and not the son who had dealt misery in the home (26:34–35). And gratitude would be apt for God sparing her people in the future from the women steeped in Canaanite loyalty to other gods and Canaanite sin (cf. 15:16). The mothers could defile the covenant line of people.

Confession, too, would be appropriate. Rebekah had taken an instigating lead in the trickery, depending on human ingenuity. Only a little reflection could prod the heart with guilt for her denial that her God was able to find a way when there seemed to be no way as He had found a way when her own inability to have a child showed no way (25:22).

Besides, affirmation of faith in God who upheld His plan in His reply to Rebekah's prayer (25:23) could be most pertinent in prayer. And intercessory appeals could suitably leap to urgent priority. She might entreat for Jacob's safety from Esau when he stood at risk of his life in every hour at home. And later, when she thought of his flight to a far country, her days could mingle prayer for his safety there with affairs in her immediate household. The probability of this rises when the reader reflects on Rebekah's compassionate involvement with Jacob in her later contact (35:8). She apparently went so far as to send her nurse Deborah on the long journey to assist Jacob and his wives, explaining why Deborah later is with them. As for herself, she may not have lived to see Jacob again in this life; an uncertainty lingers in this since only Isaac is mentioned as alive when Jacob finally returns (35:27).

For Isaac, prayer in addition to his prayerful blessings (27:28, 29; 28:1–4) could be along lines similar to Rebekah's. Jacob's might be as well, if at this point he prayed at all. At least thanksgiving would be much in order to celebrate God's grace that had upheld him despite his own deceitful acts that might have dealt him his father's disdain. Petition, too, was fitting to his predicament later when his life hung in the balances before the murderous Esau. This was not all; his heart would feel cries for help to answer the clutch of fear before the unknowns on the journey (cf. 28:20). And what of Jacob appealing with caring intercessions for the father who had blessed him and the mother who had been so concerned that he be blessed?

What can be said of principles? First, we, as Isaac, may have God's will by prayer, or miss it by choosing things of our own will. Second, God is able to work His will out His way even if He rejects a human way that seeks to get results by some human means that He overcomes while turning human will back to fit His way.

Genesis 28:1–4

A Father's Blessing for a Wife

The Background

Abraham had diligently sought for God's will in this, securing a bride for Isaac. Isaac had felt stung by Esau's marriages with women who were of people outside the national aspect of the covenant, who were steeped in worship to idols. Isaac also was by now smitten with a sense of his own folly in trying bullheadedly to force delivering the blessing to Esau. In the aftermath, having been instructed by God's own working to manage success where he would have wrought ruin, he was wiser, acting by faith (cf. Heb. 11:20). That change apparently took place even amidst the drama of his dealings of Chapter 27. "By faith" he blessed Jacob and Esau. Now he is in step to do things the right way, moving at the impulse of God.

Rebekah's timely prodding about Jacob's danger of marrying as Esau had struck a sensitive heart in Isaac (27:46). His tender sensitivity to her grief-etched words, his realizing that the meaning in life itself was on the line, came together with a passion to be true to the covenant. The final scene of Chapter 27 then opens the way quite naturally into Chapter 28.

The Blessing (28:1–4)

Five things now occur in close coordination. Isaac acts.

His calling of Jacob (v. 1). Isaac, still facing his problem of aging (cf. 27:1), requests that his blessed son visit him at his bedside.

His caution to Jacob (v. 1). Isaac's own grief, that of his wife, and his loyalty to the covenant, ignite his lips with urgent clarity. He counsels Jacob that he is not to marry a bride from the Canaanites.

His counsel to Jacob (v. 2). Following the God-blessed precedent that Abraham showed in securing Rebekah for him, Isaac points Jacob to the same family in Mesopotamia to gain his wife. These relatives have been at center stage in Chapters 22 and 24.

His conferral to Jacob (vv. 3–4). Isaac makes a prophetic pronouncement, led by the Lord, in a prayerful blessing, "the blessing of Abraham." This is none other than the covenant blessing of 12:1–3, 7; 13:14–17; 22:16–18 and other such passages in the series. The spotlight here embraces not only the blessing, and people in Abraham's line, but the land God also had guaranteed in His covenant choice. The blessing to all nations through this one nation is certainly a part of the total picture in some other instances (cf. 12:1–3) but is not mentioned here.

First, Isaac dwells on the *source* of blessing. He is El Shaddai, a description that the Lord introduced for Himself to Abraham and his people (17:1). This conveys the idea that He is, as the root thought suggests, as a vast mountain rising up to loom over the affairs of men. He is all-powerful. God gave the term to Abraham, Isaac is convinced of its resource, God later also gave it to Jacob here in 28:3 and again in 35:11, and Jacob urged it before Joseph in 48:3.

Second, Isaac lays out the *specifics* of the blessing. Spiritual and temporal prosperity, multiplication in descendants, and possession of the promised land are parts of the panorama.

Prayer, in addition to being vitally involved in the pronouncement (wishing) of blessing at this point, would also have a many-sided relevancy dealing with all of these facets of God's purpose through the centuries. Men could pray about such aspects on track with the Lord's plans, and be in step with His will in this involvement.

In a nutshell, the prayer wish bound with God's own will deals with blessing. The blessing is related to a *people* and a *place*. God is firm about these.

His commission to Jacob (v. 5). All has been said. Now, probably in a scene of teary eyes and surgings of family emotions, the covenant father sends the covenant son on a journey of several weeks. His destination, the verse shows, is the home of Rebekah's father Bethuel and brother Laban, descendants in the family of Abraham (24:24, 29, 50; 22:20–23).

And now principles leap into the spotlight. First, behind privileges in prayer is the loving kindness of God. Here He is true to the gracious intent in the covenant He had made. Second, it is only natural in the love one shares with God to pray for others, wanting them to bask in blessing. In the present passage, this is in a prophetic pronouncement, but such good wishes also can surge in normal, concerned intercessory pleading. One sees this in Numbers 6:22–27 and in Paul's examples of Ephesians 1 and 3.

Genesis 28:11–22

The Prayer of a Traveler

As almost always seems to be the case in prayer tutored by Scripture, God's promise precedes man's prayer. Jacob does not utter the prayer until the latter verses, but God's promise first, His word, is a strategic catalyst to foster the prayer. The prayer then is a response to the promise.

God's Promise to Jacob (vv. 11–15)

The account in a nutshell is simple. Jacob stops to make camp overnight while his trek is still in the promised land. Before he journeys out of the land, God speaks to him in a dream vision. He gives His declaration along with visualization that is as vivid as a modern video.

God sets up His own version of a "TV program" on the screen of Jacob's dream consciousness. By His effective power, the device would be very graphic, as later dreams to Jacob, Joseph, Egypt's Pharaoh, and a butler and a baker. The details of the portrayal relate vitally to covenant reassurance to Jacob about the land though he is to be out of the promised area for twenty years.

Towering above all, God stands and speaks. Below Him is a ladder stretching from earth (Jacob) to heaven (God). God is the one who initiated and often reiterates the covenant, from Genesis 12:1–3, 7 forward. Jacob individually represents his covenant people, chosen by God. The ladder no doubt stands for God contact, keeping in touch with His people on earth and their opportunity to enjoy access/communion with Him in the onward surge of His will. Angels, ascending and descending on the way between earth and heaven, illustrate continual contact with interest and interchange kept up between the God they serve and the covenant people to whom these angels minister. Jacob himself goes on his way to a far country on earth to secure a bride. But the far more important feature that reassures of eventual success is the way open to Jacob between earth and heaven! Jesus Christ would centuries later be revealed as the ultimate way for man's blessing with God (John 14:6). Frequent activity of angels to serve in details of God's program with men is clear in Scripture (Gen. 31:11; 32:1, 2; cf. Gen. 16, 18). This line of interchange runs into the New Testament (John 1:51) and even into the Book of Revelation (21:9; 22:8, etc.).

With such a dramatic display, God gives His affirmation of blessing. He is the covenant Lord, the God of Abraham and Isaac. The land where Jacob now lies, receiving the dream vision, is the land of 12:7 and 13:14–17, which the Lord assured to Abraham's people. He pledges multiplication of Jacob's descendants, this bearing in itself solemn testimony that Jacob will find a wife, safety, and a return in God's will for him. With this also is the promise that in Jacob's people, all families of the earth will gain blessing, ultimately to be fulfilled in Christ's salvation to people of all nations (cf. Rom. 3; Gal. 3). He the son of Abraham will secure it (cf. Matt. 1:1; Rev. 7:9ff.). God, having affirmed His assurance from the positive side, also declares it from the other. He will not leave Jacob until He has done what He promised him. To believers of a later era, He similarly vouches, "I will never desert you, nor will I ever forsake you" (Heb. 13:5).

Jacob's Promise to God (vv. 16–22)

His convictions (vv. 16, 17). Awaking, Jacob is impressed by powerful convictions of God's presence here. The place which was but a campsite of stones before is now to him "the house of God," which gives Jacob the appropriate name for it, Bethel (v. 19). It is also, as plausibly suggested by the ladder leading up and into God's presence, a kind of stairway or "gate to heaven." That is, the way is open for prayerful communion with the God who will fulfill the covenant.

This is similar to Jesus' picture centuries after this for prayer's contact with God as a door where God is available, "knock and it shall be opened to you" (cf. Matt. 7:7–11).

His ceremony (vv. 18, 19, 22). Jacob anoints the stone that has been his "pillow" after setting it up as a pillar marker of memorial. His oil of anointing fittingly identifies the spot as the place where God met with him, an audience of one, but representing his people. This campsite is "God's House" (v. 22). This is what he ascribes as the significance of the place he anoints by its marker stone.

His commitment (vv. 20–21, 22c). In these verses Jacob is praying. His aspect of prayer is affirmation—asserting in a vow what he pledges God will be to him ("my God") and what he will do in response ("give a tenth"). His prayer at the same time seems to have as its core a yearning of petition, recognizing the need of God's help. If God will be with him, keep him safe, provide what he needs, and bring him safely back to his father's house, He will be his God.

Temporal necessities are urgent in this prayer, as often in Scripture and in all of life. Jacob does not plead greeds, but needs. He also prays very much in line with, and impacted by, God's word that was just spoken. God's declaration dealt with, among other things, Jacob's critical need to be preserved wherever he went and come back to the promised land intact (v. 15). That most desperate need at the time would, of course, fit within the larger needs the declaration encompassed, the all embracing covenant program to run through the centuries. Jacob's prayer, then, was sensitive to and in accord with the word of God, a part of it (cf. John 15:7).

The prayer of commitment moves from the part Jacob sees God fulfilling to the part he sees for himself. This comes in two verses. First is the promise about his God (v. 21). Apparently God already was his God. His valuing of the birthright and the blessing (Chaps. 25, 27) would point in that direction. What he probably is saying here is that he also will be true to this commitment toward God who would do such great things for him. He could properly have no other response. Despite his failures to act like this at times, He does claim the Lord after returning to the land (33:20; 35:3, 14–15). And he claims Him to the end (49:18, 24, 25, etc.).

Second is the promise about giving (v. 22). The tenth to give back to God who gives him so much compares with Abraham's giving a tenth part of the spoils to the God who possessed heaven and earth (14:20). The point is not that God needs such gifts to finance His program. He created the earth, possesses it, and its fulness (cf. Ps. 24:1) and has resources to supply men. Jacob looks to Him for these bounties (Gen. 28:20, 21) and in all the necessary ways God supports him later. The point rather is that in view of who and what God is in His grace, a worshiping heart seeks expression in gratitude. Sometimes this is in tangible, temporal bounties. God Himself is always the far greater giver.

In the passage now in focus, God's giving of His word (His will) elicits its response in a prayer shaped by His word. Jacob is at first moved in awed contemplation of God, at His presence (He is so near), and His promises. His spirit of worship continues with his reverential commitment, which actually finds words that show how profoundly God has impacted him.

Now a statement of principles is in order. First, God's way into His presence encourages a believer to come to Him at His door (cf. Matt. 7:7–11). Second, it is an immense privilege to call the Lord "my God," speak prayerfully to Him for His care, and even give to His cause. We who received all from Him (cf. 1 Cor. 4:7) long to give back to Him and can do this cheerfully (2 Cor. 9:7). And His cause embossed on our hearts is our cause, as we live not for ourselves but for Him (2 Cor. 5:15).

A Panorama of Biblical Vow and Oath

Since Gen. 28 moves to Jacob's vow, it may be helpful at this early point to consider the comparison in prayer between a vow and an oath. Both appear frequently in the Old Testament.

Similarities between the two may suggest that they are finally the same. However, differences assist to show that they are legitimately distinct aspects in which one can voice prayer. Some main considerations can point this way, without an attempt to cover the subject exhaustively.

Similarities. The vow and the oath have in common the following, which may make it appear in general that they are finally the same when this is not exactly the case.

First, both at the root of their idea bear on dealing with God in transparent truthfulness and integrity. In either case, one is to follow through on a commitment to Him. Second, in both aspects, accountability to God is basic. In a vow, this is to do what one pledges to Him or to another in a prayerful commitment. And in an oath, it is to draw into a matter God's faithfulness and power to give certainty to one's undertaking. Third, both have at their core a determination and responsibility to complete an agenda before God or before Him and whoever else the oath involves. Fourth, vow or oath inherently transpire during some process of time and are to be pursued to the climax; otherwise, the party falls short of making good on it. Fifth, the vow may be wise in a valid purpose of heart, as Jacob's vow in Genesis 28 or David's pledge to find out a dwelling place for God on earth (Ps. 132:2–5; cf. other prayer, too, in vv. 8–9). Or a vow can be a rash, unwise, flimsy, unwise, undisciplined splurge in words, in pressured haste or careless and precipitous thought, as Jephthah's vow in Judges 11. Similarly, an oath as well may be wise and God-honoring or voice what turns out to display one's falsehood (Lev. 6:3).

The similarities, then, are apparent. Yet meaningful contrasts show that the two can truly be distinct ways of praying. Consider differences.

Differences. Hopefully it can clarify matters to set the two in contrast under each way in which they differ, point by point.

(1) Vocabulary exists for each on its own right, and it is not the same. A main word for vow is the Hebrew (Old Testament) ***nedher*** or the Greek (LXX, New Testament) term ***euche***. In either language, the terminology speaks of one binding himself to an obligation; he realizes he should show integrity to see a pledge through to the full resolution of what he

pledged. Jacob in Genesis, for instance, vowed his own faithfulness to God in exchange for God benefiting him with safety while he was away from the land of promise (Gen. 28). Later he did come back, always kept safe by God, and what he had vowed was realized (Gen. 31–35).

For an oath, one word is the Hebrew ***shebuah,*** derived from an idea meaning "seven." In Hebrew custom, the number was understood to denote completeness. In an oath, one aimed to be complete in honor, being reliable, all the way, and he appealed to the certainty that God could give his oath. One example is that of Abraham and Abimelech who agreed to an oath to act honorably toward each other in friendly, neighborly relations for mutual welfare (Gen. 21). Abraham gave the other man seven lambs as a token verification in God's name (vv. 28–32). The seven were a witness guaranteeing that Abraham will stand true to his oath. For both men, the swearing of the oath is "by God" (v. 23), invoking His name to assure certainty and fidelity.

Another custom in expressing the serious responsibility of an oath was to place one's hand on the thigh of the person the oath served. Abraham's servant enacted this gesture with Abraham to show his determination and sense of responsibility to complete the oath with God's help. He would make a long journey and secure a bride for Isaac (Gen. 24:2; cf. also 47:29).

In a covenant oath that God makes unilaterally in His own pure grace and plan, He alone stands good for the eventual fulfillment. In Gen. 15, he accommodates Himself for Abram's sake to a human, vivid custom of walking alone between two rows made by parts of sacrificed animals. In doing this by Himself, God agrees to fulfill the covenant He had made earlier with Abram (12:1–3, 7; 13:14–17) without failing. He anchors His oath by the surety of His own indestructible life and unceasing continuation

In 1 Samuel 14:39 Saul draws God's name into an oath by the words, "as the Lord lives." In that case, the oath is an unwise one out of the fleshly minded and disobedient king's erring heart. He uses God's name without sincere intent. Later, by contrast, David and Jonathan agree in a friendship oath, "may the Lord watch between you and me" (1 Sam. 20:23). Here the outlook is wholesome, and God can honor it because what His name is drawn into He Himself can honor.

Another Heb. (Old Testament) word for an oath is ***alah,*** "imprecation." It is based on the word ***el,*** a reference to God. The idea of the term is to call on God. It came to refer to a curse that involved invoking God's judgment on when he does wrong (Lev. 5:1; Num. 5:23). But, depending on the context, the same term can positively be used for a sworn oath for neighborly good, a friendly pact (Gen. 26:28; 2 Sam. 21:7).

Now, continue with differences between a vow and an oath.

(2) A vow focuses on a commitment to undertake and complete a purpose. The emphasis is, while trusting God for help as in other aspects of prayer, on self-discipline necessary on the human side to reach a goal. So Jacob's vow in Genesis 28 is a voluntary agreement to be true to the covenant Lord who has appeared to Him, and in exchange he wants God's benefit in taking care of him to bring him back safely to the land. In another case, David vows to get no rest (not let the matter go) until he has found a place, a house, that is the dwelling place of God on earth among His people (Ps. 132:2–5).

By contrast, an oath, while likewise retaining a commitment, puts its basic spotlight on drawing God's name into the intent. One *invokes* Him, due to His honor, veracity, governance, and power to guarantee a follow-through. In case of failure from the human side, one agrees to take God's equitable dealing for his breath in trust. A reader can observe 1 Kings 8:31–32, which shows the feeling that God can deal in His judgment with a person who makes an oath but proves untrue, or justify a person who keeps what he has affirmed.

(3) In a vow, a promise or pledge is essential. But in an oath, the accent falls on a penalty or a prospering, depending on whether one follows through responsibly (1 Kgs. 8:31–32). Sometimes a vow expects God to perform a reciprocal favor, as in Jacob's case in Genesis 28.

(4) A vow gives the driving force to the intention to be faithful in seeing a matter through to the finish. If one desires God to fulfill a special part in the case, this too is part of the intaent. However, in an oath, an added element the deliberate invoking of God's name to monitor, superintend and stand as the guarantee of certainty. If the person making the oath reneges, the oath maker expects God to deal with what is untrustworthy as He sees fit.

(5) Other comments on a vow:

First, a vow could be of a Nazirite version (Num. 6), in some cases only temporary and in others permanent for a lifetime. Hannah in prayer committed the son God would give her in His answer by a pledge of service for his entire life (1 Sam. 1:11, 22, 28). The son, Samuel, served the Lord all of his life. Likewise, Manoah and his wife pledged their child, Samuel, to a lifetime of dedication as a Nazirite (Judg. 13:7). Other vows could be only temporary, terminated when one had fulfilled the started period in the pledge, as Jacob's promise in Genesis 28.

Second, a vow could be good, as in the cases just mentioned, or bad. An example of a bad vow was the man who selfishly slights his needy parents by mouthing an excuse that he has made a vow putting his savings under the category of a gift to God so that he cannot touch the fund to aid the parents. Jesus condemns such selfish heartlessness (Matt. 15:3–9). Another sinful vow appears in Paul's enemies bonding in a pledge not to eat until they have murdered him (Acts 23:21).

Third, in certain, more rare cases, vow and oath can combine. This is in a special case of a vow arranged even with the added form of an oath. This is as other aspects of prayer can flexibly come together, for example, petition (one's own needs) and intercession (those of another), or an affirmation about God can be one of awe in worshipful tribute (praise) to Him, or confession and petition can both mingle in a desire, "God, be merciful to me, the sinner!" (Luke 18:13).

Fourth, when one looks back on his vow in remembrance of God helping him, it is a time to put a finishing touch of prayer on this, paying God tribute. In the Old Testament times, a sacrificial offering could combine with the voicing of praise/gratitude, or the thanks alone be mentioned (Ps. 22:25; 50:14, with a sacrifice of thanksgiving; 56:12, with thank offerings; 65:1; 66:13–14, with burnt offerings; 116:14). This is one venue of exuding with the spirit that later Scripture recognizes, "In everything give thanks . . ." (1 Thess. 5:18).

Fifth, even unbelievers who know something about the Lord can make vows before Him when they feel His pressure. For example, the pagan sailors of Jonah 1 fear they will lose their lives in a storm at sea that they realize Jonah's God has brought. They enter into pledges of dues they will fulfill to Him in return for His working to rescue them (vv. 15–16).

Sixth, a foundation upon which one enters into a vow is the keynote to be dependable. A worshiper should keep the vow (Deut. 23:21–23). So Jephthah was zealous to follow through on his pledge, even though he realized his folly of making an unqualified promise that brought him to grief when his daughter came forth, and not an animal (Judg. 11).

Seventh, a father or husband had the privilege of rendering null a vow that a daughter or wife had made (Num. 30). This, handled in responsible love, could safeguard a precious one from unpleasant results of a pledge uttered out of unwise or hasty decision.

Eighth, God did not permit a person to vow to Him what already was to be given to Him or to vow to His cause what He regarded as sinful, such as earnings from a prostitute's immorality (Deut. 23:18). When a woman of ill repute had repented before the Lord, what she had could become acceptable as a gift made in sincere love (Luke 7:36–50).

Ninth, Jesus was against traffic in private vows in any manner of irresponsibility, whether flippant, frivolous, selfish, cheap, insincere, or in any sinful way (Matt. 5:33). These bore a stamp of untruthfulness. Rather, they should truthfully fulfill what they committed to Him to do. The same principle applies to swearing in an oath, for it can be acceptable, or the mouthing of hypocrisy (Matt. 23:16–22). As in any other aspect of prayer, a vow or oath can be genuine. Jesus did not invalidate the high priest's adjuration of Matthew 26:63–64, "I adjure You [charge You, Jesus, under oath] by the living God, that You tell us whether You are the Christ, the Son of God." Jesus affirmed the reality of Who He was in His immediate response, "You have said it; nevertheless I tell you [what will show powerfully Who I am in that] hereafter you shall see the Son of Man sitting at the right hand of power, and coming on the clouds of heaven" (v. 64). The high priest immediately understood from this His claim to deity, for he lashed out with an accusation of blasphemy (v. 65).

On the other hand, Jesus does not advocate private oaths as actually necessary. A man can speak unadvisedly and sin so easily, so glibly, by heart and tongue. A believer's word should be trustworthy, straightforward, without added words (Matt. 5:33). Oaths that authorities require in judicial cases are a distinct matter as one fulfills his civil duty and is a good testimony in this way (cf. Rom. 13:1–7; 1 Pet. 2:13–15).

(6) Further comments on an oath. A prayer in this aspect or form could be pertinent in various kinds of scenarios. Abraham's servant undertook to depart on a long trek and bring back a bride for the patriarch's son Isaac (Gen. 24). In another sort of case, subjects could swear (assert) loyalty to a king (1 Kgs. 18:10; 2 Chr. 36:13). Or a ruler could voice by God's name an oath on what he aimed to do, for instance Saul (1 Sam. 14:24). God was honorable, but Saul was rash and unwise. Priests made pledges to be faithful in their servant role (Heb. 7:21). A person could affirm certainty in an oath, invoking God's name, that there was no theft or damage to borrowed property, and he could return it in good condition (Ex. 22:10; 1 Kgs. 8:31). Or one could vouch by summoning God's name that he could display integrity if accused of having lost someone's property, yet in his human unreliability, he might turn out to be false (Lev. 6:3). In another case when a husband accused his wife of sexual infidelity she had the fair avenue of clearing herself by taking an oath and proving her innocence by passing a special test in Israelite custom (Num. 5:19ff.).

Genesis 29:31–32

Leah's Prayer Regarding Children

Jacob joined his relatives, worked to gain Rachel's hand in marriage but was craftily dealt Leah, then labored again to win Rachel, fourteen years in all. He had to endure his relative Laban's trickery after the first seven years for Rachel, finding that the taste of his own medicine was frustrating.

Leah, finding herself not the object of Jacob's love as it was poured upon Rachel, was given God's help in being the wife who could furnish children.

Her Affliction before the Lord (v. 31a)

God's compassion shines in His taking note of Leah's heart-wrenching experience.

Her Assistance from the Lord (vv. 31b, 32a)

God enabled Leah to conceive and give birth to a son, Reuben, which means "look, a son."

Her Affirmation to the Lord (v. 32b)

The blessed wife in gratitude traces this boon to the Lord, giving Him credit for His sensitivity and for the affection she felt this would give her from her husband. What she says is before those of the household, apparently when Jacob is out. But it is a kind of prayer voicing her thanksgiving or highly suggestive of prayer testifying the same thing directly to Him.

Let us single out principles. First, God is touched by the prayer of a wife who wants to please her husband within His covenant goodness. Where this involves children and it is His will, He can answer with children. This also was true for Rachel and Rebekah and will be later for Hannah and the wife of Manoah, father of Samson. Second, when God's wisdom allows what we ask, or even if not for His kind reasons, in either case, a heart thankful to Him is fitting.

Genesis 29:33

Leah's New Thanksgiving

Her Addition from the Lord (v. 33a)

Leah again conceived and gave birth to a son, Simeon, which means "hearing." Her name for the baby again was in tribute to God.

Her Affirmation to the Lord (v. 33b)

Again the words she uses are apparently the essence of her heart-felt gratitude to the Lord. He has heard that she is not loved, for she presumably has poured this out before Him as Hannah would later (1 Sam. 1). God not only has heard the prayer but answered by this giving a second time. How appropriate then is the name she chooses for the infant, Simeon: "hearing." It is testimony of God's hearing that fills Leah's mouth.

A principle has already appeared under 29:31–32.

Genesis 29:34

Leah's Prayer about Love

Her Addition (v. 34a)

So far she does not have Jacob's certain love. She perseveres, apparently still praying. This time a new baby is a third son, Levi.

Her Anticipation (v. 34b)

Leah is encouraged to think that the third time will work the wonder she desires. Her heart is set on seeking Jacob's attachment in love to her. So her name for the baby is Levi, "attachment." God is good to her in giving the children, and she recognizes His answers, but her thought that love will come from just producing is not working. Love is made of more than ability to give birth and arithmetic.

A principle stands out vividly. One does not, in every case, get what he prays to receive, and while he may not grasp God's reason, the heart yet can trust that He is good. Who are we to think that we know what is best along the whole way or to doubt the One who has our finest interests at heart?

Genesis 29:35

Leah's Praiseful Prayer

Her Addition from the Lord (v. 35a)

She has a fourth son. In the flow of the context, this one reasonably is again in answer to prayer.

Her Adoration of the Lord (v. 35b)

Something new appears here! Leah has changed her focus from asking to praising. She has been grateful in the other cases but now devotes a strong emphasis to prayer in the aspect of praise. The futuristic idea, "I will praise," does not furnish information on how long her praise went on. The name of the son that celebrated God's supply was itself Judah, "praise." This would at least be a perpetual reminder.

We are not told why Leah ceased bearing here and in 30:9. It may have been because four births, all answers, have given her abundant reason to be grateful. God is allowing a time to let her continue in praise. If the reason is not along some such line, at least readers know that a sovereign God has done much for Leah.

At any rate, the spotlight shifts temporarily to Rachel. God may have desired to show that, in the situation of two women, He was not unmindful to give His attention to more than one.

How evident are principles! First, when a believer offers praise to God, he or she glorifes Him (cf. Ps. 50:23). Second, some have much within their own experience for which to praise God, as Leah for her several children. Whatever is our experience, God is great and greatly to be praised (Ps. 48:1). It is good to rest upon blessings He has bestowed, even if not all we ask, but bitter to hold it against God if He does not grant everything we specify.

Genesis 30:6

Rachel's Prayer

Her Ascription to the Lord (v. 6a)

As in other cases, here we do not read her actual prayer for help in childbearing. We do meet with her tribute to God before her household. It voices at its heart the theme of her life for prayer. "God has vindicated me, and has indeed heard my voice (in prayerful appeal), and has given me a son" through the maid Bilhah. God gets the credit, in her thinking; however it may be in line with God's will or a misconception of His working. Back in Chapter 16, Sarai's and Abram's resort to a maid, Hagar, was not really the method by which God willed to provide a son. They only produced their Ishmael; God would work in His spiritual power along His own line to give them supernaturally His Isaac! And He leads Paul in Galatians 4 to draw a distinction on this and other details of Genesis between what is of the flesh only and what is of the Spirit. When Rachel or Leah secured God's help in their use of maids, the account endorses this (30:17) as God's working in a concessionary manner. He does, He permits, what people do in their limitations as to faith, though ideally He is able to do things otherwise, more fully true to His standard (cf. Gen. 2:24). In graciousness to encourage those in need, He could give water flowing out of a rock even after Moses had *smitten* that rock, not *spoken* to it as was God's ideal, true to His word (Num. 20:7–13).

Her Affirmation to the Lord (vv. 6b, 7)

Rachel affirmed an appropriate name for the son, Dan, meaning "justice." She thought of God's merciful concession that made her feel righted or vindicated. She was commemorating God's answer to her prayer, what He had permitted.

Guidelines leap before us. First, God may graciously answer a prayer with compassion in some measure, even though believers fall short of what they really ought to be. In any matter, who among people is absolutely perfect in all the ways he should be? The bottom line is God's grace. Second, it can in some sense exalt God when a believer in some meaningful way gives Him the credit for an answer (cf. Ps. 50:23).

Genesis 30:7, 8

Rachel's Second Prayer

Her Addition from the Lord (v. 7)

This wife's method of relying on her maid, Bilhah, has its positive result, encouraging her again, a second son for Jacob. As the next verse in context will clarify, her human emotions mingled a dependence on a substitute with reliance on the Lord.

Her Affirmation before the Lord (v. 8)

The drama Rachel recounts becomes more obvious in three steps.

Her wrestling. The favorite of Jacob drew upon intense efforts in her prayer and on God to secure a baby.

She mentions her passion in this. She engaged in extraordinary wrestlings. What she testifies to is literally "with wrestlings of God (Elohim) I have wrestled with my sister. . . ." Some interpreters view it as prayerful wrestling with God that mingled with wrestlings with Leah. If so, her passion or arousal, so serious in its quest, was similar to that some years later by her husband Jacob. He, too, is said to have wrestled with God, though the word depicting that is a different one meaning "wrestle" (Gen. 32:25, 26). And the word for Rachel's having "prevailed" in her objective (30:8) is the same term that appears for God not prevailing over Jacob (32:25) and then Jacob having prevailed in his wrestling (v. 28).

Another explanation of the phrase "wrestlings of God" in 30:8 is "mighty wrestlings," god-like ones, wrestlings on a superlative scale in the realm of what God can do.

The first sense seems to capture the literal wording in a better way. It is interesting that Jacob after his own wrestling bout designates the place "Peniel," meaning "the face of God (El)" in 32:30. And when his wrestling with God leads him to win with Esau, he exclaims that he has seen Esau's face (seen this antagonist) "as one sees the face of God (Elohim)" in 33:10. The flow of the context in which Rachel and Leah take their needs to God with fervent feeling points up the possibility of this as well.

Either way, however, Rachel's wrestlings are certainly involved with God as well as with Leah, just as Jacob's would later be with God and Esau. And in both explanations her struggles rise to great intensity to gain what she yearns for, related to God's covenant.

Rachel, having such wrestlings in her wifely longings, says "I have wrestled with my sister . . ." Here now is the verb form of the noun just used for "wrestlings." It is ***pathal,*** meaning "to twist." She has twisted herself in her writhings in prayer. A form of the word appears for the "cord" of Tamar, twisted out of fibers (Gen. 38:18, 25). Rachel is recounting her agonizing efforts in seeking to produce as Leah but depending on God for success.

Her winning. She captures this in the word "prevailed." ***Yaqal*** signifies "to be able, have power, overcome, win out." Job uses this word in 42:2, "I know that You can do all things." God is able, God is adequate to prevail, God can win out, He can do what He chooses to do. Blessed by His answer to serious prayer, Rachel has gained victory.

Her way of celebrating this. As so often in the context, Rachel's tribute, crowning prayer, is the name she gives to her son. "Naphtali"; she exults in commemorating the struggle that has led to the overcoming: "I have wrestled." May the same God this believer sought out grip many more in their situations to be able to say this!

Principles stand out as if in bold face. First, God may choose to give kindly even when one of His people pray with a mixture of depending on human means and looking to Him. God knows the heart in any case. Second, prayer can count on God with great and earnest appeals that go all-out like agonizing efforts to win in wrestling. Third, God may permit intense struggle in prayer, not to say He is reluctant, but to draw a believer out to show the special value placed on an answer and to develop in such qualities as trust, patience, and humility.

Genesis 30:9–13

Leah's Blessedness through Prayer

Her Additions by Zilpah (vv. 9, 10, 12)

When Leah realized, apparently after adequate time, an inability to conceive more children, she too fell back upon a custom of the day to rectify this. She did not wait patiently on the Lord who had enabled her earlier, depending on His power directly. Still, God graciously helps those who trust Him, though so inconsistently. She found His goodness despite her failure and limited reliance. So it was with Abram (Gen. 12, 20), Isaac and Rebekah (27), Jacob (27, 32), and so on.

Two sons were born through Zilpah.

Her Affirmations before the Lord (vv. 11, 13)

In the two different births, Leah exulted with words expressing her felicity due to God's generous working. Her affirmations were in what she could credit Him for as in verses 18 and 20.

When one son was delivered, she exclaimed that she was "fortunate" or "blessed." So her fitting name for the boy was "Gad" which meant this. At the arrival of the next son, she probably cradled him in her arms in similar jubilation and was radiant. Her name would be very proper for the occasion, as she called the baby "Asher." The word derives from an idea of "going straight, forward, or right." It describes, for example, a person going straight on the path of understanding (Prov. 9:6). The ecstatic wife was saying what would be similar to English phrases, "I am just hunky dory," "I am right on," or "I feel so neat." She exuded because she felt things were so right.

Another way to capture the same essential joy that lifted Leah is to say, "How happy, how blessed I am!" For the word was used for blessedness, as in the expectation that all nations would call the Messiah in Solomon's throne line "blessed" (Ps. 72:17). The same term applies to another woman, the wife who is so virtuous in Proverbs 31:28, when her children rise up and "call her blessed." And Leah says that women will call her "blessed," one with whom, in this case, things are going forward.

What may be said of maxims here? One thing is that even when a child of God secures the object for which he pleads, it is out of His mercy that God gives it. Second, remember to pour out to God the thanks due to Him for what His power has wrought. Once our hearts become tenderly aware of His gifts, we can be praising Him all the day long.

Genesis 30:14–18

Leah's Reliance on Plants and Prayer

Her Agreement with Rachel (vv. 14–15)

Leah consented with Rachel to a little arrangement both wives thought would boost their standing with their husband. Rachel was of the notion that love apples Leah's son had come across in some secret spot could enhance her ability to conceive. So she figured it an advantage in the long run to coax these from Leah to help her own childbearing in exchange for agreeing to give Jacob into Leah's arms one night. Leah, on her side, felt triumphant in gaining the man whose love she sought in this triangle.

Much has been written about the plants' ingredients aiding fertility to some degree as aphrodisiacs today, and much against the effectiveness in Genesis 30. The love apples are not said to assist Rachel in this case; rather the passage attributes the subsequent ability of Rachel to bear Joseph to God (v. 22). So does Rachel herself (vv. 23, 24). Throughout the contextual flow, God is credited with bringing the blessing. A somewhat analogous human device to influence offspring is Jacob's in the same context in verses 31–43. In his case, he believes that he can, with influence of colors before animals in their mating season, get offspring to his advantage. Again, students of Scripture and science have reasoned that the dependence on the human method really worked, or it did not but rather *God* worked to prosper Jacob. The context itself presents the almighty God as creator and giver of life (Gen. 1–2). It is of His power that those in His covenant are blessed (12:1–3; 28:14, 15). The immediate context credits God with the prospering (31:5, 7, 9–13, 16, 42). In a vision, he shows Jacob that He is the cause of animal genes working to give Jacob animals of a color that bless him (31:9–13).

A person who relies on natural means may find help through these where it is God's will to work through them, in part. Even if a believer partly trusts in a natural device that does not of itself work and also trusts in God though with imperfect faith, God can be gracious in the result.

Her Addition from the Lord (v. 17)

God is said to be the giver of Leah's child here. He responds to her need.

Her Appreciation to the Lord (v. 18)

Her own imperfect conclusion is that God's giving is a fitting payment (wages) in reward for her motive prompting her decision to give her maid to her husband (vv. 9–13). She at least wanted her husband to have children when she did not think that any were coming from her. It is difficult to assess her opinion of God's reason. But children can be a "reward" in God's grace as a form of the same word appears in Psalm 127:3. And God can read motives at work in human minds (1 Sam. 2:3; 1 Cor. 4:5). So He can endorse aspects pleasing to Him and not bless due to aspects that do not. Certainly His perfect perception notes imperfections in whatever man he blesses, and none is sinlessly perfect. Yet as a God of covenant loving-kindness, He deals in tender compassion though those who call on Him in their needs, all are far from being as upright as He is.

Leah's words reflect:

Her recognition of God.

Her recognition of another reason. This is her own self-denial.

Her reference to the meaning. To her, it is fitting to call the son Issachar, "wages." She thinks of the baby as her reward. The name is a form of the same basic word for reward in Genesis 15:1. In a sense, due to God's grace, believers, though far from utter consistency in godliness, can receive special reward from God in this life or the next. And in a sense, reward is related to their works, words and motives. Yet finally reward is of God's generous grace, for He Himself gives all that helps men to do anything (cf. Luke 17:7–10; 1 Cor. 3:10). God could be gracious to Leah when the minglings of notions and aspects in her life were so imperfect.

Principles that are apropos here are already stated under 30:9–13.

Genesis 30:19, 20

Leah's Thanksgiving to God

Her Addition from the Lord (v. 19)

The unfavored wife bore her sixth son, again showing that fertility had been given anew to her.

Her Appreciation to the Lord (v. 20)

Her recognition. She is quite direct in voicing this: "God has endowed me with a good gift. . . ." She traces the cause of her ability to God. Her testimony, before others, is her prayerful praise to Him.

Her reasoning. She continues, "now my husband will dwell with me, because I have borne him six sons." God's help to meet her need will lead to this long-sought boon of having Jacob's love. The passage that follows does not explain what the result really came to be. It does not even mention Leah's death, though it gives Rachel's (35:19). But at least Leah felt comfort for a time.

Her reference. God's gift of a son and the cheer of Jacob dwelling with her prompted the name Zebulun, "dwelling."

After this, Leah also had a daughter, Dinah (v. 21). That name means "just" or "justice," possibly based on the mother feeling that God had rendered some justice, vindicating her even with a daughter. Mention of Dinah prepares the reader for the role she will play in Chapter 34. Though she is singled out, other daughters also were born to Jacob (37:35; 46:7).

At least one new principle emerges. Paul's counsel centuries later shows this as fitting in the present passage. "In everything give thanks, for this is the will of God . . ." (1 Thess. 5:18).

Genesis 30:22–24

Rachel's Prayer at Joseph's Birth

God's Remembrance (vv. 22–23a)

Prayer possibly is assumed as Rachel needed God's help. So verse 22 explains that God remembered her and gave heed to her. Credit accrues to Him, not to love apples she also had relied on. It is God who "opened her womb."

The writer of the account notes this reality, and in it, the suggestion that Rachel had urged this need to God.

Rachel's Response (vv. 23b–24)

Her celebration. She speaks before others in the household what is probably a matter of praise to God. "God has taken away my reproach." He has lifted the sting she felt in thinking of her inability as failing the man she loved, bringing her into disrespect. To her, Joseph's birth was a momentous occasion. She wanted to render to God tribute for it.

Her designation. The name Joseph signifies either "may the Lord add" or "He has taken away." It is Rachel's way of expressing in a nutshell her prayerful feelings, either in petition for another child or in gratitude for what God already did. That the name is followed by a petition based on its meaning seems to fit well with God adding Benjamin to Rachel later (35:17, 18). After Joseph, he was an added son.

Prayer is well-suited to each of the births since God in His covenant so frequently promises descendants. They come, ultimately, out of His giving goodness (cf. 30:20, "gift").

A guideline is clear enough. In what we think of as mundane or in what to us is momentous, giving God the plaudits is appropriate. Magnifying Him always is relevant. This can be in prayer or simply in words that exalt Him before others.

Genesis 31:11

Jacob's Prayer of Listening

Sometimes in the Bible, prayerful communication with God can come in the very brief utterance, "I am listening" (one short word, as Gen. 22:1–2). That is a good way to begin talking with the Lord when one starts to read His word, ready to hear Him (cf. Ps. 119:18).

Jacob is an example of this here.

The Rousing to Hear (vv. 10–11a)

God opens the door to prayer in a fresh stimulation, speaking in a dream. He had communicated with Jacob in a dream vision in 28:12–15, showing Himself at the top of a ladder to heaven and reaffirming covenant promises. Now He is back in another dream vision, and by His power to make things authentic, even in a dream when it is His will, can cause Jacob to respond in a way that reflects reality of his life when awake (cf. Solomon, 1 Kgs. 3).

The Readiness to Hear (v. 11)

Once God has roused his attention, Jacob is submissively available and attentive to hear. "Here I am," he says concisely. He was ready, before God, sensitive to listen.

The Revelation to Heed (12–13; also 3, 10)

God's display (v. 12; cf. 10). The visual aids include the display of animals in the flock mating. This is to show that God Himself is arranging the passing of genes to result in building Jacob's livestock venture. He is pursuing His covenant undertaking to bless Abraham and his descendants.

God's devotion (vv. 13a-c). In order to convey His devotion to Jacob and His people, the heavenly Speaker takes Jacob's mind back to a scene where His identity was a sharp reality to the man. That is at the place where Jacob himself has been so impressed by God's presence that he called the spot Bethel. All kinds of encouraging facets would spring into Jacob's mind from that time of vision and promise.

"I am the God of Bethel," the God who pledged such promises and showed such a visualization to assure Jacob. He continues, "where you anointed a pillar, where you made a vow to Me. . . ." This is a clear-cut reminder of Jacob's devotion that should be kept with the God so devoted to him.

God's direction (v. 13d; 3). His will is for Jacob to *arise*, do whatever is necessary to move in the right way, *leave* the land of sojourn, and *return* to his native land. In verse 13, it is the land of his birth; in verse 3 which Jacob is now repeating in larger detail to prepare his wives, it is the land of his fathers and relatives.

God's defense (v. 3). The God who is guiding assures that as Jacob obeys His word, He will be present to back him up. "I will be with you." Jacob's safety that was his concern back in 28:21 will be sure.

Think of principles.

The point about prayer here seems clear enough. The person sensitive to listen to God and tell Him so can enjoy His devotion, direction and defense. The God who is the initiator in Genesis (creation, covenant, etc.) is so much more attentive to see things through than the person who prays listening. A second lesson is also pertinent. Prayer should ever be with the ready spirit, "Here I am," instantly available in servant stance to do God's good pleasure.

Genesis 31:53

Prayer Invoking God's Care

Jacob does leave Laban but does it by slipping away while Laban is unaware. Surely, he could have avoided this sneaky way of departing, and God could be faithful to give him safety before Laban as He would later (v. 24). But Jacob chose to do it his own crafty way, learned from long habit.

Laban is stung, pursues swiftly, is warned by God (v. 24), and catches up with the slower-moving party of Jacob. Finally the two men pledge their peace in a covenant, invoking God to attest and help them to be true to their pact.

The Person They Invoke (v. 53)

Laban knows the right language, and at least he has this right. He proposes that they call to adjudicate their relationship "the God of Abraham . . . Nahor . . . their father. . . ." Laban himself worships other gods (vv. 19, 30). But he has been a keen listener when hearing of Jacob's God; he remembers this religion from the visit by Abraham's servant years before. What he does say about God recognizes Him as the One Jacob's forebears trusted as their own. More can be involved than Laban discerns. The God he wishes to invoke, who will be pleasing to Jacob, is the God who watches over His covenant to fulfill it.

The Pledge They Make (v. 53).

The two men enter into their covenant pledge in three forms as the surrounding context clarifies.

First is the decision and affirmation in speech (v. 53). To swear in a solemn oath of promise to meet one's obligations in the pact, to do this by an appeal to God is to call upon Him to control the undertaking. It is a form of prayer wishing His attestation and sponsorship to see this through with integrity. It is an unusual facet of prayer, but it is that in the intent of the covenant parties.

Second is the affirmation in stone (vv. 44–52). The men established a stone as a pillar marker formalizing their commitment of peace. Other stones were placed in a heap to erect the pillar more conspicuously to stand witness. Though the two men have different names for the heap based on their distinct languages, they express the idea, "heap of witness." Mizpah means "watch tower," memorializing Laban's wish (prayer) that "the Lord watch between you and me when we are absent one from the other" (v. 49).

Third is the affirmation in sacrifice (v. 54). The sacrifice by Jacob was another expression of good will, tied closely to the agreement. It possibly is a gesture of defining details for a sacrificial ratification of a covenant by the agreeing parties passing between parts of the sacrifice as in Genesis 15.

A principle is like a headline. When one invokes God as the true One to grant His care and bear witness to the honor of a pledge, and follows through on a noble intention, he glorifies God.

Genesis 32:9–12

Jacob's Prayer in Fear of Facing Esau

His Adoration of the Lord (vv. 9, 10)

His understanding of God (v. 9). Jacob sees Him as the God of Abraham and Isaac, suggesting the covenant loyalty so prominent with these men. Jacob personally may have understood quite a lot about that, even if he has not always demonstrated keen sensitivity of faithfulness to it.

His unworthiness before God (v. 10). His frank admission of unworthiness in himself is accompanied with a praiseful recognition of

God's worthiness. He humbly feels unfitted for all of what God is in covenant loving-kindness and faithfulness.

As to prayer, verse 9 reflects the aspect of affirmation, a part in prayer that rehearses before God what one realizes He is. As Scripture would increase through time, men would see many more examples of things to affirm in His presence. The Psalms are full of them, for instance, "I love Thee, O Lord, my strength" (18:1).

Verse 10 is at its core praise in prayer.

His Supplication to the Lord (vv. 11, 12)

The plea he makes (v. 11). His heart no doubt thumping with fear of the showdown with Esau, he petitions for safety. How specific! We see no wandering around the Milky Way in prayer here! "Deliver me . . . from . . . Esau." Prayer as definite and right to the point has a clear example here. Why not come right out and say it rather than beat around the bush and only hint at the need?

Jacob is clear, too, about the reason that drives him to prayer. "I fear him. . . ." And he then lays out what is in substance the aspect of intercessory prayer: "lest he . . . attack me, the mothers with the children." He comes in advocacy for these others who are his heavy concern.

Both the petition and the intersession in this case follow the words of adoring praise.

The promise he mentions (v. 12). Jacob pleads for God's bounties while pressing God's own promises. The Lord's very honor in showing integrity to His word is at stake. By His faithfulness, which Jacob has acknowledged in verse 10, Jacob now urges the safe-keeping. The promises he goes back to are a combination of 28:14 (increase of his descendants) and 22:17 to Abraham (multiplication as the sand by the sea). Quite possibly, Isaac on Mount Moriah heard God voice His promise to Abraham and shared the rich expectation with his family. The illustration about the sand by the sea was a part of that.

Jacob prays a wonderful prayer, yet seems to fall short. He *remembers* God's promises and *reminds* Him of them. How appropriate! But he does not *rest* completely in them. He is partly depending in his presents sent ahead to soften Esau, not wholly relying on God's presence. He sends his family over the Jabbok tributary near where it flows into the Jordan River south of what would later be the Sea of Galilee. Then he is alone in his vigil, a troubled man. Faces out of the past are vivid in his memory—Rebekah's, urging the trick to fool Isaac, Isaac's, squinting as he verified Esau's odor and the feel of his hands, Esau's as he skulked waiting to murder him.

Many principles surface here. First, it exalts God to let prayer be shaped by utterances true to His Word about who He is. Second, prayer with a humble rating of one's own unworthiness and accolades for God's worthiness strikes right notes. Third, a person can mingle different aspects of prayer in one kaleidoscope of utterances. Fourth, what we fear on earth can be a backdrop for fearing God whose help we seek from heaven (cf. Hezekiah in Isa. 37). Fifth, it is helpful to lean on what God has promised when we pray. We can go forward hand in hand with God. Sixth, we can partly place our confidence in things of human aid, or we can sell out totally to trust only in what God is able to do without any dependence on human help at all. God may use humans, or He may work a matter out even when all else is of no avail. Our finite minds will probably never have the fullest estimate of God, but it is good to *seek* not to underestimate Him.

Genesis 32:24–32

Jacob's Wrestling in Prayer

His Crisis (32:1–23)

This we have already seen. It all centers in the emergency of meeting Esau, coming face to face with the brother who approaches with blood in his eyes.

His Challenger (v. 24)

Perhaps the snap of a twig or a soft footfall hauled Jacob around. Something . . . somebody was stalking him in the night! And then out of the darkness a figure took vague shape, and before he could react, Jacob found himself locked in a wrestling match.

It was a "man," or so it seemed from the form, the hands that clutched, the words that he spoke. Jacob would realize before long that this was God, for he would name the place for seeing "the face of God" (Peniel). The Lord had appeared in some angelic, even man-like shape to Hagar and to Abraham. Possibly Jacob had heard of that in covenant talk within the home growing up. Readers now know it from reading and believing the Book of Genesis.

The wrestling was apparently new to Jacob. It was unless Rachel's wrestling was "with Elohim" in prayer, she had described this to him, and it had impacted him. At least in his case, prayer is coordinated with wrestling in a bodily sense. Having prayed in 32:9–12, Jacob still faces his showdown that drove him to this mood for God's help. Actual talk with God as in prayer is evident, breaking from Jacob's lips at least three times in verses 26, 27, and 29. The wrestling foe's words also show that a conversation is going on, necessitating Jacob's words of interaction. Further inclination to take this as prayer is furnished by the divine commentary on it in Hosea 12:3, 4. Jacob contended with God, wrestled with the angel, wept and sought His favor! And the association of wrestling with prayer is clearly validated in Ephesians 6:11–20. There the command to be strong in the Lord is quickly linked with wrestling, with the Satanic foes, with the cruciality of donning the right armor, and with prayer in all situations, in all seasons, in all steadfastness, and all in the Spirit for all believers.

In Ephesians, the wrestling with God in alert intensity to have His blessing for success is in harmony with the effectiveness in wrestling against what would oppose His will. It is very much the will of God for Jacob to be kept safe to fulfill covenant blessing pronounced on him. This would entail, for example, any effort by Esau to take away his life opposed to God's will. Jacob becomes in God's purposes a man brought to pray what it is the will of God to give! He prays for God-sufficiency, not winning the day by his own devices: "I will not let you go unless you bless me."

His Change (v. 25)

The visitor (God) sees that so far He has not won out over Jacob; Jacob is depending so much on his own means to win now, as he is doing to prevail with Esau—by his presents. God reduces him to weakness, touching him at the point of the ball and socket in his leg, which is a key to human strength. That changes things and ought to put Jacob on the way toward seeing that he is weak, God is strong, and he needs God's strength to face life.

God also changes him another way. God asks a question calculated to draw from Jacob an acknowledgment of his utter need of Him. Jacob's lips burst forth with a confession of what he needs, of Who he needs. "I will not let you go unless you bless me." He was not fighting to overcome God, as if really opposed to Him; He was grappling to win out in gaining His help. Back in 32:9–12, he had prayed but had not actually rested in God's giving. Now he has been brought to cry out for *God*'s blessing—what will come only from *His* working.

God then pursues him with another key question, "What is your name?" The reply is "Jacob," having its background of "heel-gripper," supplanter, man gaining his ends by his own devices. Confession of the name, and how he has lived it, puts things right out in the open. Yes, he needs the blessing, and he has won it in prayer. God says his name henceforth will be "Israel," meaning "God's fighter," and then explains the significance. To Jacob he says, "you have striven with God and with men and have prevailed." He has wrestled with God by the Jabbok; in this, he has also, as symbolized by analogy, wrestled with Esau and his four hundred. They could do him so much damage. But God assures him he has prevailed.

Already Jacob has come to the realization that the visitor is from God, for he has sought his blessing. Now, following a query about his name, and the assignment of a new name, he pursues the subject of names. He asks the visitor to tell him his name. Perhaps his hearing of various descriptive names for God piqued his curiosity to know the exact significance of this wrestler who was of God. The answer Jacob gets is "Why . . . ask my name?" At any rate, he blessed Jacob, and right away Jacob is aware of who He is. "I have seen God face to face. . . ."

His Characterization (v. 30)

Jacob is so clear about things that he calls the scene of the match "Peniel," meaning "face of God." God has met with him in his crisis with Esau; having won before the face of God, Jacob can now see the face of Esau (v. 20) and will find God has changed it to be, as in the wrestling, "as the face of God" (33:10). Both God and he won the battle in prayer; the next day's showdown would only display fruit resulting from this!

His Consequences (vv. 31–32; 33:1–16)

These are a reminder in his body (a limp), and peace with his brother. The limp would be there the rest of Jacob's days to bring his mind back to his weakness and God's strength. And going on to face Esau the following day, as he must, Jacob saw not a murderous face but a merciful face (33:10), this wrought by God. God put His own face upon Jacob's situation and made the good of His blessing presence so obvious. Jacob would learn, too, that it was not his gifts that transformed Esau's attitude, but the God who answered his prayer (vv. 8–11).

Prayer, then, has had a strategic place in the rush of human events.

Several principles bless the spirit. First, what is gained in prayer can make a profound and precious impression when we have wrestled long to receive it. Perhaps God waits to give some blessings to bring us to a sharper, greater sense of appreciation, and lovingly help us grow. Second, when God does not change us physically in prayer as He did Jacob, He can transform us in spiritual ways. Third, it is often when God brings us to a sense of our own utter bankruptcy that He most starkly can show us what His strength can do. Fourth, how blessed to see with the eyes of faith "the face of God" in prayer or in any circumstance of life (cf. 2 Cor. 4:16–18). Jacob saw God in the physical sense of His revealing Himself as a man in a wrestling encounter and also in the spiritual impact as he realized He had seen the face of God.

Genesis 33:20

Jacob's Altar at Shechem

His Buying (v. 19)

He purchases the ground he camps upon from the owner in the nearby village of Shechem in the land of promise west of the Jordan River, far north of Beer-sheba where Isaac was.

His Building (vv. 17, 20)

For himself (v. 17). He had stopped for a time in Succoth and built a dwelling, then traveled a few miles to Shechem.

For God (v. 20). First is his construction of an altar. Second is his caption for the altar. It is a testimony proclaiming the name of his God, "God, the God of Israel."

This is significant in that Jacob is fulfilling, partially at least, his promise of 28:21. There, if the Lord would keep him safe on his time away from the land, He would be his God. God promised to do that and has kept His pledge. Jacob now is taking a step toward keeping his.

A second possible motive in proclaiming his God might be a witness to let his convictions be known early. The peoples around him had other gods. The witness, if within his intent, had questionable effect in helping his people, also, to look to God. A bit later in 35:2–4, some of them have dabbled in worship of idols, and Jacob belatedly leads them to a break from these.

Jacob also attaches his own new name to the altar. He is "Israel," as in 32:28. So the name has had some impact on him, though in subsequent passages, his actions fluctuate between what testifies of Israel and what suggests the old Jacob.

What can we say of Jacob's prayer as associated with the altar? It is one of the strange silences in Genesis that after Jacob's impression about God in 28:11ff., he is not found specifically praying in Chapters 29–31, except in the few instances. Even when his wives are evidently praying about their need, Jacob is not said to pray about his or to pray for their barrenness. Yet it is wise to exercise care in what is concluded from this. Even Joseph later, the sterling example of godliness that he is, is not specifically described as praying, with few exceptions. The silences are not always clear. But after Jacob's definite seriousness about prayer in 32:9–12 and 32:24–32, it seems probable that he did pray at the altar. That does not mean that he would pray only at the altar. His experiences with God at Bethel (Chap. 28) and Peniel (32) certainly had left a deep conviction that he could speak with God far from any altar! And so is the case of Abraham, praying in Gerar (20), Isaac and Rebekah at Beer-lahai-roi (25), and so forth.

While seeking to be fair to Jacob, one does not gather the impression of a strong spiritual tone in his life as he dwelt in Shechem. His daughter Dinah would be the victim of rape by the prince there, and Jacob would do nothing on hearing the news until his sons returned (34:5). This may have been natural, as he would think it advisable to have the entire family together in any action. Yet even when he and his sons have a confrontation meeting with the leaders of Shechem, the sons and not Jacob gain the spotlight with the chronicler, at least as the situation went on (cp. vv. 11, 13ff.). What Jacob's prayer life or general spiritual fervor were, we do not know. Certainly his sons soon become guilty of deceit and murder—execution not simply of the prince who violated Dinah but all the males. Learning this, Jacob is rightly disturbed about possible Canaanite retaliation that can blot out all in his family. He is responsible for these (v. 30). Why he does not express feelings of how wrong the violation of his daughter was leaves one puzzled. The culprit sons voice this concern (v. 31); it really is their only defense, and one that must have stung Jacob, for the wrong to Dinah was a serious matter. Still, the concern does not vindicate them, for they lied, murdered, and took their anger out on a whole community for what one man did. Two wrongs do not make a right, for the Shechemite scheming to "take Israel for a cleaning" (v. 23) does not justify that Jacob's sons also fail. God could have supplied a better way.

One can wonder why Jacob lingered in this area, not going to his father as God had said (31:3) and as Jacob had intended to do (31:18). He had been concerned those twenty or so years earlier that he return to his father's house (28:21). He had not even gone to Bethel, as God would tell him to do in 35:1, when he was still dilly-dallying.

One principle looms. Let us pray at a place we can memorialize as where our meeting is with "God, the God of Israel," and "our God." And let us be sure that we are in living touch with Him.

Genesis 35:1–5

Jacob's Move in Consecration

This passage shows that Jacob's spiritual devotion of Chapters 33–34 is in need of drastic change. As He so often does in Genesis, God took the initiative. "Then God said" in verse 1. This ignites a new fire, for "Then Jacob said" in verse 2. God led him, then he led his people.

Prayer is not explicit. But Jacob's steps in leading those with him would surely engage any who are genuine in purpose to deal with God in prayer.

The Call from God (v. 1)

First, God calls Jacob to "arise," which is quite apropos after he has been lingering short of going to his relatives (31:3) and Bethel to complete his vow (28:18–22). The call at least reflects that it is not God's will for him to mark time here any longer. Certainly it is not His wisdom to allow spiritual values to slump.

Second, the guidance is to go to Bethel. That is only fifteen miles from Shechem, about a day's journey. And so, again, one can wonder why Jacob stopped short of there, a place so close, in the first place, and dilly-dallied. Jacob had spoken of God as the God of Bethel while out of the land (31:13), but has been delinquent to go all the way there.

Third, in distinction to dwelling in Shechem, Jacob is to live at the new site, Bethel.

Fourth, once at Bethel, the leading is to set up an altar to God. God Himself had set up a ladder there and reassured Jacob by covenant plans to bless him. He had also shown him His angels in continuous activity ministering to the fulfillment of God's will for Jacob and his people. And there Jacob had recognized the "house of God" and "gate of God," both assuring of a way into His presence. He had exulted that if God kept him on his journey out of the promised land and brought him back, this God would be his God. God had kept His part in the relationship. Jacob was as yet short of making good on his, all the way.

God reminds the man that He was the One who appeared to him when he fled from his brother Esau. In a situation of fear—leaving his family, leaving the land, leaving a brother plotting murder—God had graciously intervened with His presence. How relevant for the predicament of the moment that causes new fear to catch in Jacob's throat. Canaanite clans were outnumbering him and were incensed at reports of the atrocity Jacob's sons had dealt some of their neighbors. These men could mass and wipe Jacob's people off the face of the earth (34:30). How timely such a reminder from God was, for Jacob in Chapter 34 does not appear to have taken his fear to Him. It would have been so fitting to think quickly of this and depend only on Him. For in similar threats of Laban and Esau coming to force a showdown, God had been Jacob's shield, as Abraham's (cf. 15:1). Surely, the mighty El Shaddai could find a way to deal with the Shechemites without the sons resorting to treachery, and surely God could raise His defense against other Canaanites!

The call God now issued was potent. His word was enough to rock Jacob to the core and stir him out of complacency into decisive action. He must go back to Bethel, the place of the vow he had *made*, the vow he was *reminded* of (31:13), but the vow he had *dragged his feet* to keep.

The Challenge from Jacob (vv. 2–4)

This at least is to Jacob's credit. When God now calls, the man lets no grass grow under his feet! Three aspects are an exposition of the challenge.

The purging involved in it (vv. 2, 4). Jacob is moved by God through His word to provide vigorous spiritual leadership. God fills his consciousness; other gods must be put away! Separation to God is necessary. Here is a turning to God (v. 3) from idols (v. 2) as in Thessalonians 1:9 (cf. Acts 26:18–20). This would have sharp effect on any who, like Rachel with her father Laban's little household gods, teraphim (31:19, 30, 34–35), had these useless figurines with them. It is possible that such idols were thought to have power in conferring to a person family inheritance, as in Nuzi tablets of the fifteenth century B.C. excavated in the 1920s and 1930s in northeast Mesopotamia. Laban in confronting Jacob after his pursuit (Chap. 31) could have had that idea in ransacking Jacob's things in an aroused search to retrieve his gods. He would not want Jacob and his wives to show up later with those idols so as to claim inheritance. But whatever trust any of Jacob's people had in such gods, his challenge now was to break with such superstition and trust in the God of Bethel for blessing that He alone could guarantee. The separation also meant parting with amulets such as rings and earrings (v. 4). The challenge summoned the people to a thorough "housecleaning."

The purity involved in it (v. 2). In dealings here with God, two facets are the focus as to purity. One is a cleansing that is pertinent, the other is clothing that is a manifestation that cleansing is real.

Prayer in such dealings with God is vital and necessary and was quite probable here even if not mentioned. It is not easy to think a spiritual cleansing is realistic if an individual does not become *personal* with God. His earnest concern over sin (idolatry here, etc.) spontaneously finds expression in prayerful thought or words. Jacob, for example, had voiced his conviction in prayer, "I am unworthy," speaking to God (32:10). Jacob's sons later were very personal and forthright in words seeking Joseph's forgiveness (cf. 50:16, 17). And Jacob himself led them to do that. It seems sensible that in 35:2–4 this same Jacob, vigorous as his challenge was after God aroused him, would lead his people to do this before God Himself.

The change of clothing is no doubt an outward reflection of the inward cleansing and of a clear-cut new beginning. It was a meaningful tangible gesture speaking of a fresh and right endeavor after laying aside sin.

The presence involved in it (vv. 3, 5). Jacob articulates to his people the reality of God's specific past answer meeting him in his distress of spirit (28:11ff.). The Lord backed up this response by His presence that had supported Jacob "wherever I have gone." Personal testimony of that Presence has a profound impact in stimulating a resolute turnabout, leaving sin (v. 4).

It is significant, also, that when the decisive people step forth in that commitment, the Presence again is a powerful shield keeping the people safe from what they fear. God puts a great terror on people of Canaanite cities to hold back from harming them. So they do not pursue them (v. 5). He could have done this or worked some other way earlier had Jacob trusted Him. This was the Presence that had shielded Abraham (15:1; 12:17–20; 20:3–7); the Presence that kept Isaac's neighbors at peace (26:26–31); the Presence that thwarted Laban and Esau from hurting Jacob (31:24, 29; 33:1–15). How deceptive sin is. For believers who have seen so much of how God is faithful often grow cold about looking to Him in a new jam and need to learn a lesson all over again.

Genesis 35:6–15

The Commitment of Jacob

God's escort accompanied the party south to Bethel. Then the thought moves to their arrival, their altar, and their ascription of tribute to God. The passage also refers to their agony in the death of Deborah (v. 8), God's new appearance (9–13), and Jacob's acclamation of God anew at Bethel (14, 15).

The arrival and the events linked with it represent a completion for God and for Jacob, though for neither a final one. God had completed His pledge as it related to keeping Jacob while away on his sojourn (28:15). He had used His further words of guidance at many points along the way to work this completion (cf. 31:3; 35:1, etc.). As to Jacob, he had vowed that the God appearing at Bethel would be his God; he had specified his return to his father's house (28:21), and God had kept him safe at least to get to the place of the vow, Bethel. This was, for him, a major part of the completion already realized, the rest assumed by faith and in due time to be totally done in Isaac's presence (35:27).

The altar now newly put up (v. 7) renews and extends Jacob's commitment to God (his God!) at this spot. The pillar he had left as a memorial after seeing God's ladder and hearing His covenant reaffirmation may or may not have been still in its place. Thirty or more years had passed. Now before his people and with his possessions, trusting God as before, he proclaimed for the altar the honored name, "El Bethel," or "God of the House of God." The tribute was tied to God's revelation there, and this when he needed reassurance on leaving the promised land that this land would yet be his.

Mention is not made of his promised gift of a tenth, but Jacob probably followed through to complete this also. He might have done it in sacrifices from his God-given flock, in a day when such gifts to God, as Abel's precedent had been (4:4), were offered. Abraham had done so (22:13) and so had Jacob himself (31:54). Prayer, while again one of the details not noted in the narrative, could appropriately accompany worship at the altar. And Jacob knew what it was to pray to God (28:20–22; 31:11; 32:9–12, 24ff.). His aroused spiritual leadership of his people at the beginning of this chapter points to their knowing about seeking God as well.

Agony suffered in losing Deborah could have been keenly felt. For Jacob she was a love link with his mother Rebekah, who apparently had sent her those many days of journeying to support Rachel and Leah. These wives, too, would wince at the pain of grief in so great a loss. So, as is easy to understand, Deborah's burial site beneath the limbs of an oak suggested the name, "Oak of weeping." Such a memorial service as must have transpired would be felt by God, too. He was the God who showed compassion at the weeping of the boy, Ishmael (21:17), at the heartache of Leah and Rachel, and when Joseph wept in his chamber after seeing his youngest brother, Benjamin (43:30).

A new appearance of God to reassure Jacob and his people of covenant fulfillment is apropos to the context. Jacob and those with him had been worshiping at Bethel. Now the Lord responds to the new step forward in spiritual commitment. He calls Jacob's name "Israel" anew, re-emphasizing what He knows of Jacob's tenacious fighting in prayer to prevail a few years before near the bank of the Jabbok (v. 10). What He calls the man is a witness to the value that He sets on prayer that wins with Him! God help us to be like that!

Not only does God call Jacob by his new name again. He also characterizes Himself by a name, a description, the same title with which He approached Abraham (Gen. 17:1). That occasion was one of similarly repeating His covenant promises and there even giving the symbol or token of the covenant, circumcision. It was also a situation accompanied by His desire for Abraham to walk before Him and be perfect in a sound, all-out commitment. All those associations except circumcision are pertinent in Chapter 35 as well. God is El Shaddai, using a term for a mountain hulking in awe-inspiring greatness before a man, a description conveying His great power to see the promises through. As some have styled the thought, He is "the God who is Enough!" His expansive sufficiency stands as a striking stimulant to this "Israel" or any who struggle in prayer. Through Him one is able to overcome.

He dubs Jacob by a new name, He characterizes Himself, and then He confirms what El Shaddai is adequate to fulfill. In verses 11–12, He can challenge Jacob to be fruitful and multiply in descendants because His own power and promise guarantee that the covenant is bound to prosper through him and his people. The plan initiated in 12:1–3 calls for a nation, even nations and kings (17:6). Then, too, it includes the land guaranteed to Jacob and his descendants as early as 12:7. All of this could snatch the breath away. Jacob is no doubt stoked with new assurance that God's word gives. His worshipful response (vv. 14–15) is to show his commitment in two ways. He re-enacts the kind of scene he had had years before when he first saw God there. He sets up a pillar marker, pours a drink-offering on it, pours oil on it to identify it with God's confirmation, and in a second step affirms the very special place afresh. It is "God's house." And his reaction is fresh commitment.

Again it is strange that no words of prayer explicitly appear. Still, many details are suggestive that he surely would pray at such a time. How very meaningful would be prayer to thank God for His accomplishment, for safe arrival , for what the altar memorialized, for the years of Deborah's ministrations, for God appearing anew, and for so much more. And how apt to the situation to praise God as he had in 32:10 for His covenant loving-kindness, and for all He was as El Shaddai, God of Bethel

Principles can reasonably occur here. First, if we mean business with the Lord, we trust Him, and not false gods that people rely upon. Isaiah 41–48 later gives many reasons not to depend on gods that are not God but the creations from the hands of men. Second, God can give His sure signal to return to an earlier contact with Him that is more true. Let each one ask, "Is my heart ready to surge or to slump at His summons? Third, a believer who takes a clear stand for God may have a strong influence on others who need to look to Him alone. Fourth, even a leader who has failed to trust God can do an about face before God and others who know of his failure, and still have clout to lead others with him. Fifth, when a believer draws near to God, God draws near to him (cf. 35:8–9; 2 Chr. 7:14; James 4:8).

Genesis 37–50

Joseph and Jacob

Few servants of God shine for sterling character as Joseph does on the pages of the Bible. Certain names that would spring to mind could be Samuel, Nehemiah, Daniel, Ruth, John the Baptist, and the apostles John and Paul. But one of the surprising things in the Joseph story is the infrequency of direct references to his prayer. We would expect to find the Joseph chapters (Gen. 37–50) saturated by communion with God.

The main focus in all this section is on the initiating work of God, sovereignly engineering His progress in effecting steps forward for His covenant people. In the book overall, His action is foremost. He created, He commanded Adam and Eve, He brought the flood, He led Noah to pronounce a prophecy, He called Abram, He appeared to reaffirm His covenant, He sent Joseph ahead to Egypt to become a savior to His people in famine. It may be the studied emphasis in Genesis 37–50 on just the narrative of the story and God's providential control that leads the writer to mention so little about prayer.

Joseph

Whatever the reason, the narrative is rich with material suggesting a prayerful Joseph. So as a preparation for passages on the certainty of prayer (reserved for later), three lines of emphasis suggesting the relevancy of prayer can help. These are Joseph's circumstances for urgent prayer, his consciousness of God that would make prayer a native breath, and God's care for him that would stimulate prayer in quite natural ways.

His Circumstances for Prayer

Joseph appears in one predicament after another that could draw him to God in prayer, yet the passages skip over this. But the same phenomenon applies to other leading characters in Genesis. Abraham is not said to pray where prayer was extremely relevant in several of the chapters.

Examples are his crisis in Egypt (12), his temptation to resort to Hagar to gain a son, his securing of the promised son and the conflict with the maid and the other son, his great loss of Sarah and his marriage to Keturah.

The same is true with Isaac in 26:1–22. And Jacob's possible prayer life goes without note in his crucial winning of the birthright, his seeking Isaac's blessing, all of the time when his wives need God's help to conceive children, and in his stay at Shechem.

Silence about prayer meets the reader in most crises of Joseph. The situations called for God's help. Such was the lad's desperation imprisoned in a pit without a drink, waiting to be slain. Agonizing moments while the brothers bartered with caravan traders spring to mind, as does the camel carrying the boy to a far land away from his waiting father. How urgent prayer was when Potiphar's wife was using her wiles day after day seeking to entice Joseph into compromise. How relevant prayer could have been when Joseph thought of the seductress retaining his garment and rigging a case to pour into her husband's ears when he came home. Then Joseph was cast into prison, where prayer was critical for a way out.

These and many other difficult moments were opportune to draw appeals from Joseph's heart and lips, just as Jacob's peril in meeting Esau stirred him to pray.

God's Care and Prayer

Many passages spotlighting God's faithful blessing fit well with faith as in prayer that is so spontaneous with commitment. Thanksgiving in prayer, for example, would be difficult not to imagine for blessing at Potiphar's house (39:2, 3, 5, 21–23) and in the prison (40:3, 4). And God's care brightening the young man's daily life goes well with a principle of petition casting all care on God who cares (cf. Ps. 55:22; 1 Pet. 5:7).

His Consciousness of God

Joseph's tender God-consciousness bespeaks a spirit that communes with God and relies on Him. This seems apparent in several clues.

God's plan. Joseph began to have very attention-rousing convictions that God was pursuing a plan for him and his family after two early dreams (Gen. 37). This would add to whatever details his father had taught the children about God's covenant drama. The strong words of Joseph to his brothers about God sending him before the family to Egypt and God's over-arching superintendence of all the events finally for good reflect his conviction of a master plan. Even in the finish of his life Joseph is God-conscious, so much so that he is passionate to have his family inter his bones, put them in the land of the plan.

God's person. Joseph so respects the Person of God that he can react to sexual temptation with the reverential awe due Him. He chooses to do what is in harmony with His Person, what will please Him. To yield to what Potiphar's wife is lusting to indulge in is unthinkable distortion. Later Joseph can testify to his brothers, "I fear God" (42:18). This respect for the Person of God, this sensitivity to what fits with His nature and His will is decisive for Joseph's actions. He mercifully releases the brothers from prison and holds only Simeon, letting the others trek back to Canaan that God may carry forward His plans for the family.

That sort of tender prompting to do what displays respect for God suggests a heart ready to be close to Him in prayerful longings.

God's priorities. A prayerful attitude of priority for God's ways surfaces in Joseph's overall tenor of things that are important. His consistent purity shows the fruit of the Spirit that the Scripture refers to later. All nine aspects listed in Galatians 5:22–23 are obvious in Joseph. *Love* for God appears in his refusal to sin with his master's wife; a proper love for her and her husband shines there too. And Joseph loves his brothers, who had dealt him sharp heartache. *Joy* is clear when, in the prison, he asks the butler and the baker why they look so glum; Joseph apparently is cheerful. When he can name one of his sons to honor God having made him forget all his trouble and his family back home (41:51) he seems to be composed, at *peace*. He shows *longsuffering* to his brothers and is *gentle* with them. *Goodness* toward Potiphar when he will not take advantage of the master's wife during his absence is obvious. His goodness to receive his brothers and meet his family's needs even without charging them is pronounced. He is *faithful* to carry the truth to his father when he is young, faithful to serve Potiphar in a shining way, and trustworthy in prison work. *Meekness* is manifest in his submission to God's providential will (45:5–9). Finally, *self-control* is plain in episode after episode. Joseph is disciplined to integrity facing the purring temptress, keeping his composure while for a time not revealing his identity his brothers, and following through on his pledge to bury his father in the covenant land.

One further aspect points out Joseph's sharp consciousness of God.

God's provisions. Joseph was so aware of God supplying what he (and God's will) needed that he was confidently expectant. He looked to God to give him the interpretations of dreams that were from Him (40:8; 41:16). And God gave him the interpretations as a usable channel. God had supplied the sufficiency to help Joseph forget his troubles and his far away family (41:51). This was not to blank his memory of these, but to feel adequate to cope with the pain and be occupied with other things as he rested in God until His time and way became clear. Joseph would remember the dreams God had given him in his boyhood and meditate on God's covenant kindness. God's provision was strongly on his mind and lips when he said that *God* had sent him to Egypt; in his view of things, his brothers were not foremost in doing it after all (45:5–9).

Prayer in keeping close accounts with God would seem extremely cogent in a life so overshadowed by God's plans, God's Person, God's priorities, and God's provisions.

It has been the aim in the preceding pages on Joseph to dwell on evidences for him praying even when direct praying is not on the scripture pages. Now, by contrast, the spotlight changes in the next section to clear references to praying.

Before entering into that, reflect on a principle in general for prayer. Some in Scripture, like Joseph, are notably godly and probably steeped more in prayer than specific references may show. One can think of Caleb, Othniel, Jonathan, Ezekiel, Joel, Amos, Micah, and so forth. Let it be true of us, whatever some written record of us that may or may not emphasize this, that our hearts and lips are in frequent engagement with God. Another obvious guideline is that a life lived to God's glory as Joseph's was can be a life stayed on Him in prayer.

His Certainties of Prayer

Genesis 43:29. Joseph utters a prayerful intercessory wish for God's gracious dealing toward Benjamin. It is a scene in which the Egyptian leader is caught up by incredible emotional stirrings. He has just looked out and picked his youngest brother from the band of men visiting him. The sight of Benjamin arriving from a home far away after twenty years is enough to rock Joseph to the depths.

How he would love to throw patience to the wind, rush to his brother, kiss him, and clasp him in a warm hug (cf. 48:10). How intensely he must have felt a surge to speak out his heart to the young man. But Joseph summoned resolute self-control. He could not let his feelings burst forth yet. He must let the drama with the brothers be played to the mature point.

First, he seats the brothers in the exact order of their birth, a spectacle which strike them as uncanny, provoking their awe at such accuracy. Then he would give Benjamin five times more on his plate than for any other guest. This special favor would give a strong hint of unusual feeling for the youngest. That could set the brothers' curiosity ticking. From where, from whom could such feeling for Benjamin most naturally come? And Joseph's own mind would flash back through the years to the prayer of his own mother, Rachel, assuming she had shared it with him later. It was the time of his birth, an answer to her prayer and occasion for her fresh prayer for God yet to add another besides himself. God had answered. Benjamin, son of the same mother!

But here, before seating and serving, Joseph cannot restrain himself from one thing, prayer. It flows forth so spontaneously, possibly with his hand going to his brother's head or shoulder. his eyes, at least, fixing on Benjamin with love. Yet Joseph prefaces the incident with a question to the other brothers, so as to appear casual and not give away his identity yet. The prayer is one of wishing or invoking

God's blessing, in essence an expression of an intercessory desire. The probability is that Jacob had shared with his family so momentous a thing as Isaac invoking a blessing on him from God.

A kind of blessing in prayer came so naturally to Joseph's lips now. It came within a long line of prayers interceding for God's graciousness, a stream of wish utterances such as in Numbers 6:24–27 and Psalm 67:1, even as before and after Joseph's case.

God would answer the prayer. His graciousness would be shown through Joseph himself who prays, at the meal and later on Benjamin along with the entire family. God's reply would be with great provision.

A fitting outline of the prayer passage above is this: Joseph's Invitation to His Home (43:16–28); Joseph's Invocation on His Brother (v. 29); and Joseph's Interlude of Weeping (v. 30).

The time in secret, with tears flowing, is almost certain to have involved prayer. A man just coming off prayer, and being conscious of the priority God had in all things would find it relevant to pray again. Prayer in *gratitude* was apropos for incredible things—for God having at long last brought all of his brothers to him; for God having spared Benjamin heartache such as his own; for news that his father still lived. Just as timely for the situation was *petition*—for his wise steps in preparing his guilty brothers for his disclosure to them. And *intercession* would be extremely opportune—for his father to survive to be reunited; for the effect to be powerfully helpful to the brothers in dealing with God and with him about their wrong; for a reaction in the Pharaoh to go along with the will of God.

A principle pertains in 43:29. Those who know the Lord may at times pray particular blessings for people whom God has highlighted on their own hearts as special.

Genesis 48:12. Jacob wishes to pronounce covenant blessing on Joseph's two sons. More detail is devoted to this later in regard to Jacob since the present prayer has him invoking the blessing. Joseph as the focus at the moment can be summed up in two points.

First is *the blessing* itself which Jacob voices (vv. 8–20). Second is *the bowing* (v. 12). Joseph bows in worship before God whom his father is invoking. His act of deep respect for God and His will in the blessing would reasonably go with prayer thinking and possibly voicing praiseful adoration and affirmation of the respect with which he values the blessing. His sons had been born in Egypt and heard only their father's stories of the God of Israel, His covenant, and Abraham, Isaac, and Jacob. Now reality was truly facing the boys with covenant blessing, this in the very presence of the grandfather himself who was in the line of the blessing. This was a big day in their lives, as in Joseph's, and Joseph would want them to receive the fullest impact from it and from God who gave the blessing.

A principle is easy to see here. Like Jacob, we too can pray for blessing on grandchildren. Of course the same principle can relate to any member within one's own immediate human family. For most of us, a family tree even in our own generation can include many, and so right here is a potentially long prayer list and opportunity to have an impact. Our prayers would not be limited to our own relatives, but also devoted to those in the wider family of God, for the unsaved, and anything in life.

Jacob

As strange as it may seem, more specific prayers in Genesis 37–50 come from Jacob than from Joseph. The latter was very godly in his submission to God's will and played the very great role in God's will as a deliverer of the family in need. Still, Jacob or Israel is in the succession from Abraham and Isaac and is the father of the sons overall who will multiply into tribes and the nation.

It is from Jacob that the blessing of the covenant is passed on, humanly speaking. And so Jacob comes back to play a strategic role in which prayer is right at the heart.

Genesis 43:14

The plan for a second trip. Persisting famine and dwindling supplies drive Jacob to send his sons back to Egypt. He even braves the trauma of parting with Benjamin. The risk is great for his youngest son, even for all the sons. This draws him to prayer.

The prayer for God's blessing. He pleads for God's gracious blessing upon all of the sons as he will wait for their return.

First, Jacob mentions the sufficiency on which he depends. May "El Shaddai" work compassion to move the Egyptian leader. Jacob goes back to the greatness of his God as depicted by this description. God had designated Himself this way to Abraham (17:1) and to Jacob (35:11). He was the God who was big enough to do all the impossibilities within His will. He was great like a mighty mountain looming up before men. He was sufficient to multiply His covenant people, give nations from them, promise to raise up kings, and assure He would give care to His people. He was the God big enough to bless the momentous journey when so much was hanging in the balances. Yes, He was the God to whom Jacob could make his appeal.

God was adequate—more adequate than Jacob's faith came up to. For before the verse ends, the praying man shows he is not certain how things will turn out. Possibly Jacob is just showing that he supposes that God may will to bereave him of his sons, as he had once thought that Joseph had been taken. How kind of God to hear a prayer of His covenant man even when it flickers, coming short of the full faith that might be there. How often this is true of us, who trust God but still are beset by elements of uncertainty.

The specifics of the prayer. Jacob is very definite, right to the point as he had been when fearing to face Esau (32:9–12). He makes intercession for God's giving compassion to the Egyptian man in command so that the sons might receive this kind of bounty. The travelers indeed stood in dire need of God's special working in the leader. along with other problems the journey held. Monies for goods brought back on the first trip had shown up in their sacks, making them appear to be thieves. To go back now was to walk into high danger if the leader thought their explanation a tall tale.

The prayer also pleaded for release of the captive Simeon and the safety of Benjamin. The leader had made a special point of asking about the younger brother. So, who could know of the designs he might have to keep him as he had Simeon?

The scenario he fears. Jacob is so pressed by the urgency for provisions that he must order the trip. If the results prove so disastrous as loss of his sons, he is resigned to this. So be it. He hopes for something far better, and he has a God who is able, but he does not shine with the most sturdy faith. It is like this for all of God's people as they pray, at one time or many. God desires to see perfect faith, but in covenant kindness He blesses even when we fail at it.

Principles register their impact. One relates also to 43:29 and 48:12 noted above. We should pray for family members and others to be kept safe on a journey or a mission, and for God to meet their needs. In this case Jacob pleaded for his sons on a long trek. He probably also prayed, at various times, for family members in other matters—for example for Dinah and his other daughters. In all matters we may call on God for our children too (cf. Job 1:5). Here alone is a ministry that has great repercussions. Are we committed to it or shirking it and letting the ministry slip past?

Genesis 46:2

This transpires much later. The God whom Jacob trusted in 43:14 has answered his prayer despite flawed trust. He has kept all the sons safe. He has not only inclined the leader to show compassion, but he had given far, far more provision than Jacob had even envisioned. God's supply is above all he has asked or thought (cf. Eph. 3:20). Still that is not all. The leader who displayed the compassion, in God's extraordinary sufficiency, is Joseph! Unbelievable. Yes, at first (Gen. 45:26), it was. Oh, Jacob, of little faith, why did you doubt? How like the God of power this was. How like El Shaddai!

Once Jacob collects himself, grasps the mind-boggling reality of this work by God, and starts on his trip to see Joseph, God reappears. He reassures His covenant man that He will take care of him even when he goes out of the land. This is as God had shown His presence at the top of a staircase many years before when Jacob was ready to go out of the land (Gen. 28).

His remembrance in sacrifice (v. 1). Stopping at Isaac's home area, Jacob paid trusting tribute to the covenant God, his own God

(28:21) and the God of Isaac. The emphasis is on His being God of his father Isaac to underscore the continuity Jacob feels with the covenant line. He is conscious of God's covenant grace, upbeat as God's safe-keeping of Joseph and the entire family has cheered him to be. Thoughts of the covenant continuation would also be filling his mind with wondering about going out of the land.

In grateful worship the head of the family honors God with sacrifices. The movement of his devotion is in thanksgiving/praise. But it also is in seeking God's confirmation in a petitionary quest, for Jacob feels need of definite go-ahead counsel. This is the first mention of him offering sacrifice since 31:54, though the record does not always refer to instances when this or that occurred.

God's reassurance in speaking (vv. 2–4). Two points are parts of this go-ahead to the covenant head.

First is a calling of names, Jacob's and God's (vv. 2–3a). God initiates the speech, calling "Jacob, Jacob," repeating the name for emphasis as a strong attention-getter. The prompt response is "Here I am." It is not insensitive prayer being squeezed out of the man, but a sensitive reaction affirming his alertness, arousal, and availability to act at God's desire. It is brief, to the point, tenderly in a listening attitude. It is like God's own preparedness to act on a believer's behalf in His instant "Here I am" to answer prayer (Isa. 58:9, same word). He is the God who is there.

The calling of names continues with descriptions for God. True to the intent of Jacob in verse 1, the One responding to the sacrifices is the covenant God, "God, the God of your father. . . ." Jacob might well be stimulated to think back to God answering Isaac's and Rebekah's prayers, confirming His covenant, giving peace with his neighbors, and leading Isaac to pronounce the blessing on Jacob. Of strong relevance, too, since Jacob is set to leave the covenant land, would be Isaac's emphatic pledge to him that he and his descendants would possess the land (28:4). That encouragement had come also when Jacob was set to leave the land.

The reminder that this was the God of his father could also stir Jacob to quick recall of God being with him too. Over and over again God had continued His covenant goodness even to him. As he would exult in celebration later (48:15) God had been his shepherd all his life (cf. Ps. 23:6).

Such a cheering calling of names prepares aptly for a confirming of the move.

Second, God's reassurance comes in a confirming of the sojourn in Egypt (vv. 3–4). The confirming draws its force from the calling of the name that stands behind it as its guarantee. God expresses His promise in four steps. He pledges:

(1) His advancement of Jacob's descendants to see the covenant expectations through ("I will make of you a great nation").

(2) His abiding with Jacob personally ("I will go . . . with you").

(3) His assurance of a return later to the covenant land ("I will also surely bring you up again").

(4) His attention through Joseph ("Joseph will close your eyes").

These are strong reinforcements, certified by a mighty name. So the next thing for Jacob is rising to go, trusting the promise of God (v. 5).

Among many principles that fit the case is this. In all of life or in some special venture touched with awesome possibilities, we should spend vital time with God. A second, related guideline is to live in such sensitivity to the Lord that when He speaks we will hear and be instantly at His beck and call ("Here I am"). Today our main way of keeping sensitive to Him is to be ever listening to take in His written Word in Scripture saturation. When we are ready to listen, He will pour this into us and guide us wisely according to it, as in Jacob's case He guided by His Word in a personal appearance. We now also see the prayerful lesson of. Psalm 119:133, "Establish my footsteps in Your Word," and the principle of Proverbs 3:5–6.

Genesis 47:7, 10

Soon after the drama of God reuniting him with his beloved Joseph in Egypt, Jacob accompanies Joseph to pay a courtesy call on the Pharaoh. He prays during the interview!

The introduction to the Pharaoh (v. 7a). Jacob would be glad to see the potentate whose generosity God had stirred to support Joseph in his gracious care. The leader would be honored to meet the head of the family from which he had gained so wise a controller of all he had. It was without doubt a momentous interchange by two men. Each was great in his own venue, one in worldly authority over his nation, under God's providence (cf. Ps. 75), the other in God's momentous plans set on embracing peoples of all nations.

The interchange with the Pharaoh (vv. 8, 9). The head of Egypt asked Jacob how old he was. Jacob was forthright. He was 130, and this is later seen to be seventeen years before his death (47:28). He humbly and candidly sums up his life made of years few and unpleasant. He dwells on the difficulties, the dark side, when he could better have testified so richly of great goodness God had dealt. He did not snatch up and redeem this opportunity (cf. Eph. 5:16) but let it slip by, as God's people so often do. He did at least bear witness to the longer lives his forebears had, and this reflects on the bounties of their God.

The invocation upon the Pharaoh (vv. 7b, 10a). In this prayer, Jacob was definitely bearing positive impact while he had the opportunity. He blessed the host when entering and when exiting, when first introduced and before he went his way. His pronouncement of blessing was in essence a prayer wish energetic for the leader's best interests in his life and governance. It was a kind of intercessory gesture calling on God to show His hand for good. The element of prayer was of the essential spirit of praying for secular governmental leaders in later Scripture (Ezra 6:10; Jer. 29:7; 1 Tim. 2:1–2). Jacob was of this inclination, though he did not have the light that the subsequent scriptures provide.

A good principle sifts from this. A believer can pray even during contacts with unbelievers and pray meaningful things that relate to them. God may incline a pagan's heart to Himself through a gesture of kind concern. A ministry of this kind expands to various situations, such as later Scripture shows in believers asking God to give peace to Babylon (Jer. 29:7), and believers praying for kings and others in authority (1 Tim. 2:1–2).

Genesis 47:29–31

Seventeen years have come and gone in Egypt. Jacob, knowing that the shadow of death was on him, wants Joseph's promise to bury him in his beloved covenant land.

The request of Jacob (vv. 29, 30). He asks Joseph to perform the gesture of guarantee and to promise in solemn oath before God to lay him to rest in Canaan. Joseph is his choice because he will transfer firstborn rights to him (48:22), forfeited by Reuben in 35:22 (49:4). Jacob intends for Joseph to take the lead in this, even though he also charges all the sons to carry it out (49:29–32). They do, as Joseph is in charge (50:4–14).

Placing the hand under the thigh is a sign attesting that one will fulfill the oath affirmed. Abraham's servant using this custom in Genesis 24 has clarified that. It is an act signifying the idea, "Be assured that what you would do by your own power were you able I will most certainly do in your behalf, God attesting what I pledge to you."

The response of Joseph (vv. 30, 31). Joseph agrees to this burial wish, then affirms it in the oath. He places his hand on his father's thigh and invokes God's witness by prayer.

The result in Jacob (v. 31b). The aged father bows, probably in prayer as suits the great occasion. What he says might be in praise to God who had assured him in 46:1–4 and now assures him anew. Or an intercession for God's help to Joseph would fit. At any rate, he feels at rest that the Lord will bless so that all goes well.

A principle in this is reasonable, based on Joseph appealing to God in an oath prayer and others (cf. 1, 2 Sam., etc.), summoning Him to see them through to fulfill godly aims. We, too, can pray relying on Him to help us stay on a path true to good goals.

Genesis 48:8–20

Jacob utters a prayerful prophetic pronouncement of blessing on Joseph's two sons.

His asking for the sons (vv. 8–11). He appeals to Joseph to bring the sons before him to receive his blessing.

The arrangement of the sons (vv. 12–14). As seemed natural due to custom, Joseph stationed the sons with Manasseh the firstborn to Jacob's right. The grandfather then could easily place his right hand on Manasseh's head and his left on Ephraim's. But Jacob would deliberately insist on crossing his arms to lay his right hand on Ephraim to receive the greater blessing (vv. 17–19).

His adoration of God for the past (vv. 15–16a). The blessing begins with Jacob's focus on the God from whom the blessing comes. He sees himself only as God's channel to voice the blessing. His words are the prayerful essence of praise, adoring God as God of the fathers (Abraham, Isaac) and God of faithfulness in his own life. He bridges past and present, sensitive to covenant continuity. In the life of Jacob, God has been the shepherd through all his days and the redeemer keeping him safely in the face of all evil. His thoughts are steeped in thanksgiving that credits God for everything that has blessed him. In such a sense of personal endowment, he is ready to pass the baton to the future generation, his grandsons here and his sons in 49:1–28. To Joseph and his sons, a testimony of this nature from the forebear would be very encouraging. As God had been faithful to all the covenant people up to now, they could thrill in His aims to be compassionate to them.

His anticipation of God in the future (vv. 16, 20). The patriarch pronouncing the blessing, which is his own prayerful wish as well, conveys it in four aspects:

(1) Prosperity of the grandsons (16). This is in identification with the names of Abraham, Isaac, and Jacob and by an increase to

become many. God would give the fulfillment in their being called sons of Abraham, sons of Israel, and descendants of all the three patriarchs. Realization would also be in tribes filling the promised land.

(2) Perpetuity of the names (as above).

(3) Plentitude of the descendants (as above).

(4) Priority of Ephraim (vv. 17–20). God had already sovereignly chosen others in the covenant line for priority, Abraham, Isaac and Jacob. Now He exercises His prerogative again. He leads Jacob to show this by the arrangement of his hands and the assertion of his lips. Ephraim, in his later tribal territory and significance, would be the greater. The blessing given to both would give rise to a saying among Jacob's descendants wishing blessing like that shown to Ephraim and Manasseh. Consider a principle of prayer. What one prays that is in accord with God's intentions in His Word and plan he can have confidence God will usher to its answer. Solomon pleaded in his temple dedication prayer for blessings to His people even in later times (1 Kgs. 8), things God would do (cf. Dan. 6:10). And Daniel, in accord with God's Word that he had studied, appealed for the very blessings that were on God's heart to fulfill for His people (Dan. 9:4–19; cf. also Jer. 29:10–14).

Genesis 49:1–28

Another enactment is crucial to Jacob while he yet lives in the present life. Again, as God's mouthpiece, he is moved to bless, and this time he blesses all his sons. His words are a prophetic pronouncement as God moves him, coordinated with aphorisms of character his sons have displayed or the Lord shows their descendants will reflect. His own freedom to speak what he has rightly observed, or his feelings such as displeasure with Reuben's sexual wrong and Simeon's and Levi's cruelty still find expression. As in inspiration through any chosen channel, God is able to voice aspects of His will in a blend with elements the person himself feels.

The blessing is on all of the sons, each in the measure that God gives (v. 28). When Jacob curses, he curses the sin his sons committed but does not curse them personally (v. 7). The blessing through the human vehicle permits the strain of prayerful wish to blend in, as in verse 18. There, Daniel in his future development will gain success as in judging and conquest (vv. 16, 17). Yet any success should be sought in the spirit of trust in God that the prayer articulates. This is in looking to God to effect His deliverance, by His power. This is affirming in prayer one's reliance on Him.

Now it is time to look more fully at prayer in the patriarch's last words.

The call of Jacob's sons (vv. 1, 2). The father summons the sons to his bedside. He has things to speak before it is too late (v. 1), and he is earnest that they are all ears (v. 2). He mentions their listening twice.

The character of Jacob's speech. One can note several things, at least five.

(1) Its prophecy. Moved by God, who knew the future and actually planned it in covenant faithfulness (12:1–3), Jacob is enabled to speak this. He is God's mouthpiece as Noah was in 9:24–27. His words relate to what will happen to his sons' peoples "in the latter days." The phrase, as becomes clear later, is apparently elastic, since in the continuity of the peoples' future various times are parts of days later than Jacob's speech. The words can pertain to not-too-distant times or to times very far off but relevant to the descendants (Heb. 1:1–3).

Relevancy of Jacob's words, even to times of the Messiah centuries later, becomes evident when God leads Jacob to utterances about Him. This seems to be the case in 49:10. The one destined ultimately to wield the king's scepter in Judah's line is "the one to whom it is, or belongs." He is the great Shiloh. And in verse 18 the salvation for which Jacob waits is that which the Lord will effect. As later Scripture in the continuity of covenant dealings with this same people defines, His salvation is ultimately in the Messiah, and in a Messianic era (Isa. 9:6, 7; 59:16; 63:5; Acts 4:12). Far more can be a part of God's providing salvation to satisfy Jacob's longings than Jacob at that time so far grasped.

(2) Its purpose (v. 28). Jacob's intent, as God is speaking His will through him, is to "bless" the sons. The prophecy will articulate the aspects of blessing.

(3) Its plentitude. That the aim is to extend the blessing to all of the sons and their descendants is made clear in definite ways. The blessing is for "the twelve tribes" (v. 28), not only some of them. It is for all twelve, "them" and "each one."

Cursing is here, but in the wording it is directed not just against perversity, but persons—for example, against the anger and cruelty Simeon and Levi had displayed (v. 7). Yet the sin which is condemned does relate to people or their descendants losing privilege they might have had. Reuben was guilty of incest and will not excel (v. 4). Sin of Simeon and Levi leads to their descendants being scattered. Simeon would receive tribal land only within Judah's, and Levi no land inheritance in one place but scattering to forty-eight cities amidst other tribes (Josh. 19:9; 21:1–42).

Still, blessing is retained in some measure. All the peoples would have the privilege to hope in God for salvation (v. 18). All would receive benefit from kingly rule through Judah and the ultimate king in this line (v. 10). God would value the Levites' stand for His word with Moses against idolatry (Ex. 32) and set them apart to a special distinction (Deut. 33:9). They would minister spiritual blessing to people of all the sons' descendants (Josh. 21). God would give His help to His people as the Strong One, Shepherd, Stone, and Shaddai (Gen. 49:24–26), and not only to Joseph's people.

(4) Its perceptiveness. Jacob exhibits his awareness of character traits his sons had shown. Reuben was, as in his sexual failure, as unstable as water that does not check itself but runs at its own impulse without control. Joseph was fruitful (v. 22; 41:52). Judah had plunged into sexual immorality (Gen. 38) but rebounded to show leadership in readiness to risk his own future to help his father (43:8, 9; 44:18–34).

God can, of His own will, honor good qualities in a son's descendants, as leadership in Judah's line and fruitfulness in Joseph's. But He also holds individuals accountable for their faith and obedience to Him in the final analysis. His approval is not automatic, ironclad.

(5) Its prayerfulness. On the one hand, God leads Jacob to make pronouncements about the future. On the other, this is finally coordinated with His working His will in permitting Jacob freedom to voice prayerful wishes. These are evident at times.

First, prayer is clear in verse 18. The overall context entails the pronouncements of blessing in verses 3–28. The closer context is the prevailing of Daniel (vv. 16, 17). Right at this point Jacob spontaneously steadies his heart in prayer for deliverance (v. 18). "For your salvation I wait, O Lord."

The prayer is one of affirmation. Jacob declares the working of God, "your salvation." Then he also affirms the waiting that is his own part. He waits or hopes in what the Lord can do. He trusts, expecting deliverance to come from God and not by mere human efforts. Any victory by Dan, or others, ought to be sought in this source, not by falling back on human sufficiency.

How well Jacob now knew this. He is so clear a few verses later that Joseph's arms drew success from God's hands. The secret is in having strength from the Strong One, shepherding from the Shepherd, security from the Stone, sufficiency from Shaddai, the God who is enough (vv. 25, 26). Drawing from this source is the secret of blessing. Jacob had realized this at Peniel. "I will not let you go unless you bless me."

Second, prayer is also the probable idea in Jacob 's words to Joseph (v. 25). As above, the secret is to receive "from the God of your father (of Jacob), may He help you, and from Shaddai, may He bless you with blessings. . . ." A spontaneous and natural voicing of intercessory wish at these points seems to be the idea. The verbs for "help" and "bless" in the third person singular ("He") are in the imperfect aspect and have a letter ***waw*** prefix which indicates a volative idea, a wish.

God can lead a man to speak His will in the process of inspiration, and help him to blend his own prayer desire in harmony with it. The more that prayer is all that God can enable it to be the more it is an utterance of His own will, what it pleases Him freely to give. This becomes clear in many passages (Jer. 29:10–14; 33:3 with 4–18).

Third, prayer in the last speech of Jacob follows in a natural way after prayer in 47:31b and 48:15, 16. Fourth, it fits the context for Jacob to leap into prayer at times just as he can be personal in his words at other times. He speaks of "my firstborn," Reuben, "my son," Judah (v. 9), "I wait" (v. 18), and "my ancestors" (v. 26). Fifth, Jacob nearing his death can pronounce the future of his sons and infuse prayer with this just as Moses approaching death blesses Israel and intersperses his prayer with this. Moses does this in Deuteronomy 33, praying often (vv. 7, 11, 12, 13–16, 24, 26).

Prayer in Jacob's life, as the survey reveals, shows up at least sixteen times from Genesis 28:20–22 to 49:25. This is slightly higher than the thirteen times recorded of Abraham. The high probability is that for both men the times mentioned are selections focused to more notable occasions. Prayer may have marked them in more episodes than these examples.

The principle on prayer here is essentially the same as above, climaxing 48:8–20. Prayer that seeks what is truly in harmony with some specific thing God validly shows by His Word is His will can gain its answer in His timing, even if not ours. Men's hearts can blend with God's heart in agreement; as we abide in Him. We can ask what we will that His Word surely teaches is His will (John 15:7). Then we can submissively leave the results to His faithfulness as He works out the plans of His wisdom.

Prayer in Exodus

Introduction

Exodus highlights the reality of redemption out of bondage. More will be said later of this, but prayer to God finds frequent place in the forty chapters. Seeing how it is woven into the very fabric of the book is an eye-opener to the importance God and the Exodus writer attach to this communion.

As in Genesis, prayer is important in explicit references and also where nothing at the moment is said of it but in such situations in which later Scripture reveals prayer as fitting.

The direct cases meet the reader from Moses' words to God in Chapter 3 on through many of the chapters. This study soon will concentrate on these, one by one in successive steps, as they appear. At this point, a survey can help us see how prayer suits various cases.

Prayer is relevant in relation to many things of which the book speaks. Here are matters that quite readily give impetus to prayer from the human heart in other parts of the Bible, pertinent in their essence just as matches our situations today

1. God is an encouragement for prayer by keeping His promises, such as by increasing Abraham's covenant people (Ex. 1–2). God had promised to bless the patriarch's descendants (Gen. 12:1–3), and Joseph had predicted God would follow up on this after he passed from the scene (50:24–25). When God keeps His Word, this is a prompt to count on Him even in more prayer. This can issue in praise for His faithfulness, rehearsing good things of His bounty, and even requests for added blessings that such kindness inspires. Believers are more ready to trust God to bring His latest promises, as well, on to their fruition. Jeremiah will become a prime example of expectancy that God is sure to do what He pledges—for example, gather Israelites back into their own ancient land (Jer. 31–33, cf. especially 32:17).

2. God was sensitive to answer His people's appeals for help when they felt cutting lashes of bondage their taskmasters laid upon them (Ex. 2:23–25; 3:7, 9). He acted by preparing Moses to lead them out to freedom (3:17).

3. Moses utters his own first recorded prayer in his "Here I am" (3:4), answering when God speaks out of a burning bush to seize his attention.

4. God not only blessed Moses' mouth with words to be a leader (4:10–12), and provided Aaron's mouth as well (4:14–16) and even great miracles (4:17). He enabled Moses to become mighty in prayer so that he often called down new plagues on the Egyptians who enslaved his people (Chaps. 5–14).

5. Prayers related to the plagues was in view of God's care and power that set His covenant people free from Egypt (Chaps. 5–12), also protected them on their way out (13–15), and after leaving (16–18). For us today to see what God did is to sense new impetus to trust God to deliver us, too, as we pray with trust to have His help coping with the odds we ourselves face.

6. God made heaven and earth in Genesis, and now in Exodus makes the facets of His law to shape His people (Ex. 25–40). Those who trust Him are often occupied in prayer and in other ways to count on His nearness and do His will, just as Moses' prayers are to a God of awesome resource (Chaps. 3–14).

7. As God displayed power to answer prayer in Genesis, He also does, even in other ways, in Exodus. Prayer is to a God who made Moses' mouth and can help him speak, a God who sovereignly arranged to train him in a queen's home, who spoke in a burning bush, and who acted in power over various aspects of nature in the plagues. Looking to Him is looking to a God who led His people by a cloud and a fiery pillar and raised the waters of the sea to open a way out to freedom. Prayer is to a God who caused water to gush from a rock and bread to fall from the sky. It is to a God who gave His pattern from heaven for building a worship place on earth where He especially would meet with people (25:8).

8. Prayer in praise is the great theme in the celebration over God delivering His people through the sea (Chap. 15). Even where a pas-

sage's brevity is silent about prayer, those involved could well have prayed, as the midwives God protected might give thanks (1), and baby Moses' parents would feel gratitude for God saving their son's life when lives of other male children were being snuffed out (2).

9. Prayer even about details can gain impetus from the fact that God shows His concern for the minutiae of life. He cares when a man strikes another and kills him (21:12), for fairness when one accidentally puts another to death (21:13), and when a son curses his father or mother (21:17). It is on His heart when negligence contributes to a death (21:29). And He wants one to make restitution for a hurtful wrong, showing that he cares properly about it (21:33–36). He is concerned about a man being free to protect his home and family when a thief breaks in (22:2) and is kind to the widow and the orphan (22:22). When the needy cry, He is sensitive to hear (22:23), and He wants men to be careful not to bear false witness (23:1) or have their hand out for a bribe (23:8). He wants worship offered exclusively to Him (20:3–4; 23:32–33) and desires worshippers' gifts to further His tabernacle work (25:1–7; 35:4–9).

Those who pray about details can be sure God is interested, for He created the things of heaven and earth. In Exodus, He is even particular about how furniture is made, which colors are most suitable for tabernacle accessories, and the preciousness of materials used to worship Him (25:3–7; 39:1–41).

He is orderly as to tabernacle parts and focuses even on fine spices to prepare fragrant incense to use in worship. His Spirit gives skill for artistry in the tabernacle (31:1–11; 35:30–35; 36:1–2, 4; 38:22–23). In all the process of building, He shows vital concern for each and every facet. When the place of worship is completed, He fills this place where He dwells with His glory (40:34–35). An interest like this in details should excite those who pray sincerely to sense God's devotion to be involved also in aspects of their lives.

10. A big feature in Exodus is God's working of mighty miracles. This is "that you may know that I am the Lord" (10:1–2). He apparently was testifying that nothing is too hard for Him to do, a reality Jeremiah later dwelt upon (32:17). And Paul would write

that God is able to do "exceedingly abundantly above all we ask or think" (Eph. 3:20).

11. A pitiful request by a cruel unbeliever is for God to spare him pressure, and soften his way (Ex. 10:17–18). God is able, and tender to do this but makes no promises to one who defies Him.

12. Prayer is closely linked in Scripture with God's Word that directs men, as is true for us today (John 14:21–23; 15:7; 1 John 5:14–15). In Exodus, God's words revealing His will occur often. For example, He directs Moses about what to do (Chaps. 3–4), what to say to the Pharaoh (5–12), which movements to make in travels (14:1–4), and how to construct a tabernacle (25–40). We, too, have God's Word as our main light in which to pray or do anything that is His will (cf. Eph. 1:2–14, 15–23).

13. Prayer finds encouragement because God is greater than the potentate and resources of Egypt. He beats these (Chaps. 5–15). Prayer also gains uplift fromGod holding the waters of the sea (14), and His ability to distinguish between people He sees safely through the sea and the enemies He allows the sea to destroy. It can also enhance prayer to see God providing a wife (2:21), water to quench thirst, bread to satisfy hunger, victory in battle, healing (15:26; 23:25), an angel to guide (14:19), counsel (18), commands for life (20), and skill for craftsmanship. He just seems to show He is set to cover every need, as He provides also to meet our needs according to His riches (Phil. 4:19). He is a great source to consult in prayer, for we will not ask any legitimate thing that He does not have a heart to give when it is His will. These are a few things pertinent to prayer, and others will become obvious when the study later takes up each prayer passage.

The Author

Moses wrote the book, as many conservative scholars of deep learning and high repute have reasoned. They are of this conviction despite the detailed arguments of certain higher critics, for they can meet their reasoning phase by phase and show that this makes sense. One can readily find the discussions in Old Testament introduction books by R. K. Harrison, Gleason Archer, Edward J. Young, and

Merrill Unger, as well as in Exodus in *The New Bible Dictionary* and Unger's *Bible Dictionary*, and *The Zondervan Pictorial Bible Encyclopedia*, or *The International Standard Bible Encyclopedia* (an old work, or a new work in recent years).

Great prominence is given to Moses in Exodus: he had the training, and his interest as a leader of his people would make it natural that he authored the book. He could have had help from his understudy, Joshua, who served in the same tent with him (33:7).

The Date

The pivotal issue of time is not when the writing was done, but when the exodus itself (cf. Chap. 12) occurred. A wide range of disagreement exists on the date when God delivered the Israelites out of Egypt. Unger, for example, has given a careful argument in his book *Archeology and the Old Testament*. The two principal views are well known. One places the exodus ca. 1447 B.C. during the reign of Amenhotep II of Egypt's Eighteenth Dynasty. The other fixes it much later at about 1290 B.C. when Rameses II of the Nineteenth Dynasty ruled. Unger and many evangelicals favor the earlier dating. J. W. Jack, a student in archeology and Old Testament scholar, agrees in his work *The Date of the Exodus* (cf. p. 57). He says: "the early date is being more generally accepted by scholars."

One can pinpoint the date fairly closely by biblical data. First Kings 6:1 says that the fourth year of Solomon's reign was the 480th year after Israel came out of Egypt (cf. Ex. 12:40–41). Solomon's fourth year on the throne can be anchored at ca. 967 B.C. Figuring back 480 years would place the exodus at 1447. Egyptian history of that time will permit that date for, as Unger notes, such a time would fall in the opening years of Amenhotep II (ca. 1450–1425 B.C.), son of the famous conqueror and empire builder, Thutmose III (1482–1450). Thutmose was an ideal prospect to be the oppressor of the people of Israel in Exodus 1–2. Moses fled in Exodus 2 and waited in the deserts of Midian (3:23) for the death of this pharaoh before he ventured back into Egypt.

The actual exodus could occur not long afterward in the career of Amenhotep II, who probably was the pharaoh who hardened his heart and refused to allow Israel to depart. It is also quite evident from ancient records that the eldest son of Amenhotep II never took the throne of Egypt. The Exodus record explains the reason. This was the son who died in the terrible tenth plague (Ex. 12), which claimed the lives of all the firstborn males among the Egyptians.

The Background

Prayer or any other subject of the book is concerned here.

Exodus is the connecting link between Genesis and the last three books of the Pentateuch. The opening words in the present book point back to the closing chapters of Genesis and forward to the events approaching the exodus. In Genesis 46, at the invitation of Joseph and the pharaoh reigning at that time, Jacob had moved with his family from Canaan into the area called Goshen in Egypt. Exodus 12:40 states that "the sojourning of the children of Israel, who dwelt in Egypt, (was) four hundred and thirty years." Actual experiences of the 430-year sojourn are largely passed over in silence in the scriptural record. The period is summed up in two verses (Ex. 1:7–8). The people of Israel, the biblical data says, "were fruitful, and increased abundantly, and multiplied, and waxed exceeding mighty, and the land was filled with them."

This prosperity invited disaster. "There arose up a new king over Egypt who knew not Joseph." This new king saw in Israel's powerful race a surging threat to his own sovereign security. His strategy was to begin efforts to keep Israel under his thumb. Set in operation, his policy at first was slave labor, the first anti-Semitism in recorded history. Later, when this brutal oppression failed to check the growth of the enslaved people, the pharaoh's mind thought up a new plot. This time he sought to stop the population boom at its very roots by a policy of infant murder—killing each Hebrew male child at the time of birth.

When Hebrew midwives defied the king's command (1:17–21) and kept the male babies alive, the Egyptian leader became even more cold-blooded in treacherous efforts to stop the nation's rapid rise. Now he issued a strict manifesto that would turn the nation into a "spy system," for the life of every male child born to Hebrews was to be snuffed out quickly in the Nile River. The Israelites were under terrific pressure, and the future loomed black with terror and tragedy. The nation that had developed from Abraham and through which the covenant blessings must certainly come according to God's promise was poised on the brink of eventual extermination. If the nation was to survive and God's pledge of redemptive and regal blessings be fulfilled, then God Himself must now powerfully intervene with saving action. The stage was set for the strategic appearance of a deliverer. At this critical point God introduced Moses into the gripping narrative (Ex. 2–3).

The Theme

Due to the key position of the book in the unfolding drama of redemption and God's kingdom purposes, it is possible to state the theme in two ways.

First, we can trace the theme historically. Exodus describes the historical and geographical placement of the people called Israel. Still in Egypt when Genesis closes, they are brought out of the land of bondage by the powerful hand of God and led to Mount Sinai where He positions them for their march to the land He had promised (cf. Gen. 12:7; Chap. 15).

Second, it is more deeply significant to trace the theme doctrinally. Four words would quickly sum up the book in a nutshell: deliverance, journey, law, and tabernacle. Deliverance of Israel from bondage in Egypt (Chaps. 1–15) illustrates, in the historical arena, the redemption of men from the dominating clutches of sin and death in the New Testament. The hinge chapter of this section, 12, depicts the Passover lamb and the blood of that lamb, which is a vital God-given type of the redemption He planned to accomplish by His great Lamb, Jesus Christ, in the New Testament (cf. John 1:29; 1 Cor. 5:7).

The journey experiences of Israel (Chaps. 15–18) graphically show God's provision and protection for His people. Law in Chapters 19–24 is the expression of God's will for Israel throughout most of the scriptural record until it should be perfectly fulfilled by Christ (Matt. 5:17; Rom. 10:4). Experience of the tabernacle

(Chaps. 25–40) gave to Israel a material evidence and a tangible pledge of God's eternal purpose to dwell in the very midst of His people, revealing Himself and being glorified in this, as an earlier teacher, H. C. Woodring has said. Significantly, tabnernacle truth may be traced throughout the entire Bible from Exodus to Revelation 22. God's giving of tabernacle truth at this particular point in history instructs us, for He dwells in the midst of a people here who are, as Woodring added: partakers of Patriarchal promises (cf. Ex. 39:42, "children of Israel"); participants in the Passover (cf. Ex. 12 and 1 Cor. 5:7); pilgrims in the wilderness (no tabernacle in Egypt, but one after separation from the world, Egypt); possessors of priestly prerogatives (cf. Ex. 19:5–6; Rom. 9:4–5).

Redemption, then, is the book's theme. However, it is not an end in itself, but only the divinely intended means of accomplishing His purpose. His aim centers in the fulfillment of the kingdom program through which He will manifest His sovereign authority through His Messiah/King. Before Israel can fulfill the provisions of the original promise God made to Abraham (Gen. 12) and amplified frequently in the Book of Beginnings, she must truly be constituted a nation with blessings herself. Then she can sustain the ministry of "a kingdom of priests" who share the blessings of God in the kingdom, in which believers of all nations also will share (cf. Dan. 7:27).

The Book of Exodus traces the redemption of Israel and the divine equipping of the nation for the ministry in which it was later in a large degree to fail miserably.

The Outline

I. The Liberation of Israel from Egyptian Bondage (1:1–15:21)
   A. The Bondage under Cruel Oppressors (1:1–22)
   B. The Preparation of a Deliverer—Moses (2:1–4:31)
   C. The Contests against Pharaoh for Liberation (5:1–11:10)
   D. The Passover and Redemption out of Egypt (12:1–15:21)

II. The Preservation of Israel in Wilderness Testings (15:22–17:16)
   A. The Preservation from Thirst (15:22–27)
   B. The Preservation from Hunger (16:1–36)
   C. The Preservation from Thirst Again (17:1–7)
   D. The Preservation from Military Loss (17:8–16)

III. The Organization and Regulation of Israel (18:1–40:38)
   A. The Consolidation in the Wilderness (18:1–27)
   B. The Covenant at Sinai (19:1–34:35)
   C. The Construction of the Tabernacle (35:1–40:38)

The attention turns now to each prayer passage as it occurs.

Exodus' Continuity with Genesis

The Focus of Exodus

A Focus on God's Covenant Plan

Prayer has its vital role in close coordination with God's will in developing His covenant plan. He pursues fulfillment of His promise to bless Abraham's descendants and people of all nations (Gen. 12:1–3).

So the book is immediately about the business of showing the Lord's faithfulness in this purpose. Like a novel that explodes with action on the first page, the account leaps quickly to this concern. The scene is in Egypt. People of the plan are multiplying, filling the land. Joseph has died, and time has shot through the years. A new pharaoh on the throne does not know the Israelite leader and feels no favor for his people. He suspects that the Israelites as a group of foreigners increasing so rapidly might pose a threat to Egyptian security, rising against the rulers.

Curb their power now, the pharaoh says. Keep them so safely under Egyptian power by severe servitude that they have no chance to do anything but submit and eke out an existence. A strong taskmaster force can police them and hold them in powerless subjection.

However, the man in power did not reckon on the One in power championing Israel's cause. God keeps His covenant. He prospers Israelites to keep multiplying just as He guaranteed to Jacob when He led him to Egypt (Gen. 46:3). "I will make of you a great nation there." He even works extraordinary protection in the women having babies, despite a special, evil Egyptian policy to murder male children at birth.

To uphold His promise, God could bless by multiplication of human births as He had blessed Jacob in animal births (Gen. 31), and more so. He also blessed Hebrew midwives with families of their own as a fitting reward after they honored Him by helping protect Hebrew families!

God was true to His covenant in blessing Amram and Jochebed (cf. 6:20) by protecting their infant (2:1ff.). This child, Moses, rescued by a princess from the palace in God's providence, would become God's leader for the covenant people.

A Focus on God's Redemptive Plan

Prayer here has its setting in the drama of God redeeming His people out of bondage into freedom on their trek to the covenant land. Redemption is the special main theme in this tumultuous narrative of God's covenant loyalty. The account spotlights redemption by *blood* (12:13) and redemption by *power—God's power* (15:13).

In this work for His people, God develops His theme of redeeming a people as He redeemed Jacob (Gen. 48:16). And God had prophetically announced in embryonic form His plan eventually to be worked out through the seed of the woman (Gen. 3:15). He would crush the head of the serpent, finally the greater Serpent. By this He would be the Victor over the one who led in the fall into sin and, over that sin, in redeeming from sin.

Exodus describes redemption out of bondage by great acts of power and the blood of the passover lamb. God in the latter aspect was preparing an illustration of His principle to bring, eventually, the great Passover Lamb who would effect redemption in the most ultimate sense through offering His own blood (Isa. 53:6; John 1:29; 1 Cor. 5:7). The offerings of animal sacrifices in Moses' day and in the rest of Old Testament times would prepare for the final offering. They pointed to the one greatest sacrifice for their fullest significance, as in Hebrews 1:3, 9:14, 28, and 10:4–10.

Prayer is interwoven in much of the Exodus story developing its historical picture and building toward this even greater future significance. This will soon be obvious.

The Circumstance of Grief

Action mounts fast in the context. By quick brush strokes, the writer paints the scene. The covenant people are in grievous affliction under brutal Egyptian persecution. Yet the Lord preserves male children, with Moses as the greatest example. More years drag by, and the infant grows up in the court of the potentate. He knows his mother who lovingly cared for him and realizes he is one of the Hebrews. Yet his own fleshly zeal to rescue one of his people precipitates his flight as a fugitive to another land, among Midianites.

His kinspeople continue to suffer grief in cruel bondage. It is in this circumstance that prayer becomes a cry of agony from their lips.

Exodus 2:23

Desperation in Prayer

The Cry for Deliverance (v. 23)

Prayer as God desires it is a two-way matter. The people's cry in their "SOS" for help did not bounce back from a ceiling of bronze. The account makes this clear.

The Concern for Deliverance (vv. 23–25)

God's receiving of the cry. The prayer "rose up to God" and "God heard. . . ." It is quickly apparent that the efficacy of the appeal is not out of human merit; at least the focus is not on any human reason other than an entreaty of need. The receiving is, rather, for another reason.

God's remembering of the covenant. Grace reigns. God finds His motivation within His own bounty of loving-kindness or gracious compassion, in covenant zeal. He shows integrity to keep His promise. "He remembered His covenant with Abraham, Isaac and Jacob." His own plan, His will is the foremost concern in His answer to prayer.

God's graciousness is again the focus in 3:7, one of many examples. He is aware of griefs His people feel in their trials and aroused about those who deal sinful persecution to them as the taskmasters do here.

Prayer for rescue is not, in this case, explained to be with a pleading of the covenant. But whether the sufferers here did this or not, God's own fidelity to His plan and will points up a cogent principle for prayer. Come to God pleading His promise, putting the need on the legitimate ground of His own purpose and honor. Pray keeping in step with Him, and let Him take things the way He wants them to go.

God's resolving to deliver (2:25; 3:4–22). God is prepared for action in verse 25. The next thing we read shows He is in action. He is working His miracle to seize the attention of the man He will send to lead His deliverance! He is present, in a burning bush, speaking to get His deliverance plan underway.

The prayer that drew this action is now followed by another prayer, this time from Moses. God's own *sign* in the bush and *speaking* His word out of the bush are the stimulations for the next prayer in 3:4. As is often to be the case in Scripture, hearing the word of God begets sensitivity to pray in line with this to the God of the word.

Observe principles of this passage. First, God in mercy and covenant love answers cries of grief from His people. Second, a right hearing of God's Word can stir the human spirit to pray to God in accord with this (cf. John 15:7).

Exodus 3:4

Moses' Prayer of Availability

God's Getting His Attention—His Power in the Bush (3:1–4)

God draws His answer to the prayer in Egypt from a land outside of Egypt, Midian. It is to the southeast, beyond the Red Sea. Moses who had failed to help his people through his own power and way will be back to help them in God's power and way.

The fire in the bush, not consuming it, is an outright miracle. That fits very naturally—or supernaturally!—into the flow of thought in Genesis and here. A God who can create heaven and earth and all that is in them can manage fire in one bush! And a God who can perform all the great works of caring for Abraham, Isaac, and Jacob in His covenant power would find a miracle the order of the day.

Of course, the point was to gain Moses' rapt attention to a thing so unexplainable on any natural scheme. God wanted him to be all eyes, then all ears to listen. First, He shows the miracle, then He has the man's complete and astounded attention and availability. Then comes God's message, His mandate. At the same time, when God would soon be working many miracles to encourage His people and outdo all the power of Egypt, starting Moses off with a miracle was rather apt.

Moses' Giving His Attention—His Prayer at the Bush (3:4)

"Here I am" is the simple, spontaneous prayer of availability and attention for what God will say. A principle is apparent. When God speaks His word, and a person hears, his next heartbeat should be in prayerful readiness for what God has in mind. This attitude can open the way for further listening to the word to grasp the will of God.

God's gaining of Moses' attention and Moses' giving it continues. This flows into further prayer—Moses talking with God—in a series of excuses to opt out of obeying what God wills for him. Due to the length of this series, it seems best to see it as a unit.

Guidelines are relevant here. First, the God who answers prayer is able to work miracles when it is His choice. Second, a good prayer to God is "Here I am," indicating a heartbeat to hear what He says.

Exodus 3:5–4:31

Moses' Prayers Making Excuses

The Lord reveals His plan to use Moses in delivering His people, counsels him to cast aside five excuses, presses for his obedience to take on the assignment, and supports him before the Israelites.

The Revelation of God's Purpose (3:5–10)

His caution about holy ground (v. 5). The praying person is to talk with God showing deep respect for who He is and not take Him lightly. The right spirit is one of awe, not thinking of God being "near" as if He is on the same level, but having due regard for His greatness. And by removing his sandals, Moses is sensitive to the wonder of God's holiness, rendering honor to Him. To receive God's word and to talk with Him is a very special privilege, set apart, "on holy ground." God desires him to approach in this spirit.

The commitment to Moses' people (v. 6). God introduces Himself as the covenant God of Moses' own father and earlier of Abraham, Isaac, and Jacob. Images Moses might have of God's faithfulness to his people in all these past stages of their history would challenge him now about His faithfulness. Stirred with the immense respect God taught in verse 5, the man felt a humility that could not gaze upon such a great God.

The coming to deliver them (v. 7, 8). God has seen, is aware, and has come to the rescue.

The commissioning of Moses to lead (v. 10). The shepherd of verse 1 is to come to God, be God's man sent to the head of a nation, and bring God's people out of Egypt. That involves a big God and a huge task, confronting a mighty pharaoh of a powerful nation. Moses has felt awed, but is not yet so compelled by God's authority that he is confident to take on this great a challenge. Excuses wave warning flags across his mind.

Resources for God's Purpose (3:11–4:17)

Moses urges five pretexts for backing out, but God has a ready resource to give victory in place of each retreat. The passage is a dialogue of prayers and answers as Abraham and the Lord (Gen. 18) Jeremiah and God (Jer. 14–15), and Habakkuk with God (Hab. 1–2).

Moses' unimportance (3:11). Compared with the mighty pharaoh, Moses is of no consequence, a shepherd going up before a sovereign. Further, God's candidate is smitten with a sense of his unimportance among Israelites, absent for forty years, a man on the dodge when he left. Surely he is unfit to have a big place in the scheme of Egypt or of his people.

But when God assigns a task, He enables. His answer to Moses' prayer question of excuse is His own sufficient presence (v. 12). Sufficiency to fulfill His will is admittedly not in Moses, but it is in the Lord Himself. "Certainly I will be with you. . . ." And God will not only be with him to carry out the purpose. He will bring His people all the way out to the nearby mountain the shepherd could gaze upon, Mount Sinai. There, as a delivered people, they will be free to worship Him.

That should have convinced the doubting excuse-maker. But he quickly had another reason that tacitly infers that God is making a mistake.

Moses' uneasiness about God's name (v. 13). He is reluctant over having the right name of God to convince his people he is for real. His prayer draws God's answer, the fact of His permanence. God is the great "I Am" (v. 14ff.), the timelessly self-existent God. Abraham had called on Him as the El Olam, "the everlasting God" (Gen. 21:33). In this role, He is not only sufficient to rescue the present generation from its trouble, but able for all generations (v. 15). He had been the help of Moses' people through all of the past and would be there as God for all the future times.

God's "track record" of permanence was mind-boggling. Such sufficiency ought to set Moses confidently on his way. He could obey and expect great things. But God's permanence was not enough to turn his train of doubt.

The unbelief of the people (4:1). Moses shifts from his own smallness and God's name to the unbelief he fears from others. They might *scoff him out of sight* for popping on the scene with such grandiose claims he is not able to back up.

God's answer to this question of prayer consists in proofs of His ability (vv. 2–9). He shows His chosen leader five miracles to authenticate His power. These exhibits deal with unbelief in Moses and what he might encounter in his people. He changes Moses' rod into a serpent, changes the serpent back into the rod, makes his hand leprous, restores it to normality again, and turns water to blood.

For one who comes in prayer believing in God's power, such miracles are not to be explained away but acknowledged. God is

God, whether in original creation (Gen. 1:1) or in smaller parts of the scheme later.

Even after this amazing demonstration in five acts, Moses drags his feet. He can acknowledge an all-powerful God in one breath and think in the next of another excuse in prayer. That God's power in these five examples already answers his next excuse does not disrupt his skewed thinking.

Moses' unskillfulness (4:10). Now he trots out this evasion. "I am not a man with words," not the man to speak persuasively before a pharaoh and his court. He may have thought of just not being a commanding speaker, or eloquent. It may have been his inferiority complex in this realm after forty years in another line of work, shepherding. Or he may not have felt he was sharp in Egyptian language after the absence and figured Aaron was current in it.

But God did the impossible five times before his eyes and a sixth at the burning bush. He could change any "impossibility" he met.

That Moses "was a man mighty in word and deed" (Acts 7:22) may allow for unskillfulness *at first*. Its focus can then be on what he became as time went on, God working a great change in him.

God's resource answering this prayer excuse is His provision of adequacy for Moses' mouth.

One final excuse is on Moses' lips in prayer. It finally comes to this.

Moses' unwillingness (v. 13). He would exempt himself just on this ground. He simply is not the man, no matter what. He suggests that the Lord send somebody else He could choose.

That is crass rudeness and disrespect. Of course, all of the reasons Moses advances are permeated by tacit disrespect for who God is and what He is able to do. This, now, is just plain dodging of God's will, betraying an unwilling spirit.

No wonder the Lord was angry! But even in this, He displays longsuffering with the irresponsible candidate. He provides a way yet to do His will. He models patience and also gives the partnership of Aaron to help Moses (v. 14). In 7:7 Aaron, at eighty-three, is three years older than Moses. Once this team begin their leadership and the narrative progresses, Moses moves more and more up into the place of singular command. From the seventh plague on (9:22, 23), he takes the lead.

God will use Moses to coach Aaron as to the words, and Aaron is to speak them (vv. 15, 16). Still, Moses will go before the pharaoh as the man in charge, having God's authority in decisions, with Aaron as his speaker (7:1).

The Responses to God's Purpose (4:18–31)

By Moses (vv. 18–26). This is what springs immediately out of the prayer dialogue. He is partially obedient, at least on his way to Egypt. But disobedience in one key matter causes God to bring him to a reckoning to render full obedience

This is the scenario in the strange incident of 4:24–26. At a campsite, God is about to take Moses' life. This may be in sudden violent illness or in a vision confronting him so obviously that his wife is aware of what displeases God. Moses is to speak to the pharaoh about Israel as His firstborn son and about pharaoh's firstborn son (vv. 22, 23). The issue over the importance of the firstborn to God should have caused Moses to think of his own son and circumcising him in obedience to the covenant sign God commanded in Genesis 17.

The son needing circumcision is probably the second son, Eliezer (18:4). For if Gershom the first son (2:22) was not yet circumcised, *both* sons would need this at the camp. The wife circumcises only one son, so he must be the second, Moses' failure being in a dilly-dallying neglect of this act, a token of the covenant. How could he be fit to talk about God's son and pharaoh's son when he was no example as to his own son as God's leader? God made sure he was cleared to go to Egypt as an obedient model.

Obvious here are key principles. God is fervent for obedience in His servants. He also wants prayer to be blended with His word, with sensitivity about other issues in His will.

By Aaron (vv. 27, 28). When God leads a person to do His will, and this involves any other person, God is able to work in the other also!

He is able to be faithful at both ends, doing the full job. He is not a halfway god.

He sent Moses, and He sent Aaron. And He backed up His promise that Aaron would meet Moses (v. 14).

Aaron was on the move, prompted to go in obedience. The two men met, and Moses filled Aaron in on God's plan, both the words and the signs He had given them to do.

By the elders (vv. 29–31). The report of the two leaders evoked the elders' obedience. Aaron apprised them of God's words to Moses and worked the miracles for them to see.

Three things are said of the Hebrew elders. They *heard* God's word showing compassion about their trials, *believed*, and *bowed low in worship*. The latter act suggests that they prayed meaningfully, giving thanksgiving to God.

It is with these notes of obedience by the leaders, and their prayer of gratitude that God puts into full operation His plan before the potentate of Egypt.

Several principles compel attention. First, guard against a deceitful heart that seems ready to hear God at one moment but can try to back out later. Second, deep respect is the apt prayer attitude in the holy presence of God. And in reality, we always are in His presence and should pray "without ceasing" (1 Thess. 5:17), our minds fixed on Him (Isa. 26:3). Third, no prayer excuse is adequate to opt out when God plans a work for us and provides His sufficiency to carry it out (cf. 2 Cor. 3:5). Fourth, the person who goes in the path of God's bidding can always find the provisions of His blessing. We are not simply there for Him; He is there for us, and prayer can be ever finding out His greatness.

Exodus 5:22, 23

Moses' Prayer under Attack

The Appeal before Pharaoh (5:1)

This is the start of the drama in Egypt, introduced by prayer. Moses and Aaron present their case before the supreme leader in Egypt.

Their claim is that the God of the Hebrews sent them with His request. So it is a contest in power between God and the pharaoh.

First comes the *request*, "let My people go." The *reason* follows, "that they may celebrate a feast to Me in the wilderness." It is a big request, involving so many people, possibly near two million based on the 600,000 men alone in 12:37. The request is also big from the standpoint of the One who presses it, bigger than the pharaoh realizes! And it is big considering the reason, to worship the God who alone deserves this.

The Affliction from Pharaoh (5:2–19)

The potentate insults God. He challenges Him as if, because he personally does not know Him, He is unworthy of his compliance. He will have to learn the hard way.

Affliction jumps to a new level of horror as the pharaoh piles it on the Hebrews. Now he forces the slaves to search for their own straw in brick-making. They feel the heat and the grief.

The Attack from the Foremen (5:20, 21)

Hebrew foremen over Moses' people, answerable to the taskmasters, were at their wits' end over the agonizing bind. They attacked Moses and Aaron with blistering words of blame for making the suffering even more galling. In effect, they voice a wish for prayer—an imprecation (curse) invoking God's discipline on the two trouble-makers.

The Anguish of Moses' Prayer (5:22, 23)

Feeling the blast of blame, the new leader presses his anxiety before the Lord. He, in turn, throws all the blame up to Him.

His prayer first accuses the Lord in two questions. Why has God *harmed* the people with even worse trials? And why has He *sent* Moses with what seems only a cruel pretense of providing help?

Second, Moses prays in affirming. He declares two things as they stand at the moment. God has permitted the pharaoh to do *harm*, and He has not *delivered* the people.

A prayer of intercession pleading yet for help would be so fitting here. But fear drives faith into the deep shadows for the moment.

The Answer from God (6:1–8)

How gracious is the answer God gives. No chiding is here. He has no cutting words for His servant. God says, in essence, "You haven't seen the half of what I will do yet. I'm just getting started. You'll see." He offers two encouragements, just as His word is so often the best answer to men's anxiety in prayer.

The compulsion He will bring (v. 1). God will bring so much pressure to bear on the pharaoh that he will let the Hebrews go. More than this, he will be anxious to have them go! Pharaoh flexed his muscle briefly in Chapter 5. Now he is in for a lesson on how the really Mighty One can work!

The covenant He will honor (vv. 2–8). God gives a strong reassurance, determined to keep His word of promise to bless His people. This answer is rich with encouragements that big things are about to happen.

(1) His *Person* stands as surety behind the covenant (vv. 2, 3). He is the Lord, the covenant maker and keeper who had called Abram and pledged His blessing. He appeared to the patriarchs in the role of God Almighty, or El Shaddai (as Gen. 17:1, etc.). He had been like a mountain towering as a resource before puny men. But He had not made Himself known as the Lord Jehovah (v. 3).

This needs clarifying. He had been called the Lord a number of times in Genisis but had not acted in an intense and multiplied display in that particular covenant sense. At least He had not done so dramatically in a powerful demonstration of the covenant fulness that the name Jehovah connotes, as He now is prepared to do. By a cluster of awesome acts He will perform in the capacity of Jehovah showing His covenant care for His people. The likes of this series has never been seen in the covenant history.

(2) His *Promise* of the land (v. 4) is a matter of honor He stands aroused to fulfill. He will bring His people out of Egypt to take them to this covenanted land.

(3) His *pity* is real for the people He sees in bondage. The pity is an aspect of His covenant compassion.

(4) His *performance* to deliver and to possess the people as His very own is on His agenda (vv. 6–8). He assures His bringing them out of the trial and redeeming them by power. His outstretched arm will be over them to defeat the persecutors, shield His people, and escort them out into freedom. Great judgments are in His plan, to be displayed in the ten plagues and the overwhelming victory over Egyptian power at the Red Sea.

He intends to possess *them* as His people and have them possess *Him* as their God. Surely after this they will, as He says, "know that I am the Lord your God. . . ." As He said He would make Himself known in His role as Jehovah (v. 3), so He will. And this is, in mighty demonstration, related to His being the One "who brought you *out* from under the burdens of the Egyptians." It also is bound with His finishing the task—bringing them *into* the promised land.

Such a word from God got Moses "jump started" again (v. 9). But it was not as it ought to be. The people were still hurting from the lashing bondage and smitten with despondency. God would find His leader reverting to an old excuse (v. 12). How little the powerful word of God sinks in sometimes, whether to Moses' heart or our own.

What of principles in this case? One is that God can be long suffering to bless even when one's prayer charges Him with unkind motives. A second one is, keep ever in mind that the God of prayer has all power to answer.

Exodus 6:12

Moses' Reluctance (6:10–30)

God's directive (vv. 10, 11, 28, 29). Full speed ahead is God's will given to Moses. But the leader again drags his feet.

Moses' doubt (vv. 12, 30). He trots out the former excuse, "I am not a man with words," as in 4:10. Only this time he is into the work a ways, and he thinks it is just the way he had feared it would be. His people have not listened to him, and how will the pharaoh, in view of his inability? So he is back to square one.

God's Response (7:1–5)

In a nutshell, without panic, He says He will take care of everything in two ways. One is His hardening of Pharaoh (v. 3). The other is His hand on Egypt (3b–5), performing mighty miracles to spring His people free.

The Results (7:6–25)

These are in two phases. First is the obedience of the messengers (v. 6). Finally they are getting back to the work. Second is God's ordering of the miracles (vv. 8–25). God grants Aaron miracles of his rod becoming a serpent and swallowing up serpents of the court magicians. Then He brings the first plague, water turned to blood.

A principle is this. How often a praying person can voice the same old flimsy evacuation from responsibility, yet God is big in power and in pity to make a servant usable.

Exodus 8:8

Moses Prays for the Pharaoh

Pharaoh's Appeal for Prayer to Remove the Frogs (v. 8)

Things are getting too tough for the man who had fancied he had all power. Egypt's strong man is suddenly aware of his inability. Humbled, he asks Moses to pray on his behalf for the frog plague to be removed.

Moses' Asking in Prayer (vv. 9–12)

Before he prays, Moses gives the dignitary the honor of pinpointing the time when the frog scourge will cease. In this way, in the pharaoh's eyes, Moses allows God's answer to be all the more impressive. The prayer will specify the *time* (tomorrow) and one other detail that Moses himself adds. Let the removal of frogs be from every place except the *Nile*.

The effect all of this should register on the pharaoh is obvious to Moses. Egypt's master should come out of his trouble knowing that God is greater than any other.

Once out of the pharaoh's presence, Moses sought God's work in the actual intercession.

God's Answer to Prayer (v. 13)

Specific prayer according to God's will secures God's specific response. God *did* it, and the frogs *died*!

Pharaoh's Antagonism after Prayer (v. 15)

As soon as the potentate was sure of relief from the pressure, he did not *heed* God but *hardened* his heart to Him. *He* insisted on being in charge! Of course the Lord had known and said this would be the result. How like many another heart that will clamor before God for good things but to indulge selfish motives, receive these, then turn against Him. Haughtiness reigns, not humility that gives thanks to His glory.

But who really reigns? God quickly shows who.

God's Advance in the Plagues (vv. 16–19)

He just steps up the difficulty. He brings on a plague of gnats or lice, some kind of small creatures that even the clever magicians cannot handle. They find that they are suddenly unable to copy the miracle with their own counterfeit version. The creatures are too tiny and scurrying in too many directions to manipulate by sleight-of-hand artistry. At this point, skilled fingers cannot control the effects. Beaten as they also will be later when they suffer from boils (9:11), the magicians can only testify to the pharaoh. "This is the finger of God" (v. 19).

This made no impression on the hardened leader. He did not listen to the acknowledgment of his own team members. His prayer wish, the answer, and God's next step only met with his further hardening in verse 19. But God turns the heat on him up another notch.

Two principles are pertinent. First, when we pray specifically, God's answers can also be very specific. Second, a hardened heart misuses God and is treacherous in prayer, but God is never at a loss.

Exodus 8:30

Another Prayer for the Pharaoh

Prayer comes in the flow of events, as so often in the Bible.

The Proposal for Sacrifice (vv. 1, 20; cf. 25–28)

God sends His two representatives before the royal throne with His own request. The pharaoh has required the Hebrews to serve *him,* but God demands he let them go to serve *Him*. An obvious challenge is implicit. Let the national head submit in humility to a service to One more worthy.

Sacrifice to the Hebrews involved lambs, as God had provided a male of the sheep, a ram, for Abraham in Genesis 22. But shepherds and their flocks were an abomination to the Egyptians (Gen. 46:34). So when the pharaoh concedes that they sacrifice but demands that it be in Egypt (Ex. 8:25), the Hebrew spokesmen reject his halfway measure. They will not be forced into the jeopardy of sacrificing in hostile territory, *in Egypt* where nationals could detest their acts and stone them (v. 26).

To this the pharaoh comes back with another curb that leaves him still in charge. Go outside the land, but do not go far (v. 28). He leaves himself an ace—a chance to bring them back to serve him!

The Plague of Flies (vv. 21–24)

Two stages are actually involved in relation to the flies. First, the pharaoh did not heed Moses' earlier request in 8:1 to let the Hebrews go worship. As a consequence God sent the flies. This pressure caused the Pharaoh to summon the Hebrew advocates and offer his measure of sacrificing *in* the land, then the measure of sacrificing *near* the land. He follows this up with his appeal for prayer to gain relief from the Lord.

The Plea for Removal (v. 28)

"Make supplication for me," he pleads. He himself had no relationship with God and no faith with which to ask. Besides, he was a proven antagonist of God. The principle the psalmist would later pen was true of him. "If I regard iniquity in my heart, the Lord will not hear me" (Ps. 66:18). Like the Philistine Abimelech who needed Abraham's prayer (Gen. 20), the Pharaoh was dependent on the prayer of a man who had audience with God.

The Prayer for Removal (vv. 29–32)

Four movements capture the scene here.

The agreement (v. 29). Moses offers his promise of prayer for God's relief of the problem, then a precaution against the ruler reneging on his permission to leave Egypt.

The asking (v. 30). The advocate dismissed himself (and Aaron, v. 25), sought a place to pray and made intercession for God's stopping of the fly swarms.

The answer (v. 31). God's response to a specific prayer was a specific answer, "as Moses asked." It was not only definite but complete against the flies, for "not one remained."

The antagonism (v. 32). The habit in a hardened heart reasserted itself right away. God had kept His part; the pharaoh did not honor his, not permitting the people to go worship God.

A principle here is one that occurs often in Scripture. Some who have no open door to God will try when it seems to their advantage to get to Him through a person whom God hears.

Exodus 9:27–35

Moses Prays for a Storm to Cease

Resistance by the Egyptian throne-sitter leads to disease on livestock, boils on people and animals, then a thunderstorm.

The Awfulness of the Plagues (vv. 1–26)

The disease blight was awesome in verses 1–7. It took the lives of all the Egyptians' livestock, all out in the field since some are still alive later in verses 19–21. But God spared every animal of the Hebrews.

In this plague, the pharaoh is not said to call for prayer. His heart was simply hardened again, and this is not defined as by *himself* or by the *Lord.*

As hard-hitting to the economy as the livestock death had been, the next plague was felt even more severely. Boils afflicted people and animals, resulting in sores that must have brought excruciating pain every move they made (vv. 8–12). This time, the problem was so severe against even the magicians that they were too much in agony to try their arts before the pharaoh. The scene ends with God hardening the pharaoh's heart; he bucked letting the Hebrews go on their terms.

At the monarch's further resistance, God then brought bone-rattling thunder and pelted Egypt with rain and hail (vv. 13–26). Fire of jagged lightning shot down amidst slashing hail in greater severity than Egypt had ever seen. The hail pounded on men and animals that had not been brought in as warned. It ruined plants, such as all the flax and barley, and it split trees.

God held the plague away from His people, but the terror to the pharaoh and the nationals evoked his urgent summons for God's messengers.

The Appeal for God's Removal of the Hail (vv. 27–28)

Pharaoh's confession (v. 27). The heat is getting to the man. He feels it so much that he mouths his first confession of sin. In fact, he acknowledges his *personal* sin and his *people's* sin as offending God.

He has, for the moment, come off his lofty throne to humble himself before the Lord and His ambassadors. He realizes the wickedness was an affront to God and acknowledges His honor. He says, "the Lord is the righteous one."

The confession was, in *principle* what confession in Scripture ought to be, two-sided. It should be the person's acknowledgment of sin, and also his acknowledgment of God's righteousness. But for the pharaoh the confession was not in *purity* what it ought to be. His insincerity is quickly apparent when the pressure is off and he is again hardened (v. 35).

Pharaoh's cry (v. 28). He pleads for prayer to secure relief. God's frightening thunder and hammering hail have overwhelmed him and the subjects who depended on him. The cry that breaks from his lips is accompanied by a concession that the Hebrews can go.

The Agreement to Pray (vv. 29–30)

Moses' *promise* that he will pray and the terrors will cease is accompanied by his *point* to ponder. Such mighty acts by God to wield the powers of heaven on the earth and His power to still them ought to prove a point. The earth is the *Lord's*, not Pharaoh's. Moses voices, with his promise and his point, a *perception* about the pharaoh. He discerns that the leader and his officials are not sincere in conceding (v. 28) that the Goshen populace may go. They do not know a genuine fear for God that mean's business (v. 30). Moses' perception will have its proof in verse 35.

The Asking in Prayer (v. 33)

Calling on the Lord. Moses was true to his word. After exiting the palace, he extended his hands to the Lord and expressed his intercession.

Ceasing of the storm. In the ears of the pharaoh the last deafening peal of thunder rolled across the skies. His eyes saw the abrupt cutting off of the silvery hail. The crash of ice on the royal roof and courts stopped, and sheets of driving rain no longer filled the air. In their wake, a great calm came, broken only by sighs of relief.

But the stillness was brief. As soon as safety was clear in the pharaoh's mind, he answered the stillness with sin.

The Antagonism after Prayer (vv. 34–35)

How often the changes men guarantee in peril they repudiate in peace! Pharaoh illustrates that here, relaxing in God's help but soon rebelling in his hellishness. His cabinet and other officials sinned right along with him. He led the double-cross, his heart being hardened.

"So they think they'll run out on us, do they?" he probably thundered to his attendants. "No deal! Get word they stay right where they are!"

Consider two principles. First, Moses was not the first to pray for God to control a storm, but such incredible action is easy for a God who made heaven and earth. If we can believe Genesis 1:1, we can believe other miracles by the same God. Second, one can see great acts of God and serve Him all the more, but another can see what He does, feel it soothing, yet plunge on in sin.

Exodus 10:17, 18

Another Farce in Prayer

If the pharaoh thinks he is in command, he is in for a rude awakening. His show of power is but momentary, for the One truly in power has, in a deeper sense, sovereignly effected the hardness that He might be honored in the acts of control (10:1).

The respite for the Egyptians and the delay for the Hebrews will not be long now. For God's further displays will follow in rapid-fire sequence.

The Administering of Locusts (vv. 1–15)

God sends His message right back to the king who had broken his word. He appeals for a halt in the insincerity and a humbling before

His word (v. 3). Resistance will draw a plague of locusts. These will destroy plants the storm left and fill the Egyptian houses.

The plague and others after it will be to defeat Egyptian pride but far more. For God's people, such miracles will live on in accounts to other generations of God's might, making mockery of mere human power. The purpose is to glorify God, "that you may know that I am the Lord" (v. 2). God who keeps His promises will fulfill His word of 6:3, 6–8 that He would display Himself as Lord.

Denial at the throne of the Hebrew advocates' full proposal (vv. 7–11) results in God keeping His promise of locusts (vv. 12–15). Beaten again in his contest for power, the Pharaoh has to eat humble pie.

The Appeal for Removing Locusts (vv. 16, 17)

The pharaoh's confession. He acknowledges his sin a second time, in this case against both God and His messengers. He admits in humility (cf. v. 3) his need of forgiveness from God and them. He conceded that he had offended both.

The pharaoh's cry. Again, he is at their feet, so to speak, utterly in need of their intercession to God to let up. His magicians cannot stop the locusts. He cannot call the shots and get results. Only God is able. The place he is in can be the best of places, the place of utterly depending on the Lord. Only one problem is latent here, however. The genuineness of spirit God desires is again absent from the suppliant's heart (v. 20). Yet God is very longsuffering.

The Asking in Prayer (v. 18)

Moses did something that by now was getting old. He went out from the pleading unbeliever and took his intercession to God.

The Answer to Prayer (v. 19)

God did two things that relieved the Egyptians. He *changed* the wind, for He made all things and can control what He created. He commanded the wind to a higher velocity and sent it laden with the locusts into the Red Sea. He even *cleared* the land of all the creatures. He is able to be compassionate on people and complete in answering the prayer of a true intercessor.

God is kind, but man can be deceitful. So he is here.

The Antagonism after Prayer (v. 20)

God hardened the pharaoh's heart. He also hardened his own heart as some verses in the larger context clarify. Although only the Lord grasps just how these factors coordinate in consistency, apparently they do.

The leader again stopped the people of Moses from going. His roadblock was but temporary. This is clear in Chapters 10–12. God answers the latest resistance by the ninth plague, darkness on all the land except where His people are clustered. In the pharaoh is no appeal for a removal, only adamancy of heart (10:27, 28).

This hardness is defined as involving God's sovereign action in his thinking, his unwillingness to let the people go, and two other things. He is so angry that he blasts the ambassadors from his presence ("Get away from me") and bans them from ever showing up there again, on threat of death. To this blistering hate, Moses has a reply that seems long overdue.

"You have one thing right," God's man says. "I shall never see your face again!" They would not meet in the present life, and not in the next. The pharaoh's choice was more momentous than he realized. It drew a curtain of finality between his own hopes and the God who gives hope.

God tells Moses of one more plague, the tenth, in Chapter 11. Death of the firstborn is now imminent (vv. 1, 4, 5). Then it comes in Chapter 12. First, God directs heads of Hebrew families to slay a lamb for each household and apply the blood over the doorway. This means safety for each home when God's angel brings death of a firstborn son where blood is not applied. God is also preparing an advance picture of His eventual greater Lamb. His Son will give His blood and take away the sin that brings death (John 1:29; 1 Cor. 5:7; Eph. 1:7).

Safety in the Egyptian setting is clear by God's guarantee in verse 13. He says, "when I see the blood I will pass over you." This gives rise to the idea of the slain animal as a "passover lamb" and, centuries later, Christ being the greater Passover fulfilling the principle (1 Cor. 5:7).

The preparation made, God brings the tenth plague, death of the firstborn of men and animals. Death reaches into every home lacking the blood, from that of the scepter to that of the slave (Ex. 12:29). Terrified, the pharaoh gave orders for the Hebrews that his own people strongly endorsed. He apparently did not see Moses' face but dispatched officials to talk with him (11:8). Let these people who had sought to leave the land be gone—all of them and their animals (vv. 31, 32). The final plague, most costly of all, left the Egyptians utterly convinced. Their urgency was so intense that they could not encourage the Hebrews out of Egypt fast enough.

Principles arise from this. First, when a person thinks he has seen God's last ability to act, He still is able to come back with more. Nothing is too hard for Him (Jer. 32:17, 27). Second, God can deliver people from a situation of bondage by acts of power and deliver spiritually by blood. He says: "When I see the blood, I will pass over you" (12:13; cf. Eph. 1:7).

Exodus 12:32

The Pharaoh's Last Appeal for Prayer

After this leader's pattern of insincerity, it is difficult to be confident of his sincerity running deeply here. He has asked for prayer several times, along with promises to let the people go. Each time he has quickly worked against God being free to bless him, though God has exercised longsuffering.

Now comes his final contact with Moses and a last bid for prayer. God's pressures brought against his rejection have brought him to another stage of desperation. This time, at least, he will (at the moment) let the Hebrews go, no strings attached. And with this he implores blessing. Possibly this is in prayer for a sure let-up of calamity for himself and his people. They are caught in the throes of immense suffering, losing their sons, and need safety from any further stroke.

The Egyptian leadership is getting a taste of the pain they had previously plotted for these people. They had sought to kill the Hebrews' sons. And the pharaoh seeking blessing on himself is soon to stage a hot pursuit to rob the departing people of blessing. "If I regard iniquity in my heart, the Lord will not hear me" (Ps. 66:18) could well be the wisest verdict on his two-faced dealing.

Anyway, God does not bless him. His vaunted chariotry is wiped out by engulfing waters of the Red Sea. God does, in grace, hold out blessing for those of Egypt who come to Him in faith. For His covenant with Abraham extends blessing to those of all nations (Gen. 12:1–3).

Principles can teach us here. First, how much better to pray in true submission to God than with unbelief, insincerity, double-mindedness, and deceit that waits to go against Him. Second, the person who prays and yet actually is calculating to buck God is on a path to his fall or utter ruin.

Exodus 14:10

Prayer in a Death Trap

Pharaoh's armies close in on the people of the exodus, there seems to be no way out, and the entrapped people pray.

The Chase by the Egyptians (14:1–9)

God's positioning of His people (vv. 1, 2). He put them where they had the impassable sea beyond and menacing armies behind. They had no way out. In their trap and in human weakness, their only way out was up.

Pharaoh's pursuit (vv. 3, 4b, 5–9). The man whose word never was trustworthy in this account had his armies right where they could close in and force the people back to slavery.

God's purpose (vv. 4c–d). God seeks to be honored through what He will do in beating the power of Egypt. He desires the Egyptians to realize that He is the Lord. That can be in salvation, which is not the point here, or even when people are unsaved but acknowledge His sovereign power and right. The latter is probable here. In the moments of their defeat in the sea the soldiers would see his Godhood. And after death they would also acknowledge this when the unsaved bow in subjugation and confess the Lord for who He is (Phil. 2:10, 11).

Of course other Egyptians back at their homes would know the Lord was God when they realized their armies had come out dead last.

The Cry of the Israelites (vv. 10–12)

To the Lord (10). They see themselves to be in a situation without hope apart from the Lord's intervention. Their *panic* leads to their *petition*. The prayer seems to be in unbelief, however, in contrast to the faith Moses displays before them.

To Moses (11, 12). They come with a "sour grapes" attitude. First they pin the blame. He is responsible for leading them into the trap (11). Second, they prefer the old life in Egypt, bondage and all (12). For as their logic goes, a live slave is better than a dead fugitive.

The Challenge from Moses (13, 14)

The price of leadership for God can entail taking much blame. Moses has had moments of failure and moments of faith. Never has he shown greater faith when his people needed it than here. God helps him rise to the occasion. What he says is right to the issues.

Banish your fear! (13a). "Do not fear," he shouts above the buzz of unbelief. In this he repeats the Lord's own counsel to Abram (Gen. 15:1), and the admonition that occurs more often than any other in

God's word. It is so frequent because men do fear so often, and need God's strength.

Behold your Fighter! (13b, 14). Good counsel is here. The leader meets the crisis by going to the Conqueror. God has always won in every episode Moses has seen since following Him out of Midian. The sufficiency of the Lord has begun to sink in.

His voice peals out the way when there seems to be no way.

Their part is simple: "stand by . . . see . . . keep silent." In other words, trust and give it to Him. *God's part* is sufficiency. They are helpless in themselves, but because He is what He is and can do what He can do, they can win.

He *appeals* to them just to see. God will save, and He will do it today, when they need it. When he appeals, he also *assures*, for faith sees what God can do and acts upon it. He assures them of two things. One is the utter *victory* over the enemies; they will never see them again, they will not hurt them or take them back into bondage. The other is the *Victor* who assures the victory. Behold your Fighter! "The Lord will fight for you. . . ." He will be completely able. He will win the victory "while you keep silent," unable to beat such odds.

The Consequences of a Sufficient Lord (vv. 15–31)

The Lord whom Moses trusts brings His people through the trial safely. At the same time He brings the Egyptians down in an overwhelming victory. His delivered people are beyond the waters that threatened; the enemy that posed so great a peril is under the waters, totally defeated, dead.

Such a demonstration by the Lord has its effect on the people He delivered out of trouble. He had answered their prayer cry, not because they deserved it or believed as they should, but in covenant faithfulness to His promises, in grace. He had also been honored by Moses' faith in Him as Israel's fighter and acted as a warrior consistently with it (15:3).

Consequences in the people are threefold in 14:31. They "saw" the overwhelming power of the Lord in victory. They "feared" Him in the awe of profound respect. And they "believed" in Him and in His servant Moses. The men join with Moses in prayer through a praise song (15:1–18), and the women worship in their own special praise celebration (15:20, 21).

The praise to God calls for a distinct place on its own, though it is actually part of the immediate consequences

Now principles can come front and center. First, why pray with unbelief when we can pray believing a faithful God? Second, a believing leader can stand tall with his challenge to trust God who does not fail. Third, when a need is now, God is able to act on time (cf. also Gen. 22:11). Fourth, when God wills it so, His act to deliver His own can also mean doom to those who defy Him.

Exodus 15:1–18

Moses' Song of Praise at the Red Sea

God's superlative victory caused Moses and the men to exult in prayer that took the form of praise. The praise is a "song" (vv. 1, 2) that Moses composed and led, giving adoration to God. It celebrates His *Person* as majestic, different from all gods, and His *performance* in working miracles (v. 11).

Praise for What God Is (vv. 1–3)

Preeminent over the enemy (1). He is highly exalted over the foe, great in excellence (v. 7) and has flung each Egyptian horse and rider into the sea. His victory is a rout, an overthrow of those who lifted their hand against His people (v. 9), a mighty display of His arm stretched over the enemy. His hands held out had brought the Egyptians to let His people go (3:20) and have just been majestic in power again (15:6, 12, 16).

Powerful (2a). He is "strength" in action, not as the powerless gods of Egypt that he defeated (12:12). What He has just done at the sea shows that He is majestic in power (15:6).

Personable (2a). Not only is He strength; He is, for prayerful Israelites, "my strength and song and . . . salvation." Of course He is personable to the people overall and to individuals as the God of the covenant bringing blessing He promised. The people praise Him for being "my God" and "my father's God." In the latter case, for Moses for example, He is the God of Amram (6:20) and much earlier Levi (6:16).

Proficient (3). He is not only a God who promises. He is one who performs. The picture so fitting for Him here is a "warrior," for He just went forth to meet the pharaoh's soldiers. And His leader, Moses, had shouted, "the Lord will fight for you . . ." (14:14).

Not only do the people praise Him as a warrior but as "the Lord" in name. He had specifically defined His action for them in Egypt as showing that He is the Lord (6:3–8). He would be known for mighty works demonstrating in a hitherto unprecedented way His *covenant* care to keep His word. His Lordship in pursuing His plan had come into awesome display.

Praise for What God Does to the Enemy (4–12)

Praise is so profuse that those just rescued from being destroyed (v. 9) stack aspects one on another for what God did to the enemy. He has *cast* them down, *covered* them, *conquered* them, *consumed* them, *congealed* the sea to defeat them, *confounded* them as to their strategy, and *challenged* praises of those who beheld what He did and view it as a tribute to Him.

Praise for What God Does for His Own (13–18)

Adoration goes on with blessings God confers on His own people.

He guides them (13). He has redeemed them out of bondage, the theme of the book. In doing this He has led them with strength to His holy habitation. The praise speaks of His bringing them to the mountain He intended (3:12) as already as good as done. Or it may mean He has guided them this far on the way to the destination. His guidance has been obvious in His power clearing the way in Egypt, His direction by the pillar of cloud and fire (13:18, 21), and His passage for them through the sea.

He gives them fear by their enemies (14–16). Rahab in Jericho would testify forty years later how her people had heard of the Red Sea act by Israel's God and was in fear of Him (Josh. 2:10, 11). Travelers in the area, desert bedouins, and shepherds may have passed on the news.

He grants them the land of promise (17). Praise can confidently expect God to fulfill His pledge (6:8). It is just a matter of time, and He will not fail.

He governs them (18). "The Lord shall reign forever and ever." He has already proven His governing of His people by an administering of events to spring them free. He has reigned over His creation, causing water to become blood, controlling flies and locusts, commanding thunder, lightning, rain and hail, lording it over darkness, having charge over death. He has reigned over all the gods of Egypt (12:12), and shown a greater kingship than the mighty pharaoh of Egypt. Even the winds, waves, and pillar of cloud have obeyed His authority.

A summary (19). This gathers the essence for praise as a fitting conclusion. It also ties in with verse 18 immediately. As God's entire deliverance shows, and as verse 18 aptly puts things, God does reign. "For," to wrap it all up, He reigns in the plunging of the enemies into sea, and the passage of His own over a dry sea bed.

So ends the prayer captured in a song of praise to God.

Which principles for prayer can we draw? First, our "Red Sea of trial" can be God's "Rescue Sea" to us and "the Sea of Rout" to those who are against Him. Second, praise suits God for all He is as well as for acts he performs in blessing and in judgment. Third, God's "hands on" faithfulness assures His people's safety, so it is good to say to the heart, trust Him (cf. Ps. 56:3). Fourth, elation due to God's great help can put praise into a song that erupts on the lips.

Exodus 15:20, 21

A Prayer by the Women

Fully in accord with what the men (15:1) have expressed, the women are filled with God's worthiness. Unable to contain their sentiments, they exult in their own special version. Miriam, a few years older than her brothers Aaron and Moses (cf. Ex. 2:4–8; 7:7), leads the praise. She is in her eighties by now.

The Prelude of General Praise (1–19)

This distinct prayer is in review above.

The Participation of Women in Praise (20, 21)

The prophetess (20). Miriam is called "the prophetess." This brings her function into prominence before her *family* relationship with Aaron. As certain other women in Scripture, she is God-gifted with special ability to speak God's word in prophecy and proclamation, as in praise. She is using her gift in leading the "women's seminar" here.

The participants (20). Other women join Miriam in a public demonstration with timbrels (thumped hand drums) and dancing in joyous victory.

The praise (21). Miriam leads in the words. All beat out an accompaniment on the drums and participate in lively movements to show their excitement in the Lord. Their *exuberance* is clear in the thumping, dancing, and song, "Sing to the Lord. . . ." Their *exaltation* of Him is clear-cut, "to the Lord" in tribute for "He is highly exalted." The glory is His alone. They are emphatic in placing the praise where it belongs, all to Him and none to self. Their *exhibit* of reason igniting their praise is something fresh and vital, His victory over the pursuers.

The Hebrews' enemy made planned its attack to "destroy them" and plunder what they had (v. 9). But their "warrior" stopped the plot by flinging horse and rider into the sea—all of them (14:23). So the enemy did not *destroy*; instead, it *dropped* in the waters like a stone (15:5), like lead (v. 10).

As is often true in Scripture, especially in the Psalms, the praise is for *Who* and *what* God is and for *what* He has done. The women dwell on His *worthiness* as the exalted One, and also His *work* in helping His people. The men, as in the previous verses, adored Him for *what* He is (1–3) and the *work* He has done (4–19).

Principles are plentiful. First, women who see God's mighty work can celebrate Him in their own special ways. Second, joy in the heart can put a dance of excitement in the steps as people pray. Third, instruments for beautiful sound can combine to magnify God with jubilant hearts, vibrant lips, and energized liveliness. Fourth, prayer can celebrate God for the many things He is—creator, shepherd, rock, redeemer, warrior leading in victory, and so much more.

Exodus 15:22–26

Prayer for a Drink

A three-day trek without finding water brought the Israelites to Marah. There prayer occurred again.

The Problem the People Faced (22–24)

The crisis itself (22, 23). After three days of travel in the wilderness, they were thirsty. The crisis was even worse when the water they finally found at Marah was bitter, not drinkable.

The complaint against Moses (24). As the people had done before, they took out their frustration on their leader. He was to blame for getting them into such a predicament. They grumbled against him for not seeing that they had no water.

Moses' Prayer and God's Provision (25, 26)

The prayer itself (25a). "Then he cried out to the Lord. . . ." It is not said, but Moses had a great background for a prayer of faith. So far the Lord had never failed him in a crisis. From the burning bush when his people were in a crisis to the Red Sea when the enemy could have wiped them out, he had seen the Lord always come through. Only a few days before he had composed a song of praise to God who did great exploits.

It is an encouragement in prayer to have one's memory filled with what God is and what He has done. The Psalms are rich in this. But much that is there recounts what the many episodes in His dealings with men, as here, have shown Him to be. Moses' own song has just been saturated with momentous consolations.

The provision (25b, 26). God's answer to prayer is in giving healing in two ways and in testing the people.

(1) The healing He provides. It is in water fit to drink in place of the bad. So He works a miracle related to *drinking*, then uses the occasion to promise blessing in healing from *diseases*. He shows Moses a branch which, when poked into the water supply, He uses to produce normal water. God can use means but this remains a supernatural work, just as He could have a rod thrown down and change it into a serpent, or a serpent into a rod, or water into blood.

The Lord sees chronic unbelief and sinful obstinacy in the complainers. He graciously utilizes the present provision to meet the immediate desperation for a drink. But He also uses the drama as an object lesson illustrating His overcoming of a greater problem bitter to face, pollution in the form of diseases. He is able to heal sicknesses as well. But He wants the people to trust and obey His word in being available to His provision as He is available to them.

(2) The testing He plans (25, 26). As He satisfies them in the need of the moment, a larger issue faces them. Will they believe and keep His word so as to be spiritually receptive to His overcoming problems in another physical realm? The stomach pain that foul water can cause possibly is a natural springboard into the bodily trial

that the diseases of Egypt can bring. They can well recall the boils upon man and beast not long before.

Trustful hearing of His word and obedience in doing what He says is His counsel for availing themselves of His healing blessing.

Principles flash to the mind. One is that God can quench any kind of thirst in the right way, physical or spiritual. Another is that God can heal from physical sickness in many times and ways when it is His will.

Exodus 17:4

Prayer again for a Drink

God had recently provided to meet the people's basic needs in their journey—guidance, safety from pursuers, drinking water, and bread. Now when they encounter another lack of water, their immediate reaction should be prayer and trustful expectation that He will be their supply again. Instead, as is such a chronic human inconsistency, they are back to forgetfulness, unbelief, and grumbling.

The Problem (1–3)

Lack of water at Rephidim is part of it. Another part is *looking* to the wrong source, Moses himself and not to the Lord who has been their sufficiency time and time again. A third aspect is their *lashing out* at him for not supplying water. He rightly asks, "Why do you quarrel with me? Why do you test the Lord?" He is their human leader, but providing in impossible situations is not his domain but the Lord's. By looking just to him, even lashing out blaming him, they are insulting the Lord.

They just keep trying to lay a guilt trip on the leader. Why has he brought them from Egypt to kill them, their children, and their animals by thirst? Their focus is on *man* alone, not on the *God* who has never failed them. But in ignoring and bypassing Him they are testing Him by living life as if He makes no difference.

Moses' Prayer (4)

His concentration on a solution. He asks God what he shall do to this people. Though he does not come right out with the need for water, he apparently had this *problem* on his heart. He simply voices a deeper problem, really; it is the *people* who do not trust him with their problem. God, of course, knows the entire prayer need!

His concern over a stoning. The leader senses and fears the rashness of the people. Bent as they are on looking only to him, not the real source of the answer, they are liable to take their unbelief out on him with stones. Given the attitude of criticism that inflames the people, this is a valid possibility. Moses seems to be faltering a bit in trust, too. He does not forthrightly challenge his hearers to see God's provision, as at the sea. He is absorbed with safety as much or more than supply, not boldly expecting provision but questioning what to do.

God's Provision (5–7)

The answer to prayer is in two phases.

The walk with the rod (5). God directs His servant to *pass* before the people, *pick* some of the elders to join him, and *proceed* with his staff to a rock in Horeb. The rod is, significantly, the signal instrument God had used in his hand when turning the Nile into blood and other miracles. So this suggests that His miracle work is about to occur again.

God does answer prayer, and He is gracious to the undeserving. He also uses willing people who intercede and ask for His mighty acts.

The water from the rock (6). God bountifully meets the need as He uses three stages here.

(1) The stand of God. He says "I will stand before you there on the rock. . . ." He is present to supply the need; He backs His servant; He is the One answering the emergency, not finally the servant. The people had doubted His presence (v. 7), and He certainly asserts it here.

(2) The smiting by Moses. God instructs the rod-carrier to strike the rock. It is a simple act, a dramatic device, an emphatic gesture to *capture attention* and to *center anticipation* on God's answer to prayer.

(3) The supply for the people. God promised that water would flow out, and the people would have a drink. Nothing says here that water did pour forth, but Scripture later gives us the commentary that it did (Ps. 78:15, 16). The Psalms passage describes it as *abundant*, and the need here to satisfy nearly two million people overall (cf. Ex. 12:37) plus livestock (17:3) called for it. So it was not only a supply, but a sufficient one.

One other point relates here too.

(4) The slogans about the place. Due to the people's distrust, Moses attaches slogan names by which to remember the campsite. It will be called ***Massah*** ("testing") and ***Meribah*** ("quarreling"). For them it left a legacy of faithlessness, for God one of faithfulness.

Out of this, principles arise. First, however we voice a prayer God knows more of our total need than we may utter and can give even more (cf. Eph. 3:20). Second, prayer not only can gain water from a rock to slake thirst but any other thing that is God's kind will to give. As creator of all He controls all and can manage it to do what He desires by accomplishing what does not seem possible. Fourth, time and time again, God's answers to prayer are in the largeness that grace shares when men do not deserve anything.

Exodus 17:8–16

Prayer with Hands Lifted Up

Another momentous incident took place at Rephidim, where God supplied the water.

The Surprise Attack (v. 8)

Amalekites struck stragglers in Israel's long line of people on the move, either to Rephidim or when leaving it. That they hit the

Hebrews in this way is made clear in a later reference back to this (Deut. 25:17–19).

These ambushers were descendants of Esau. Esau's firstborn son was Eliphaz, and Amalek was a son of Eliphaz (Gen. 36:12). He had become a chief over one of the Edomite bedouin tribes and was a desert raider.

God's Summons to the Battle (8–9a)

Moses, as God's spokesman, mustered a quick fighting force to shield the travelers. He appointed Joshua to do the actual enlisting and commanding of the soldiers. So far, apparently, Israelites had held the raiders off, and renewed attack was expected the next day.

But Moses does not depend on human brawn to suffice against the enemy. He was learning that *the Lord* would fight for them (14:14).

God's Sign of the Victory (9b-13)

To assure victory, Moses promised to take a position atop a hill looking down on the battle. His vigil there possibly would permit the men engaged in warfare to see him and be encouraged to expect to win. It also would allow him information about how the battle was going and any strategic adjustment he could make to relate to the outcome.

But the strategic factor in the place of vigil was the staff (rod) Moses lifted toward heaven. It was "the staff of God in my hand." The significance of this to some has been merely that the lifted staff would stir the morale of the soldiers. While this human factor could be a part of the overall picture, the staff's main purpose was as a sign of depending on the Lord. Moses was interceding to Him for the power and the victory. What factors show this?

(1) *Lifted hands* often bear significance in God's word. Men lift up hands toward heaven, to God in prayer (Ps. 28:2; 141:2). Moses has lifted his hands to the Lord in prayer in 9:29, 33.

(2) The *lifted staff* had been a frequent God-given signal for Moses in Egypt of what *God* was about to do to meet a need of His people. Moses lifted up his hands with or without a mention of the staff in representing God (7:19; 9:23, 33; 14:12, 21, 26). And *God's*

arm or hands gave the power that won (3:20; 7:5; 8:19; 15:6). So if Moses' raised staff was a signal of God's arms giving the power for His people's good, the same would seem to be true here.

(3) *The Lord*, finally, is Israel's *shield* and *sword* for victory (Deut. 33:29). The Hebrews' sword (Ex. 17:13) won because God's was helping them.

(4) *God's power* must be the reason why verse 11 defines Israel's victory surges as always when the staff was up, and losing the battle when it was down. Moses was at a distance from his soldiers and had no power in himself to give them. *To God,* distance and power were no problem.

The final victory is also related to the hands being up with the staff (vv. 12, 13).

(5) *God* is the One who pledges to defeat Amalek in verses 14, 15. So He must have done so in this context itself.

(6) Moses gives *glory to the Lord* at the altar related to the victory (v. 15).

It appears clear that *God* is the source of Joshua's triumph, and *Moses is depending on God.* His raised staff is a signal or sign symbolizing that, and outwardly picturing his *intercession.*

God's Swearing of the Enmity (14, 16)

God follows up the victory over Amalek with His plan to deal more fully with this enemy. This comes in four steps.

The recording of it. Moses did write it, both here and later (Deut. 25:17–19).

The reciting of it. It is to Joshua because he has just led in Israel's defeat of Amalek. He also will be the one to contend with Amalekites when Israel under his command invades the promised land. God later definitely tells Joshua to finish off this people after he gains rest in Canaan (Deut. 25:19). He fails in this task since Amalekites are still fighting Israel in three chapters of 1 Samuel (15, 27, 30).

The renown of it. Moses recognizes the Lord's renown in the present victory and the future defeat of the Amalekites. He also savors the latest help to his own people. He shows this by building an altar and calling it Jehovah-nissi, "The Lord is my banner." This is the essence of praise, in proclamation, but the passage does not say he put this into prayer too. He probably did.

Guidelines can finish this. First, true prayer lifts heart and lips to God and gains its triumph from Him. Second, God uses objects by which He displays His power to those who pray—a tree (Gen. 2), a rod, a bronze serpent, a fleece, a mantle (2 Kgs. 2), a sundial (Isa. 20), and so on. The power is not in the object but in the Omnipotent. We need not the article; we do need the Almighty.

Exodus 18:10

The Praise of Moses' Father-in-law

Before the reader in this account are Jethro's coming, commitment to God, and counsel to Moses.

The Coming of Jethro (1–8)

A priest from nearby Midian where Moses had shepherded, he came to the Hebrew camp bringing Moses' wife and two sons. They had stayed with him while Moses was leading his people in the exodus.

Moses filled the visitor in on "all" the Lord had done against Egypt and for His people. He testified of the hard situations they had come against and how the Lord had always delivered them. It was a testimony of power, of greatness beyond any god.

The Commitment of Jethro (9–12)

Such a giving of God's word, in effect, made a profoundly transforming impression on the man.

In his prayer (9–11). He *rejoices* in God, uttering a blessing of praise toward Him. Though he speaks it before Moses, he apparently is voicing what in essence he intends for God. It is adoration prompted by the Lord's delivering graciousness.

As Jethro rejoices, he even *recognizes* the Lord as supreme over the pharaoh, over all Egypt, and over all the gods (11). It is quite probable that the great work of God has persuaded him to the point of conversion. If so, he is a believer now.

In his sacrificing (12). Jethro seems genuine in worship here as well. He himself takes the initiative, marking the occasion as if deeply in earnest. He presents a burnt offering in thanksgiving and other sacrifices. The verse describes him as doing this "for God" and "before God." This observance grows out of the impact he feels from God's grace, and is more than thanksgiving for being with Moses and his people.

The eating and drinking before God seem to be as genuinely worshipful as when Israel's nobles ate and drank before Him (24:11).

The Counsel of Jethro (13–26)

What the relative of Moses suggests grows out of his praiseful realization about the Lord. It seems to misunderstand the flow of thought, or overlook it here, to say that Jethro is a man of the flesh passing out worldly advice wrong for Moses. Rather, the connections indicate legitimate, good counsel.

Counsel is clearly the idea in verse 19.

His insight about the load (13–18). Moses, he discerns, is taking too great a load of leadership on himself.

His input for the leadership (19–23). Jethro's management plan calls for organization. Get qualified people who can arbitrate different issues. Distribute the work to many, and utilize their capabilities. Take the massive load off one man who is covering all the work.

God's plan for dividing service capacities to various gifted people in the local church is similar. It works to the good of the "body" or group and many receive an opportunity to be used of God (Eph. 4:11–16).

Moses' implementation of the leadership (24–26). Moses found that the counsel was profitable. He himself still judged greater issues, but the remaining matters were the responsibility of leaders over thousands, hundreds, fifties, and tens.

The advice that was wise flowed out of a man the Lord prepared and to whom He gave ability. It came, it would seem, out of real conversion and a spirit of worship that was focused in prayer.

The passage suggests a principle. A servant of God who lives in trust and praise can be a servant with counsel that issues in success.

Exodus 19:8

Prayer in Representing Others

This is only a brief mention of Moses' prayer of advocacy for his people at the end of verse 8. It falls within a section of many chapters where most of the focus is on *God speaking* in giving His law and details of His tabernacle (Chaps. 19–40). *Man* speaks quite seldom in all of this because the great emphasis is on *God's* words.

But since Moses represents God's word to the people and the people before God here, his prayer is important even if but briefly noted. The discussion of the moment is only on the immediate relation of prayer in 19:8 to its flow of thought.

God's Appeal to His People (3–6)

His exhibits from the past (3–4). God encourages Moses on Mount Sinai with what He has done up to now for His people. He has *beaten* the Egyptians who held them in bondage, *borne* the Israelites on eagles' wings as it were, and *brought* them out to Himself to worship Him freely.

His encouragements for the future (5–6). First, the *part* He is giving them for their good is that of obeying His Mosaic Covenant. He will reveal that in large detail, with many laws that are for their welfare in various aspects of life (cf. Rom. 7:12, 14).

Second, the *privileges* He wants them to enjoy are rich in prospect. They are three—being His own possession uniquely among the nations, constituting a kingdom of priests (a domain having priests representing them to God), and a holy nation.

Third, their God is the One who has *prerogatives* over all the earth, so He is totally adequate to see all His purposes realized among all nations. His covenant with Abram had not only its personal aspect to Abram but its national plan and international span (Gen. 12:1–3).

That is a lot to encourage them if they walk in obedience.

Moses' Answer for His People (7–8)

Their promise to the Lord. Cocksure, the people pledge full obedience to God's word. They repeat this in 24:3, apparently basing it only on their own resolution and good intentions, not reckoning their utter need to trust in God's resources. Only a short time passes before they are denying the Lord and looking to the golden calf to be their help (Ex. 32). How like Peter centuries later, so insistent that He would be true to Jesus, then denying Him three times. And how like any believer, when he is glib about obeying God but a sinful failure when he gets his focus on self and not on the trustworthy Lord.

Moses' prayer to the Lord. As an intercessor for the people, his prayer is one of affirming their promise.

God's Aftermath with His People (9ff.)

What God says after the brief interchange and prayer actually covers the rest of Chapter 19 and in Exodus most of the detail in Chapters 19–40.

This in general is a context saturated with God in three ways, summarized here.

His presence. He is with Moses and the people he represents. He had been the God present with Adam and Eve in the garden, present to help Eve in child-bearing (Gen. 4:1), present in walking with

Enoch and Noah, present in covenant constancy with Abraham, Isaac, Jacob and Joseph. He had been present in preserving Moses, present in the bush, present as the great "I AM," present with Moses and Aaron before the pharaoh, present with his departing people in a pillar of cloud and fire.

He had been present in victory at the sea, giving water, giving manna, giving military victory, giving better organization.

Now He was present in a cloud and fire in the mountain, at Moses' tent of meeting, and in the tabernacle (25:8).

His precepts. God is with His people, giving them His word in laws to be obeyed.

His provisions. In grace God continues His compassion of the covenant with Abram and his descendants. The chapters are steeped in this grace. A few examples reflect this. One is God's gracious spirit of seeking man's welfare in laws for their blessing, laws that reveal thoughtfulness for their good. These are in many aspects of life that are made sweeter by doing things as God commands or counsels.

Another illustration is God's furniture in the tabernacle. Each item is calculated to have its role in ministering God's grace to people. The bronze altar serves in God's forgiveness by sacrifice; the laver for cleansing of priests who represent the others and in principle teaches cleansing of anybody for serving God. Inside the holy place, the golden lampstand illustrates God as light for His people in all of life; the altar of incense, access to God in fragrant prayer; the table of showbread, God's grace sustaining His people with food and all things.

The veil depicts God's holy separateness from people sinful since the fall. Yet He is graciously near in His presence so very close by in the Most Holy Place, gained by sacrifice and by supplication (incense) as in Leviticus 16. In that Most Holy Place, the Ark of the Covenant, a chest, was the place where He graciously invited sprinkled blood and rising fragrance of smoky incense to forgive His people. Under the lid of the chest was a copy of His law, the ten commandments, summarizing the essence of His moral standards with which His grace provided help to those who kept any aspect of it or broke it.

Still a further example of grace is God's positive answer to Moses' prayer for Israel's preservation after the golden calf idolatry (Ex. 32). He continues His covenant will in blessing this people as He pledged to the patriarchs, and uses the prayer as a channel in line with it! Chapters 33–34 are saturated with His grace in His dialogue with Moses.

God's presence, His principles, His provisions—all relate closely with prayer. Prayer enters into His presence in coordination with His word; His precepts detail the aspects of life that can all become matters of prayerful obedience or prayer in confessing disobedience. And His provisions are helps to be experienced in prayerful living—affirming them, petitioning for them, interceding for others, thanking and praising God for them.

Later Scripture is stocked with countless examples of prayer directly relating to the law or facets of it—love of it, thanks for it, joy in it, requests for enablement to honor it, and so forth. Psalm 119 is a special concentration on such prayer, as are many other psalms (1, 19, etc.). Even later books of the Pentateuch exemplify prayer relating to God's law and offerings to glorify Him (cf. Deut. 26:1–12).

Now a principle is pertinent. Prayer that is kept in close relation to God's precepts is prayer that God can honor (cf. 1 Sam. 12:23–24).

Exodus 19:19, 23

Moses' Prayer and God's Thunder

God's leader represents his people in prayer to God while the people stay down below, at a distance.

The Preparation of the Lord for His Coming (15–20)

God promises Moses He will "come" in a thick cloud and speak in such volume that the people will believe in him as the leader (v. 9). He repeats that He will "come" in verse 11, and in verse 17, Moses led the people out of the camp near the mountain to "meet with God." Then God descended (18), or came (20).

The Precaution of the Lord for His Coming (21–22)

The Lord tells Moses he is to make sure the people are controlled from coming too near in curiosity to gaze, for they could die for it.

The Prayers of Moses on Sinai (19, 23–25)

The Advocacy. Moses is concerned about how the people will meet with God if they are not permitted to come up because of the boundaries holding them at a distance. This is in verse 23. He had earlier prayed in verse 19, but his words there are not given. God answered prayer both times, in two ways.

God's answers. The first answer, relating to Moses' advocacy in verse 19, is *the caution.* The second answer, responding to the concern in verse 23, is *the clarification* (24). The people cannot come up into the mountain, but Moses and Aaron can. And God repeats the caution of the people not getting too close. Then Moses descends to deliver the answer to his people.

Moses later made other trips into the mountain for other stages of the revelation (Ex. 20–23, 24–32, 34).

A principle is evident. An intercessor who stays close to God can call down His answers of blessing on His people.

Exodus 22:21–24

Prayer When Afflicted

The Context of God's Laws

Prayer mentioned here occurs in a flow of thought where God is detailing His law to Moses for Israel (Ex. 20–23)

The Caution against Personal Wrongs (21–22)

Against the aliens (21). As God is gracious, His people are to be gracious. They are not to take any unjust advantage of a stranger, an alien. A good lesson for them to remember, in a spirit of compassion, is God's kindness to them when they were aliens in Egypt. There they also had gotten a taste of what it feels like to suffer at the hands of nationals, which ought to temper them.

Against the alone (22). Likewise kindness is the principle toward other people at a disadvantage, the widow and the orphan. Compassion again, not cruelty, is to reign.

The Consequences of Such Wrongs (23–24)

One consequence not mentioned here is the blessing on the person who acts with mercy.

The focus, however, is on two other results. One is the Lord's *answer* to the hurting person who prays, the other is His *anger* toward the persecutor. Both amount to one thing, His response to prayer.

God's answer to prayer (23). Prayer may or may not be the recourse of the person misused. But should he cry out to the Lord, the Lord pledges certain action. This, as far as the wronged party is concerned, will bring a sense of righteous redress.

God's anger toward the persecutor (24). This takes the injustice seriously enough to call for tough action. Hard-fisted dealings to run over others is grievous in God's evaluation, as the reaction shows. God is not only angry. He will kill the perpetrator of the crime with a sword. This might, in a case of an individual or a group, be done through civil leaders appointed (cf. 32:27, 28). Or in a case of the wrong permeating the nation involving a very large number, God could fulfill it through a conquering nation. Babylon would be His instrument wielding the sword as in Ezekiel 21, God doing it with His "sword" but the invader using it.

God will not just be angry and execute the men who deal in such heartless crime toward others. A third factor ought to be weighed in avoiding this shameful injustice. The guilty, when punished in death, would be hurting their *own* families. Their wives would be left widows, their children fatherless. And it would be by their own wrong. God could take care of the widows and orphans through gifts of the caring among His people.

Prayer in this case, and God's response to it, is very serious. Sensitive meditation on how He means business should have a wholesome effect, and probably did in many cases over the centuries.

Here is a principle: God feels for the hurting believer who prays and wants to help in a compassionate way (cf. 55:22; 1 Pet. 5:7).

Exodus 30:1–10

Prayer Rising as Sweet Incense

All of the items of furniture related to tabernacle ministry would suggest prayer to a God-conscious person in Israel. But one piece may be mentioned especially. It is the Altar of Incense placed centrally inside the Holy Place, immediately before the veil, between the Golden Lampstand and the Table of Showbread.

That the incense is symbolical of fragrant prayer raised to God is evident. One thing that points to this is the language about incense in scriptural commentary. The psalmist longs for his prayer to rise as incense (Ps. 141:2). A writer of proverbs calls prayer of the godly as God's "delight" (Prov. 15:8), like the sweet fragrance pleasing Him in the incense. For the high priest took a firepan of coals, sprinkled incense on the coals, carried this into the Most Holy Place, and let the incense smoke ascend in God's presence (Lev. 16:11–15). He also took with him blood to atone for sins of himself, his family, and all the Israelites. God accepted the blood and the incense.

In Scripture much later, incense symbolizes the prayers of believers (Rev. 8:2–5). Besides all of these considerations, the rising of the smoke with its fragrance quite naturally fits with the person lifting up parts of his body to God in prayer. He can lift up his hands (Ex. 9:33; Ps. 28:2; 119:48), his heart (Lam. 3:41), his eyes (Ps. 123:1; John 11:41), his face (Ezra 9:6), his voice (Prov. 2:3), and his soul (Ps. 25:1).

When this is kept in view, the altar is very significant.

Specifics for the Altar (30:1–6)

God wants all parts of the tabernacle made according to the pattern He gives (25:9, 40). This is true, then, of the incense altar. He lays out the details carefully, calling for full compliance. What us true of physical aspects is true also of the spiritual ministry in prayer that it signifies. Any approach to Him in prayer is to be with reverence sensitive to His word. The person is to experience His nearness in the way He shows.

Service at the Altar (30:7–10)

The service associated here is to be three things.

One of attending to sweetness (7–8). The motions the priest went through illustrated and were to be accompanied by prayer.

(1) The presenting of fragrance (7a). Verses 34–38 give the prescription for ingredients to make the incense sweet. As it arose to God its delightfulness would please Him.

(2) The place of fragrance (6a). The altar, its hot coals, and its incense were to be "in front of the veil" into the Holy of Holies, into God's presence. Verse 6 specifies not just His *presence* but the nearness in relation to His *pardon*. It is near the ark of the testimony, the chest inside which His word and will was represented. The lid of that chest was the place where the high priest sprinkled blood to atone for sin (Lev. 16:11–15).

The principle this suggests is clear enough. Prayer should ever draw near to God who is holy, to His mercy to cover the one who is unholy. Then we can have holy fellowship with Him.

For priests serving in the Holy Place, incense at that altar always would suggest prayer. Prayer ought to saturate their ministry there and in every phase of tabernacle worship.

But for the high priest, Aaron and later men in this line, there was the added ministry. Only the high priest could go past the altar, through the veil, into the Holy of Holies. This was one day a year, the Great Day of Atonement (Lev. 16). As shown above, he would offer blood and let incense taken from the altar rise to God.

(3) The perpetuity of incense (7b-8). Every morning and evening were the times of ministering with the incense. This bracketed the entire day. Once a person saw the significance of coming to God with fragrant prayer, he, like the priest, could come and come any time. Later Scripture mentions even evening, morning, and noon (Ps. 55:17), and seven times a day (Ps. 119:164), seven to represent completely saturating the day with prayer.

(4) The prescription for incense (34–38). God is discerning about what will delight Him. He very carefully lays down the principle of compounding the fragrance only out of a special blend or recipe. This is no doubt because it is to be special *to the Lord*, not on any level just with fragrance for human enjoyment (v. 37). To take what is to belong to God and direct it to self was an insult to the One worshiped. This amounted, at that time, to an invitation to death (v. 38).

Two of Aaron's sons learned that God means what He says. Nadab and Abihu offered "strange incense," apparently of a counterfeit mixture. God's instant taking of their lives lifted a caution to others that this was very important to Him (Lev. 10).

The point in this prescription brings us back to the nature of the service at the altar. It is a second thing.

One of avoiding strangeness (9). This is clear above. But more is involved than already mentioned. The full picture is one of avoiding not just strange incense but putting there the burnt offering, meal offering, or drink offering. God specified the bronze altar in the tabernacle yard for these ministrations. That possibly was to be very careful about keeping distinct the great emphasis of each tabernacle item and its service.

Prayer is not to tolerate any foreign elements, unpleasing to God. As He is particular about the ingredients for the physical incense, His Word in many places also defines the ingredients for prayer that delight Him. These, among other things, include coming in faith, in love, in purity of motives, and so on. Even the ministering priest was to wash his hands at the laver before coming into the Holy Place, depicting cleanness of heart to approach God. For God leads one of His psalmists to say, "If I regard iniquity in my heart, the Lord will not hear me" (Ps. 66:18).

The ministry at this altar is also associated with a third reality.

One of atoning for sin. As already summed up above, the altar, while itself having no offerings for sin, was closely related to these.

The priests prayed there for the Israelites, as in asking God's blessing in Numbers 6:22–27. And the high priest, as noted, took incense from there one day a year and carried it into the Holy of Holies along with blood of offerings (Lev. 16). God was satisfied with the blood of atonement. He also received the incense fragrance and the supplication that accompanied it in faith seeking His acceptance.

A principle is based on the sweet incense God had His people use in mixing spices that relate to prayer. He wants His people to set high value on coming before Him so that their prayer is with fragrance, and He regards trustful prayer as sweetly acceptable. Psalm 104:34 later says, "Let my meditation be pleasing to Him." Another psalm expresses the yearning that "the meditation of my heart be acceptable" (19:14). How sweet His words can be to our taste (Ps. 119:103; cf. Jer. 15:16), and our hearts and words to Him can be delightful. So, as Psalm 141:2 phrases it, "may my prayer be counted [fixed, set] to/before Thee as sweet incense. . . ."

Exodus 32:11–13

Moses' Intercessory Appeal for Sparing Israel

Prayer occurs after Israel's idolatry in worshipping a golden calf has set the stage. Moses has been on Mount Sinai for forty days and forty nights, receiving God's law. God sends him back to the encampment to confront the sin, and a series of prayers follow in Chapters 32–33.

The Sin (32:1–6)

Impatience over Moses' long absence was the beginning of the sin. People of the camp put pressure on Aaron to provide a god who would take them on their way. How quickly they gave up on the Lord and Moses, His leader. Their own will, not waiting for His, prompted their impatient demand. Aaron yielded and led in the sin of making a golden calf the people could see as their god.

Though the Lord was on Aaron's tongue (v. 5), associating Him with an idol image was a total misrepresentation of Him and a denial of His glory. It gave credit for the deliverance out of Egypt to an image, not the Infinite One (cf. v. 8). Frivolity rather than a spirit of true worship prevailed (v. 6), and with it, a mood out of control (v. 25).

The Summons (32:7–10)

God dispatches His advocate back down the mountain to deal with the idolatry. He expresses His grief at the people's obstinacy and makes a proposal to Moses. His anger can issue in His destroying the offenders, and He can make of Moses a great nation to continue His will.

This may be simply a test to give Moses an opportunity to show true loyalty to God and His people and not seek renown for himself. Of course, God could assure fulfilling His will in the covenant promise by yet another means if Moses failed, but He also could enable Moses to respond in true commitment to His people and God's promise. He enables Moses to meet the test.

God had already planned to send a leader in the line of Judah (Gen. 49:10). He also had pronounced, through Jacob, other details He would make good on to the descendants of the different sons. He would not fail in these. And so He could cause Moses to respond to do His will, His prayer being implemented as part of fulfilling that will.

The Supplication (32:11–13)

Moses pleads a case before God for preserving Israel, based on three arguments true to God. Here, then, is his threefold plea.

God's power over men (11). God's own power has delivered the people from Egypt and brought them this far. It is His own ability that is at stake. The prayer is focused on things that mean everything to God, and He is touched by the things of His own honor.

God's perception among men (12). Why should the Egyptians be allowed a pretext for taking glory away from God? They could impugn His motives for bringing His people out of Egypt, evil rather than good. It would seem to be pointless, also, for Him to go to all the trouble to deliver them, only to destroy them.

This does not mean, of course, that God had not thought of these things. Moses is not being smarter than the Lord and saving His plan from a mess if He did it His way. Again, God is permitting His prayer warrior the privilege of reasoning out what God already knows and having a part in His ongoing plan.

God's promise to men (13). Moses pleads with God to *remember* His people and the covenant pledge He Himself gave to them. The prayer logic is the honor of His own *self* behind His promise and His own *promise* itself. His honor is at stake, nothing less. Moses is zealous to respect His glory. What He had promised as His will, let Him fulfill!

God's own glory in Himself and in His word are often the core of intercessory prayer in Scripture. The very will of God is laid upon the heart and tongue of His servant. He gives His will to be the praying person's will (cf. Phil. 2:13).

The Sequel (32:14–35, etc.)

God's answer to the prayer will be one of sparing the people through whom to carry on His own will. He has simply brought Moses to pray in harmony with that will. He deals out discipline on 3,000 as a warning to the rest of the possibly two million people (cf. 12:37). This finally is merciful to the majority. But He continues His program with the nation itself.

A principle emerges. An intercessor of God is on good ground in stressing God's power, His knowledge of a great plan, and His promise of blessing for those who are the objects of prayer.

Two other prayer passages in the context are worthy of individual attention.

Exodus 32:30–32

Moses' Prayer for Israel's Forgiveness

The Prelude to the Prayer (30)

Moses' discernment of the great sin. He calls it "great" three times, beginning in verse 21.

Moses' desire for a great solution. He longs for atonement for the people, a prospect that drives him to prayer.

The Pleading in the Prayer (31–32)

His confession of the great sin (31). The intercessor calls the sin "great," seeing it as an enormous ugliness against God. He also affirms the nature of the sin, making a god of gold. This itself shows how it is great or of grievous character. The "god" is a terrible affront to God. Certainly such acknowledgment is an *agreement* with God's verdict, the heart of confession as in 1 John 1:9.

His cry for forgiveness (32a). The advocate's concern is so deep a burden that he does not complete his thought. His mind leaps on, and words are left out. He says "if You will forgive their sin," then apparently meant "I will be grateful" or something of that nature. But his emotions run so high that he jumps on to a related possibility, "and if not, please blot me out from Your book. . . ." He realizes that, as far as he perceives, God could choose not to spare the people overall. If He does, Moses' identity with his people is so deep that without them, he himself does not desire to go on in this life either.

God counsels Moses that it is those who have sinned that He will blot out—remove from the register of those alive on earth (cf. Ezek. 13:9). This does not, in this case, include Moses. So God does not deal as Moses is supposing, but as *He* wills.

The Postlude of the Prayer (33–35; 33:1–3)

God's doom on the guilty (33). God's principle is one of individual accountability (Deut. 24:16). He brings temporal judgment on the person who has sinned, fairly, and not on the one who has not.

God's direction of His people (34; 33:1, 2). First, He gives His *approval* to go on to the land of promise. This is His will, and He is committed to carry it out. Second, He gives His *angel* to guide Israel to the land. Angelic ministry in the covenant outworking was prominent to Abraham as in Genesis 16, 18, and 22. And it was the same with Jacob in Genesis 28 and 32. So it is here and is often evident in the rest of the Old Testament and in the New Testament.

God's discipline on His people (34–35). God does fulfill His covenant promise of giving the land. But when He sees it as fitting, He deals out discipline on a disobedient people for sin. His reference may be a summary of His principle as carried out on the 3,000 in this chapter, verse 35 attributing to *God* what He had done through the *Levites* here. The principle would also bear upon other cases in the wilderness wanderings and later, as in Numbers 11 and 14.

Principles abound. First, sin may be great, yet the one who prays for forgiveness can lay hold of God who is greater than all our sin. Second, God fills in prayer even when our burdened hearts fail to follow through with full wording. He knows all that is in the heart (cf. Ps. 139:1–4). Third, even when one pleads with God to forgive people in a group, God reserves the right to bless whom He wills and blot out from life those He wills. He, of course, has the full picture on every individual and can make the soundest and fairest decision.

Exodus 33:12–34:28

Moses' Further Intercession: Dialogue with God

This exchange between the advocate and the Lord is closely related to the prayers in Chapter 32.

Moses' Plea (12, 13)

Petition for his own person. He appeals to God to let him know His ways. His reason is "that I may know You," similar to Paul's quest in Philippians 3:10. He also longs to find grace (favor) in God's sight, to have power with Him for His purposes, to be usable.

Intercession for his people. First, Moses is concerned over which people will go, that is, who will survive with him and who will fail to go on due to discipline. Second, He is burdened for God to remember them as His people.

God's Answer (14)

This is clear-cut in two details. First is His accompanying Presence. Second is His assuring peace. Grace to Moses himself, responding to his petition, is evident in his realization at the end of verse 12, as well as in 14.

Moses' Second Plea (15, 16)

His ardor for God's presence (15). He has his values straight. If God will not show His presence going with the people, Moses does not care to go. God's presence is the priority. So all believers, in prayer, should long to see God's presence in the way they go!

His argument for God's presence (16). Moses yearns to see, as he has already seen, God's miraculous displays along the way. This is crucial in a couple of ways, which are keys to him. One is that God's powerful presence will show His vindication of Moses' leadership and acceptance of the people. The other is that such clear-cut manifestations of God's blessing will mark Israel as distinct from all other peoples.

God's Answer (17)

His pledge. He gives His promise of His presence to demonstrate that this people is special among peoples.

Moses' prevailing. This, God says, is the human reason or means He is using for giving the blessing. Prayer of a right kind has power with Him! At the same time, of course, His own prior will and plan included blessing the covenant people (Gen. 12:1–3, etc.). As He so often makes clear, He works His will in His servants. They plead His will and involve themselves passionately in it.

Moses' Third Plea (18–23)

His asking for God's confirming (18). It will help Moses' confidence if God grants this guarantee of His presence now. "Show me your glory."

God's answer by His confirming (19–23). To encourage Moses, the Lord does three things here.

First is the passing of His glory. He does not show Moses a full, direct look at His glorious being, for no man can see this glory face to face and live through such a breath-taking experience. He does show him His presence in another sense, letting him see Him from behind, in some less direct manifestation of His light.

Second is the proclaiming of His name. This name, the Lord of powerful covenant exploits to help His people (6:3), would be a great boost to Moses after 3,000 died, and he had been pleading for God to go with them.

Third is the proffering of His grace and mercy. God promises it in 33:19 and proclaims it in 34:6, 7. He shows compassion, as in forgiving abundantly, yet no man can take wrong advantage of Him, for He brings sin to an accounting.

Moses' Fourth Plea (34:8, 9)

His *attitude* in verse 8 is one of bowing in worship, showing due reverence for the Lord. His *asking* in the next verse is in intercession for three favors. He seeks God's presence for Israel in its journey, His pardon for their sin (he includes his own), and His possession of them as His people.

His God is a big God. He asks big things. And His prayer is fed by God's own word. Every blessing He seeks here God assures in His words that have just freshly impacted him (33:17; 34:6, 7).

God's Answer (34:10–28)

It is "yes," for the prayer is according to His word, according to His will. God pledges miracles nobody on earth has seen to help His people and verify to others His presence with them (10).

He also calls them to obey His word (11–23, 25–26, etc.). He intends to drive out their enemies from the land He gives them (11, 24). His house will be in the land to receive their firstfruit gifts (26). In Moses' return to the mountain, He writes the ten commandments to replace those Moses shattered in horror at the golden calf sin (28). The subsequent record also shows His presence, possessing and pardoning His people. At the end of the book, His glory fills the completed tabernacle (40:34, 35), and His presence in the pillar of cloud and fire went before the people (36–38).

Moses, the man of intercession, shows he is a man of doing the will of God. The reader comes often to a verse such as 40:16: "according to all that the Lord had commanded him, so he did."

Meditate on principles, this suggests. First, it is a very large privilege to feel a burden that drives one to pray for people who are very dear to God and to the intercessor. Second, one intercessory appeal can follow another, and prayer traffic never presents an overload to jam the circuits before God. Third, prayer that is aright, knitted to people and to God, pleads in line with heart goals that are the passion in God's own covenant intent. Fourth, it pleases the Lord for a servant who loves Him to beseech Him to manifest His presence (cf. John 14:21–23). We have His Word on this. Fifth, of a big God with a big plan, ask big things (cf. Jer. 33:3; 32:17, 27). He can do the seemingly hard things just as readily as the things that by comparison seem easy.

Exodus 39:43

A Prayer of Blessing on the Workers

It is fitting that the final prayer in Exodus is Moses' invocation of blessing on those helping make the dwelling place of God.

The Performance of the Work (35:20–39:42)

God had specified that every part of the tabernacle be built "according to [His] pattern" shown to Moses (25:9). All of this is now completed. The prayer that crowns it relates to the entire work.

The Prayer on the Workers (39:43)

The authentication by the blueprint. Moses *checked* all the work and confirmed that everything was just as in God's specifications. He must have felt exhilarated in approving it, realizing that God endorsed it.

The appreciation in the blessing. Moses' reaction is a prayerful intercession invoking God's blessing of appreciation on the people who participated. He is asking God to bless them in accord with their doing His will. They receive their God-given sense of honor, reward, or distinction. This is, in principle, what Jesus would later says can be true even after all of life's work. "Well done, good and faithful servant, . . . enter into the joy of your Lord" (Matt. 25:21, 23).

The prayer is followed by God's pertinent guidelines for service at the tabernacle and compliance with these (40:1–33). After this, God's glory cloud filled the dwelling place. His presence shown in this way and in His pillars guiding Israel to new campsites complete the Book of Exodus (40:34–38).

Principles are relevant here, and can finish comments on the book. First, one is always on track asking God to bless His workers who have diligently done what is on His heart. Second, God's glory is profuse when people move spiritually to His heartbeat and prayer dwells on things precious to Him (cf. John 15:7–8).

Prayer in Leviticus

It will be seen shortly that prayer is integral to this book even if not often explicitly mentioned. First, normal matters of introduction help orientate the reader.

The Title

Leviticus derives from the Greek word ***Levitikon***, "pertaining to the Levites," the title The Latin Vulgate translation used. However, much earlier than that the Jews knew the book by its first word, the Hebrew ***waggigra***, "and he called" (1:1). For it was a custom to name many books by the first word.

The Author

Moses is probable. The opening words enhance this, "And the Lord called to Moses and spoke to him out of the tent of meeting. . . ." The book has fifty six references to the Lord revealing the laws directly to Moses. We see the recurring phrase "And the Lord called to Moses" or "spoke to him" (1:1; 4:1; 5:14; 6:1, 8, 19, 24) as late as 27:1. Besides, the authenticity is upheld almost constantly by such repeated words to Moses as "speak to the children of Israel," "speak to Aaron," "the Lord spoke," "I am the Lord," or "I am the Lord your God." One also sees "the Lord commanded through Moses" (4:13, 25; 7:36, 38; 27:34), and Moses is the overall leader (9:1) giving commands (9:5), the one most natural to have charge over the writing. More detailed evidence for him as the writer is developed in detail by books of Old Testament introduction from R. K. Harrison, Edward J. Young, Gleason Archer, and Merrill Unger.

The Date

Conservative scholarship sees the date during the period 1447–1400 B.C. We need to distinguish the time when the events of the book occurred historically and the date when the writing was pursued or completed. Yet the writing was most naturally within the same time. Events of the book transpired during a very brief span, the month that went by as we compare Exodus 40:27 and Numbers 1:1. Things in Leviticus followed quickly after completing the tabernacle and God filling it with His glory in Exodus 40 a year after the exodus, ca. 1446. Moses could have finished writing the book soon after this as he kept abreast of recording things important to God's covenant people.

The Background

Leviticus goes on with the narrative of Exodus without a break. Once the tabernacle was ready for use and the Lord showed His presence in it, He "called to Moses and spoke to him from the tent of meeting . . ." (Lev. 1:1).

In Exodus 25–40 the author speaks about the formation of the tabernacle, and in 40:34ff. God's glory permeated it. Significantly, then, He is ready to furnish more guidance for His people from 1:1 forward. The reader moves from the formation of the tabernacle in Exodus to the functions of the priests and other people in this center of worship. Another way to put it is this. Exodus 25–40 shows the construction, and Leviticus adds to this further instruction about the nation's use of the tabernacle. The purpose is to prepare people to worship God in holiness, for "You shall be holy because I the Lord your God am holy" (Lev. 19:2; 20:26).

Before the place of worship was built, the Lord spoke in Exodus from "the mount that burned with fire." But now in Leviticus the Lord indwells the tabernacle and speaks out of it. In this light, the Israelites are addressed in the book as a people separated to God by redemption and not separated from God as the other nations. Since the Lord is actually in the midst of His people at the outset of the book, the account goes on to reveal the provisions or grounds of true holiness by which the people, now redeemed out of Egypt, may have access to His presence and engage in fellowship with Him. In this context, prayer will be the heartbeat.

After finishing the tabernacle, the inhabitants of Israel remained in their camp at Mount Sinai for another month and twenty days (cp. Ex. 40:17; Num. 10:11). Then they set out on a trek toward Canaan, the land God intended them to inhabit. So the Book of Leviticus and Numbers 1:1–10:10 occurred during this period after completing the tent but before resuming travel to the threshold of the land God had promised (Gen. 12:7).

The Theme

Repeated key words help in grasping the main focus. For example, "holiness" occurs ca. eighty-seven times, "before the Lord" about sixty, and"atonement" in around forty five places. The book's central emphasis, in this light, is the holiness of God and the standard of holiness on His heart for His redeemed people. The principle is evident in 19:2 and 20:26 by direct statement, "You shall be holy (set apart) because I the Lord your God am holy." The book explains the offerings and cleansings by which the people of the holy God can experience holiness and walk in fellowship with Him.

The Outline

I. The Provisions for Holy People (1:1–10:21)
  A. The Sacrifices (1:1–7:38)
    An introduction (1:1–2) leads on to five different offerings—burnt, meal, peace, sin, and trespass (1:3–7:36)—then a summary for the offerings (7:37–38).
  B. The Priesthood to Lead in the Worship (8:1–10:21)
    Pacesetters are consecrated (Chap. 8), tabernacle ministry begins (9), and a special sin of two priests is condemned (10).

II. The Practices of Holy People (11:1–25:55)
  A. The Holiness in its Functions (11:1–15:30)
    This is traced in relation to clean and unclean food (11:1–23), physical contact that can contract uncleanness (11:24–47), a woman's purification after a childbirth (Chap. 12), in leprosy (Chaps. 13–14), and in

cleansing from sexual impurities for men, then women (15).

B. The Holiness Related to the Day of Atonement Once a Year (16)

C. The Holiness in its Functions Continued (17–22)
This deals with holiness among the people in general (17–20), then among priests who lead in matters of holiness (21–22).

D. The Holiness in National Feasts (23–55)
Maintaining holiness is shown as related to the Sabbath day (23:1–3), six different feasts during the year (23:4–44), tending the tabernacle's holy lamps and table of showbread (24:1–9), a case of punishing a blasphemer (24:10–33), and God's will for special years such as the Sabbatical (seventh) Year and the Year of Jubilee (49th year).

III. The Prospects of Holy People (26)
If Israel remains holy, God will give blessing (vv. 1–13), but if they become unholy without repentance, He will bring chastisement (14–39). If they repent after chastisement, God will restore them (40–45).

IV. The Presentations by Holy People (27)
Focus is on the presentation of eligible things—persons, animals, houses, and fields in a desire to please the Lord (vv. 1–25), then the principle that pertains to other things, such as firstborn animals, devoted things, and tithes (30–33). Then verse 34 concludes the book.

The Relation to Prayer

Prayer fits in several ways.

(1) It is the response to the Word of God. The book places a great emphasis on the Lord's Word specifying details vital to tabernacle worship. For example we see the recurring phrase "the Lord . . . spoke" (1:1; 4:1; 6:1, etc.), and what is said in chapters is often a running account of the guidelines He spoke. Some exceptions are 9:1, where Moses spoke,

relaying God's words, and instances of doing what Moses directed (vv. 5, 8–24), or the writer narrates the episode of Nadab and Abihu sinfully offering a different incense than God specified (10:1ff.).

God's words and acts to men are a catalyst for their words or acts toward Him. An example is in their response of giving Him thanks (7:12–15).

The focus in the book is predominantly not on prayer but on details about matters of worshipful life and service. Much about different offerings (Chaps. 1–7) is followed by priestly acts (8–10), and other matters as in the outline (cf. above). But the minutia of directions for various outward facets of life and service assume inward sincerity, if things are as God wants them to be, as in a prayerful response to the Lord. Even the thanksgiving in 7:12–15 does not explicitly mention words spoken to God in prayer related to the sacrifice. But later Scripture understands the gratitude as having inward delight and words. One can see this in "a broken spirit, a broken, contrite heart" (Ps. 40:6–10; 51:14–17; cf. 34:18; Heb. 13:15). The chronicler says that the Lord seeks to show Himself strong to those whose heart is sound toward Him (2 Chr. 16:9), and even when the Ten Commandments appear the Lord wants those who "love Me and keep My commandments" (Ex. 20:6). If done rightly, so-called holy facets of service should represent a worshipful seeking of God "with all your heart and all your soul" (Deut. 5:29). Where that is true, it quite spontaneously would, among other things, evoke prayer in gratitude, rehearsing of precious truths from God, sensitive tenderness to confess sin, pledges to do God's will, requests for strengthening, and prayerful intercessory concerns seeking blessing for others too.

One can go through each section of the Leviticus outline and readily see how a godly heart can respond to this truth with sincere prayer. It is pertinent in each offering of Chapters 1–7 to pray in the instance that most spontaneously fits the case, whether a crying of heart and lips for dedication and thanksgiving that God accepts it (burnt), offering one's possessions or property (meal), longing to be forgiven (sin, trespass), or appreciation (peace). In details about priests (Chaps. 8–10) a leader or a lay person could quite relevantly give thanks for such guidelines, for opportunities of ministries, and for God accepting and using any sincere leadership. In portions on cleansing from bodily flows, it is meaningful to thank God for caring about details, and speak to Him in desire for the benefit. On the yearly Day of Atonement (Chap. 16), prayer would be apropos by the high priest to carry out faithfully his representing of the people within the most holy place, and for the people represented to thank God for forgiveness, and offer themselves afresh to God in a sensitive, heart-searching stand against any sin. In the times of feasts, it would be spiritually natural to draw near to God with fresh gratitude, affirming what this feast vitally means, and asking for the Lord's way of responding to this in the truest, complimentary godly motives and acts (cf. on Ps. 51:16–17, 19 the place of outward offerings yet the priority of inward godliness that could make these delightful to God).

Certainly, then, prayer of a right sort is a spiritual reflex response to God's Word. It also can be a proper clinging to God in fellowship in view of who He is in giving His words (cf. Deut. 4:7–8).

(2) The Person of God. God is many things, holy, truthful, worthy, compassionately caring in covenant fidelity, and so on. Prayer is a natural reflection to His Person in several ways.

a. One way is a sensitive respect that will seek harmony with Him, for His delight. One sees this immediately even in the opening chapters. There, worshipers can offer Him gifts with the accompaniment of fire that lifts "a soothing aroma" to Him (1:9, 13, 17; 2:2, 9; 3:5, 16; 4:31). The focus of a heart in sync with Him is not just on what one himself gets out of the worship, but what God gets out of it because it is pleasant and acceptable to satisfy His heart. True devotion to God would find it a spiritually natural reflex to pray in such holy worship. This could be in various aspects along which prayer might trace its reality with God—for example in affirming love to Him (cf. Ps. 18:1), petitioning for guidance to be pleasing to Him, interceding for others whose needs are known, acknowledging sin and forsaking it, and presenting words of thanks.

Cases of cleansing could relevantly be prompts for prayerful intertwining with the heart of God. So could any kind of thing in

Leviticus. Offerings recognize God and can be accompanied by giving the heart's affection anew to Him. Priestly service, as well as all other service in principle, could be given with the heart, and its words, just as when offering God any contribution or skill in usefulness for His sake (cf. Ex. 35:5, 21–22; 36:2). Foods God gives men to enjoy, and the ones He sees not as for their good (cf. Lev. 11:46–47) can be a basis for words of appreciation to Him. Feminine hygiene in child bearing is a possible occasion for rehearsing details of life, so important to one's heart, with God (cf. 12:6–7). So can any sexual hygiene and directions for cleanliness be good venues for taking matters to the Lord in prayer.

It is crucial for the person who fixes his heart on God to have a single eye to do what pleases Him. The focus can be to have an outlook that seeks to deal with matters by an uplook to do His will. The path of life, true in Leviticus long before our Lord Jesus Christ walked the earth, is essentially the narrow way that He would teach (Matt. 7:14). It is the way God wants; it is the way He leads; it is the way that inclines to Him. It is life for His sake. And it is in respect for Him that fixes the gaze of the soul on His mind, and prizes it, in whatever matter His guidance covers. How different is the way of respect that has true communion with Him in doing what He counsels rather than showing disregard and disrespect that bypasses and degrades Him.

b. Prayer is pertinent, as was already mentioned, in times of remembrance before God, and can even expand into a spirit at all times appearing in grateful words. Some would be ready to give praise/thanks. In restating God's law Moses says, "He is your praise and He is your God" (Deut. 10:21). The psalmist later would put this in the perspective that "great is the Lord and greatly to be praised" (Ps. 48:1; 145:3). Every matter of God's counsel in Leviticus, seen in a receptive and tender spirit, can become an occasion in a proper way for thanksgiving, or some other facet of prayer.

Thanksgiving as linked with the Peace Offering in Leviticus 7:11–15 can pervade the life in always relating to God in some meaningful relationship. That is as true in this Old Testament book as often in the Psalms, or in the New Testament (cf. Eph. 5:20; 1 Thess. 5:17).

In the five great offerings of Leviticus 1–7, prayer, even when not immediately stated, is very cogent. Later Scripture helps us see the valid saturation with prayer. For example, prayer is strategic with the burnt offering (Ps. 20:3–5; 51:16–17; 4:5). It is natural to the meal offering (Ps. 20:3–5; 96:8). Even in the day when Moses restates the law (Deut. 26) it is already clear that prayer in grateful tribute to God is vitally germane. For a worshiper within the covenant recognizes that God is the giver of his many blessings (vv. 1–11). In verse 10 part of a prayer that fits the case is, "And now behold, I have brought [to the house of God, v. 2] the first of the produce of the ground which Thou, O Lord hast given me."

Prayer suiting the peace offering is distinct in Leviticus 7:12–13. One thanks God for the peace God has given in the covenant relationship. David, when he confessed his sin of numbering the people (2 Sam. 24:10), presented burnt offerings and peace offerings (v. 25). For the sin, offering prayer is completely suitable. For prayer is vital in any dealing with sin before God. The psalmist later is clear about this (Ps. 32:5; 38:18; Ps. 5), and so is other Scripture (Prov. 28:13; 1 John 1:9). For to make offerings outwardly without the heart, devotion, faith, and genuine inward worship would never be acceptable to God (cf. comments later on Ps. 51:16–17). The same is true of the final of the five offerings in Leviticus 1–7, the trespass offering. This is relevant when one has in some way defrauded God or man, that is, trespassed on rights that are due them. To deal with the sin, the person needs a relevant way to resolve what is offensive, and must reach God, to whom, ultimately, the guilt offends. This is in prayer. The one who has trespassed needs also, of course, to make whatever honorable restitution is pertinent to another person, whom he defrauded. Jesus focused on this in Matthew 5:23–24 to make things right with the other as well as with the Lord.

c. Prayer also can be relevant in the aspect of confession.

One confesses sin when sensitive to his or her need. This direct prayer to God would naturally fit cases of sin and trespass offerings (Lev. 4–5). It also could apply in dealing with cases of sexual emissions, in instances where one acknowledges desires or acts that have been impure, and not pleasing to the Lord (Chap. 15). And in Leviticus 16 the high priest would on the Day of Atonement once each year offer blood for his own sins and the sins of fellow Israelites whom he represented when entering the Most Holy Place. On such an occasion, too, those sensitively responsive to God would join him in heart and in words by their own dealing with the sin and their heart cry to please the Lord.

Even in a future day when the people repent of sin, they can confess it and find God's covenant mercy (26:40–42). In principle that people of Israel in Moses' day could learn from this to acknowledge their sins at any time now, for the need to confess can be true of themselves, each personally, in their own day. Daniel would see that it was applicable in his own case and that of his fellow-Israelites, so he confessed sin (Dan. 9:4–19).

Finally, prayer is meaningful in Leviticus in terms of an intercessory aspect.

d. One can summon God's blessing on others. This comes into the picture in 9:22–23, where Moses and Aaron blessed the people. They desired God's blessing to impact those they were representing before Him. In servant spirit their focus was on others. The same is true in "the Lord bless you" in Numbers 6:22ff., and the principle appears in many intercessory vigils throughout Scripture. Paul expresses it in detailed requests for God's benefits to other believers (Eph. 1:15–23; 3:14–21).

Now the focus can be on passages about prayer as they appear in the book.

Leviticus 5:5

Confessing Sins

Chapters 4–6 develop the matter of dealing with sins in daily life through offerings and confession. Two great offerings relate to the sin, depending on the differing nature of each specific sin.

First, the *sin offering* avails in 4:1–5:13 for sins of failure in *one's own life*. These can be sins of which a person is unconscious that he is sinning at the time. He is unaware that he is failing, and deliberately going against God's will.

He may, for instance, through his human weakness, slip into a sin of ceremonial defilement touching some unclean thing before he thinks things through. Or he may swear idly on the spur of the moment. Examples are laid out in 5:1–4. Or he may sin even when conscious that he is doing this, yet do it in human weakness. One such wrong is in refusing to testify in a case where he can be of help. He holds back knowingly due to some human fear (5:1).

Second, the *trespass offering* is effective in 5:14–6:7 and 7:1–7. It differs from the sin offering in covering cases of *fraud against God or people*. Due to violating another's rights, it is necessary in such a case to make restitution, whether to God or the human. This is aimed at making things right with the offended party. Trespasses are sins done in error or unwittingly at the time, such as forgetting to fulfill something due to God (5:15), or committing a wrong knowingly but again due to human weakness. One might hold back on giving a gift to God that is really due Him. Or he might commit fraud against a person's rights, as in theft, trickery to take advantage, or a matter of trust (6:4). To fail in a case of trust would be to deny falsely that he had ever borrowed an item he had failed to return, or lie claiming it had been stolen.

In case of sin requiring a *sin offering* or a *trespass offering*, confession in prayer is necessary. The example in 5:5 pertains expressly to the former, but the same principle applies to both.

The Committing of Sin (5:1–4)

Examples of sin are clear here, whether refusing to testify as a witness, contacting a dead body, or swearing in an oath to do something he should not do.

A distinction becomes obvious between the *act* of sin itself, and the subsequent *awareness* of it being sin (v. 4). Once the true nature of what he has done smites the person's conscience, it is time to deal with the sin!

The Confessing of Sin (5:5)

The offender against God needs to acknowledge the sin as sin, and bring a sacrifice to offer in covering it. He comes to the officiating priest, first confessing and giving the offering as a substitute in his place, then having the priest confess and offer on his behalf.

Such confession involves prayer to God. The person would say, in effect, "I have sinned, doing this in Your sight, and I need Your forgiveness. I bring this offering with its blood to cover the sin." The priest would offer for him, and take his confession to God, giving him on God's behalf a confidence of God's satisfaction. This would be as specific by the individual as the prayer in presenting a gift to God with thanksgiving (Deut. 26:1–11).

The Covering of the Sin (5:6–13)

A confessing person dealt very specifically with the sin. He brought a *sin* offering for his *guilt* (v. 6), a lamb or a goat. At the same time he also brought a *burnt* offering (v. 10). The first sacrifice dealt with the sin by blood, the other was consumed entirely on the bronze altar. This second phase in offering was an acknowledgment that like the animal offered, his entire life was dedicated to the Lord. He was yielding everything, holding back nothing from devotion to Him.

God's grace allowed for *any* sinner to be able to follow the steps. If a person was poor, having no lamb or goat, he could bring two turtledoves or two pigeons, one as a *sin* offering, one as a *burnt* offering (v. 7). If extremely poor, he was free to offer a tenth of an ephah of fine flour, serving for the sin aspect and the yielding up entirely to God.

The sacrifices "cover" or "atone" completely, satisfying the Lord. So the sin is "forgiven" (v. 13). At the same time the offerings in illustrative principle picture the ultimate sacrifice by Christ which cleanses from sin (1 John 1:7). Believers today can *confess* sins, *depend* on the blood of Christ for *forgiveness*, and be *cleansed* from all sin (1 John 1:9). Christ who fully gave Himself to God is a burnt offering in their place, and they offer themselves in entire renewed yieldedness to God.

This leads to principles. First, it is always right to acknowledge to God any kind of sin one feels guilty about, even any trespass against others' rights. Second, a prayer of affirmation can join with confession and the cry, "I need Your pardon," or "I give this offering as I recognize my sin, and I desire that You cleanse me in Your sight." Third, God made it possible even for a very poor person to present an offering within his means—two doves or pigeons, or a small portion of ground grain. All can come. Later, the offering Jesus Christ made atoned for all, whether wallowing in wealth, or writhing in poverty, or those in between.

Leviticus 7:12

The Peace Offering of Thanksgiving

So far, this study has mentioned three of the five great offerings in Leviticus 1–7. These are the *sin*, *trespass*, and *burnt* offerings. Another presentation in the five was the *meal* offering of 2:1–16 and 6:14–23. It was given in recognition that one's *possessions* or *things* belonged to God, in distinction to the burnt offering acknowledging that his *person* (life) was wholly the Lord's. The flour or grain or meal was a testimony of his recognition that all his produce, given by God, belonged to Him (cf. Deut. 26:1–11).

One other great offering rounds out the five. It now becomes the subject here.

The Sacrifice Related to Peace (7:11)

The person in Israel could offer this animal in any of three categories. One was in *thanksgiving* to God (v. 12), another linked with some *vow* the person fulfilled and gave God tribute for, the third a *voluntary* offering. The last of these arose out of one's own spontaneous desire to credit God for His blessing of peace, though no specific incident stimulated it. The second and third kinds appear in 7:16.

Any of the three occasions involved prayerful communion with the Lord in thought and in word.

Leviticus 3:1–17 also describes the peace offering. A male or female animal was allowed. Christ is the ultimate offering, combining in Himself all human fullness, the strength of the male and sweetness of the female. He is the perfect human, in all completeness.

Offerings in these categories could be cattle (3:1), sheep (v. 6), or goats (v. 12).

The Significance Related to Peace (7:12–15)

"Thanksgiving" to God is the chief idea. It is mentioned four times in verses 11–15. The person brought his offering to the priest, and prayed in gratitude. On his behalf the priest prayed and offered his sacrifice.

The thanksgiving was related to peace that was a blessing of God within His covenant kindness.

Parts of the peace offering, the richest portions, were burned. They became God's alone. So in Christ, the greater offering who made peace for men with God (Rom. 5:1). God saw on the cross the richest innermost value. Christ *is* our peace, He *made* peace, and He *preached* peace (Eph. 2:12ff.). Colossians 1:20 says He "made peace through the blood of His cross." Likewise in the believer who prays in thanks for His peace, God delights to see the richest innermost attitudes, feelings, yearnings, passions toward Him.

Other portions of the peace offering could be eaten (7:15–18). The offerer took these home for a joyous celebration in thanksgiving to God for His peace, peace based on blood. When one was at peace with God, living with a jubilant spirit, he could offer the sacrifice of thanksgiving (Ps. 116:16, 17). And today the believer can live in light of all God's benefits, offering a sacrifice of praise to God continually (Heb. 13:15). This is "the fruit of his lips" in prayer, giving "thanks for all things" (1 Thess. 5:17).

Principles jump to the fore. First, as in the meal offering, one can give all that he has over to the Lord who gave it (cf. 1 Cor. 4:7) in thorough dedication. Today this can entail land, produce, animals, home, vehicle, business, job, clothing, abilities such as speaking, singing, artistry, writing, mechanical know-how, and so forth. Second, a person should celebrate with thanksgiving the peace he enjoys from God's provisions. This could be in anything, even a successful harvest, growth of a herd, prosperity in work, or help to fulfill a vow (pledge).

Leviticus 9:22, 23

Prayer in Blessing Others

Aaron and priests of his Levitical line are consecrated to their spiritual ministry in Leviticus 8 and their service inaugurated in Chapter 9. It is on this momentous occasion that Aaron and Moses, as sacrifices are offered, bless the people they lead.

The Presentation of Offerings (9:1–22)

All is done in orderly fashion. With Moses taking the lead, the priests consecrated in Chapter 8 now offer sacrifices for themselves and then for the people they represent.

The Prayer About Their Effectiveness (9:23, 24)

Prayer played a vital role in the priests' ministry to God and to the people. In 1 Chronicles 23:13 the summary is given that God set Aaron and his sons apart as holy to fulfill three things. One was to burn incense before the Lord, a ministry already seen (cf. Ex. 30) to relate strongly to prayer. Another was to minister to Him in a myriad of connections that would reflect and redound to His glory. The third was to bless His name. This blessing would be in such facets as Numbers 6:22–27 spells out (cf. there).

Aaron and Moses both are said to bless the people in Leviticus 9. As in Numbers 6:22ff., this is probably a prayer invoking God's blessing on them. The prayer is spoken before the people and to them (in their hearing and to their joyous benefit), but more so to God. An illustration that can well suggest the tenor is that of David later in blessing the Lord and His people (Ps. 28:9). He blesses the Lord in *thanksgiving* (v. 6) for His help (v. 7). He also *intercedes* for God saving His people, blessing His inheritance, being their Shepherd and carrying them!

Similarly in Numbers 6, verse 27 defines the kind of prayer the blessing entails. For "they shall invoke My name on them," and in answer to prayer for His blessing, "I will bless them." Specific intercession gains His specific response.

God's response in Leviticus 9 assuring that He will bless is accompanied by a manifestation of His glory. The glory appeared to all, probably in splendid light from His glorious pillar of fire. His fire also consumed the burnt offering and fat, depicting the full dedication of the priests and that to which they called the people. Other offerings included the sin and peace offerings. God's endorsement of the offerings with His signature, His presence, caused the people to *shout*. His glory was here as on the day when He filled the completed tabernacle. The shout is no doubt in praise, exulting in appreciation to God for His approval in grace. They not only shouted but fell prostrate in deep reverence, probably in prayer continuing the praise.

What of principles relating to this? First, we can appeal to God to infuse us or others with grace. Paul later would begin and end letters with this intercessory gesture for the Lord's enrichment, strength, discernment, or whatever variety of gracious help fits each life. Second, we ought to be always bestowing spiritual caresses on God as we tell Him that we recognize His glorious beauty and worthiness of plaudits.

Leviticus 16:12, 21

A Leader's Ministry in Incense

Aaron as high priest led Israel's worship on the Great Day of Atonement which was set one day each year. In fulfilling his service, among other things he brought blood of sacrifices and also incense into the

Most Holy Place. By these two actions he was representing the Israelites' sin and also relating the incense sweetness before God on their behalf.

The Representing of the Israelites' Sin

Aaron made at least two trips into the Most Holy Place, into the presence of God, on that special day. On his first entrance he sprinkled blood of a bull for himself and his family, and let incense smoke rise over the Ark of the Covenant in fragrance before God. The second time in, he sprinkled blood from one of two goats for all Israel's sin, and let incense fragrance rise again.

The first goat was slain, and he took the blood in to sprinkle on the mercy seat, the lid of the chest called the Ark. This sought God's *atoning* for sin. Over the head of the second goat he confessed Israel's sin of the year, and had an assistant lead that goat away into a remote desert place to release it. By this he illustrated God's *removal* of the sin far away, never to be remembered against the people again.

Confession was a big feature on this day (v. 21). Aaron confessed all sins of those in the community during the entire year. In case any sin had not been dealt with in the regular offerings through the year, this day's sprinkling of blood covered even those of the nation that were otherwise uncovered (cf. v. 33). As the high priest carried out his intercessory ministry for them, seeking reconciliation with God, the people probably were with him in spirit, seeking the Lord in prayerful contrition and confession.

That such elements gripped the people is a fitting expectation. For they observed the day by fasting, "afflicting" themselves (v. 29), apparently in serious self-denial and seeking of God.

The Relating of the Incense Sweetness (16:12, 13)

When the high priest walked into the Holy Place on the two occasions, he paused at the Altar of Incense momentarily. There he took a pan, filled it with burning coals from the altar, and sprinkled incense on these. Then he took the incense pan as well as blood already obtained from the offering at the Bronze Altar outside, and entered the Most Holy Place. He sprinkled the blood on the mercy seat seeking God's reconciliation for sin. The incense smoke ascended from his hot coals, bearing the fragrance of the spices prepared true to God's formula (Ex. 30:34–38). The sweet smell illustrated the sweetness he prayed God would find in his advocacy by blood for reconciliation and cleansing.

The Removing of the Sin (16:21)

As noted already, the first goat was used to depict reconciliation for sin, the second goat to illustrate removal of it. This drama of removal was saturated with prayer. For the high priest confessed the sin over the second goat's head. When the attendant had led the goat far away, he returned to the camp without it (v. 26). This pictured the sin as gone!

Principles make their impression. First, it is a precious and moving privilege to have the sin of one or many put upon Christ and its penalty utterly paid. It also is a boon filling the heart to realize that God has taken sin away, never to be an issue to mar our relationship with Him. What grace! Second, as the high priest represented those of Israel before God, each believer priest today can enter boldly into the most holy presence of God and be directly acceptable. This is by the blood of Christ shed for him (Heb. 9:9–14; cf. 10:10, 14, 17, 19–22). Third, as Israelites afflicted themselves, mourning and repenting over sin, we now can make serious turnabouts to God in situations as these come up.

Leviticus 19:24

Praise for Fruit God Gives

This account tells of growing a tree and praise to God who gives the fruit.

The Prohibiting of Fruit from the Self (v. 23)

One of God's guidelines is here. When an Israelite plants a tree, he is not to eat its fruit for three years. Then on the fourth year, again, he is not to eat but to praise God. The point seems to be to focus the heart on giving credit to Him rather than on enjoying the fruit himself, at least this early.

The Praising for Fruit to God (v. 24)

The fruit has come from God, as in creation (Gen. 1). So, the principle is to pray in *acknowledgment of God* and in *appreciation to God.* He gets all the credit. Such a spirit of rendering gratitude to Him is illustrated later. When a farmer of Israel brings fruit God has given him to God's house, he is to thank Him in prayerful acknowledgment (Deut. 26:1–11).

The Partaking of Fruit for Oneself (v. 25)

By the fifth year the tree has reached some maturity. Now the one who follows God's counsel obediently can partake of the fruit God has given him.

One explanation of this is a natural one from gardeners. A tree can bear more abundantly if blossoms are nipped off in the earliest years. A second is to teach self-denial. The fruit is thought of as "uncircumcised" in the earlier years, in a condition analogous to that of a male child who is "uncircumcised." Then the dedication to the Lord renders it "circumcised," with a recognition that God gives the increase as He multiplies Israel to fulfill His covenant (cf. Gen. 12:1–3; 17).

A guideline is evident. Whatever fruit of any sort God gives us, physical or spiritual, it can be a catalyst for offering gratitude to Him. We can pour forth thanksgiving words to Him in all things (1 Thess. 5:17), and season prayer in everything with new bursts of gratitude (Phil. 4:6).

Leviticus 26:40

Confession by a People in Dispersion

Verse 40 refers to confession of sin after disobedience to the Lord has resulted in His giving Israel over to conquest and dispersion to the enemies' land. The whole context needs to be in view to place the prayer in its setting.

The Call to Obedience (1–2)

God summons His people to commit themselves in three great particulars. First, the obedience is to His own person, to worship only Him and avoid different expressions of idolatry as substitutes for Him (v. 1).

Second, He desires them to observe His sabbaths, holding fast to channels and times of drawing near to Him (v. 2a). And third, He is passionate that they center their lives in Him through due worship at His sanctuary (v. 2b). In both verses, His call to obedience ends with His right to their steadfast affection: "I am the Lord." This is a reminder of His identity as the covenant-keeping Lord of Exodus 6:3, the Lord who had done awesome wonders in Egypt to deliver them out of bondage into freedom and spring them on their way to His promised land.

He alone deserved their worship, and this because of who he was and what He had done to display it.

The Contrast over Obedience (3–39)

In a nutshell, this long passage sets in contrast two ways and their results. The first is the way of *obedience* to God, and the blessings He bestows on those who obey (3–13). In this way He gives them prosperity in their toil (4, 5), peace (6), prevailing over enemies (7, 8), and His presence (11–13).

The other way is that of *disobedience* (14–39). God first mentions the possibility of disobedience (14, 15), then the perils of it (16–39). The perils are many and menacing; wise meditation on God's word could save the people many a heartache! God mercifully seeks to lead them away from these—sickness (16), loss of crops (16), defeat (17, 25), hardened heavens and earth (19), frustration in their efforts (20), disasters from beasts (22), hunger in siege (26), ruin of their worship centers (30) and cities (31, 32), dispersion from the promised land (33–39), and so forth.

Prayer would be vital in relating to any of these. As an example, *peace* could be a matter of prayer (cf. Num. 6:22–27), whether in intercession by the priests, petition by the rank and file for it, affirmation in having it, and thanksgiving/praise for it.

Confession with Obedience Again (40–45)

Three elements are clear-cut in this.

Their acknowledging of sin (40). This would feature an agreement as to the sinfulness of what they had done, and that they were wicked in doing it. They would acknowledge disobedience in themselves and also their forebears which they have copied, and show awareness that the wrong was "against Me."

Solomon later would pray along similar lines for Israel when he publicly dedicated the completed temple (1 Kgs. 8:47–53). He prayed that if his people disobeyed, went into captivity, confessed and returned to the Lord, He would bless them. Jeremiah prophesied of Israel's distress in enemy conquest, calling for confession and guaranteeing God's bringing them back to Zion (3:12–18). Daniel confessed his and his people's sin and interceded for God's restoration of the people, the city, and the temple (Dan. 9:4–19).

Their attentiveness to God's way (41). The Lord also looks for a genuine humility and real integrity of motive to return to Him. True confession, as He sees it, is not just a mouthing of words in trouble but a heart desiring His way and returning to it desiring to follow it. As other Scripture would clarify, God Himself must work to energize hearts to do this (Ps. 80:3, 7, 19; Jer. 24:7; 31:18).

God's answer according to His covenant (42–45). From His own standpoint, with His commitment, the Lord will fulfill His gracious covenant with Abraham to bless his descendants (cf. Gen. 12:1–3, 7, etc.). He pledged and He cannot fail to honor the promise of His own plan, His own will. He does discipline the disobedient (Lev. 26:43, 44), and they lose blessing they might have had along the way. But the covenant with the nation is steadfast and always will be continued. And the plan that is sure in the guarantee of His own covenant He will fulfill even by using, at times, the prayer of His people coming into alignment with His purposes. His will, and their prayer, intertwine as He works within them to will and to do of His good pleasure (cf. Phil. 2:13).

An interesting phrase repeated here in verse 45 takes the reader back to verses 1 and 2. God said, in calling the people to obedience to His will, "I am the Lord." Now in certifying His fulfillment of His covenant will, He closes with the same affirmation, "I am the Lord." He is the covenant-keeping Lord! When other nations control His people far from their land only the "Lord" is able to assure answer to prayer for restoration. And He pledges surely to do it.

Key principles suit the passage. First, as God called His ancient people to focus on worship to Him at His sanctuary, He wants believers now to meet together for fellowship in Him (Acts 2:42) and encourage one another (Heb. 10:25). Second, God honors those who obey, most of all with a glad sense of His dear presence (Lev. 26:11–13; cf. 1 Sam. 2:30; 2 Chr. 16:9; Ps. 84:9–11; 1 Pet. 3:12). But those who dishonor Him miss out on His favor and make themselves liable to various kinds of grief that center in their walking away from Him (cf. James 4:2–3) Third, the way of holiness is also the way of wholeness. in genuine well-being. The verses in Leviticus 26:3–13 share various facets of life made full as God is able to make it.

Prayer in Numbers

Introduction

Prayer will be evident soon, but first one can become orientated to key matters before the concentration on communicating with God.

The Author

References in this book and in the New Testament infer that Moses the great leader of Israel was responsible for the written record. This is not contrary to any proven fact. True, some like G. B. Gray (*ICC*, p. xlii) posit unhistorical material and view the book as a composite of several documents centuries later than Moses' day. Gleason Archer, R. K. Harrison, Merrill Unger and E. J. Young quite reasonably answer the denials that Moses wrote the document, and give positive arguments that he did. A great host of evangelical writers stand in this tradition.

Moses as the obvious, overall leader of his people was a natural choice as writer (11:1; 16:25–26). He recorded journeys from Egypt until the people of Israel were poised ready to enter the land God had promised (cf. Gen. 12:7). This was in Numbers 33:2–49. The book ends on the summary note that God gave commands and ordinances via Moses to the Israelites before they crossed the Jordan to possess the covenant land (36:13). The book's first verse begins a pattern of saying more than eighty times that "the Lord spoke to Moses" (cf., for example, 1:48; 2:1; 3:1, 5, 11, 14, 40, 44; 4:1; 6:1; 8:1, and as late as 35:1, 9). Another frequent phrase is "the Lord commanded Moses" near the outset (1:54; 2:34), throughout (8:20; 15:23), and near the end (36:2, 6, 10, 13). The only portion within the thirty-six chapters not expressly attributed to Moses is the account of Balaam and Balak (Num. 22–24), but that is natural since Moses is not in that account.

The Date

The chapters cover thirty-eight years (cf. 1:1, 18; 36:13), and give a record during Israel's wilderness wanderings after the exodus out of Egypt. This is before they go into the land of Canaan. With an early date for the exodus, ca. 1447 B.C., the thirty-eight years would fall between ca. 1445–1407 B.C.

The Title

The fifth word at the outset of the book, ***bemidhbar,*** gave Moses' people the Hebrew name for the account. This means "in the wilderness," a description that fits the contents better than the name the LXX Greek translation assigned, ***arithmoi,*** of which the Latin *numeri* and English *numbers* are translations. The latter title is apt since the book has two numberings of the people, the first (Chap. 1) just before the outset of their journey from Mount Sinai (cf. 10:11), and the second at the close of the treks covering thirty-eight years (Chap. 26). Other main numberings are the three branches of Levitical servants (4:34–49), military musters from different parts of the camp (Chap. 2), twelve scouts sent to spy out Canaan, one from each tribe (12:1–16), the total that died when God judged Korah and other rebels and 14,700 others (16:49), the 24,000 who died in a plague (25:9), the figure for animals captured from the Midianites in booty (31:32–54), and the listing of starting points and new camps in stages of journeys from the exodus until Israel waited near the Jordan to enter the land God had promised (Chap. 33).

The Setting

As the Hebrew name suggests, the account depicts the wilderness journeys. Numbers 1:1–2 explains that Israel, while yet at Sinai, took a census in the second month of the second year after leaving Egypt. At this time they received God's further directions (Chaps. 5–10). The number in the initial census was 603,550 (1:46). Then, on the twentieth day, nineteen days later (10:11), the population left Sina. The book gives the record of Israel's movements from the final nineteen days at the mount where they were in Exodus 19–Numbers

10:11 until the arrival on the plains of Moab east of the Jordan River in the fortieth year after the exodus (Num. 22:1; 26:3; 33:50). The second numbering was 601, 730 (26:51). Both census figures, for men, would indicate a total population, with women and children, of approximately two and a half million.

The explanation in 14:34 is that the forty years of wanderings were for the forty days in which Israel's scouts spied out the promised land, and all but Joshua and Caleb would not believe that God could fulfill His promise to them. In their eyes, the task was out of reach due to giants and high walled villages they had seen. God had the unbelieving scouts die by a plague (14:37), and only the two who believed that God was greater than the giants and the lofty walls gain passports to enter the land (v. 38).

The Value

The document is important to the canon of Scripture and significant for several reasons. Prayer, as other themes, fit with these.

(1) Numbers explains the cause of the lengthy delay in entering the promised land (unbelief, cf. Chap. 14). It also gives the reason why God does not permit Moses to go in (20:9–13).

(2) Rich spiritual lessons and applications to believers of the New Testament era are plentiful here, since Christians insofar as they sin also experience wanderings.

(3) A wealth of background is laid here as in Exodus, Leviticus, and Deuteronomy for grasping the many allusions later in the Bible to Israel's history and laws.

The Theme

It is fitting to see the theme as the wilderness wanderings of the people in Israel due to their unbelief in God's promises to give them the land in covenant faithfulness. These promises are frequent in earlier Scripture, for example, in Genesis 12, 15, 17, 26, 46, Exodus 6, 7, and so forth. When the writer sums up the years of wandering (Num. 33), he repeats over and over the phrase "and they departed" to show that the people were often on the move as a wandering group.

The Outline

- I. The Preparations for the Trek (1:1–10:10)
  - A. The Preparation for Functional Organization (1:1–4:49)
    This includes the census (Chap. 1), campsite (2), and charge for the Levites who are leaders in Israel's worship.
  - B. The Preparation for Spiritual Life and Obedience (5:1–10:10)
    God gives provisions to deal with defilement and sin (5), Nazarite vows (6), priestly ministry (6:22–8:26), observing the Passover annually (9), and marching signals when Israel must move to a new campsite (9:15–10:10).
- II. The Trek to Kadesh Barnea and Israel's Rebellion (10:11–14:45)
  - A. The Order of the Groups for Travel (10:11–35)
  - B. The Complaint of Many and of Moses (11:1–35)
    The people complain (11:1–9), then Moses complains to the Lord (11:10–15), seventy helpers are selected to share responsibilities (11:16–17), and God provides meat (11:18–35).
  - C. The Presumption of Aaron and Miriam (12:1–16)
  - D. The Spying Out of Canaan (13:1–14:45)
    A report of scouts who have gone throughout Canaan features wide-spread unbelief that God condemns and faith by two of the scouts. Due to the unbelief God allows Israel to wander thirty-eight more years before a new generation will enter the land.
- III. The Wilderness Wanderings to the Plains of Moab (15:1–21:35)
  - A. Instructions for Life Once in Canaan (15:1–41)
  - B. Rebellion led by Korah, and Judgment (16:1–50)
  - C. Instructions to the Priesthood (17:1–19:22)
    God approves of Aaron's priesthood over upstart rivals, then gives directions to the priests for leading Israel.
  - D. Problems During Wanderings (20:1–21:35)

- IV. The Prophecies of the False Prophet Balaam (22:1–25:18)
    - A. Balak's Scheming to Turn the Lord from Israel (22:1–24:25)
      This features a proposition to gain Balaam's support, and the prophecies Balaam utters.
    - B. Balak's Success in Turning Israel from the Lord (25:1–18)
- V. The Preparation for Entering Canaan (26:1–36:13)
    - A. Preparations for Conquest and Division of the Land (26:1–27:13)
    - B. Regulations for Offerings and Vows (28:1–30:16)
    - C. War with Midian (31:1–54)
    - D. Settlement of Some Tribes East of the Jordan (32:1–33)
    - E. Summary of Journeys from Egypt to the Plains of Moab (33:1–49)
    - F. Briefing for Dividing Canaan (33:50–35:34)
      This includes details for possessing the land, boundaries of it, officials for apportioning, directions to set up forty-eight cities for Levitical leaders, and instructions to designate six cities of refuge where Israelites could seek justice.
    - G. Inheritance by Women (36)

The Relation to Prayer

Cases of explicit prayer are soon to follow one by one. It bears saying at this point that some prayer in this account, as in other Bible books, is *specifically articulated*, whereas in many instances it is not mentioned but its high probability can be *safely assumed* as spiritually natural to details in the book. One could go to other Bible books and find the same phenomenon, where other details fill the record but prayer no doubt would be the apt current of hearts and lips in such matters. Many are the examples (cf. Gen. 1, 5; Ex. 1; Ps. 1; Matt. 1, 10; Rom. 2, 13; 1 Cor. 2, 3, 4, 6, 8, 9, etc.; Eph. 4; Col. 2; Titus 2; 1 Tim. 3, and such passages).

Specifically articulated cases in Numbers. These will soon follow, case by case. At the moment, one can summarize examples of prayer's different chief aspects that the writer mentions.

(1) Petition. Moses, for instance, pleads for God to permit him to go into the land, but God has taken his privilege away due to his sin of striking the rock in anger in Numbers 20. He also complained due to his strain at the burden the dissatisfied among his people posed for him (11:10–23). Balaam mouthed his prayer as the phony who profess to know the Lord often do, for these can learn the words and fulfill their form of godliness (22:10–11, 34).

(2) Intercession. Some examples are calling in God's blessing on others (6:22–27; 10:35–36; 27:15–17), summoning His judgment (14:1–3), and so forth. God often spoke to Moses in the privacy of his tent of meeting, and he prayed to God (7:89). He interceded for God's blessing on his people *before* carriers took down the ark of the covenant to move to a new camp and also *after* they assembled the ark at the later site (10:35–36). At another time, he pleaded in advocacy for God to spare Miriam when the Lord smote her with leprosy after she and Aaron spoke against Moses. Aaron confessed his sin and interceded to Moses for Miriam's healing, and Moses' appeal to God gained this freeing from the leprosy (12:1–16).

The great leader kept interceding for his people in various cases, for example in 14:13–19 and 27:5. And in 27:15–17, he even prayed that God would provide a man to be the next leader, and the Lord answered by naming Joshua (vv. 18–23). A further case is Moses beseeching the Lord to spare Israel when He has begun to take some in death for complaining in unbelief (21:7). And the law-giver voices a prayer on behalf of the daughters of Zelophehad in Manasseh's family group when they request rights to inherit a portion of land (27:1–11). Moses' testimony for interceding to help his people lived on in Israel. He is one man of prayer later Scripture honors for prayerful effectiveness (Ps. 99:6; Jer. 15:1). Many examples behind this would be cases in Numbers.

(3) Confession. Owning up to sin before the Lord is clear enough in 5:7 and would also be pertinent in dealing with the Lord with offering sacrifices to atone for sins and trespasses.

(4) Praise/Thanks. This is an accompaniment when thanking God in connection with peace offerings (7:17, 23, 29; cf. Lev. 7:13, 15). It also would be extremely fitting after God gives victory in battle, for example against Midianite cities (Chap. 31). It suits the case when thinking of what the census figures reveal about how God has increased His covenant people (Chaps. 1, 26). The relevancy of magnifying God and being grateful in all things of life comes to a copious expression later in the Psalms and in the New Testament (cf. Phil. 4:6; 1 Thess. 5:17), but for those in Israel sensitive to the Lord, it is probable in many a case even where the record does not take note of it.

(5) Affirmation. God even honors a corporate prayer by Israelites, which they probably present through priestly leaders, who often represent them (21:2). This is in stating a vow, pledging to destroy Canaanite cities if God will lift them to victory over the southern Canaanite King of Arad. God delivers them, and they follow through on their promise. Vows, which involve prayer, also find mention in Nazirites being on stints for the Lore (6:2), and in other cases (30:1–16).

(6) Questions. It is natural at times to pose questions in prayer to the Lord. Moses mingles questions about God allowing difficulties he has to face from the people with affirmations such as his inability, and a petition that God might put him to death a way out of the trouble (11:10–15). In another instance, Moses and Aaron fall on their faces before the Lord, asking God if the entire congregation must die for one man's (Korah's) rebellion (16:22).

(7) Oaths. Such a case is the woman accused of adultery. She can take an oath before the Lord, undergo a test, and prove to be innocent of the suspicion, or be proven guilty (5:19). In such a case, her prayer is one of calling on God to be her witness that her claim is genuine. Prayer also would be natural even in accounts which do not mention it.

Safely assumed. The godly, seeking audience with God in whom they trust, and the ungodly when merely thinking of matters before God or uttering words He cannot accept would pray in a great variety of situations. Some probable scenarios occur at many a point.

A few cases are before and after battles, asking God for help in disputes, in the priests' worship, and when the godly in the rank and file speak to their Lord. Other likely instances are in appeals to God to grant safety and provisions on travels, asking for success when hunting for Red Sea animals to secure skins for the tabernacle, and just praising God for His excellence, power, truth, and countless blessings.

It would be impossible for a book of thirty-six chapters to refer to every instance of prayer among more than two million people with their varying situations over around thirty-eight years. Even the multiplicity of offerings for individuals (cf. Lev. 1–7) would suggest countless utterances of prayer, plus regular offerings God specified for the whole community—morning and evening daily for approximately 13,870 days, also on the Sabbaths, the seventh years, the festivals, and other occasions. Gratitude to God from sensitive hearts could exult in His increase of the nation's population as He had promised (Gen. 15), wisdom for fair dealings in countless inter-personal relations with family members and neighbors, help in work routines, hunting, supply of food and water, help with gaining forage for livestock, safety from other desert peoples, and His pardoning sins, and so forth. Even His blessing in cases of so many journeys (Chap. 33) would be germane in prayer—for strength, guidance, provisions, success in caring for the animals, dealing with sinful attitudes, and the like.

Moses could express his gratitude for the Lord's prompting to include details He wanted in His record, and for insight of the leaders to make apt decisions in hundreds of scenarios. Another impetus to prayers, in the lives of priests, is confession of their own sins so that they could maintain fellowship with God and be spiritually usable to help others in their spiritual needs.

Prayer was relevant even when the writer was not specific in cases that say a person fell on his face "prostrate before God, or men fell on their faces." It is interesting that quite often in Scripture, such a phrase is accompanied by reference also to prayer. This is true with the singular, face, as Abraham (Gen. 17:17–18), Moses (Deut. 9:18–20), Joshua (Josh. 5:14–6:2), Jesus (Matt. 26:39), and a leper Jesus healed (Luke 17:16). In the plural (faces) prayer is sometimes explicit (1 Kgs. 18:39; 1 Chr. 21:16–17; 2 Chr. 7:1–3; Neh. 8:6; Rev. 7:11; 11:16–18). Where falling down appears without a direct reference that prayer accompanied it, prayer could again be spontaneous before God, whether with the singular "face," as when Moses "fell on his face" in concern for God's will being flouted and men's peril, as during Korah's rebellion (Num. 16:4), or the plural "faces," as when the congregation shouted and fell as fire consumed a burnt offering and fat (Lev. 9:24), or Moses and Aaron in reverence and concern when the people complained and blamed their leaders (Num. 20:6; cf. 14:5).

Of course, these are all humans falling before God, and different from cases of humans falling before an angel, as Manoah and his wife before a celestial visitor (Judg. 13:20), David in the presence of Jonathan (1 Sam. 20:41), Abigail in a meeting with David (1 Sam. 25:23), and King Saul before Samuel (1 Sam. 28:14).

Another phrase that comes with prayer appears twice in Numbers (16:22; 27:16). Moses and Aaron fell on their faces and spoke to the Lord as "God of the spirits of all flesh" in the first case. And in the later instance Moses, with no reference to his falling before the Lord interceded for "the God of all flesh" to appoint a leader, his successor over the entire congregation (cf. the significance of this later when detail is given on prayer in 27:16).

As a background to prayer or any other facet of spiritual life, the book points to quality care to keep worship at a level worthy before the Lord. This appears quite safe to assume in regard to several things.

(1) Watchfulness to offer to God sensitively (28:2). This is apt rather than nominal indifference or careless complacency.

(2) Personableness. One can note God's desire that worship be "to Me" (28:2) and at least eleven times in Chapter 28 where "to Me" or "to the

Lord" appears. It apparently is meaningful to the Lord that worship be personal to Him in light of who He is and what His will is.

(3) Regularity (28:2–3). A habit in keeping up the worship is evident. This would include some devotion each day (v. 3) and not a hit-or-miss affection.

(4) Pervasiveness. Prayer should even be through the day, as in morning and evening (28:4). This blossoms into full, explicit expression as the psalmist writes what ought to be normative, and probably was for some (Ps. 5:3, morning prayer; 119:164, seven times a day, or a completeness in turning to the Lord).

(5) Fragrance that will please the Lord (Num. 28:2, 27; cf. Ps. 141:2). This is worship deliberately intended to be a delight to God, not a so-called worship that is of a foul odor to Him, so to speak. It follows from the priestly example of sending up sweet incense to Him from the Altar of Incense. The same is true in the New Testament, where a believer is to have the ambition to be pleasing to God (2 Cor. 5:9), to learn what is pleasing to Him (Eph. 5:10), as Jesus' life was a fragrant aroma to God (v. 2), and to please Him in all respects (Col. 1:10; cf. 1 Thess. 4:1). Another way to say this is to do everything—and amid this would be prayer—in the name of the Lord Jesus (Col. 3:17, 23).

(6) High quality. This is apparent in offering to God what is "free of defect" (Num. 28:3. 11, 19, 31). It is not "any old thing will do" when worshiping God, but giving the best. He is not a God of the leftovers, or the discarded, or the third rate. This teaches, in prayer and any part of the spiritual life, to approach God with what will honor Him and show respect. In the cases in Numbers, the offering ought to be the quality kind, and the heart and lips behind this gift should draw near to God with prayer of quality devotion.

(7) Fidelity to one's word. Transparent truthfulness is important to God (Num. 30:2). When one makes a pledge to God, he should follow through, true to his word. In that day, as in the New Testament day, believers' acts should reflect what is "holy, just, and good" (cf. Eph. 5:9). God stands by His Word; so should those who pray any legitimate thing before Him, or do anything in His service.

(8) Trust that God is able. An example is Numbers 11:10–35. God responded to the people complaining to have meat and Moses' prayer asking how he would secure meat to feed the enormous numbers in Israel, at least 600,000 men besides women and children, perhaps a million and a half (v. 13). Moses thought about the impossibility of the animals the people had providing enough meat to keep feeding so many mouths, or fishermen catching enough fish from such sources as the Red Sea. God asks, "Is the Lord's power limited (His hand short)? Now you will see whether My word will come true for you or not" (v. 23). Then the Lord caused a wind to blow in quail three feet deep for a day's journey out from the camp, enough for a month's supply (31–35). It was a lesson to Moses that he can trust God to be able when one prays. Others in Scripture would celebrate God's power to do incredibly great things, for He has all power, among these Eliphaz (Job 5:8–9), Jeremiah (32:17), and Paul (Eph. 3:20).

After this general introductory survey on prayer, it is profitable to turn to individual passages in Numbers that in some way mention prayer. These are now before us, passage by passage.

Numbers 5:21

Prayer in an Oath of Judgment

Two broad sections are before the reader in the Book of Numbers. The first shows God's preparation of Israel for its trek to the promised land (1:1–10:10). This includes a census of the tribes in Chapter 1, the campsite in Chapter 2, the charge to the Levites (Chaps. 3–4), and the concerns for spiritual life in obedience (Chaps. 5–10). After this, the second part of the book describes the wanderings in the wilderness (10:11 to the end, and Deuteronomy).

While still at Mount Sinai as in Exodus 19–40, the people received God's directives for various issues in an obedient spiritual commitment (Chaps. 5–10). One of these is the subject in the present prayer passage, a ritual for proving adultery (5:11–31). God wanted His people to be holy in all their relationships, to be set apart to moral soundness as He is (Lev. 19:2). One of the urgent aspects of this, even among His ten commandments (Ex. 20:14), was a pure life free of adultery. That issue is relevant here.

The Problem of Suspicion (vv. 11–15)

A wife cheats on her husband, goes to bed with another man, and her husband suspects unfaithfulness. He has no witness who caught her in the act and no firm evidence that proves her guilt. Yet he is jealous in concern that things be right. In his eyes, she may have wronged God, himself and herself, another man, and all the community by a grievous offense. Or she may be innocent and, if so, needs her purity to be put beyond suspicion.

God has a procedure by which He promises to expose the truth in such a matter. So the husband can avail himself and his wife of this. He brings her to the priest to whom God has given a proving method.

The Proving of Sin (vv. 16–31)

Her standing for the test (16). The priest directs the wife to stand before the Lord. Her sin, if guilty, is ultimately before *Him* and against *His* commandment (Ex. 20:14). Not only that, but *He* is the giver of the proving method, and *He* will work the result that is proof.

The success of the test will be by God's miracle of exposing the truth. This is just as He works other miracles as He leads Israel—the plagues in Egypt, the passage through the sea, the giving of water, healing, bread, victory, the death judgment on Nadab and Abihu (Lev. 10), and smiting Miriam with leprosy (Num. 12:10). God worked many miracles in a period when he was maintaining purity and peace of the one people through whom He was preparing for redemption.

Though this ritual has seemed like heathen magic to some, it was not. God forbade magic (Deut. 18:9–13) and defeated experts of Egypt who tried their magic (Ex. 7). Looking to the lifted Brazen Serpent also might seem like magic for healing, but it was of God's power (Num. 21). The serpent had no inherent power to transmit healing or life; only God did. And only God has the power to expose the truth in a suspected woman, not the ritual, though He uses the procedure as He used the hoisted serpent.

His solution in the test (17–26). In the ritual, the priest has the wife drink water muddied by desert dust, hold a grain offering, drink the water, and take an oath that she is innocent. Her oath, and his own, are both in effect a form, albeit an unusual one, of prayer. In the case here, it is before the Lord and an invoking of His curse or blessing as He exposes His verdict, her guilt or innocence.

The seeking of the truth (27, 28). This, as above, is finally in prayer inviting God to reveal the woman's purity or impurity. The wife being proven utters the prayerful oath, and the priest does also. Both understand that the words summon God to make the truth clear and to bless the wife or bring a curse on her if guilty. God apparently would do right away, during the brief ritual, making her stomach swell as a sign of her illegitimate pregnancy and causing her thigh to rot, possibly meaning a miscarriage. Some see a God-wrought premature birth, an untimely one (cf. Job 3:16; Ps. 58:8, 9). The word for "waste away" is from ***nepel*** which means "to fall," and the Hebrew letters can denote to be "born" (Isa. 26:18).

The thigh is the place in the body for procreative power (Gen. 46:26). So the idea is probably an untimely birth God provokes to display the wife's unfaithfulness.

Possibly the grain offering has the significance of denoting the wife's conviction that whatever she possesses belongs to the Lord, as the grain offering in Leviticus 2. In this case, as God possesses and gives success to grain to grow, He possesses her body and her procreative capacity. It all really belongs to Him and is to be for His use and to His praise.

The success of the test (27, 28). If the wife is innocent, God will bring neither of the two exposures of verses 21 and 27 on her. His answer to prayer would cause her innocence to be obvious. She would be cleared and free, and He would bless her with legitimate children (28). But if she has been false to her husband, she must bear her guilt, and her husband be free from guilt (31). She could be put to death as an adulteress (Lev. 20:10). That detail of the law is different from God's principle in New Testament times, as in Matthew 19:9. It is either divorcing of the guilty party (some view it) or continuing the marriage with loving forgiveness as Hosea's marriage illustrates (others say).

It is now time to shape principles. First, integrity is crucial in any prayer. In the case here, it is when one appeals to God to be the witness and monitor that what one says is true. Second, even when hard to grasp, an ancient device to show up innocence or guilt could work when God's power exposes the truth or the consequences. At other times, also, God was able to lay sin bare and convict or clear a person through other methods—the Urim and Thummim, lots, and others. He could, when He desired, show Achan's guilt, or cleanse Naaman of leprosy after a seventh dip in the river Jordan, or cause a needle to go back against the norm on a sun dial. It is a privilege to serve the God who is always sufficient to do what is His will and not fail, whether we can explain how He does it or not. This suggests a third principle, that of humble faith that puts away doubt in favor of His unfailing ability.

Numbers 6:22–27

Leaders Praying for Those They Lead

While Israel is still at Mount Sinai, before striking out for a new campsite, God gives Moses a message for His priests. They had been consecrated and inaugurated in their spiritual leadership in Leviticus 8–9.

God's Assignment of Priestly Prayer (22, 23)

Moses is to instruct Aaron and his sons to "bless" the sons of Israel. That the blessing is more than a wish, even intercessory prayer calling blessing upon them becomes evident in the following verses.

God's Aspects for Priestly Prayer (24–27)

These come in an initial summary, then four specifics that the leaders are to pray about.

Summary (24a). First is a general, sweeping invocation, "May the Lord bless you." It is an actual asking of blessing upon the people.

Safety (24b). "May the Lord keep you," or preserve or guard you. This could have its answer in temporal, bodily details, as in preservation from illness (cf. Ps. 91) and battle (Lev. 26:7, 8). God promised safety from diseases to those who obeyed Him (Ex. 15:26). It also could entail safety in having food to sustain them (Lev. 26:4, 5). But the safety could also be in the spiritual dimension of life, as God provided to guard Abram from greed for Sodom's spoils (Gen. 14:22–24) and prepared him for his greatest of all tests (21:33).

Shining (25). "May the Lord make His face shine on you." As the priests and all Israel had God's light in Egypt and in the pillar of fire going with them, they also had the light of the golden lampstand in the Holy Place. They would also have light shining on their paths spiritually as He enlightened them on points of His word and helped them obey. The psalmist would be able to say "The Lord is my light" (27:1) and reference to His light in spiritual blessing is a rich vein running through the psalms (18:28; 119:105).

Today believers know the Lord as the light-giver (Eph. 5:8–14; 1 John 1:5, 7). The person seeking God could himself pray what his leaders had taught him by their prayer, "Make your face shine on Your servant" (Ps. 119:135).

Smile (26a). "May the Lord lift up His countenance on you." In this is a desire for God's acceptance, approval, amity in true refreshing friendship, and cordiality. The writer of Psalm 4:6 caught the significance of this longing, petitioning God to "lift up the light of Thy countenance upon us." In his context, this was by relief when in distress (v. 1), by hearing his prayer (3), by giving gladness (7), and by peace related to His safe-keeping (8).

The range of blessings in Psalm 4 suggests that God can show His smile in favors touching *any* aspect of need.

Serenity (26b). "May the Lord give you peace," was a blessing leaders were to invoke on those they served. That was clear in Psalm 4. Believers could be receptive to His peace and have it in the path of loving obedience to His word (Ps. 119:165). In a corporate fulfillment of peace, the same principle of obeying was a key (Lev. 26:6).

Surety of blessing (27). The leaders' role is to pray for the people; God's promise is a sure answer. Of course, many other parts of His word define His way. His blessing is coordinated with the people's receptivity by sensitivity to His word (Lev. 26:3–13).

Principles are evident. First, one vital ministry is interceding that God will bless those for whom pacesetting leaders pray. Second, the scope of blessing points out that it can be relevant to pray about all things that might enrich lives (cf. Phil. 4:6, 8).

Numbers 7:1–88

Prayer with Tabernacle Offerings

A leader for each of Israel's twelve tribes presents, for his tribe, offerings for the tabernacle recently completed. Prayer is associated with every offering, prayer by people of the tribe, by the tribe's leader, and by the officiating priest.

The Presentations by Tribal Representatives (1–88)

One by one, the tribal leaders bring the offerings, a unit of verses devoted to the kinds of offerings in each presentation until all twelve have contributed.

Each presentation includes four of the main offerings that Leviticus 1–7 described.

The Prayer That was Related

With all of these offerings, prayer would be a fitting accompaniment. The grain (meal) offering would entail prayer affirming that *possessions* such as grain were given by the Lord and thanking Him for His provision, as the clear example in Deuteronomy 26:1–11. With the burnt offering, prayer would acknowledge dedication of the Israelite *persons* to God as being His to be completely for Him as the offering was.

Pardon for sin when confessed was the significance of the sin offering, as was seen in Leviticus 4–5 and 16. The fourth offering, the peace offering, was linked with *peace* for which the offerers rejoiced, thanking the Lord. This was evident in Leviticus 7.

When of a right spiritual attitude before the Lord, the people, their tribal presenter, and the priests would invest these aspects of prayerful worship with the offering. Every offering was for Him who met them in tabernacle worship (Ex. 25:8), and every one was joined by communion with Him. Prayerful worship of Him was a part of everything, as it should be for His people today. Christians are to "pray about everything" (Phil. 4:6) and "pray without ceasing" and "give thanks in everything" (1 Thess. 5:16, 17).

One principle stands out: gifts to God in the offerings should reflect lives dedicated to Him as Lord over all things. This was true for Israel overall and the ideal for each individual, who should take it to heart and live wholly for the Lord. The New Testament essence of this is in 2 Corinthians 5:15.

Numbers 7:89

Moses' Prayer after the Offerings

When all twelve tribes have brought their offerings, their foremost human leader, Moses, enters the tabernacle to pray.

Moses' Representation of Israel Before God (89)

He climaxes the giving of tabernacle offerings with this entrance. The verse says that he goes in to pray, to speak with God, but the emphasis swings not to what he prays but to what God says to him.

A principle is here. Sometimes when a believer comes to God to pray, it is good to place the focus on just listening to His word. Still, since he goes in to pray, it is possible and likely that he did pray, or God was aware of the aspects of prayer on his mind. Moses would wish to pray along at least three relevant lines. First, it was fitting to *affirm* that the offerings of Israel were completed, second to *thank* God for putting this in the people's hearts, and third to *intercede* for a further follow-through in a worshipful attitude.

God's Revelation about the Spiritual Leaders (Chap. 8)

Now that offerings have just provided for priestly tabernacle ministry, God directs Moses to set the Levites apart for serving with such provisions. Aaron and his sons had been chosen and inaugurated for priestly service in offerings (Lev. 8–9). Now God provides other Levites to assist them in various facets of the total leadership duties.

God gives instruction for Aaron lighting the golden lampstand in the Holy Place (vv. 1–4), and the Levites are cleansed for their service in a special ceremony (5–26). Here are the principles of light for serving God and the cleanness that is vital in fulfilling such ministry. Both principles would pertain to Levites in leading, here, and to all the people they lead as they follow the same necessities.

For *any* servant of God, the Lord is the light (Ps. 27:1), and cleanness through God's word is a priority (Ps. 119:9–11).

Two principles are of note. The first is that a leader after God's own heart can find good things to pray when he pleads advocacy for others before the Lord of heaven. The other is that God wants cleanness in both those who lead and those who follow in spiritual issues of life. This is in, "be clean, you who bear the vessels of the Lord" (Isa. 52:11). Any believer is to be clean in his life with God (cf. Ps. 24:4; 51:10; Matt. 5:8, "blessed are the pure in heart . . .").

Numbers 10:35, 36

Prayer for God's Blessing in Travel

Whenever Israel's camp would move to a new site and the Ark of God's Covenant was carried on its way, Moses' prayer here is a fitting one. He asks for God's help in commencing a journey and in concluding it, and of course all along the way and all the time.

Prayer in Commencing a Trip (v. 35)

Moses petitions God for two things he depends upon for the good of God's people.

"Rise up, O Lord." The prayer focus is right on what was God's will. For in 9:15–23, the Lord's glory cloud was "lifted up" when He was leading His people to journey to a new campsite. When the cloud stopped and remained in a place, He wanted them to set up camp (9:17). They were to move only according to His guidance. So in 10:10, 11, when He set out, they set out. The prayer principle is that of praying in sensitive alignment with God's will as He reveals it.

To pray "rise up" is to petition God to go before His people to ask that His presence be shown. God promised that presence (Ex. 33:14), and Moses passionately longed for it (v. 15). He set a high priority on the presence in all Israel's movements, just as God wanted to show His presence in the tabernacle (Ex. 25:8) and in the pillar of cloud and fire.

The prayer invokes that presence to lead on in the next phase for His people.

"Rout your enemies." This, in effect, is Moses' appeal in Numbers 10:35. As the Lord had overwhelmed the Egyptians and later the Amalekites (Ex. 14, 17), need would arise for Him to protect His people from other desert peoples. He had promised Israel that when they would trust and obey, He would lead them in routs of enemies (Lev. 26:7, 8). In this, too, Moses prays in line with God's will.

By the same principle Ezra, much later, would pray for God's protection from enemies while his people journeyed (Ezra 8:21–31). God gave full safety.

Prayer in Concluding a Trip (v. 36)

When the next stage of the journey ends at a new camp, the prayer advocate asks that the Lord "return." He does not mean that God has at any time left His people; he only means that just as He has been with them in the journey to this point, He will be with them here as well. As God has shown that where the guiding cloud stops, they are to stop (9:17), so let Him be there with them.

Of course, God's will is to do that—to be near them in His glory cloud, present to meet with them at the tabernacle (Ex. 25:8), and present as each item of furniture symbolized. As the Lampstand gave its light, He was their light. As the altar of incense depicted His desire to receive their worship as a sweet fragrance, so He would be with them.

In representing his people, Moses' "bottom line" in the intercessory concern is *the blessing of God's presence*. The passionate value He fixed on having the sense of God's nearness was clear in his earlier prayer of Exodus 33:15. If God's presence would not be with them, he did not want God to lead them from Sinai!

Just as He sought *God's presence* with them, he modeled bringing *his own presence* before God in prayer. And this was a high privilege the priests and people could learn more and more to practice as well.

Which principles are cogent? First, as we pray about everything (Phil. 4:6), it is important to prioritize God's being with us in making a moving to a new home as He leads and knowing His nearness when we arrive. Second, ask if you have forgotten anything before leaving, and be certain this is not the Lord.

Numbers 11:2

Prayer in the Midst of Chastisement

God had answered Moses' appeal in 10:35, 36 for letting His presence be realized on the trek. Now, at a place that will draw the name Taberah, "burning" (v. 3), distrustful complaint leads to God's judgment, Moses' prayer again, and a remedy.

The Complaint of the People (v. 1)

God's prayer-answering care along the way and constant displays of sufficiency for any situation should have been met with praises as at the Red Sea (Ex. 15). But it is one of the dark blemishes on Israel's history that here, as so often, the reaction was bitter unbelief. The people, probably weary from a three-day journey (10:33), were chafing, unwilling, and impugning the faithful ability of God. He could have given them perfect rest of body and spirit, but they were not receptive.

Grief to God was the order of the day. He had never failed them, but His sufficiency was rebutted by such a hurtful attitude of blaming. So, as He had disciplined some in death for the Golden Calf sin and issued a warning of judgment (Ex. 32:34), He teaches them that principle again. His judging fire smites on the fringes of the encampment, drastic but merciful in contrast to a wider judgment. It stirs them, in fear, to cry to Moses for advocacy to plead God's deliverance.

The Cry of Moses to God (v. 2)

No description of repentance meets the reader. But Moses goes to the Lord in desperate concern, usable in the midst of crisis. God responds in mercy, causing the fire to die out and further damage to be averted. The power of availing intercession has forceful illustration.

The Commemoration of the Prayer Incident (v. 3)

A place receives its name in Israel's history to mark what happened there. Taberah is fitting, meaning a "burning," and it ought to burn in the memories of the untrustful. Many a Taberah of that people, as for those later who name the name of the Lord, might well have been a Berachah ("blessing"). Those who take the lesson seriously, and live it out, can see God change many a place in life to a blessing rather than a burning.

One principle is that a godly person's intercessory prayer can have a great effect to resolve a crisis. Another is that it is so much better to pray trusting God for His blessing than blame Him and suffer needless misery.

Numbers 11:4–34

Prayer to a Sufficient God

Here, now, is an incident following right on the heels of the "burning" in the camp, betraying the unbelief in a sufficient Lord.

The Problem of Sufficiency (4–15)

A mixed multitude that had attached themselves to Israelites in Egypt, and Israelites, in general, fell into this sin. They grew unthankful to God for daily manna, treated His gift with contemptuous "griping," and were lustful for meat. They exhibited their insulting dissatisfaction toward God by rating His provision as inferior to foods they had eaten in Egypt. And their craving to satisfy their greed by something better than what God thought best led even to whining tears. Both God and Moses were aroused by this unbelief in God's sufficiency.

As was his spiritual reflex, Moses went to the Lord in prayer (11–15). What he says under pressure shows failure but not the unbelief the people are demonstrating. His sin, rather, is in permitting himself to be so distracted by his own insufficiency that he does not triumph in God's sufficiency. And so, blinded for the moment, he misses the whole point, as his eyes are turned too much on himself.

He speaks to God as if God lays the burden of meeting Israel's needs on him. God had already shown him time after time, in deep crises, that His miracle-working sufficiency could provide, no matter what the need. He loses track of that, as many other leaders of God had done. "Where am I to get meat . . . ?" he asks. Of course he could have said, "You have shown your servant that You can provide. So, I look to You. You know just what to do and how to do it."

Later this beleaguered advocate admits, "I alone am not able to bear all this people. . . ." How right He is! It would help him here to summon from his memory that God had carried His people as on eagles' wings to Sinai (Ex. 19:4). God had supplied a way through the sea when there was no way. God had furnished good water when there was no water. God had given manna from heaven when there was no manna.

Sadly, Moses was smitten with self-pity as well as missing the point. He felt at the point of despair, so unfit to solve his people's problem that he invited God just to let him die to have the burden off of him.

It is at this point that God in great compassion shows Moses once again who is sufficient to provide a way.

The Provision for Sufficiency (16–34)

God's answer to prayer is twofold.

Men to share the ministry (16, 17, 24, 25). Moses' feeling of inadequacy at being overwhelmed by so many people's needs is met by God providing seventy men to help. He had similarly received help at God's counsel through Jethro (Ex. 18), and the present supply probably does not contradict that. As some believe, the current provision can be for this crisis in particular. God gives the men ability to prophesy, possibly in praise of His adequacy as would fit the situation, to show the people He authenticates their leadership. These seventy, called *outside* the camp to a meeting, plus two men *inside* the camp show God's authority. By appearing in different parts of the large camp (estimated at a million and a half or more, cf. Ex. 12:37), these could spread a sense of God's authority more than Moses alone could.

Meat to supplement the manna (18–21, 31–34). God also provides quail blown in by the wind, exhausted from flight and struggling no higher than three feet in the air. He shows His miraculous supply by the bringing them at a precise time, by so many and for an entire month to feed so many people. So He demonstrated that His power was not *limited* (v. 23). As far as His Word says, He did this special thing only on two occasions, in Exodus 16 and here, whereas His manna was provided daily for forty years.

God does something else. He deals firmly with many of the lustful. This is a rebuke to chronic unbelief about His meeting needs, designed to make them wiser toward resting in His sufficiency rather than darkening their lives with distrustful greed. By His own power, and not from diseased quail, He inflicted the guilty with a severe illness (33). Rather than being unloving, He had the right to work a drastic difficulty, which was apparently needed to get their attention. Even in days of the New Testament church, He can utilize discipline in weakness, sickness, or death to speak to the greedy and issue a general, helpful caution to those lax about His meaning business (Acts 5:1–11; 1 Cor. 11:30–32).

So God's answer to Moses' intercession is His sufficiency in the two provisions, men and meat. Psalm 78:17–33 is a commentary on the nature of Israel's deep failure. It is one of sin and rebellion (17), putting God to a test (18), and insulting His glory in unbelief (19, 22): "Will He provide meat for His people?" (20).

Principles abound. First, a leader for God is never sufficient alone to provide for the needs of those he or she leads. That person leads best who looks to God, who is adequate, and does not imagine that things depend only on any human ability. Second, sometimes people spurn those who would lead them spiritually in good things God can provide. Their way is not the way of blessing with eyes on the Lord, but the way of complaining and lusting for what they fancy would be better. Third, certain problems find resolution by getting more people serving rather than one leader supposing he has to do it all. Fourth, the God who answers prayer can meet needs through a miracle and discipline those who need a jolting call to get right with Him.

Numbers 12:13

Prayer for Healing Leprosy

The Problem (1–12)

The speaking against Moses (1–3). This is a criticism of Moses that is a pretext by Miriam and Aaron. They accuse him of violating God's law in marrying a Cushite woman. Their wrong amounted to far worse than this, for verse 2 explains that the attack really is designed to satisfy their greed for power, and jealousy of Moses' authority from God. They are hungry for high recognition on a level with Moses; God has spoken through them also!

Lack of proper humility and teamwork surfaces in this, as well as a hateful spirit in place of love. Often, as here, sin is a jumble of several discordant and self-glorifying aspects that work against bringing honor to the Lord. It is plain that the disunifying effort by the two leaders, Miriam of the women (cf. Ex. 15) and Aaron of the priesthood, is a deeply hurtful one, and God draws a serious assessment of it.

The summoning of the parties (4–9). Yes, the sin was so drastic that it aroused the Lord to call the three involved to the tent of meeting, Moses' tent, and not the tabernacle (Ex. 33:7). He also spoke to them out of the cloud of glory. And He addressed His firm words to the two offenders after having them step forward.

Here is the sum of God's rebuke. When it is His will to use a person to receive prophecy, He has a way to do this, in a vision, by a dream. But His using Moses is very distinct. He speaks to him directly and also permits him to behold His form, as He showed Moses an indirect glimpse of Himself as He passed by in Exodus 33. Since God chose to give Moses this privilege, what crass effrontery and disrespect (for God and for His man) for the two to speak against His servant.

It is plain that God is angry at the two.

The smiting of Miriam (10–12). God departed, but a short time later when His cloud moved away, the three in the tent made a startling discovery. Miriam was leprous! Aaron, now respectful toward Moses, implored him for his and God's mercy and confessed their sin. He asked for the healing of Miriam, the removal of the condition that was like death's rottenness.

It is hard to know why Aaron was not also smitten. Miriam may have been the ringleader as her name is first in verse 1, but this is not certain. At any rate, the one case of leprosy had its hard-hitting effect on both sinners.

The Prayer (13)

Moses' advocacy. He intercedes with immense feeling, crying out to the Lord. These are not only leaders in Israel, Miriam highly regarded by the women, but they are his own sister and brother. His prayer is a direct request, straight to the point of need. "O God, heal her, I pray!"

When a person is on praying ground, and praying in God's will, no long prayer is necessary on a given matter. God hears without an excursion around the Milky Way or eloquent language.

God's answer (14, 15). He is merciful in sparing Miriam, so the answer is "Yes." But He also makes clear that her sin was a very shameful one, as when one in authority over her, her father, would spit in her face in disgust. She is to experience her shame in a seven-day duration outside the camp, a humiliating thing but no doubt attended by serious rethinking and repentance.

Finally, however, God compassionately brings soundness back to her body, and she is reinstated in normal life.

The prayer is an example of definite prayer by a person praying in God's will, and of God's firmness yet kindness in answering affirmatively.

Guidelines occur readily. One is to learn to get specific in prayer and come right to the crux.

A second one is to be sensitive to God so that when a problem arises one can be a part of the solution and not the difficulty. A third one is that God can restore a person who sins but may give him a serious time to come prayerfully to a deep change of heart.

Numbers 14:13–19

Prayer in Overcoming God's Test

Moses' prayer is set in a flow of the people testing him and the Lord posing His own test. The people speak of stoning him and Aaron, and God proposing He spurn the people and develop a nation out of a remnant.

The Circumstances of the Prayer (1–12)

This stage is set in two parts.

The pathetic failure of the people (1–10). God sees the same sin in Israel that has cropped up over and over, like a record skipping, repeating the same lines. He voices this in verse 11. A new crisis challenges them to trust God, as is clear in Chapter 13. It is the report by ten of twelve scouts who returned from spying in the land of Canaan. They spoke negatively of threats they had seen, giants who made them seem like grasshoppers by comparison, and high-walled towns. The scouts saw Israel as no match against such a problem, and the danger seized the Israelites with panic, spelling their doom.

Caleb and Joshua stood against the tide, hurled out a positive challenge that God could win against the peril, and urged trust in Him to be greater than the obstacles. But the crowd, darkened by unbelief in God (v. 11), was now certain of imminent disaster before the swords of the enemies (3). Rather than face the challenge relying on God's sufficiency, they were ready to discount miracle after miracle He had done in every crisis. The urgency of the hour was to choose a new leader and return to Egypt.

This is when Moses and Aaron went to God in prayer (v. 5). They fell prostrate before the Lord in utter prayerful reliance on Him. At the same time, Caleb and Joshua again sought to plead with the unbelieving, pressing strong arguments that fell on dull ears. They urged the *productivity* of the promised land, which God's word (Ex. 3:8) and their own scout's report attested. Implicit in this is the *promise* of God to give the land. With this, they also focus on the *presence* of God to be with His people, bring them in, and give them the land. They also assure the hearers of the enemies' *powerlessness* to win against God and them.

Along with strong words about God's *ability* for certain success, the two scouts warn against *attitudes* of wilting before the opportunity. Let the people not fight as rebels going counter to God's will, and not fear the foes who will fall before God's sufficiency.

The only reaction this provokes in hearts of unbelief is a murmuring about stoning these who exalt God. But in the Lord whose faithfulness is impugned, another reaction is clear. He confirms His presence by His glory shining in the tent that Moses, Aaron, and Joshua use, probably with light from His glory cloud (v. 10).

The possible forsaking by the Lord (11, 12). Speaking to Moses, God voices two things. First is His *concern* over the people spurning Him in all that He is as sufficient, rejecting in unbelief "all the signs" that had proven His ability. Second is His *consideration* of sending pestilence on them, disowning them, and making a new nation of Moses. Apparently the last detail would include others who, as the context defines, would join Moses—Caleb and Joshua (24, 30) and all under twenty (29, 31).

God has promised His sure word to continue a plan with Israel, and He can do it different ways. But His words are evidently a test of Moses' commitment to His will, similar to the test in Exodus 32. Moses would pass the second test as he had the first, in both showing firm intercession to see God's people spared.

The Content of the Prayer (13–19)

What the prayer warrior pleads is what will glorify the God he addresses. He does this in a pair of arguments.

God's fame (13–17). He is zealous to have his God's power continue to have force with the nations that hear of Him. So far, He has succeeded big time before the Egyptians, but should He not follow through in helping Israel, the Egyptians and Canaanites will undercut this with a lie, stripping God of glory. They will construe God as failing in *power* to take His people all the way, and as failing in His *promise* (vv. 15, 16). His glory in sufficiency and veracity is on the line.

God's forgiveness (18, 19). Moses throws a strong emphasis on the covenant loving-kindness of his God. His advocacy is saturated with God being a forgiving God, for he urges this three times. To pardon His people for sin is according to His love, which is "abundant" and "great." At the same time, the intercessor is perceptive that God morally fulfills His *pardon* in balance with His *perfection*, dealing justly toward sinners and sin.

Another detail the man of prayer highlights is God's past consistent practice in forgiving Israelites (19). His consistency in practice accompanies His character in pardoning. Moses pleads His "track record." And of course what God has done over and over is true to His Person and His promise guaranteeing the covenant.

The Consequences of the Prayer (20–24)

God's answer to prayer is right in line with Moses' points, according to His will which the intercessor pled.

Pardon to the people (20). "I have pardoned them according to your word," the Lord assures. This is, first of all, according to God's word. For He *is*, as Moses argued, a God of fame and a God of forgiveness!

Promotion of His glory (21). The people as a group are forgiven, and not struck with disease or disowned (cf. v. 12). But God will uphold His glory at the same time. This is in letting them reap what they have sown; their unbelief robbed Him of glory and so He will consistently uphold that glory, letting them gradually die over the remainder of forty years, the older generation not entering the land. In another sense, too, the earth will be filled with His glory: through retaining Israel in its younger generation He will continue His covenant plan. Through their descendants God will provide the salvation His Abrahamic Covenant forecast, and He will be glorified in all the earth.

Passport to the remnant (22–38). The unbelieving generation will be kept from the land. But to Caleb (24), Joshua (30), and those under twenty (29, 31), He will give passports. Miriam and Aaron would die first, and Moses by sinning in Chapter 20, would have his passport cancelled, and die first as well.

Though removing the older generation over the years seems harsh, a true perspective shows it fitting. The unbelief that drew the cancellation was a great sin. It was great in being against a great God, denying the glory that was His (cf. v. 21). It also was great in its persistence in the face of great authentications of His sufficiency. In verse 22, God scorns the people for testing Him ten times and not hearing His voice. They had seen the shining of His glory and the signs of His power. The ten times could be ten as a figure for *completeness* of evidence, or ten literally, as is reasonably the case. For if one counts the occasions when Israel met God with unbelief he finds ten: Exodus 14:10–12; 15:22–24; 16:1–3; 16:19, 20; 16:27–30; 17:1–4; 32; and Numbers 11:1–3; 11:4–34; 14:1–3.

As an immediate witness to the enormity of the unbelief and a warning to Israel as a whole, God disciplines the ten negative scouts with sudden illness and death (14:36, 37). They were ringleaders in rejecting His glory. His distinction between unbelief and belief registers also in sparing the two positive men, Joshua and Caleb (38).

Moses' prayer will gain God's persistence in His work with Israel. God tested him, found him willing, and worked His will in aligning his prayer with His plan. The disciplinary steps do not stop the covenant plan itself or cause God's will to change.

At the same time, God firmly sticks to His word that the unbelieving generation will die out before forty years pass. Israel will mark time in wilderness wanderings rather than going on immediately into the land. He backs this up. Here, He lets Israelites, still not serious about His word, be defeated when they bullheadedly insist they will defeat enemies and go on into the land themselves (40–45).

This is a situation with many prayer principles. First, set the heart so that after it has seen God do mighty things, it will not slip into unbelief when a new crisis breaks. Second, when we do not refuse to pray and trust in a big God, obstacles will not tower as threatening sure failure. Third, step wide of the unbelief that finds a scapegoat to blame—often a spiritual leader. Fourth, prayer that trusts cares for God's reputation before the watching world, His upholding His glory by showing pardoning mercy, yet His just dealing. Finally, God's answers are consistent with His faithfulness. For as one properly praying expects, He forgives, acts in glory by equitable judgment, and assures some of entering His promised blessing.

Numbers 16:15

Prayer against False Offerings (Korah's Rebellion)

Here is the scenario. Korah leads 250 Levites in a rebel bid to gain ascendant status in offering as priests rather than submitting to God's will in an assistantship role. They insist on prerogatives Aaron and his sons have, unwilling to be content with attendant ministries to support the priests. At the same time, some Reubenites, such as Dathan and Abiram, also challenge God's will in regard to the leadership order.

Prayer is at the heart of this.

The Rebellion before the Prayer (1–14)

When the upstarts challenge Moses and Aaron (1–3), Moses evidently went on his face before God in anguished prayer (4). His prayer also surfaces in verse 15.

It may have been while in prayer that Moses gained God's direction for his next move. If so, verse 4 is only a summary that he went to prayer, leaving out what was said in exchange with God. He is clear that the rebels want priestly privileges (10). In this, he summons Korah and his followers to appear before the Lord with incense in pans. The Lord will demonstrate whether he approves *their* offering or that of *Aaron* and his sons.

At the same time, Moses also called Dathan and Abiram to come for a confrontation, but they refused. They also accused him of two failures—misleading them into the desert to die and mastery without right to it (12–14). The rejection of God's sufficiency and resistance to His will perpetuates the terrible unbelief God had dealt with in Chapter 14. In the face of this insult, Moses goes ahead leading in God's discipline.

The Request of the Prayer (15)

He pleads two lines of concern. One is an intercessory request that the Lord reject the rebels' offering of incense. God had given priests the incense ministry to depict that which would be of fragrance pleasing to Him. But the rejecters here cannot have incense God would accept. They have no God-given right as priests, and their sinful attitude shuts out their prayer (cf. Ps. 66:18). The intercession will receive God's "yes" answer shortly in repudiating the false.

Moses' second aspect of prayer is his own petition, a *review* of his pure motives before men and God. He is blameless in regard to profiteering through his leadership, and in relation to any injustice. God will answer him in this as well, vindicating him.

The Response to the Prayer (16–35)

God's answer to Moses' prayer (4, 15) stimulates further prayer, this time by both Moses and Aaron (22).

The answer is a strong "yes" to Moses. God is ready to consume many, as Korah and his henchmen stand ready for the showdown. So Moses and Aaron issue an urgent appeal in the form of a question prayer (22). If one man is in the wrong, will God deal with the whole congregation? Later, God clarifies this in a clear-cut way (Deut. 24:16), and here, also, He differentiates the guilty He will judge from others in Israel who will be safe (v. 24).

When Israelites listen to God's instruction and draw back to a safe distance from the offenders, God causes the earth to cleave and plunges the guilty into the gap. Their families, apparently in complicity with their rebellion, die also as Achan's family would in Joshua 7. God is God, and His entire creation story as well as His covenant dealings show He is able to work miracles. He can separate water at the sea and send it crashing down on Egyptians defying His power, and He can separate the earth and drop God-opposers into the crevice. One is as easy as the other to an all-powerful God.

Coordinated with the catastrophe of the cleavage was the fire from God that consumed the 250 men wielding incense God repudiated (v. 35).

The Reminder to Israel (36–40)

God's verdict simply verifies His choice of Aaron and his sons for priesthood. The point is crystal clear in verse 40. What has just happened must be a reminder to Israelites that He authenticates only Aaron and his sons for such ministry. His word given to these priests through Moses earlier (Lev. 8–9, etc.) stands.

The Repetition of Sin (41–50)

One of the strange things in the wilderness wanderings is the repeated sins of Israelites along the same lines. On the "next day" (41), the whole congregation is grumbling against Moses and Aaron. By an odd twist of facts, what *God* has shown His full validation of beyond any reasonable shadow of doubt, the people now blame on the two human leaders. *They* are the cause of deaths for Korah, Dathan, Abiram, and their families, and the spurious claimants to priestly rights.

Yet *God,* who originally chose Aaron and his sons and had just confirmed them now, acts again. His glory appears from the cloud over the tent of meeting (42) and He cautions Moses and Aaron to get clear of the people before He consumes more of them (45).

The two men go, as by spiritual reflex, to prayer. They are on their faces, apparently interceding for their people (45). No detail appears on the prayer, but Moses may have gotten his procedure from God. He instructed Aaron to fill a censer pan with live coals, sprinkle incense on these, bring them to the people, and make atonement for them. The fragrance the smoke would have, rising toward God, was symbolic of intercession gaining favor with Him. For having begun a plague among the thousands, He now protected those yet alive from the 14,700 who suddenly died. The division was marked off from where Aaron took his stand, the dead in one direction from him and the living in the other. The censer ministry here was, in its principle of effectiveness, not finally in the object Aaron held but in the prayer it symbolized. And so it was the *God* to whom the incense arose who helped Israel, just as their *God* delivered them when Moses' hands were lifted to Him against Amalek (Ex. 17:8–13).

Authentication of rightful priests in God's sight continues in Numbers 17. There, God causes *Aaron's* rod to blossom, showing His approval, not the rods of men from other Israelite families God had not designated for *priestly ministry.*

Three principles stand out. First, godly prayer can appeal for God's work to remove bogus claimants to spiritual leadership. Here God does it by a miracle, but He also uses other ways, such as showing them up as spurious (cf. Rev. 2:2–3), illness, their having to live with disrepute from bad decisions, and so forth. Second, God can honor a believer who requests Him to back up motives that truly are pure in service. Third, even when God works by incredible ways to approve one's ministry, He may find that some people put a false spin on this and are fault finders. So further prayer may be necessary to gain God's way of dealing with those who stand against Him.

Numbers 20:6

Prayer and then Terrible Sin

God had never failed to supply what His people needed. This consistency, time after time, should have prepared them to take their latest problem in stride. It was no real problem after all, not with the presence of the great God. But unbelief again led the Israelites to a host of other sins. Moses and Aaron prayed, God met the need completely, but Moses himself committed the blunder of his life.

The Discontent of the People (1–5)

Miriam's death (v. 1) may have had its effect to discourage the people, or it may have played no significant role in their failure. The *passing* of Moses' sister was followed by the *problem* of supply (2–5). Smitten by a chronic spiritual malady of complaining, the people now fixed on their lack of water rather than God's proven ability to take care of them. They protested against Moses and Aaron, firing their darts of discontent.

Moses, for example, was to blame for leading them into a place where death summoned them. Not sensitive to count their many blessings from God and look positively for further ones, they foolishly thought they would have been better joining those who died in the recent plague (Chap. 16). They figured the old life in Egypt held its advantages in grain, figs, water, and so forth. Sin-filled thinking darkened their minds with a strange forgetting of the terrible bondage, and God's multiplied blessings.

The Directions from the Lord (6–8)

This is where prayer comes in, a bit late but in the leaders, though not in the crowd.

The seeking of help (6). The two leaders, as they often did, threw themselves prostrate before the Lord. They sought, and He shined, His glory coming from the pillar of cloud over their tent.

What they said in prayer is not included in this case. It would well have been some kind of exercise about the need of the hour. All the emphasis is thrown on God's solution itself.

The simplicity of help (7, 8). God gets right to the point. It is clear that He wills to be gracious, meeting the need of water. There could be no easy mistaking of His directions for supplying water. "Take the rod . . . you and . . . Aaron assemble the congregation . . . speak to the rock. . . . You shall in this way bring forth water for them. . . ."

The Disobedience of Moses and Aaron (9–11)

Close obedience characterizes Moses at first. Many a believer obeys in part. For full obedience, the ranks thin. He took the rod as directed, and he and his brother assembled the throng. So far, so good! But after this, he swings a sharp turnabout and disobeys in the rest of the incident. How so?

A number of elements fuse. First, he is so heated with anger at the people that he loses control, calling them rebels rather than simply being God's agent in gracious supply. Second, he shifts the focus from the providing God to themselves, "shall *we* bring forth water for you . . . ?" That throws the emphasis on *self* instead of the *sufficient Lord*, and takes away from His glory. Third, whereas God said explicitly to "speak" to the rock, Moses "struck" it with the rod twice, intensely angry.

Further clarity on why God viewed the sin as so great comes in His own word later. The two men were both guilty for *not believing* the Lord (v. 12). They apparently failed to trust Him to have His right to act graciously if He chose to. In verse 8, all that He said was positive and generous. He would give water. The unbelief is the heart of failing to *sanctify* God as the kind of God He would display Himself to be, even in the face of Israel's guilt (cf. v. 13). Unbelief in what God *could* do was not the fault; unbelief in what He *should* do was the problem. Psalm 106:32, 33 offers the commentary that Moses, losing his cool to a hot-headed hatefulness, "*spoke unadvisedly,*" or rashly. God defines that the two men "*rebelled* against My command" (Num. 20:34; 27:14). And Psalm 105:42 provides the insight that in giving the water, God "remembered His holy promise, and Abraham His servant." So the sin had the inset of *insensitivity* to God's covenant will.

Careful tuning of a prayer warrior to God's word was a necessity. When God, in an earlier, similar need for water, said "strike the rock" (Ex. 17:6), to strike was to follow His word. But when He now said "speak," to speak was to do His will.

The Discipline of the Lord (12, 13)

What immediately follows is God's emphasis on the *character* of the sin and the *consequence* of it so drastic for the two leaders.

The character of the sin (12, 13, 24). This is a part of the above. Suffice it now to say that the two showed wills running at cross-purposes with God's will. Their wrong was deeply serious in that it shouted disrespect toward the Lord and had ever the more gravity in its distorted modeling before all of Israel.

It is an interesting but sensible point that while sin is sin and always serious, God views it as having greater influence against holiness the more prominent the sinner is among His people. This is why He prescribes offerings for sin in Numbers 4 that are related to the influence an offerer has. An offering for a priest or for the people overall is a bull or ox; for a civil leader, a goat; for a common person, a lamb or goat; for the poor, two pigeons or two doves; for the very poor, an offering of fine flour. And in Leviticus 21, priests who lead others spiritually are expected to rise to good modeling standards.

No wonder, then, that God saw great gravity in the sin by Israel's top overall leader and its highest leader in spiritual ministries.

The consequence of the sin (12). God had cancelled the passports of both men into the promised land! Aaron would die soon after their sister Miriam (vv. 28, 29), so God had Moses commission Eleazar as the successor to be high priest (23–28). And Moses would also die before Israel entered the land (Deut. 34).

Both men were saved and safe for eternity, but their sin drew a disciplining forfeit of certain earthly privileges. It can also cause them to be diminished in some equitable degree as to special reward eternally (cf. 1 Cor. 3:8, 15).

One sobering lesson is that even when faithful in a pattern of prayer, one needs to be ever vigilant so as to triumph over grave sin. Though the person prays earnestly to God and obeys in some details, he may lose sensitivity to the fact that the work is *God's* and to do it *the way of God's word* is imperative. A second maxim is this: in ministry we need patience with people who fix their eyes on the problems and not on God who is able to deal with these. Third, when the problem is of a "no water" kind, prayer can draw in God's provision. Fourth, prayer does not claim good success when one undercuts it by imposing self when the believer should set God alone apart to glory and follow His way of blessing others. The solution is to trust in His sufficiency, love, and Word. Fifth, disobedience ruled when God did not say "Strike the rock," as in Exodus 17:6, but "speak to the rock" and Moses chose to strike. Sixth, the more eminent a leader is, the greater the hurt of his sin can be in God's view. For He looks at a person's position in terms of its spiritual impact on others and on Him in setting Him apart for what He is like.

Numbers 21:2

A Vow in Prayer

An attack of an enemy on Israel became the setting of a vow in an appeal to God for help.

The Victimizing of Israel (1)

One of the desert kings led his army in a strike that netted him some prisoners of war.

The Vow of Israel (2)

It is to Israel's credit that they met the raid trusting in the Lord. They entered into a vow pledging that, for God's deliverance against this foe, they would destroy the enemy cities. The wickedness of the attackers, as peoples are in God's appraisal in Leviticus 18, was probably justification for God's move against them. He also had said in His covenant with Abram that He would curse those who cursed Abram's descendants (Gen. 12:1–3). And He had acted already to defeat the Egyptians (Ex. 14) and the Amalekites (Ex. 17).

A vow was one form prayer could take, as in Jacob's agreement with God at Bethel (Gen. 28:20–22) and, much later, Hannah's pledge (1 Sam. 1:11, 27, 28). The bottom line in a vow was a very important principle of character, integrity in honoring one's word, the person praying, and the God answering prayer. Once one made a vow to God, his word was to be trustworthy as he wanted God to be, and he was to avoid insincerity or rash words (Deut. 23:21).

Vows were not only prayer at the beginning, but led to prayer in thanksgiving for answers at the end (Ps. 22:25; 50:14). A worshipper thanking God for His answer could do this with an accompanied peace offering (Lev. 7:16).

The Victory from God (3)

Integrity did reign here. God kept His part when He "heard" the prayer favorably and "delivered" the enemy in an utter rout. The Israelites honored their part when they "utterly destroyed" those hostile to God and to them, as well as their cities. God would lead His people in many similar victories later in taking the promised land. Joshua 12 gives a long list of conquests.

Two principles are bold in the text. First, when a praying believer agrees before God to do something, his claim should be truthful, leading to keeping his pledge. Second, it is fitting to offer the Lord thanks for help He has given to see an intent through.

Numbers 21:4–9

Prayer for Healing

The Problems (4–6)

Two aspects are defined as problems.

Supply (4, 5). The dragging out of the wanderings fulfilling God's extension of the trip due to Israel's unbelief in Numbers 13–14 was wearing on the people. Impatience gnawed at them over the delay and frequent trials. So they vented this wickedly against both God and Moses. A theme song they had often had on their lips surfaced again, distrustful expectation of death when they saw no immediate water or food besides the manna. Ingratitude was compounded in their hearts, for they were not giving thanks for the daily miracle of manna.

Serpents (6). Not by chance but by God's choice a new trial was given to discipline the complainers and challenge them to faith. God sent fiery serpents of some kind, whose bites led to many deaths. He is God, and has the right to bring discipline, as He did in the church at Corinth centuries later, in weakness, sickness, and, in some cases, death (1 Cor. 11:30–32).

The Prayer (7)

The fervent appeal for prayer. The complainers humbled themselves when so many among them were dying. First, they confessed their sin against both God and His leader (cf. v. 5). They were specific about the sin surfacing in evil speaking. Joined with acknowledgment was a request for intercession that God would take the serpents away.

The faithful action in prayer. Moses got right down to business about praying. He did go to the Lord in urgency for the people. How different he was from many a believer, getting a plea for prayer. He says he will pray, then lets the matter slip his mind in the traffic of a busy life. The person who takes God and others seriously in love insists on strong measures. He cultivates disciplined earnestness to make intercession one of life's passionate priorities.

God's Provision (8, 9)

The erection of a solution (8). God's way of deliverance is simple. Four aspects are in it, all quite evident.

(1) Likeness. A bronze figure Moses is to prepare is that of a serpent, having a likeness to the problem dealing out death, the serpents.

Of course no potency attaches to the physical object itself. It is of no value that is *intrinsic* but is effective only by God's *investment* according to His purpose and power. *God* is the success in objects He chooses to use, whether a tree in a garden, a lifted rod, a rock, a serpent, an altar, incense, and others.

The likeness is easy to see between this problem for Israelites and the similar problem of a greater sickness, sin, that brings death (Rom. 5:12). Since Jesus Himself explicitly drew the analogy, it is certain. "As Moses lifted up the serpent in the wilderness, even so must the Son of Man be lifted up . . ." (John 3:14). The serpent was in the likeness of the problem, identified with it. And in His case, the greater problem was sin that had smitten men, and on His cross He was "made sin for us" (2 Cor. 5:21) that we might have life rather than death.

(2) Lifting. In the wilderness, lifting of the bronze serpent is evident in several ways. One is setting it on a standard. For a camp so widespread with at least an estimated million and a half or more, it was imperative to see the emblem from far off. People had died and others were dying, no doubt at home and needing a solution they could look at from their distance. Jesus bears this out, saying "as Moses lifted up the serpent. . . ."

The analogy Jesus focuses on is Himself later lifted up on the cross. Not only is that the case in John 3:14 but in 12:32: "And I, if I be lifted up, will draw all men to Me. . . ." His death on the cross was the solution that removed death from men spiritually, eternally (John 3:15, 16).

(3) Looking. The solution was for "everyone who is bitten," none excluded. It was his "when he looks at it. . . ." God in this case gave physical health. It was not by any works in any way, only in the simplicity of *looking* to receive what He gave.

Similarly, the solution to the greater malady, sin and eternal death, is by looking. As Jesus phrases it, looking means *believing* in Him who died, unto eternal life (John 3:15, 16).

(4) Living. By looking, "he shall live." Living physically in the desert incident illustrates living eternally by the believing look at Jesus Christ and His work on the cross. Again, John 3 is very plain about this, on the authority of the very One who would be lifted up.

The efficacy of the solution (9). True to God's directive in answering prayer, Moses made the solution in the *likeness* (a serpent), *lifted* it on the standard, and when "any" person would *look,* he *lived.* It worked in every case when one looked, when he looked at God's solution and not depending on anything else.

Even in the wilderness episode, the *looking* involves *believing.* To take the God's only remedy required commitment in trust that His word was true, that He would do what He said, and that the way would work. Not to look was not to believe in His provision, not to take it seriously, but to trust in some other way, or needlessly perish even with a simple answer in reach.

The passage places the whole famous scenario in a crucial flow with prayer.

Vital guidelines flow forth. First, trustful prayer could prevent many a disciplinary act God brings on His people. For they could draw near to Him and find out His heart in the way of blessing. Second, God's servant who prays as He desires brings a request to Him seriously, fervently, and punctually. Third, when God's Word imparts an answer of clarity on what to do, it honors Him to follow through as He points the way. Fourth, the people looked in faith to a raised serpent that God said to look to, and lived physically rather than being judged. In an analogy that Jesus would draw (John 3:14–15), those who look in faith to Him who was lifted up on the cross for their sin can live eternally.

Numbers 22:10, 11

Prayer of a Religious Hypocrite

The strange prophet Balaam prays three times in explicit words in Chapters 22–24. Perhaps he also prayed in other meetings with God where mention is made only of what *God* said.

Here are the definite occasions, each seen separately.

The Plot against Israel (1–7)

Wanderings through the desert have now brought God's people to the area of the Moabites east of the Jordan River, northeast of the Dead Sea.

Israelite victories versus Arad, the Amorites, and Bashan in Chapter 21 laid panic in Moab's King Balak and his people. In cahoots with the Midianites, he hit on a plot to curse the victors and ensure his own conquest of them. He dispatched a delegation to summon a prophet named Balaam of Mesopotamia, whose fame reached across hundreds of miles. He will secure another in Balaam's string of successes when the prophet pronounces against Israel. To lure the man, he offers wages for his services.

Several reasons make it apparent that Balaam's status was what we would call unsaved. He was not a true prophet of God.

What are the reasons? The clearest is Scripture's commentary appraising him later. Numbers 31:16 shows that Balaam was actually against God's people, maliciously informing Balak on a way to work Israel's downfall. He said in effect, "Even if God will not permit you to defeat them in battle, here's a tip. Do it through your women seducing them." He could not move *God* away from His people, but he maneuvered to move His people away from Him through the women and their idol-worship.

Joshua condemns Balaam in God's three direct counts (24:10). (1) God did not will to listen to Balaam's request to curse, showing how He regarded the prophet's aim; (2) Balaam had to bless Israel, this being contrary to his own scheme; (3) God assesses His answer denying Balaam as a deliverance of Israel from his hand. He was out to ruin God's people.

Three New Testament passages are very condemning as well. God leads Peter to say that the prophet went astray, having "loved the wages of unrighteousness" (cf. Rom. 6:23). He adds that a donkey "restrained the madness of the prophet." Jude 11 condemns the man as following a way of "error" among examples of those God rejects. Peter made his remarks in that kind of flow too. Finally, Revelation 2:14 strongly repudiates Balaam.

The context in the Book of Numbers gives its own evidence that Balaam did not know God genuinely. God told him in no uncertain terms that His will was to bless Israel, but Balaam came back time and again, trying to get that changed. He was saying, in effect, "I know what you said, but how about a second opinion from you." Balak's persistent upping of the stipend if Balaam delivered on the curse found his price! God's allowances for Balaam to go to Balak were only concessions in view of the man's hankering to have his own way. In 22:22, God in actuality was angry at his going and in verse 32 says "your way was contrary to me." The matter was so serious that if Balaam's donkey had not turned three times from going on, "I would surely have killed you . . ." (v. 33).

How, then, could Balaam speak God's blessing on Israel and even give discourses of God's word beginning in 23:7, 23:18, 24:3, 24:15, 24:20, and 24:21? God's word answers this. God can reveal truth to the unsaved to serve His purposes, as to Abimelech (Gen. 20), the pharaoh (41), Laban (41), Caiaphas (John 18), and even Balaam's donkey! He also led Nebuchadnezzar and Darius to acclaim Him (Dan. 2–4, 6), even Cyrus (Ezra 1), and it is uncertain that they were converted.

Balaam's Prayer

He *petitions* God to curse Israel, and also *purposes* to fight against this people himself and drive them out (v. 11). It is a case of a misguided prayer out of one's own self-serving will. In its very core, it runs directly counter to God's will to bless Abram's people and curse those who curse them (Gen. 12:1–3).

God's Plan (12)

God's answer is a flat denial, an emphatic "No!" What He says is His will in His own word. It is a lesson to others who pray to God. Yes answers out of God's firm approval must be sensitively in line with His word, true to His will. And so it is a summons to the asker to be steeped in His word and plead what He can stand behind. This may be in direct statement as here, or in principle. Where one is not able to see His word approving a current desire, his move that will always prove wise is to yield the desire to God, trust Him for grace, and insist on going His way.

How different for Balaam. He keeps trying to work angles to effect a change in God's will. How tragic his blunders in refusing to submit his own will to be changed by God!

Principles are rather evident. First, a false prophet can wrest prayer against God's desires to seek selfish ends, but it can lead to his spiritual end in ruin. Second, God does not honor prayer that He regards as the subterfuge of sin (cf. Ps. 66:18).

Numbers 22:34

An Insincere Confession

The Context of It (21–33)

What is going on is fairly evident. It can be summed up in two thoughts. Both reflect on the perilous state of Balaam's heart.

The arm-twisting. It has already been noted that God has made His will ever so clear: "do not go" (12). For He wills to bless and not curse Israel, and He will not tolerate a prayer opposing this.

At first, Balaam did refuse to go (13). Later, Balak's spokesmen came raising the reward. That put a new twist on things, for Balaam's will really was to feather his own nest. He was on to a way to do it. He speaks fine-sounding words about obeying God, but with a catch. "Don't leave," he implores the visitors, "and I will see if God can work this thing out for me to go" (19). How like the squirrel that wills to get its paw out of the jar, but also wills to retain its grasp on nuts in it, and so is actually trapped in its own will. In his own density, Balaam no doubt thought he had won the day by a bit of arm-twisting.

Again, it is true that God has made His will known and now lets Balaam go only by concession (20). The passage again makes the matter plain. God was angry at his going (22), so angry that His angel barred the way to teach Balaam a lesson if he would hear. Balaam, though, did not have as much sense as his jackass, which had a perception of God erecting a roadblock and refused three times to keep on that way.

The anger. God's anger is obvious. So is Balaam's. God's concerns a man insisting on his own will, not His. Balaam's arises out of the donkey keeping him from following his stubborn will. He vents the anger in merciless brutality to the animal. Both the animal and the angel who blocked the way rebuked him. Balaam was so evil that he would have killed the innocent donkey had he brought a sword. The angel would have killed Balaam if the mount had not balked but gone on.

The Confession (34)

Under pressure, Balaam acknowledged, "I have sinned." It must not be a really sincere confession, for scriptural appraisals of him are all negative. Not only that, but what he admits does not flush out all the truth. He says, "I did not know that you were standing in the way against me," but nothing of God telling him at the start not to go, and his angling to get a change in this. He is a very dull learner or, as is more likely, has sought to revise God's will all along to have things *his* way. He already knew it displeased God to go, yet he tries to come out smelling like a rose. If it now displeases the angel and God, "I will turn back."

God again let him go as he had his heart set on. He goes on to reveal His will through the inferior instrument, as sometimes He did with others in Scripture. Since He overruled that Balaam would speak His word, He gets the glory.

Balaam utters one more prayer, in 23:4. He simply affirms that he set up altars and offered animals on each. These, donated by Balak (vv. 2, 3), would not be burnt offerings having genuine acceptance before God. And the passage does not say that *God* told Balaam to do this specifically. God does use the occasion, and does so after offerings like these, to give His word to the Moabites through Balaam. Still, He could even use the donkey! The later scriptural evaluation of Balaam shows that he himself was unsaved. And he would not be the first man to give God's word without knowing God in reality.

Guidelines summon the mind. First, a person can tweak prayer to maneuver God *his* way, but if he keeps this up, he can be on his selfish path to destruction. Second, one can even offer sacrifices with prayer, to make things look legitimate, but God discerns counterfeits and rejects sham worship.

Numbers 27:5

Prayer about Inheritance Rights

The Plea of the Women (1–4)

Five daughters of Zelophehad, a man in Joseph's lineage who had died, request the inheritance their father would have had. They are thinking of the future after God gives Israel the promised land.

Their plea shows *faith* in God fulfilling His covenant guarantee, and also *fortitude* to prepare for days to come.

The Prayer of Moses (5)

Moses did not speak off the top of his own head, but went to God in prayer to seek His will. He was a true intercessor for his people, even in a concern of one family, and God would use him to set their hearts at rest.

The prayer matter is one of many examples showing God's interest in temporal details of life as well as spiritual issues. Much in the law witnesses to this care about all things in human need. Centuries later, the psalmist was aware of this. "Cast your burden on the

Lord, and He will sustain you" (55:20). Even later, Peter could write, "Casting all your care upon Him, for He cares for you" (1 Pet. 5:7).

The Permission of God (6–11)

Its definiteness (6, 7). The five sisters were requesting in line with God's will. Moses was to transfer their father's portion of land to them, for they had no brothers to lead over it.

Its details (8–11). Moses was to incorporate this prayer answer as a part of the law on land rights. When any man would die without sons, his inheritance would pass to his daughter, or if no daughter, his brothers, or if no brothers, his father's brothers. If even that is not possible, the nearest relative left would have the inheritance.

Later, 36:1–13 qualifies that these women who get the land must marry within their tribe. This was God's caring safeguard that the land would not be lost from the tribe, for each tribe would receive definite portions in Joshua 13–22, and such a statute would minister to tribal unity.

Principles show up clearly.

First, when God answers prayer, He encourages His people by His care about every facet of an issue. He thinks of everything in order to assure the good of His own. Second, it can be quite valid to beseech God for help to secure what should be temporally one's right. For God upholds what is fair and truthful.

Numbers 27:12–23

Praying Oneself Out of a Job

Miriam and Aaron have died in Chapter 20. Zelophehad has passed away. The generation aged twenty and older whom God had barred from entering Canaan due to the unbelief in Numbers 13–14 is gradually thinning during the forty years in the wanderings. Now Moses' death looms after a few more incidents and his giving of the law again to the younger generation (Deuteronomy).

God's Announcement of Moses' Death (12–14)

The concession to see (12). God permits His leader to climb into Mount Abarim, a name for the northwest mountains in the Moabite area. There, overlooking the Dead Sea and Jordan Valley, he will gaze out on the promised land God will not allow him to enter.

He would, after death, see some of it in the Mount of Transfiguration (Matt. 17) and all of it in the distant millennial kingdom.

The coming of his death (13). Soon after this view, Moses would die, as Aaron had.

The cause of his discipline (14). God reminds him of his sin in striking the rock in Numbers 20. This sin was great, causing so great a discipline as not leading his people into the land. God defines it as in Numbers 20. Moses had *rebelled* against the Lord's command to *set Him apart* before the people's eyes as the gracious covenant God He was.

The Advocacy for a New Leader (15–17)

The recognition of who God is (16a). It is good, when praying, to come in light of who the Lord is. Here, Moses is aware of Him as the Lord, the covenant Lord who had demonstrated His faithfulness to His promises. He also knows Him as the God of the spirits of all flesh. In relation to what he will request, that is highly pertinent. It reflects on God's *creation* (He made all men), on His *comprehension* (He knows them all), His *control* (He has rights over all, in His will), and His *care* (He cares even as a shepherd in verse 17).

The request for what God can do (16b). He intercedes for God to appoint a leader over Israel as his successor. As the God he has recognized, He would be sufficient to do this, and pick the right one.

The reason for Israel's good (17). The *point* of a leader is to have a man who can appear before the people and give them direction. The *picture* of it is to prevent the people from being unprovided for and unprotected by having a shepherd.

The Answer in Joshua (18–23)

God's instructions about the leader (18–21). Joshua is the choice. Number one among his credentials is the focus here. He is a man "in whom is the Spirit." It would seem unnecessary to say he has a human spirit. The more likely meaning is the Spirit of God empowering for service, as the Spirit who enabled men of Israel to prophesy in Numbers 11. Deuteronomy 34:9 says Joshua has the spirit of wisdom, the same expression as Isaiah 11:2 where the Spirit of Wisdom is on the Messiah.

Joshua was a good appointee for other reasons too. He came to his opportunity here by way of *soldiery* (Ex. 17:8–13), *service* (24:13; 33:11), *scouting* (Num. 13–14), *supplication* of Moses (here), and the *sovereignty* of God (here).

Moses is to lay his hand on Joshua in personal identification and endorsement and also in symbolizing a transfer of authority (20). The inductee is also to stand before Eleazar the high priest, who will seek God's will for his leadership, and before the congregation he is to lead.

Moses' installation of the leader (22, 23). He simply follows through with all God had directed that he do.

The Spirit was probably *already* on Joshua for his service close to Moses up to now, and *attested* (Deut. 34:9). But in the present commissioning ceremony, the putting of authority on him (20) would be to *authenticate* God's endorsement of him publicly to enhance acceptance of his role. It would be to *authorize* him in this new, broader service as having the stamp of God, Moses, and Eleazar on him, and the right to the people's approval.

Several lessons about prayer are evident here. First, Moses prays in submission to God's will, even though he no doubt aches at missing the privilege to lead his people in. God's will is more important than a servant's desires. Second, this leader also prays in light of who

God is, as Abraham and Jacob often did, and also the psalmists. Third, his prayer is right to the need, not a beating around the bush. Fourth, his prayer reflects both his sensitivity to God's care and his own care that the people have a shepherd.

Still other principles join these. Fifth, one can pray for another to carry on what needs to be done after he is gone. Sixth, ask in faith that lays hold of God's power, control, knowledge, and concern. Seventh, pray to gain what is best for God's interests. And eighth, God often shows as here that He can supply His kind of ready leader to take the work forward.

Prayer in Deuteronomy

Introduction

The Author

Moses wrote the book as a part of what has become the Pentateuch. The document itself claims him as its author (31:9, 24–26). And Moses is prominent as the leader formulating the thought all the way through. Of course, Mosaic authorship has faced relentless denial by critics, yet has never been reasonably disproved. Evangelical scholars have set forth copious evidence to support Moses, for example Merrill Unger, Edward J. Young, and Gleason Archer in their Old Testament introductions.

The Date (1:3)

Forty years of wandering in the wilderness are almost over. The fortieth year, indeed the eleventh month, finds Israel east of the Jordan River, a few miles from the crossing into the promised land in the Book of Joshua. With an exodus ca. 1447 B.C., the date is 1407 or a bit later (cf. below).

A journey of but a few days could have brought the people of Israel to the vicinity (cf. v. 2) had they obeyed God in Numbers 13–14. But they rejected His sufficiency, and He disciplined them with another thirty-eight years of waiting (cf. 2:14) for the unbelieving generation to die. The wilderness had become a vast graveyard.

Moses evidently finished what he intended to write shortly before his death. A close associate, possibly Joshua, his understudy, or another leader close to him, added the account of his death to complete the record (34:1–12). Since a new generation is waiting on the very threshold of Canaan after the forty years of wandering (1:1–5; 4:46; 29:1), the book must have been composed during the brief time there before the great law giver died. The statement in 34:10

seems to imply that the appendix was written after some time had elapsed from the date of Moses' departure, between ca. 1400–1407.

The Title

God's central idea here is captured in the title we use for the book. ***Deuteronomion*** was the designation in the LXX or Septuagint Greek translation of the Old Testament during the inter-testamental centuries. The Greek title means "second law," an apt label in view of three things. First, 17:18 shows the book is giving law. Second, the content includes many details of God's laws on facets of life lived to His glory, as in Chapters 5–26. Third, 31:9 characterizes it as the "book of the law." That it is a "second" law comes from the fact that Moses, who stated the law a first time at Mount Sinai (Ex. 29–Num. 10:10), is now giving it afresh, after wilderness wanderings, to the new generation. Having missed the first giving of the law, the younger generation, now mature, needed to hear it afresh before they went in to possess the covenant land. The purpose is that they can obey this law, living as God desires. The "second" law is not a new law but the exposition of the same, old law. Yet it is not a mere repetition or copy of it, but a hortatory description, explanation, and enforcement of the most essential contents of the covenant revelation and covenant laws, with many appeals to live in accord with these.

The Hebrews, according to their custom, named the book after the opening words, ***Haddebharim,*** meaning "The Words."

The Theme

The great emphases in the book help show the currents. Moses reviews and reminds concerning past blessings, and warns the new generation to cling tenaciously to God and avoid idolatry. He exhorts them to love and live obeying God, and assures of blessings in the promised land as they obey. Some things God adds to what He already has given to them (29:1).

What, then, is the major thrust? It is this: Moses, shortly before Israel is to invade the promised land, expounds God's law anew to the generation, which was so young, under twenty, when God gave the disciplining sentence of forty years wandering, allowing time for the old generation to perish (Num. 13–14). None of the survivors, except Joshua and Caleb, can be older than fifty-eight now. Those old enough to hear the law originally at Mount Sinai have all eventually died, and God has seen to this to carry out His verdict. The law now is not literally a "second law," but second in the sense of being a current exposition of the first and remaining law. It is an explanation of the law's most essential elements and an appeal to obey the Lord. It is time for a new and right start in the land God gives to Israel as He pledged (Gen. 12:7). As fits the rehearsal of the law, Deuteronomy refers back to details in Genesis through Numbers around 260 times. The rest of the Old Testament refers to things in Deuteronomy about 350 times. And the New Testament quotes or alludes to details here nearly 100 times. Jesus drew His three responses to the tempter from Deuteronomy 6:13, 16; 8:3; and 10:20 (Matt. 4; Luke 4). The chief commandment—to love God and love thy neighbor as oneself—cites Deuteronomy 6:5 (Matt. 22:37, 38). Other related key words or phrases are "be careful to do" (6:3), "fear [show reverential respect for] the Lord (6:13, 24), pursue "what is just" (16:20), "keep the commandments" (4:2, 5; 10:13; 11:8, 13–14, 22–23; 30:16), "listen to His Word" (12:28) or "voice" (13:18), remember they are a holy people to the Lord for His own possession (7:6), "serve Him" (10:12), exercise humility in light of God's grace (9:3–6), and be watchful to worship (12:5–19, 23).

So, the theme has two complimentary aspects. One is negative, to *prevent* a repetition of the tragic sin that was the earlier generation's blunder (Num. 14). The other, positive, was to *prepare* the people for a daily walk committed to God and His will in the new land. True to this theme, "love" appears more than a score of times, and "obey" about ten.

To see the flavor of the book and how prayer can fit in, observe a few of many superb verses that reveal facets crucial in entering and living in the expected land. They are to *go in and possess* (1:8); *God will fight for them* as in Egypt (1:30); *God has been with them, they have not lacked* (2:7); God took them to be *a people of His possession* (4:20); *God will not forget His covenant* (4:31); if they would *obey*, it would *be well with them* (5:29); *they should love God with all their heart, soul, and might* (6:4–9); God *led them* forty years *to humble them, testing them to know what was in their hearts* (8:2, 3).

The Outline

This is based on six addresses the book gives.

I. The First Address—Looking Back (1:1–4:43)

II. The Second Address (4:44–26:19)
Moses introduces this (4:44–49), then states testimonies (5:1–11:31), statutes (11:32–16:17), and judgments (16:18–26:19). Civil legislative laws for justice (16:18–21:13) are followed by legislation for various social situations (Chaps. 22–26).

III. The Third Address—Cautions to Avoid Judgment (Chaps. 27–28)

IV. The Fourth Address—Details of the Covenant (29:1–31:13)

V. The Fifth Address—The Song of Moses (31:14–32:47)
Introductory words (31:14–30) are followed by the song in Chapter 32 (cf. prayer in it later) and a historical supplement (32:45–47).

VI. The Sixth Address—Pronouncing Blessing on Israel (32:48–33:29)
An introduction (32:48–52) precedes the blessing (Chap. 33).

VII. A Historical Appendix of Moses' Death (Chap. 34)

The Relation to Prayer

At least nineteen of the thirty-four chapters mention prayer. Words to God surface in at least twenty-four cases. The people are to live by prayer. In this they can respond sensitively to God's provision that satisfies, uttering their thankful blessing to Him for the land He has given with its bounties (8:10). The Lord is their praise (10:21), and they are to fear Him, serve Him, cling to Him, and swear by His name (10:20). Prayer to God also fit quite spontaneously with key words such as walking by His Word (5:33; 6:17; 12:28), loving Him (6:5), and being holy to Him (7:6). One of the best reminders of how prayer is so very a propos is in 4:7–8, "For what nation . . . has a god so near to it as the Lord our God whenever we call on Him?"

Various aspects of prayer leap into view: intercession (1:10–11), petition (3:23–29), summoning God's attesting witness (4:26), praise/thanks (8:10; 10:21; 14:22–29; 16:1–17), appealing for God's curse on wrong (23:4–5), engaging in vows (23:21–23), and affirming truth (26:1–11; 30:10).

Prayer is *plain* in passages soon to follow. It is *probable* as well, from many of the people, in apt opportunities even when the writer is not exhaustive to specify it. Not everything can be mentioned all at once, and it need not be. This principle is true in any book of the Bible. Prayer is provocatively natural when crying out of human need for help in battles (2:32–36; 3:1–7), for countless reasons to offer a celebration of thanks that God is not lacking (2:7; cf. Ps. 23:1), when confessing sins, when rehearsing matters in fellowship before the Lord, or when voicing appeals to God to meet needs over the entire spectrum of human weakness. Numerous examples become obvious later in the Psalms. One instance in Deuteronomy of a case where prayer is not *explicit* but *probable* is in Chapter 15. When one frees a slave in his seventh year of service, he is to give the emancipated person a start for his or her own flock or produce (vv. 13–14). The thing that motivates this is a tender memory of God freeing this people from their own slavery in Egypt (15). It would be a tender impulse here to yield the heart to God and exclaim, "I thank you for setting us free, and now in a spirit that this teaches me, it is my privilege to set him (or her) free."

Many more scenarios are apt, but it is time to view individual passages on explicit prayer one by one.

Deuteronomy 1:10, 11

Prayer for Promised Multiplication

The Fulfilled Blessing Moses Sees (10)

What God promised in His covenant with Abram (Gen. 15:5) is already a reality. He has multiplied this people as the stars of heaven. Another illustration of the increase is that they have become numberless as the particles of dust on the earth (13:16).

The Future Blessing Moses Seeks (11)

The person who encourages it. As Moses did in his prayer of Numbers 27 when asking for a successor, he prays now. It is good to repeat in prayers elements that glorify who God is. Here, Moses honors God and shows the people how to honor Him. He remembers that He is the Lord, the covenant Lord as in Exodus 6:3, who did such exploits for His people in Egypt. And with this He exalts Him as the God, the almighty One. As He has been to the past generations, He is now to the people ready to enter.

The petitions that express it. He intercedes that the God of prayer will *increase* His people a thousand-fold even beyond their current numbers. And He asks that He will *bless* them, aligning this with what God's word has pledged as His will. Probably the blessing includes the multiplication but is broader. If so, it covers *all* aspects of life God specified as blessings (Lev. 26:1–13). God would mention these again in Deuteronomy 28:1–14. So Moses has saturated this aspect of his advocacy, as well, with the will of God.

That is a sure way to pray.

Principles suggest themselves. First, we also can intercede for God to multiply our family as this suits His will. Second, we can plead that He will increase the spiritual family of believers. This is in accord with His Word, which expects multitudes from every tongue, tribe, family, and nation to be in heaven (Rev. 7:9). It is also in harmony with His electing some, for He can answer by drawing (John 6:44) the ones He has elected before the foundation of the world (cf. Eph. 1:4). Third, we may ask God to save Israelites and multiply the number of those who will be in the church with saved Gentiles today (cf. Eph. 2:11ff.) and be in the millennial phase of His kingdom reigning with Christ (Rev. 5:10; cf. 2:26–28). Fourth, we can even ask ahead of time for salvation of many in the future tribulation period, for God will save the 144,000 of Israel (Rev. 7:3–8; 14:1–5), some other people of ethnic Israel who are a part of the "Woman" (Israel) of Reveleation 12:1ff., and also many Gentiles at that time.

Deuteronomy 1:45

This, actually, is a review repeating details already involved in Numbers 13–14, so it can be read along with that passage and the comments on prayer there.

Deuteronomy 3:23–29

When God Said "No" to Moses' Prayer

This review goes back to detail already given in Numbers 27. God has permitted Moses to climb and see the promised land from afar, but prohibited him from leading Israel in. He said "yes" to his prayer for a successor, and asked him to commission His choice, Joshua. Some details left out in that account now fill in blanks there, and some aspects there are passed over here.

This review will be quick, going into detail only on the supplementary details.

Moses' Appeal (23–25)

His reveling in God (24). He pleads (v. 23) this argument before God. The Lord has started something with him; he would like to see it finished with him still leading. God had shown His great power in miracles unparalleled by any god.

His requesting of God (25). He wants a passport to enter the promised land, and describes it wistfully.

God's Anger (26)

Moses' desire is fervent in prayer, but God's denial is firm in answer.

As the Numbers 14 and 27 accounts explain, God's anger arose because of *the relation to His people.* Moses had not modeled God's grace in that critical situation, and it had not set Him apart as the kind of God He was. So God's response was the *refusal of the passage* into Canaan. Moses reflects on the truth. God was "angry," "would not listen to me," and said "Enough! Speak no more to me of this matter." Moses did not lose his salvation, but he did forfeit, in some measure, opportunity for further service.

God's Answer (27, 28)

Moses desires and God denies, but He also directs. He is still gracious to His servant in answer to prayer.

The look He allows (27). God let him ascend into the hills of Abarim (Num. 27), here Mount Pisgah because it is a particular place there. He could enjoy the land by a distant gaze, but not enter it. The look must have been sad from one standpoint (he had forfeited so much by disobeying!), but joyous from another (he was so favored to gain this privilege).

The leader He approves (28). Numbers 27 covered God's choice of Joshua and Moses' commissioning of him. An added detail here is that God had Moses encourage and strengthen Joshua for the field general task of going against many enemies.

Here are guidelines from this for prayer. First, prayer may be earnest, even from a very godly believer, but may not gain God's "yes" answer where He sees factors that incline Him against this. The reason might be some disobedience, or God's will being otherwise, for example when a man prays a certain woman will become his wife, yet God says "yes" instead to another's prayers to receive her, and has a woman who is His wise will for the first man.

Second, God may permit a believer sweet opportunity even when He denies one specific request. He later denied David's petition to build a temple, gave this privilege to Solomon, and gave David many other privileges. Third, one may ask and not receive a role it is God's choice to confer upon another, in this case, Joshua, and in David's situation, Solomon. Fourth, whatever God shows is His will, or not His will, one of His children should trust Him to get past the hurt and rest in His will as right and wise.

Deuteronomy 4:7

Prayer to a God Who is Near

This is a celebration for the God who hears prayer whenever His people appeal to Him.

The Call to Obey God's Commands (1–6)

Moses urges that this people steep themselves in the word of God and obey it. This, of course, is the atmosphere of effective prayer in verse 7, as often in Scripture. A life aligning with what God says not only is the way of blessing with *Him,* but the way of blessing that is a testimony before other people (v. 6). For those who see them occupied in obedience will be impacted. They will testify that God's people "is a wise and understanding people."

The Closeness of God to their Call (7, 8)

As a way of focusing attention on the blessing of a life close to God in obedience (1–6), Moses asks two questions about His closeness in prayer.

What nation has such a person? (7) He wants them to answer both questions with a resounding "no nation!" Here, no nation has a God so near when His people call to Him in prayer.

God had shown His nearness to prayer cries at the sea, when there was no water or no food, and in every other need. The privilege Moses holds before them is an unparalleled one. It ought to light a fire in them to draw near to the God who is so near.

What nation has such precepts? (8) As the Israelites stand alone as the only people having the God of the *presence*, they stand alone in having the God of *perfection*. Out of His righteousness, He had given righteous aspects filling out His whole law. This, too, should be a motivation to draw near.

Prayer in *calling* on the God who is near could be a key factor in *conducting* themselves in the law of the God so near. The word itself was not far away but very near, "in your mouth and in your heart, that you may observe it" (30:11–14).

The Caution of God for True Commitment (9, 10)

If the people avail themselves properly of prayer and the word, their commitment will be shaped along lines Moses spells out. They are to exercise care to remember and commit the truth to their children in family worship and example (9). This is worship only of God (15–19), not of any image. If they disobey, God will scatter them from the land (25–28). Even when dispersed from the land, if they seek Him genuinely (which would involve prayer), He will answer in mercy and not forsake them or His covenant.

To assure them of His help even in such a crisis, let them take seriously the great things He has done for them in the past (32–38). This ought to draw them to reckon seriously that God is God, and there is no other (39). And with this would be a real obedience to His word (40).

A principle is very comforting here. God is also very near believers today who have access to Him (Eph. 2:18; 3:12; Heb. 10:19–20). They can draw near in full confidence of faith (Heb. 10:22), even come boldly before His throne of grace (Heb. 4:16).

Deuteronomy 4:26

Prayer in a Call for Witnesses

Prayer in this sense is rather rare in Scripture. Moses challenges his people to obedience. He calls on heaven and earth to attest what God is sure to do if they disobey. What he warns will happen is what he is impressed by God's will to pray for as the consequence. Prayer, as often in Scripture, comes into alignment with proclamation.

A Challenge to Obey (1–15)

As surveyed in relation to 4:7, prayer occurs in a context spotlighting the obedience to which God draws His people. Past obedience has resulted in freedom from discipline even in death (v. 4). God had brought such death on those who fell into intermarriage and idol-worship with the Moabites in Numbers 25 at Balaam's evil designs, as Numbers 31:16 later explains. When the people enter Canaan, it is strategic that their walk is one of obeying the Lord.

A Call to Witnesses of Disobeying (26–28)

Moses summons or invokes witnesses from two realms to testify as to what rightfully follows if the Israelites disobey God.

First is the calling itself. The leader calls on heaven, God, and probably His angelic messengers who carry out His will. Such calling is an aspect of prayer. It appeals to God to bring His imprecation (judgment) necessary to uphold His honor against defiance. The prayer is not capricious, vindictive, or unloving. It is in accord with what a glorious God must do and has a right to do when men drag His word and name in the perversion of sin. This is as true in 4:26 here as in the curses God faithfully warned Israel would meet disobedience (Lev. 26), and further cautions them about in this new statement of His law (Deut. 28). It is as true as in the twenty or so imprecatory (curse) psalms such as Psalm 109, and the imprecatory prayers of the Book of Revelation—by men in 6:10 and by an angel in 16:5.

Moses' calling on God in prayer for His attestation to rightful action is steeped in a true grasp of God's word. In what ways? First it accords with God's *Person* as a "consuming fire, a jealous God" (v. 24). He must act firmly against sin, bringing the fire of judgment against what is defiant of Him, being jealous in righteous passion for what is good. He is the God of glory, not a wimp without moral backbone who can go along with anything. Second, Moses' call on God fits with God's *precepts,* or will for what is right, as in verses 27 and 28 here. He had made known in His ten commandments His zeal for worship as God alone and His will against worship of any other God (Ex. 20). And in Deuteronomy He shows that His action against allegiance to false gods must be strong (7:4; 8:19, 20). Third, Moses' prayerful call is sensitive to God's past practice against false gods (4:3).

The second realm of testimony Moses summons against disobeying is the earth. This is earth in the sense of *people* outside of Israel who hear His word when Israel obeys and who testify to the good impact the word has on its subjects (4:6). People of other nations also come to know of Israel's sin, a scandal leading to God expelling them from their land. This is clear in Deuteronomy (29:24–28; 1 Kgs. 9:8, 9). And it is clear in God's prophets centuries later, when people of other nations testify, just as Moses' prayerful call summoned them to do (Jer. 22:8, 9).

Second is the consequence that Moses called for. Both heaven and earth would testify that disobedience to God had its consequence in scattering from the land. This is already evident above.

It is astounding how sin has such powerful influence and sad consequences. At the same time, what Moses realistically prays in case of disobeying need not occur. The people had privileges unprecedented among men, which could avail for blessing rather than judgment (4:32). Five extraordinary assets to boost them appear in 4:33–39.

These are God's *declaration* of His will (33, 36), His *deliverance* of Israel (34a), His *demonstrations* by miracles (34b), His *deity* shown (36, 39), and His *devotion* in choosing this people (37).

A principle here can boost the spirit. We who know the Lord today can pray that God will be near those who obey Him, in line with His desire to be strong to them (2 Chr. 16:9; Ps. 84:9–11). The flip side is to pray that He will be far from those who deny Him a place in their lives. Scripture says God is near the godly spiritual leaders (Num. 16:10), near believers who are broken hearted (Ps. 34:18), near by His salvation to those who fear Him (Ps. 85:9), and close to the godly, though the ungodly are far from Him (Ps. 119:150–51; Eph. 2:11–12). He is near to all who pray to Him in truth (Ps. 145:18). His saints are near to Him (148:14), people are to call on Him while He is near and still offering salvation (Isa. 55:6), and when a believer draws near to Him, He draws near to that believer (James 4:8).

Deuteronomy 8:10

Prayer Blessing God with Thanks

Giving thanks for gifts God provides in the promised land should be a spontaneous and frequent response for a sensitive people. The capsule statement about gratitude in 8:10 joins other passages in this rehearsal to the generation that will go into Canaan. It is a theme in 12:5–19, 14:22–29, 16:1ff. (cf. v. 11), and 26:1–11, and shows how prayerful thanksgiving for God's goodness should saturate all of life.

God's Provisions of Bounties (1–9)

How much this people has to fill its thanksgivings to God! Moses mentions primers that elicit gratitude. One is God's leading for forty years (2), having its high purpose of humbling them to be more receptive to Him, testing them, and assaying what really was in their hearts. Another was His supplying manna (3), again with its strategic purpose of teaching them that man does not live by temporal bread alone but by His word. Still a further one was His sustaining them in all their needs. Examples are clothing that lasted and feet that did not swell from journeys (4).

All these gifts were in fatherly kindness to discipline them as a human father in caring for his son. God had told Moses that Israel was his "son" in Exodus 4:22.

The latest of God's provisions is His escort into the land He promised, where His bountiful gifts ought to call forth thanksgivings in prayer (7–9).

Their Prayer about Blessings (10–18)

God tells them ahead of time how to react to plentiful blessings—it is in like manner. As God has provided, so they are to pray, steeping their lives in thanksgiving for the gifts.

The context is packed with attitudes that express gratitude. One is humility that sensitively gives the glory to God (14) rather than proudly stealing the credit themselves (17). *God* is the One who "is giving you the power to make wealth." This giving spirit offers faithful verification of His covenant goodness (18), not their own prowess. He reminds them of this so that they will not lose *God* in the midst of His *gifts* (11–14).

Thanksgiving that blesses God who confers the blessings is the secret of life in verse 10. As He continues the blessings, they are to keep up the giving of thanks. The counsel is of the same essence as God's counsel through Paul to *rejoice* always in the Lord (1 Thess. 5:16), and *render thanks* in all things (v. 18). Paul adds there, as Moses makes clear, that giving thanks "is the will of God . . . concerning you."

God's Punishment for Betrayal (19, 20)

Two tragic things are a part of Moses' loving warning.

The worship of spurious gods. Should the people *forget* their God who gives the bounties and *follow* false gods, the consequence is sure.

The woe that will come. Here is a solemn *affirmation*: in false worship they are to perish. What Moses prayerfully called God and men to attest in 4:26 is now a direct proclamation. The perishing is also a result of failing to keep God in focus by thankful prayer, as in 4:10.

With the affirmation of God's certain judgment comes an *analogy*. The demise of Israel in the path of sin will be like the perishing of other nations before them (20). These illustrations, as they see them, ought to provide loud wake-up calls to avoid sin's pitfalls themselves. The wake-up would be in returning to the way of thankful prayer (10).

Consider principles for prayer. First, let life be a continual flow of "thank you" notes to God for His myriad bounties (cf. 1 Thess. 5:18; Heb. 13:15). Second, avoid the great let-down in a life given over to man-made gods (cf. Isa. 41–48; 1 Cor. 8:4–6), and the let-down at the end for those who are devotees to false gods, for the gods, which are not gods, and those who worship them will perish in the judgment by the true God.

Deuteronomy 9:18–20

Prayer for a Sinning Brother

Most of the passage about prayer is a review of Moses' prayer to spare Israel after their sin in the Golden Calf episode. Already surveyed in Exodus 32, it need not be repeated here.

But Moses now mentions a new element not included in the Exodus 32 summary: "I also prayed for Aaron at that time." The present exposition will outline the passage, but expand on the prayer for Aaron.

Moses' Appeal

For Israel (18, 19). See Exodus 32.

For Aaron (20). First Moses mentions *God's anger against Aaron*, which is part of the anger in Exodus 32. God could have taken Aaron's life right there in discipline, as He later takes some believers at Corinth (1 Cor. 11:30–32). That would be discipline in death and a loss in some degree of special reward, not default from salvation itself. Loss of reward with salvation itself still intact, not loss of salvation, is clarified in 1 Corinthians 3:8, 10–15.

Second, Moses emphasizes *His advocacy for Aaron*. He asked God to pardon Aaron and preserve his life. His safety was included with Israel's in general in Exodus 32. For this, we go to Deuteronomy 10:10, 11.

God's Answer (10:10, 11)

Now the divine sparing of Israel, and Aaron with them, becomes apparent as in the Exodus account. Moses mentions two aspects in the answer to prayer.

One is God's *preservation*, "the Lord was not willing to destroy you." The other is God's *presence* going with Israel, as is clarified in Exodus 33–34. God's answer is very specific. He permitted a *continuation* of the journey toward the covenant land, and gave a *certification* of Israel entering it, just as He had promised. The plan was sure, and God even prompted Moses so that his prayer was aligned with the plan and ensured of its "yes" answer.

Principles are clear here. First, prayer arising out of being saturated with God's promises (His word and will) is prayer certain of God's encouraging response. Second, one great ministry of a serious intercessor can be in pleading longer opportunity for so-called people of God who fall away into idol worship, and yet can still get right with the Lord. Third, another vigil of a person who cries in spiritual advocacy is for a particular, professedly saved individual who slides, hopefully only temporarily, to an idolatrous delusion. In such a case, one pleads that God will bring the person in certainty to Him, forgive and protect the life from having gone astray, and work true faith before it is too late. Fourth, God's merciful clemency, in some cases, to answer concerned prayer is an amazing elixir to the spirit that such ministry can have part in the salvation and usefulness of a person.

Deuteronomy 9:25–29

Prayer to Preserve Israel

Prayer in this case is a review again, this time of Israel's sin in not believing God to enter the land, and again involves intercession for sparing Israel. It is not necessary to repeat the details, since the discussion of

Numbers 13–14 already covered that. Verses 25–29 here repeat arguments Moses pleads before God to gain Israel's preservation.

As noted in Numbers 13–14, the Lord did answer the prayer with a "yes" for most of Israel. At the same time, He raised a firm warning to Israel about trusting His sufficiency. He barred that generation aged twenty and older from going into Canaan, and took the lives of the ten unbelieving scouts. He also allowed enemies to defeat Israelites trying to force a way to Canaan while waving aside His word.

Cf. principles on 9:18–20.

Deuteronomy 10:8

A Special Role of Prayer

God entrusted to one tribe, the Levites, a special ministry of prayer for people of all the tribes.

The Sanctification of the Levites

God set apart men of this tribe for special spiritual service to uphold all of Israel. Detail on this was a part of the study in Leviticus 8–9. The Levites' *concern* for the holiness of God in the Golden Calf scenario and God's *choice* of them in Deuteronomy 33:9 were included in that review. The Leviticus passage also explained their *consecration* to the special privilege in a public ceremony.

The Specifics for the Levites

Here is a quick summary of the spiritual ministries God gave them in three areas.

Carry the ark. Certain Levites were put in charge of transporting the Ark of the Covenant from one campsite to the next. God gave them directions for doing it with reverence to Him (Num. 4:1–20).

Commune with God in holy service. They were to "stand before" the Lord, ministering in His presence in all they did.

Call for spiritual blessings. Their ministry "to bless in His name" was one of prayer, seeking God's blessings for all of life for His people. Specifics in what they prayed for are clear in Numbers 6:22–27, and they representatively cover the sweep of life's needs. Their own ministry of modeling prayer for their people was to be joined by the people's sensitive prayer as in Deuteronomy 26:1–11.

The Substance of their Inheritance

This is evident in verse 9.

What they are prohibited from. God does not permit them the regular temporal allotments of tribal land. This is to help them focus on the very special privilege He does grant them, and carry it out in a way that glorifies Him.

Likewise, it is, today, a high privilege to be set apart in God's leading for service as spiritual leaders, so God calls on one in such a capacity to fulfill the ministry to His credit and one's own (Col. 4:17). And in the entire body of believers, each Christian is to concentrate in exercising his God-given contribution to the others (Rom. 12:6–8).

What they are privileged in. Their opportunity is very great: "the Lord is his [the Levitical tribe's] inheritance." This is the rich bounty God has given. Access to Him in a representative and advocating sense and articulating aspects of His spiritual blessing to others is the heart of it. The Levites' lives are absorbed in this atmosphere, in the presence and principles of God. This sets them apart from others in Israel who are occupied with many other temporal necessities that do not permit this full-time concentration.

Before leaving this passage, it is good to go back to the prayer aspect of being channels of blessing. Any leader who is in a ministry that especially models the values of God to others ought to make any sacrifices to be a pace-setter in prayer. Tragically, this is too often only acknowledged as an ideal, not applied as an insistence. Leaders may not pray as much, and sometimes less, than people they lead who themselves let the details of life all but blot out prayer. Instead, those who model God's will should make it a passionate priority to go often to prayer and be steeped in prayer. And this practice, as they themselves point out the way, should saturate the lives of the believers they lead (Eph. 6:18–20).

One other thing, and remarks on 10:8 and its context must suffice: the seriousness of this life that includes much prayer is derived not from its being a helpful idea, it flows from it being "as the Lord your God spoke to him" (9). *God* is the originator of the ministries that are so much in prayer. The Levite reaction in fulfilling these, or sloughing off from them, will be no less than a reflection of the value they place on God!

A principle can counsel us: a believer can be thankful that God separates some of His people and uses them in a special, full-time ministry such as praying for others. Here, priests in the tribe of Levi became developed in this all-out labor. They appealed to God to bless, whatever the needs across the entire spectrum of life. Today, faithful full-time Christian leaders do this, and any Christian, a believer priest (cf. 1 Pet. 2:4–10), can be exercised and effective in a role of "praying for you." Paul perceives this as an engagement, in some degree, that all of the saved can experience (cf. Eph. 6:18–20).

Deuteronomy 10:21

God is "Your Praise"

This is one of the finest statements in a book of astounding messages. It is not easy to plumb the depths of such a concept, but it is possible to say a few things to clarify it. First, the context of God's faithfulness prepares readers for it, and verse 21 itself rivets attention on the occupation due to God.

The Acts Done by God

Moses fills his context with God's exploits as a background leading up to verse 21. He gave the ten commandments (1–5), set the Levites apart to their unique ministry (8, 9), answered prayer in saving

Israel from destruction after sin (10), and gave clearance to go on to the promised land (11).

That is not all. All in the heavens and earth belongs to God (14). He loved this people from all the earth (15). He is God of gods and Lord of lords, a God of power and of integrity (17), of justice and love (18). In light of all this, verse 21 is part of an appeal for an appropriate response in worship.

The Adoration Due to God

In verse 20, the focus is on what they *should do for God* as a fitting acknowledgment. This embraces an awe in respecting Him, faithful service to Him, fervent steadfastness toward Him, and staking all on His name, that is, what He is and stands for.

Then verse 21 puts its spotlight on what *God is to them*.

This comes as two points for them to meditate on so as to render to Him the service verse 20 articulates.

His place in their hearts. He, unique above all gods and lords (cf. v. 17) is all in all to them.

(1) "He is your praise." The idea is that God is the lone object of their praise, as in Psalm 109:1. He is the appropriate One to receive their praising acknowledgment. This is for all that He is and all He has done as in the examples of the context. All that they can give praise for centers in Him, the possessor of all (v. 14), the giver of blessing (8:18). He rightfully inhabits the praises of Israel as the psalmist will say later (Ps. 22:3).

As the praise of the people, God is everything as related to all true prayer, for every aspect of prayer other than thanks or praise should be an acknowledgment of His praiseworthiness. Confession of sin has its prompt in His being what He is that the worshipper wants to align with. Petition and Intercession have their origination in the praying person recognizing God's will and seeking things that fulfill it. Affirmation of His truth issues from respect for Him and a desire to be in accord with Him.

So all these and other aspects of prayer are tacit acknowledgments that to God belongs the glory.

(2) "He is your God." No other god is. In fact, He repudiates every false god in His ten commandments. He defeated all the gods of Egypt by His miraculous work (Ex. 12:12). He did His will in delivering His people from Egypt, and no gods or magician tricks could stay with Him, do what He did, or undo His work. He was Israel's God at the sea and when they needed water, food, victory, organization, law, and all things.

He alone, then, deserves the place in their hearts as Object of their praise and as their God.

His performance in their history. In what He is in Himself as God and Lord (v. 17) and in what He has done to help Israel He certainly can lay singular claim to their allegiance. Here the focus is on His performance, which had been an exhibit of His worthiness to praise and His very Godhood.

What has He done? One emphasis is His *miracles*, so great and awesome, which their own eyes have beheld. Even with the passing of forty years, the new generation, aged fifty-eight and younger, would have many who were children or teenagers in Egypt, at the sea, at Sinai, and in the earlier wanderings. They could remember personally seeing God perform miracle after miracle. So, Moses can say, "which your eyes have seen."

Another focus is His *multiplying* of His covenant people (22). Once, in Jacob's own day, they were only *seventy* (Gen. 46:27). Now in some fulfillment of God's promise to multiply them they are as the *stars* in being of a great number. This, to His credit, is what "the Lord your God has made you."

This passage is one of many that recounts many things to praise God for, even for Himself. Psalms 146–150 mention numerous promptings for thanksgiving/praise as well. God is the believers' praise, and the person who prays can find in His "Prayer Book" many ideas to keep prayer spiced with the incense of praise.

Now attention can center on principles. First, prayer in much praise fits the case of a God who can be all in all—in who He is, what He has done, and what He plans yet to do. It is similar to Paul later speaking of Christ "who is our life" (Col. 3:4) and "to me to live is Christ" (Phil. 1:21). Second, "God is great and greatly to be praised" (Ps. 48:1), so "He is your praise" can in some vital degree be true for all His special spiritual leaders and for everyone who knows Him. Some are pacesetters, yet all to whom "He is your God" applies can give their lives to the pace.

Deuteronomy 12:5–19

Rejoicing in Prayer

This passage prepares for prayer in directing the people, once they are in the land, to bring gifts to their worship center and thank God for His provisions.

The Stand Against Other Gods (1–3)

Devotion to God (1). The Lord calls for a steadfast fidelity to Him through following His word. He gives them the land and they are to give Him their loyalty. He focuses on the positive before the negative. This is as Paul the apostle would put the matter in 1 Thessalonians 1:9, "You turned to God from idols. . . ."

Destroying of gods (2, 3). These are, in the perspective of God's word, not gods at all. They are not genuine; they are part of a great misconception, even a deception in human minds. They do not deserve devotion; they are fit only to be destroyed. So God leads Moses to call for their total removal from the land of promise. His people are to destroy the *places* of vain worship, the *objects* used in misguided devotion, and the lifeless *idols* or images themselves.

This is what God commands when they conquer the peoples in the land. And he wants them to be resolute about the gods so as to "obliterate their name from that place" (3).

Some would label this intolerant and unloving, but this is because they are not submissive to the true God and fair to His legitimate love that must be vigilant against things that mislead and ruin men. His way, the way of genuine love, cannot stand by and be spineless when deceptions keep people in bondage to a lie; it must act to point them to the truth He gives.

The Seeking of the True God (4–19)

Rather than giving guidance permitting worship places and gods wherever impulse dictates, God guards His people in genuine love, ambitious for their real welfare. They shall not go the way of their own inclinations, which may be quite illegitimate even if they are sincere but sincerely wrong. Instead, they are to act diffently toward God, and worship Him alone as in the Ten Commandments (4).

This is in seeking Him at the worship center He indicates, which at first would be at Shiloh and later, in David's day, at Jerusalem. Steadfastness in this would guide them to worship the true God and keep them unified in giving Him the glory due Him.

Coming to the center from wherever they live in the land, they are to bring their various offerings (cf. Lev. 1–7), tithes, and other gifts to the Lord's work (6). In their honoring God's guidance, *prayer* is a saturating element. The passage says three times that they are to "rejoice" before the Lord (7, 12, 18). This is in "all your undertakings in which the Lord your God has blessed you" (7). This is in thanksgiving for God's blessings in all things. And so it is of the same essence as Paul's challenge to "Rejoice always" and "in everything give thanks" (1 Thess. 5:16, 18).

Prayer is apparent in other ways here, too. It would accompany various offerings in verse 6. In the *burnt offering*, the one sacrificing was symbolizing his own complete dedication to God, which would quite fittingly be in affirmation of his desires toward God and in thanksgiving for the privilege. The *peace offering* was joined with thanksgiving for peace and other bounties God's covenant kindness gave. The *meal offering* was a prompt for affirming one's appreciation to God for all the produce He had given, and for all things of His blessing. The *sin* and *trespass offerings* combined with confessing sin and thanksgiving for God's pardon.

Offerings for vows (11) also came with affirming one's pledge to God, petitioning for His help, and thanking Him for the faithfulness on His side.

The jubilant spirit before the Lord here is a theme that recurs in Deuteronomy. One such passage is 14:22–29.

Guidelines lift off the page to greet readers. First, for those who know the true God, He is the One to rely upon in prayer, and all so-called gods are unworthy of confidence. Second, it is natural for people to feel a rush of joy before the Lord when they realize the majesty of His person, the things He has accomplished, and the designs He has to fulfill. Third, prayer is vital in all the offerings as one is exulting in God, having His forgiveness, being dedicated to Him, or realizing the peace He imparts.

Deuteronomy 14:22–29

More Rejoicing in Prayer

This is very similar to 12:5–19. God's people receive His teaching to express their joy to Him in tithing various things.

Gifts to the Lord (22–26)

Prayer is a big factor in this as the people "rejoice" before God (26), as in Chapter 12.

The presenting of tithes (22, 23). Gifts to God in thankful credit for His blessings cover the whole of life. The people are to bring to God every year a tithe of all their produce from both plants and animals. He wants them to be grateful in all of life.

The purpose of tithes (23). In this is a great lesson the offerers are to learn: the opportunity to remember from whom the blessings came enhances their fear (worshipful awe) of Him always, for all of life and all of their days.

The personalizing of tithes (24–26). In any case the worshipper is to journey to the central place of worship. Even if it is too far away to bring animals or a load of produce, the person who means business with the Lord can exchange his offerings for money, go to the center, and use it in his own and his family's expression of joy to the Lord. The benefit accrues to God, whom they acknowledge (23), and to *the ones grateful* to God (26).

Gifts to the Levites and to Others (27–29)

The spirit of giving to the Lord with joyful and thankful prayer also extends in principle to giving to Him to help the needy. Worshippers are to give sensitively to sustain the Levites for their concentrated spiritual leadership, and also to various people in need. In the latter groups are aliens residing in Israelite land, far from home and often having particular problems, as well as orphans and widows.

Contributions from those giving to the people, but intending these to God above, all can manifest prayerful thanksgiving for what He, first, has given. They also can reflect faith working through love in compassion (cf. Gal. 5:6), as in Jesus' parable of the Good Samaritan (Luke 10:25–37).

The same essential principle of gifts to God in thanksgiving is at the heart of Deuteronomy. Other principles join this. One is that the person who trusts the Lord and who presents contributions to Him who bestows so much to His people can live in joy (cf. Deut. 8:18; Eccl. 5:19; 1 Cor. 4:7; 1 Tim. 6:17). Another is that special joy comes to worshipers in conferring gifts on spiritual leaders to boost these who minister to them. A third one is to take up the privilege of giving to help meet needs of the poor, which is a kind of giving for the Lord's sake, too. Jesus would say, "It is more blessed to give than to receive" (Acts 20:35). This is the spirit that Jesus taught (Luke 6:38) and displayed (2 Cor. 8:9). Such a giving life can be one vital aspect in "pure and undefiled religion" (James 1:27; cf. 1 Tim. 6:18), and in being like Christ.

Deuteronomy 16:1–17

Still More Rejoicing in Prayer

The Israelite worshipper had God's guidance as to what to bring to the central worship center as offerings for great feasts—Passover,

Weeks, and Booths. At these, prayer would have a very prominent part, seasoning all the interaction with God.

The Feast of Passover (1–8)

This observance was joined with the seven days following it, the Feast of Unleavened Bread. God's aim was the remembrance of His bringing Israel "out of Egypt," a phrase that appears four times here. Leviticus 23 gives the panorama of seven great feasts.

Passover action included offering a lamb (v. 2), as in the first Passover in Egypt in Exodus 12. Also foremost in the observance was eating unleavened bread to recall the haste in leaving Egypt (3), when the quickness allowed no time to leaven bread to enhance its taste. This reminded worshippers of the "affliction" in bondage and in not having normal bread due to the departure.

Prayer would also be vital at the Passover in *thanksgiving* to God for deliverance from death and from bondage. And it would be meaningful in rehearsing or *affirming* to God what they know He did for them. Such prayer would spring up in hearts attuned to God during all the eight days, and in the special solemn assembly on the final day (8).

The Feast of Weeks (9–12)

Seven weeks after the Passover this feast was set. Held on the day after seven weeks, on the fiftieth day, it also was called "Pentecost," meaning "fiftieth." Further it was called the "Feast of Ingathering," since it commemorated gathering grain (v. 9).

Thanksgiving in prayer was a propos here since the person brought a freewill offering from his crop as a gift to God in gratitude for His giving the produce (10). So the time was one to "rejoice" (11) with the family, servants, Levites, strangers, orphans, and widows. How could a heart sensitive to the Lord's goodness not run over with gratitude when one remembered His springing Israel free from slavery (12)?

The Feast of Booths (13–15)

Prayer in thanksgiving saturated this observance, too. The occasion was one to "rejoice" for God blessing the crop and prospering in all the work of the hands (15). It was a time of high joy in God, similar to the American "Thanksgiving Day" worship meetings of Christians.

One other detail about a prayer-stimulating phase of worship is included (16, 17). All the males in Israel are called to appear during the three feast times just reviewed, each with a gift for God's work. The giving is taken for granted as the appropriate expression and ought to be *spontaneous* in the desire of each heart. At the same time, it is *sensitive*, allowing each to offer the amount he is able to give. And its *standard* is the level on which, first, the giver has himself been supplied by God's gifts.

Any man's tender reflection on what He has received from the Lord should prompt him in turn to give. And the giving would join, quite naturally, with prayer *affirming* God's kindness, *thanking* Him, and *interceding* for His blessing of the gift in the use He would make of it. A good illustration of how prayer fits strategically with giving to God meets the reader in 26:1–11.

A principle is apparent. Joy in prayer that linked hearts with God was a flavor not only in daily matters and offerings, it was a saturating factor during worshipful feasts that memorialized God's provision to His people.

Deuteronomy 18:16

Prayer Answered with a Prophet

God does not want His people to be impacted by those who peddle a spurious message (9–14), he desires that they listen to a person He raises up who has a sterling message (15–22). He will raise up a prophet as an answer to Israel's prayer.

The Rejection of Phoniness in Religion (9–14)

God's point is simple. He does not will for His people, once in the land, to imitate sins or gravitate toward false teachers who entice into sin. Those claiming His name are to be separate from pagan peoples, their belief and behavior distinctly wholesome as He appraises values. The principle of being set apart to a holy life is as Paul also articulates it (2 Cor. 6:14–18).

The caution. God-pleasers are not to participate with the practices or the people given to sinful things (9–11). Some examples of what God detests and they are to detest are put on display. Child sacrifice, black arts, witchcraft, interpreting of omens, the sorcerer's art, casting spells to manipulate, fortune telling, and claiming to contact the dead are all under God's censure.

The censure. Verse 13 shows God's sharp rejection of such things by stating His view of *people* who practice them and the *poison* He sees in the things. He appraises both as "detestable." Since God is so strongly opposed to the people and the poison they accept, He will "drive them out before you." He has already shown in 4:25, 26 that if Israel practices such evils He will expel them from the land.

The challenge. God wants His people to be very *different* from those who do not know Him (14), strongly *devoted* to all that pleases Him (13). "Blameless" is the way He wills for them to be. Leviticus 19:21 put it another way, "You shall be holy, for I the Lord your God am holy." He desired this for His own glory, their good, and the testimony before other peoples (4:6).

"Blameless" in Old Testament thought is not a state of achieving perpetual sinless perfection. It is a good testimony of a consistent pattern of life devoted to God and His values, even though sin does occur and God forgives (cf. Ps. 119:1, 9–11, 176). He had given provisions for forgiveness in the sin and trespass offerings (Lev. 4, 5). The godly person persists in living to please Him, not having arrived at final perfection but marked by a refreshing direction.

The Raising of a Prophet (15–22)

False values and practices have their spokesmen to mislead. God will provide a spokesman for true values and practices to lead His people the right way.

The promise of God (15, 18, 19). He pledges to provide a prophet, a proclaimer of His will. The *promise* is according to a certain present *profile*, like Moses whom they now can attest is God's authentic leader. Moses says "like me," because He faithfully gives what God assured him, "like you."

Such a leader will meet certain credentials. He will arise out of *Israel*, God assures putting His in his mouth *His true message*, the words He desires, and he will *speak all* God wants him to give. Moses himself had met these criteria, except in the episode in striking the rock (Num. 20).

The prayer to God. As so many things are in Scripture, the raising up of this spokesman is God's answer to prayer (16). What is already God's will in a plan that has no surprises to upset Him, He prompts people to pray. Their will becomes a blend with His, His will is lived in them.

At Horeb or Sinai, God's voice out of the mount and cloud had been so awesome that the people were afraid. They had heard the thunderclaps, seen the fire, heard the warnings of death if they crossed the boundary, and voiced a prayer (cf. Ex. 19). What they petitioned was that they would not hear the voice or see the fire attended with the peril of possible death. What they are not said to have gone on to pray God has filled in. He takes things on to their real intent (cf. Rom. 8:26, 27). They wanted, instead, to be able to approach God through a leader representing them.

God had been answering the prayer through Moses. He will answer it even further by giving them a leader *like* Moses.

The prayer is in *principle* answered in each true prophet God gives the people—Samuel, Elijah, Elisha, Isaiah, Jeremiah, and others. It is in God's *perfection* realized far above all other examples in Jesus Christ, His greatest messenger. This is as the early Christian leaders recognized (Acts 3:22–26).

The Reckoning on False Prophets (20–22)

Prophets who advocate a spurious message without God's authority will die. Such was the temporal end of false prophets Elijah confronted on Mount Carmel (1 Kgs. 18), and such was God's dealing with Hananiah (Jer. 28:17).

A true prophet will be marked off from the false by the fulfillment of what He speaks, so the false prophet's unfulfilled word will betray his false colors. Deuteronomy 13 clarifies that even if God permits a false speaker's word to be fulfilled, His people are to appraise his message in the final analysis by what is clear in His word (vv. 1–5). His word, not experience, is the final bureau of standards.

Now a principle comes into focus, stated from our present vantage point. High gratitude in prayer can celebrate that God promised and gave a great prophet, Jesus Christ. He, in the pattern of Moses, but greater than Moses, has shared God's message as other true prophets have, and this is quite distinct from false voices. Christ Himself is "the way, the truth, and the life" (John 14:6).

Deuteronomy 21:8

Elders' Prayer for their People's Forgiveness

The Finding of a Corpse (1)

Someone comes across a human corpse lying outside a city and showing evidence of having been struck to death.

The Function of Elders and Priests (2–7)

Elders. Leaders of the city that measurement shows is nearest the victim carry out the procedure. They provide a heifer as an offering for sin. The heifer must meet certain qualifications: never been worked and never worn a yoke. They break the animal's neck at a running creek in a valley where the land has not been plowed or sown.

Priests. These sons of Levi officiate by God's appointment and authority. Under their spiritual leading, the elders wash their hands over the heifer. This is a sign that they attest that they did not commit the sin (crime) and did not witness it. The action is a picture illustrating that their hands are clean of the wrong.

The Forgiveness Upon Confession (8, 9)

The seeking of it. They are not guilty themselves, but somebody presumably in their area is, so they seek forgiveness in a general coverage, similar to Israel's high priest seeking pardon for all Israel once a year on the Day of Atonement (Lev. 16).

Their prayer is right to the point, and not an excursion around the world. They plead forgiveness, plead God's redemption for Israel as a whole, and plead freedom from any guilt. They apparently desire that coverage by the sacrifice's blood should avail for those in their city, and innocent people should not be held accountable as having a hand in the sin.

The sequel of it. The forgiveness is granted after the sacrifice and confession. God gives a certainty of a covering.

The animal's death seems to depict death that actually belongs to the one who committed the sin, but at the same time those not guilty of it arc guaranteed clearance before God. They were tender to God's standards—careful to "do what is right" (9)—in dealing with sin in prayerful sensitivity to God.

Here is a broad principle. Leaders in spiritual things may need to pray confessing sin in their community when they do not know who is guilty but feel a human accountability before God. In the best way they can they close with the wrong. In this they show respect for God by seeking His forbearance and offering a sacrifice. It is one way of reflecting a sincere desire to be right in His sight. Today, to refer to the sacrifice Christ has made at the cross would be a testimony that exalts His provision for any who will receive it.

Deuteronomy 23:4, 5

Prayer of a Selfish Man

This is a capsule review of Balaam's selfish efforts to gain God's curse against Israel. The detail need not be repeated (cf. Num. 22–24). Briefly, some things here ought gain notice. God was not willing to answer the hireling's prayer because it was opposed to His covenant will to bless Israel. Second, God worked a blessing, not a curse, despite Balaam's repeated efforts. Third, God's dealing with Israel was because "the Lord your God loves you."

Principles fit the case. Believers who reflect on this can learn much. Study God's word and bring prayer sensitively into harmony with His will already clear there. If it is clear, deal firmly against selfish desires to talk God into aligning with self's cravings. Take comfort, too, in God's faithfulness to fulfill what He has promised in blessing. Rest in His love, a very great love that has the believer's true interests in His heart (Eph. 2:4–6).

Deuteronomy 23:21–23

Prayer in a Promise to God

A vow in prayer was a subject earlier (cf. Num. 21:2). Only a brief sketch of what is now said along the same line ought to suffice.

The Promise in a Vow (21, 23)

It is helpful to note that the praying person "promised," and also that this is to "the Lord" and "from your lips."

The Performance of the Vow (21, 23)

God desires integrity in those who pray. One can observe the *counsel* to carry out what is promised, and the *character* God sees in going back on one's word. It is "sin" and God will deal with the believer about his slip-shod word. Follow-through is a part of truthfulness.

The Permission Not to Vow (22)

A person may have other sin to deal with God about, but should he hold back from making a vow he is not prepared to honor, this particular decision is not sin. He has not spoken what is untruthful and unreliable in this matter, at least.

Guidelines are apparent. The point is to pray in purity. A great ability is dependability. Prayer can, by sinful gravitation, become a light thing spun off the lips without genuine commitment. Paul could tell the Ephesian believers that the fruit of light as God evaluates things is in the realm of "all goodness, righteousness, and truth" (Eph. 5:9). Fruit and not fakery is what God wants in all of life and in prayer that relates to "everything" (Phil. 4:6).

Deuteronomy 24:15

Prayer Incited by Injustice

Moses deals briefly with a case much like the one on prayer already in Exodus 22:23. In both cases, a cry goes up to God from a person dealt an injustice.

Pity toward a Servant's Poverty

The counsel is to show compassion toward a servant by giving him the remuneration he needs, and promptly. It should be on the same day the work is done, before the sun sets, probably due to the need for food before the next day.

An urgency in the worker's situation seems evident in two clues here. One is his *circumstance*, a condition of poverty. The other, closely related, is his *concern* over payment to make ends meet if the one he serves delays this. Possibly living from day to day, he will "set his heart on" the postponement. It puts him in a crisis.

The Preventing of a Servant's Prayer

Two steps can intertwine.

A step of pity. The right move of the master is to be forthright about paying the same day. This could be an expression of heartfelt mercy that pleases the Lord. It would, in Galatians 5:22, 23, be "fruit" of a right walk with the Lord in "love" and "goodness." It is having the other's true welfare in view and upholding it.

A step of prayer. In this case, the godly action just mentioned would prevent prayer! That seems strange, but on reflection it is not strange at all. Should the poor man be denied his right, it would be a rather spontaneous result for him to cry out to God about the predicament that puts him in. He needs help, and the unthoughtful, perhaps heartless action of the master would register to God as sin. This is before God, but also before the desperate servant, and could come before the civil and spiritual leaders as the case in 21:1–9 did.

A principle is sensible. The right move before God and the proper testimony before men is to show compassionate thoughtfulness. This would be like the Lord who had often seen His people "between a rock and a hard place" and dealt in loving-kindness. "You shall be holy, for I the Lord your God am holy" pertains in all of life (Lev. 19:2).

Deuteronomy 26:1–11

Prayer in Giving to God

Thanksgiving in prayer here is the theme already spotlighted in Chapters 12, 14, and 16. Detail on the prayer itself is developed more in the present passage.

The Presenting of a Gift (1–3a)

A nutshell of the idea is that a man of Israel is to bring firstfruits of his crop as a gift of gratitude to God. He comes to the central worship center, which in the early days in the land was at Shiloh where the Ark of the Covenant rested (Josh. 18:1).

God's prior giving. By the time the Israelites fulfill this trip of gratitude, God will have given them the land. This giving is mentioned four times in the eleven verses. A larger conception than even this is that for the God who created the whole earth, it all is His (Ps. 24:1).

Man's privileged giving. The prompting of gratitude stirs a man's heart to give his firstfruits to the Lord who gave so much to him. The very soil out of which his fruits grow is a gift. The power to have success making a living is His gift (8:18). The man feels compelled by such blessing and wants to express himself to the One blessing him, so he *takes* a token gift of the fruit in a basket and *travels* to the tabernacle to give to the Lord. His *time* is a willing sacrifice. He will not be entrapped in self-indulging ingratitude and forgetfulness toward the source of his good things.

The Praying with the Gift (3b-11)

The access to God's priest. He goes to the person God has designated for spiritual ministry to His people. It would be disobedient, even defiant, to go to any other. Even in this, he means to do things the way that honors God. The passage, given before Israel entered the land, is commanding him, and his response is one sensitive to God's direction.

The acknowledgment of God's provision. Prayer is now in session. It is composed largely of *affirmation* or recognition of what he has (entry and residence in the land) and what God has given. Things he says to the priest, intended directly for God (10, "You, O Lord"), are of a nature that also reflects a spirit of *thanksgiving*.

He is to review God's *multiplying* of his people (5) and His *might* in delivering them from bondage into the land (6–9). His provision in the land is bountiful, "a land flowing with milk and honey." To such credits to God he is to add that his own *motivation* is to render appreciation to the God of such kindness (10).

The *commemoration* of God's goodness itself suggests a thankful strain in the prayer, then even more gratitude follows. The worshipper leaves the gift basket "before the Lord" at the tabernacle and goes on worshipping. He has brought his family with him to share in the worship and also invites an alien to share in this impact. Together these "rejoice in all the good things the Lord your God has given you and your household." A keynote in this is thanksgiving to the Lord, a spirit as in Paul's call to "rejoice in the Lord always" and "give thanks in everything" (1 Thess. 5:16, 18).

Here "all the good things" would gather in the totality of life's blessings. A godly father and godly family could carry the spirit of the special acknowledgment of God from the tabernacle to all the daily tasks. Giving thanks in all things would be, for them, "the will of God" as in 1 Thessalonians 5:18.

Deuteronomy 26:12–15

Praying about a Tithe

Affirmation in prayer about obedience in giving to God leads on to *supplication* in prayer asking God for further blessings.

The Sensitivity about Provision for the Needy (12)

God wants His people to practice unselfishness in tender care of those with special needs. This is love in action, the kind of quality God Himself displayed in finding this people in desperate plight in Egypt and giving His help.

The payment of the provision. This was a special gift every third year to God's work, provided to support Levitical ministry and those with particular hardships.

The people for the provision. In the latter category were strangers far from home in a strange place, not part of the natural Israelite fabric of family help. Others were orphans and widows, obviously without normal support. They, too, needed to eat as the end of verse 12 shows. The spirit that would reach out to them with help was the spirit Jesus Christ would develop in His Good Samaritan parable. A heart aflame with love would be sensitive to "Who is my neighbor?"

The Speaking in Prayer to God (13–15)

The affirming of present obedience (13, 14). What God has counselled His people to give is set apart for His blessing of others. It does not belong, really, to the giver, and he should not think selfishly as if it does, so he rightly submits it to God's work and can affirm in truth that he has given it. He acknowledges that his giving is what God's own gracious word has prompted. He can further say honorably that he has not withheld any of it to indulge his own supposed needs.

The asking for prospective blessing (15). Prayer is apt after such giving in love to God and man. It can be a confident prayer, refreshed by the fragrant touch of God's own presence. Two facets make up the prayer.

First is the giver's *request for the future faithfulness.* He petitions God's seeing, "Look . . . from heaven. . . ." He can know, with obedience, that what God sees He can approve. And he also petitions God's success, asking that He bless His people and the land.

Second is the giver's *recognition of the past faithfulness.* This emerges in three thoughts. God the greater giver had given His *provision* (a gift), He had given in *plenitude* ("a land flowing with milk and honey"), and all this in fidelity to His *promise* to the fathers.

An interesting principle of prayer surfaces. It is that of giving prayerfully in sweet accord that is fragranced by remembering God's own greater giving. Paul, centuries later, would speak to the Corinthians about generous giving and close with thanks to God for His indescribable gift (2 Cor. 9:15). He also gave them this great example: "For you know the grace of our Lord Jesus Christ, that though He was rich, yet for your sake He became poor, that you through His poverty might become rich" (8:9).

Two principles are germane. First, giving to God is fitting since anything men bestow is what He Himself in some way has already generously given (cf. Deut. 8:18; 1 Cor. 4:7). We are custodians of what belongs to Him (Ps. 24:1) and He has first shared. Second, the way a believer is in his best moments of gratitude should be the way he is all of his moments. His is the privilege, not of the tight fist but the open heart and the open hand.

Deuteronomy 27:1–8

Prayer in Joyful Thanksgiving

As Israel is poised to enter His promised land, the Lord calls them to erect two memorials when they have conquered the peoples there. These are stones of *Scripture* (His law) and stones of *sacrifice*. Prayer is strategic in this in thankful rejoicing before the Lord (v. 7) and as related to the sacrifices their worship includes (5–7).

The two memorials are part of a commitment to allegiance to Him.

The Erection of the Memorials (1–6a)

Two memorials are strategic here.

Stones of Scripture (1–4). The *inscriptions* on the large stones are the words of God's law. The *idea* their use conveys is blessing or cursing, depending on whether Israel obeys God in the land or not. Moses had said earlier that God was setting before the people a blessing or a curse (11:26–32), and he will enlarge on the theme in 27:11–26 and Chapters 28–30. A third point also needs to be noted—the *illustrators*. These are three segments of Israel, six tribes standing on Mount Gerizim to bless the people, six on Mount Ebal to curse them if they disobey, and the Levites in the valley to shout out the blessings and the curses.

The second memorial follows.

Stones for sacrifice (5–7). Stones compose an altar for two kinds of offerings. First, the *burnt* offerings, in being totally consumed, were a picture signifying complete dedication to God. Prayer would be vital in it, affirming before God the intent and petitioning Him to be pleased. *Peace* offerings were in recognition of peace with God, and were accompanied by thanksgiving for that peace.

Simplicity was to characterize the altar in its being only of uncut stones as in Exodus 20:25. It makes sense that the simplicity throws the focus on the altar not being of human polish but purity in worship. Not ingenuity but integrity in devotion was the idea. God did not want human finesse to distract the people from pure and simple sincerity.

The Expressions of the Meaning (6b-8)

These are, largely, clarified above. To these expressions one thing further is added. Verse 7 is clear that God wants prayer to permeate the people. His will is that they "rejoice" before Him, which would be in praise/thanksgiving in sensing the impact of His word on the stones and work the sacrifices depicted. He Himself was the greater *burnt* offering completely devoted to them, and the *peace* offering giving them peace. How much the people then grasped of the full meaning as those with the New Testament see it we do not know. But they could sense the ideas of dedication and peace, and they knew that the ultimate in both was realized in life with God.

The blessings and curses themselves gave much to stimulate prayer. Aspects of prayer related to naturally to blessings were thanksgiving, petition for more blessing, confession when they failed of blessing, and the like. Curses could easily cause rethinking, with petition crying out for help and confession as a way back to blessing (cf. 4:29–31).

As to principle, the same realities can shape us in godly prayer today. These are Scripture that guides our steps for God (cf. Ps. 119:105), and sacrifice that ever gives ourselves over to God who gave His sacrifice for us (cf. Rom. 12:1–2; 2 Cor. 5:15).

Deuteronomy 30:19; 31:28

Invoking God and Men as Witnesses

This use of prayer is already the subject in 4:26. See the principles there.

Deuteronomy 32

A Song of Prayer

Other songs in prayer were in view in Exodus 15. Now Moses develops his second great song after Exodus 15. God gives it to him to *pen* and for all Israel to *participate* in (31:19). As they take it on their lips in a prayerful response to God, it has a two-fold significance, affirming their *commitment* to God and His word and the *consequences* that God shows will overtake them if they spurn Him. And so it is a witness (31:21), a witness of God and men on earth (4:26; 30:19; 31:28).

God commands Moses to write the song and teach it to Israel (31:19). So he does write it (22), speaks it (30), and completes speaking it (32:45). The people evidently took it on their own lips (31:19) and the obedient took it to heart (32:46). They then would recall its words from memory and possibly by the help of Joshua or the priests (reading it to them), the elders, and God. So they could pass it on to their children (32:46), and the prayerful words repeated over and over.

The song has several parts coordinating various themes in prayer.

The Appeal (1, 2)

Moses and the people also join in this later appeal to God and men to hear what they pray. They want the truths of the prayer to refresh them spiritually as the rain and dew physically refresh the earth. A similar picture in Isaiah 55 draws an analogy between the rain stimulating the earth to be fruitful and God's truth refreshing hearts.

The Acknowledgment of God in Praise (3, 4)

The prayer is obviously exalting God here. It exalts His greatness—His Person, work, and ways. His Person is faithful and righteous, and so His ways just. If there will be any default it will be by the people, not by such a God, and this from their own lips.

The Affirmation of God and Men (5–43)

Three things gain affirmation here: Israel's sin, God's care, and His compassion.

Their corruption (5–6, 15–35). This is not only affirmation of their sin but a confession of it. It acknowledges that the people have been perverse and crooked (5), ungrateful (6), betrayers of their heavenly Father (6), scorners of God (15), idol worshippers (16), people who forget God (18), and people worthy of His judgments (19–35).

Details of judgment, known and given by God for the song (31:19), appear to reach prophetically into the future sweep of Israel's idolatry and His necessary curses on them, as in Chapters 27–30. For example, the prayer acknowledges God's judgments in famine, plague, destruction by the sword, and beasts (24, 25). God who inspires the prayer is eternal (33:27) and knows the future.

His care (7–14). God's portion and inheritance is His people (9); He gave them His care in the wilderness as an eagle cares for its young (10, 11), even bore them on eagles' wings (11; Ex. 19:4). He guided Israel, generously meeting their needs (12–14).

His compassion (36–43). This, too, with God's help, reaches into the future compassion God will display. When they come to the end of their resources, and their false gods are of no help, God will show them who is really God. And so we have:

(1) An affirmation of compassion in His *vindication* of Himself over the gods (36–39).

(2) An affirmation of His compassion in His *vengeance* on Israel's enemies, who are also His adversaries (40–43). As He had pledged in His covenant with Abram, He will bless Israel and bless those who bless them and curse those who curse them. By God's help in referring to what will occur in the future, those who pray envision His retributions against other peoples. Great sections in the Prophets carry this theme onward, naming specific peoples (Jer. 25, 46–51; Ezek. 25–32, etc.).

Although vengeance is sure on adversaries, the prayer song expects victory in joy for some from the nations, along with God's people (43). They can rejoice with His people, for though He avenges sins He also atones for His land and His people. The covenant with Abram anticipated people of all nations being beneficiaries of blessing, and later Scripture often develops this theme (cf. Dan. 7:27; Zech. 8:20–23).

A principle can be drawn.

Prayer that the Lord distills can be prompted in the human will, impressed by God's will, and borne along in His leading. This, too, is a frequent theme in His word as men pray for things that God proclaims in other passages as His will (Jer. 29:11–14; 33:18; Dan. 9:4–19). For God is able to work in men to will and to do of His good pleasure (Phil. 2:13).

Deuteronomy 32:48–52

Prayer that Gets a "No" Answer

Two lines of thought relate to this passage.

The prayer of Moses. Reference to the leader's passionate prayer is omitted here, but the passage is a review of 3:23–28 where Moses does mention his petition for passage into the land of promise. God gave him a firm "No" because of his sin in Numbers 20. The prayer needs to be kept in mind as part of the total picture here. With it, another point is vital.

The passing of Moses. While the account in Chapter 3 put heavy emphasis on Moses preparing Joshua to lead the people in, the present review focuses attention on Moses' death after seeing the land from afar. First would be his gaze, then his going. And as in Chapter 3 and Numbers 20, God mentions his sin as the reason that cost him present entry.

In the context at this point, the passage fits with Chapter 34 in referring to his death, but it also serves a second purpose of preparing readers for Moses' final blessing in Chapter 33 on each of the tribes before his climb to look and to die. God will use him in a prophetical and prayerful roll-call of blessing before he turns the leadership over to Joshua to take the people in.

A guidepost for life is evident. Guard the heart with all diligence (cf. Prov. 4:23a), for sin has a high price tag. It can cause forfeiture of blessing we would later prize, yet by then the way into blessing in a particular respect is closed. This can apply in countless human relationships of the present life, and also applies in gaining certain aspects of special reward in the next life (cf. 1 Cor. 3:10–15; 2 Cor. 5:10).

Deuteronomy 33

Moses' Final Prayers for His People

Three aspects so often recurring in prayer mingle in this rich series of Moses' blessings. One is *affirmation* or celebration of God's truth in His presence. Another is *intercession* with specific requests for different tribes. And the final aspect is *praise* to God.

Moses can be God's channel for praying blessings upon his people just as he often has done and as the priests did (Num. 6:22–27).

The three aspects of prayer above are now the focus.

Affirmations of Blessing (2–5, 12, 18, 19, 22, 23, etc.)

These are parts where Moses simply rehearses truths about God or people of Israel. This is as the psalmist affirms that he loves God, his strength, and his other blessings (Ps. 18:1, 2).

Relating to God (2–5). Moses celebrates God's coming to this people in their wilderness trek to bless them. He came as *the light of sunrise* flashing forth, breaking across the darkened earth. He came *as a holy one* from a heavenly council of angelic holy ones. He came *as one who loved this people*. And He appeared *as King in Jeshurun*. The word is a descriptive nickname for Israel meaning "the upright one," probably meant as a designation of what He wanted the people to be, as He was upright (32:4). God can be called King for several reasons. One is that His *signature* is on a level all His own in working mighty miracles. He did this in reigning at the sea (Ex. 15:18), in victory over nations (Ps. 10:16), and in commanding the Noahic flood (Ps. 29:10). Another claim to Kingship is His *superiority* to all gods and lords (Deut. 10:17; 33:20, 26). He is possessor of heaven and earth (10:14; cf. Gen. 14:19). Further is His *splendor* or majesty shown by riding across the heavens to help His people (Deut. 33:26).

To describe God in such magnificence is not only to affirm what is true but to adore Him in praise.

Affirmations continue.

Relating to Benjamin (12). Moses begins with intercession but blends this into affirmation of what God does for Benjamin. God *shields* this people and *supports* them in faithfulness between His shoulders. Of course, He gives these benefits to all of Israel (33:29).

Relating to Dan (22). God grants this tribe *safety* in avoiding disaster. The last clause can be read, "springing away from the serpent (not Bashan)," or may mean *stability* in conquering and operating from a home area in a part of Bashan north of the Sea of Chinneroth.

Relating to Naphtali (23). This is a prayerful affirmation of the tribe's satisfaction in God's provision, and in this way a tribute to God's credit. It also is an invitation for this people to take possession of the area in Canaan that Joshua will allot to them.

Appeals for Blessing

These are intercessory prayers for divine blessing on various tribes. Only Simeon is left out, possibly since it will get its possession within Judah's land area and in a sense be absorbed into that portion (Josh. 19:1–9).

A key word can summarize, in essence, the benefit Moses pleads for each:

Reuben (6). The advocacy is for God's *sustaining* of the tribe, possibly suggesting that they would be hard hit by a difficult threat, decimation, and need God's help to prosper.

Judah (7). Moses asks for *success* by God's blessing in battle.

Levi (8–11). *Strength* by God's help versus hateful opposition is the intercessor's appeal.

Joseph (13–17). For Ephraim and Manasseh, the advocate implores God to gain *success* in fruit-producing and in battle.

Zebulun and Issachar (18). The two combine in Moses' advocacy for *success* in daily life (going forth and staying at home), and *supply* from toil in the sea and on the land.

Gad (20, 21). Moses asks for blessing in *securing* Canaan, for this tribe, though living east of the Jordan, would fight to help Israel conquer Canaan (cf. Josh. 22:1–6).

Asher (24, 25). Benefits Moses pleads are *supply* with plenty, illustrated by an extra supply of oil to dip the foot in, more than just to apply in anointing. He also asks for *security*, illustrated by having bolts of iron and bronze to secure their area.

Adoration for Blessings (26–29)

In a fitting tribute, Moses draws his prayers of blessings to a close with praise to God. He sees Him as worthy on at least seven counts.

Splendor (26). The God of Jeshurun (Israel idealized as the upright one) is incomparable. For example, He shows His elegance and majesty in riding across the heavens like a king in His chariot.

Support (27). He is, as the eternal God (Gen. 21:33), two things for his people. He is a place of lodging, One to abide in, and He is a lift as His arms are beneath them to support them. No wonder Moses can be confident in His ability to answer the intercessions!

Strength (27). He provides His own strength in driving out the enemy and bidding His conquering people to "destroy."

Security (28a). He is praiseworthy for letting Israel dwell in security.

Sufficiency (28). Moses adores Him for establishing Israel with bountiful provisions of food and drink.

Salvation (29). As Israel's God is incomparable (26), God's Israel is incomparable. This people are blessed beyond those of any nation, being saved by the Lord. The salvation is no doubt both in God's temporal deliverance from Egypt and other enemies and in His spiritual deliverance through sacrifice. Their redemption by *power* and by *blood* was the theme of Exodus

Shielding (29). God deserves this praise for being His people's *shield* and *sword.* He had told Abram, "I am your shield . . ." (Gen. 15:1). He had been this for the first man of the covenant and for the descendants He also promised to bless. His shield protected them in battle, and His sword prevailed for them as it had against Amalek as Moses prayed (Ex. 17:8–13).

For battle and for behavior in all of life the people who would trust God would enjoy victory. Their spiritual salvation was not by works of merit, though God's law said much about works. As He intended, He did not design the works for gaining merit but for manifesting a walk of faith. He imputed righteousness in grace through faith (Gen. 15:6). The behavior in obeying His laws would be a product of faith, supplied by His grace enabling them.

Many clues bear out that He did enable the godly (cf. Ps. 119:1). He would fight for them (Deut. 1:30); He supplied for them, without lack (2:7; 8:3); He was near when they prayed (4:7); His word was near (30:14); He was compassionate (4:31); He gave them power for all their undertakings (8:18); He led them (8:2; 32:12); He carried them as on eagles' wings (32:11); He gave them light (33:2); He loved them (33:3); He lifted them (33:27); and He gave them a way of confession and cleansing (Lev. 4, 5).

His blessings were a key of grace to godliness, and godliness of life empowered by His grace led on to blessings (Deut. 27–30). The godly walk did not merit the blessings, but it was a life of appropriating blessings by faith. The blessings in daily life could be forfeited and replaced by judgments. This was not because the works ever merited favor, but because the people kept their eyes on God as the source faith could draw on for a continual supply of gracious help.

Principles in Deuteronomy 33 can bring remarks on this book to their finish. First, a life filled with God's blessings can deposit its treasure in one's last days along many rich paths of prayer. Second, one way for a life to leave a great legacy of love is to confer its testimony of intercessory prayer. Third, cultivate breadth in prayer to embrace every group in a leadership ministry and cry out for what is apt to each. Fourth, let praise to God grow in the human heart and caress God's majesty that is so immense and so varied. Fifth, praise for what God is can infuse the heart with fresh confidence to expect what He yet can do.

Prayer in Joshua

Introduction

The Author

Joshua or somebody strategically close to him did the writing. Joshua, of course, would not have recorded his own obituary notice (24:29–30), as Moses would not write his (Deut. 34). But Joshua could have authored most of the book. Several factors point to him. First, we see the recurring phrase "the Lord spoke to Joshua," and he is the successor to Moses (1:1; 3:7; 4:1, 15; 5:1; 20:1, etc.). Second, Joshua relays God's commands to Israel and would be the natural one to write of them (1:10–15; 3:9–13). Third, the people accept this man's leadership (1:17–18; 4:8). Fourth, Joshua continually takes the lead (2:1; 3:5–6; 6:6–8; 7:2–3; 11:16–20). Fifth, the Lord appears to Joshua to give him direction as the leader (5:13–6:5). Sixth, the Lord's commanding Joshua is compared with His commanding Moses (11:15; cf. 1:9). Seventh, Joshua charges his people to be faithful after his death (Chaps. 23–24). Eighth, the book says that this stalwart wrote certain things (18:9), and penned words of Israel's covenant in a record (24:26).

The Date

Much of the book could be finished before Joshua's departure. With Israel's exodus ca. 1447 B.C. and entrance into the land ca. 1407, completing this conquest would be not long after ca. 1400. The part added after Joshua's death (24:30–33) carries on to the deaths of the elders and Eleazar the high priest who survived Joshua. Rahab of Jericho was still living at the time 6:25 was finalized. The book is certainly before Solomon's day (16:10; cf. 1 Kgs. 9:16), even pre-Davidic (15:63; cf. 2 Sam. 5:5–9). A book in the main done by Joshua could be retouched and updated during the era of the judges.

The Title

The book is called "Joshua" because of the exploits of the man with that name. "Yahweh saves" or "Yahweh is salvation" is the meaning of the word, which is fitting in view of the salvation (deliverance) that the Lord accomplishes for Israel in the book. He has been "fighting for you" (23:3, 10). He gives the land He had promised (Gen. 12:3) for Israel to possess, or yet to possess in further victories after Joshua's day (24:8–13) as an inheritance (23:4–5). God was faithful to fulfill every promise He had made to Israel concerning this land, at least in initially putting them in it (21:45).

The Theme of the Book

Four concepts sum up the theme, the third taking the most space.

The promise. God promised Abram and his descendants the land of Canaan (Gen. 12:1–3) and keeps His word to give it to them here. He had reaffirmed His pledge to Isaac, Jacob, and Moses, and now does to Joshua (Josh. 1:2).

The presence and power. God had been present with all the patriarchs in Genesis and with Moses and his people in Exodus, Numbers and Deuteronomy. Now He says to Joshua, "I will be with you; I will not fail you or forsake you" (1:5). As the Lord who fights for Israel (Ex. 14:12) and is the supreme warrior (15:3), He now appears as the captain of His own host to lead His people to victory (5:15–6:2; 23:3–5).

The possession. This is the main theme, often repeated, whether His giving of the land (1:2) or His guaranteed possession of it (1:6) or the two combined (v. 11). Joshua's forces do possess the land in the sense of general, overall conquest (11:23). God challenges His people to possess all the individual areas (13:1–7), pledging that as they act to obey He will drive out the enemies (v. 6). The possession could have been complete, yet Israel did not in faith claim every pocket of resistance, as Judges 1 shows.

Possession takes up most of the book, as follows.

I. The Commission for It (1:1–5:15)
II. The Conquests to Gain It (6:1–12:24)
III. The Claims to Enter Into It (13:1–22:34)
God leads Joshua to allot a portion of the land to each tribe, and special city areas for the Levites within the other tribal areas. He also assigns portions to Caleb and himself.
IV. The Challenges with It (23:1–24:33)

Even more is involved in the theme.

The passion for God. All the other three key aspects above are of great importance. But at the heart of this all, God calls Joshua to be steeped in His word and obedience to it and to Him (1:8). That this is not only for the leader but for all those he leads is clear in the last two chapters. Joshua summons the leaders (Chap. 23) and the entire nation (24) to a passionate faithfulness to the Lord.

Parts of the great leader's stirring exhortations are negative and parts are positive. Joshua's challenges are to guard against intermarriages with pagans (23:12) and idolatry (23:7, 16). Positively, he appeals to the hearers to *love* the Lord (23:11), *cling* to Him (8), *keep* His law (6), *fear* and *serve* Him (24:14). Five of the vital aspects appear in one verse (22:5), and two in another (24:24). Joshua is a good model, and can call his people to do as he does. For "as for me and my house, we will serve the Lord" (15).

The response Joshua incites is the people's pledge to keep up this passion for God (24:16–28). And during the rest of his old age and the lives of elders surviving him, the people do serve the Lord (31).

The Outline

A four-point outline of the book was already apropos above as a help to discerning the theme.

The Relation to Prayer

Much of the book devotes attention to developing the theme. But prayer relates to them all. Direct references to prayer occur fewer than ten times as God gives the land He guaranteed. But almost every instance of prayer has some strategic bearing on themes foremost in the book. Observe some examples.

5:13–15. Joshua's prayerful exchange with the Lord fits with the Lord's commitment to lead in the conquests of the entire book.

6:26. Joshua led in having his people affirm in an oath before the Lord, a kind of prayer pledge, not to rebuild the destroyed Jericho or to receive dire consequences for violating his agreement. The prayer was an avowal claiming God's witnessing attestation that it would be kept, and if not the guilty party would lose his firstborn son in laying the city foundation and also suffer death of his youngest son when he erected the gates.

7:6–9. The Lord responds to Joshua's prayer concerning Israel's defeat at Ai by showing that sin is the problem. Obedience is vital in faith that gains the victory, for though God in *grace gives* them conquest, He acts in consistency with His holiness. Joshua's intercession stresses God's great name of honor and power before the nations. God answers with the need to deal with sin on the way to the victory that will uphold that name.

9:14. Travelers from Gibeon are the only Canaanite people that hoodwink Joshua's invaders. Strategic in this failure is the Israelites' neglect of prayer sensitive to seek God's guiding counsel. This definite statement of being remiss suggests that in many a case in the chapters where He positively blesses, prayer was probable even if the writer is not explicit to include it, at least by the genuine worshipers. This is as even the godly Joseph must have been much in prayer though the focus is on other details and not on his communion with the Lord (Gen. 37–50).

Opportune cases where prayer was feasible in Joshua are: in relation to battles, in priests being spiritually in sync with God to lead in strategic matters such as in Chapters 3 and 6, wisdom for Joshua and others drawing up boundaries for portions of the land for the tribes (Chaps. 13–22), affirming God's presence and Word which quicken and inspire to courage (cf. Chap. 1), and appealing for divine aid in clearing and utilizing land allotments.

Other pertinent venues for prayer are for God's fulfilling His promises, as He does (21:45), continuing engagement to obey God in matters relevant to worshipful lives as spelled out in Exodus–Deuteronomy, and any manslayer fleeing for a city of refuge entreating God to give an arrival safe from an avenging relative, and for a favorable verdict by elders and the congregation at the trial, if the death was not premeditated (cf. 20:6), Still other probable instances are in the manslayer asking help to be patient to wait for his trial and for the death of the high priest before returning home (Chap. 20), peoples settling east of the Jordan praying about their sincere intent in building an altar commemorating their bond with Him and His people west of the Jordan (Chap. 23), and Joshua beseeching God to help his people after him be true to their pledge to keep close to Him.

Prayer was appropriate to seek God's blessing on Joshua's final challenges to his countrymen (Chaps. 23–24), in the people affirming their continuing fidelity to worship only the Lord (23:6–8), gaining strength to love the Lord (23:11), and expressing gratitude for God's help delivering them out of Egypt when they prayed (24:6–7).

10:12. This is strategic as a bold prayer summons for God to work a miracle enabling Israelite victory. God gives the mighty miracle in the heavens as a sign that this triumph, even all the conquests in the book even when they do not speak of prayer, are by *His* power.

14:13. Joshua's prayer blessing in the allotment of a land where Caleb would have to overcome giants underscores the power of God helping to conquer. It is a tribute to Caleb as an example of looking to God to be with him and give the victory, and a scenario of the need of God's success in the whole conquest.

22:6–7. Joshua "blessed" the Israelites who settled east of the Jordan. Prayer is relevant in his calling down God's blessing on them.

22:21–24. People of the tribes in land east of the Jordan voice what is possibly at its root an attitude that drives them in prayer. When probed as to the motive behind their altar near the river in a place other than the tabernacle, they call into reckoning what God knows, whom all Israelites should worship. They laud Him as "The Mighty God, God, the Lord, the Mighty One, God, the Lord" in words honoring His praiseworthy nature. He, they declare, is One who knows that their aim is pure. It is not a rebel act to turn away from Him, for if so they ask "may the Lord require it" in judgment (v. 23). The altar is not one on which to offer sacrifices which ought to be presented at the tabernacle, but to witness that they belong to the same Lord and have a portion in Him just as those west of the Jordan (24). It attests that they will offer sacrifices to the Lord at His recognized worship center (27).

22:33. The people west of the Jordan "blessed" those east of the river after the latter convinced them of a sincere loyalty to them and to the Lord as the reason behind setting up an altar in the river basin. The blessing was prayer in an outpouring of praise.

24:7. Joshua's challenge to be faithful to God in the land is prefaced by such examples as this. He had answered the Israelites' prayer in peril at the sea by the awesome defeat of the Egyptians. Joshua cites the Lord Himself as saying, "your own eyes saw what I did. . . ." Such power and care by the faithful God sets up verse 14, "Now, therefore, fear the Lord and serve Him . . . and put away the gods. . . ." The answer to prayer shows a God who is absolutely worthy of their whole devotion in the land.

This introductory survey hopefully opens the way to look successively at each prayer passage in the book in more special detail.

Joshua 5:13–15

A Briefing Session in Prayer

Just before Joshua is to lead his people against the first city of the conquest, God engages him in a final briefing session to encourage him.

His Seeing the Lord (13)

A man suddenly appeared to Israel's leader. Three things are strategic in what Joshua saw.

The place. It was near Jericho. How pertinent that shortly before His people's surrounding of the city, the Lord appeared for this crucial contact. It is easy to see the relevance to the first victory in the promised land. The Lord would be ever so clear about the connection in 6:2.

The Person. Joshua did not at first know who the figure was, at least in his first of two questions (13). He would know by the Lord's direct identification in 6:2, "See, I have given Jericho into your hand. . . ." And he may well have known in 5:14 where he fell, bowed, and called the visitor "my Lord."

The picture. The figure gave a picture of his activity at the moment, that of a drawn sword ready for battle. Joshua would not have to do much searching of his memory to remember the words of the leader whose understudy he had been. Moses had said in his final words that the Lord was the sword of Israel (Deut. 33:29). Joshua had also been present to join in Moses' song of Exodus 15 that saw the Lord as the warrior par excellence (v. 3), and could still have ringing in his ears Moses' shout at the sea, "The Lord will fight for you . . ." (14:14),

To a later generation of Israel, God through Ezekiel would paint the picture of Himself as a warrior wielding a glistening sword (Ezek. 21). In that case it was not to use in Israel's help but in judgment against them for their sins. God would fight against them by using the Babylonian army.

His Speaking with the Lord (13, 14)

This passage becomes one example of prayer in the form of a *question.* In fact Joshua asks two questions, and the second realizes who the visitor is, the Lord or at least a messenger (angel) representing Him.

His concern over his intent. He asks if the man is in the fight for Israel or for their enemies. The newcomer's answer is that he is captain of the Lord's host. That in itself would tell Joshua the fighter was friendly. For as Moses' apprentice and a man attentive to God's word, he knew the Lord's *commitment* in promise to give Israel the land, and His *commission* to himself to take possession.

His capitulation to his instruction. The brief reply to his prayer is all Joshua needs. He throws himself prostrate before the captain, an act of deep reverence as his people have done before the Lord (Num. 14:3). And his second question in prayer breaks from contrite lips. "What has my lord to say to his servant?" He seems by his posture and his address to lordship to recognize He is before the Lord Himself. His first question was to know the swordsman's *side* in the warfare, the second is to know his strategy for it.

God's command in holiness (15). The Lord's *request* of Joshua is that he take off his sandals, as He told Moses before the bush that burned (Ex. 3:5). The *reason* is that the place is holy, set apart as very special by the presence of God. If Joshua had any grain of doubt who this was, it vanished now. His *response* is complete obedience and rapt attention.

God's Specifics of Victory (6:1–5)

Joshua is listening in alert receptivity to God, a watchful attitude that often accompanies prayer in Scripture. Of relevance now is the *preparation* of Jericho for siege (1), and the captain's *proclamation* of a sure victory with details on how to appropriate it. Soldiers and priests (these carrying the Ark symbolizing God's presence) are to encircle Jericho once a day for six days. A sevenfold encirclement on the seventh day is to be followed by the priests' trumpet blast, the people's loud shout, city walls tumbling down, and Israelites rushing up and in to take possession.

Prayer to God has been vital in all this prelude to the conquest. Prayer is not repeated in the text before each successive city is taken, for this passage before the first city is representative for the entire conquest.

Principles are evident here. It is legitimate to ask a pertinent question respectfully in prayer, as often in Scripture. Complete submission to hear and do God's will also finds an illustration. We, too, need to come in this kind of holy awe to hear His word and follow His strategy.

Still further guidelines are recognizable. First, God can help His praying people by weapons in physical battle or by His Word, "the sword of the Spirit," in spiritual warfare (cf. Eph. 6:17–20). Second, questions in prayer never offend God when they reflect respectful desire to find out His intent and leading. Third, to talk to God in holy, reverential awe is to submit to the power that gives the victory. Fourth, a heart to hear God's Word during prayer is as important as the tongue is to speak. Fifth, the time spent in trusting prayer before an undertaking is strategic for success in the time that follows this up.

Joshua 6:26

Prayer in an Oath

After capturing Jericho, Joshua requires his people to subscribe to an oath not to rebuild the destroyed site.

The Capture of the City

Background for this pledge is the conquest of the city and destroying it by fire.

The Commitment to the Oath

An assumption is that Joshua gained his authority for not rebuilding Jericho from the Lord. God could have said more detail to him than the book has recorded.

He calls his people to prayer in an oath. In taking the oath, they invoke the Lord as a witness to attest their promise and confirm He will bring on them a curse if they are disobedient to the promise. The spirit is, as in certain other passages (Ruth 1:17; 1 Sam. 3:17), "May the Lord bring a curse on me if I build this city." The curse is, "May the Lord require the death of the firstborn and youngest son of anybody who rebuilds it." A high price is put on being truthful.

The prayer in the form of an oath is answered in 1 Kings 16:34. Hiel of Bethel proved to be untrue. He built Jericho, and did lose his two sons to death. And that is said to be according to the word of the Lord through Joshua.

A solemn principle in this is to follow up with actions that are true to a valid promise one voices before the Lord. However, if one has uttered some rash and unfaithful kind of vow he should discern his error, confess it as sin, look to God for mercy, and repudiate one's whim as untrue to what the Lord Himself would want. The latter, a kind of foolish intention arising out of one's own error, is exposed later in Jephthah's troubling vow (Judg. 11).

Still other principles are here. One is this: to appeal for God to attest and monitor a pledge is to honor His truth as a great support to assure man's own integrity. Another is: what God puts in the heart to pray He is able to perform, whether quickly or after a long time.

Joshua 7:6–9

Passion in Prayer for God's Concerns

Joshua is an example of this here.

The Circumstances (7:1–5)

Joshua had apparently gotten word from God, nowhere recorded, that all the booty in Jericho was to be devoted to the Lord. Nothing could be kept for individual purposes (6:17). Disobeying this, Achan of the tribe of Judah held out and hid some of the things for himself (7:1). Then Israel's soldiers were soundly beaten by defenders of the second city, Ai.

The Consternation (6)

Joshua and the elders were in deep anguish, seeking God in prayer for a resolution to the calamity. They showed their grief by three customs—tearing their clothing, falling before God's presence at the Ark, and putting dust on their heads.

The Concern in Prayer (7–9)

Joshua prayed along four lines.

Failure before the enemy. He falters here, now questioning God's faithfulness, rather than questioning respectfully as in 5:13–14. He is copying some old sins of his people complaining to God. Why has He brought His people into the land to let them fail like this and be destroyed? It would have been better not to follow the Lord's will, and stay outside the land!

God is very gracious to His people's foolish words in prayer, as here.

Flight from the enemy. Rather than chasing the enemy as winners, the Israelites have fled from them as losers. Joshua can see only continued flight, apparently. At the moment it does not occur to him to do the wise thing—trust the God of great things for more great acts.

Finishing as a people. The Canaanite peoples will get the word soon enough, mass, and wipe Israel out. Israel's name will be lost in death. Joshua goes against the principle of God promising blessing to His people in the covenant with Abraham and in Joshua 1.

Fame of the Lord. Now Joshua comes to the greatest threat. What will God do for His great name when He has been dishonored by losing all His people? Joshua violates the principle of counting on God to be totally adequate to look after His own honor and also keep His word to His people.

The Counsel of God (7:10–15)

God answers graciously. He does not view the unwise remarks in prayer (sin) as necessitating forfeiture of leadership, as in Moses' sin in striking the rock. While not condoning the unbelieving attitude, He is compassionate toward His leader's concern that comes from human weakness but reflects care for His people and for Him. So He patiently counsels Joshua along three lines.

"Rise up!" Rather than crying the blues, Joshua needs to get up and deal with the real problem.

Realize sin is the issue. The reason for defeat is not that God has made a mistake bringing the people in, or that He is inadequate. It is sin. God informs Joshua of the sin that has violated His "ban" against private use of Jericho's goods, which were to be devoted to Him.

Remedy the real problem. The people must consecrate themselves to God to be fully obedient, removing the things of the "ban" that have been secretly hoarded. The sin must be rooted out, the things under the ban burned as they were supposed to be, and the guilty punished as an example that obedience is very important.

The sequel shows that Achan and his family are exposed as guilty. These are punished. God counsels a drastic step in the early days in Canaan as an object lesson to get the attention of all Israel. Let them be sensitive to His hatred of disobedience, and His meaning business about full loyalty to Him. An action that seems so severe is no more so than the discipline against a group in the Golden Calf idolatry, or against Korah for rebellion. The God who knows more about loving-kindness than we will ever know is also a God of righteousness. And He has the right to do as He deems best when it is time to judge, whether in the Genesis flood, in the plagues of Egypt, at the Red Sea, here, or at the final judgment.

Principles for prayer are clear enough in Joshua 7. One is that it is the act of a fool to use prayer to blame God. A related one is to pray with sensitivity to find God's wisdom. Joshua did not yet know that sin was at the root of the defeat, but God was willing patiently to enlighten him. Today, with a completed Scripture, wise prayer is along lines sensitive to discovering God's will in His Word, not in a new revelation.

A further guideline is evident: a man's fears in prayer may fall short of what God is or is certain to accomplish, but in covenant love God still can work the good He sees that the heart has in view. A final principle is that the reason why God is not blessing may be special sin in the camp, but prayer can gain God's remedy.

Joshua 9:14

The Sin of Bypassing Prayer

Here is an unusual passage about prayer. Joshua and those he leads neglect prayer, and get "burned."

The Ploy of the Gibeonites (3–12)

While Israel is pursuing its conquests to possess the land, their fame spreads quickly. One city, scarcely seven miles northwest from Ai, fears inevitable destruction like Jericho and Ai. So the leaders hit upon a lying trick to fool the invaders into a peace covenant.

Gibeon is the city. Its people were Hivites or Horites who had a long residence in Canaan even as early as Esau who married into the group (Gen. 36:2, 20). The ploy is for an envoy to go to Joshua's forces and pretend they are no threat to them from within the land but travelers from a far off place irrelevant to their conquest, which only desires peace.

The lie is accompanied by clever deceptions to make it work. A long trek will appear convincing when the conquering people see the Gibeonites' worn out clothes and wineskins, and check their stale bread.

God had directed His people to make peace only with peoples outside the land desiring peace, who were no nearby threat (Deut. 7:1, 2; 20:11–15). They were to enter into no peace covenant with those in the land (Ex. 23:32), but destroy them completely. The reason was that survivors could entice Israelites into worship of false gods (Deut. 20:18). Closely tied with this was the extreme wickedness of Canaanites (9:4, 5; 18:12), ripe for accountability with God. They could be a moral cancer to work Israel's gradual ruin.

Gibeon's device worked. Joshua and his men were hood-winked by the plausible claims of the travelers, and the deceptive appearances of a long journey. They were drawn into a covenant bond by taking gifts from the envoy.

The Prayerlessness of Israel (14)

No time was devoted to seeking God's counsel. God's leaders did not go to the high priest, Eleazar, for a consultation of the Urim and Thummim to be clear about the Lord's guidance. Prayer to move according to God's word had no place. And so, as the saying goes, "haste makes waste." They leaped to their decision, entered into a covenant of peace, and gave their oath in prayer calling God to attest it. In this case prayer was a bit late and also their will, not God's!

What the leaders of Israel failed to do is an old failure in God's people. The motto too often is, "go ahead with the business at hand" without a thought of prayer. Discuss the church deal without prayer, or only a brief token prayer tacked on, merely going through the motions of custom and not a passionate conviction! Rush right into the impulse to marry, take out the church loan, or give time to all the aspects of the Christian camp except serious prayer.

It was three days later before the men of Israel discovered the truth; the travelers were from about seven miles away (16)!

The Pledge of Israel (15)

Sealing a peace pact had been taken care of. Israel was not prayerful, but they were prompt. The arm of the flesh can move at swift impulse. Israel at least kept its foolish word; it pledged to let the Gibeonites live, and 11:19 remarks that this was the only city in the land they made peace with rather than destroying. It was a failure, but to Israel's credit once stung they did not make the mistake again.

A part of the covenant ceremony was a form of prayer. It involved an oath invoking God's witness to the agreement and His judgment if the Israelites went back on their word (cf. 6:26).

So, prayer failed, but not Israel's firm commitment to honor, which meant that Israel was in it for the duration.

The Pronouncement versus the Gibeonites (16–27)

Israel kept the peace treaty. They felt foolish, however, at having been duped by a tall story.

Did the Israelites track the envoy back to their city, or go with them to learn how they had been deceived? The method by which the truth dawned is not clear. But it is clear that God's people were zealous to be true to their prayer before the Lord, though grumbling against the leaders.

Also clear is that the tricked found a way to judge the sin of Gibeon's men. They subjected this people to be wood cutters and water carriers, a curse that was perpetual. It was an expression of God's will, "cursed be Canaan" (Gen. 9:26). Gibeon, spared, became a part of Benjamin's land area (Josh. 18:25). Joshua consigned it to be a Levite town (21:17). Centuries later, Gibeonites served Nehemiah in rebuilding Jerusalem (Neh. 3:7).

Principles occur. First, pray seeking God about everything, and leave nothing to neglect's blunders. Second, if you have failed in bypassing prayer, God still is there and the way is open to see that it does not happen again. Third, if believers permit prayer to slide, they can bounce back with prayer that does things right, and be glad.

Joshua 10:12

Prayer for a Miracle in Battle

The prayer failure and later prayer pledge in Chapter 9 set the stage for this prayer passage.

The Coalition of Canaan Against Gibeon (1–5)

News about Israelite demolishment of Ai as well as Jericho and then the peace pact with Gibeon aroused five Canaanite kings to mass against Gibeon as a traitor city.

The Commitment of Israel to Gibeon (6–11)

Joshua answered Gibeon's appeal for help by bringing troops against the besiegers.

The slaying by Israel (6–10). God did two things strategic to this warfare. He showed His own commitment by *counsel* guaranteeing a full victory (8), and followed up by His *confounding* the coalition soldiers (10). This time Joshua acted at God's word, probably given in a prayer consultation, and made the right move. The result was as God pledged, a great rout and pursuit of the foes.

The stoning by Israel's God (11). God further assured the victory by a miracle. He rained hailstones on the fleeing enemies, killing more by the stones than Israel had by the sword. That this was a miracle is clear in several ways. The *source* of the hailstones is said to be God; their size is large, unusual; the *slaughter* is beyond what Israel could do; the *selectivity* is distinct, only on the foes; their *swath* is broad, even reaching to other cities; their *setting* is in company with another miracle, the sun standing still; and their *similarity* is to other stones God will fling on the defiant during His future wrath (Rev. 16:21).

Prayer occurs again in the very heat of battle.

The Cry of Joshua to God (12–14)

His appeal itself (12). Joshua said this in the hearing of his soldiers, so he may have shouted the prayer out loudly. Possibly he pealed it forth to be heard above the crash of hail.

The prayer is "to the Lord," though heard also by his fighters. God is the great warrior (Ex. 15:3) and the captain who leads in battle (Josh. 5:13–6:2). So the cry is to the ultimate Commander of the soldiers and of the skies. Joshua may have intended, "Lord, this is what I pray. O sun, stand still at Gibeon, And O moon in the valley of Aijalon."

He prays not only in light of God's *counsel* pledged to the battle (8), but to His *covenant* to help his people. He also prays, finally, in view of God's *creation* and *control* of His universe. He prays trusting in an incredibly great God. And he prays in light of God's *commitments* to Israel in the past. He had worked mighty miracles in the plagues, opening the sea, providing manna dropping from the heavens and water gushing out of the rock, holding back the Jordan's waters, and throwing down the walls of Jericho.

God in His will often invites prayers for great things (Jer. 32:27; 33:3). His people speak of Him doing great things (Ex. 15:1–21; Job 5:8, 9; Phil. 4:19).

God's answer (13). The results of the prayer are threefold.

(1) The stilling of the sun and moon. Some have tried to explain this on a natural level alone. It was an eclipse that hid the sun, keeping its heat from Joshua's weary soldiers. Or it was only language of observation, that is, it just seemed to the men that the sun and moon stopped as God helped them do in one twenty-four hour day what would take longer. Others say it was lavish poetic depiction, not literal fact.

Such ingenuity fails to do justice to what is said (vv. 13, 14). So some see a local, not universal, refraction of the sun's rays, as God brought darkness on Egypt but not on Goshen where Israel was. The refraction would be similar to the event at the North Pole when the sun remains visible for all twenty-four hours by a slight dip of the pole or by a miracle of the refraction of rays.

An outright miracle by an almighty God answering prayer fits the verses and the entire flow of the Bible from Genesis 1:1 on. The God who created heavens and earth can control what is done in them, without any strain on His ability. Joshua, moved in the Lord's will (cf. v. 8), is inclined by the Lord to ask for something big, as Isaiah would challenge King Ahaz to do (Isa. 7). He commanded the sun to delay (Heb. "be still, be silent, leave off"). It did, the moon delayed consistently with this, and God gave his troops more time to complete the battle. Verse 11 shows that the victory was gained in the shade. The enemy, on the other hand, was unable to benefit from the long day due to the pressing Israelites and the other miracle, the hailstones, helping the pursuers.

(2) The success of God's people. They won with God's supernatural help. Defeat of the Canaanites was a phase of God's just judgment on people steeped in sin (9:4, 5).

(3) The scripting of the miracle. Someone in Israel, writing in a Book of Jashar, meaning "upright," commemorated the miracle. The word "Jashar" may be related to the nick-name of Israel and of Israel's God, "Jeshurun" (cf. Deut. 33). The book is possibly the same as the book called "Wars of the Lord" (Num. 21:14). Since the other passage naming the Book of Jashar (2 Sam. 1:18) records David's lament song of the bow, using poetic lines, the book may have been a Hebrew compilation of songs honoring Israel's battle leaders, their exploits, and their God.

The acclaim (14). Such a day was unprecedented. So was God's creation of the world. God here heard the voice of a man praying for a mighty act, and gave a "yes" answer. This adds one more attestation that "the Lord fought for Israel." And so it again confirmed His covenant faithfulness, and fulfilled His immediate promise of an overwhelming win (v. 8).

At all such times in the conquest, the people of Israel had reason to pray in thanksgiving. This would be as Paul later expressed it, "in everything give thanks" (1 Thess. 5:18). The prompt for gratitude in this case was that in battle against all of Canaan's kings, "the Lord fought for Israel."

Now principles surge to the fore. First, a flurry of biblical bases can lie behind a prayer of power. Second, others may hear a person's prayer of power, yet the God of power works what is sought, not the human. Third, the God who answers always has the power to do things thought impossible. Whether He does them or not depends on His will and His prompting of a person to ask in accord with that. Fourth, if God can do such great things, what is He able to do with any believer's smaller problems? Fifth, all of Canaan's kings and armies put together could not stop one God, the true God, from victory.

Joshua 14:13

Godly Joshua Prays for Godly Caleb

When Joshua has secured overall conquest of the land (11:23), and rejoiced over 31 kings defeated (12:24), he can assign land inheritances to the tribes and individuals (Chaps. 13–22).

This sets the scene for the re-appearance of Caleb, who with Joshua had believed God in scouting out the land, and gained God's passport to enter it (Num. 13, 14).

His Recall of Past Behavior (6–8)

Caleb recalls with Joshua God's blessing upon the two at Kadesh-Barnea. Only these, among twelve scouts, had returned to Israel with a report showing faith that God could give the land. This, Caleb testifies, reflected what was in his heart (7), an inward badge of honor God could read. While other scouts struck panic in their people against going in, "I wholly followed the Lord my God."

It is exhilarating when one has walked with God. He or she is refreshed to look back on that rather than unbelief and failure.

His Rejoicing in Perpetual Blessing (9–11)

Now Caleb savors the taste of blessing in the way of faith.

God's commitment for the land (9). Moses had given God's pledge of the scouted land as an inheritance. Caleb is focusing on the portion coming to him and his family. Again he mentions wholly following the Lord, but this time it is in the words of Moses and of God.

God's certification in his life (10, 11). The man of faith emphasizes two things.

(1) His *span*. God has kept him alive these forty-five more years since he had been forty at the scout report. This itself is a tribute to God. He had kept His promise that Caleb and Joshua would live to go into the land. The entire unbelieving generation above age twenty were consigned to die before entry, and they had.

Caleb's present age of eighty-five adds up correctly, a total of his forty at the report and forty-five since it. It also shows that the thirty-eight years that completed Israel's forty in the wanderings left seven up to his present moment for the conquest. With an exodus around 1445 B.C., the report was in 1443, the entry in 1405, and Caleb's present request 1398.

(2) His *strength*. Though eighty-five, Caleb can claim the vigor his body had at forty. He was similar to Moses, whose manly strength was not drained to prevent his trek up Mount Pisgah (Deut. 32:48ff.).

God had certified His blessing in Caleb's *span* and *strength*. Though the passage does not refer to it, this would be bountiful reason to go to God often in thanksgiving.

His Request for Prospective Blessing (12)

The God-honoring scout evinces an awareness of three things.

His request is all of these.

Specific about the promise. He asks for the inheritance the Lord specified at Kadesh-Barnea, which he had set his heart on while scouting.

Sensible about the problem. He knows that to capture his area he will be going against a great challenge. For the territory he wants is a region of giants, Anakim, "long-necked" men. And it is an area of strong fort-like cities. He is asking for a place of high challenge, fully aware of what he is going against.

Caleb had the spirit captured in the famous song, "Faith looks at the impossible, and cries it shall be done!"

But has Caleb become somewhat loony in these forty-five years? How can he think so big? It is because his mind is set along a certain line.

Supernatural as to the power. He can cry "give me the place where the giants are" because it is the place where His God is greater than the giants. If it is the Lord's will, as he trusts, "I shall drive them out" and this is with the Lord's backing, "as the Lord has spoken."

Did he later conquer his area? Yes, Judges 1:12–15 reports that he did! And right here in Joshua 14, verse 14 sums up that Caleb did possess the land. The Lord did not fail him.

All of this connected flow of thought leads to Joshua's prayer on that occasion.

The Result in Prayerful Blessing (13)

Joshua "blessed him" in a prayer of conferring territory to him, and so Caleb received Hebron. The blessing was a form of prayer, as the blessings the sons of Aaron invoke on the people of Israel in Numbers 6:22–27. It is in this spirit: "I appeal to God to make good this blessing to you, as He wills," a form of intercessory prayer.

After Caleb's defeat of the giants, he had his inheritance, which the writer confirms is still intact at the time he writes some time later. For the third time in the passage, Caleb's secret of success is honored: "because he followed the Lord God of Israel fully." Another significant detail is that Caleb's area is named after the greatest man among the giants. The world has its great men, as it assesses greatness. Even greater is a man such as Caleb, great in the estimate of God. And one final note is that after the conquest that delivered the land to this man of faith, the land had rest from war.

This prayer passage is the last until Joshua 22. However, Joshua's blessing in a kind of prayer for Caleb's sake possibly reflects a prayerful spirit attending *all* the claims in Chapters 13–22.

Beacons for prayer flow out of this. First, Caleb is a good example of a believer who looks at daunting obstacles and sees them grow smaller as he beholds the God who is undaunted. Second, prayer can call God's blessing on another by His grace being given (cf. Eph.

6:24). God can confer such a boon by possessions to use for His glory, or a venue of service, or an ability to be fruitful, or health, or any other aspect of help.

Joshua 22:21–29

Prayer in the Attitude

Soldiers of Reuben, Gad and half the tribe of Manasseh left their lands east of the Jordan to help others of Israel conquer west of the river. When battles had been won, they went back to join their families to the east. On the return trek it occurred to them that, divided as their lands were away from their kinspeople, they might be thought of as not in unity with them. So they constructed an altar by the Jordan.

News of the monument spread like wild fire in Israel, provoking suspicion of these eastern tribes devoting worship to other gods. This incensed the tribes west of the river, and a delegation came to call the eastern Israelites to an account.

This is where prayer appears to enter the picture.

The Provocation by These Tribes (10–20)

Israel dispatched an envoy of priests to face the eastern tribes. Phinehas, son of the high priest Eleazar, and a priest from each of the other tribes made the trek. The showdown occurred in the region of Gilead east of the Jordan.

The dignitaries from the west launched an accusation before learning the true motives. To them the altar represented rebellion against God in rivalry against His tabernacle altar, sin so serious that it could bring God's judgment as when 24,000 died over idolatry at Peor (Num. 25:9). Then all Israel might have to suffer the consequences.

The Motivation of These Tribes (21–29)

They clear themselves of guilt and explain their real motives prompting the memorial. The first thing they do is point attention to God in a kind of praise. Their words are filled with tributes to His greatness, dear to their hearts. He will attest the validity of their intent—the true worship given to Him. He is, to them, "The Mighty One, God, the Lord, the Mighty One, God, the Lord!" They say the descriptions of God twice for intensity and emphatic effect. He alone is worthy. They call Him to validate the purity He knows, and call on Israel also to know the true purpose for setting up the altar.

The site is not even one of sacrifice, in rebellion against God's stated will that Israelites offer at His central dwelling place. If they have put up the altar to defy God in such a way, they invoke God's judgment on them (23). This is a summons in calling on Him in prayer.

Then they spotlight the pristine purpose. The altar is not for sacrifices competing with those at the tabernacle in Shiloh, but to stress unity with the western kinsmen in worshiping the Lord. It is a memorial of "witness" reassuring them that they have part in the same Lord and will bring offerings to the right place in obedient respect (27).

The Validation by Israel (30–32)

Aware now of the legitimate motives, the priestly delegation breathes a sign of relief. Now they are confident that the act is not one to invite God's judgment, but one to cause celebration because this brings honor to Him.

The Jubilation of Israel Before the Lord (33, 34)

Prayer again leaps into expression. When the priests return home issuring a good report, the people of Israel *bless* God. That is to say, they pray voicing jubilation. This would suitably be in *praise* for who He is, worthy of unified worship by western and eastern peoples. And it could be in *thanksgiving* for the worship He had inspired in their countrymen.

The principles here are priceless. First, it is strategic to hear the evidence before impugning others' motives. Second, it is crucial to clarify prayer motives if this will promote unity to the Lord's glory. Third, it is helpful in a prayer life to set down memorials at times to witness desiring a part in God. It can help the person himself, and give joy to others. Today it may be done using prayer memory cards at the breakfast table, putting pictures on the wall in memory of the Lord, and the like. Fourth, it is right for believers learning of others' steadfastness in God to express jubilation to God. Too often, the proper zeal of others is used as a pretext for envy at their testimony, as if they think of themselves as superior.

Other principles also are relevant. One is this: it is a blessing to people whose prayer can sincerely call on God to attest that their allegiance to Him is pure. Another is that it is an inspiration to be sincere when testifying to oneness of heart with others who pray to God. And a final guideline is cogent: it is a blessing to witness those whose hearts are devoted to God and who offer Him praiseful gratitude for what He means to them.

Joshua 24:7

A Cry of Fear in Prayer (cf. Ex. 14)

Joshua in his extreme old age (23:1) is challenging the leaders (23) and all Israel (24) to remain steadfast in the Lord. He reviews some of God's acts of faithfulness in their past, and in this reminds them of their fathers' cry in peril when the Egyptian pursuers locked them in a seeming death-trap.

In this way, Joshua in his closing challenge has memory of prayer as one of the urgencies on his heart. In the light of the God who answered prayer at the sea and was faithful in many other ways, he calls his people to look to Him in respectful awe and serve Him (14).

One final principle can finish thoughts on the book. It can be a fresh trumpet signal to pray just to recall past prayer when God has heard and answered by His rescue.

Prayer in Judges

Introduction

The Author

No potential writer is mentioned, and scholars can only make guesses as to a possible candidate. The Talmud and early Christian tradition choose Samuel, a reasonable possibility. For Samuel would distinguish himself as a priest and prophet as the days of the judges, when Israelites had no king (cf. 21:25), merged into the early days when they did have a king (cf. 1 Sam. 7–15).

The Date

The words of 17:6 do suggest a time after Israel's monarchy has begun: "In those days there was no king in Israel." The phrase occurs four times (cf. 18:1; 19:1; 21:25). Also, the fact that Jebusites still have control of the city that would become Jerusalem (1:21; 19:11–12) implies a date before David's army captured this site (2 Sam. 5:6–9; 1 Chr. 6:5). Internal evidence in these ways points to a date during the initial times of the united kingdom (1050–1000 B.C.), possibly by Samuel during the reign of Saul as king.

The Theme

Apostasy, or failure through sinful compromise, is a dominant focus. The first three chapters establish spiritual departure from the Lord soon after Joshua died in 1:1. Israelites left altars to pagan gods in disobedience to the Lord (2:2). They committed evil and served other gods (2:11–13), did not listen to judges God raised up to help them (2:16–17), did not continue to serve the Lord even after He used judges to lead them to victories (2:18), and went through a cycle of prayerful cries in repentance, God's defeat of enemies, and their own chronic slide back into sin. In this they repudiated the challenge of Joshua 22:5—to obey God's commandments to love the Lord, walk in His ways, hold fast to Him, and serve Him with all their heart and soul. They also violated what Israelites themselves pledged, to serve God and obey Him (Josh. 24:24).

In the midst of this, another theme also is persistent. It is God's power to deliver, displayed through the various judges. These God raised up in different sectors of the promised land at various times against enemies there. They were not judges as in courtrooms today, but leaders in arbitrating civil questions and in military action, and sometimes gave counsel (cf. 4:5 and the chart of these leaders below). God's graciousness to prayerful cries for help is shown by such phrases as "the Lord raised up a deliverer" (3:9), "the Spirit of the Lord came upon him" (3:10; 6:34; 11:29; 14:6, 19; 15:14), "the Lord routed" an enemy (4:15), and "the Lord is with you" (6:12; cf. v. 16).

The Relation to Prayer

Two broad orientations help in approaching what the book says about prayer, or any subject. These are the main emphasis (i.e., the theme), and a synopsis of steps in the outline.

The significance. This comes into focus by emphasizing the theme of sin (perversity) and God's sufficiency (power) in delivering from sin's effects.

(1) Sin is quickly evident in summaries of the era in 1:1–3:6. These provide a general preparation for the book, and from them five expressions of sin become obvious. The five are:

One is the *incompleteness* of faith in obeying God's directive to possess tribal inheritances allotted in Joshua 13–22. The passage gives examples of this failure to trust God enough and go all the way in conquest (1:19, 27–34). And so the enemies still had a foothold and remained, as God had warned, to be thorns in the Israelites' sides.

Second is *ignorance* of the Lord in the new generation after Joshua and the elders died (2:10). With this was a forsaking of Him (2:12, 13).

Third is *inattentiveness* even to listen to the judges God raised up to lead them, and in this a failure to be receptive to God's word (2:17). At times the people are receptive to God's word (cf. 2:4).

Fourth is *idolatry* in giving devotion to gods of Canaan, rather than to the true God (2:11, 12; 3:6, 7, Chaps. 17–18). This is not only clear in the introductory chapters, but at various times throughout the book, as illustrated in the bizarre drift from God in Chapters 17–21.

Fifth is *intermarriages* with pagans who influenced Israelite commitment to false gods and corrupt practices (3:6).

Sin is obvious at times in men God raised up as leaders. An illustration is Gideon, who after great exploits in God's service, delivering his people, succumbed to idolatrous self-worship in making an ephod such as the high priest alone was to wear (8:24–27). Samson was ensnared by lust for a Philistine (16:1, 4). A Levite priest from Bethlehem is an example of what seeking God in prayer ought not to be, in a life sold out to idolatry and available for hire (17:7–13; 18:1–6). Prayer appears evident in 18:5, "Inquire of God," and that the priest did make some religious inquiry, even if it were a mockery, seems reasonable from his answer giving guidance in verse 6.

(2) God's sufficiency to deliver from the enemy is an even greater theme than sin. His power to free from defeat and bondage under enemy control is evident along at least three lines.

First, the reader frequently sees statements that when the Israelites cried to God for deliverance, *He raised up a deliverer*. He frees them in 3:9 (and cf. other cycles of sin and prayer in chart below). Second, statements in these cycles also say that *God gave them rest* (3:11, etc.).

(3) Prayer is frequent. Words communicating with God begin in 1:1 with an inquiry to secure guidance in battle and end in 21:2–4 with weeping over the threat of the tribe of Benjamin being blotted out. About 25 references to prayer appear, these in 13 of the 21 chapters.

Prayers come in a variety. Some are petitionary pleadings for God to work deliverance (3:9, 15; 4:3; 5:31a; 6:6–7, 17–18, 36–39; 10:10, 15; 16:28), or petitions to gain information (13:8, 15).

Other aspects of prayer are praise (5:2, 3, 9; cf. 20:28; 21:4), affirmation before God of truths (5:4–30; 6:15, 22; 15:18), intercession (5:31b), a vow (11:30–31), questions pressing to receive guidance (1:1; 13:11, 12, 17; 15:18), or confession (10:10; probably 2:4).

The Outline

A structure and overall synopsis of the book flows like this:

I. Introduction and Summaries (1:1–3:6). This describes trends of the era, such as conquests when the tribes possess their inheritances, and sins that work against their full or continued blessings.

II. Cycles of Sin and Deliverances by the Judges (3:7–16:31). A chart below provides a convenient glance at the main details under twelve leaders.

III. Samples of Sin During the Period (17:1–21:25). The writer furnishes some cases that illustrate the recurring statement that there was then no king over Israel and "every one did what was right in his own eyes" (17:6; 21:25; cf. 18:1). More can now be said of the cycles of sin, judgment, prayer, and deliverance. These come in Section II. above, which develops seven different cases or cycles. "The Lord raised up" some deliverer is a phrase which often recurs. The deliverer is called a "judge." Judges did not rise to leadership over the whole of Israel, but in particular areas of the tribal inheritances that were the "hot spot" at a given time. The chart shows this.

Since the judges were in various specific areas, it is not possible to figure a chronology of the total period strictly by adding the different years in all the cases. There were undoubtedly overlaps in the times of judges' leadership in the different areas. However, Judges 11:26 mentions 300 years, and it is possible to figure plausible parts of the picture. The 300 years fit within a larger span of 480 years (1 Kgs. 6:1) from Israel's exodus (Ex. 12:40, 41) to Solomon's fourth year, ca. 965 B.C. Here is a possibility: 38 years from the exodus to Heshbon; 300 from Heshbon to Jephthah in 11:26 here; possibly 5–6 more years for Jephthah (cf. 12:7); 40 for Samson; 20 for Eli; 20 for Samuel; 15–16 beyond that for Saul; 40 for David; and 4 for Solomon, making 476–480 years in all.

The chart shows details of the sections in the book, all of which develop prayer featuring Israel's cry and God's answer.

Sin	**Judgment**	**Prayer Leader**	**Area**	**Years**
Idolatry	3:8, Mesopotamians; 3:9	Othniel	Judah	40
Sin	3:12, 13, Moabites, Ammonites, Amalekites, Philistines; 3:15	Ehud	Benjamin	80
Sin	4:2, Jabin of Canaan; 4:3	Deborah, Barak	Ephraim	40
Sin	6:1, Midianites; 6:6	Gideon	Manasseh	40
Sin	No verse, Canaanites;	Tola	Ephraim	23
	10:1, 2; 10:3–5	Jair	Manasseh	23
Sin	10:6, Ammonites,	Jephthah	Manasseh	6
	Philistines; 10:10, 15, 16	Ibzan		7
		Elon		10
		Abdon		8
Sin	13:1, Philistines; 16:28	Samson	Dan	20

These are the cycles in the Book of Judges. Other judges are Eli and Samuel (1 Samuel). It is now time to look at prayer passage by passage.

Judges 1:1

Prayer for Guidance in Conquest

This seems to be a prayer relating to all the individual tribal conquests of their specific land allotments. It is in a spirit of seeking God's will in how to initiate the possession of each area. Going to God for His leading in battle is also important elsewhere (20:27–28).

Israel's Asking for Guidance (1)

The circumstance of the prayer. It is after Joshua's death at 110 (2:8; cf. Josh. 24:29). Since general possession of Canaan was achieved in the Book of Joshua while the leader still lived (11:23), Israel has waited some time before starting the more thorough possession of particular inheritances. But the time need not be lengthy, since Joshua was already quite old (Josh. 23:1).

The content of the prayer. It is a good prayer, seeking the will of God. The people are sensitive to His input on which tribe should make the first penetration to root out the Canaanites.

God's Answer in Guidance (2)

His plan for Judah. God answers in consistency with His choice to give Judah leadership among the tribes (Gen. 49:8–12; cf. 1 Chr. 5:1, 2). Judah is to possess its area first.

His pledge to Judah. God says, "I have given the land into his hand." The possession is as good as carried out, by God's promise.

Israel's Appropriation in Possession (1:3–36)

Their prevailing over the enemies. Sensitive to God's direction that Simeon's area be within Judah's (Josh. 19:1), Judah's leaders invite Simeon's warriors to join in the possession.

At Bezek, conquest was successful against the king, Adoni-Bezek, who acknowledged God's retribution on him to be just (7).

Next to fall was Jerusalem (8), then Hebron (10) and its environs. Caleb's inheritance was here. He promised his daughter Achsah to the man who conquered Kiriath-sepher, and Othniel claimed the prize. Other victories followed, such as in the Philistine cities Gaza, Ashkelon and Ekron (18).

The secret of conquest is in verse 19: "Now the Lord was with Judah, and they took possession of the hill country. . . ." But the victory sweep was incomplete.

Their problem in the valleys (19). Despite wonderful triumphs, Judah's men seemed to have failed here in faith to possess fully. The verse says, "but they could not drive out the inhabitants of the valley because they had iron chariots."

Of course, *God* was as able in the valleys as in the hills! He had not had any problem with the chariots of Egypt, or the army of Amalek, and the thirty one kings of Joshua 12. Similar failures to go all the way in faith and its victory are noted for Benjamin, Zebulon, Asher, Naphtali, and Dan (21ff.).

The lack of faith is one valid explanation. At the same time, to be fair, to some degree the Lord Himself chose not to give complete victories for another reason (Deut. 7:22). He saw wisdom in permitting some peoples to remain to keep the wild animal population from becoming a hazard. Still a third explanation is that God gave Israel only partial success to test them even with Canaanites still around (Judg. 2:21–23; 3:1, 2, 4). He wanted the new generation now coming on to have further opportunity to learn to fight well. And He tested His people to see what was in their heart. Would they be true to Him and not succumb to false gods, if temptation still urged its enticements? The writer shows in 2:2, 3 that disobedience by going soft on idolatry is one reason for His not driving the enemy out.

Before leaving this theme, further details in Judges 2 have a vital bearing. The new generation after Joshua's death does not know the Lord and His mighty works (10). They show this by worship of other gods and forsaking the Lord (11–13), even disobeying Him by persistent idolatry and rejection of His judges (16, 17). And compromising intermarriages with the idolaters (3:6) gave impetus to the apostasy.

Prayer in 1:1 is on a right note. A principle is a propos: those who pray need to guard their spiritual lives as time passes, prioritizing the presence of God who gives victory, and not forsaking Him. In the months and years of battle with the enemy, they need vigilance to keep close to God (cf. Eph. 6:10–17), or the power that prayer can have is worn thin or lost.

The particulars of other tribes (21–36). Seven other tribes besides Judah and Simeon receive mention of partially possessing their areas. Dan even beats a retreat (34), and later will migrate to a new tribal possession at Laish north of the Sea of Chinneroth (Galilee), as in Judges 18.

Judges 2:4

Confession

Certain clues indicate that this passage reasonably includes prayer. This will soon become evident within the exposition.

The Conviction (2:1–3)

The Angel of the Lord scores the people for their sin. The remonstrance is set against a backdrop of God's gracious faithfulness to deliver them out of Egypt and into the promised land (v. 1), and His appeal to worship Him, not pagan gods (2). Their response has been disobedience by falling into league with those devoted to other gods and letting their idol altars remain to entice them. God's reply to this is that He will not drive the enemies out; rather, they will be obstacles to thwart the Israelites, and their gods a means of drawing them into heathen worship (3).

The Confession (3)

The blunt words from the Lord stimulate hearts to acknowledge their sin. They show this by lifting up their voices, probably in confession, and showing how they are moved by their weeping. To posit prayer here seems feasible in light of two considerations. First, the same phrase, "lifted up their voice and wept," occurs in 21:2, where the record includes actual words in prayer (v. 3). Second, the people sacrificed to the Lord (2:5), as those in 21:4 built an altar and offered sacrifices.

The sacrifices in 2:5 would reasonably be as those in 21:4—burnt offerings and peace offerings. Significantly, as in Leviticus 1, burnt offerings included the entire animals as a display of the entire devotion of those whom the gifts represented. In such a case, a return to whole-hearted spiritual dedication to God was the idea. The peace offerings were in a tender spirit of thanksgiving for the peace God made possible by His gracious goodness (cf. Lev. 7:12–13).

The Change (6–7)

A heartfelt and prayerful repentance seems evident from clues here. The people went from this fresh meeting with God to serve Him all the days of Joshua and elders who outlived Joshua. After this repenting generation died, a new cycle began of the next generation drifting into sin (10–13, 17), God allowing enemies to defeat them (14–15), and subsequently raising up judges, giving deliverance (18). This in turn was followed by further cycles of spiritual backsliding (19).

In their plunge into sin, the people's "groaning" (2:18) possibly was even expressed in prayer crying for another deliverance, as in the pattern of 3:9, 15; 4:3, and so forth. The pressure might be a means of jolting them to come to their senses, as is often true in human lives.

Principles follow from this. First, keeping close to God is the norm to find His triumph over obstacles, but those who drift to other reliances forsake their own blessing. Second, as in the burnt offering, God desires a sinner to dedicate himself wholly to Him in undivided devotion.

Third, as in the peace offering, the Lord wants people to experience His peace and exult in thanksgiving to Him.

Judges 3:9, 15

Desperate Cries for God's Help

The cases in 3:9 and 15 will be examples of a pattern here. Later instances are integrated with exposition of Deborah and Barak (4:3) and Gideon (6:6–7).

The Testing (3:1–7)

The fact of it (1–4; cf. 2:21–23). God in giving conquests in the land allowed some Canaanite nations to remain, to test the faith of Israelites in different places. The test was whether they would obey His Word given through Moses, and by faith in this gain further victories (2:22; 3:4).

The failure under it (3:5–7). First, a survey of Canaanite enemies is given (5). These are Hittites, Amorites, Perizzites, Hivites, and Jebusites. Second is a review of a slide by the Israelites (6–7). They contracted marriages between their daughters and sons with pagan partners, capitulated to serve their idol gods, and in general committed what was sinful in the Lord's appraisal. In this they forgot the Lord and wrote Him out of their lives.

The Trauma (3:8–30)

In the present chapter this comes in two examples.

The first case is in relation to the king of Mesopotamia, an invader and claimant to a part of the land (8), and the second instance is against the Moabites (12). Both examples follow the same pattern.

The pressure. In verse 8 God was angry due to His people's sin, and He permitted the Mesopotamians to conquer them. In the second exhibit, when the Israelites again did evil, God allowed a coalition from Moab, Ammon, and Amalek to defeat them (12–13).

The prayer. In both situations the people in jeopardy "cried to the Lord" (9, 15). This was obviously prayer beseeching Him to break the enemy domination and set them free. In the first case, God mercifully empowered Othniel to be the judge, leading His people to break the Mesopotamian yoke (9–10). This allowed a rest as free people for forty years (11). In the second case, the Lord brought Ehud into command as the judge; he killed Eglon the Moabite king and led Israel to gain its freedom from the federation. Ehud's accomplishment gave his people rest for eighty years (30).

These are displays of God's merciful kindness to answer prayer with victory in battle.

His people turned their backs on Him in pitiful disloyalty, but apparently God used the pressure He put upon them to bring them to repentance. They became tender before Him as in 2:4 and 21:4. In both cases the delivering judge died (11; 4:1), and after a long time people of that area, probably a new generation not tender to God, drifted again into denying the Lord (3:12; 4:1).

Consider principles. First, when God allows obstacles in life as tests we ought to face by faith and allegiance to Him, we should seize the opportunity to stay close to Him (cf. Deut. 8:2). Second, even where failure has darkened a life, God is merciful when hearing a sincere cry for rescue out of the human mess. It is better to look to Him than continue in a defeated existence. Third, God in compassion is able to answer prayer by raising up a leader to help in a crisis.

Judges 5

A Prayer Song of God's Victory

Songs in prayer have already appeared at great moments in Israel's history—after God's overthrow of the Egyptians at the sea (Ex. 15), and before going into the promised land (Deut. 32). Now Deborah and Barak have led Israel in God's great victory over the Canaanites (Judg. 4).

Aspects of prayer are distinct in the song. The prayer is a song of *praise* exalting the Lord for His help (3). It confers *blessing* on Him (2, 9). At times it is an *acclamation* of tribute to God for His work and for people He used. At times, Deborah and Barak, who sing the song, directly address the Lord (4). Both *petition* and *intercession* combine in verse 3.

The Prelude to the Prayer (Chap. 4)

Canaanites oppressed Israel and held them in bondage for twenty years (3). People of Israel cried out in prayer (3), and God moved Deborah, a prophetess, with a command to go against the enemy (4, 5). She summoned Barak, who was reluctant to take the lead (8). He was willing only if Deborah went too; it was plain to her that he was not willing to be manly, and she said that though he went, the Lord would defeat the opposing king, Sisera, by a woman (9).

Ready to attack the enemy, Deborah still was taking the lead in her battle *cry* to attack and her *confirmation* that God would give the victory (14). Barak and the army surged into action, and the Lord routed Sisera's host. Sisera himself escaped alone to the tent of Jael, a woman who let him collapse to rest from his battle weariness and then killed him with a tent-peg driven through his head. In Barak's lack of faith to go into battle, God did turn the enemy leader over to a woman to defeat. All Barak could do was enter the tent, gaze upon the finished king, and probably feel the smiting of his own heart for so small a faith (22).

God, ultimately, was the giver of victory (23). It is on this note that the song is so appropriate.

The Praise in the Song (Chap. 5)

The two leaders laud God with praise for raising up leaders and their people to press the attack (2), and for things He did in Israel's history. They remember things that today would be in believers' prayers from the scriptural accounts: His faithfulness in the wilderness trek (4, 5), during times of earlier judges (6), and in their own day.

In the last category the praise is for Deborah's rise in difficult times to help her people (7), and for God's help though Israel lacked weapons (8). Tribute is paid to the commanders and soldiers (9, 12–18), to the Lord (10, 11, 28–30), and to Jael (24–27). The song even includes a detail the angel of the Lord gave the singers, a curse on those not willing to fight together with their people (23).

As a conclusion to the prayer song, the two leaders break into petition for two things (31). First, they pray for *success* the Lord can give against all His enemies. In the analysis, all who oppose Him will perish, so the request will be answered. Second, they intercede for the *shining* of those who love the Lord. That, too, God is sure to answer with a "yes." In some sense He can do so in the present life (Ps. 119:105), and after this life His people will shine "as the stars" (Dan. 12:3) and "as the Sun" (Matt. 13:43).

Principles surface. First, prayer crafted to song and music can ring within the spirit and also be a delight to God (cf. the Psalms). Second, a prayer song, like other Scripture, can be a kaleidoscope expressing a variety of parts in talking with God. Third, a prayer worthy at God's throne can exemplify case files that exult in His triumph, and expectations in Him that abound with hope. The same is true in songs of Exodus 15, Deuteronomy 32, 1 Samuel 2, and the many examples in the Psalms.

Judges 6:7

A Prayer in Desperation

Seven years of Midianite control left Israel devastated of produce, animals, and homes, due to retreat to mountain hideouts.

The Pressure from the Midianites (1–6a)

Overwhelming numbers of soldiers filled the land during the invasions. The enemy came to keep Israel in subjection by destroying crops and taking animals they needed for a reasonable livelihood.

Moses had married Zippora from Midian. Now, possibly a century later, these people were enemies of Moses' people. Moses' forty years as a shepherd had been followed by forty years in Israel's wilderness journeys and some years into the era of the judges.

Joining the Midianites were Amalekites, who had been Israel's enemy in Exodus 17:8–13, and other desert marauders to the east.

The Prayer of the Israelites (6b, 7)

Crying in desperate prayer for God's help is, as the chart earlier shows, an illustration of what happened over and over in the sin cycles.

God's Proclamation to the Israelites (8–10)

God has sent a prophet, whose name is not identified, to reason with His people. The Lord speaks through him (10).

God has delivered them (8–10a). The message stresses two things. First is a focus on what He has done for Israel. He sprang them free from bondage in Egypt, then gave them victory to possess the land He promised. Second is a reminder of *Who He is* and, in light of this, how they should not fear the enemy. The victory could continue to be theirs except for one thing.

They have disobeyed God (10b). This follows up the sin that prefaced the account in verse 1. No mention is made of Israelite repentance, although smarting from such pressure it is probable in some degree. The spotlight is turned on another theme, God's gracious answer to prayer, by raising up Gideon to lead in shaking off the enemy yoke.

Now reflect on the principles. First, God is amazing even in tender mercy (cf. Ex. 34; Ps. 103), for He answers prayers of the needy who throw themselves on Him. How great is His compassion in helping those who take His blessing, then "double cross" Him, and appear back at His door pleading a new crisis! Second, how painfully men suffer what sin costs them, when they could pray always with true reliance on God and walk in blessed success (cf. Josh. 1:8; Deut. 1:8; 1 Sam. 2:30; John 14:21–23)!

Third, God often answers men's prayers through other people (cf. Gideon here), shaping them in faith to display how He can bless. Fourth, even one of foggy misconceptions such as Gideon can be led out of these and rise to greatness in being the Lord's useful channel. God frequently uses the unlikely to be His understudies to do the unbelievable—Abram, Moses, David, Elisha, Jeremiah, Amos, Jonah, Peter, Saul of Tarsus, and others. For little is much when God is everything.

Judges 6:11–24

Prayer in Dialogue with God

Prayer has already sometimes appeared as a conversation with the Lord. Abraham did this, for example, in Genesis 18, and Moses in Exodus 3–4 and 33–34. A later notable illustration is Jeremiah in his Chapters 14–15.

The Appearance of an Angel (11, 12)

This is the Angel of the Lord, later identified as the Lord Himself (14, 15, 16, etc.). He had appeared often before, as in Genesis 16 to Hagar.

The coming is to Gideon, son of Joash the Abiezrite. The latter name is from Abiezer, a son of Manasseh (Josh. 17:2), as a family had grown up taking their designation from him. Gideon is an example of the Midianite pressure. He is beating wheat out of the stalks in a wine press in a dogged effort to get it hidden before the enemy could grab it.

When the messenger speaks, his emphasis is on the Lord's *presence with Gideon.* He says more to drive this home as the dialogue progresses. At the same time he compliments the farmer, calling him a valiant warrior. This seems to be in anticipation of what he will make Gideon as time passes—a man of strength to lead his people out of the crisis.

Gideon's Asking about the Circumstances (13)

He is perplexed. If the Lord is present with His people, why the servitude to an enemy? Why has He not worked miracles as in the fathers' days? The *question* form of prayer quickly leads to the *affirmation* form. Rather than performing miracles to deliver Israel, the Lord has deserted them into oppression. Gideon's complaint is often repeated, "What have you done for us lately?"

One answer was already obvious in the unnamed prophet's words (10). It is not clear that Gideon was one of the audience who heard these. The present visitor takes another tack with Gideon.

The Lord's Answer of His Presence (14)

Now it becomes clear that the angel is "the Lord." He calls on the man of Manasseh to go in his strength and free Israel from the tyranny. The strength He is speaking about appears to be that of His own resource, for He asks, "Have I not sent you?" That is, you will have all that you need if I the Lord am sponsoring your effort. But Gideon is slow to pick up on the certainty of victory.

Gideon's Appeal to His Own Weakness (15)

Triumph that seems obvious in God's presence and power is brushed aside by the threshing man. The thing on his mind is not God's mighty power but his own pathetic weakness. That is all he sees. How could *he* do this preposterous thing, deliver Israel? He has two counts against the plan, both ruling him a bad risk. First, he hails from a family of nobodies in Manasseh. If that does not disqualify him the second surely does, for he is his father's youngest child.

Gideon sounds like Moses mouthing his five excuses (Ex. 3–4).

The Lord's Answer about Full Resource (16)

He makes two points about a sure victory. First, His *presence* guarantees it. However incredible the odds, it only takes one to win if that one is God. His presence in blessing had been the secret of success for Abraham, Isaac, Jacob, Moses and Joshua. Now it is all Gideon needs. And so the Lord can give his second assurance. His *pledge* is a rout of Midian "as one man." The Lord can defeat 135,000 soldiers

(8:10) as easily as He can stop one man (cf. Isa. 37:36). Since now it finally sinks in that the battle is the Lord's, not just Gideon's, Gideon is ready to talk on that basis.

Gideon's Asking for a Miracle (17, 18)

If God truly is ready to show such grace to him, Gideon requests a sign confirming that *God* really is the one giving the pledge. He is a careful man, a timid man. Possibly behind his caution is the thought that if he gets Israel's hopes up that he will lead in victory, he must be sure. Otherwise he will place them in still greater peril, if not death, and step forth to ruin himself.

Moses had needed signs to give him courage against the pharaoh. Gideon needs them also.

The Answer of the Lord to Wait (18)

The visitor agrees to remain until Gideon has time to go get an offering to lay before him for his sign. This would involve at least an hour or two. The Lord's *consent* to wait to perform a sign is followed, in due time, by His *consuming* Gideon's animal and bread offering (20, 21).

This done, the Lord vanishes from Gideon's sight.

Gideon's Acclamation of the Lord (22)

God's consuming of the offering has brought Gideon to a recognition. The Lord Himself is the messenger he has beheld.

It is frequent in God's word, and surely a blessing to God, that those who pray call out His name. How often in Abraham, Jacob, Moses, and David this facet in prayer recurs! Just to meditate on who He is and acclaim Him is one of the main phenomena in utterances to Him. It can be a fragrance like Aaron's sweet incense to God, and a tonic to the one praying. Just to think of who He is boosts the spirit; it also helps in other parts a prayer may include.

God's Answer of Peace to Gideon (23, 24)

Peace in the heart is one of the great by-products resulting from prayer that God honors. This is why God showed Paul that in praying about everything, the peace of God that surpasses all human understanding does guard duty over the heart in Christ Jesus (Phil. 4:6, 7).

Here, three steps stand out in Gideon's prayer life.

God's poise. He gives, with the sense of His presence and the power of His action, a sweet balm of restful composure. It must have come to Gideon's consciousness like the refreshing of a gentle rain bringing verdure in the earth. All was well to the man who had been living in awesome anxiety of the invaders as he toiled to save the little wheat he could.

God's promise. The poise is based upon the promise. A man whose life had been one of fear need no longer be in turmoil. God pledged, "you shall not die." It was a reassurance that, having seen the Lord in some sense face-to-face, Gideon would not perish. And in its wider context, it quite possibly also braced Gideon against the very real danger of death at the hands of the enemy. Now he could be sensing that the Lord had not really abandoned His people (13), but was the very giver of peace in the face of perilous threat.

Gideon's portrayal. The man visited with such encouragement feels a powerful prompting to portray this Peace-promiser. He *constructs* an altar to His honor and *calls* it "The Lord is Peace." This tribute to God joins many others so far in Scripture, acclaiming Him as so many things—the Most High God, the everlasting God, the God of Bethel, the Strong One, the Stone, the Shepherd, the great Shaddai, the Banner streaming over Moses, and on and on.

It is a key principle in prayer to testify to God in thanksgiving for what He is and does. It is also helpful yet to others to lift His blessedness high to enhance their worship too. It is like the theme in Psalm 107, "let the redeemed of the Lord say so . . . ," and for so many reasons! In Gideon's case the testimony continued to bear influence when a writer penned this episode.

Still another principle is that prayer can be carried on, at times, in dialogue with the Lord. In Gideon's day the Lord appeared personally at His will. After Scripture is complete, praying can intersperse words to God with listening to words from God already in His word. This expression springs from the word of Christ dwelling richly (Col. 3:16).

Yet other principles appear. One is this: when what we see is weakness, God can lead us to do what others see as strength. Gideon learned this; so did Paul (2 Cor. 12:7–9). Further, when we believe that the battle is the Lord's, we can see Him break upon the enemy in winning power. A final principle is that God is worthy of the names His servants put on places of worship to honor Him, here, "The Lord is Peace." In Exodus 17, God is Moses' banner. And we see other facets about Him summed up in names of churches: "The Way," "Covenant Church," "Grace Church," "Church of the Open Door," "Church of the Good Shepherd," "Hope Memorial Church," "Church of the Rock," and others.

Judges 6:25–40

Prayer Fervent for Certain Confirmation

Gideon further *proclaims* God's glory, *prepares* for attack, and *prays* for assurance in the famous episodes of the fleece.

Gideon's Proclamation of God's Aloneness (25–32)

Acting on God's directions, Gideon tears down his father's altar to the false god Baal and erects over it an altar to God's glory. This, with help of a bull to pull the altar down and ten companions, also included a bull for a burnt offering. This offering, fully consumed as in Leviticus 1, was Gideon's picture of full human surrender to God.

The next morning, men of the area expected Gideon's father to discipline his son. Instead, Joash felt moved to an extraordinary reaction. He asked if a god worth anything was so weak that he needed the men's help. And he affirmed death for any who took it on themselves to contend in place of Baal's inability. In response to an act as defiant as the ruination of the god's altar, if Baal were worthy of any worship at all, he ought to show power on his own behalf. The implication is that if he is unable, none should count him as a god to honor.

Joash's reaction gave rise to his new, second name for his son, "Jerubbaal." The meaning is "Let Baal contend against him," which, when used of Gideon, would be to recall over and over the failure of this god before God. Before the battle against the Midianites, this is a battle of the gods, and God wins. He triumphs as He would later for Elijah on Mount Carmel (1 Kgs. 18).

The Preparations for Attack (33–35)

Midianite soldiers with Amalekites and others massed in readiness to crush Israel. Three points form the emphases. First is the *massing* of the enemy, second the *might* of the Spirit of the Lord coming as clothing upon Gideon, and third the *mobilizing* of Israel's fighters. Gideon summoned the men of the area, and also dispatched messengers to call other able men of Manasseh and three other tribes.

The enduement by God's Spirit upon Gideon is also in this book said to have come on Othniel, Jephthah, and Samson. Since even other judges also acted in God's power, they too probably enjoyed this blessing for their successes. An example is Ehud, whom God raised up in answer to prayer and who told the enemy he had "a message from God for you" (3:20). Ehud told his people that the Lord had given the enemy into their hands (3:28). Likewise, Shamgar's extraordinary ability, striking down 600 Philistines, seems to be from the Lord (3:31), just as Samson's in single-handed victory over 1,000 (15:15).

The Prayers for Assurance (36–40)

Gideon has seen God's sign already in a flame of fire consuming his offering and heard firm promises that He is with him to assure victory. Still, he seeks two further confirmations that God will guarantee success, both by signs relating to his fleece.

The problem in this. It is just this. Has he not had sufficient witness to go ahead confidently? Is he failing in faith, and due a reprimand?

One approach is to blame him and call this a failure. Many have taken this path. Another is to say he showed timidity and some lack of a sturdy faith, as all believers do more or less, but that God did not think of him as a failure. That this can be the case is possible along several lines. First, God nowhere speaks negatively of his prayers; to the contrary, He acts positively in each case to provide the further encouragement. Second, even Moses needed several steps by the Lord to prepare him for facing his own people and the Egyptians. Probably most potential leaders would. Third, God Himself volunteers even a *further* sign in Chapter 7. He dispatches Gideon to scout out the Midianite camp and lets him overhear an enemy dream of God and Gideon defeating the invaders.

The prayers. First the petition is for dew on the fleece and dryness on the ground about it. The next morning God gave this exact answer, a miracle, just as His care of His people in history had involved miracle after miracle. Still, Gideon asked for the opposite, dew on the ground but dryness on the fleece. Again God worked it precisely.

Needing confirmation may not seem reasonable to some. From the Lord's standpoint, utter power puts victory against the enemy beyond any doubt. But from a new leader's perspective, given the difficulty men share in coming to complete faith, it was a different matter. It had, by Gideon's time, been a long while since God gave victories in Joshua's day and in the period of certain tribes reviewed in Judges 1. Men can lose the sense of God's triumph over enemies under the gradual dulling influence of sin. Not only that, but the sheer magnitude of the invader was awe-inspiring. A leader would need to be very, very certain of his assets before venturing to risk himself and his countrymen against such a huge fighting force (cf. 6:5; 8:10).

Those who pray face two problems. One is in mustering full faith in God, even though He is overwhelmingly sufficient. The other is in adequately overcoming the tendency to maximize the power of the odds that seem against victory.

This is, for the moment, to Gideon's credit, no matter how human fears weighed on him. Once God gave him the two fleece displays, he moved in prompt, early obedience fed by his new assurance (7:1). Even then he would be glad for yet more reassurance (7:10–15), and God would show tender regard for his fear, without rebuke.

Meditate on guidelines. First, the power is not in the object, but in God who uses it. This is true of the tree (Gen. 2–3), the rod of Moses, the brazen serpent, Aaron's rod that budded, the breastplate, the Ark of the Covenant, Gideon's fleece, Elijah's mantle, the sundial of Hezekiah, and so on. Second, the Spirit, all powerful, can do astounding things when He works through a weak human channel who prays. Third, when a servant of God needs a confirming gesture, such as in a fleece, God can meet him in ways to nudge him on to unfaltering steps of faith. God graciously chooses the way that reassures, and does not rebuke.

Judges 7:15

Prayer in Grateful Awe

Prayer itself waits until verse 15, but actually the entire context flows in close relation to prayer in Chapter 6 and here.

The Temptation of Human Resources (1, 2)

God speaks to Gideon while his army is encamped south of the enemy. He acts to guard against His army of 32,000 (v. 3) having a pretext to boast in victory that *their own adequacy* had won the day. As in Psalm 20:7, some trust in horses, some in chariots, and one can quickly add his own brawn and brains. But the right attitude is to remember the Lord trustfully.

The Trimming of Human Resources (3–8)

Gideon's troops dwindled to 300 by two causes.

By dismay. The commander permitted any soldier who was afraid to fight to go home, so 22,000 dropped from the ranks.

By drinking. God felt that 10,000 were still too many. For when they won, they could too easily assume that their own prowess was the edge, and take the glory from Him. He gave Gideon a test to eliminate the majority. Only "everyone who laps" like a dog should be retained. So, 300 did this, scooping water up with their hands as a dog uses its curled tongue as a dipper. This posture showed discipline in alert readiness for instant battle. By contrast, the 9,700 who sank to their knees to drink were unfit, "dropping their guard" to surprise attack. Their stance would require too long for them to get up and defend.

So 300 men remained to go up against at least 135,000 (8:10).

The Triumph by God's Resources (9–25)

Despite God's reassurances, Gideon was still quaking in his sandals to lead his contingent against an army so overwhelming. God gave him another encouragement of victory in verse 9, one of nine between 6:14 and 7:14. Yet the Lord realized His servant's human fear, and provided him with one last confirmation. He sent him to scout out the Midianite camp. While he lay in hiding, he overheard a sentry's dream told to a companion.

God had given the enemy soldier a dream of Israelite victory to spread apprehension in the ranks. In the dream, a loaf of barley bread tumbled into the resting camp, flattening a Midianite tent. The dreamer's partner came up with the interpretation right away, helped by the Lord to grasp the fitting picture. Grain was what the Israelites had that the enemy liked to take, and so grain was the apt subject to depict a turnabout victory over the invaders. The sword of the Lord and of Gideon would defeat the outsiders.

Back in concealment, Gideon bowed in worship. Prayer was undoubtedly the core of this. Quite rightly the leader expressed *adoration* in thanksgiving and praise to God who dispatched him to the outpost and divulged this dream as a symbol of triumph. Thoughts and words formed in the silence of his scouting stealth overwhelmed Gideon with encouragement. As God assured in verse 11, his hands were strengthened, his heart as well. Gideon and a servant stole back to their own camp, realizing the truth the psalmist would later put into words: "You did make me bold with strength in my soul" (Ps. 138:3; cf. Isa. 40:29).

The *summons* to the scouting mission and the *strengthening* for the attack is followed by a *strategy* to hit the enemy by surprise. All 300 men surround the enemy at 10 p.m. (v. 19) with trumpets in their right hands and torches inside jars in their left. At a signal, they simultaneously blow the trumpets, shout "For the Lord and for Gideon," then shatter the jars so that the lights flash all around.

At the changing of the guard for the 10 p.m.–2 a.m. shift, the timing was opportune. Guards just spelled would report all was utterly quiet; they would return to their tents, and the new guards would take up sentry, completely assured the night was safe. Inside the tents, still moving about in the darkness to get bedded down, the retiring guards could be mistaken by awaking men as attackers already inside. The loud crash of noise—trumpets and shouts—against the former stillness would strike terror into men who were so surprised. Glaring lights every direction their panicked faces turned in the confusion would only add one awful message. The enemy, massed in overwhelming numbers locking them in a death trap, would make short work of them. As body struck body in the chaos, men took the body as an enemy, whether in tents, in brush, or on the trails. Every man's sword slashed to save himself, with little hope of seeing the light of another day.

The Lord Himself "set the sword of one against another even throughout the whole army" (22). Gideon's prayer of praise-filled awe was followed by pursuit, capture of several leaders, and their execution.

Later, to his credit, Gideon declined an Israelite offer of kingship, exalting the Lord as their rightful king (8:23). But he was inconsistent. He asked for gold trinkets, made an ephod, placed it in his city Ophrah, and it became an idolatrous snare to him and his family. In some way it may be connected with the offer of kingship and a halfway honoring of God. He would not accept kingship to guide the people in further triumph, but he would grant them another means of God's blessing, one tainted by pagan notions out of his father's household. Instead of allowing the ephod to be, as

God willed it, a prerogative of His high priest giving guidance (Ex. 28:6–35), Gideon associated it with himself, independently of the priest. And so it lost its real relation to God, who should give the guidance and get the glory, and became an object worshipped in itself, in idolatry.

Rather than helping his people in the end, Gideon hurt them. His was a contribution that did Israel much good (8:35), but he did not go all the way in faithfulness, trailing off in idolatry and multiplying wives (30). He did not lead his people to give God the glory (33).

Principles bid for attention. First, the God of all resources can win even when He shows His servants He does not need the vaunted resources they might fancy offer the best hope. Second, human servants that God uses are not perfect, consistent examples, but flimsy, variable figures who bounce from the godly to the ungodly. So Gideon, and so Abraham, Moses, David, and others. If God waited until we were absolutely perfect, He could not use us until He brings us to ultimate glory. He uses the weak things to accomplish mighty things, and to Him properly all the glory belongs. Paul said, "we have this treasure in earthen vessels [pots of clay]," limited human bodies (2 Cor. 4:7).

Judges 10:10, 15

Confession after Idolatry

This is another episode in the sevenfold cycle of sin, confession, and deliverance. After Gideon, the untrue kingship of his son Abimelech, and judgeships by Tola and Jair with continued idolatry, Israel lifted desperate cries to God for rescue from Ammonite oppression.

This adds little not essentially summed up about such cycles earlier, but it introduces Jephthah's judgeship. Prayer, not only of the people in general, but by Jephthah, enters the picture now.

The Pathetic Defection from the Lord (10:6)

Worship of gods from five areas replaced a true allegiance to the Lord who had done so much for Israel.

The Painful Distress before the Ammonites (10:7–9)

Eighteen years of servitude to Ammonites in the area of Gilead caused anguish. Added to the regular domination were special strikes by attacking Ammonite forces penetrating into Judah, Benjamin, and Ephraim. The agony was intolerable.

The Prayerful Desire before the Lord (10:10–16a)

Confession of sin (10, 15). The acknowledgment is right to the issue. In it is an awareness of Who the Israelites have wronged (the Lord) and what they have worshiped (the Baals). Verse 15 shows further elements. One is readiness to receive whatever discipline God may feel is wise for them, not as punishment but as ministering purging to cleanse (cf. John 15:2b). Second is a request, a petition for rescue from the enemy thralldom.

Confrontation over sincerity (11–14). At first the Lord reviews the chronic insincerity of the past, His deliverance time and again, and Israel's idolatry. He also refuses to play along with the syndrome of selfishness that is more concerned about the distress to them than the defection that offended Him. By His hesitation, God wisely lets them weigh their motives.

Contrition in seriousness (16a). Now the people mean business, in some reality at least. Three aspects mark this. Two are by the confessing people—sweeping away false gods that have been no help, and serving the true God. The third is by God; He is ready to answer prayer.

The Powerful Deliverance By the Lord (10:16b–11:33)

God's covenant compassion was in action. He raised up Jephthah as His leader and gave a significant victory, "a very great one" (11:33). The section includes the *ascendancy of the leader* (10:16b–11:11), *his arguments with Ammon* (11:12–28), and *his answer for Israel* (11:29–33).

This moves to the Lord's answer of the prayer in 10:10, 15 by deliverance, and within it a new prayer by Jephthah.

His power in the Spirit (29). God is faithfully answering prayer, preparing His leader. The Spirit of the Lord came upon Jephthah, clothed him with sufficiency, as He had done for Othniel, Gideon, and probably others like Shamgar, Deborah, and Barak.

In prayer as prayer ought to be, Scripture often coordinates the Spirit, the word (cf. vv. 15–27 here), and prayer, as in Ephesians 6:17, 18.

His prayer (30). This is prayer expressed in the aspect of a vow. Jephthah pledges his own fulfillment to God if God will give what he asks. As God is to act without failure, so is the one framing the vow. In Jephthah's case, feeling the human pressure of producing for the people he leads, it is a foolish and unnecessary pledge. God had often responded to prayers that did not extend vows. It is unwise to bargain with God when one cannot control details to meet his hopes.

If God gives victory over Ammon, Jephthah will offer to God the first thing that meets him from his home when he returns.

His prevailing (32, 33). God's answer in victory was a double answer—to Israel's prayer and to Jephthah's.

His Pledged Deal with the Lord (34–40)

The vow Jephthah entered into was a rash one, but having made it, he kept it at great cost to his daughter. She shocked him when she was the first to meet him from his home, and he must have been instantly jolted into realizing how hasty his little "deal" had been. While it had been legitimate to pray for help in battle, his terms had not been careful in light of possibilities.

He had vowed to offer what met him as a burnt offering (31). He did follow through in giving his daughter, and she submitted to this. Two main views explain this differently. Some reason that he turned the girl over to be a perpetual virgin. Verse 31 is rendered, "shall surely be the Lord's, *or* I will offer it up as a burnt offering." The view sees virginity in verses 37 and 39 and escapes his offering the daughter in death, for human sacrifice was against God's will (Deut. 12:31).

The other view says that he meant a "burnt offering" and, startled when the daughter came forth, felt obligated to see the vow through. The translation of a simple Hebrew letter ***waw*** involved in verse 31 is far more often "and," in Old Testament usage, not "or." Also, the word for offering is normal for a "burnt offering." This act came in an era of bizarre acts, even inconsistencies by leaders whom God otherwise empowered. He did not condone *all* that a man He used did. Gideon (8:27) and Samson are examples. This view sees the daughter as sad because death would prevent marriage and children (37, 39). It agrees that God was not pleased with Jephthah's rash pledge, or his offering. Jephthah was to blame.

Whatever the solution, the incident came in a dark time when many human decisions were not what *God* prompted. Still, God uses people who are very imperfect, then and now. Scripture faithfully tells the truth, whether decisions are by His direct leading or men's foolish failures.

A principle of prayer is to be very careful in making promises to God. If one has erred, it is better to line up with God's word, acknowledge the wrong, and humbly seek God's mercy, rather than force through an act that His word condemns. In the first view, Jephthah still was inconsiderate of his daughter's opportunity for fulfillment.

Judges 13:8

Prayer for Parenting a Son

Parents of the child who would grow up to be the mighty Samson hear of his birth from an angel and ask for more of God's will regarding him.

The Announcement of Samson's Birth (1–7)

Another cycle of Israelite sin, God-inflicted servitude to an enemy (this time forty years), and need for a deliverer is the setting.

An angel told the mother-to-be that her barrenness will be broken by her having this son. He is to be a Nazirite (cf. Num. 6), so special restrictions pertain to the woman's pregnancy and the son's life. She shared with her husband Manoah, of the tribe of Dan, what God's messenger told her.

The Asking for God's Will in the Son (8)

Manoah *petitioned* the Lord to allow the messenger to come again, this time to "us." His *purpose* is to receive counsel on what to do in God's will for the boy. Probably the *provocation* of such a prayer was even with special urgency. An extraordinary announcement of a son ahead of time in itself suggested that the son was meant for an extraordinary career. The parents longed to fulfill their submission to God entirely.

The Appearance of the Angel Again (9–23)

This, now, is the answer to prayer. One needs to remember that the prayer itself had been prompted by God's will in the first appearance.

For the second time the heavenly messenger appears to the woman, but she has summoned Manoah so that both can meet with the angel. Manoah takes the lead in the dialogue prayer that follows.

First, Manoah *presses the visitor with questions*. Is this the same person who made the promise to Manoah's wife? Yes. Taking for granted that the promise will be fulfilled, what are the heavenly designs for the son, that is, his style of life and his service? The reply focuses on the Nazirite plan.

Second, Manoah *petitions to prepare a kid* for the messenger. The response is that the visitor will not eat this as food, but can accept it as a burnt offering meant for the Lord. It would appear that the visitor is God, as Manoah will later realize (22), but at this point Manoah only knows the guest is from the Lord, not that he is the angel of the Lord. The designation has often meant the Lord Himself, as in Genesis 16 to Hagar and Judges 6 to Gideon.

Manoah presses a third query in prayer, "What is your name?" and explains his good motive in asking. They wish to honor him properly when the promise is fulfilled. To this the messenger responds with his own question, which implies that this is the Lord. "Why do you ask my name, seeing it is wonderful?" Jacob in wrestling with the angel had gotten a similar mysterious reply about the name, apparently a name finally incomparable for the human mind. Manoah's sense that God was there (21, 22) may well have started to form here, to be definite in a short time. He offered the burnt offering on a rock.

As the angel visiting Gideon had struck fire to his offering and consumed it, the angel now ascends in this flame. In both cases, the visitor then vanishes.

More prayer apparently follows. The two people fell prostrate in worship, probably in praise affirming something of the majesty of God. Then, filled with a sense of this majesty, Manoah was able to say to his wife, "We shall surely die, for we have seen God," that is, seen something of His splendor, up close. As wives often do, she had a bit of wisdom apt for the moment. If the Lord meant to kill them, He would not have received their burnt and grain offerings. He also would not have shown such splendors nor spoken such informing words—in short, answered prayer.

The coming and ministry of Samson is in this way prefaced by God's revelation and prayer within His will.

The Arrival and Advance of the Son (24, 25)

God brings the child, a son as promised. His name, Samson, is from a word meaning "sun," and the parents may or may not have thought it fitting in view of the bright career. After all, God had done extraordinary things in announcing him, and in some way a bright future beckoned.

In a way undefined, the Lord blessed the boy as he grew toward manhood. Above all, verse 24 clarifies, there came a time when the Spirit of the Lord was evidently stirring him. In some fashion He was moving the young man to act in His power. When the Spirit has been mentioned in the Book of Judges, it has always been in relation to God moving one of His judges to deliver His people.

One principle of prayer in the angelic appearances has been clear. Manoah prays seeking the will of God according to the word of God, in this episode by a messenger from heaven whom he comes to realize is God. Another guideline is evident. It is natural to ask God questions when one does not grasp how He will work, and God does not put this sincerity down. A final maxim is a propos. God's name is "wonderful" beyond what any mortal can understand. The depths of perfection, beauty, and power of His majesty are more than mind-boggling (cf. Job 38–39; Isa. 40; Rom. 11:33–35).

Judges 15:18

Prayer to Satisfy Thirst

Samson is well into his career when God now gives him a marvelous victory over the Philistines and he becomes thirsty from the struggle.

His Exploits in War (14–17)

Samson had turned 300 foxes loose in Philistine grain fields, carrying torches on the tails between 150 pairs. The fiery destruction, itself suggested in Samson's mind by a Philistine father taking away Samson's bride, drew enemy retaliation. Samson killed many Philistines who attacked him (8), but his own people later turned him over to the enemy. He burst their bonds by mighty surges of his arms, grabbed a fresh jawbone of a donkey, and killed 1,000 more.

His Entreaty for Water (18, 19)

Four steps sum this up.

The request itself. After a battle that may have taken several hours, as soldiers kept coming on, Samson felt a raging thirst. So he prayed, the tenor of this being the essence of a thankful tribute to God for victory and then a petition for a drink. The petition comes in a question. God has shown His favor by such a deliverance against the Philistines. If so, how can it be consistent with such favor for the instrument God has empowered to die, lacking a drink, and fall into enemy hands after all?

God's resourcefulness. God's answer is by a miracle, causing a hollow place in the earth to split and flow with water. This act of power fits consistently within the pattern of great provisions an almighty God of creation and covenant has been supplying all along for His people, often in relation to prayer.

His refreshment. A mighty warrior must have had a mighty thirst to quench. Finally he felt his drained strength returning. God's answer was deeply satisfying.

His remembrance. Samson was so impressed by this miracle, on top of God-given strength to deliver his people, that he fitted a name to the place. It was related to prayer as the "spring of the caller." At the same time, the name would remind those who heard it of the God who answered the caller.

Three principles are prominent. One is that prayer in a new need can receive its encouragement in a great thing God already has done. The one who prays needs to recall His faithfulness in his own life, or in His Word, and take heart from this. Second, Samson called specifically for what he needed, no beating around the bush (or the battlefield). Third, as often stated, God is not *appalled* by a question that gropes for an answer, but *affected* to work a compassionate provision. He is a good example of His own counsel to give even an enemy food or drink (Prov. 25:21; Rom. 12:20), and His pledge of reward for giving a cup of cold water in His name (Matt. 10:42).

Judges 16:28

Prayer for One Last Victory

Samson was, by God's endowment, "the Hercules of the Hebrews," a mighty Tarzan able to do extraordinary things by his physical prowess. Yet he did not live up to his full potential, for he played with sin and squandered away the secret of his success. The final scenes of his life are these scenarios.

His Pathetic Compromise (1–20)
His price of compromise was the beauty of a woman. He fell the way many men have fallen, giving in to a bodily appetite for pleasure in illicit sex. First he seeks out a prostitute at Gaza, and his God-given physical strength helps him escape from the city patrol later. Then he lounges in the lap of Delilah at Sorek. She plies her wiles, winds him around her finger, and pries from him his secret of strength. It is his hair, a sign of his Nazirite dedication to God. When he sleeps in her betraying embrace, she snips the hair off, and once awake he is powerless against the Philistines she has lurking to pounce on him.

He did not know that the Lord had departed from him. Of course, he had departed from the Lord beforehand.

His Painful Calamity (21, 22)
How fitting are God's judgments so often in Scripture! Samson squandered away the opportunity to fulfill God's maximum blessing in his life by his compromise of the eyes. He kept yielding himself to sin, here a little, there a little. Finally, sin's boomerang did him in. His eyes had been the focal point of nourishing the sin. Now God permitted the enemy to take away his eyes. He also was bound with chains, slapped into prison, and made a grinder of grain.

Somebody once remarked that "sin binds . . . sin blinds . . . sin grinds." Samson found it all out the hard way.

Their Prayerful Credit to False Gods (23–25)
Philistine conquerors and their people praised their god, Dagon, as if he had delivered Samson over. The situation was turned upside down. God had judged Samson; Dagon had no power at all. But the God who could have given Samson continued victory and gained His people's praises was replaced by a god that was no god.

Amidst the praises, some Philistines thought of a second idea. Let praises turn to pleasure. Let Samson be brought in chains to perform where they could jeer at him.

His Prayerful Calling on His Own God (26–30)

The area. The place to which the Israelite hero was brought was between the pillars. This is strategic in light of archaeological discovery clarifying Philistine architecture in their great public halls. A second story had balcony railings from which assembled guests could look down on a scene below. Two pillars below were strategic in supporting the upper floor.

The appeal. Samson knew this architecture. He asked the attendant guiding him in his blindness if he could feel the pillars and rest upon them.

The assembly. The victory celebration had lured a full house. The top leaders of the enemy were assembled, and in addition to those below, about 3,000 men and women gazed down on the former Hebrew muscle man.

The asking of God. God had announced Samson ahead of time and reared him to be His judge against the enemy. Samson had forfeited much of what he might have done. But now, in one last prayer, his whole heart is in the asking. Just once, just this time, is all he pleads. He petitions for God's remembrance of him, of his personal plight and possibly his purpose in God's will. He also asks for strengthening, as he has known it before, one against a thousand. At one time, in dying, he asks for an avenging on the wicked enemy. They were exceedingly corrupt (Lev. 18), ripe for judgment. And they had done a very wicked thing to Samson, putting out his eyes.

First he appeals to God, and then he acts with God's strength that has come again. Grasping the two middle columns so vital to the whole structure's stability and balance, his muscles bulge with all their might. The pillars buckle, and the entire structure gives way in turn, the second story collapsing in a roar and an outcry.

More Philistines perished in this one episode than all Samson had stopped in battles.

Prayer principles? A simple one is that, with contrition of heart, a believer who has lost former usefulness to God may still pray to be used again, as God wills. God is not through with us in this life until He is through with us. A second and greater principle is to deal with sin resolutely and early in prayer with faith's obedience. If so, the believer can realize victories all along, not have them held up until so late, or never gain the great ones.

Judges 17:1–6

Prayer Compromised with Idolatry

Chapters 17–21 of Judges give examples of flagrant sin. These were during the era when no king reigned and every man did what was right in his own opinion, even if skewed (v. 6; 21:25). Prayer in the present case illustrates a bogus use of the Lord's name in prayer, while steeping the life in details of idol worship that denies Him. This went on in Israel, as it so often does today.

The Prayer Mouthed (1, 2)

A son of a woman in Ephraim's tribal territory named Micah stole silver from his mother, but returned it, confessing his wrong. He wanted to be free of the prayer curse she had uttered against the thief. Getting her 1,100 silver pieces back, the mother elatedly seeks to turn her curse prayer into a prayer for blessing.

She mouths an invocation of the Lord's name that appeals to Him to give blessing to her son. God is willing to forgive and fill with blessing. But in this case the prayer is from a life soon seen to be infested with things that are as sinful against God as the theft. Candidly, things the people in this home are tolerating are thefts too—robbing God of the worship and obedience due only to Him.

So, the prayer is counterfeit, saturated with sin, and as in Psalm 66:18, the Lord will not honor it.

The Phoniness Manifested (3–6)

What inconsistency! While pretending to pray for the son's blessing from God, the mother fosters false worship that brings God's rejection, not help. At least five steps of outright disobedience to His word are manifest. First, the woman has dedicated all 1,100 pieces to the Lord, but insincerely trims that to 200 pieces, even this for a God-insulting purpose. Other sins are the images which the Lord repudiated in the ten commandments, the gods that also are rejected in the ten commandments, the ephod such as God authorized only for the high priest, and consecrating an Ephraimite in place of a son of Aaron to be priest.

The ephod was clearly the high priest's wear (Ex. 28), and only those in Aaron's line were by God's will to serve as priests (Ex. 28:41; Num. 3:10). Having a private priest wherever one chose was in violation of God's directive to set apart forty-eight special cities as Levite residences.

A principle is obvious for prayer. The kind of prayer God hears with blessing is in obedience to His will. This is in a worship true to Him, not undercutting Him while mouthing prayer before Him. He does not tolerate men giving His glory to another, as His servant Isaiah says later (42:8).

Judges 18:5–6

Prayer by an Idolater

A Levite priest named Jonathan (18:30) who moved from Bethlehem to Micah's home in Ephraim's territory (17:5–13) shows that so-called worship can be a counterfeit. This was apparently also the case with Balaam, a false prophet, in Numbers 22–24. (cf. that passage), and later with certain scribes and Pharisees in the ministry of Jesus (Matt. 23:14; cf. 6:5; Luke 18:11; 20:47).

The Setting (17:5–13)

Micah hired the Levite to serve as his own priest, urged on by his philosophy that "the Lord will prosper me, seeing I have a Levite as priest" (13). Five Danite scouts visited Micah during their search for land where the tribe could settle. The Levite told them that Micah had hired him as his priest, that he had found a nest egg (18:4).

The Seeking (18:5–6)

The request. The spies of Dan jump at their opportunity. They ask the priest to "Inquire of God" whether their present direction in scouting out the land will be successful. It is not said but seems probable that these scouts had not asked God for guidance before even setting out on their journey.

The reply. The passage does not explicitly say that the priest prayed to God. One possibility is that the priest thought fast and pretended to gain the Lord's answer. Another is that he complied by seeking the Lord's wisdom to protect his pride as a spiritual leader before the visitors. The latter assumes prayer, or else fakery. If prayer, it is that of a compromising man who is not serving God in one of the 48 cities for priestly ministry, but has sold out his soul to idol worship. God is emphatically against false gods (Ex. 20:3–5; Josh. 23:7–8; 24:15, 23; Judg. 2:2, 12, 15), hears those who fear Him (Ps. 33:19), is far from the wicked, and honors the prayer of the righteous (Prov. 15:29). The priest keeps his wits about the contact with God that the visitors request, is opportune, and comes through with a glib response crafted to please. At the same time, the Lord in providence can answer mercifully to give an inheritance to the Danites, in spite of the false worshiper's failings and the Danites' sins. They were guilty of not trusting God to help them possess the original land given as their inheritance near the Mediterranean in Philistine territory west and northwest of Judah's claim (Josh. 19:40–48; Judg. 1:34–36). How different they were from Caleb, for example, who looked to God in faith for help to conquer lands (Num. 14:7–9; Josh. 14:6–14; 15:14–17). The people of Dan were spiritually adrift to fall into still other sins (cf. below).

The Levite "yes man" gives the Danites counsel, "Go in peace; your way is before the Lord" (Judg. 18:6), or "has the Lord's approval" (NASB). When Dan's fighting men get their scouts' report and are en route to Laish, the five scouts steal the idols and other objects of worship from Micah's shrine (v. 18). They superstitiously put their trust in these things, as Laban had depended on his idols (Gen. 31). The Levite again prostitutes himself for hire, going with the Danites in a sinful service as their idolatrous spiritual leader (19–20). A threat of death to a pursuing Micah sends him back home empty, having lost all around, without the genuine God and stripped even of his worthless gods (22–26). What he put his confidence in was a pitiful denial of what his name means, for Micah is a contraction of Micaiah, "Who is like Yahweh?"

After taking control of Laish, the army gave the rebuilt city the new name Dan, set up a religious center infested with idolatrous objects, and trusted in these as well as in the counterfeit priest (27–31).

Principles for prayer are not difficult to see. First, how wise to worship only the true God at whatever cost, yet how foolish to follow the lure of worshipping false gods. Second, a person may fancy he is in a way of grand success while in false worship, but the truth is that sooner or later he must give an account to the One who really is God. Third, one who is for hire to whoever has the highest bid for his services as in prayer is serving self, not God. Fourth, those who do not follow the Lord to gain victory by faith in Him (the Danites) may have a worldly triumph, but it is just self-deceiving without God.

Judges 20:18, 23, 26–28

Praying in Failure, Then Success

An interesting example here shows two cases of prayers followed by defeat, then a third prayer that gains victory.

The Atrocity in Benjamin (19:1–30)

A gang of Benjamite hoodlums in the town of Gibeah take turns ravishing a visiting Levite's concubine, using her until she is dead.

The Levite sends messengers with a macabre summons to the other tribes to avenge the atrocity. He dispatches a part of her dismembered body to each tribe, with the messenger supplying only some details to stoke a fire to right the wrong.

The Assembling against Benjamin (20:1–17)

An army of 400,000 masses, hears the Levite's complete details, and sends investigators throughout Benjamite territory to confirm the crime and demand a handing over of the guilty. A refusal leads on to war.

The Appeal for God's Will (20:18–48)

Prayer now precedes the warfare.

The prayers that fail (18–25). Two of these occur.

(1) The first prayer (18–22). The men of Israel, probably some representatives, went to Bethel to inquire of God. All they do is ask who will go first in the battle. God's answer is Judah, as in Judges 1. The result, however, is disastrous, as Benjamin strikes down 22,000.

(2) The second prayer (23–25). This time it is said of those who prayed that they also wept until evening, and prayed in a question seeking whether to engage in battle. God answered to go, but again the result was a calamity as 18,000 fell.

What was wrong when God had answered their questions the first two times, yet they had suffered such defeats? It is not altogether clear, but some clues seem to provide a plausible explanation.

The prayer that avails (26–48). This third prayer vigil in verses 26–28 is marked by new indications of seriousness in those who pray. Sincere weeping can be a part of seeking God's will, but more. Now fasting all day shows a sacrificial quest to have the Lord's leading. More than that, the prayer summit is impacted by the first offering of sacrifices. And, significantly, these involve burnt offerings, completely consumed, symbolizing the worshipers' total dedication of themselves. And with these are peace offerings, associated with gratitude for peace with God through His faithfulness (cf. Lev. 7:13).

A greater seriousness seems evident. A real dedication appears to enter the scene. It is similar to the principle of meaning business with God in 2 Chronicles 7:14 in self-humbling, prayer, seeking His face, and doing an about-face from wicked ways. God will hear, forgive sin, and heal the land.

Another new detail, not mentioned before, is a specific seeking of God's mind through consulting His priest. Phinehas in the line of Aaron leads in prayer, seeking the Lord's leading whether again to fight the Benjamites (28). He gets God's answer for Israel to attack, and His pledge of a victory.

Results of prayer are far different this time. Victory is present, and it is great, bringing the conflict to an end. Benjamin's numbers add up reasonably to the 26,700 (v. 15). For 1,100 fell the first two battles when Benjamin won, and verse 48 may be a part of that figure; 18,000 fell in verse 44, 5,000 in verse 45, then 2,000, in verse 45; 600 survived in verse 47, adding up to the 26,700.

Principles vital in prayer are apparent. Pray in real, aroused seriousness. Also, fasting is often a vital element in examples of God's word. Third, true-hearted dedication to God (Rom. 12:1) as well as thanksgiving (cf. Phil. 4:6; 1 Thess. 5:18) are facets on which God sets much value.

Judges 21:2–4

Praying for God's Will, Yet Doing Man's Will

Prayer in the aspect of a question is prominent here.

Their Prayer for God's Counsel (2–4)

Their previous plan (1). The men of tribes dealing with Benjamin about sin had pledged by oath not to "give" daughters to marry any of the 600 surviving Benjamites (cf. 20:47). Prayer was possibly a part of the oath itself, as often. Now they realize that the remnant can fade as a tribe unless the men have wives. Benjamite women had died in the total sack of Gibeah (20:37).

Their present prayer. A meeting convenes at Bethel because God's ark is there at the time (20:26, 27). Delegates give some time to prayer ("until evening"), sitting "before God" as He met with them via His priests and the ark of His presence. Their concern was evident in tears and words. Weeping in true submission does touch the God of tender mercies, as later in Hezekiah's tears when life seemed at an end (Isa. 38).

Then the question presses their sadness and caring about Benjamin. Though they dealt forthrightly when the tribe would not face up to sin and get right with God, they still did care. Why has this happened, that one of the tribes so long important to God and in Israel's kinsman bonds should be missing, or virtually cut off (v. 6) from the tribal fullness?

Their passion for God's interests and Israel's even motivates offerings (4). The significance of the two kinds is no doubt the same as seen in the prayer burden of 20:26.

We do not read of God giving His will in a clear answer to the prayer. What His counsel would be is difficult to say as His wisdom is so far beyond our own. We do discover, however, that Israel apparently does things its own way by its own wisdom as the chapter continues.

Their Planning by Their Own Counsel (21:5–25)

It does not take the delegates long to figure a scheme. They are still concerned for the Benjamites (7). Since some of Manasseh, in the Jabesh-Gilead region east of the Jordan, had not cooperated in discipline on Benjamin, Israel destroyed the inhabitants except for 400 women who had never been married. These women they gave to the Benjamites, but 200 still lacked wives.

Israel could not break its pledge (1) and provide their own daughters to the other 200. They maintained the sanctity of the vow, keeping their word. But they advised the remaining men of Benjamin to wait in hiding near an outdoor dance in Shiloh and each grab a wife from the young women who came to the dance.

The passage does not give God's approval of destroying Jabesh-Gilead or of the device to snatch wives. So the Israelites act on the logic that they do not "give" wives and violate their oath, but can give them in another sense by taking advantage of families in the Shiloh area. So can be the reasoning of men, and 21:25 explains the surprising maneuvers of men. They can even find a scheme to get around an oath, yet keep the oath. They can look good in their own eyes and convince themselves that they look good in God's by keeping a pledge they made.

A couple of principles sift from this. First, we sometimes need long periods before God in searching prayer to know and follow His wisdom. Such extended vigils may not be seen often in our day of rush, but they are frequent in God's Word and in church history. The examples can challenge us to take time to be holy, even in prolonged grappling to establish our steps. Second, those who pray may forfeit God's direction if they cease too quickly to inquire of Him and fall back on their own scheme. It is better to wait and be sure, for haste can make waste.

Prayer in Judges has at times been exemplary, at other times self-serving. The book is filled by many twists in departing from God (cf. "Introduction"). So the human plan that follows the last prayer passage fits in with the strange climate so frequent in dark times.

Prayer in Ruth

Introduction

The Author

Samuel is a possibility, as the Jewish Talmud attributes the book to him. Today few accept this, but it can be the case. It is true that 1:1 appears to look back to the judges era as a thing of the past, yet Samuel was toward the end of this era and had a long sweep of time to look back upon. Also, reference to a custom in former times (4:7) appears to thrust this writing into a later era. However, this note could be to a custom which was quite old by the time of Ruth in the days of the judges (1:1). God had given it in His law generations earlier. Third, the genealogy carrying on to David (4:22) may have been updated during David's day in a writing primarily by Samuel. That Solomon is not added to the list may suggest that the writing, or the updating, was before he became king. An updating by a later person is possible as Moses' death could have been added to his writing (Deut. 34) and Joshua's death to his (Josh. 24).

The Date

The times when Naomi and Ruth lived in Moab and came to Bethlehem can be earlier than the later date when a writer penned the accounts, or the record was updated as in 4:22.

The original events were during the days of the judges (1:1), in a span from Joshua's death around 1385–1380 B.C. to Saul's kingship starting around 1050 B.C. Some believe that Naomi wrote the account, and a much later hand extended the lineage to David. The date of writing the bulk of the book might be quite early or later, depending on who was the primary author. In any event, the authenticity of the book to be in the biblical canon need not be in any doubt.

The Title

The eleven times that Ruth is mentioned by name provide a pervasive reason to call this "the Book of Ruth." It is not certain what the name means. Further good support for the title is pertinent. Ruth chooses to worship the Lord and turns away from Chemosh, the god of her Moabite people (Num. 21:29). She insists on staying with her mother-in-law, Naomi, to make her future with her when Naomi returns to her own land. Once there, Ruth faithfully gives herself in labor to provide for both. Her gratitude to Boaz for his courtesies during the harvest puts her in a shining light (Ruth 2:10, 13). Boaz prays for the Lord's blessing on her for her kindness to Naomi (2:12) and later to him (3:10). And after becoming his wife, she is mother of the child Obed, who is in the family line to King David and later the Messiah (4:17–21; Matt. 1:1–17, espec. v. 5).

The Context of the Book

This briefest book so far in Scripture is set "in the days when the judges governed" (v. 1). That is not further defined within an era stretching from after Joshua's death around 1385–1380 B.C. until the time of Samuel and Saul around 1050 B.C.

It does not affect the message of the narrative to pinpoint the exact time of the famine in Bethlehem (v. 1) or the Lord bringing it to an end (6). The theme is the same regardless, *redemption* of a man's *land* to keep it in his family after his early death, and *redemption* of the family to keep the land for his heirs. The *land* and the *lady* (Ruth) gain this redemption in Chapters 3–4 as the drama mounts to its apex.

The Contrasts with the Book of Judges

When the reader reflects on the survey of the two books both in the same era, it is easy to see marked differences in the emphases. Some of these are:

Judges	**Ruth**
Tribal concerns (sin, deliverance)	Family and Personal
Redress of bondage	Romance
Liberty from enemies	Love between two people
Judges leading	Kinsman leading
Conquering of foes	Caring for family
Compromise to gods (often)	Commitment to God
Power in God's plan	Pedigree in God's plan
Military actions	Domestic actions
Set throughout Israel	Set in Bethlehem
Miracles	Providential working
Battlefields	Barley and wheat fields
Pressure the norm	Peace the norm

The Concerns and Theme

Natural to the book is the focus of redemption. Boaz, a wealthy relative, *redeems* both Naomi and Ruth, in addition to the family property that Naomi inherited. Boaz, by analogy, depicts Christ, who is the believer's ***menuchah,*** "resting place," and ***Goel***, "Kinsman Redeemer." J. Vernon McGee, a famous Los Angeles pastor, now deceased, shows that such a redeemer have five traits: be a near relative, be willing to carry out the redemption, have the ability to do it, be free himself, and have the price of redemption (*Ruth, The Romance of Redemption*).

The Old Testament idea is based on a custom in which a family member could deliver himself or another in the family from duress (Lev. 25:47–49). He was the ***Goel***, that is, "redeemer." According to Leviticus 25, he could be a brother, uncle, uncle's son, or some other blood relative. The redeemer, if he chose to take this obligation, could pay to effect a freeing from a debt to retain one's land safely in the family, or purchase one out of slavery; or a person who is able can redeem himself (49). Jeremiah 32:7–15 illustrates a case of a relative redeeming land to keep family rights to its inheritance.

Other themes are interwoven in the Book of Ruth. One is God's faithful covenant love in keeping His pledge (Gen. 12:1–3) not only to natural descendants of Abraham who believe (cf. Gen. 15:6), but those of all nations who trust in Him (Dan. 7:27). This theme reaches on into Romans 4, Galatians 3, Ephesians 2, and Revelation in the New Testament (cf. Gal. 3:26–29; Eph. 2:11–22; Rev. 7:9ff.). Ruth was from an outside nation, the Moabites, but emphatically gave herself to God (Ruth 1:16–17), as even Boaz attested later (2:12). Another theme is the walk of faith that bears fruit in a life faithful to the Lord. Abraham displayed this (Gen. 22; James 2:21–23), and Ruth does as well.

With its perspectives, the book is like a bright star shining through a cloudy sky coming in the often dark times of Judges. At least seven concerns emerge: (1) It instructs Israel and also believers today about David's family lineage, tracing the blood-line leading to the ultimate king fulfilling God's prediction of kings (Gen. 17:6; Ruth 4:17–22). (2) It spotlights virtues of its chief characters, commending devotion, love, the loyalty of Ruth and the kindness of Boaz. (3) It illustrates an actual case of the Kinsman-Redeemer custom in Israel. (4) It gives a historical link between the time of the judges (1:1) and the time of the kings as it mentions David, though possibly being set in Gideon's day when a famine prevailed (Judg. 6:3, 4; Ruth 1:1). (5) It is a vivid example of a Gentile accepted upon faith into the blessing of the covenant. (6) It points out the faithfulness of some in a period of widespread unfaithfulness. (7) It lifts up the ideal of pure and simple love and wedlock, which is a flash of light against the midnight of the era reflected in Judges 17–21.

The Outline

Four segments trace the sequence.

I. The Resolve of Ruth (Chap. 1)
II. The Resourcefulness of Ruth (Chap. 2)
III. The Request of Ruth (Chap. 3)
IV. The Reward of Ruth (Chap. 4; cf. 2:12)

The Relation to Prayer

Ten utterances of prayer in the four chapters show faith in the ordinary experiences of home and field. These illustrate how prayer was woven into the fabric of everyday existence for the godly in Israel. Given this window into the times, these may well reflect the far more pervasive place prayer had in many lives than the selected examples mostly drawn from *leaders* in Judges.

Nine of the ten are intercessory prayer wishes invoking God's blessing (1:9; 2:4 twice, 12, 19–20, twice; 3:10; 4:11–12, prayer in four aspects; 4:14b-15, a wish in two aspects). The remaining tenth case is a voicing of blessing to God who is worthy of praiseful exaltation (4:14a).

Ruth 1:9

Naomi's Intercession for Her Relatives

The Adversity a Family Faced (1:1–5)

Elimelech in famine had taken his wife and two sons 75–80 miles away from Bethlehem to find sustenance in Moab. The sons married Moabite women. All three men died within a ten-year period, leaving the wife Naomi and her two daughters-in-law in a difficult predicament.

The Advice Naomi Gave (6–8a)

Seeking survival, Naomi started back to Bethlehem where she could rejoin family. She had also heard that God had given encouraging times back home, and there she might find hope. She counselled both daughters-in-law to remain in their native land, with their mothers. The counsel leads into prayer.

The Appeal Naomi Made to God (8b, 9)

Here is intercession in the form of an invocation appealing for God's work in caring for the two kinswomen. It is in two phases.

The general request (compassion). Naomi pleads that the Lord will show kindness in their future, a sweeping request for their welfare. She leaves the details to the wisdom, power and love of God. Her advocacy in their interest takes wings in the encouragement she feels about God being kind to them as they have been kind to her husband, sons and her. This in principle is consistent with the Lord promising blessing on those who bless His people (Gen. 12:1–3). It is not that the kind deeds *merit* His return in a kind of pay plan, contrary to grace. Rather the deeds show a general disposition of kindly regard toward His people, and Him.

The specific desire (contentment). Naomi prays that the Lord will arrange circumstances so as to lead the women into new marriages, and contentment in satisfying domestic needs. As Abraham could pray for the good of people in Philistia (Gen. 12, 20), Naomi can for the welfare of these so close to her heart in Moab.

The Answers of the Women (10–18)

The conviction of the two (10). Both preferred going back with Naomi to her people. This may or may not indicate that Orpah, who eventually remains in Moab, had made a commitment to this people and to their God while in this Israelite family circle in Moab. At any rate, God would still be able to work in her life in this unlikely place, though her spiritual status is uncertain.

The counsel of Naomi (11–13). She insists on their finding their future in their own land. Twice she says "return," and once "go." She is not trying to get rid of them in an unlovely way, but thinking in a considerate way of their good. Whether her counsel is finally best is open to debate since the Israelite circle of influences to trust God would be so much an advantage.

Naomi's focus is on the women's possibility for marriage. Why should they accompany her away when she can give them no husbands? Even if she herself had a husband and raised sons, it would require years of waiting, with hardships. She rates her own predicament harder than theirs since she is older, and they at least are young enough to have hope to remarry. Her prayer and counsel drifts into feeling sorry for herself, embittered about the life the Lord has now dealt her. Even in prayer, one needs to erect watchful guards. It glorifies God to saturate the prayer life with confidences in God's goodness now and faithfulness in the future, not indulge in self-pity that amounts to God-dishonoring whining.

The choices of the women (14–18). Both kinswomen wept in strong passion about this crucial choice. It was difficult to part with this mother-in-law, also threatening to face the future.

(1) Orpah's choice. It is, as mentioned, not certain what her choice would mean spiritually. It may have been in the final analysis for the gods. That would be the saturation in the pagan land. At

least that is the conclusion Naomi draws from Orpah's turning back: "back to her people and her gods." It also is the rather natural contrast to Ruth's clear-cut conviction for God. How weighty the value choices people make at the places of going on, or going back!

(2) Ruth's choice. Three things mark it out.

First, her *persistence* is obvious. Even when Naomi gazes back where Orpah is already going away (observe "has gone back") and encourages Ruth to join her, Ruth is firm. She asks Naomi not to keep up the talk about going back from her. Her mind is made up. The utterance of it is one of the most dramatic value choices in all of God's word. "Where you go, I will go, and where you lodge, I will lodge. Your people shall be my people, and your God, my God. Where you die, I will die, and there I will be buried." This lady is going all the way! She puts where she stands beyond all doubt.

Second, her *prayer* is firm as flint (17b). "May the Lord do so to me (i.e., work in accord with this choice, in blessing) or worse if anything but death parts you and me." It is an oath prayer, a pledge of her follow-through and a yearning for God's part in blessing it. Negatively, it is a desire to face discipline if she fails to stick with it.

Third, Naomi's *perception* of Ruth's choice is unmistakable, as is her *permission* to go with her.

The Arrival in Bethlehem (19–22)

The adversity has been faced so far. The advice has been given to go back. The appeal has been pled before God for the two women. The answers they give are initially the same but later issue in quite different choices. Ruth's own appeal to God is sincere and laden with spiritual resolve. So now the mother-in-law and the daughter-in-law take the road to Bethlehem.

They go in late April, for it is the time of barley harvest. They arrive as the center of a stir after Naomi has been away about ten years. She voices again her conception that El Shaddai (the strong God) has given her a bitter portion. Having gone away full (better off than she had realized, with a husband and two sons), she is back empty. How lacking she is in perception, for with her is one of the finest flowers that ever bloomed in Israel, this young woman Ruth who loves her and loves God. How full Naomi actually is with such a kinswoman and such a God, El Shaddai. Yet she permits her life to be shadowed by the negative as she mentions even a second time that the Lord is down on her.

As the story progresses to other scenes, Naomi will see how good God really is. And she will realize the treasure she has in this woman who insisted on never leaving her.

At this point we can sum up principles relating to Ruth 1:8–9 and 11. First, one vital gesture our intercession to God can make is a bid that He show kindness to another person. Second, prayer can generously seek a temporal, common grace asset even for those in pagan homes. This could be with the hope that one out of a believing home could influence the marital partner to worship the true God (cf. 1 Pet. 3:1).

Third, it must honor the Lord when sincerity draws His name into a proper ambition as the moral monitor in one's keeping true to the aim. Fourth, seek through prayer to be loyal all the way to death to another who follows God.

Ruth 2:4, 12

Three Prayers Wishing Blessing

A pair of prayers appear in a barley field as Boaz the boss returns to his workers with a greeting and they respond in kind. A third comes in verse 12. Such wishes today, as in any time, could be mere comments of friendliness simply following a habit. In that case they would not be a form of prayer. As has often been clear in this study already, invocations in effect calling on God to confer His blessing on others are a valid form of prayer. In the mouth of those conscious of God's presence in all of life's aspects, they are not a mere form or facade, but intended to invite God's action.

Today such utterances might be politeness alone, or real prayer. The motive or intent remains a key.

Prelude to the Prayers (1–3)

Whereas Chapter 1 brought the account to the arrival of the women at harvest time, Chapter 2 shifts to a scene in the field. Its focus is immediately on the harvest boss, and the relation he will cultivate with Ruth.

The drama moves in three phases here.

The profile of Boaz. He is defined right away to be a relative of Naomi in the family of her deceased husband Elimelech. This sets the stage for the movement toward his kinsman work of Chapters 3–4. He also is described by the expression, *ish gibbor hayil*, sometimes translated "mighty man of valor." The phrase can be a compliment in any or all of four realms. (1) Strength, sometimes physically; (2) a sterling standard of moral life, either a man or a woman as Ruth in 3:11 and the woman in Proverbs 31:10; (3) soldiery in standout prowess (Judg. 6:12; 11:1); or (4) stature in the social sphere as one influential and respected.

In Boaz's case, (2) and (4) fit the book aptly, and (1) is possible although strength physically is never mentioned.

As a farmer of some success, hiring workers, Boaz is enjoying blessing God promised to those who obeyed Him in faith (Lev. 26; Deut. 28). This is in contrast to judgment for sin as often in Judges.

The purpose of Ruth. She had no lazy bone in her body. She desires to glean grain. And she is aware of a need to find favor from a farmer who will permit this. Perhaps her husband or Naomi had told her of the kindness God taught Israelites when harvesters left some grain for the poor, to help them (Lev. 19:9; 23:22). She no doubt also knew that the unmerciful could cast aside this custom.

The portion Ruth chooses. It is not clear that Ruth went right to the field of Boaz. Whether immediately or in due time her gleaning was in that portion. *God* must have blessed her by guiding her although *she* was not yet aware of it. The answer Naomi had prayed for her in 1:9 was beginning to come into shape, by a different way than Naomi had realized. And Ruth was receiving early movements in the blessing supplying what she longed for in her own prayer of 1:17. Naomi, at home, may have been praying again as well, before her prayer of 2:19.

The Prayers of the Harvesters (4)

The greeting of Boaz. It is actually what he prayerfully bids God to do for his workers. "May the Lord be with you." Intended out of a godly generosity seeking God's blessing, it is as much a prayer in essence as when the priests uttered the "may the Lord" invocations of Numbers 6:22–27.

The greeting of his crew. Like begets like. They, in turn, greet the boss with a prayer for His blessing on Boaz. Such a prayer, wishing from the heart God's compassions, could have preceded and followed their daily work and been an invocation in their thoughts and lips even as they worked. Certainly it is so with godly workers today, who appreciate godly leaders and uphold them in their yearnings before the Lord. This can be a spice of life, a tone, a relish as one lives in a sense of God's presence and seeks to pray His blessing for all things.

The connection with prayer continues as the verses flow on.

Boaz's Pleasure with Ruth (5–17)

His interest (5–7). The new woman among the crew attracted the boss's eye right away. He inquired of his foreman whose young woman this was. He had never seen her before, and wondered how he could have missed her, and which family she was from.

If Boaz caught his breath when he first saw Ruth, the foreman's answer no doubt quickened his heartbeat. She was not just anybody. She was attached to Naomi, and single. For "all the city" had heard of Naomi's return, and details had reached Boaz, as is clear in 2:11. He just had not seen the young woman until now, and it had not dawned on him this was the same person.

So, this day she had come to his field! Boaz lost no time.

His invitation (8–11). Boaz spoke to his workers, then was drawn right to the woman. His words to her were kind. He did not want her to shift to another field, but to glean after his reapers. He assured her his servants were under his orders not to interfere with her work. More than even that, the drinking water was for her too.

Ruth is overwhelmed by such courtesy. She throws herself prostrate before the boss in respectful gratitude. She is totally impressed that the man would show such kindnesses to her, a foreigner.

Boaz graciously explains. He has been told of her many deeds to help Naomi after Ruth's former husband died. Boaz knows of her sacrifice, leaving her initial family and the land of her birth, also of her brave venture coming among a people she did not know.

His invocation (12, 13). All this leads the man to utter words meant as a prayer, words spoken to Ruth for her benefit but beyond her to God in her presence. It is like a believer today speaking in conversation with another person, then voicing a prayer out loud heard by the person and God.

Boaz is zealous for the Lord's attention to give Ruth reward for her labor. God answers that prayer in blessing her work efforts with His success, as in the favor here and later before Boaz. And the essence of it could go on in her work the rest of her life. Boaz also prays desiring her wages to be full. Certainly God made them so with food in the field (14), help in getting more grain that she herself was free to gather (16), Boaz's additional gift of grain (3:15), his hand in marriage, a child, and so much more.

In his prayer for her blessing, Boaz asks for fullness, and certainly God's answer is bountiful. Added to the physical supply given her would be the joy of a man she loved and of a son, Obed. And more than even this was the presence of the God she had chosen in Moab. Boaz is mindful of that spiritual relationship and all it held. The blessing he interceded for on her behalf was from "the Lord, the God of Israel, under whose wings you have come to seek refuge." That wingspread is a picture of a God who is sufficient in His presence, provision and protection. Boaz conceived of His God, her God as like a great bird, perhaps an eagle (cf. Ex. 19:4; Deut. 32:11). God was her asset, as the eagle with its mighty, extended wings drew its eaglets near, brought them all they needed, and shielded them from harm.

Ruth's again is deeply touched by such compassion. She is stirred by his favor that is a comfort when she needs it, his words that have lifted her. And all this, she humbly reasons, comes to a woman who has no relationship with Boaz, as his maids do (cf. v. 8), no link by which to expect any help.

His interest continued (14–16). Boaz's courtesies extend even to inviting Ruth to the meal the workers enjoy. He gives his own hospitality to satisfy her, and orders his workers to help her do especially well. These acts of cordiality prepare for the next prayer.

Four principles emerge. First, it honors the Lord when one sincerely prays "The Lord be with you" or "bless you." This is similar to the New Testament appeal, such as in Paul, for God's grace to be with believers (cf. Gal. 6:18). Second, prayer to God on one person's lips can prompt reciprocal prayer on others' tongues. Like begets like. Third, it is in harmony with God's Word to pray that He will give recompense to honor a believer's work (cf. 1 Sam. 2:3, 30). Fourth, the person who prays aright can also expect that God's blessing for one's labor will be full.

Ruth 2:19–20

Naomi's Two Prayers to Bless Boaz

The Provision for Both Women (17, 18)

Ruth reports home at day's end with enough grain to supply both Naomi and herself.

The Prayer of Naomi for Boaz (19, 20)

At first, the mother-in-law invokes God's blessing on whoever the owner of the field was where Ruth gleaned (19). She did not know yet the identity of the man. Of course God did, and He would answer the prayer. God always knows everything when His servants pray though they do not! His answers can leap far beyond what the intercessor imagines (Eph. 3:20).

Probably that general prayer prompted Ruth to supply more information. The man Naomi had prayed for, she explains, was Boaz. Then Naomi prays a second time for God's blessing on him. She requests this in light of Boaz's "kindness to the living [Naomi and Ruth as well as others] and the dead [his deceased relative, Elimelech, and two nephews]." His kindness had not *merited* God's favor, for the blessing was of grace from a God of an unconditional covenant to bless. But the man's kindness had *manifested* God's own gracious character by faith that obeyed, and of course God would bless what was consistent with Him, all in grace.

Naomi is quick to come to a crucial point. Why, the relative is not only kind, "he is one of our closest relatives." It will not take Naomi much longer to think the thought God no doubt God moves her to think, the fitting possibility of "match making" in 3:1–4. The purposes being worked out are not just those of people; they are God's, who inclines them so that His will becomes theirs.

The Persistence of Ruth (21–23)

The women agree that it is wise for Ruth to continue gleaning in the harvest of Boaz. The days pass on through barley harvest in late April and early May and into the wheat harvest of late May and early June.

Reflect on principles. First, even when a person asks God to bless another whose identity he does not know, God Himself knows how to direct the favor. Second, one way to pray is for God's benefit in grace to rest on a member of the family.

Ruth 3:10

Prayer on a Threshing Floor

An interesting study is that of places where people pray in Scripture. Adam and Eve prayed in the garden, Abraham out under the stars, Jacob on the bank of a creek, Moses by a burning bush, Joshua outside his camp, Gideon at a winepress, Samson in a Philistine court, and Jonah in a great fish. In the case here, Boaz prays on a threshing floor, no doubt in whispered tones to keep Ruth's reputation safe.

Ruth's Presence on the Threshing Floor (1–9)

Naomi's resourcefulness (1–4). Thoughts that have ticked in the woman's mind, no doubt at God's own prompting, now take sound in words. She has wisdom to counsel Ruth on what she should do.

It is clear here that Naomi is lovingly considerate. She seeks Ruth's security so that she may realize the fulfillment a young woman yet can enjoy (1). Boaz is a kinsman, and he can take Ruth in marriage his mind is inclined to, carrying on the inheritance of Ruth's husband who died. Naomi's sage advice is for Ruth to get herself all dolled up and follow a custom of uncovering a man's feet.

The kinsman right goes back to God's merciful provision for families in Leviticus 25. When a husband died, his brother could marry his widow and redeem his property to keep it in the family, lest she was unable to pay debts. More of this appears in Deuteronomy 25:5–10. Should the male relative nearest in line forfeit the right, the next in line could act on it. Here it will turn out that Boaz is the second in line, and when the first or nearer family member declines, the door opens to Boaz. A person who was such a redeemer (from the Hebrew ***goel***) was a "protector, vindicator" who upheld family rights (cf. Job 19:25).

The custom of a man spreading his covering over a woman was a gesture of willingness to marry her (Ezek. 16:8). The practice is still known among Arabs today. In a far greater sense, God clothes those who become members of His redemptive family with garments of righteousness (cf. Isa. 61:9; Rev. 3:4–5; 7:14; 19:8).

Ruth's readiness (5–8). Apparently she has fallen in love with Boaz by now, and is ready to follow a custom regarded as decent. She is prepared to do all that Naomi had counselled. So she dresses up, not in any indecent fashion, but evidently normal good clothing with a mantle big enough for Boaz to give her a gift of grain later. Boaz, having finished his evening meal, retired near the pile of grain. Ruth came quietly, uncovered his feet, and lay down beyond his feet (cf. 8).

A charge of impropriety is misguided and unreasonable. To uncover the "feet" means just that, not uncover the "waist" or entire body for sexual intimacy as some falsify it. It was an act to awaken the man when his feet became cold. Ruth's position beyond the man's feet was uncompromising, a place of submission and of petition, which suits her purpose for being here. Boaz esteems her for her sterling character (10, 11), for his phrase for her excellence (11) is that which describes the virtuous woman in Proverbs 31:10.

Her request (9). As planned, the man awoke probably from the cold his feet felt, and sensed that somebody was nearby. He bent forward (Ruth was not beside him!) and for the first time was aware that it was a woman and that she was lying modestly beyond his feet.

He did not recognize Ruth in the darkness. "Who are you?" was natural. She replied, "I am Ruth your maid. So spread your covering over your maid, for you are a close relative." That is not being immodestly forward. It is acting on opportunity, following the urge of good counsel and love, but not out of place. Nor does Boaz draw back thinking the woman a bit pushy. She has given him a straightforward answer, free of any deceit as to her request. Her drama is not lust but a longing reaching out for a legitimate relationship and opportunity to share with him a fulfillment in their interest (love) and his future (land inheritance).

How does he react to all of this?

Boaz's Prayer on the Threshing Floor (10)

The prayer itself. He recognizes Ruth's act as a refreshing thing, worthy of blessing from the Lord. For this his prayer invokes God's attention to her, seeking favor for her as he himself has so generously given in Chapter 2.

After his brief prayer, he explains. What he reads in her present brave gesture is a showing of kindness. And it is even greater kindness to him than she showed in the barley and wheat fields. The prospect of marriage with her is, in his esteem, a great prize. He commends her that her kindness is unusual for a woman in that she has not sought a relationship with any of the young men, poor or rich. It is gratifying to him that if wealth was what drove her she might have sought that and a younger man too. That he feels she might realistically pursue such a course may suggest that he thought her beautiful.

His plans (11f.). This is closely related to the prayer and the explanation of it above. Boaz does three things.

(1) He consents to marry her. He is as ready as she, and love must be inspiring his answer, "yes."

(2) He compliments her further. In fact, he pays her the highest compliment of all his people in the city! They are convinced, as he is, that she is a "woman of excellence." Just as he is a man of excellence (2:1, man of valor), Ruth is what Proverbs 12:4 and 31:10 describe as a woman of the highest praise.

(3) He concentrates his efforts for her. He wants to marry her according to the redemption custom. One problem, however, he must be honest about, for he is a man of character that she well respects. Another relative is closer than him and by law has the first choice.

That must have hurt him when he said it. Perhaps he swallowed hard. How much praying he did that God would clear the way the passage does not say. It would have been a matter of high motivation for him, no doubt. And the words must have hurt Ruth, too. She, too, would have a lot of thinking and praying to do. Boaz assures her he will concentrate on resolving this matter.

Boaz displays his tender regard for Ruth by carefulness to protect her good name. He will not allow her to be thought impure by people learning of her being at the threshing floor and not knowing her real motives, or his. He bids her goodbye while the darkness is still concealing, and sends her off with a lavish gift of grain.

A principle of prayer here is to pray (10) in line with what God's will in His word shows He would be pleased to do. Another is to pray matters that touch one's personal life very dearly, for we are human and have some valid human joys that encourage prayer to

God. These need, in discipline, to be placed in the right perspective with what we can desire in His will and what is good for another person. A third guideline is to let prayer for the opposite gender be sincere and pure. Fourth, prayer for another can be a celebration for that person's qualities that please God.

Fifth, consistent upholding in honest ways of the person prayed for can show godly sincerity. Sixth, in prayer for one with whom romance is in the air, focus on aspects that prize the will of God.

Ruth 4:11, 14–15

Prayer in Relation to a Kinsman

The Procedure of the Kinsman Redeemer (4:1–11a)

Boaz presented the matter to the nearer kinsman in the presence of ten witnesses. The relative at first agreed to exercise his right, but Boaz then qualified the case by further detail. The present redemption was not only of the *land* but of the *lady*. At this the relative backed out. To draw another person, Ruth, into the transaction with its possibility of future children would complicate the man's existing inheritance due to his immediate family. He must have had another heir, or heirs, who would then have their portions divided into lesser shares if he carried this matter through.

A custom was brought in to seal the freedom given Boaz to marry Ruth and redeem the land. The nearer relative took off his sandal. The sandal was a symbol of the foot walking in it to possess the land. To remove the sandal and hand it to another man was a sign of removing from oneself the right to inherit the land, and acknowledging it goes to another. Boaz asked the ten witnesses to attest officially his legal receiving of the right to the *land* and the *lady*.

The Prayer of the Witnesses (11b, c)

Not only the ten elders of verse 2 but all the people at the court session became witnesses. They pray corporately, possibly as a spokesman articulates what they all feel. And the prayer is a single invocation, though it specifies two details.

For blessing on the posterity (11b). This is primarily with regard to the woman Boaz agrees to marry. They invoke God's blessing to give Ruth vitality in having children. The prime analogy they adduce is Rachel and Leah from whom Jacob's twelve sons and the tribes sprang.

For blessing in the prosperity (11c, 12). Now the prayer focus shifts more to Boaz. May God help him have success in material things and in renown in his area, Bethlehem. And may his house (descendants) be analogous to that of Perez who was born to Judah by Tamar (Gen. 38). The significance of this, as the Lord seems to prompt their prayer in accord with His will, is that Perez (18) is in the genealogy leading to David (22). God would know the significance in His plan for Perez and his line as it fitted with His will to raise up kings in Abraham's line (Gen. 17:6) and Judah's (49:10). He would bring this on to David, though those in Boaz's day did not know that. The writer, later bringing the account up to date in David's day, long after Boaz's transaction, would be aware of it.

The prayer, then, is for great blessing on Boaz and Ruth in the plan of the God who answers.

The Provision of a Son (13)

The wedding followed, and the two enjoyed the intimacy God had willed (cf. Gen. 2:24). By God's enablement, Ruth conceived; it was not merely a foregone conclusion resulting from human ability. The two welcomed a son. Another prayer is natural on this glad day.

The Prayer of the Women (14, 15)

Here the prayer involves a blessing giving praiseful credit to the Lord (14a), then one intercessory wish invoking God's benefit in respect to two details.

Women rejoicing with the couple speak to Naomi, their words at this point actually voicing a prayer. First, they express *thanksgiving* to the Lord on behalf of the grandmother especially. They credit Him with the son, a redeemer who will carry on the family tree and the inheritance. After this recognition of God, they *intercede* that the son's name will become famous among his people. Of course it did, for Obed's presence in the kingly genealogy (21) would be before his people, even those of all nations (Matt. 1:5).

In another facet of their intercession, the women summon God's blessing that this child will be a tonic to Naomi in her older years. May the Lord work that he is a restorer to rejuvenate her life (grandmothers often can identify with that) and a sustainer to make her senior days fulfilling. The bitterness she has known (1:13, 20) can be overcome by joyful sweetness. How well these praying women have come to know the preciousness of this jewel, Boaz's bride, to Naomi also. Ruth loves Naomi and is proving better to her than if she had seven sons, a number to express blessing that is full.

The Pedigree of the Son (16–22)

A heart-warming love story and chronicle of God's faithfulness in providing a kinsman redeemer closes with a genealogy linking Boaz and Obed back with earlier men and forward as far as David. In the larger context of God's word, the movement is on even to the greater David, the King Himself, Jesus Christ, "son of David, son of Abraham" (Matt. 1:1, 5).

It is significant that the list runs on to David, and that other Scripture continues it to Jesus the son of David. For all that Boaz is in the book as the kinsman redeemer of his day is an illustration of Christ as an even greater Kinsman Redeemer. He is truly in the right line that God marked out, that of Judah, for His coming king (Gen. 49:10; cf. Ezek. 21:26, 27). And He is the Redeemer for those of Israel and all peoples of faith God promised to bless in His covenant with Abraham (Gen. 12:1–3). His plans for the people of faith who would comprise His bride would form an even greater love story than the beautiful love book of Boaz and Ruth.

Principles flow from the passage. First, prayer for a marriage can quite aptly dwell on God's blessing in children, provision of things needed (cf. Phil. 4:19), and the two being useful where God puts them. Second, season prayer with thanksgiving (Phil. 4:6). Third, faith's vision can stir prayer for God's blessing even years later in a life's impact, and even in the farther future (cf. Solomon in 1 Kgs. 8).

Prayer in 1 Samuel

Introduction

The book opens in the latter days of the judges, nearly three centuries after the start of Judges and after the Book of Ruth.

The Author

Only God, the holy angels and the people of the ancient time know who wrote 1 and 2 Samuel. Tradition in the Jewish Talmud regards a portion of our present 1 Samuel as by the prophet and priest by that name (Baba Bathra, 14b). This is possible since he was the greatest spiritual leader in Chapters 1–25, and 25:1 mentions his death. Inspired Scripture claims that the acts of David are written by Samuel, another prophet Nathan, and a seer named Gad (1 Chr. 29:29). Samuel might have completed 1 Samuel 1–24 before his death in 25:1, delving into the days of David's rise toward kingship (Chaps. 16–24). The other writers could have written their parts of 1 Samuel 25–1 Chronicles.

A problem in the Samuel view, at least after his death, is 1 Samuel 27:6. The writer mentions that King Achish of the Philistine Gath gave David Ziklag, which "has belonged to the kings of Judah to this day." This assumes that time has moved long past Samuel's day and well into at least the United Kingdom succession of Judean kings.

The Date

With authorship by Samuel and others after him, the time of writing might have covered the span of ca. 1000–950 B.C. A later date, such as late in the kings era, seems improbable since the two books nowhere mention the fall of the northern kingdom and its capital Samaria in 722 B.C. However, as early as 1 Samuel 11: 8, the record mentions Israel and Judah as distinct entities (cf. also 17:52; 18:16;

2 Sam. 5:5; 11:11; 12:8; 19:42–43; 24:1, 9). A writer after Samuel's death in 25:1 may have made insertions in the record that came to him, as would be natural in updating the account.

The Title

The books we know as 1 Samuel and 2 Samuel were, in their earliest existence, one unit in the Hebrew scriptures, "The Book of Samuel." This in itself appears to assume, quite early, Samuel's prominent role. Later the Septuagint Greek translation ca. 150 B.C. divided the material into Books of the Kingdom A and B, viewing our 1 and 2 Kings as the third and fourth books of the Kingdom. Centuries after this, the Latin Vulgate translation put the name "Samuel" for both books. The first use of 1 and 2 Samuel was in the Hebrew Bible in the Christian era, ca. 1448, and the distinction came into the English Bible.

Samuel's name over the books is reasonable in light of the very early Hebrew recognition as well as the man's prominence as a leader in Israel (cf. the theme below).

The Theme

Several emphases pervade 1 Samuel.

One is the rise and ministry of Samuel, the great priest and prophet, renowned for his spiritual leadership of his people as in 1 Samuel 7, 12, 15, and so on. His name would be revered later for his effectiveness in prayer (Ps. 99:6; Jer. 15:1), and he led Israel from the days of the judges through the transition to the kings, Saul (1 Sam. 9–31), and David in his gradual rise to power beginning with his early anointing (16:8–13).

A further main current on its own is Israel's clamor for a king and God's initially giving them the kind of king (Saul) who titillated their own hasty, surface instincts (Chaps. 7–10; cf. 9:2; 16:7). This came about despite such earlier sentiment as Gideon's to be a judge and not a king (Judg. 8:23), and wisdom in 1 Samuel itself about God being their king, whom they were in effect rejecting (8:7; 12:12). Later, God gave them His kind of king, David. For they were not wrong in wanting a king, but in their motive of wanting one in place of the Lord. God had earlier shown His own plan to give them a king in the line of Judah (Gen. 49:8–12), and scriptures had mentioned kings as in His intent (Gen. 17:6, 16; 35:11). Deuteronomy had even mentioned cautions to honor when they should have a king (17:14–20). And Hannah in her song to God's honor, voices the first specific expectation of the Lord's "anointed" one on the throne (2:10; cf. 9:6).

A related theme is David's rise in the favor of God and Israel to be the king. God leads Samuel to anoint him in his teenage years (16:1–13). In this passage several things stand out. God says of Saul "I have rejected him from being king" (v. 1), "I will send you to Jesse . . . , for I have selected a king for Myself among his sons" (1), God's specific bypassing of David's brothers (6–10), Samuel asking if Jesse has yet another son (11), God's acceptance of David (12), Samuel's anointing of David (13), "the Spirit of the Lord came mightily upon David from that day forward" (13), and so forth. David gains popular acclaim (18:7–8, 16), and has God's support to prosper (12, 14; cf. 13:14; 15:28–29).

With the above thematic lines, God works in sovereign power to accomplish His will. His power is obvious in answering Hannah's pleading for a son (1 Sam. 1–2). It appears in His defending the Ark of the Covenant as He topples the Philistine god before it and brings pressure on those who wrongly hold the Ark (Chap. 5). He has the ability to reject Saul and bring David on toward kingship. He brings thunder and rain and answers prayer with victory in battle (Chaps. 7, 12; cf. also Chap. 30). When David goes against the human odds in fighting the mighty Philistine champion Goliath, the Lord gives his anointed one a complete victory (Chap. 17). In that account, verses 45–47 stand out in exalting the Lord. In various further episodes God works to protect David against Saul and show him favor over this king who is on his downward slide due to sin (24:1–22; 26:1–25). And the Lord's power even causes Samuel to reappear after he has died (28:8–25).

The Outline

I. Samuel—the Last Judge (Chaps. 1–8)

II. Saul—the First King (Chaps. 9–15)
He is disqualified by his offering (13:1–23), his order (14:1–52), and his obstinacy (15:1–35).

III. The Rise of David and Decline of Saul (Chaps. 16–31)

This develops the emergence of David as God's choice for king (16:1–19:17), then David's exile and Saul's eclipse (19:18–31:13). Most conspicuous here is David's movements fleeing to escape Saul, the two times he spares the life of the king who would snuff out his own life, and Saul's death.

The Relation to Prayer

This is evident in several ways.

Prayer's permeation. More than fifty distinct references to prayer occur from 1:10–11 to 30:8, and explicit prayer is mentioned in at least twenty-three of the thirty-one chapters. Some of these are not listed separately later as sections devoted to prayer. An example is 9:13, which is a passing reference to Samuel coming to "bless" the sacrifice. In such a case, Samuel would pray, that is ask (invoke) the Lord's blessing on the offering. There also are instances of people vowing before the Lord. These, too, would be instances of prayer. One can see several cases (for instance, 19:16; 20:17).

Prayer's parts. Several normative aspects of biblical prayer appear. Examples are easy to find, as follows.

(1) Petition. Hannah appeals to have a son (1:10–11), and David seeks guidance from the Lord (30:8). As can be seen below in (7), some questions are in effect a way of making petition for God's counsel. And another kind of petition is in David's asking that the Lord forbid him from hurting Saul, God's anointed king (26:11). Wish prayers of "may God give a certain blessing" occur (cf. David's "may my life be highly valued in the sight of the Lord," 26:24).

(2) Intercession. Samuel is a stand-out example in beseeching God on behalf of his people (Chaps. 7, 12) and praying all night in grief over Saul's sin and rejection from being king (15:11).

(3) Praise/thanks. This is an underlying impetus driving Hannah's prayerful song in 2:1–10. Her magnifying of the Lord often comes in reciting or affirming what God has done. David blesses the Lord in a tribute of thanksgiving/praise for His sending Abigail to meet him with kindness (25:32), and shortly after this blesses Him for His help in letting the evil Nabal die (vv. 38–39).

(4) Confession. Saul acknowledges his sin to Samuel, and probably through this great spokesman of God to the Lord Himself, whom he disobeyed (15:24–25, 30).

(5) Affirmations. Hannah recounts things about the Lord (cf. 3), and Samuel declares his instant availability to hear when the Lord speaks, the Hebrew ***hanani,*** "Here I am" (3:4, 6, 8). Later, this leader repeats words of Israel's clamor to have a king in the presence of God (8:21).

(6) Calling for God's blessing. Samuel calls for this favor to be on his people when he leads in sacrifice at a town called Zuph (9:13). Earlier, wish prayers are evident ("may the Lord") on the lips of Eli (1:17) and Elkanah (1:23). This is actually a form of point (2) above, Intercession.

(7) Questions. Prayer in Scripture is often in this form. Examples in 1 Samuel are frequent, not in upstart challenge to the Lord but in sincere desire to receive His input for guidance. One prime case is Samuel's questioning when he feels danger before King Saul in going to anoint David as God has directed (16:2). Another instance is in people of Benjamin inquiring of the Lord if Saul has come, and the Lord's answer that this man, reluctant to take the throne, has secreted himself away among the baggage (10:22). Urgency relating to battle moves men to ask God what move to make (Saul, 14:37, 41; David, 23:2, 4, 10–12; 30:8). The priest Ahimelech and other priests met death at Saul's evil order for inquiring of God to help David (22:10, 15)

(8) Vows. These binding obligations are rather frequent on the Old Testament pages, as they are here. Hannah pledges that if God will help her give birth to a son, she will dedicate him in a Nazirite vow to Him all of his life (1:11; cf. her integrity in 28). Elkanah traveled to the tabernacle in Shiloh to offer a sacrifice and pay a vow, that is, complete it faithfully (1:21).

(9) Oaths. These have in common with vows that they are pledges that obligate a person. Yet they are a bit distinct in two respects: they are a kind of petition appealing to God, and they invoke Him to witness to the integrity of a pledge and bless or judge in accord with this. Saul, pressed to win in battle, bound his soldiers under oath, invoking God's curse on any who took time out to eat when he felt it urgent that they push hard at every moment to win (14:24). David swore to Saul by invoking the Lord as the guarantee he would keep his word to protect the family of Saul once the kingship passed to him (24:21–22). And he apparently affirmed in an oath with God as his witness to protect a man who told him where to find camping Amalekite raiders he pursued (30:15).

Prayer's power. God is able in answer to prayer to give Hannah a son (Chap. 1), supply victory to His people when Samuel cries to Him (Chaps. 7, 12), and guide those who need direction in battle. He has power to answer Samuel's all night prayer (15:11) by bringing the disobedient Saul to the end of his kingship (Chap. 31), to bring Samuel back from the dead to talk with Saul (Chap. 28), and to preserve David alive to become the king.

In various ways in 1 Samuel, then, prayer is vital at the very heart of events. The birth of the strategic man who transitions from the judges to the kings is a matter of prayer. Much in his ministry is carried out with prayer at the core. God's announcement of Samuel's prominent role in His work comes in a context of prayer (1 Sam. 3). Strategic battles are won in prayer (cf. 1 Sam. 7, 12). Samuel is convinced he would be sinning if he ceased to carry on intercessory prayer for his people (12:23). He leads in the transition from judges to a king (1 Sam. 8) in prayer. The great king, David, is announced to Samuel in his prayer conversation with the Lord (16:1–3). David prayed for guidance in his military steps (23:2–4, 9–19; cf. 2 Sam. 2:1). Samuel was a model in prayer (12:18–23, etc.), and long after his lifetime stands out as an honored example in prayer (Ps. 99:6; Jer. 15:1).

At this point we can begin to look in on cases where prayer occurs in the book's record.

1 Samuel 1:10–28; 2:1–10

Prayer for a Son

Hannah's Prayer for a Son (1–11)

A Levite who was a resident of Ramathaim-zophim (Ramah for short) about six miles north of Jerusalem had two wives, one of them unable to bear children. The place this family came from meant "the heights of the Zuphites," one branch of the Levites. The barren woman, Hannah, suffered much from the other wife Peninnah's jibes about her inability and probably insults of inferiority. So during a trip to Shiloh to present offerings to God, Hannah took her prayer burden to God at the tabernacle amidst tears of anguish.

She promised God that she would devote the boy to His service as a Nazirite (cf. Num. 6:1–8). This came in a vow form of prayer, a pledge. If God would give her a son, she in turn would devote him totally to God.

Principles of prayer are clear. One is that a believer can pray about anything, everything (Phil. 4:6). Another is to pray fervently in sincerity. This can be accompanied by tears that are not a put-on but a genuine expression of grief as even God's Son would pray with tears (Heb. 5:7). Finally, prayer with a promise is legitimate when a person is genuine and follow-through is faithful. Rash promises not thought through well, as Jephthah's, need to be screened out.

Eli's Perception of the Prayer (12–18)

The high priest watching Hannah's moving lips misjudged her to be a drunken woman. Hannah clarified that her actions really only displayed great distress. Eli believed her and wished her God's answer to her prayer. She then felt encouraged (18).

Eli's priestly wish is itself prayer in its intercessory aspect. It is in the form of a blessing invoked. He prays God's peace upon Hannah, one of the facets of blessing in priestly prayer of Numbers 6:22–27. The reason this woman can feel at rest is because Eli calls for God's answer to her petition. She trusts God that it will be so, for she responds desiring to find the favor he, too, has pled for her. And the peace he requested for her has its answer in the confidence consoling her.

God's Provision of a Son (19, 20)

In answer to the prayer, "God remembered her." Hannah became aware that He had given her the ability to become pregnant, and she lived with a joy of expectation. Just as she had asked, the answer was a son. In gratitude to God, her name for the baby was Samuel, "the name of God," for she had asked this son of God and devoted him to God. A principle is that when we pray we always need to do it "with thanksgiving" (Phil. 4:6).

Hannah's Presentation of the Son (21–28)

When she had weaned the boy (cf. Gen. 21:8) at two or three (2 Macc. 7:27), Hannah brought him for dedication to God at Shiloh. As a part of her worship led by Eli she offered a bull in death to fulfill her vow, the death symbolic of her offering her son's life entirely to the Lord. With this was a meal offering symbolic of dedicating what she had to God.

Hannah testified to Eli in verses 26–27 that God had answered her prayer of verses 10–11. The Lord had been faithful. She now in gratitude was making good on her phase of the agreement.

This passage also mentions prayer in saying (v. 21) that Elkanah went to the tabernacle to pay his vow. He as well was fulfilling a commitment he himself had made to the Lord in prayer.

Hannah's Praise for the Son (2:1–10)

A praise song is the expression of the woman's overflowing heart. It follows in the rich history of exultations by Moses and the men of Israel (Ex. 15), Miriam and the women (Ex. 15), Moses and Israel (Deut. 32), and Deborah and Barak (Judg. 5).

Her rejoicing in the Lord (1). Hannah may well have prepared her sentiments ahead of time in writing, or vividly remembered them in recording while yet fresh. They came to be incorporated by the chronicler in due time.

She stresses her exultation and the Source from which it flows. Her heart is really thrilled in giving tribute to the Lord. Her horn is exalted, a picturesque way of saying that her power in success has its explanation in the covenant Lord. She feels vindication against those who oppose her, as Peninnah had done, this because of God delivering her from her inability.

Her reasons in the Lord (2–10). All of the favor shown to Hannah prompts her to exalt God for reasons that flow out of her lips.

(1) His preeminence (2). He is incomparable. He is this in holiness, set apart to His character and will, and He is this in power (a great rock). She says more about His power in verse 4, shown *against* with strength those who oppose Him and in *assisting* those who are weak, who trust Him.

(2) His perception (3). It is useless to speak arrogantly, as if one has assets by his or her own sufficiency. Peninnah had done this in flouting her superiority, as Hagar had earlier (Gen. 16). Pride finally counts for nothing. For God knows the truth. He discerns motives, and dependence as in Hannah's prayer to gain His assets. He weighs actions as on scales, and sees things according to their real character. So He is able to work consistently with motives that are yielded to Him.

(3) His provision (5). God is able to change things to the very opposite of what they are. For example, those who have been full can become empty and in desperate need, those who have been hungry satisfied. Now, to bring the analogy over to Hannah's own case, it is like this: the one who was barren is enabled to have seven children, possibly the number seven as picturing complete satisfaction. Hannah would later have three other sons, and two daughters, a full household (2:21), even these an answer to prayer (2:20). By contrast, a woman with many children can begin to languish. So the truth about life before God leaves no valid room for sinful pride.

(4) His prerogatives (6–8). Hannah is filled with pictures of God's ability to change everything. He is praiseworthy in that He can kill or make alive (he gave life in her womb when there was no way!). He makes poor or rich (cf. Deut. 8:18). He humbles and exalts. He is in control of everything, for instance the pillars of the earth, a picture of His upholding the earth securely. He does these, and other examples she exults to name.

(5) His protection (9). God, as He has done for Hannah, keeps the feet of His godly ones. He has guided her in a pathway protected from what has hurt her but now plentiful in things that encourage her. The success of a person, such as herself, is not by personal power but a gift from God.

(6) His prevailing over enemies (10). Defeat is sure for those who oppose the Lord; He will thunder against them. What Hannah says is true, though she did not know yet of God's thunder to defeat the Philistines (7:10). Everything is sure to get its proper judgment, for God will judge the ends of the earth (the people there). Hannah, praying in the will of God, said more than she fully understood. So do the other godly, whose God is able to do exceeding abundantly above all they ask or think (Eph. 3:20).

(7) God's promotion of His king (10). Hannah is led by God to pray in His will, that of Him who had announced kings in the line of Abraham (Gen. 17:6) and Judah (49:10). The king of His own choice, exalted to the throne, would serve by God's gift of strength and wield authority that He bestowed. Hannah's praise song also includes prayer's aspect of affirming His will, which she does frequently in the verses.

Within the books in which Hannah's own son will play so great a role, God would bring forth His anointed and place him on the throne (1 Sam. 16:1–3). What God prompts the woman to voice in prayer is a strategic detail in the plan He is unfolding. No doubt the God whom Hannah extols as so sufficient put such things in her mouth as she prayed. It is a privilege to be close to God, trusting Him, and have one's prayer in accord with His will. Today a principle in this is to know God's word, and be shaped by His guiding influence to pray more and more things true to His Person and purposes.

Principles for prayer are plentiful. First, God is able to answer prayer for a child when it is His will, for He is the author of life. One can see this in Abraham, Isaac, Leah and Rachel, and Manoah and his wife. Second, God is a God of the specific, so one can be particular with Him in prayer. Third, if one agrees with the Lord to do an honorable thing, it is a good testimony to be true to the pledge. Fourth, God can hear sincere prayer even though some person falsely reads a wrong into the act.

Fifth, a person who has put a wrong idea on a prayer can listen to truth and correct the error. Sixth, when God answers a person's prayer it can be a blessing to somebody else when the recipient testifies of this. Seventh, celebrate with gratitude to God for the answer. Eighth, prayer in thanksgiving can expand into other aspects as well—rehearsing glorious things that exalt the Lord, affirming truths about what God is (3), and what the buoyed up heart yet expects of Him (9–10).

1 Samuel 2:20, 21

A Priest's Prayer for Children

On later worship trips from Ramah to Shiloh, Hannah brought new robes she made to keep up with the growing son she visited.

Eli's Appeal for Children (2:20). Since this was, for some years, an annual gesture of love, Elkanah and Hannah possibly heard Eli's prayer blessing from year to year and not just once. As God had given the priests such roles as blessing the people for spiritual good (Num. 6:22–27), Eli prayed asking God to give Hannah children after Samuel. He prayed in light of her honoring the Lord in giving her son over to God's service at the tabernacle. This is one outworking of the principle God Himself highlights a little later in the context (2:30), "those who honor Me, I will honor. . . ."

God's Answer of Children (21). God did answer Eli's prayer, and no doubt a prayer in the heart of Elkanah and Hannah in accord with the priest's. In due time He blessed their home with five other children through Hannah. Although many other details also do not find their way into the record, the way things went for Peninnah is left to silence.

An interesting principle is that Eli was to some extent usable in prayer despite God's judgment, in context, on his priestly family's place in His service. The tragedy is that along with his good points, Eli tolerated some very bad ones and, like Samson, was not as useful as he had the potential to be.

His good points were his interest in prayer, as for Hannah in 1:17 and 2:20, and his concern for the Ark (4:13–18). Shadowing his career as a spiritual leader was his weak-hearted failure to manage and discipline his sons. They brought shame to God's service while Eli went along with some of it (2:12–17, 27–36). God sent a man of His mold to rebuke Eli personally, and announce removing leadership blessing from his line. With this is God's pledgc to raise up a faithful priest whose house He will bless (2:35). Eli's sons did die (4:11), as did other priests in his line at Nob (22:9–20). Also, Abiathar did not prosper under Solomon (1 Kgs. 2:26f.), though the priesthood of Zadok did (2 Sam. 19:11, etc.).

Principles attend this. First, one valid way to pray is to invoke specific blessing on another from God. Where it is His will, God is pleased to answer appeals of this kind. Second, when a person gives in faith to God, God is the great giver. In this case He already had given Hannah life, Himself, a husband, and an answer to prayer. Yet in her worshipful life He gave even other children, and the son Samuel whom she devoted would be an investment to return rich dividends (cf. Eph. 3:20; Phil. 4:17).

1 Samuel 3:4–18

A Boy Talks with God

God appears to the boy Samuel in the tabernacle three times, and in each an exchange occurs between the Lord and His young servant.

What the Lord Said Three Times (4–9)

God spoke to the boy who had begun his rest for the night in the tabernacle near the Ark, probably in a little side chamber that served for priestly quarters.

The Lord's voice came three times, at intervals, but Samuel was not used to hearing Him speak audibly and did not realize it was the Lord. It is a rare case of a person hearing God but not yet being aware that what rouses him is from the Lord. The boy simply assumed it must be Eli summoning him, as he was used to doing. He does say "Here I am" (Heb. ***hanani***) to God, as Abraham had said this for instant availability to Him (Gen. 22:1). However, Samuel did quickly go to the priest, and on the third occasion Eli finally realized that the voice the boy was hearing must be from God. So Eli gave Samuel counsel about how to respond when this recurred. Assume it was the Lord ("if He calls you," 9) and say to Him, "Speak, Lord, for your servant is listening."

What the Lad Said the Fourth Time (10)

Samuel lay down again, and heard the voice calling. This time the writer adds the detail that the Lord "stood" when He called, indicating that He was apparently present in bodily form. This is reasonable, since the Angel of the Lord had often appeared. Now He calls Samuel's name twice, probably to place special emphasis on it and to get him wide awake.

Samuel follows Eli's counsel.

His invitation to speak. Now the lad realizes, as Eli had explained, that he was dealing directly with the Lord. So he responds with a welcome to God's word. In principle, each believer needs to do this as he comes to God's word (James 1:21). This is in a spirit of alertness, freshness, and submissive receptivity to the impression with which God desires to incline the heart.

His inclination to hear. God can speak and Samuel is serious in his commitment to deal with His word. He is all set to listen. His attitude is that of being "your servant," sensitive to be moved by His word, prepared to act on it.

This is the spirit of Psalm 119:18, "Open my eyes, that I may hear wonderful things out of your law." It is the tone of obedience, of promptness to credit the word by its due weight and take it seriously.

What the Lord Said on the Fourth Time (11–14)

Now that He had riveted Samuel's attention, the Lord announced judgment on Eli's priesthood. This follows up His word through one of his human messengers delivered to Eli in 2:27–36. Here the Lord clarifies that Eli not only knew of his sons' sin but was sharing sin himself in not rebuking them. The sin this family condones will not be atoned for by sacrifice or offering forever. This may mean that none of Eli's house were genuinely saved, or some were not. Or it may indicate that the sin does not affect their eternal salvation but their continuation in their role of leadership, their priestly usefulness under God's blessing.

Fulfillment of the prophecy did not in all aspects occur right away. Eli and his sons died in Chapter 4, but this line of priesthood endured in Ahijah during Saul's reign (14:3). About 130 years later, Abiathar of this family tree was rejected and Zadok's line established in the priesthood under David (1 Kgs. 1:7, 8; 2:27, 35). Zadok was in the line of Eleazar, son of Aaron, and the prerogative remained in his family during the rest of Israel's kingdom. The sons of Zadok are also God's stated choice in the time of the future rebuilt temple ministry (Ezek. 44:15).

The prophecy God is giving on His initiative and in response also to prayer meets with Samuel's obedience in aspects pertaining to him. When Eli questions him, probably nervous as his conscience is disturbed by God's prophecy in 2:27–36, Samuel forthrightly divulges the Lord's message.

Eli himself prays in verse 17. He asks what the message was, and invokes God's action on Samuel if he hides anything from him. It was God's will for Eli to hear the message, so the priest is within God's will in this prayer. And Samuel scored high on the test. Eli, despite his failures that draw God's displeasure, now is resigned to His will. His prayerful wish is, "let Him do what seems good to Him."

In days after God's appearance, Samuel's prayer, and His message, God confirmed two things. He was *present* with Samuel, and He was *pleased* with him as a prophet as He confirmed to Israel that Samuel was His channel of authority.

What of prayer principles? One is that an older person who knows the ways of God can give help to a young one on how to pray. Another is that the God who knows all things and hears prayer knows us by name. Third, we need to come to God and His Word with a heart cry, "Speak, Lord, for your servant is listening." Fourth, the person who will obey God's Word, whether it is pleasant or bitter, will have power in his word before God (cf. 2:30; John 14:21–23). In this, the praying person acts best by responding to God even when His will is tough; let the heart say, "let Him do what seems good to Him."

1 Samuel 7:1–17

Samuel's Prayer for Israel's Victory

Israelites move the Ark from Shiloh to Kiriath-jearim about ten miles west of Jerusalem. It set there twenty years (v. 2), during which Samuel grew into maturity and greater ability as the Lord's leader. Several related steps occur here.

Israel's Renewal before God (1–4)

The situating of the ark. This, as above, is for twenty years.

The seeking of the Lord. All in Israel "lamented after the Lord," seeking Him in complaint due to their distress but so far not effectively gaining His blessing. They needed to repent.

The solution by Samuel. In verse 3 the prophet challenged his people to return to the Lord. This must not be skin deep but with all their heart (cf. Jer. 29:13) in genuine devotion. It will involve not only a return to Him but, as a part of sincere earnestness, a turn-about from worship of idols. They cannot get away with offering God a two-faced devotion, extending one hand to Him professing worship to Him while keeping a tight clutch on idolatry with their other hand. He insists on being alone in their allegiance. This is the ideal to see victory over the Philistines.

The separation to the Lord. The people react to Samuel's message seriously. Their devotion involves censure of idolatry and commitment to the Lord, a full and real about face. It is, in spirit, like that of the Thessalonians in Paul's day who turned "to God from idols, to serve the living and true God" (1 Thess. 1:9).

Now that Israel seriously means its approach to God, things can be different.

The Requests to God (5–9)

Samuel is ready to do spiritual business with a prepared people.

His call to prayer (5). He summons the repentant to Mizpah and promises to pray for them as a group there.

Their confession (6). As a sign of their reality, the people drew water and poured it out before the Lord. This seems to picture their self-denial of everything dear to them in a desire to be fully given to Him. Another indication of their spirit is their fasting. A third is their confession of sin that offends God. They want to make a clean sweep, and let nothing stand between God and them to block blessing.

Their crisis before the enemy (7). Philistine leaders, counting the Israelite massing a surge to national unity and poise for military attack, mobilized their troops to fight. News of the enemy approach struck consternation in the minds of the Israelites.

Their cry for help (8, 9). The people cried to Samuel, who had pledged himself to pray when they gathered. They desire that he keep up prayer appeals for them, for deliverance from the enemy. Samuel first acted with a burnt offering, wholly consumed as a sign of his people's whole-hearted devotion in verse 6. Then he lifted his voice in a cry to gain the Lord's protection.

God's Rout for Israel (10–14)

The sound of thunder. God rolled a crash of thunder across the sky just at the time the Philistines prepared to attack. Taking this as an ill omen, the enemies were confused, probably in indecision about whether to strike with confidence, or retreat fearing Israel's God was dooming them.

The smiting of the enemy. A result was Israel's pursuit of the Philistines and routing them as they fled.

The stone of praise. Samuel set up a stone on the battle site and called it Ebenezer. This means "stone of help." a memorial honoring God for His help in saving His people. This was a visual way of expressing the praise he felt for God's answer to his intercession in verse 9. It followed in the line of memorials God's people had erected through their covenant history, for example Jacob's stone of tribute to the "God of Bethel" (Gen. 28).

The subduing of the enemy. After the twenty years of Philistine oppression (2), God kept the enemy in defeat all through the days of Samuel. They would attack, but the Lord re-asserted His strength to beat them back. Captive cities were regained for Israelite possession, possibly in subsequent battles or else negotiations which are not recorded in the detail.

Effective prayer can have far-spanning results in blessing, as here. Samuel no doubt rekindled his ministry in fresh prayers as the days passed. This was acting on his conviction that to fail to pray for his people would be sin against God (12:23). Samuel's special altar to the Lord (7:17) is suggestive of continued prayers. New days bring new trials, and the urgency for God's help is continual.

Did others in Israel pray, or did they leave this completely to Samuel? The most probable answer is that many prayed, following up the repentance, but some could be more faithful than others persisting in this walk with the Lord. Some turned away, as Chapter 8 makes obvious.

Principles abound. First, power in prayer with God is found in submission that yields to Him the whole heart, not a nod to Him along with allegiance to idols. Second, one can be more confident to plead blessing for God-professing people when they are sincere before him. Third, clear a prayer path to God of things that might hinder as roadblocks. Fourth, a person who prays effectively to God is one He can use greatly to bless others. Fifth, praise to the Lord is always apt, as when He answers an intercessory concern. Sixth, where an intercessory ministry flourishes, God's power can thrust back the enemy. Seventh, using a place of prayer (altar, etc.) in faith and persistence can be a springboard into seeing great things from the Almighty. Eighth, when God does His work, it is often a result of a leader and those he leads praying.

1 Samuel 8:1–22

Prayer Clamoring for a King

Israel's Plea for a King (1–5)

Two currents of thought flow here.

The defect of Samuel's sons. By now Samuel had grown old, as 7:13 had already spanned his lifetime. He and Eli have been the last of the judges. Now Samuel's sons are unfit for judgeship, a travesty forfeiting respect by Israel. They gain dishonor due to their perversions of justice that repel those looking for a fair decision.

The desire for sovereign security. No judges are apparent, so the people's reaction is to resort to the desire to have a king like those who rule and lead other nations. Samuel's response to this craving is displeasure, and he takes the crisis to God in prayer (v. 6). The next verse, giving God's counsel of what Samuel is to do, suggests the lines along which his prayer must have pleaded. Quite naturally, he uttered petitions directly in search of wisdom, or pressing questions to gain guidance on what he should do. At the very least these would fit the case, even if praise/thanksgiving magnified God for past help.

The Perception of the Lord (7–18)

God has three aspects in His answer to the prayer.

His admonition. He admonishes Samuel to permit the people the choice they insist on forcing—their will and not God's best, which He would reveal in Chapter 16. The case is like that of Psalm 106:15, "He gave them their request, but sent leanness into their souls."

His attitude. Why does God give clearance for kingship, since He here rejects Israel's desire? He tells Samuel that the people have not rejected him, but God from being their king (7). They repeat the pattern that has long been chronic for Israel, forsaking Him and serving other gods (cf. Judg. 1–3, etc.).

The *idea* of their having a king, one chosen by God, is within the will of God itself. He had predicted kings in the line of Abraham (Gen. 17:6) and Judah (49:10), and approved this (Deut. 17:14–20). It is not the *idea* of a king that displeases God, but the people's *intention* to indulge their own will in having one. Their attitude was at enmity with God's. They were forsaking *Him* as the object of their confidence, the God who had thundered and protected them in Chapter 7. Their wickedness was great (12:17; cf. 12:12) as it was a heart failure of serving false gods (8:8), something besides the Lord. Their vesting of confidence in a human king was just another indication that their trust was not really in the *Lord*. It has been well-said that their sin was not in desiring a monarchy, but a monarchy *in the place of* a theocracy.

It is significant that Saul, the first king, was from the tribe of Benjamin, not Judah as God had said His certified king was to be (Gen. 49:10). The fact that Saul was not from Judah suggests an Israelite readiness to fulfill by fleshly wisdom God's original, right intention of a kingdom. This is similar to Abram and Sarai at first fulfilling by their fleshly way the desire to have a son, getting an Ishmael and not an Isaac. Israel, too, reflects impatience, not willing to wait in trust for God's time and way. This is also as Jacob who was not wrong in desiring the blessing, but wrong in the fleshly way he used to gain it.

Here God was willing to spend a generation on Israel's mistake to demonstrate that He could fulfill His true desire for a king when He was ready. Later He designates David from Judah (16:1–3) and gives him the promise that through his lineage would come the king to establish his house forever (2 Sam. 7:12–16). He Himself allows to Israel their will, Saul (1 Sam. 9:15–17; 10:1, 6, 9, 10). Yet His permitting to men their wrong preference (10:23, 24; 12:13) is in contrast to His providing a man after His own heart (13:14).

His alerting of Israel. God's answer to Samuel's prayer includes a warning of the problems Israel will suffer from having a king. The king would require their sons as soldiers, appoint people to do his plowing, reaping, weaponry, and cooking, grab the best lands to confer to people he favored, tax the people, and so on. This counsel even moves to Israel's future prayer (v. 18). When the people would have a king, they would cry out in prayer, hurt by the leader's oppression, but God's answer would not be to relieve them of kingship.

His aversion to Israel (18). Prayer finds mention again in Chapter 8, as in verses 6 and 21. While Samuel is briefing his people on details summing up life with a king (11–17), he adds frankly that the Israelites will pray, that is, "you will cry out in that day . . . but the Lord will not answer you, . . ." They will have to live with their choice and its consequences. It is as when an egg breaks and spills upon the floor; one cannot gather it back into the former state, but has to deal with it as it is.

The arrogance of Israel (19). They think they know better. They refuse God's counsel through his prophet/priest, and re-emphasize what is their own choice. How often people have repeated this kind of decision that they must have what is their own conceit.

God's answer to prayer makes no difference to hardened hearts. But note more on verse 19.

The Persistence for a King (19, 20)

God's viewpoint that the people had rejected Him from being king (7) is illustrated here. The throng repudiates Samuel's words, therefore God's, since Samuel is only a channel delivering His words to them. They desire to be "up" with all the nations in being led by a human king, not unique in being led by the heavenly King.

The Prayer of Samuel (21–22)

God's "servant" (cf. 3:10) repeats this rejection in conversing with God. This is a prayer in the aspect of affirmation, or rehearsing truth. Samuel does this after listening to hear things correctly and represent them rightly, nothing twisted. God answers by instructing him to give them that for which they clamor, to appoint a king. He says, "Tell them 'have it your way.'" Chapters 9 and 10 then explain God's giving them Saul, a man who fully appeals to their human tastes and misconceptions of greatness. His great handsomeness and height are the qualifications foolishness approves (9:2), whereas later God would place His value on the heart devoted to Him (16:7). Samuel anoints Saul with oil to set him apart to kingship (10:1), and God gives Saul His Spirit to assist in leadership.

Now glean the principles. First, God can do His will even when He lets people get a taste of their own foolish will and learn the backlash their "know better" spirit insists on having. Second, a given matter of prayer may be God's will, yet the impatient can work against God's right way to provide it and get something else. An example may help. It is His will for a person to have a marriage partner, yet that person demands his own choice not in sync with God's wisdom, and in his own timing, and botches his life for a time. In a rare case, the same person, who has gone through a bitter divorce, may marry the one God has reserved, His will, and see it work out to His glory through grace. But he could have had this answer without the way of heartache.

Third, no matter how a godly person warns praying believers of what they can face as they are rigid to have things their way, the counselees may have to learn the unpleasant consequences. Fourth, when believers must maneuver things to their own liking and they do not heed God's way, they not only discount His will but push *Him* aside.

1 Samuel 9:13

A King "Tailor Made"

We can trace three movements about this in Chapters 9–10.

Saul's Search (9:1–13)

Two references to prayer meet the reader here (9, 13).

Saul, who would fill the bill for a king, is coming front and center. He makes a trek to find his father's donkeys, and a focus is on what a magnificent specimen he is (9:2). It was a custom at that time when a lay person inquired of God he would go to a seer, or prophet, who notably was felt to have effective clout in prayer (9). So Saul seeks out the famous spiritual leader because his reputation is honored—what he says God has told him comes true (v. 6). Young women tell the seeker of donkeys and his servant that Samuel is due in the local city to "bless" the sacrifice (13).

When a priest blessed a sacrifice, he prayed to petition God to bless the offering, receive it as pleasing, and hear thanks for His grace. One can review the significance of the offerings in Leviticus 1–7 (cf. Introduction there).

Samuel's Solution (9:14–10:13)

Two things happen quickly.

The answer to his request (9:20). Samuel tells Saul the donkeys have been found and are safe. He mentions far more than animals; he turns the emphasis to an anticipation. A most desirable honor is set for Saul and his family, an intimation that he is to be the king!

The anointing for his royalty (9:22–10:13). The prophet places Saul in the seat of honor at a banquet (9:22), gives him a special portion that exalts him at the feast (24), and the next day poured anointing oil on him from a flask. In this ceremony, Samuel must have awakened Saul with the question, "Has not the Lord anointed you a ruler over His inheritance?" (10:1). He also tells him that the Spirit of the Lord will come upon him to enable him to lead his people (6). Later, God transforms the new king to suit him to kingship (9), and the Spirit helps him to prophesy among a band of prophets (11).

Even a further intimation of prayer occurs in 10:8. Samuel forecasts that he will meet Saul again at Gilgal and officiate at burnt and peace offerings. As in Leviticus 1–7, the import of this relates to prayer in this way. It was spiritually natural to pray in dedication to God when one's burnt offering, completely consumed on the altar, pictured his own full dedication to that pleased God. And the peace offerings signified peace within the covenant bond, which for minds in sync with this stimulated thanksgiving (cf. Lev. 7:13).

The Sequel (10:14–26)

One phase of this is mundane, the other momentous.

Saul's answer to his father (14–16). The anointed king once back home reported only Samuel's assistance in finding the donkeys. It was an incomplete answer, truthful as far as it went, just as God's answer for Samuel to give is later (16:1–2). What Saul said satisfied the family member about the burning issue most at stake immediately for him, though it kept back the detail that Saul was the king.

Samuel's announcement to Israel (10:17–26). The point most relevant to the present study is the prayer that is obvious in verse 22. Samuel receives the privilege of making the news of a regal choice known to Israel at Mizpah. He reminds them about their rejection of God who has been their deliverer, better than any human king (19), and with elimination by the custom of lots shows that Saul from the Tribe of Benjamin is their royal leader (20–22).

Prayer leaps into the scene (22). It also emerges in 11:13. For later, at Gilgal, those of Israel install Saul in his high position. This drama was accompanied by peace offerings, which were with prayer in thanksgiving (cf. Lev. 7:13). Consider in more detail the inquiry before God in 10:22.

But first review principles from this episode. One that can impact prayer is that God knows where something lost is, and can lead the person to it. Often He does, yet sometimes He may not, should He gave some other purpose intended for good. One may lose valuable notes for a Bible message, finally have to prepare notes again, profit greatly from the new study, and grasp things better. Second, in whatever one offers to the Lord, it is appropriate to look to Him in grateful and freshly dedicatory prayer.

1 Samuel 10:22

Prayer for a Man's Location

Calling for a gathering for Saul's inauguration, God signals the people to Mizpah by Samuel's instructions.

Saul's tribe, Benjamin, was selected by lot for kingship, and the lot further narrowed the choice to his family. But Saul was missing. The people prayed asking if the king had arrived yet, and God answered by telling them the exact place where they would locate him, by the baggage. In this way identified, Saul was ushered into the limelight to be the king.

Consider a principle that relates here.

This illustrates God answering prayer with a "yes" in His kindness, yet giving people what they in rejection insist on getting. Careful reflection to be sure of God's word that had specified Judah (Gen. 49:10) and sensitive ambition to have only His will (cf. 7:6) could have helped Israel wait for God's way.

1 Samuel 12

Avoiding Sin by Prayer

Five verses are explicit about prayer in Chapter 12 (7, 10, 17, 19, and 23). Most potent among these is Samuel's belief in verse 23. It is sin not to pray for God's cause and God's people. And even verse 5 suggests the probable prayer behind it. For Samuel invokes (reasonably calls upon) the Lord as witness, and Saul as one who can testify, that he has been a faithful leader.

Samuel's Pleading for Vindication (1–5)

The judge and prophet/priest reviews his faithfulness as God's leader from the perspective of his old age. He also does this on the verge of the shift to leadership by a king. He calls on his people to reflect on his wise pattern.

Prayer will play a big role in the later part of the chapter.

His review of his modeling (1–3). The new leader has already begun (cf. Chaps. 10, 11). Samuel is in his last days. He asks the people to think soberly of his example, for this is wise to remember and hold up as a standard.

He asks questions designed to draw their answer, "none." Never has Samuel cheated them to pad his own profit, or oppressed them by injustice. A principle for prayer is simple. The person who will count before God and others in prayer needs to realize the relation of prayer to all the currents of spiritual faithfulness. He should take care of his entire act, and not expect respect from God or men if his is not an all-around commitment. When a prayer warrior has had his whole life together, a testimony honoring the Lord, the impact can be great, as Samuel's is.

Their reflection on his modeling (4, 5). Now the people answer Samuel. His testimony has been sterling, a worthy one before all. His *worthiness* as they attest it leads Samuel to proclaim God as also the *witness* of it.

His Panorama of Israel's History (6–13)

After the review of his own exemplary life, Samuel reviews Israel's history to show them the faults they need to avoid in the future. The man of high values is pleading with them to take note and be careful about faithfulness (cf. v. 7). God had answered Israel's prayers in Egyptian bondage by sending Moses and Aaron to lead them out of distress. Later they often drifted, prayed to Him in troubles, and He delivered them in the days of earlier judges. After this their prayer was a clamor for a king, so now God has granted them a king.

His Prayer about Their Sin (14–18)

The ball is now in Israel's court, so to speak. They can yet fear the Lord, serve Him and find blessing for their king and themselves. Or they can rebel against the Lord and find His hand dealing them judgment. Let them recall the illustration from their forebears. At this moment, Samuel prays to the Lord for a sign to expose how great a sin God esteems the hankering for a king in place of Him to be (17).

Samuel pleads for thunder and rain from heaven, probably as a sign of God's action from heaven against sin. When God answers the request with the heavenly sign, the people greatly feared both the Lord and His servant.

His Proclamation of God's Will (19–23)

The people fear so much that they are smitten by an immediate prayer burden.

The request for prayer (19). They feel they totter on the verge of death due to God's provocative sign via powerful thunder and lashing rain. They confess their sin of having asked for a king, and see it fitting with the pattern of past Israelite sins.

His reassurance in His plan (20–23). Samuel bids his people to cast aside terror of impending doom. Yes, they have indeed sinned. But now their move is to see that their act is in positive steadfastness to God with all their heart. He reassures them of God's own steadfastness based in two guarantees. First, His *Person* is a pledge. His great name is committed to them, and He will not violate His character. For if He did He would lose more than they, the very faithfulness of His reputation. Second, His *pleasure* of His own covenant will in making Israel a people for Himself is a certification. He will not act in dishonor to His word in covenant.

The covenant inviolability goes back to such a foundation as God's ceremony ratifying its sureness to Abram in Genesis 15. There He had verified by the honor of His very life that on His own faithfulness He would see the covenant through. He would fulfill it unconditionally, in grace. Its reliability would depend on Him who walked between the sacrifice parts, and not on Abram. Let His very life be dismembered like the sacrifices should He ever fail to be true to what He promised!

The reflection of Samuel. Here is one example showing why Samuel would be so honored by Israel as a model of greatness in prayer (Ps. 99:6; Jer. 15:1). Not only is *God's* commitment a reassurance to Israel; *Samuel's* also is. He reflects, for their encouragement, on his unswerving loyalty to seek their blessing. This, too, is in the form of a prayer. May it be far from him, by God's grace, ever to sin against God by ceasing to pray for His people. Commitment to the *Lord* entails for him commitment to God's *interests*.

Rather than failing them by curtailing his praying, Samuel pledges them that with continued intercession will be His instruction in the will of the God who hears prayer. This will is like a pathway, a trail of what is good and right. Centuries later Paul would see the fruit of light, of God, as in all goodness, righteousness, and truth (Eph. 5:9).

A faithful servant of truth must also be candid and speak the unvarnished truth. So Samuel is prompt to brief Israel on the other side of this.

Their Ruin in a Way of Disobedience (25)

If Israel persists in catering to sin, ruin must be sure from God's disciplining hand. Both they and their king will be swept away in the judgment. This prophecy points to its fulfillment in God's judgment bringing Assyria to devastate Samaria in 721 B.C. and Babylon to wreak the end of the southern kingdom in three phases during 605, 597, and 586 B.C.

Several principles invite attention. First, God often shows mercy (cf. Ps. 103) in giving kind answers to people who are not consistent and dependable. He can be very gracious in efforts to nudge them along with encouragement and give them further opportunity to grow. Second, one of the lessons we learn in prayer is that we often do not learn in prayer, but continue along our own paths and for our own sakes. Third, we work against effective prayer in many ways: sin that has its demanding way may be selfish indulgence, divided loyalty, sloth, or some other version of catering to one's own will (cf. v. 10). Fourth, since God made and controls the universe, prayer has often gained His help by sending rain. His power can do this, though His purpose may or may not be to work this way (cf. v. 17). Fifth, it is always true that God answers prayer in harmony with His own character and honorable purposes in some benefit He intends to work (cf. v. 19). Sixth, in verse 23, when God gives a person a role in ministry to others it is a sin not to intercede for their welfare. Likewise in verse 23, prayer for God's will in a given situation should always be in unison with His will in His Word.

1 Samuel 13:9, 12

Praying that is Out of Place

Saul prays on one occasion here, but two different verses relate directly to it. He shows disrespect in speaking to God, and then Samuel voices disdain in confronting him.

The Disrespect (1–12)

Saul's act (1–9). The king mobilized his fighters against Philistine invasion, but pressure drove some Israelites to hide wherever they found refuge, and some retreated east of the Jordan. Saul grasped for the

Lord's help. When Samuel did not come in the seven day span he had specified (cf. 10:8), so the impatient king acted with presumption. He himself presented the burnt offering (9–10), an interference into Samuel's priestly ministry. According to God's word (cf. Lev. 7:13), prayer had a vital relationship to this, in uttering to the Lord a dedication of one's entire life, just as the offering was consumed totally on the altar. Shortly after, Saul refers back to his prayer, seeking victory God could give as he supposed devoted all to Him.

It was prayer arrogantly taking the priestly privilege to himself, and showing disrespect for God and His word, and Samuel the priest.

Saul's account (10–12). Now Samuel has arrived, seen what Saul has just done out of place, and is dealing with him point-blank. Saul greets him as if all is just as it should be (10). But God's spiritual leader asks for an explanation. The king, ready with his glib defense, supposes he can smooth it all over. His rationale is along three lines that put pressure on him—his soldiers' flight, Samuel's lateness as if he blame shifts to him, and Philistine mustering to attack. So, he reasons, he can be clear of any fault, since it was high time for the prayer, for he had felt "I have not asked [in petition] the favor of the Lord." That he had prayed, done the "spiritual" thing, ought to make everything right.

It all has the rosy ring of legitimacy, given his self-willed view of things.

The Disdain (13–14)

Samuel's perspective cuts sharply against the king's. What Saul did was foolish. For it was in disobedience to God's command, as in Leviticus 1–7, a context of commands, and His command through His mouthpiece, Samuel (1 Sam. 10:8). In the latter passage, the prophet/priest was plain. Samuel would make the offerings, Saul was to wait for him and not run ahead of him, and Samuel would show him what he should do.

Not only was the out of place offering foolish. It brings Saul into such disdain with God and with His spiritual servant that not just a battle but the kingdom is at stake. The words must have hit hard, "now your kingdom shall not endure," and "The Lord has sought out for Himself a man after His own heart, and the Lord has appointed him as ruler over His people." This is "because you have not kept what the Lord commanded you" (14). Of course a further reason is that God sovereignly had His own previous will that a king in the lineage of Judah should reign (Gen. 49:8–12).

Having spoken the disdain, "Then Samuel arose and went up from Gilgal" (15), and Saul was left to deal with seed thoughts that he was on his way out.

Guidelines are inherent. First, a person should guard against usurping the ministry that God has given to another. Second, when one is brought to account for a wrong in prayer or anything else, he should deal with disobedience squarely, get right with God and others, and not try to slide off with glib, self-made evasions.

1 Samuel 14

A Carnal King's Prayer for Guidance

Saul was a man who impressed others from his youth, especially in handsomeness and height (9:2). Soon after his royal career began, he started downward on a trail of sins that disqualified him before the Lord. Chapter 13 has already been vivid about one of his sins, his disqualification by his offering.

Others offered in days when the people were far from the tabernacle. Gideon did (Judg. 6:15), but Saul surely sinned in disobeying Samuel's specific instruction to wait for him to come and offer (10:8). The impatience was a sin, as was his lack of faith to trust in God's timing (13:8–14). Possibly the summary of Saul's offering is simply generalized, not mentioning priestly help though it occurred (cf. 2 Sam. 24: 25; 1 Kgs. 4:4; 8:63). If so, the king still sinned in his attitude of forcing the offering ahead of God's will.

Now in Chapter 14 Saul's second disqualification is in view.

Saul's Ascendancy Over the Philistines (1–31, 47, 48)

The king's son Jonathan and his armor bearer climbed up to attack a Philistine stronghold high in the rocks. They defeated about twenty enemy soldiers (14), and the Israelite army also gained a great victory putting Philistines to flight (20–23).

In the midst of this drama, Saul in prayer charged his fighting men to keep a rash oath (14:24). Like Jephthah, he let the impatient fear and urgency of the battle press him to a hasty demand. He foolishly invoked God's curse on any man who ate before evening, for he wanted every man to focus only on getting the win. It turned out that his own son, weary from the hard fighting and unaware of the vow, ate honey he found in a grove of trees (27). Saul would soon have to deal with his impetuous requirement.

Saul's Acts of Worship (32–42)

His provision for sacrifice (32–35). Exhausted from battle and extremely famished from Saul's unkind denial of food, the soldiers butchered cattle amidst the spoil. They ate the meat with blood still in it. This was a violation of God's law. He had called Israel to a respect for the blood as the life principle strategic in picturing His atonement for sin (Lev. 17:11). Saul, whose rash order had led to this dire hunger, now does what is right. He has a stone rolled near, upon which to drain blood from the meat. He also built an altar to the Lord in a step to seek His favor after the episode of misusing the blood. Presumably soldiers offered animals on this altar to pacify Saul's desire to be within God's good graces.

His plan to surprise the enemy (36). The king devised the strategy of a night attack on unsuspecting Philistines. The priest whose word carried weight advised seeking the Lord, which was the right counsel.

His prayer for strategy (37). Saul had already formed a strategy. Now, at the priest's intervention, he pauses to ask God's direction on what to do. His prayer is for the right move, whether to attack and whether God would give victory. His recourse to seeking God's will seems to be an afterthought of a man rushing ahead to fulfill his own plan. Saul is like the man who wondered if it was God's will to accept a pastorate at a certain church. He told his wife to stay downstairs and pack, and he would go upstairs and pray.

His perception of sin (38–42). God did not answer the king's prayer of verse 37 that day, and this would appear to be to permit time for Saul to deal with the oath he made in verse 24. So he perceived the delay as indication that something needed attention. He remembered his oath and in some way discovered that what he had invoked from God had been violated. Possibly this insight came by the high priest's Urim and Thummim providing guidance. Or it may be a casting of lots that narrowed possibilities finally to a focus. He can use lots as he does in a further prayer attempt (41–42).

Saul is again impetuous and rash. Even if his own son violated what the army had said in oath, he will put him to death. His mouth kicked into motion before his brain was engaged. Then, shuddering in shock, Saul has to deal with the cast lots narrowing the guilty one to Jonathan! This stunning fact can remind one of David's anger at a man Nathan described, and Nathan's shocker in telling David that he was that man (2 Sam. 12).

Saul's Attempt to Fulfill the Oath (43–46)

Put on the spot by Jonathan's confession, Saul sees himself trapped by his own hasty oath. His pride is at stake before his men. He resolves to go through with Jonathan's execution to save face. Even his son can die if his own ego is bolstered.

His insensitive reaction. At first Saul is insensitive to who the man is who went against his vow. He puts that aside, and also is insensitive to the wrong of righting a wrong with a greater wrong, the slaying of a man who only ate food when hungry. He would be bull-headed and defend his ego. He was insensitive to the will of God that Jonathan and his armor-bearer had carried out in bravery that risked death (9–14).

Saul's words in verse 44, as those in 24, follow a form of making an oath, and an oath involved prayer in speaking to God as he had uttered words to Him in verses 37 and 41. He was saying in verse 44, "[I pray invoking God for His action], may God [who is my witness that I will follow through] do this [bring a curse as in verse 24?] to me and more as well, for you shall surely die, Jonathan."

Israel's insistent rescue. The men around Saul were on to the bullheaded folly of his course. They recognized Jonathan's valiant and strategic pace-setting as God's key to gaining the victory (45). Now they utter their own oath, calling in prayer on God who lives to stand as their witness, they resolve to protect their champion's life. Saul backs down.

Principles in prayer are plain enough. Seeking God as at an altar ought to be part of a total commitment to know His mind. One should not rush ahead in a self-willed scheme and only inquire of God later. Suppose a person has erred making a foolish vow, thinking lightly about the welfare of others. It would be better to confess sin and let the vow go than to compound wrong by insisting on doing one's will to save face. Second, it is of extreme importance to take time thinking through on promises made to God. This would all opportunity to form them within His counsel and not in the vacuum of erroneous human thinking under pressure. Did Saul ask for counsel of the priests before leaping into the vow? Did he reflect in an all-around recalling of God's principles to weigh his impulse by these?

Saul has already disqualified himself by his offering (Chap. 13) and now also by his oath. Yet ahead in his plunge downward are disqualifications by his obstinacy toward God (Chap. 15), his oppression of murderous hatefulness toward David (Chaps. 18–26), and his occultism visiting the witch of Endor (28). The obsession to kill David, in itself, is made up of a dark pattern involving about twenty insistent steps. These show a man bent on framing his own ruin.

A principle in verse 24 is this. Carefulness wisely makes certain that what one summons God to attest is God's will. It should not be our own conceit to maneuver out of a bind, and against the sensible benefit of those we involve in the situation. A principle also pertains to verse 37. Ask is it really God's leading that we prize through prayer, or is prayer a formality that conceals a heart rigid to have things one's own arrogant way? In verse 41 a guideline occurs: In the Old Testament one could make a valid, God-fearing pledge in good faith and truth, or use it to serve a foolish design. God knows the difference. How much better to seek God's help in normal petition or intercession and trust in His great faithfulness!

1 Samuel 15:11, 13, 24–25, 30

A Godly Man's All-Night Prayer and a Carnal Man Mouthing Prayer

Samuel prays all night in grave heartbreak, mourning Saul's sin, and after this ordeal the disobedient Saul greets Samuel as if all is well. His greeting is a form of prayer.

Saul's Compromises in Disobedience (1–9)

God used Samuel to give the king clear instructions to carry out. Saul did not obey these but did things his own way.

God's directions (1–3). Samuel was God's mouthpiece, speaking ever so plainly to the king. He identifies himself as the man God sent to anoint Saul to his leadership. Now he calls Saul to receive his present ministry as also from the Lord.

The prophet's words are pointed. God wants Saul not only to defeat the Amalekites, but destroy them utterly. This is a just mission, for Amalek is ripe for judgment. An Amalekite army ambushed Israel during its wilderness journey, and God answered Moses' prayer by leading Joshua to victory over this enemy (Ex. 17:8–13). Later God specified through Moses that Israel, after getting into the promised land, was to destroy this evil nation (Deut. 25:17–19). Now Saul is the leader to fulfill God's will.

God insists that Saul be unsparing, that he wipe the enemy out to the last man, woman, child, and animal. Nobody and nothing is to remain alive.

Saul's disobedience (4–9). Saul triumphed, but spared Agag the king and the best of the sheep, oxen, lambs and other animals. He saved what he preferred, substituting his will for the will of God.

Prayer comes in this atmosphere of rebellion.

Samuel's Confrontation of Disobedience (10–23)

God gave the directive in this episode. Now He takes the initiative in a showdown with Saul over his partial obedience.

God's arousal of Samuel (10, 11). The coming of the Lord's word about Saul is the first emphasis. God pierces right to the issue. He is grieved that He made Saul king since Saul has "turned back from following Me. . . ." He is not admitting a mistake, for He does not make any. Rather He is expressing the pain He feels in the role of Saul so far. Saul's *attitude* of turning against God is joined with his *action* in not doing what God commanded.

God's hurt is shared by Samuel.

Samuel's agony in prayer (11). When a person is resolute to see God's will done, he is grieved (cf. 16:1) to hear of another not doing it. God's passion is in Samuel, and the news of Saul distresses the prophet. His agony is so intense that he prays all night. He displays full identity with God's will. He joins others in the Bible who are said to pray all night, such as Jacob (Gen. 32:24–32) and Jesus (Luke 6:12).

What did Samuel cry to God? The passage does not elaborate. It would be relevant that he make *intercession* for Saul to rectify things in any partial way he yet might. At the same time he probably *petitions* God to give him wisdom in dealing with the king the next day. Also likely is *intercession* for God to raise up His own choice to be a good king. If so, God's summons to anoint a king in 16:1–3 is an answer. Saul may have *affirmed* the rightness of God's will, and his sorrow in the king grieving God.

Samuel's accountability with Saul (12–23). Several things occur rapidly during the confrontation.

(1) Saul's calling for blessing (13). At first the king is glib and "spiritual." Everything is just right. He meets God's man with a prayer wish, an invocation of God's blessing on him as if all is well, yet insincerely. A person living in disobedience to God can put up a front that is ever so smooth and positive, yet it is a façade.

(2) Saul's claiming of obedience (13). How falsely the words fell on Samuel's ears. "I have carried out the command of the Lord." The principle to watch out for in one's own life is alleging the doing of God's will as a cover-up for doing only some of it and indulging self-will in the rest. God sees right through the sham.

(3) Samuel's convicting Saul of sin (14–23). The prophet cuts right to the obvious. If Saul has obeyed, what is the meaning in the bleating of spared sheep and the lowing of spared oxen? Carnality can be ingenious in its rationalizing, as Saul's now is. The people, he says (not acknowledging that *he* led in this) but passing the buck brought the animals. Even then, the sparing was for a "spiritual" purpose—to sacrifice to the Lord. But, to smooth everything over as fine and dandy, "the rest we have utterly destroyed."

Samuel then is up front about the Lord's view of this, freshly emboldened by his vigil in prayer the night before. Why the decision, when taking the battle spoil, to do "evil in the sight of the Lord?" Why did Saul fail to obey the Lord? Saul is still glib, trying to bluff his way out of the tight place. He *did* obey; he went as God sent him to do, brought back Agag (he got the leader!), and put all the others to death. But "the people" took some animals, and did it for a good reason, to sacrifice. Saul fails to confess that *he* was guilty in that, as leader responsible over the people (v. 9).

At this point Samuel's answer is convicting. He reasons with Saul to bring him to confession. Does the Lord have as much delight in burnt offerings and sacrifices serving man's own scheme as in obeying Him? The truth is, to obey is better than sacrifice, and to heed more valuable than the fat of rams offered. For, on the other hand, rebellion such as Saul's is as evil (cf. 19) as divination. And insubordination rates as iniquity, as evil as idol-worship. Saul has rejected the word of the Lord, in its place insisting on his own will. Because of this the Lord has rejected him from being king.

Saul's Confession of Disobedience (24–31)

Finally the truth registers, and the king faces the light.

The acknowledgment (24). "I have sinned . . . transgressed the command of the Lord and your words." With the confession comes the cause at the root, "because I feared the people and listened to their voice." It was a collapse where faith could have held him up (cf. Hab. 2:4). Fear reigned instead, and Saul put more stock in what the people said than in what God said.

Later Scripture would explain that the fear of man brings a snare. The principle is that the spirit needs to foster the sense of God as having precedence and power over people we can fear.

The appeal to save face (25). Saul has confessed, but seems more disturbed about how he will appear in the eyes of those he leads than in God's eyes. The same fear of man above still sways him. He wants Samuel's pardon, and probably God's in which Samuel leads. With this he wants Samuel to act a lie, return with him, smooth everything over to look normal before others, let him worship the Lord as if all is well.

The announcement of a new king (26–29). At first Samuel declines to go. His reason is, "you have rejected the word of the Lord, and the Lord has rejected you from being king over Israel." Turning to leave, Samuel felt a tug and heard a rip as Saul's fingers clutched at his robe to hold him. This ripped robe then became for Samuel a picture of the Lord having torn the kingdom from Saul to transfer it to a neighbor.

He cannot change the decision, but must respect God's honor. God as the Glory of Israel will not lie or change His mind, as a man can.

The accompaniment of Samuel (30, 31). Saul confesses again, but urges a second plea for Samuel to accompany him. This will honor him before the leaders and the masses. Graciously Samuel did go through with this, though surely without any lie in compromise.

Samuel's Completion of the Obedience (32–35)

God's command for dealing with the Amalekites had not yet been fully obeyed. Samuel is careful to attend to this.

The punishment on Agag. The enemy king felt that, due to the delay and his safety by Saul's decision, he would live. But Samuel recognized his wicked acts against others, and dealt with him as he had done to them. He deserved a death sentence and got it. So will all who reject God and His way, even if not until after temporal death, in the intermediate state and in eternity (cf. Luke 16:19ff.) and ultimately at God's Great White Throne (Rev. 20:11–15).

The parting of Samuel and Saul. The two parted, each to his own home. Samuel would not see Saul or have any dealing with him before the prophet's death. He *would* see and speak with Saul after death in an unusual act of God before the Witch of Endor (1 Sam. 28).

The pain that lingered. The grief over sin that kept Samuel praying all night, and been on his heart in confronting Saul now persisted as a painful burden. "Samuel grieved over Saul." The sin was a grief to God as well (Eph. 4:30). The Lord knew pain in His permission to Israel to have *their* kind of king, and had seen this lesson through. But His own choice, now to be revealed, is David (16:1–3).

Principles now are in order. First (v. 11), a prayer tryst of many hours can be by one's own agenda, an exercise in fleshly zeal, or in genuine, godly burden for God's work and some leader and others affected. Of course the latter is true here. Second (v. 13), God knows when a person just spins words of prayer out of a disobedient heart and off sinful lips. Honey on the lips will not resolve poison in the heart. Third (vv. 24–25, 30), confession to God is due when one has pushed aside His will to have his own way (cf. Ps. 51; Prov. 28:13; 1 John 1:9). Fourth (vv. 32–35), a time may come when God or a true leader of His parts company with a person who does endruns around the Word and is only open to what is on his own disobedient terms. Even Jesus would teach hearers to turn away from the insistently unreceptive. So would Paul, and so his counsel (1 Cor. 5, "from such turn away").

1 Samuel 16:2

Prayer for Guidance in Anointing David

God charges Samuel to anoint one of Jesse's sons to be king. Samuel obeys, anointing the son God chooses.

The Announcement of a King (1–5)

Samuel's pain. The prophet still suffered as he had hearing news of Saul's disobedience, and in confronting him with God's rejection. Samuel was sensitive for Saul's life in caring love, deeply involved with Israelites he had served, and grieved at the sad state of affairs as God did.

The Lord, however, is moving on. He asks how long the grief must continue. Samuel's suffering is understandable, but he needs to buck up, put the hurt in the past and dwell on God's will in turning from Saul's kingship. God is not defeated. He has plans that will brighten the scene.

God's plan. He directs Samuel to fill his ram's horn with oil to use in anointing and visit Jesse's family. There God has a man to anoint as the new king.

Samuel's prayer. Marking out a new king poses a threat to Samuel. He petitions God in the form of a question. How can he go and anoint a king? For the present king, hearing of this, will retaliate quickly to avenge the threat against his own security. This is a valid concern for safety, and God is ready with a solution.

A principle fits here. We may pray without knowing a way to do an act in work for the Lord, but God can answer with an effective plan. It may be wise to wait in trust, keep on praying, and let the Lord distill the guidance that fits the case.

God's provision. He tells Samuel to do the anointing in connection with announcing his purpose to sacrifice, and inviting Jesse's family to attend. The purpose Samuel will state for his visit to Bethlehem is itself the truth. It does not go into all the reasons. Saul would, as Samuel fears, react with murderous intent, and has no right to know all the detail.

Here is a principle. God can lead a person to do what is certainly truthful, yet not divulge all facets about the entire truthful picture (cf. also Jer. 38:27–28). A given party or audience may not need to know the full detail, or may be liable to react disastrously, against what is wise.

Samuel invited Jesse and his family, and also elders of Bethlehem to the sacrifice. The elders at first suspect that the prophet and judge has come on some matter of judgment (cf. 7:16), so they are uneasy. But Samuel puts them at ease with his invitation.

When David is anointed, the guests possibly only think that it marks the boy to be a trainee as a prophet under Samuel's supervision. So word of the anointing would not cause Saul to slap a death price on Samuel or David.

The Anointing of David (6–13)

The choices God passes by. At first Samuel assumes that any of Jesse's first three sons would qualify to be God's choice. Eliab, Abinadab and Shammah come before the prophet, but the Lord tells Samuel not one of them is His man. He counsels Samuel not to prefer a man on the criteria of his appearance, or his height (7). This is man's way, to judge on such bases (cf. 9:2). But God's preference is based on His seeing the values that guide a man's heart.

The choice God prefers. When seven of Jesse's sons pass by and God says "no," Samuel asks if Jesse has another son. The father mentions the unlikely one, the youngest, left at home to tend the sheep. When the boy, David, arrives he is "ruddy," possibly meaning he has a reddish countenance. He also has impressive eyes and a handsome appearance. God tells Samuel to anoint this son.

Oil from the horn is applied to David as his family and the elders look on with a sense of wonder. Then in some way it became obvious that the Spirit of the Lord came upon David in power that day and afterward. This may have been in an increased wisdom in speaking in a commanding way, or in his overall carriage summoning respect.

The prophet whose concerned prayer for safety was being answered by a faithful God returned to his home.

A principle from the entire episode of anointing David is as follows. A faithful servant in ministry for God may see some discouraging things, but sooner or later God can bring what encourages. In Samuel's service, several matters in the experience with Saul could be disheartening, but anointing David, God's choice for king, could bring an upbeat spirit to a praying man.

1 Samuel 17:37

Saul's Prayer of Well Wishing

Here is one of the frequent intercessory appeals to God to help another. In his case it is Saul praying in support of David against an incredible Philistine man of war.

The Challenge to Israel (1–30)

Enemy soldiers from Philistia posed a grave threat that inflicted terror in the Israelite ranks. The foremost opponent was a giant named Goliath, a man between eight and nine feet tall (v. 4). Clad in massive armor (5–6) and wielding a super spear (7), he hurled out a challenge for a fighter from Israel to settle the battle, one on one, winner take all (8–10).

The proposal seemed entirely impossible for any Israelite soldier to take up. In fact, it sent shudders through the men fighting with Saul, for "they were dismayed and greatly afraid" (11).

Into the camp facing this crisis David came from tending the family sheep. He delivered food from his father three of his brothers who were soldiers, and a gift for the commander of the thousand these men served. When he reached his brothers on the battle front, Goliath made his latest imposing challenge (23), and the shepherd boy saw his countrymen flee back from the threat (23–24). The soldiers told David that the man who could kill the frightening warrior would the king's gift of riches, his daughter in marriage, and freedom of family rights in Israel (25). David's interest brought his oldest brother Eliab's rebuke at an upstart even thinking of taking up the challenge (28). Despite this put down, the boy pursued the possibility.

The Conquest for Israel (31–56)

Prayer soon will be mentioned.

David's willingness to go against the mammoth man led to soldiers telling Saul, and Saul calling the lad to taLuke The confident youth somewhat confidences the king that he might have a fighting chance despite his inexperience and Goliath's long record and string of victories. Among the boy's credentials were wins even against a lion and a bear that tried to kill one of his the flock he shepherded (34–36a). He boldly believes that he can beat the human opponent also since the battle is finally against "the living God" who can take up the challenge (36).

At this point, Saul sees a ray of hope, and is willing to thrust David out to meet Goliath. Prayer surges on the king's lips in verse 37: "Go, and may the Lord be with you." This is in effect uttering an intercessory appeal intended to gain the Lord's support. How much faith Saul puts into this possibility is uncertain. One thing is sure. David trusts in the One whose might is beyond that of the Philistine hulk, and certain details show that he himself no doubt prays to the Lord who hears.

How is this evident? One clue is the youth's dependence on "the living God" (36), whom he later tells the giant is up to the task. Goliath advances only with human weapons such as "a sword, a spear, and a javelin," but David comes "in the name of the Lord of armies," those of heaven, and also "the God of the armies of Israel . . ." (45). Another evidence in the same verse is that Goliath stalks forth to face not David, finally, but the One "whom you have taunted." Third, the representative for Israel goes with firm conviction based not in himself but in what the Lord "will" do. He "will deliver you up into my hands, and I will strike you down . . ." (46). Fourth, David sees the outcome as far more momentous than a victory for himself, or even for Israel. This is in the objective "that all the earth may know that there is a God in Israel" (46), in addition to this assembly of Israelite soldiers seeing fresh evidence that "the Lord does not deliver by sword or by spear, for the battle is the Lord's and He will give you into my hands" (47).

Enough said. The young man who ventures all on the Lord's sufficiency steps into action. He deftly fingers one stone from his shepherd pouch, and fits it into his sling. His practiced arm gives the sling a whirring motion, and the unerring missile imbeds itself deeply in the giant's forehead. He staggers, unable to brace himself on those mighty legs, for he has no hope. His huge body topples and lies in oblivion, quite still. The bigger they are, the harder they fall. Israel's God is indeed the victor, and David as His soldier who dares to believe is the new champion in the Valley of Gath.

Saul and his soldiers find their breath snatched away by this stunning event, but soon will pursue the Philistines to gain a great triumph. The lad who has beaten all odds now himself towers over the massive frame, and plunges his sword in, probably into the heart. He finishes the seemingly impossible feat. With God all things are possible. God and a person who trusts Him form a majority.

Reflect on a guideline. Even a person of questionable harmony with God can pray with a wish that one will have God's favor (so Saul). Others may be praying out of pure hearts; the possibilities here are Samuel, David himself, and other godly people in the populace of

Israel. A second principle is evident: God in His faithfulness is greater than an unfaithful man who prays for a part of His will.

1 Samuel 18:3

Prayer that Love Knits

A "covenant" here between Jonathan and David mentions no prayer, however 2 Samuel 21:7, which comments back upon it, assumes an oath. And that normally was in prayer. Hence it is taken that way here.

The Setting of the Love (1–2)

Shortly after David was victor over Goliath, an interview with King Saul was followed by Saul's son Jonathan sensing a strong heart bond of love for David. As for Saul, he chose Israel's military hero for an appointment in royal service (2). David found himself on missions for the king, and he performed these so well that Saul designated him his military commander (5). This announcement met with the applause of others in Israel, and with those in governmental service.

The Sealing of the Love (3)

Readers are told that Jonathan made a covenant with David due to the prompting of friendship love. The emphasis is on Jonathan's part, possibly because he is the son of the king, and David at this point only a young shepherd, a poor man (cf. vv. 18, 23), just installed as an army appointee under the king's authority.

Years later, 2 Samuel 21:7 refers back to this wholesome oath as by both men, when David in fidelity to the pledge shows favor to Jonathan's son, Mephibosheth.

A covenant can be ratified by an oath, as God had done this in Genesis 15 in His "blood covenant" with Abram (cf. Heb. 6:13–18). Often when men make an oath in Scripture, they swear or confirm their strong resolve to keep their word by invoking into the agreement the name of a greater, the Lord (cf. Heb. 6:16). In seriousness to follow through their prayer appeals to the Lord as witness. He knows all things and can bless for faithfulness or punish for violating the agreement. A godly persisting to honor the pledge is true of some, as of both Jonathan and David in this pact.

The context flows on.

The Sign of the Love (4)

Again the focus is from Jonathan's side, for the same reason as earlier. As a token or his sincere aim toward the friend he admires, he presents a gift, as Abram had laid out parts of sacrifice in Genesis 15. In this case, the sign of allegiance involves Jonathan's cloak, armor, even his sword, fighting bow, and belt. Nothing is said or denied about David contributing anything of substance, as his father had sent gifts to Israel's commander in Chapter 17. What is highlighted is the sign offered by the party who was "well heeled," in the king's family.

The Suspicion with the Love (6–30)

Saul begins to harbor suspicions of David as a threat to his throne. This grows due to several factors, such as women honoring David for military conquest (6–9), David's increasing favor after military exploits, and Saul seeing David survive battles despite his plan to have the enemies strike down the man, and the evidence that the Lord was with David. Other reasons can be added from later chapters, such as Saul's sensing Jonathan's loyalty at certain points to David.

The passage points to principles. First, two or more people who serve God can bond their hearts in an agreement to follow through on what is pleasing to Him (cf. Ps. 34:3). Second, when one or more people enter into a pledge invoking God to witness and monitor this, it should be with truthful sincerity and trusting follow-through.

1 Samuel 19:6

Another Oath

Jonathan befriends David by seeking to persuade his father not to seek David's death.

The Situation of the Oath (1–5)

The fiend's angle (1a). Saul required Jonathan and all who served in his court to take David's life.

The friend's advocacy (1b–5). Not sharing his father's unloving designs, Jonathan persisted in his keen love for David. He even informed God's anointed but fugitive choice for king of the plot and the need to be watchfully alert and in hiding. He promised to bring further news to his friend when he could learn anything new about Saul's vendetta. And he went to bat for David by a deliberate effort to persuade his father to drop his evil intent. His reasoning goes back to the Goliath episode. David had risked his life for Saul and Israel in that contest, God had given His people a sweet victory, and even Saul had been ecstatic. David has done no sin to offend Saul, and Saul is sinning in his design against an innocent man, void of any proper reason.

The Statement in the Oath (6ff.)

Jonathan had success, at least in temporarily persuading Saul to go back on his evil "hit man" idea. As a result, his father feels conviction which impels him to utter his pledge. He invokes the fact, "as the Lord lives" and can stand as witness that he is truthful, "he shall not be put to death." It is a temporary reprieve, for it will not be long before the vacillating Saul goes back on the avowal he swears and is head hunting again. Jonathan perceives the tenuous nature of his father's word (20:13), and Saul soon proves his word is not true to his oath (19:11, 14, etc.).

The king's breaking his word comes even after David returns to the court and leads Israel in a great defeat of the Philistines (8). Saul is moved by an evil spirit, and hurls his spear to pin David to the wall. David evades the death attempt, and escapes (9–10). Then David flees and foils Saul's designs to have him taken from his home and killed.

In this case, a man's prayer is shown up for the undependable utterance that it is, a mere temporary whim or a shallow pretense.

A principle is obvious. In making a prayer oath (pledge) calling God in as witness to the truth of it, one should follow this up honorably. God is truthful, and wants us to be truthful. In the present case, Saul would later turn out to be untrue and drag the honor of the God he drew into the agreement into the dust. Indeed this king guilty of unfaithful mouthing would seek to nail David soon after he had spun the oath off his lips (19:9), then over and over again (vv. 11, 15, 20, 21, 22; 20:31–32; 23:21–26).

1 Samuel 20:3, 12–13, 16–17, 42

Prayers in Vows Friends Make

Saul's son, Jonathan, becomes a steadfast friend of David while the latter is evading Saul's maneuvers to kill him.

The Pact of Jonathan and David (1–9)

The initial oath of hearts in 18:3 is followed by other pledges of the friends' hearts.

Unlike his father, Jonathan affirms his readiness to do whatever he can to help David. So David broaches a way of revealing Saul's intent toward him. If Saul is curious about David's absence at a meal and asks where he is, Jonathan is to say he has gone to Bethlehem for an annual sacrifice. If Saul acts pleasantly about this, they will read it as showing no bad intent, but if he explodes with anger it will reveal his intent on evil, and feeling thwarted from it. Jonathan agrees to inform David if his father plots to hurt him.

The proposal is based on a lie. David shows much obedience to God in the steps of his life, but various instances of sin as in his fabricated reason here (and cf. 21:2). God is of purer intent than to bless sin, yet He watches over his own with tender mercies His heart can show even when they are out of step with His will. The shepherd's lies are links in a chain of events, which later result in Saul having many priests slain (22:9–18), as David himself comes to realize (22:22). And how variable the fickle human heart can be in its deceit (cf. Jer. 17:9). David can pray, affirming by the name of the Lord and on truth such as He lives (20:3), yet turn into truth when he fancies a personal advantage. Indeed "all have sinned and come short of the glory of God" (Rom. 3:23), and like David need His pardoning mercies.

The Pledges of Jonathan and David (10–17)

Prayer surfaces twice in verses 12–13, and twice again in 16–17.

Jonathan's. The king's son has a plan to give a signal to David in the field. But first he utters a prayer in an oath of his sincere intent. A part of this is in verse 12. He invokes (calls on) God to be witness attesting his truthfulness that he will bring out news to David if Saul means good toward David. Another part of the oath, in verse 13, is that Jonathan calls on God to be the monitor to discipline him if he fails to bring David news that Saul devises harm. A third facet of his prayer is an intercessory appeal to the Lord to keep David safe as He has been with Jonathan's father, and bring judgment on David's enemies (v. 16). The Lord had helped Saul by blessing him in his earlier days (cf. Chaps. 9–12).

God frequently answers this prayer with a "yes" later. For example, He spares David from Saul's missions to capture this fugitive (Chaps. 24, 26, etc.), eventually puts down enemies, and exalts David (cf. 2 Sam. 1–6).

David's. In return, Jonathan has David pray before the Lord (17) to be gracious to him and his family when he rises to power (cf. vv. 14, 15). David would keep up his faithfulness to his friend in protecting Jonathan's father (1 Sam. 24, 26), honoring Jonathan after he died (2 Sam. 1), and even after the friend's death showing compassion on a relative in Jonathan's linage, Mephibosheth (2 Sam. 9). What both men commit to do in a covenant of friendship they express in prayerful pledging "in the name of the Lord" (42). The latter verse refers back to verse 17 as a case as having "sworn to each other in the name of the Lord." This is a form of solemn petition in prayer that calls on the Lord to stand as witness attesting to the integrity of their agreement.

One of the great elements of this prayerful exchange is the affection the men show to each other as they pray together. Jonathan's love shines in 1 Samuel 20:17, and 2 Samuel 1:26 vouches for this love to David and David's heart reciprocating it.

The Plan of Arrows (18–42)

This is drawn into the account here since it is a vital follow-up to the prayer commitment.

Jonathan lays out a plan to signal David by shooting arrows. It is in two phases. If the king's son shoots arrows to one side of David's hiding place and sends his servant to retrieve them, it will signal good favor from Saul. Perhaps this is fitting because in such a case David would know he can be safe near the side of the king. But if Jonathan shoots arrows beyond David, it will show Saul's evil intent, and direct David to flee beyond the plotter's reach.

At the king's meal on the second day after this, Jonathan's word of David's trip stirs violent anger in Saul. The king accuses Jonathan of preferring David to him, and says that as long as David lives he is a threat to Jonathan reigning on the throne. He commands his son to bring David to him to be put to death. Jonathan asks what wrong David has done. This opposition further inflames Saul's anger, inciting him to hurl his spear at his own son to thrust him through.

Jonathan has himself entered into David's lie about a reason for being away.

After this exchange of oath and vow, Jonathan keeps his rendezvous with David. His arrow past David is a vivid message to the man in hiding about Saul's murderous vendetta. Jonathan then sends his attendant home none the wiser. David can safely reveal himself to Luke After the two men have kissed each other, David departs on the fugitive trail from Saul. Prayer springs again into the account, for He goes with Jonathan's reminder of their pledge voiced before God (42), a lingering fragrance to encourage the wandering man's thoughts.

Now we can focus on principles. First, one could make an oath by the surety of God's life and have a sincere motive in contrast to deceit as in the oath of Saul (19:6). Second, God weighs men's actions (1 Sam. 2:3), one can feel assured of His certain judgment, as David does (24:12, 15; 26:23–24), and admit God's fidelity as Saul does (24:19–20). God knows what is going on in each heart.

Other principles join these. Third, in prayer one can realize and invite God's dealings with him as these are in line with what He deems faithful. If sincere, such prayer testifies of one's own heart set to act in step with God. Fourth, in a mutual prayer pledge two believers make, each assumes his own moral commitment to carry things out with integrity. David later keeps fidelity by generous bounties of property, hospitality, and love to a man in this friend's family line (2 Sam. 9:1–13). God is honorable in being dependable, and honored when His people finish things in truth.

A fifth principle also occurs. It is acceptable (42) to jog one's memory so as to encourage him by the sanctify of a promise voiced in prayer.

1 Samuel 23:2, 4

The Fugitive's Fib

This is a case where no statement of prayer appears. Still, Scripture shows that prayer did occur. This is based on three lines of evidence. One is Doeg's *accusation* (22:9), another is Saul's *assumption* that prayer did occur (22:13), and a third is the priest Ahimelech's frank *admission* that he prayed at David's request (22:15).

David's Appearing (1–2)

In flight to escape Saul, young David visits the priest Ahimelech at a town called Nob.

Weakness shows up again in the fabrication to explain his appearing when the priest naturally thinks he should have provisions while serving King Saul. David concocts a tall story about carrying out a special assignment for the king that has resulted in hunger for himself and those with him (cf. vv. 4–5; and Matt.). The priest, convinced, shared consecrated bread right off the altar (v. 6).

David's Appeal (3–9)

Prayer does occur in requesting, via the priest's inquiry before the Lord, the guidance David needs (cf. above). The summary record mentions other things for which he appeals: food (3) and a weapon (8), but only eventually fills in that the priest inquired of God for him.

The food at the place of worship was normally for priests serving there. Jesus later defends David getting loaves from the Altar of Incense, as a case of God allowing compassion due to special human hunger, relaxing the strict letter of the law (Matt. 12:3–4). After securing food, David also asks the priest for a weapon, again lying with the cover-up that he had left hastily due to his urgent mission (8). Accepting this, the priest gives him the one thing he has, the sword of Goliath kept there (9).

One hitch in David's visit will lead to a disaster later for the priest who helps him and other priests.

David's Accuser (7)

One of Saul's servants, Doeg of Edom, is eavesdropping on the episode, and will give David's visit away to Saul (cf. 22:9–10). This will inflame Saul's fury to wipe out any who aided the man he is determined to eliminate.

A guideline is relevant. Due to sin in the world, when a spiritual leader prays to help or does some other good work, he may have to suffer or die for what is right. In this case, Ahimelech, the priest, prayed to God, inquiring for David, if Doeg's report is correct (cf. 22:10). In this possibility, the content is not stated, but it makes sense that the priest interceded for God's help to David's on his journey. Besides this aid, the priest supplied David with a weapon, the sword David had taken when he defeated Goliath, and gave him food. The evil Saul would readily take all this as aiding and abetting, and be inflamed against the priests.

1 Samuel 22:10, 13, 15

A Case of Showing Prayer Occurred

Two references now point back to assume prayer in Chapter 21 (cf. the first paragraph there). We can summarize this briefly.

The Charge

Doeg the snooper lodges the charge against David in the ears of Saul (10), and Saul buys into it as true (13).

The Consequences

Saul presses the priest on what he construes as a sell-out to the king's enemy (11–19). Ahimelech has believed David's lie, is innocent, and answers the king candidly. Saul charges him with the prayer to help David (13), a case of a man serving his own selfish interests by faulting an intercessory kindness. The priest, thinking David had been serving Saul, walks into the trap. He simply replies assuming David has been faithful which ought to please Saul, he even is the king's son-in-law, and is honored among the king's people. He sees his prayer as a natural service, just one more instance of what his valid priestly service has been all along. And he is innocent of any wrong, so the king can fell at rest.

The upshot of the affair is Saul's engaged order to his men to execute Ahimelech and other priests of his family line. When the men decline this atrocity on the basis of respect for the Lord's priests, Saul finds a man ready to carry out his "dirty work," Doeg the informant. This "hit man" slaughters eighty-five priests. As if that evil scene was not enough, he even exacts a toll on the entire priestly city of Nob, piercing through men and women, children and infants, and besides these the animals.

One man who escapes death and flees to David is Abiathar, a son of Ahimelech.

In this dark scene, Ahimelech when "called on the carpet" in a trial before Saul may be denying that prayer to help David was one of the things that took place in the interchange of Chapter 21. If so, it is his word against the informant Doeg's, true in a bid to save his life, or a lie if he actually had prayed.

Principles become noticeable. First, those close to God or thought to be are often approached in Old Testament passages, or today, to ask God for answers to help in various cases (cf. 23:1–2, 4, 10–12). These are guidance in battle, whether a besieged city can be a safe haven, help in illness, on and on. A guideline is that a spiritual leader can have impact by interceding to God. This ministry can be for temporal helps or eternal welfare (cf. Rom. 10:1). It is of utmost cruciality to be on "praying ground" with the Lord so as really to count in these opportunities. And in a normal life the cases can mount to mind-boggling numbers, so that the amassed spiritual fruit can be incredible (cf. John 15:8, "much fruit," and 15:16; Phil. 4:17).

The Conscience

David's conscience smites him on hearing of the mass murder. He has to recount profound bleakness, "I knew on that day, when Doeg the Edomite was there, that he would surely tell Saul [cf. 21:7]. I have brought about [the death of] every person in your father's household" (22:22).

A principle is apparent. David's prayer, trafficking in a lie he spun, had exacted a terrible price others had to pay. Suppose David had trusted in the Lord for a means of securing food and weaponry. Imagine what might have been had he stood for truth with his prayer, and looked to "the living God" as when he faced another threat to his life, Goliath.

Other guidelines also appear. First, prayer may occur even when a biblical text does not include the details it mentions. God, of course, is fully aware of when a person prays though we may not perceive prayer, just as He hears our prayers when others are not aware of these. Second, in the busy course of life, another may hear prayer, apparently said aloud, even when the ones praying do not detect this. This is similar to imagining that what we do is private when at times another, without our knowing it, has seen.

1 Samuel 23:2, 4

Prayers for Guidance in Battle

David and a band of men who have joined him are living in the wilds eluding Saul. At the same time the Philistines pose a threat as they long had been. Twice David prays seeking God's wisdom on whether to attack the Philistines or not.

The Philistine Situation of Danger (1)

David's first prayer. News from his men about Philistine pressure and plunder at Keilah stimulates his calling on God (2). He petitioned for counsel. The prayer is in the form of a petitionary question. Should he strike the enemy? God possibly conveyed this answer through the priest Abiathar. This spiritual leader had recently joined David (22:20–23), and could seek guidance through the Urim and Thummim within the breastplate fold of his garment, the ephod. Abiathar is said to have the ephod (6, 9). The answer David received was "go" (2).

David's second prayer. Reluctance of his men prompted David to confirm God's will by a back-up prayer (5). His men live in jeopardy of death in their fugitive state, and going to battle against the mighty Philistines raised a threat of dying even sooner.

David was urgent to find the Lord's direction (4). Again God's answer was to attack with the guarantee that He would give the victory. Sure enough, the result was an overwhelming win against the Philistines, and setting Keilah free of subjugation to the enemy.

Observe principles here. The prayers illustrate how God chose to guide His people at that time. A principle is relevant here. Today, still praying for direction, believers discern God's guidance through less direct means—sensitivity to Him as they weigh truths of His Word prayerfully, counsel of wise people close to Him, assessing circumstances He uses, and the like. Though God is flexible in not choosing to use the same means as in David's day, His leading is just as real. And believers now have far more of His will filled out in His Word than David and Abiathar had, with the benefits that spring from this.

Had God told David via His means (the Urim and the Thummim) not to go, it would save him and his men. So, either way, appeal for His will in prayer was a wise value choice.

1 Samuel 23:10–12

Prayer for Information Giving Safety

The prayers related to attacking the Philistines were unusual. Now further prayer for information ahead of time is also very special.

Saul's Expectation to Capture David (6–8)

David's stay in Keilah inspired in Saul the craze to trap him within the city and force his surrender.

David's Entreaty for Wisdom (9–12)

Word reached David of Saul's designs, and this too prompted him to pray.

His request for God's ephod. David seems immediately to think of deciding God's guidance via the ephod, that is the Urim and Thummim, placed inside the garment's fold over the priest's breast. This suggests his use of the same method in verses 1–5, for the priest had just come among David's men.

His request for Saul's deployment. He asks for God's confirmation whether Saul will try to besiege him if he remains at Keilah. God answers "yes," showing that the scouting report David had received was correct. This information leads to a second part of the prayer.

His request for Keilah's decision. Will Keilah's pressured leaders hand him and his men over to Saul if they remain here? The Lord says "yes." So David knows to flee to safety away from the city.

David's Escape Before the Siege (13)

Flight by the band of about 600 sprang them into escape from Saul. Advised of their departure, Saul gave up the chase at this time.

It is mind-boggling to think of God's sovereign plan and what would happen if believers go on the way they are going, or if they change to a different course. In David's case, God gave information as a means of preserving him. Should He have permitted Saul to capture him, He could even then have worked a way of escape to carry his sure purposes forward with David.

Now principles can receive their due. What of believers who do not have definite information in advance? They can still insist on doing right and rest in God's faithful care, entrusting the keeping of their lives to Him as to a faithful creator (1 Pet. 4:19). Even when God has permitted believers to be in trials He has been versatile in ways He has chosen to protect them. He kept Jacob safe with Laban, Joseph in Egypt, Moses as a baby, His people at the Red Sea and David in the contest with Goliath. The surest place in all the world is walking in the will of God, as God's further keeping of David from Saul in verse 14.

1 Samuel 23:21

Prayer that God Will Not Hear

A word about prayer that the psalmist would express later is true in principle with Saul. God sees that Saul regards sin in his heart, and the Lord does not hear him in a "yes" way (cf. Ps. 66:18). God in merciful forbearance can permit things to work out even when men do not do what pleases Him, as even in some of David's failures (cf. an example in 1 Sam. 21:2).

The Plot Against David (19, 20)

Ziphites twice notified Saul to betray David's location (cf. also 26:1–5). They were people of David's own tribe, Judah, in the desert area where Jeshimon is southeast of Hebron near the Dead Sea. Chalky hills were infested with many hiding places for fugitives.

Here, the Ziphites side with the reigning king, apparently regarding David as a traitor to the government. They promise to turn Saul's quarry over to him.

The Prayer of Saul (21–23)

Here is an example of an evil prayer, hatched against the will of God. It comes as no surprise when one reviews Saul's sinful disqualification by his offering (1 Sam. 13), by his rash order (14), his obstinacy toward God's will (15), and his oppression against God's anointed man so far. When a man turns himself away from listening to God's will, "even his prayer is an abomination" (Prov. 28:9).

The king mouths a prayer calling blessing on those informing him of David's hideout. What he invokes from God is not what God commits Himself to do. The prayer is driven by wretched ugliness, a spewing of carnality and self-will. As soon as it spins off of Saul's lips, his next words are a command to go confirm David's campsites so that Saul can move in to kill him.

The Preservation of David (24–29)

David, receiving a report of Saul's new pursuit, again evades his clutches. God Himself works providentially to pull Saul back when he is about ready to close in and snatch David. He does it by having a messenger reach Saul with news of a crisis. Philistines have raided, and Saul's fighting force is desperately needed to repel the enemy.

A principle is shaped in all of this. When a believer is doing the will of God and trusting in Him, God is able to protect him even against those who pray for his downfall. Today, God's people are the objects of carnal prayers from within the so-called Christian circle. But also pitted against them in spiritual warfare are outsiders seeking Satanic help to stop them. This embraces not only enemies sold out to heathen superstition, but purveyors of cultic delusions, evil plotters in phases of the New Age Movement, and opponents pushing devil worship. These are but a few. The warfare is real, and the enemies always involve Satanic hosts who manipulate them. It is imperative for the believer to be vigilantly dressed always in the whole armor of God, depending on His power to stand against the stratagems of the devil (Eph. 6:10–17). And strategic with the parts of the armor and the power of God is prayer (vv. 18–20) in relying ceaselessly on God.

1 Samuel 24:12, 15, 19, 22

Prayer in Sparing a King

David is able to get two opportunities to kill his pursuer, but in both he holds back in godly grace. Here is the first of these episodes, the second yet to come in Chapter 26.

David's Compassion on Saul (1–7)

Prayer comes first in verse 12, and it is good to see the flow of thought preparing for that.

Saul prowled the desert haunts with 3,000 select fighting men, goaded on by a mania to snuff out David's life. The king sought out a cave where he could relieve himself, possibly meaning to ease bodily pressure or to rest in the coolness from the oppression of a tiring trek. He was not aware that David and his men lurked in the deeper, dark recesses.

Men of the fugitive band whispered advice that David kill his enemy. Instead, he only crept up in silent stealth and cut off the outflung edge of Saul's kingly robe. David's tender conscience smote him even for this act of disrespect for the king. He told his men, probably in a low tone out of Saul's hearing range, that in respect for the Lord he would not harm Saul. For as evil as the king had proven to be, he was still the leader the Lord's had once anointed. David would not tolerate his men to taking violent advantage of the unwary pursuer.

David's Challenge to Saul (8–15)

Saul went away unsuspecting of danger. There from a distance David shouted a challenge, and Saul whirled about to gaze back at him. David was respectful of the kingship, calling the would-be murderer "my lord the king." He even bowed to honor the office Saul stood for.

Then David told the king the falsehood of claims that he meant Saul harm. Even in the cave he could have plunged a spear through him, with men urging him to kill, but he displayed mercy. His noble reason was his high regard for the kingship from God. Then he must have shocked Saul by lifting high the cloth cut from Saul's robe, a proof of his good intentions.

Prayer comes at this point (12). David invokes God's judgment between Saul and himself. He calls for *God* to avenge the wrong Saul has done in His time and His way. Let God do that in His own way and time, as is God's will elsewhere (Deut. 32:35; Rom. 12:17). *David himself* will not presume on God's prerogative. He does not lift a finger to hurt the man on a mission to snatch away his life. Later, in verse 15, David voices his burden a second time. May the Lord judge as fits His own will in this rift between the two men. And may He take note and uphold the cause of David, falsely persecuted as he is, and keep him safe from Saul.

Principles of prayer flow richly here. David calls for God to work His good pleasure, and is passionate not to intrude his own. He pleads that God will see and bless him in his innocence. And he petitions God to protect him. Not a single word of hatefulness, spite, or retaliation sours the prayer. He is at rest to leave vengeance to the Lord, to effect as He knows fits the case.

Saul's Confession to David (16–21)

This, too, includes prayer.

The acknowledgment (16–19). No doubt David was shouting from a distant vantage point, for Saul asks if it is David's voice. Murderous as he has been, he calls David "my son David," and sobs loudly. The king is still in possession of his life, which had been in jeopardy in the cave. The compassion shown him could lay its potent impression on him, at the moment at least, even as a man with murder in his heart at one moment but favor at another. His tongue is loosed to confess that David is more righteous than he has been, showing kindness in place of his wickedness. David has shown a rare attitude, not piercing out his enemy's life when it was within his reach.

Now prayer returns.

The advocacy (19b). Saul mouths his prayer that God will reward David with good as a suitable return for the fugitive's mercy. However carnal a person's heart may be, if what he prays is in the line of God's will, God will show mercy to the merciful.

The appeal (20, 21). This calls for prayer. The thought ticks in Saul's mind that David is sure to be the king (20). This prompts his request that David will pray in an oath before God, for his sake. What he desires is that David, when on the throne, will spare Saul's descendants.

David's Confirmation (22a)

David responds in his own prayer. It is in the form of an oath, a pledge or guarantee before the Lord. It calls for God's attestation of what he promises, His blessing in keeping true to carry it out, and His equitable judgment should David go against his word. All of this is to assure from himself, and with God's help, that his word is worth something.

A principle of prayer in this instance is easy to see. The person calling on God to attest and assure an undertaking needs to think through on what he agrees to do. He also needs to be ready to honor his word and the name of the God he has invoked to stand as a witness. Years later, David shows kindness to a man in Saul's line, Mephibosheth, for the sake of Jonathan (2 Sam. 9:1–13).

1 Samuel 25:22, 32, 39

A Man's Prayer with a Woman

David's evading of Saul's searchers drew him to various desert hideouts. The setting here is near Carmel, a site about seven miles south of Hebron, not far west of the Dead Sea, south of Jerusalem.

A Review of the Situation (1–31)

David has dealings with Nabal, a rich stock-raiser whose name means "fool" and who was a tight-fisted man, rock-hard against mercy. The wife of the evil man, Abigail, turns out to be of sterling character and shows kindness later to David and his band.

David sends men to Nabal with his cordial greeting, itself a prayerful wish of peace (v. 6). He reminds the stockman that his men have treated Nabal's shepherds kindly, and never stolen from his herds. But living in the wild, David and his men need help, and he is asking for some gift from Nabal in fitting gratitude for the safety to his enterprise.

Nabal is stingy, not willing to give any token of friendship. He insults the visitors' leader, David, by asking who he is (he was very uninformed, or wilfully cocky, and mean). He discounts David's family, and insinuates that he has broken away from his master, as if failing Saul. He speaks of his own possessions only in proud, selfish terms of "my . . . my . . . my . . . my," showing he has acute "I" trouble.

David's outfit returns to report Nabal's dealings. David then takes 400 of his 600 men to stage a raid on Nabal. In the meantime, one of Nabal's young men had sensed his boss's wrong, and gotten word to Abigail of impending danger. Unlike Nabal, he felt the visitors had been cordial, had shown respect for Nabal's property, and even formed a protective buffer for Nabal's men. He bluntly tells the wife that her husband is "such a worthless man that no one can speak to him" (17).

Abigail springs into action to save the day. She gets foodstuffs together in large gifts on donkeys, probably with help from workers on hand (cf. 19). Then she sends the donkey train ahead of her with the men to intercept David's band.

How strategically things come into place. Before Abigail arrives, David does two things. First, he *realizes* that Nabal has decided evil toward him in return for the good David has dealt to him (v. 21). Second, he *resolves* in an oath prayer to deal with the evil "tight wad" by wiping out his entire outfit of men before the next day. It is a vindictive prayer of the flesh. He summons the Lord's working to bring what his own feelings regard as justice on his enemies. He has hit the trail to a showdown when his eyes light on a strange sight. A woman is coming to intercept him with a donkey train.

It is difficult to defend David for such a vengeful intent, and using God's name to give it clout. Oaths men make do not always express God's will. Still, in His providential care God keeps David back from carrying out the bloodshed.

A principle at this point is vivid. We should screen our prayers watchfully, and sift any malicious intent in a sensitivity to do as God's Word gives proper warrant.

As David draws up in surprise, Abigail falls before him in respect, a striking contrast to Nabal, and shows class in taking the blame herself. She beseeches David to hear her out. Abigail's husband, she acknowledges, is a worthless man, a "fool" living up to what his name means. She is prayerful in her plea in verse 26. She invokes the Lord who lives to grant His attestation to what she says. He has providentially kept David from avenging himself, probably meaning she has heard of his noble act in sparing Saul. She also can be referring to his leniency to Nabal so far. Her desire is, may God give David victory over his enemies, even Nabal. She pleads that the men will accept her gift packed on the donkeys, and that forgiveness be extended to her as she selflessly shoulders the blame in place of her husband.

Abigail compliments David. She desires his house to be an enduring one, for she sees him as fighting the Lord's battles, doing the will of God. She expects no evil to be found in David all his days, a good gesture, and a broad hint to deter David from violence in this case. She is unaware of the sins David was yet to fall into as the years went by. She is well-informed about David's anointing, for she expects him to be the new king, and has heard of good things spoken about him (30). She does not want David to spill blood now that would be a grief to trouble him later (31).

Such wise and generous words evoke a response in the leader of the fugitive host.

The Recipients of His Blessing (32, 33)

David's words form a prayer of blessing or thanksgiving/praise. They trace his blessing to the Lord who gave it (cf. also 39). It is good to speak words that exalt God in the presence of others, if they are genuine. David also praises Abigail herself.

The Reasons for His Blessing (32–34)

Two reasons are apparent behind David's praise.

God's providence. He exalts God for His providence in working to turn him back from bloodshed by this narrow escape.

Abigail's perception. He has praise for the woman's keen wits in grasping how the situation really was, recognizing the wrong done, and throwing herself so boldly into preventing calamity. She had ministered him a huge favor in this forthright trip to meet him before he fulfilled his revenge. He discerns both God's restraining hand and Abigail's brave act as worthy. His early passion would have led him to wipe out every man.

David also is thankful for Abigail's gift. He accepted the gracious supply of food and gave his staunch promise of peace.

The Result for Nabal And Abigail (36–42)

The entire episode reads like a John Wayne action thriller of the wild west.

Nabal. Once back home, Abigail found her husband having a feast and in a drunken stupor. He was so out of it that he would not be able to understand if she told him of his narrow escape. When he was sober the next day she told it to him straight, and the shock put such fear in him that he suffered heart failure. Ten days later he was dead.

Abigail. When David heard a report of Nabal's death, he exulted in praise to God (39). God had mercifully protected David from snatching justice into his own hands. He had dealt justice to Nabal His own time and way. And He was ever so thorough.

The next scene reveals a contingent of men delivering David's proposal to Abigail to be his bride. She was rid of a drunken bum and a hard-hearted husband, and now free. She gladly accepted David's offer, and went to him attended by her wedding party of five maidens, this itself a sign of the wealth left to her.

The story seems happy. A sad note comes at the end, in the review of David having another wife at the same time. God's blueprint for marriage, the way He *wanted* it to be, was one man and one woman in a bond of unity (Gen. 2:24).

Observe further principles out of this.

This failure of David points up a principle. God honors the prayers of His people even when they are so short of spiritual perfection. He knows who follows Him in some genuine degree of faith, and in great compassion is real to them even in times when they are far from being altogether what He wants. Still, He wants His people always to strive to do His will more closely. A second principle is that God knows how to work out justice better than we do. So we should leave this to His plan and His time (cf. Rom. 12:19, 21). He even allowed Nabal's hired servants to live. At the same time He preserved David from his own quick trigger vendetta and rush to get on with things.

1 Samuel 26:11, 19, 24, 25

Prayer as David Spares Saul Again

First David held back from killing Saul in Chapter 24, when he had him in a cave, not suspecting peril. Now he gets a second shot at stopping the pursuer.

David's Action Toward Saul (1–12)

A tip from the Ziphites drew Saul again to the region of Jeshimon near Hebron and the Dead Sea. He came over the desert with 3,000 men to roust David out of hiding. David stole upon the sleeping soldiers of Saul and located Saul at the supposed safe center of the night camp. David again passed up an opportunity to kill the king, or to allow his man, Abishai, to do it.

David's reason again is his respect for the kingship, under God. He expresses faith in God's sufficiency to take care of Saul, whether by smiting him directly, or natural death, or in battle (10). Then, in a whisper near the sleeping king, David prays. May the Lord keep him from hurting His anointed leader! It is a brief petition expressing God's will.

He and his companion Abishai grab Saul's spear and water jug and slip out of the camp. God Himself, the passage shows, kept the enemy soldiers in a sound sleep (12).

David's Appeal to Saul (13–20)

Reaching a peak of safety, David shouted down at the soldiers. He chides the now shocked Abner, the general, for not guarding his master from danger. He hoists the spear and jug as signs that he had been right beside the king while he lay helpless. Saul, as he had done in the first sparing, calls David "my son." David pleads his innocence of any effort against Saul, and asks the king to break off his hateful pursuit.

If the Lord has stirred Saul to pursue, David is ready to present an offering to be right with God (19). The offering would be accompanied by prayer. Indeed, prayer is intimated here in "let Him accept [lit. "smell" the aroma of] an offering. . . ." The idea can be, "I ask Him to receive" the sacrifice. But if this is not God's motivation, but instead men have wrongly aroused Saul to construe David as an enemy, the appeal in prayer is different. He pleads that the Lord will curse them for their sinful hurt to him. For they have shut him out into the wilds far from acceptance among those who are the Lord's inheritance (His people). He is far from God's presence at the tabernacle, as if cast out to worship other gods.

Saul's Acknowledgment (21)

Confession pours from Saul's lips as it had in Chapter 24. It had been insincere there, as it would prove again to be here. What good is confession if nothing is changed in the sin one is confessing? An empty promise is all the insincere king can give. He asks David to return, and gives a lying promise not to harm him. This comes with admission of playing the fool and falling into a grievous mistake.

David's Answer (22–24)

The pursued man emphasizes two things.

His reassurance of God's reward. David declares that the Lord will repay each person for his righteousness and faithfulness. He does not emphasize the negative, the retribution or else diminishment of reward sure for sinful misuse of the life. God deals reward in grace, not merit, but in His grace honors the fruit that He can approve by distinguishing the person in some equitable degree of reward (1 Cor. 3:8; cf. Luke 19:12–27). He will deal retribution in punishment to the unsaved but reward to the saved (Dan. 12:2). The true believers will receive special reward for their "work" He can endorse, or see their reward reduced in a manner God sees as in equitable accord with unfaithfulness (1 Cor. 3:10–15; 2 Cor. 5:10).

David did not necessarily know all of this in his day, but he had the essence of it in view. His words ought to have struck Saul's heart with powerful conviction.

His request for deliverance. David would have to be still shouting to be heard down below. Prayer is unusual, for David is praying in a yell (24). He petitions the Lord to set high value on his life, and spare him, as he has valued Saul's well-being and left him untouched. Even beyond the present situation, he petitions God to deliver him from all distress.

The Lord would answer that prayer. He would spare David's life until he would die of a ripe old age. And He would deliver him finally out of all distress into eternal bliss (cf. Ps. 16:10) It also is true that along the way God would let him face unpleasant consequences when such sins as adultery and numbering the people caused a backlash of pain. God does answer prayer; He also permits men to reap what they sow, ever teaching needed lessons even in this.

Saul's Anticipation for David (25)

Shouting back as he stares up the slope, Saul utters words that are partly a prayer of affirmation, and partly a prediction, in truth.

He invokes God's blessing on David ("may you be blessed") as God would surely give this, for it was God's will whether Saul prayed or not. His prayer is a wish, a call to God that His will be done, that He deliver the blessedness. Saul also predicts what he must know is God's purpose since Samuel had told him plainly that God would give the kingship to another (15:28). David, he expects, will accomplish much and prevail. Truly he would, in victories, in prayer, in writing many psalms, and in royal projects.

What are the principles in prayer? One of these is to pray in line with God's will (11) and equitable dealings (24). Another is that even a knowledgeable but very carnal person can utter prayer that has the wording of God's will (25). This points up the urgency both to *live* in God's will and *pray* in it, as David is doing here and Saul is not.

After the dramatic awakening of the soldiers, David goes on his way, and Saul to his place. They would never meet again in the present life. David would soon rise to the throne, and Saul would go downhill to his tomb, his life so empty of God's guidance that he would resort to a woman of a familiar spirit. There he would meet the stiff rebuke of Samuel's message: the Lord had become his adversary and would take him out in defeat (28:16–19).

1 Samuel 28:6, 10, 15

A Demonic Substitute for Prayer

Prayer occurs in Chapter 28 in three ways. First, the disobedient Saul tried to pray but God did not answer (v. 6). Second, he prayed in a bogus way as he vowed safety to a medium by invoking the Lord's name (10). And third, Saul tells Samuel, who comes back from the dead to speak with him, that God "answers me no more" (15).

The Circumstances (1–7)

The invasion by Philistines (1–5). When this foe massed in a threatening mobilization, Saul summoned soldiers from all Israel to Gilboa. A scan of the enemy encampment struck great fear into a man who already knew terror after the Spirit had left him. (5).

The inquiry in prayer (6). The panicking king did not know how to face the invaders successfully. His stiff-necked acts had raised up barriers between himself and the Lord, but he needed help. So he "inquired of the Lord. . . ." He was not on praying ground, for he did not honor the Lord and the Lord could not honor him (cf. 1 Sam. 2:30; cf. Ps. 66:18). The result was that "the Lord did not answer him," and this was in three ways that the king attempted.

(1) God's refusal. God did not give him counsel, in the first place, by dreams. In some instances in ancient Israel the Lord did give revelation either by voice or by pictorial vision or both, in dreams. Jacob received reassurance this way (Gen. 28:11ff.), as did Joseph (Gen. 37). After Saul's day, Solomon would (1 Kgs. 3). The all-powerful and resourceful God is able to make His will known distinctly even by this method (Num. 12:6), when He wills. Second, God offered no response by the Urim (cf. Num. 27:21), an object in the fold of the high priest's ephod over his breast. How this worked is uncertain to us, but one suggestion is that the Urim meant "lights" and the Thummim "perfections." Possibly God caused the object to light up to answer questions "yes" or "no." Abithar the priest had fled to David (1 Sam. 22:20–23), so he was not accessible to Saul, and could not have validly complied with him anyway, if in spirit with Samuel rejecting the king. And third, Saul could obtain no help from the prophets, for Samuel whom Israelites consulted (1 Sam. 7, 9, 12) had died (25:1), and had cut Saul off from contact (15:15–23). The school of prophets Samuel probably established would no doubt reject Saul as their most honored example had done.

It was desperation time for Saul. He was between a rock and a hard place.

(2) Saul's resort. The king groped for counsel with which to cope with the warfare. He asked his servants to locate a woman who was a medium, who could supply information to him. They knew of a medium at En Dor. Saul clutched at this possibility. In this, he did an about face, going against the policy he himself had made to ban those who set up shop to contact demons and pretend to get in touch with the dead (28:3; cf. v. 9).

The Mosaic Law rejected mediums and spiritists (Lev. 19:3; Deut. 18:11), and directed that both kinds be put to death (Lev. 20:27). Their traffic led people to bypass God, as in legitimate prayer, and seek information from other sources.

The Consultation (8–14)

The appeal. Saul sought to deceive the woman he visited by disguising who he really was. He surely knew that she would not dare do business if she perceived her night guest was the king who was out to get people of her craft. His request was that she engage in her conjurer act to bring back from the dead a person with whom he could speak. She was cagey against danger to herself, and reminded him that Saul had shut down people who did this sort of thing. That ought to have stopped the king's illicit effort.

The assurance. Saul swept this roadblock aside. He did it by affirming a vow. In this, he glibly and illegitimately invoked the name of the Lord, whose word he had so often gone against, as even then. This was a kind of prayer, but he had no right God would support to traffic in His name, and pledge by His life as his witness of truth, that he would protect the woman.

The appearance. Satisfied, the woman was willing to go ahead. She only must know whom her visitor wanted brought forth. Saul specified Samuel. She acted to do her usual thing, to work in accompaniment with a demon within her, who could pretend and impersonate Samuel to make it seem he himself was there. But when God by His almighty power did an unusual thing and brought Samuel's spirit back from the dead, it disrupted what she expected. So she "cried out," startled, shocked, and in terror at a power overwhelming her own. Quickly identifying Samuel with the Lord he served, she perceived who in the land chiefly had sought Samuel, had been cut off from him, and would want to be in touch with him by her God-opposing method. Saul!

The king reassured her she need not fear him. She then went ahead and described the appearance she saw as that of an old man clothed in a robe. Saul was instantly aware that he had achieved his mission. He was in touch with Samuel, and he bowed with reverential respect to honor the prophet.

But Samuel was not at his beck and call.

The Condemnation (15–19)

God's servant got quite pointedly to the bogus consultation.

The reason for the request (15). Why has Saul interrupted Samuel's state after death by bringing him up? That Samuel himself did appear seems most probable for several reasons.

First, the woman's shock shows that this was beyond what she expected even in what an evil spirit was able to do; it was counter to this, of God. Second, the following account represents Samuel as actually speaking to Saul. What he says is in complete accord with what Samuel has said in the scripture earlier (Chaps. 13, 15, etc.).

The response of Samuel (16–19). Rejection of Saul is crisp and direct. The Lord has departed from the king and is his adversary (16). He has taken the kingdom from Saul and given it to David. Saul disobeyed God (cf. Chap. 15), so the Lord has confronted him by allowing him to be in the predicament without help. Further, the Philistines will win the battle, while Saul and his sons will be with Samuel, either meaning generally in the place of death whether saved as Samuel is, or unsaved, or saved even though so disobedient.

The Consternation (20–25)

For Saul in the rest of his time with the sorceress, two things are true. He has an empty misery in his utter dismay as doom is before him (20–23a), yet after some persuading an encouraging meal to give him a lift from his wrung-out weariness (23b–25). Even the physical satisfaction is only a brief respite; during the battle "tomorrow" (v. 19), which comes quickly in Chapter 31, he will die.

Principles of prayer are clear enough. First, one ought to repent, confess, and seek God's merciful forgiveness for disobedience, not plunge more deeply into a life against His will. Second, one ought to use God's name in prayer to honor Him, not mouth words using that name to try to salvage a personal agenda (cf. v. 10). Third, the same essential things can be started another way. We please God when we do things in sensitive harmony with His Word, not in doing what runs counter to it. Fourth, God has the power and wisdom to do what seems impossible, yet He does it to accomplish His will, not to help a self-willed person (cf. 1 Sam. 2:30). In this case, God does a rare thing, the only time in the Bible. He allows a person to come back from the dead, not to aid Saul but to oppose him, and show once for all His power even over a false and disobedient attempt to contact the dead (cf. Merrill Unger, *Biblical Demonology*, pp. 144–152).

1 Samuel 30:6–8, 15

Prayer in the Face of Heartache

While still fugitives, David and his band returned to their encampment to make a stunning discovery. Amalekites had plundered, taking their wives and children captives.

Sorrows of a Great Loss (1–6a)

Three things portray the extreme gravity of the situation. One is the *capturing* of the men's families. A second one is the *burning* of their homes. Another is the *stoning* of David the men are talking about because he is the leader, and his orders pulled the men away, permitting the catastrophe.

Solace in a Great God (6b-8)

It was a high crisis for David. He had help to cope with it in two ways.

By the gift of power. When he could have fallen apart, David "strengthened himself in the Lord his God." Was this one occasion when he experienced the reality of the words he would write in Psalm 138:3? "On the day I called Thou didst answer me; Thou didst make me bold with strength in my soul." In the same psalm he is confident, "The Lord will accomplish what concerns me" (v. 8).

Like Jacob in meeting Esau and Moses in facing the Red Sea David found God to be sufficient when the crisis swirled around him. A person who walks with good in the good times also finds it safe to walk with Him in the bad.

David had help in a second way, coordinated with the gift of power.

By the guidance in prayer. Power did not just come automatically. It came as David went to the source of power, in prayerful desperation. A godly person in a predicament does not just think of the alarms; he meditates on the Almighty. David asks Abiathar who had joined him (22:20ff.) to bring his priestly ephod (breast apron). His reason, as in 23:9, was that inside the fold of this breastpiece were the Urim and Thummim, objects God used to furnish guidance in some way for His people. With Abiathar consulting there to see God's will, David prayed for guidance.

"Shall I pursue this band? Shall I overtake them?" As He had gained God's guidance in other situations (cf. Chap. 23), he secured it in prayer this time. God said, apparently through Abiathar, to pursue. He guaranteed recovery of all that the men had lost.

Success in a Great Victory (9–19)

David, with 400 men, clung to a resolute pursuit and came across a straggler left behind by the fleeing raiders. David, in a kind of prayer, swore by oath to him that he would not harm him if he led the pursuers to the Amalekite camp (v. 15). It is not said that David made this oath, but it is apparent that he must have. He appealed to and invoked the name of God as his witness, to guarantee his commitment to keep his part of the agreement.

An overwhelming victory included slaying most of the marauders, and regaining the families and spoils. David gave some of the spoils to 200 men who had pursued part of the way before dropping out due to exhaustion. He also sent a gift to elders such as in Judah, whose areas had suffered from Amalekite attacks. This was a testimony of fairness and no doubt won greater acceptance for David en route to the kingship after Saul's death. That death in 1 Samuel 31 and 2 Samuel 1 sets the stage for David to return from exile and reach the throne.

He will rise to kingship as a man of God, a man of prayer.

Lessons in prayer again are evident. Instead of going to pieces under pressure when his men spoke against him, David stayed on top by God's power and found His way out of difficulty in answer to prayer. Second, the promise God makes in His word to the praying person He is faithful to fulfill. Today, His people can search His written word for what He says to guide their steps.

Prayer in 2 Samuel

Introduction

Comments before 1 Samuel relate to 2 Samuel as well. For, as stated, this second book originally was part of a single unity with the first one, all one book. Together the accounts developed the beginning of a kingship in Israel with Saul and then David's reign as God's choice. The kingdom theme is evident in several verses (2 Sam. 5:10, 12; 7:4–17; 8:6).

As to author, date, title, and theme, cf. the "Introduction" in 1 Samuel.

The Outline

David comes to the throne in Chapter 2, and 2 Samuel is in two divisions, developing two contrasting emphases in David's career.

His Triumphs (Chaps. 1–10). First David reigns over Judah alone (1–4), then over all Israel (5–24). The focus in Chapters 1–10 is on his crowning (5), capture of Jerusalem to become his capital (5), construction of a palace (5:11, 12), conquests over the Philistines (5:12–25), changing the Ark's location to Jerusalem (6), concern to build God a house or temple (7), and is further conquests (8–10).

His Troubles (Chaps. 11–24). David's sin of adultery with Bathsheba (11) is the pivot here as his career begins to decline. Some key events in this section are the sin (11, 12), his son Amnon's rape of Tamar (13), his son Absalom's revenge against Amnon (13), David's relations with Absalom, including the latter's revolt to seize control of Jerusalem (15–19), Absalom's death and David mourning it (18, 19), and David's last days as king (20–24). In this final part, highlights are David's confidence in God's covenant (23:1–7), the courage of his mighty men (23:8–39), and his sin in taking a census, followed by God's chastisement (24).

One of the most strategic passages is David's desire to build God a house (temple), and God's promise, instead, to build David a house (dynasty), kingdom, and throne forever (7:12–16). This kingship in the line of Judah carries on God's aim given through Jacob (Gen. 49:10). It also stays consistently in the line of Judah via David, which is the focus at the end of the Book of Ruth. God eventually fulfills it in Jesus Christ, the ultimate king in Judah's and David's line (Matt. 1:1; Acts 2:30–36).

The Relation to Prayer

We see prayer in different ways.

The accent on it. One can say that the book is fairly saturated with utterances to God. At least forty references to prayer occur from 2:1 right to the end in 24:23–25. Words of the Lord appear in at least sixteen of the twenty-four chapters.

The aspects of it. At least eight aspects or parts of prayer are present. These can be seen in review.

(1) Petition. These can ask for guidance as David seeks God's leading about a city of residence to await his time to be king, and learns the place is Hebron (2:1). It can appeal for God's blessing in dealing with a famine (21:1). Petition in the form of David's question whether to go to war against the Philistines is apparent in 5:19. In 22:4, David prays for God to deliver him from his enemies.

(2) Intercessory vigil. These can plead for the Lord's judgment on others (3:39), or quite the opposite for benefit, as when David "blessed the people in the name of the Lord" (6:18) The latter seems to be in the spirit of a wish for God's bounties, as in Numbers 6:22–27. Honored by the covenant God pledges with him to bless those in his lineage, David prays the very thing God had declared is His will (cf. 12–16), "may the house of your servant David be

established before you" (26). What a man in prayer has spoken God surely will do in such a case, for what God has spoken He surely will do! Prayer hitch-hikes on the will of God here as in other parts of the Bible (cf. Jer. 29:10–14; 33:3; Dan. 9:4–19).

(3) Praise/thanks. David exemplifies this when he magnifies God (7:22), and calls on the Lord "who is worthy to be praised" (22:4). And in 7:18–29 David responds to the "Davidic Covenant" of 7:12–16 with one of his finest statements of humble gratitude for such God's showering him with such a bright prospect (7:18–29).

(4) Question. Sometimes this blends with petition, or what is in effect a petition comes in this sort of approach to God, as in (1) above. David's entreaties for light to help him take the right steps are framed in inquiries to move at the impulse of God (2:1; 5:19, etc.). At other times, straightforward questions are on the tongue. An instance is when David savors the covenant God has made with him (7:12–16) and asks in overwhelmed humility, "Who am I, O Lord God, and what is my house, that You have brought me this far?" (v. 18). He follows up with other questions in grateful awe (20, 23).

(5) Confession. Examples are in David acknowledging his adultery to God (12:13), and his arrogant dependence on human military might seen in numbers (24:10).

(6) Affirmation. Just rehearsing truths in prayer is sometimes the focus in prayer. David, as recipient of God's covenant, not only praises Him and asks how he can have a right to such bounty. He recites how this blessing touches him in such words as "You have spoken also of the house of your servant concerning the distant future" (7:19), and "For the sake of your word, and according to your own heart, you have done all this greatness to let your servant now" (21). The king pours forth still other reviews of God's action, as he sits praying in awe (cf. 21b, 22, 24, 27, 28, etc.).

(7) Vow. Absalom said he had made a vow before the Lord (2 Sam. 15:7–12). It appears to be a sinful ploy, a part of a cunning pretext to cover up an opportunity to work a treacherous plot of murder. When a man plays fast and loose with God, he is actu-

ally working against Him and weaving a pattern toward his own judgment. Eventually Absalom's deceitful selfishness results in his hanging (18:9–10). In sense his hanging in the tight fork of a tree limb was an accident, and in another it was a boomerang on the ego-driven course; he went and got himself hanged!

(8) Oath. One specifically invokes God's monitoring to bring retribution on him if he fails to follow through on an act or design that he pledges. This kind of prayer inviting God's action can be used for good, as in David's case here. He boldly summoned God to smite him if he went against his commitment and ate food before he finished his mourning to honor the military leader Abner. It was a strong way of showing respect for the one who had been put to death (3:35).

The assumptions of it. In some passages that do not explicitly mention prayer, it can be assumed that prayer did accompany what is said. An example is in David's mourning with weeping over the deaths of Saul and Jonathan (Chap. 1; cf. Ps. 30:10–12). Prayer would be natural here in thanksgiving, especially for the love bond with Jonathan, affirmations about the careers of this father and son, and intercession for God's blessing in throne rule after Saul's demise. Even petition would fit in asking for God's timing to be king since God already had had David anointed (cf. 1 Sam. 16), and had given direct anticipations from the lips of Samuel (Chap. 15, etc.).

Another instance strongly likely to feature prayer comes with David's presenting burnt and peace offerings (24:25). According to Scripture, the peace offering was to be given with prayer in thanksgiving for peace in His covenant dealing (Lev. 7:13). And prayer fits closely with the burnt offering, a gift totally consumed, picturing the offerer's total dedication to the Lord (cf. Lev. 1:3ff.).

Let this summary suffice to open the way into looking at specific passages where talking with God occurs.

2 Samuel 2:1

Prayers for Further Guidance

David had previously prayed for God's guidance of his steps in battle (1 Sam. 23). Now he pleads for his first steps after being on the run from Saul away from his people, for the report of Saul's death has come to him in Chapter 1.

The Petition for Specific Guidance

David prays twice in very specific terms, and God answers him just as particularly. The principle is, pray definitely and get definite answers in God's will.

What he asks. Now that Saul is no longer present to bar him from Judah, he asks whether he should go up to one of Judah's cities. It is a very natural, legitimate request.

How God answers. "Go up" is a direct answer.

What he next asks. Narrowing things down, David asks in which city he should make his residence. It is God's will he wants.

How God answers. "To Hebron" makes things very clear.

David and his band of men bring their families to various sites in and near Hebron, west of the Dead Sea and south of Jerusalem. Leaders of Judah visit David, broach the proposal that he be their king, and anoint him for his reign. His first kingly act follows their news that men of Jabesh-Gilead gave honorable burial to King Saul.

2 Samuel 2:5, 6

Prayer of Blessing in God's Will

This is a prayer invoking (calling) God's blessing on the people who showed decency to Saul.

The Conveying of the Blessing (5)

David dispatched an envoy to express his prayer wishing blessing on the men.

The Cause for the Blessing (5)

The prompt for the prayer was the kindness and respect shown to the deceased king.

The Content of the Blessing (6)

David's wish for blessing is in two parts: the first a prayer to God; the second his own sentiments.

The Lord's will. He prays in the Lord's will for Him to honor with His loving-kindness and truth those who honored His anointed king. David is consistent with his high respect for Saul's kingly office, under God, in 1 Samuel 24 and 26 when he spared the leader's life.

His own will. David pledges his own decision to honor those of Jabesh-Gilead for their act. They have shown goodness; he will display goodness to them. Remarkable in this is a complete freedom from a vengeful motive to dishonor the king whose efforts to kill him had dealt him so much heartache. A spirit of love such as Paul would express centuries later controls David: "Love is kind" (1 Cor. 13:4).

David also exhorts the city leaders to carry on faithfully and stresses Judah's recognition of him as king.

Principles suit this. One is that as a person seeks God's will he can invite His blessing on believers who did a thing that He can honor. This is expressing what the mind of God thinks, and what is His will. A second guideline is very close to this: to pray effectively to God, the supplicant must pray seeking harmony with what He is like.

2 Samuel 3:29–39

Prayer for God's Judgment

Now, in contrast to the episode above, David's prayer is for God's judgment, not His blessing.

Abner's Pact with David (6–21)

The commander of Saul's army is incensed against a stinging charge that he has slept with one of Saul's wives. Saul's son Ish-Bosheth, who had set himself up as king succeeding Saul, accuses Abner of this, and Abner takes it as tantamount to accusing him of designs for a coupe to seize the throne. Now carrying out a vendetta against Ish-Bosheth, he swings his loyalty to David.

Joab's Provocation by Murder (22–27)

David's commander arrives back from battle and tells David that Abner's friendliness was a spy's deceit. Snatching justice into his own hands, Joab calls Abner back, catches him off guard, and stabs him to death.

David's Proclamation of Innocence (28)

It was not David's will but Joab's own deceitful plan that Joab privately carried out (37). David avows his own and his kingdom's innocence of sin in the atrocity.

David's Prayers of Cursing and Vowing (29, 35)

Two parts are involved.

The invocation of a curse (29). He prays that the blood of guilt fall on Joab and his line. David is either sinfully vindictive to implicate others besides Joab and Abishai (30), or in God's will. If the latter, it recognizes the guilt of others who themselves also sin. At any rate, David invokes judgments, willing that some in the family line suffer from a discharge, leprosy, lameness, death in battle, and hunger.

The insistence on a vow (35). While mourning Abner's death, David fasted all day in regard to food. The people perceived his sincere concern. David prayed, calling on God by oath to judge him if he broke his promise to abstain from food before sunset. Of course God would see the untruth if David violated his promise, and judgment would pertain to having less in his degree of special reward, and not a loss of salvation (cf. 1 Cor. 3:13–15).

Abishai, Joab's brother, had participated in the murder, too (30); David prayed that the Lord would, in His timing, bring fitting retribution on each evildoer (39), both brothers and others in the family who deserved it (29). He commits the justice to the Lord, who knows all the truth to carry it out.

Now we can reflect on principles. First, a believer in grief over a hideous wrong can appeal in an oath for God to judge him if he violates a spiritual pledge he makes. This is a way of saying that he is serious in underscoring his sorrow over what has happened. It also is true to the principle that a believer's prayer should be in accord with God's will; God indeed will appraise and judge even a believer for his works in relation to an equitable effort to give him his reward (cf. 1 Cor. 3:10–15; 2 Cor. 5:10; Eph. 6:8).

A second guideline vies for attention. Prayer in true heartache can also beseech the Lord to deal justice as fits the case with those behind evil. Of course, this, too, is in sync with God's will, for He indeed weighs actions (1 Sam. 2:3) and will judge evil as well as good (cf. Rom. 2:3, 5–6). He may do this in the present life or in the life to come. So to pray in this way is to ask in accord with His moral will. Third, prayer can express humility in one's own inability to make a proper adjudication, and confidence that in His timing God will unfailingly take care of this.

2 Samuel 5:3

Prayer in a Covenant Agreement

David apparently prayed, for this was "before the Lord" (cf. 6:5, 14, 16, 17, etc.). It was the occasion of David accepting kingship over all Israel, and no longer Judah alone.

The Appeal to Accept Kingship (1, 2)

David has reigned over Judah seven-and-one-half years and was thirty-three when officials of Israel sought him as king over the whole of Israel. They seek his leadership for three reasons.

His pedigree. He meets the qualification of being one of their own, of Israel, as a man from the tribe of Judah. They do not say so, but before the Lord this lineage in Judah was the line He had specified long before (Gen. 49:10; cf. 1 Chr. 5:1, 2). He was qualified, whereas Saul was of the wrong tribe, Benjamin—also really Israel's choice, not the Lord's.

His prowess. They remember David's proven military skill leading Saul's army before Saul had made him a fugitive (1 Sam. 18:5, 13, etc.). David also displayed this leadership while a fugitive.

God's preference. The men of Israel appear to be aware of God's choice pronounced by Samuel (1 Sam. 13:14) and recognized by Abigail, for example (25:30). And Saul himself, before his men, had acknowledged that David would be king (24:20). Now that Saul is gone, an envoy from Israel can voice this boldly.

The Agreement to Accept Kingship (3)

David's covenant with his people probably included different aspects of prayer. One would be his *affirmation* of accepting God's will, another his *thanksgiving* that God has brought him safely to this privilege. Still further aspects could be his *invocation* of God's blessing to carry out the kingship, and his *oath* pledging to do his best. The agreement included, then, not only his *pact* with his nation, but *prayer* before the Lord.

After this momentous meeting came thirty-three years of leading his combined people (5).

The Anointing to Assume Kingship (3)

It is possible that the delegation that anointed David king called on the high priest, or else Nathan the prophet (cf. 7:2). Samuel had died (1 Sam. 25:1), and David had looked to Abiathar at key times when he sought God's leading (1 Sam. 22:20; 23:9, etc.).

Two principles of prayer are easy to see here. David and the delegation of Israel, at least on this occasion, carry out the transaction seeking God's will. All is saturated with His presence, "before the Lord." God's word, in this case about His choice of a man to be king, is uppermost. Jesus would later say, "If you abide in Me, and My words abide in you, you shall ask what you will, and it shall be done to you" (John 15:7), done God's way.

Verses immediately after this show that David *captured* Jerusalem from the Jebusites, made it his capital, and called it "the city of David" (6–9). He also had a palace built. Not all was as it should be, however, as he yielded to fleshly thinking, like so many others in authority, continuing to multiply wives. This trend had begun much earlier (1 Sam. 25:43). A principle is apparent: God is willing to use imperfect people (He finds none in this life totally free of sin), though He never compromises as people do. So David "became greater and greater, for the Lord God of hosts was with him" (2 Sam. 5:10). Even David, in some humility, discerned that the blessing was not just to *him*, but for the sake of God's *people* (12), the people the Lord of covenant grace had pledged to bless.

Another principle joins the one above, and it is this. Prayer with the eyes on God fits well in accepting a role as a leader, whether it be as king or any other position.

2 Samuel 5:17–25

Two Prayers for God's Will in Battle

Philistines, hearing of David's coronation, invaded to test the new king.

David's Search of Counsel (17–19)

His asking. In a way similar to inquiries for God's will in 1 Samuel 23, David used the question aspect in prayer. He was very specific. Should he go against the enemy? Would God assure victory?

God's answer. He answered both queries, "go, and I will give victory."

God's Surge of Conquest (20, 21)

God kept His promise by victory. David exemplifies a principle of prayer in giving the credit to the Lord, acknowledging him in *thanksgiving*. His picture is that of an overwhelming flood that sweeps upon the enemy "like the breaking through of waters." So he gives the battle site a name that means this, "Baal-perazim." The God of prayer won, the gods the Philistines depended on lost, and David's army carried the idols away.

The enemy made another strike soon after.

David's Search for Counsel Again (22, 23)

A maxim is in this. The person who trusts God in prayer must be ever vigilant, for the enemy keeps coming, and the believer can never relax his guard.

The new pressure. The Philistines advanced again. Some learn slowly. The enemy persists; so must God's praying servant.

The new prayer. A principle is that we can never rest on yesterday's victory. David went to God in prayer for the new crisis. He no doubt sought His counsel through Abiathar (cf. 1 Sam. 23:9–11), whose items within the ephod God would use to indicate His guidance.

The new plan. God is a God of variety and many possibilities. This time He gave David a different strategy. Rather than a frontal assault, he was to circle the invaders and come at them in front of a stand of balsam trees. These were Baka-shrubs that exude (run) with a lot of resin. Positioned there, David and his troops were to listen for the sound of marching in the tops of the trees, then attack—for the sound was God's signal that His own unseen hosts had gone ahead of David's soldiers to lead in the victory. This was as the Captain of the Lord's host led Joshua's army (cf. Josh. 5), and as Elisha of a later day would see heavenly warriors arrayed to help him (1 Kgs. 6:16–18).

God's Supply for Further Conquest (25)

Implicit in this is another principle: God does not fail to keep His word. When David obeyed forthrightly, God gave him another great victory. In this case He worked *with* David's army, though when He chooses He can work entirely on His own *without* any human effort. He had done the latter against the Egyptians at the Red Sea, and He would help Judah's later king, Jehoshaphat, against invaders (2 Chr. 20). Both were in response to prayer, as here.

Consider further principles. First, God wants to guide His people, so it is pleasing to Him that they consult Him for the way He wants to lead. Second, when a person follows God's counsel, God backs him up and treads a pathway to success (cf. 2 Chr. 26:5; Prov. 3:5–6). Third, one victory can lead on to another for a person who prays in harmony with the God who is able.

2 Samuel 6:5

Prayer in Praise for God's Presence

David and his people celebrate when he has had the Ark of God's presence brought to Jerusalem.

The Carrying of the Ark (1–4)

Going with a great host of his people, David has the Ark transported from the house of Abinadab. It had been detained there, about ten miles west of Jerusalem, since God's pressure caused the Philistines to return it (1 Sam. 7:1).

Four things stand out here.

David's desire. He was aroused to move the Ark into "the city of David," which now was the capital and center for all of Israel.

The designation of the Ark. It was called by the Name (2), meaning that it was "the Ark of the Lord." The significance of this was not only the perception of the covenant meaning in the Name, and His faithfulness on behalf of the people He had chosen. It also was the presence of God (cf. Ex. 25:8) represented, for He "is enthroned above the cherubim." Of course He created heaven and earth and was present everywhere, but He chose to manifest His presence in a special sense here, so this meant much to Him and to His people.

The defect in the moving. Zeal for God while ignoring obedience to God is a sinful thing. God had specified that Levites, sons of Kohath, were to carry the Ark with poles through rings hoisted on their shoulders (Ex. 25:14, 15; Num. 30, 31). This was not narrow-mindedness but a call for due respect in careful transport.

God's word is set aside here. The saying is true, that "Haste makes waste." Instead of being sensitive to God's guidance, men showed disrespect, loading the Ark on a cart as the ignorant Philistines had done (1 Sam. 6:7, 8). When the cart tilted at a rough spot, Uzzah reached to steady it, putting his hands on the Ark.

The Chastisement Over the Ark (7, 8)

God counted Uzzah's act as an example of careless irreverence and insensitivity to His word. It was possibly one instance that brought to a head for Israelites their indifference to doing things His way during the entire project. He would not tolerate a sloppy attitude of "any old thing is good enough for God."

Uzzah was not the only person who faced discipline for a sinful course or act throughout God's dealings with His people. Other examples were Nadab and Abihu (Lev. 10), Korah and others (Num. 16), Moses when he struck the rock (Num. 20), and much later, Ananias and Sapphira (Acts 5). God's judgment would not mean eternal rejection for those who were genuine believers, but He registered a strong warning to the many to be sensitive to His will.

The Custody of the Ark at a House (10, 11)

Such strong censure of the low standard Israelites were tolerating stung David. His anger (8) was probably against himself for permitting a shoddy standard to prevail under his insensitive leadership. For a time he kept the Ark at a private house along the way, afraid to bring it the rest of the way.

The Celebration Over the Ark (5, 14–16)

While the Ark was being transported before and after the discipline, David and his people were praising the Lord. Praise can glorify God. True, it is possible to praise God with glib spins of the tongue while disobeying His word. God through Samuel had told Israel's first king, Saul, that to obey is better than to sacrifice. If prayer is not mingled with true respect for His word, its value as worship is tainted. God wants His people to get their act together so that their worship is pure. And He acts sharply to call it to their attention. Though He shows discipline to one, He displays great mercy to the many left to profit from the lesson.

Prayer will be more directly stated in verse 18. But how is it feasible in verses 5, 14–16? First, the celebration "before the Lord" with various musical instruments suggests it, as prayer often occurs in the Psalms to such accompaniment (cf. Ps. 150). Second, the leaping and shouting in exultation adds to this; true worshipers would most naturally direct the credit to the Lord from their hearts and lips.

It is not certain that verse 9 has prayer in view. When God disciplined Uzzah in death (cf. 1 Cor. 11:30–31), David was afraid of the Lord. He hesitated about further movement of the ark.

His words may simply be to himself as he ponders what to do, or a query to God for the right steps to take. What he says can fit either way, "How can the ark of the Lord come to me?" He had thoughtof moving the ark on its way toward Jerusalem, for his desire was to exalt Him (v. 2). But the method used in the transport had not worked, so his question could very easily be ultimately in quest of correcting guidance.

The Comfort to Move the Ark (12–16)

Having made a deep impression about the wholeness of worship, God showed by blessing the household keeping the Ark (vv. 11–12) that He meant good to Israel. This encouraged David to bring the Ark the rest of the way.

Now God moves those who carry the Ark to bear it as He has directed. In effect, He is showing David an answer to his query of "how" in verse 9, whether that was prayer or simply a man questioning within himself. The cart method has been put aside. Another detail about "how" in David's reverence is his sacrifice after those carrying the Ark had gone six paces. And during the transport, the king and his people are dancing before the Lord—not dancing in any lustful impulse but in joyous excitement in celebration of God's presence that the Ark signified. The jubilation included shouts and trumpet blasts in gladness.

The Consecration after Moving the Ark (17–19)

David had the Ark set in the Most Holy Place in a tent prepared for it. Then as king he led, no doubt via priests (he was sensitive to God's word now), in burnt and peace offerings. The first signified the Israelites' complete dedication to God (if hearts were genuine). The second was in thanksgiving for the peace God gives with His blessing.

Another highlight was David's prayer for all his people (18). This was probably closely associated with the offerings, after they had been devoted. He "blessed the people in the name of the Lord." This was an intercessory prayer. He was invoking or appealing for the Lord's blessing. Solomon, too, would lead the people in a similar way at the dedication ceremony of the completed temple (1 Kgs. 8). The blessing asked for was possibly along the essential lines of the priests' blessing in Numbers 6:22–27 (cf. the discussion there).

It also was of the essence of what Paul prayed in blessing believers (Eph. 1:2) and in his frequent advocacy for God to give grace to believers, ending many of his letters (Gal. 6:18, etc.).

A final gesture of King David was a gift to each of his people. This consisted of three cakes, bread, dates, and raisins to take home as a token of his good will. It was a considerate act after their tiring trek accompanying the Ark's transport.

Shortly after, David arrives home seeking to "bless his household" (v. 20). It is not said, but this may well have been in the afterglow and in the prayerful spirit with which he had prayed with the others. If so, he intended prayer to ask blessing for loved ones who had stayed home.

At any rate, his wife Michal met him with "sour grapes," sharp with criticism, as her spin on his public uncovering of himself of his outer garment was that it was undignified and shameful. Her accusation is one that he feels he can answer validly; he has acted in worship "before the Lord" with an intent pure to celebrate His worthiness. He is confident that he has shown humility, and women who appraise things fairly will see humility and not wrongdoing. However, a distance came between himself and this rejecting wife (23).

A key principle for prayer in all of this emerges. Pray in thoughtful sensitivity that is serious about honoring God's will. This is so distinct from trying just to slide by, carelessly indifferent toward the standards on which God sets value. Second, we, too, can praise God in shouting and leaping when we think of all that speaks to our hearts about His presence with us. Third, we may prayerfully receive further guidance from the Lord after waiting, and when people involved are ready to do things His way. A fourth principle is to exercise discretion in how we worship, yet however decently we think we do this, we still may suffer disapproval from some.

Fifth, one can pray in accord with God, yet feel hurt from God bringing a setback when others within a total work disobey Him. This was true at Ai (Josh. 7) when Joshua and his people obeyed, but Achan and those complicit with him disobeyed. God looks at the total picture, and in a group a cooperating obedience can be vital. Sixth, wise times for prayer are during a work for God and when it has been completed as supplicants seek His blessing.

2 Samuel 7:1–29

Praise for the Davidic Covenant

David is fervent to build God a temple, but God proclaims His passion to build a house for David and Israel. Filled with encouragement, David praises the God of the covenant.

David's Passion to Build a Temple (1–3)

The prayer does not come until verse 18, but in the flow the verses before are a vital part of the episode.

David has constructed his own palace in Chapter 5. Now he tells Nathan the prophet his longing to build a temple for the Lord. Thinking that he grasps God's will, Nathan answers that he should go right ahead.

Nathan's Proclamation of God's Will (4–17)

The *thought* is God's will, but not the *timing*. David's son, not himself, is to carry out the project (13).

The builder is to be David's son (4–15). God faithfully enables Nathan to correct his first word to David. The Lord had dwelt, as it were, in a tent during Israel's wanderings, and until now He had never faulted His people for His dwelling in a tent. Now He pledges that instead of David providing Him a house, He will confer great blessings on David and all His people.

What He promises is incredible.

(1) Pre-eminence of David himself among great men of the earth. In his own day he became great as an empire builder prospered by God. And God would cause His name to be a household word to Israel and to Christians in blessing "the throne of David."

(2) Placement for Israel (10). Since His people were already in the promised land, the prediction through the prophet Nathan must look on to placement after being disrupted. This will be in the days beyond the Babylonian Captivity (cf. the pledge of restoration God gave Moses: Lev. 26; Deut. 28). Prophets later than Nathan would enlarge on this and place it not only after the dispersion to Babylon, but also in days more ultimate than that (Jer. 31–33; Ezek. 36–37, 39, etc.).

(3) Peace for Israel (10). God will grant peace from all enemies, free from their disruption, peace such as they have not had from the earliest days in Canaan under the judges. This aligns with the time of (2).

(4) Prospering of David's house (11–15). God pledges to build David's house (dynasty on the throne) in his immediate son's day, and this line even forever. This son, who will turn out to be Solomon, will build a house (temple) for the Lord (1 Kgs. 5–8, etc.). The Lord assures discipline of the son when he sins, but steadfast maintenance of His covenant loving-kindness to bless the Davidic line on the throne (cf. Ps. 89).

The blessing is to be on David's seed (16). In the key verse, 16, God guarantees to prosper David's house (dynasty), kingdom with people under kingly government, and throne (authority). Since this is "forever before Me," it must leap on past any time when kings in David's lineage do not reign and endure again perpetually in the final analysis. God faithfully pledges this even for a time after the Assyrian and Babylonian exiles, when His people will be reunited in their ancient covenant land under a king, never again to be uprooted (Jer. 31–33; Ezek. 36–37, 39; Amos 9:11–15).

Final fulfillment in David's line would be in the greater or ultimate Son of David, the Messiah/King, Jesus Christ (Jer. 23:5, 6; Ezek. 34, 36; Dan. 7:13, 14, 27; Matt. 25:31–46).

David's Prayer of Submission (18–29)

David sits before the Lord, greatly encouraged by God's promises (v. 27). His prayer includes two movements.

His sense of his own insignificance (18–20). In the total scheme of things, he feels quite unimportant, in humility. The impact of God's grace overwhelms him. Certainly the blessing is in that grace, and not for any merit in himself or his house. He is astounded that God has brought him this far and even pledges to bless his house forever. Aware that he does not deserve this, he is amazed that God, knowing him, would still bless.

Such humility is a good principle for any of us to live by as we ceaselessly think of God's goodness.

His sense of God's significance (21–29). Here his prayer is in two currents.

(1) Adoration (21–24). He just focuses on why God blesses. He does so for the sake of His own word (will, or plan), and His own heart (covenant kindness). So, all David can do is exalt the Lord in adoring praise. God is great to have such a big plan, spanning the past and all of the future, and the ability to carry it out. No god compares with Him. No nation is blessed the way Israel is in being redeemed and having His power assuring the land.

(2) Asking (25–29). David intercedes that God will perform what His plan prescribes; that is, he prays that God will carry out what is His will. His confidence fueling the prayer is that God is God, His word is truth, and He has made an inviolable promise on His own honor. As a result, he finds himself borne on the stream of God's will, praying that God will do all that He has guaranteed. May God's will be fulfilled for David's house, and realized forever.

Principles flow from the passage.

First, as often in God's Scripture, promise and prayer here blend into one. What God has promised is itself the best; this is the kind of blessing that His servant who ventures all on Him longs to have. It is the essence of what someone wisely expected, "God always gives His best to those who leave the choice with Him."

Second, in some cases what we long for in prayer God chooses to do through another, yet with His good reason. The temple builder would not be David, but Solomon. Third, whatever a praying believer longs to do for the Lord, God is able even to do more for him. Fourth, God gives some blessing to the believer even though He disciplines him for sinful failure. Fifth, God guarantees some matters, such as the Davidic Covenant, by His own gift of grace that will not fail to see it through. Sixth, God's pledge to fulfill this covenant rightly elicits praise by David or any other believer. And seventh, it gives a heart poise to pray that God will bring to realization what He vouches, what He will surely do.

2 Samuel 8:11

Prayer in a Dedication to God

It appears quite probable that while no mention of prayer occurs, it would most reasonably be on David's heart and lips.

The Defeat of Enemies (1–6)

Victories come to David's fighting force against Philistines, Moabites, Ammonites (cf. v. 12), Amalekites (12), Arameans near the Euphrates, and Syrian hordes. The summary of triumphs stretches over a broad sweep of territory west, southeast, and far to the north of Jerusalem.

Behind David's battle success are two things. On the human side is an army of skilled fighters, obviously, as he had had while fleeing from Saul. And on the divine side, the writer puts in his record "And the Lord helped David wherever he went" (v. 6; also cf. 14). David will give credit where credit is due in what follows.

The Dedication to the Enabler (7–12)

Spoils of warfare become objects the conqueror's men carry back home. Among these are shields made of gold, probably a gold overlay since solid gold would be formidable in weight. A great supply of bronze came with the wins. From the visiting Toi, king of Hamath to the north, came gifts of silver, gold, and bronze. The victories, plunder, and goodwill gifts lead on to prayer, so natural in verse 11.

David dedicates this increase to the Lord, whose presence and power had given the conquests even as He had gone before Joshua (cf. Josh. 5:13–6:2), and the victory to David over Goliath (1 Sam. 17). Why assume prayer? It would fit the case for a man of prayer to honor the Lord in prayer in gratitude for His help. Such plaudits to God in prayer would be rather spontaneous when He triumphed over other nations, as nearby in 7:23. Besides thanksgiving, words of affirmation to God would be apropos: "O Lord God [cf. 7:18], You worked that we could have this treasure, and it is Yours. May Your name be magnified!" (cf. 7:26).

Principles are obvious. First, let us discern behind the success of another of God's workings, as the writer has done here (8:6, 14). Second, the godly person individually should dedicate victory to his Lord, realizing as David had earlier done, "the battle is the Lord's" (1 Sam. 17:47). Third, what God can do with a man who trusts Him can be a testimony to others, even far and wide, as David's exploits to a far-off king here.

2 Samuel 10:12

A Prayer for God's Will in Victory or Defeat

Joab was not in a good light when David prayed for God's discipline on him for taking justice into his own hands in Chapter 3. He looks better in this scene.

The prelude is a kindness of David, spurned by the king of Ammon. Joab, who commands David's forces, deals with a war threat.

The Provocation by the Ammonites (1–5)

King Nahash of Ammon died, and David sent an envoy to Nahash's son Hanun, the new king, with a kind outreach. Hanun's cabinet members swayed him to read the visit as a spy mission and to humiliate David's ambassadors by shaving half off each man's beard and cutting off their garments at the hips. It was a stinging insult to David as well, and realizing this the Ammonites secured war allies from Syria and other areas.

The Preparations for Battle (6–11)

Joab found his army trapped between Ammon and Ammon's allies, so he sent a separate fighting force against each of the two. He led the soldiers who met the Syrians and other allies.

The Prayer Before Battle (12)

Final words from Joab to his brother Abishai, who led against Ammon, were in part a *challenge* to be courageous for "our people" and for the cities of "our God." They also were in part a *prayer* before the two men and their divisions parted.

Joab's prayer is one of invoking the Lord's action in the warfare. He calls on Him to "do what is good in His sight." That sounds like Joab was resigned to defeat or victory, not asking in faith expecting to win for sure. Surely he knew that God had, for His purposes, not given victory to Israel in every battle. On the other hand, his intent may have been for the Lord to lead to victory, viewing this as His will, good in His sight. This is natural, for *His* people and *His* interest were on the line.

Whatever Joab's intent was (probably the latter), even sincere prayer is not God's only factor in what He wills. Other considerations that a person in prayer may not be giving the weight God gives may prompt the Lord to permit defeat. Such instances as the two battles in Judges 20 come to mind. In the final analysis, God does what He wills, not what praying people insist on as inevitable. They need to be submissive to *His* right to do as *He* sees best (for He ses better than they), and not feel that *they* can play God.

Prevailing in Battles (13–19)

As it turns out, two battles follow. In the first, Joab's assault on the Syrians was a rout, putting the enemy to flight, and Ammon's army also fled back into their city fortifications. Later, the Syrians regrouped to mount a threat, and David led his troops to meet them. His army again gained a rout, killing 40,000 horsemen and even Shobach the commander. This instilled fear in Syria, which submitted to a peace treaty.

Principles grow out of this. First, God may allow defeat even when His people pray, as He sees details that may not factor in with what He sees as best, all things considered. Second, and related to this, we should trust Him as wise and kind whatever His answers are, and rest with the conviction of His faithfulness. Third, God does know how to give truly good things when we pray (cf. Luke 11:8–13). What appears good to us may not be good to Him, and He looks out for us better than we can for ourselves.

2 Samuel 12

David's Sin and Prayerful Confession

The king who had enjoyed so many triumphs (2 Sam. 1–10) falls into sin, confesses, and is forgiven, but will have to reap from seeds his folly has sown (cf. Gal. 6:8).

The Committing of the Sin (11:1–12:12)

Not just sin but a series of sins disrupt David in this passage. A sinful attitude can bring a chaos of sins.

Lust (11:1–3). While Joab led Israel's army against the still-hostile Ammonites, David remained at his palace. This in itself is not necessarily sinful, as he was responsible for many duties and also stayed home at certain other times. Rising from a late-afternoon nap, David's gaze from his roof fastened on a woman bathing at a residence nearby, below. She was possibly in a patio, not realizing her privacy was being violated from the unexpected angle that the roof gave.

A burning of lustful desire excited David. He was, as James 1:13–15 would later portray, being led away, enticed, and drawn into a sinful act. He *saw* the woman, no sin in itself, for he could have turned away resolute to put no deceitful thing before his eyes. Then he *fondled* her in continuing thoughts, entertaining himself by her beauty and desirability. Lust was now rampant, insistent to grasp its prize.

Implicating others in the wrong. David sent and inquired about the bathing beauty. Now he was drawing a servant or servants into awareness of his sin.

Heedlessness to a warning bell. The report came back that should have arrested David from his lust. She was the wife of another man, even one of his soldiers risking their lives. God's word against adultery might have snatched him back from his sinful bent (Lev. 20:10). But lust was an obsession now to gratify, blinding him to all else.

Stealing. David became guilty of even this other sin, of taking what was not his. He sent messengers now, so that, for sure, several knew that sin's playground was in the king's heart—and he took the woman. He committed the theft of another man's wife.

Unrighteousness. That he "took her" adds more to what David already was doing in a burning insistence on things not right. He was deeply into doing things against God's moral law (cf. Ex. 20) and also misusing a sacred trust as his means, his authority as a king.

The deed was far along, and David kept at it. Bathsheba came to him at his royal, powerful will, and he went to bed with her in *adultery*. He indulged in his little pleasure, and it would cost a big price tag—to himself, to Bathsheba who would mourn, to Uriah who would die, to a child who would die, to Amnon and Absalom who also would resort to flagrant sins, to Nathan who would mourn, and to God who was grieved (11:27). As someone has said, "secret sin on earth [here secret to some] is open scandal in heaven." And what of the servants who went at the king's command to demand that the woman yield to the summons.

Deceit. The steps of sin continue. David learns of Bathsheba's pregnancy (11:5), and practices deceit, or further deceit, in a scheme to cover up his wrong. In this he summons Uriah from battle and commands that he spend time with his wife, thinking this will explain the baby later. But he fails when Uriah valiantly abstains, thinking of his comrades' hardship in battle. Then David gets Uriah drunk to fog his mind so that he will surely go home, but still the soldier holds back from his wife. A desperate David resorts to something even more drastic. He sends Uriah back to war carrying a sealed message for Joab to put him where Ammonites will be certain to slay him. Murder is in David's heart. This way, David can later say the baby is Uriah's, and Uriah will not be there to question this.

Even then the sins have not stopped. A bit after this, David *puts a sugar-coating over the murder* by trying to make it appear that Uriah's death was just an ordinary thing in fierce battle (25). Bathsheba mourned for her husband, but David seems to be sinful here too, this time in *callousness* to the incident. Nothing is said about the king himself mourning his soldier's death.

God, displeased (11:27), sends His prophet Nathan to confront David. He tells the king a story of a rich man who took another man's only ewe lamb to satisfy his own will. David explodes with indignation against the rich man.

Then God's spokesman peals his thunderclap. "You are the man!" He tells the stunned adulterer that the bottom line is this sin: David has *despised the word of the Lord* (12:9). That word had been very clear against the two sins Nathan now names, murder and adultery, as well as others.

God as a result will let the sword trouble David's house. Indeed the violence of Amnon in ravishing his sister Tamar, and Absalom's murder of Amnon would be examples. In family life a bad model (David) can sow disrespect, contempt, and self-will in others of the family. David did his sin in secrecy from most, and God will bring troubles before all Israel (12), including evil from his own family and another man of the family (Absalom in his revolt) taking David's wives (11).

The Confession in Prayer (13a)

Caught dead to rights by God and Nathan, David acknowledges that he sinned against the Lord. Detail on his confession and plea for cleansing appears from his own hand in Psalm 51, also Psalm

32. That he sinned against "the Lord" puts the focus on the ultimate One he wronged. It does not deny sin against Bathsheba, Uriah, and others. Similarly in Psalm 51 he says "against Thee, Thee only, have I sinned."

The Clearing from Guilt (13b)

God's word from Nathan is, "The Lord also has taken away your sin." As in 1 John 1:9, "If we confess our sins, He is faithful and just to forgive us our sins, and to cleanse us from all unrighteousness." The one who confesses receives mercy (Prov. 28:13). Psalm 51, again, gives great detail on David's desire for clearing, and 32:5 says that when he confessed God forgave him.

More Consequences of Sin (13c, 14)

Nathan told David some results of the sin above.

That David will not die for this episode of sin is God's pledge. But the child of the adulterous union would die. God's reason in this is to show His enemies who blaspheme Him over this matter that He hates sin and does not take it lightly. The product of the sin will be taken. In some measure this will uphold His honor.

The Lord struck the child with illness (15), and a week later the infant died (18).

The Concern in Prayer for the Child (15–23)

David shows deep concern after the baby born of his adultery becomes ill.

His prayer during the illness (16). He inquired of the Lord on behalf of the little one. This very naturally would have entailed certain aspects in prayer. Aptly, he would intercede for the child's recovery if God willed it. Also he would petition for mercy to himself in any way that would right his heart fully and clear any hindrance to God healing the child. Possibly he also would affirm his desires to do God's will rather than cast it aside as he had done. And praise for God's Person and ways would be very apropos as well.

Prayer here is accompanied by fasting with regard to food (16, 17), and denying himself comforts by lying contritely on the ground. Both are no doubt sincere expressions of humility, submission, and brokenness before the Lord (cf. 2 Chr. 7:14). They are not attempts to run up merit points to coax God into line with self-will, but forms of all-out receptivity to His grace.

When David realizes God's answer is in taking the child's life, he rises and washes (he had not taken time to do that for a week). He also anoints himself, changes into clean clothes, worships at the tabernacle, and later eats.

His worship (20). This, at the Lord's tabernacle that David had had set up in 6:17, undoubtedly includes prayer. It would be fitting to praise God for His will now made known, affirm his submission to it, and thank Him for his own hope of joining the child when it is God's time (cf. 23). Again, Psalm 51 reveals more fully his wholehearted spirit in prayer.

That David expects to go to the child has received different interpretations. Some say it means no more than that he knew he would go into the afterlife as the child had. Others believe that as he felt he would be with the Lord in death, received with the saved (Ps. 49:15), the child would be in that place. In the second view, he felt God would be gracious to the child, who had been unable to believe personally but dealt with in the equity and kindness of God.

Further probable allusions to prayer occur twice in verses 21 and 22. In 21, the servants may refer back to prayer in verse 16 when they see that David there had fasted and wept (probably including prayer, cf. Ps. 51) while the child's survival was uncertain. Yet now when the boy is dead David has gotten up and eaten. In verse 22, David has an answer to what seems to be inconsistent. While the child clung to life, he had fasted and wept (probably in prayer). This was because he was gripped by what was possible. The Lord "may be gracious to me, that the child may live." This appears to assume that intercessory pleading for God to spare the child had been a part of his spiritual vigil in verse 16.

The Comfort in the Grace of God (24, 25)
Comfort comes in three aspects.

From David to Bathsheba. The king had been forgiven and had a tender heart before his Lord (cf. Ps. 51). Now, sensitive to God's will again, he is able to minister comfort. This is to the woman he wronged. How might he comfort her? Possibly it was in various kindnesses to encourage her; in talking with her about God's mercy that triumphs over sin, and about God's will being good; he also could tell of his desire for her fulfillment in having another child. He may have honored Uriah in some way that lifted her spirit. Another comfort would be in his acceptance of her after their heartache, for she would be alone without Uriah if David put her aside. And finally, his new sexual favor, now in the marriage bond after God renewed his motives, could enhance her.

From a son. A son is born to them, whom David names Solomon ("peace"), for he felt peace with God after confession (Ps. 32:3, 4). In God's leading, Solomon would enjoy peace in his career (1 Kgs. 5:4).

From the Lord. However God lifted their spirits when sin was first dealt with, He encouraged them even more now. He sent Nathan as his messenger to voice His love for the new son, and His name for him, Jedidiah, "Beloved of the Lord"). Like the name Solomon, it may have a two-way reference. David and Solomon were both beloved in God's covenant commitment. Though He would discipline for sin, He would not take away His loving kindness from them (2 Sam. 7:15).

Which principles for prayer suggest themselves? One is that a strong prayer walk sensitive to God can be an asset against falling when temptation comes. It may be significant that shortly before David fell spiritually, we do not find a single focus on his prayer life (Chap. 10). When his eyes fall on the woman below, he does not turn away; he does not look to God for help to put out the fire. He just keeps meditating on her, not the Lord! Even after David sent to learn of the beauty, he had time to do an about-face and avoid a snare in the path he pursued.

Another principle is clear. Even when he has taken advantage of the woman, David remains hardened to repentance for nearly a year. For the birth appears to occur before he repents, or at least before he is *said* to worship God. In the long interval, sin after sin is spawned in his cover-up deceit. He should have dealt with the sin of adultery immediately. That could have meant the sparing of Uriah's life and preventing a host of evils.

Third, when David at last gets around to it, his confession stands as a helpful pattern for other believers (2 Sam. 12; Ps. 32, 51). Fourth, when God has answered "no," as in taking the child's life, it is best to submit to that and go on to live life from there, as David does. Fifth, when it is God's will for a leader like Nathan to confront sin boldly, it is best to be forthright however it may sting. Helping people win the battle in coming back from sin is no place for spiritual cowards. Nathan could be up-front, even if loving, for the God who sent him also strengthened him.

Yet other principles accrue. One is that a sin may be a link in a chain of wrongs; one sin yielded to can make it easier to succumb to another, and this to still another. Another is that even when a wrong desire is met by glaring stop lights, one in a lust trip can rationalize and tromp on the accelerator. An additional one is that when one enters into adultery, he hurts the other persons in the marriage union, and potentially many others.

Further, it is crucial to delight in God's Word and obey it rather than despising it and trafficking in disobedience. We also need to remember this guideline: however awful sin is, God can pardon, yet sin forfeits so much of what might have been for God, others, and oneself.

Finally, repentance may be late after great damage, yet it is a turn back to God and to good, and is still better late than never.

2 Samuel 13:31

Prayer in Mourning

We meet with another passage that omits specific reference to prayer where it is a really probable accompaniment in a strong gesture of mourning. The action moves swiftly here.

The Report (1–30)

Various things precede the prayer. One of the royal family, Amnon, rapes his beautiful sister Tamar after tricking her by a pretense of needing her help when ill (1–19). Absalom hears of this wrong and plots the death of Amnon. When his treachery has the unsuspecting man go with others to a sheep-shearing task, he calls for henchmen to murder the rapist. The deed done, they flee (20–29).

The report pierces the heart of David, but exaggerates what really happened. He hears that Absalom had killed *all* of David's sons (30).

The Response (31–36)

David ripped his garment, a custom in reacting to shocking news and feeling utter grief. He had done this at news of King Saul's death (1:11). A Bible reader sees this frequently in the Old Testament as a gesture of shock, horror, or grief. Reuben tore his clothing when he found that Joseph was gone from the pit (Gen. 37:29), Jacob when smitten by the report that a wild beast had slain Joseph (37:34), and his sons when searchers turned up Joseph's cup in Benjamin's bag (44:13). Jephthah recoiled at his vow going awry when his daughter came to welcome him home (Judg. 11:35). Tamar, having been raped, shows utter despair and shame by ripping her tunic, putting ashes in her hair, putting her hand to her head, and sobbing disconsolately (2 Sam. 13:19). Other cases join these (1 Kgs. 21:27; 2 Kgs. 5:7; 6:30; 11:14; 18:37; 19:1; Ezra 9:3, etc.).

David also prostrated himself on the ground, and his servants joined in his consternation by tearing their garments. The heartbreak and posture, as in 12:16, most feasibly involved prayerful cries to the main refuge, God. This was the case in Joshua 7:6–9, for example. A natural aspect of prayer would be questions, "Why, Lord? How could Absalom do this to his brother, and snatch the law into his own hands?" Another part of prayer could be confession, for David had heard of Amnon raping Tamar (13:21), but despite anger seems to have let things ride without any kind of discipline. Now in sharp pain he could voice his part of the blame. Yet a further relevant facet of prayer would be petition, beseeching God for wisdom on what to do. And David, as would be so pertinent, could have felt proper concern for the violated Tamar, which would prompt tender intercession for her welfare.

Jonadab, David's grandson, offers some measure of consolation. He informs the king even during his show of dismay that the atrocity did not claim the life of the other grandsons, but only Amnon. Absalom had targeted only this one who forced Tamar. Before Jonadab has finished speaking, he spots the king's surviving sons arriving home from the trip. David and the returned sons and royal servants weep together (36). It would be surprising if a vital part of this, too, was not prayer. The result of the episode for Absalom was his sojourn for three years to keep a distance from his father David's possible retaliation. However, David, in due time, felt comfort, and he did not seek to punish Absalom.

What of principles for prayer? One is that God understands the anguish that events hurl at the human spirit, and we can honor Him in a sincere display of deep hurt. This would not have to call for the same custom, such as pulling our clothing apart. Second, others can enter into the grief that one feels, and in the New Testament this is part of life in Christ's spiritual body (1 Cor. 12), a sharing of burdens others feel (Gal. 6:2–5).

2 Samuel 14:11, 17, 22

An Oath and Two Wish Prayers

The Prelude to Absalom's Return (1–20)

Two prayers surface here.

A general of David, Joab, finds that the king has good wishes toward Absalom. So the general sets a plan in action to get Absalom back. He locates a woman who has a similar problem to plead with David by using her own story. What is happening to her son has an analogy to David's attitude toward his son, Absalom. In her account, which appears to be true (cf. vv. 15–16), one of her two sons killed the other. Now the family pressures her to hand over the guilty son to be executed. Aroused by her heartache, David guarantees he will see that no harm befalls her living son.

A part in this account is David's oath in verse 11. Using this form of prayer, the king swears by the very fact that the Lord lives (a sure thing) that he will protect the son. This is David's heart intent in prayerful conviction before God.

Then the woman running interference for Joab presses to her point. If David so insists to help *her* son, why does he fail to bring back *his* own son from exile (13)?

Light dawns on David, and he questions the woman until she admits that Joab put her up to this approach (18–20). The woman voices the second prayer in the passage (17), an intercessory appeal or wish, "may the Lord your God be with you."

The Problems in Absalom's Return (21–33)

True to the woman and convicted by the application she makes, David asks Joab to bring Absalom back. Found out in his design, the general falls down before the king and blesses him. That is, whatever the state of his heart, he prays, asking God in a wish prayer to bless David, with the focus more on gratitude to David for his order than an emphasis on the Lord.

Difficulties soon emerge in Absalom's return. David freezes out his son, holding back from any personal meeting with him, even for two years (24, 28). Tired of waiting to have a bid into his father's presence, Absalom asks twice for Joab to visit him, but Joab ignores him. To provoke action, Absalom has his men torch Joab's barley field, and this brings Joab to confront him. Joab listens to him, seeks the king's favor to allow a visit, and so David gives the invitation for his son to come. Temporarily it would appear that problems are resolved when David kisses his son.

Now it is time to review principles. It can be right to utter a strong guarantee of one's actions as David did to protect the woman's son, if one is sincere to keep his word. Second, it can be an act of sincere love to pray that God will be with a person in blessing as the woman prays for David. Joab prays this for David also, and it is a valid way to pray if, again, one's intent is pure before the Lord (cf. Ps. 66:18). One sees intercessory wish prayers for blessing at the outset and end of many of the New Testament epistles. One needs to do a heart check to be right with God so as to pray in a way pleasing to Him (Ps. 34:14–15; 1 Pet. 3:12).

2 Samuel 15:7, 8

Deceit in a Prayer Vow

David's son Absalom was creating treachery in fertile minds. He had ambitions to grab the throne at his father's expense. Sin has its own ingenious ploys.

The Clever Pretense to Fulfill a Vow (7)

The principle the psalmist would later express was pertinent in essence for Absalom: "If I regard iniquity in my heart, the Lord will not hear me" (66:18). The writer of that psalm goes on to clarify that *he* himself is not doing this, so God does hear *his* prayer. Absalom asked leave of David under the lying excuse of going to Hebron only to fulfill a vow. His subsequent conspiracy that temporarily gains him the throne, and also his falsehood to the content of the vow, expose his heart in its misusing prayer.

The Component Parts of the Vow (8)

Since a vow includes the pledge of the one praying and the part he wants God to do for him (cf. Jacob, Gen. 28), both are relevant here.

The Lord's part. Going on a sojourn to Geshur of Syria, Absalom prayed that the Lord would keep him safe to get back to Jerusalem. In return for safety he made his own promise.

His part. "I will serve the Lord." God brought Absalom safely back, giving him Joab's escort and David's approval (14:21–23). Before fleeing to Geshur, Absalom had snatched justice into his own hands and murdered his brother Amnon for raping Tamar (13:20–33). So when Joab brought Absalom back from his fugitive sojourn, David permitted him safety but refused to see him personally for two years, then kissed him in reunion (14:24–33).

In the two years following the reunion, Absalom plotted treachery against David's kingship (cf. 15:7, "four years" rather than "forty"). So, when he claims intent to fulfill his vow "I will serve the Lord," his design is already a proof of his sin against serving God.

When David okays Absalom's trip to complete his part in the vow, the son uses the time away not to fulfill the vow but to entice many to support his insurrection. In a short time, news of his massing for attack leads David and his followers to retreat from Jerusalem to safety.

Principles of prayer are obvious. A person should get his act together, as in telling the truth, in coordination with being effective in a prayer pledge. God is no narrow-minded ignoramus who irresponsibly isolates His "yes" answer to prayer from a person's motives and his lifestyle. Paul clarifies that "truth" is a vital part of one's armor in a warfare standing against sin in prayer (Eph. 6:14–20). Second, the person who tries to traffic in prayer while actually living for deceit is on a slippery path headed for ruin, not success, unless he repents. Absalom's path leads to getting himself hanged where he is helpless, a victim of enemies who pierce him to death (18:9–15).

2 Samuel 15:31

David's Prayer to Void a Fool's Actions

A report of his former priest/counselor Ahithophel's double-cross to side with Absalom prompts David's appeal to God.

The Report of the Defection (31a)

The notable priest, Ahithophel, had made the momentous decision to join the conspiracy (15:12). After a time, a messenger reaches David with news that his counselor is among the enemies.

The Request for the Defeat (31b)

A good principle of prayer is vivid here. When confronted with a hurt that deeply wounds, a wise recourse is to take the heartache to God. What David himself pens in Psalm 55 shows his readiness to follow this path. The psalm is partly about friends who become turncoats. David prays that God will defeat them, but his resolve for himself is, "I shall call upon God," who "will save me" (16). He counsels others also, "Cast your burden upon the Lord, and He will sustain you . . ." (22).

Living by such a conviction, David asks that the Lord will "make the counsel of Ahithophel foolishness." How apt, for the priest's name means "brother of foolishness." Esteemed for a time to give counsel as if one inquired of God's word (16:23), the priest made a wrong turn and never got back. He turned out to live up to his name, as Abigail's husband Nabal (fool) had lived up to his. God answered David's prayer by making his adversary's counsel foolishness. Late in the traitor game, Ahithophel's counsel was not honored, he saw "the jig was up," and committed suicide (17:23).

A principle of prayer here is this. David, though rocked by his counselor's defection, prays not for his death but for defeat of his unwise counsel. The sweet discipline of tender mercy tempers prayer.

2 Samuel 19:7, 13, 23

A Saturation of Prayer

Joab prays, swearing in an oath in the name of the Lord as his witness (7), and David pleads for God's action against him if Amasa refuses to become his army commander (13). Later, David swears in a promise he makes, probably "before God" as in verse 7, to preserve Shemei's life (23).

Calling on God these three times mingles with the context of David's restoration to his kingly rights in Jerusalem. Absalom, who had gained control at Jerusalem, has died and David is mourning (1–4). His military commander Joab persuades him that his demeanor makes his people feel dispirited. For he makes it appear that he loves those who hate him such as the followers who backed Absalom, and hates those who love him, those who have been loyal to him. He ought rather to encourage his supporters since they did what was for his good. So Joab advises the king to go out, be available to his people, and speak tenderly to whoever visits him.

Joab's Prayer (7)

This utterance to God comes amid the commander's words above appealing to David.

Let David "speak kindly to [to the heart of] your servants," Joab pleads. Then comes the prayer, "for I swear by the Lord," by appealing directly to and invoking His name as witness. Witness to what? Joab continues, that "if you do not go out, surely not a man will spend the night with you. . . ." This is probably because David's men, though they respected him, were not in favor of his attitude that appeared more favorable to the Absalom crowd.

David leads a swell to reinstate him in Jerusalem (19:11ff.). He had evacuated the city when Absalom's revolt swept him in to take over (15:14–16:23), and gone east of the Jordan.

It is during this movement back to the throne city that David's first of two prayers in this chapter occurs.

David's First Prayer (13)

Amid events of the return, David chooses as his new military commander Amasa, one of the favorites at Jerusalem and in Judea. He speaks to those of Judea who come forth to meet him at the Jordan the words of the prayer. He wants them to report to Amasa that in prayer he swears in an oath he will make this man the army leader to replace Joab. In the oath, a strong affirmation of resolution, he asks God, whom he summons in as witness his integrity, to "do to me and also more" should he allow anything to cause this oath to fall through. He invites God to deal firmly and justly with him for any such turning back from the decision. This is a way of stating the intention with his most serious human guarantee to carry it out. Such words should show Amasa that he means business, help him accept with confidence, and swing the loyalty of the Judeans (15). He could go into Jerusalem with great unity in his support.

Shemei, a man of Benjamin who had cursed David on the king's exit from Jerusalem (16:5–13), now does an opportune about-face. He comes with a large following of people from Benjamin, and these pitch in to help David's household cross the Jordan and please the returning king in other ways, too (16–18). Shemei begs David to accept his confession of sinning against him. So, despite counsel to have the man executed, David tells Shemei he will be safe.

David's Second Prayer (23)

The man on the move to resume his place in Jerusalem swears in a second oath. This time it is to assure Shemei. In prayer, David guarantees what he affirms. His stout assertion of the oath is probably, in this context, "before the Lord" as the oath of Joab is in verse 7, and as David's first oath (v. 13) brings God in as witness, "May God do so to me. . . ." If this is an accurate grasp of the words, prayer fits the case well enough.

Which principles are appropriate? First, the person who trusts the Lord when things have gone awry for him may later see God's will is to put him back into prized privileges. Second, when one makes a pledge in prayer, he should be resolutely true to it unless God shows him it was not right in His sight.

2 Samuel 21:1, 7

Prayer to Put a Famine in God's Perspective

A three-year famine drove David to prayer to see if some cause needing correction might lie behind the pressure.

The Problem David Perceived (1)

Reflection on God's word apparently suggested to the king that some sin that grieves God might be at the root (cf. Lev. 26:19). If so, he was zealous to set it right. Sensitivity to God's will is a vital element in effective prayer.

The Prayer David Prayed (1b)

His entreaty. He sought the Lord's presence, evidently at the tabernacle and in respect for God's priest, Zadok or Abiathar (19:11). He had gone to the house of God often (7:18; 12:20). He aspired to dwell in that house all the days of his life (Ps. 27:4), saying "Thy face, O Lord, I shall seek" (8). Sadly, he apparently missed many of those precious times in his indifference after adultery and murder (2 Sam. 12).

Seeking the Lord's presence, longing to see His face in the vision of trust, could fit well with any aspect of prayer. In this case, as he realized that sin might be behind the famine, a spirit of *confession* was relevant. With it, sensitivity would voice *affirmations* of God's faithfulness, men's wanderings, and "I love you, O Lord" (Ps. 18:1). *Praise/thanksgiving* would be much in place in any meeting with God. And *intercession* for Israel's welfare which the famine puts on his heart relates meaningfully.

God's explanation. God gives David the perception he needs. He answers that the famine's cause is one of Saul's sins in an incident that Scripture has not recorded up to here. Saul had broken Israel's covenant of peace with the Gibeonites (Judg. 9) by putting some of Gibeah's people to death. This must have been a blood-bath along lines similar to Saul's treachery in ordering eighty-five priests slain at Nob (1 Sam. 22:17–19). He had shown the Gibeonites, in effect, that God's Israel was not true to its word, and this reflected on Israel's God, who is truth.

The Plan David Pursued (2–14)

His seeking of counsel (2–6). David asked Gibeonite leaders what would clear the wrong. They proposed that he turn over seven of Saul's family for them to execute.

His sentencing of descendants (7–9). David selects seven men he marks for death to right things with Gibeah.

His sensitivity to another covenant (7). At the same time David is true to his earlier promise in a prayer oath to protect those of Jonathan's house (1 Sam. 18:3; 20:12–17; 23:18). He spares Mephibosheth. Greater detail on the covenant oath in prayer appears in 1 Samuel 18:3.

The sequel (10–14). Two movements occur here.

(1) The grieving of a mother (10). Rizpah, a concubine of Saul and mother of two among the executed seven, honors the dead. She spreads sackcloth on a rock and keeps a lonely vigil near the hanging corpses, driving away birds and beasts.

(2) The gesture of David (11–14). Hearing of the mother's stint from barley harvest (late April) to the rains (around October),

David honors her long devotion. He has bones of Saul, Jonathan, and the seven men interred decently in their own Benjamite tribal area.

David followed up his prayer with a faithful life. He was true to a covenant with Gibeah, true to a covenant with Jonathan, and kind to a grieving mother. A right prayer walk before God coordinates with fruit living within His will (Eph. 6:10–18). God had also said "them that honor Me, I will honor" (1 Sam. 2:30).

God's Satisfaction (14)

David did things he knew to do to please the Lord, and others did what David commanded (14). This forthright zeal to honor God's will met, of course, with His action to bless. The Lord was moved by entreaty, David's prayer in verse 1 (perhaps others prayed also, when hit hard by famine, as in the Judges era), answering the cry by removing the famine.

Principles leap to greet the reader.

First, David would memorialize his own principle in Psalm 37:3–5. When a believer moves to "trust in the Lord and do good . . . cultivate faithfulness . . . Delight . . . in the Lord" and "commit" his way to Him, the Lord responds. In some way that He feels wise in His purpose, He will "give you the desires of your heart" and accomplish these (cf. John 15:7).

Add to this other principles. First, God even has power to remove a famine, for He is the creator and sustainer of the universe, and nothing is too hard for Him (cf. Jer. 32:17, 27). Second, if God is not giving blessing, as during a famine, meditation to see if sin and spiritual disobedience are at the root is a path to harmony with Him.

2 Samuel 22

David's Prayer Song of Praise

The "sweet psalmist of Israel" (23:1) wrote many entries that are in the Book of Psalms. One of those, Psalm 18, is also incorporated here in the context of his career, and 23:1–7 is still another.

His Circumstances in Praising God (1)

It is the testimony of the verse that David prayed the words to God. Perhaps he wrote these thoughts before voicing them to the Lord, or was later empowered to remember and record them accurately. Either way, the Spirit of God moved him (cf. 23:2, 3), speaking by him. His was an experience of "praying in the Spirit" (Eph. 6:18), but more than this, being inspired by God.

The setting that stimulated the prayer song was God's rescue of David from all his enemies and from Saul, possibly about the time of 2 Samuel 1 and 2. God's faithful guarding of his life was the cause for praise.

His Comparisons of God in Praise (2, 3)

God, to him, is such a bastion that David calls Him "my rock . . . fortress . . . deliverer . . . shield . . . horn of my salvation . . . stronghold . . . refuge . . . savior." He feels safe within the protecting sufficiency of God as one could feel inside an impregnable fortress, or behind a shield big enough to ward off all attacks. God is his "horn" in that He has potency like a strong animal with a horn that gives mastery over other animals. He is a "stronghold," like the famous Bent's Fort, the first thick-walled outpost against Indian attack west of the Mississippi River. Built ca. 1832, it was along the Arkansas River near the present La Junta, Colorado. It seemed so invincible that Indians never assaulted it.

His Call to the God of Deliverance (4–20)

David calls in prayer on the Lord, knowing that He is worthy of his praise. In situations that threatened like sure death-traps, he cried for help, and God answered from His heavenly temple.

God's response came with a shaking, possibly in mighty thunder (cf. v. 14 as when Samuel prayed; 1 Sam. 7, 12). Fire streaked from God's mouth, possibly a picturesque way to describe fiery lightning flashes in a frightening storm. Verse 12 envisions a storm. God came on the wings of the wind, a poetic depiction of swift action. God's arrows, streaks of lightning shooting along the heavens along with thunderclaps, caused panic that helped rout the enemy. The Philistines had faced such terror in 1 Samuel 7:10.

David, in great danger as a man caught in a flood, felt God answer his prayer "SOS." The Lord lifted him into safety, away from his enemy, setting him in a broad place, no longer feeling the tight squeeze of being entrapped.

And why did God do this for David? It was "because He delighted in me," in grace. No wonder David's heart sings in praise!

His Concord with the Lord of Praise (21–28)

In commitment to God's will, one finds the way of blessing through prayer. This is not because a person's faithfulness *merits* the benefit. It is because the faithfulness *manifests* by God's empowering grace a heart open in fellowship to receive His ways. God Himself gives the grace to make His servant pure, and "With the pure Thou dost show Thyself pure" (27).

His Celebrations to the Lord of Praise (29–51)

God is worthy of praise for His gift of light that is like a lamp making the way clear (29). His power makes the person able to run through a troop in victory, and leap over a wall (30). God's gift of sure-footed stability provides the believer the grip not to slip (33; Hab. 3:19; cf. Eph. 6:14). Like a mountain animal that does not easily lose footing on treacherous paths, God helps him go safely (cf. 2 Sam. 22:37). God even trains the hands to win in battle, supplying strength to the arms (35). His help is the secret that makes David great (36), and His power furnishes the victory against enemies (40; cf. 1 Cor. 15:57). He even turns the enemies back in retreat (41); James 4:7 says that when God's servant resists in His strength, the devil will "flee from you."

David also is grateful that God delivered him when people contended against him (44). Pastors over people, even all believers, can know this encouragement. When David led his band home to Ziglag they found that Amalekites had raided, stripping the camp of the men's families and spoils. The men murmured about stoning David, whose leadership got them into this predicament. He strengthened himself in the Lord (1 Sam. 30:6; Ps. 138:3) and led a pursuit. They regained the families and spoils, and David had honor again with his followers.

Now the praying man knows the Lord lives, is blessed, and is exalted (47). This flames his heart to give thanks, to sing praises to His name. At the very end, the song-writer acknowledges the covenant zeal of God behind his blessings. God shows covenant kindness to the king He anointed (cf. three anointings, 1 Sam. 16; 2 Sam. 2:4; 5:3). He also displays covenant compassion to the people of David forever (51). These are his Israelite descendants and, in a wider application, people of like faith from all nations. God's original covenant with Abram expanded to blessing for "all nations" (Gen. 12:1–3).

Take to heart the principles. First, a song to God is one way to press one's prayer. Second, what one writes out can honor the Lord with vital currents that are sincerely from the heart, or it can be dead ritual of just going through the motions. Third, if a prayer is in sincere godliness, colorfully vivid expression can be a part of the devotion. Why not celebrate the worthy One with the very finest words if these are the outflow of a pure heart? Fourth, praise is fitting, for God is great and greatly to be praised (cf. Ps. 48:1). Fifth, it is good in prayer to trace blessing to the covenant compassion that a promise-keeping God is faithful to keep up.

2 Samuel 23:1–7

Another Song of David's Praise

Some describe these "last words of David" (v. 1) as a psalm of praise, a prayer. Others do not. In any case, what David wrote here exudes *affirmations* that truly credit the Lord with worthiness to be praised. If not prayer, it is the essence of the kinds of points that quickly kindle the heart to exult in prayer.

A few examples are ready at hand. David says things for which he is deeply thankful to God. God raised him on high to be His king, anointed him, gifted him to be Israel's "sweet psalmist," and made him a channel to speak His word. He let David rule righteously in reverence for Him, and let his career be as the light of sunup. He made an everlasting covenant with David, and will cause it to prosper. These stimulants to prayer in praise/thanks set a believer so greatly in contrast to the unbeliever whose sphere of life is outside this special grace.

The quick summary prepares us for a closer exposition.

The Claim to His Inspiration (1, 2)

His humble pedigree. He is the son of Jesse, a sheep-raiser, taken from tending the flock. Even when the Lord pledged His covenant to bless his house, kingdom, and throne, David responded, "Who am I . . . what is my house, that Thou hast brought me this far?" (7:18). Here in Chapter 23 he did not say, but could have, that even when Samuel first sought to anoint a man from Jesse's family he was the youngest and last to be brought before the prophet (1 Sam. 16). God took him from the pasture and the sheep (2 Sam. 7:8).

His high privilege. He is declaring now that in contrast to his lowly place in life, God has highly blessed him. He raised him to a lofty role, with the God of Jacob annointing him. He endowed him with ability to be "the sweet psalmist" usable to his people. The Spirit of the Lord spoke by him, inspiring what he wrote for Scripture. As a psalmist, he wrote more that would be a part of God's psalter than any other. His privilege of penning what God led him to say is a high one.

The Character of His Reign (3c–5)

Writing what God prompted, what did David say in this case? He spoke of what a rule under God is like.

Its attributes. David's own rule, tutored by God, has in some degree been one of dealing with others righteously and in respect for God,

His word and will. He did fail badly at times, as in his adultery/murder and in taking a census. But overall his people recognized a whole-hearted devotion to the Lord that could be held up as a comparative standard for later kings (1 Kgs. 11:4; 15:3). Best of all, the Lord measured his career with high honor, in grace (1 Kgs. 9:4).

A prime instance of David's righteousness came in his zeal to set right Saul's breaking of a covenant that had promised peace to the Gibeonites (2 Sam. 21). His fear of God surfaced in that episode, as in his passion to bring the Ark to Jerusalem, his tender prayer over God's covenant (7:18–29), and his repentant pouring out of water when men flung their lives into jeopardy to get him a drink (23:13–17).

A God-honoring rule also has its analogies.

Its analogies. David paints a portrayal of God-honoring rule in two facets. A righteous rule is analogous to morning light breaking across the landscape on a cloudless day. The scene is resplendent and also refreshing, pure. The second facet is tender grass on a meadow reflecting sparkles of the sun in myriad raindrops.

David breathlessly exults in these conceptions. Prayer springs from his heart in the form of a question: "Truly is not my house so with God?" That he asks a question calling attention to what is true and is not denying that his house is so seems verified by his next statement. He builds on what is the case ("For . . ."). True, he himself has fallen at times and needed God's forgiveness. But God in covenant grace has prospered his kingdom to be in some measure resplendent and refreshing. To God be the glory!

The Covenant of His Hope (5b–e)

David's confidence in his kingdom being worthwhile is based not on anything in himself. It flows from God's sponsoring covenant grace that assures success (cf. 7:9, 16). He rejoices in God doing several things with regard to the covenant.

His sponsoring of it. He "made" it, taking the initiative to build David a house in response to David's ambition to build Him a house. Behind this was the very promise of God (2 Sam. 7:12–16).

His securing of it. Due to God's reliability, the covenant was "ordered in all things, and secured." God cannot lie or fail, and so the covenant will be fulfilled entirely.

His saving in it. David's salvation is safe in the purpose of God to bless him unconditionally in grace. Of course his deliverance and that of his descendants rests upon what the Lord is and what He does, all worthy of praise (cf. 22:51 and that whole chapter). Centuries later the writer to the Hebrews would express similar confidence with regard to God's covenant with Abraham (6:13–19).

His satisfaction in it. All that David can desire that is worthwhile is found in God's covenant determination to bless. God's pledge of 7:9–16 was filled with assurance to meet his fondest pure desires.

The Contrast in Those Without Hope (6, 7)

David brings his last words to a close by portraying how different is the lot of those outside covenant blessing, the unsaved. This he clarifies in three aspects.

Their rejection (6a). God had told Abram that whoever cursed him or his descendants would be under His curse (Gen. 12:1–3). David agrees, moved as he is by the Spirit (2 Sam. 23:2). Some, he describes, are "worthless," unprofitable (cf. Matt. 25:30; Luke 12:46–50), void of faith and submission to God. Not only are they without worth, they are without God's welcome. Instead, He must thrust every one of them away in rejection as one casts thorns away (cf. Ps. 1:4–6; 145:20; Matt. 13:40–42).

The reason (6b-7b). It is clear. Those outside the covenant blessing are not manageable, submissive, of a nature to be received. As a man cannot take thorns in hand, God cannot take people whose nature is set against Him. Other Scripture supplies detail that they do not believe (John 3:16; 5:24), have no delight in God's word or fellowship with His people (Ps. 1:4–6), nor love to God (Ps. 145:20), and are contrary to God (Rom. 2:5).

The retribution (7c). Finally, David ends his writing career reflecting on the punishment God must bring on those whom He cannot receive. He describes the retribution in two details.

(1) Its fullness. The wicked will be completely or thoroughly punished. Other Scripture enlarges on this as eternal, unending, and carried out without the possibility of escape from it (Matt. 25:41, 46; Rev. 14:9–11; 20:11–15).

(2) Its fire. As thorns are cast into fire, those outside God's blessing are in fire. Whatever the reality this analogy of fire pictures, it is awful, painful, and conscious. It must be so since the fire is not quenched (Mark 9:42–48), and the picture is used of its smoke going up forever, therefore from fire not ending (Rev. 14:9–12). The destiny of the blessed is eternal, and the destiny of the wicked described in direct contrast to this is also eternal (Matt. 25:46).

As early as Moses' song of deliverance at the Red Sea, Scripture speaks of God's fiery retribution on the wicked (Ex. 15:7; cf. Deut. 4:24). This testimony continues through to the end (Rev. 21:8).

When 2 Samuel 23:1–7 is viewed as a prayer passage, or closely related to prayer, what principles are evident? The verses can point to praying with humility (1), gratitude for privileges (1), and reverence toward God (3). Also clear is the value of righteous dealings (3), encouragement from God's light and refreshment in doing His will (4). Other principles are praise for His covenant, today the New Covenant being central (5), and faith in God to prosper His will (5). Finally, here is reason for a prayerful life in God's word to snatch the unsaved back before they go into the eternal fire (7; cf. Jude 23).

2 Samuel 23:17

David's Prayer of Tribute to Sacrificial Men

Camped in battle against Philistine invaders, David spoke words that prompted daring by three of his mighty men listed in 23:8–12.

His Request for a Drink (14, 15)

Philistines had seized occupancy of Bethlehem. David voices a wish to satisfy a raging thirst. If only somebody would bring him a drink from the well near Bethlehem's gate! The longing of an honored king was all it took to inflame the zeal of valiant men.

The Risk of Three Warriors (16a, b)

Many are the stories of heroism in annals of the nations. In Mexico, the lieutenant of the invading Cortez named Pedro de Alvarado fought off Aztecs at the rear of his army until only he was left behind. Then, wounded and in full armor, he sprinted and leaped across an eighteen-foot chasm of water along a dike, landed safely, and escaped with his soldiers. A monument was erected there called "Alvarado's Leap." America's Tennessee soldier, Sergeant Alvin York, a Christian, crawled through grass advancing on a German machine gun nest in the Argonne Forest in 1917. Others lay shot to death around him. Several of the enemy raced down the slope to get York because his Enfield bullets were picking off machine gunners. He whipped out a pistol and shot the attackers in rapid-fire succession, captured the major, and forced him to order surrender of his men. York took 132 to General Lindsay, his brigadier commander, who said the mountaineer had captured the whole German army. "No sir," the modest Tennessean replied, "only have one hundred and thirty-two."

In 2 Samuel 23, three similar heroes respond to David.

Their past heroism (8–12). Adino defeated 800 in one battle, Eleazar cut down Philistines until his weary hand clung fast to the sword, winning a great victory. Finally, Shammah defended a field in a mighty victory against Philistines.

Their present heroism (16). The three broke through Philistine defenders (cf. 22:30), bore water from the well back through the ranks of the enemy, and brought the water to David.

His Refusal of the Water (16, 17)

Twice we read that David would not drink.

His tribute in pouring. He poured the drink out to the Lord in honor of the trio's bravery and devotion. He sees the water as representing the blood of the men. For every step in their fight through the opposing ranks placed their lives at jeopardy. Desire for a drink has fled, replaced by awe at the incredible devotion.

His testimony in prayer. He prayed, apparently out loud, to the Lord. Part of his prayer is affirmation. He cannot bring himself to gratify his thirst selfishly by what could have cost men their lifeblood. Then comes a question. Shall he indulge his desires for pleasure so lightly as to partake of what represents the most precious thing the men have? As the three had grown in stature before their king that day, he must have become greater in their eyes than when they raced to fulfill his longing.

Values in prayer spring before us. One is the sacrificial aspect that the praying person can express in so many ways. As David was sacrificial to men who risked their lives for him, believers can be sacrificial to God who sacrificed His Son for them, and also to other believers who put their lives on the line for Christ's sake (cf. Phil. 2:30). One of the greatest sacrifices a believer can make is a consistent devotion before God in praying. When that develops into a lifetime of commitment, it is all the greater.

A second principle is to keep one's eyes alert, watchful for acts and trends that can become the substance of prayer that pleases God and does men good. Third, it shows character in prayer and in all of life to honor others who do exploits that inspire admiration.

2 Samuel 24:10, 17, 23, 24–25

Prayers of Confession and Repentance

David insists on numbering his people from one end of Israel to the other, Dan to Beersheba. He vests his faith in numbers in a list rather than in his Lord.

David's Request for Numbering the People (1–9)

Comparing the account with its parallel in 1 Chronicles 21, three causes are behind David's move.

His own desire (2–4). He commands Joab, his army commander, to get the census so that he can know the number. Joab advises against the project, but David's insistent authority wins. That David's ambition was sin is the Lord's verdict, David's own in verse 10, and Joab's (cf. 1 Chr. 21:3).

Satan's desire (1 Chr. 21:1). Satan put the desire in David's mind, as he deceived Eve; he is a master at using "schemes" and "flaming missiles" (Eph. 6:11, 16). Paul spoke about not being ignorant of the evil strategist's "devices" (2 Cor. 2:11).

God's desire (2 Sam. 24:1). Possibly the Lord detected a focus on trusting natural things, and not Him. That had usually been the problem with Israelites. That He moved David is not contradictory to Satan doing it and David willing it. Scripture often shows that God as the ultimate authority is said, at times, to do things that He does through other agencies as they insist on these. An example is His moving armies of the world to the campaign of Armageddon (Rev. 16) to bring a showdown during the future tribulation period. It is clear that the armies are also moved by demons, and that they do what they want to do. God permits this in His overall plan to bring a reckoning, allowing Satanic forces and men to express evil within them.

David's Repentance over Numbering the People (10)

Recognition of sin is vividly clear. David shows this in three ways: his *conviction* (his heart troubled him), his *confession* ("I have sinned greatly"), and his *contrition* ("acted very foolishly"). His prayer here, like that when God brought him to task over his adultery and murder (2 Sam. 12; Ps. 51), shows that he is aghast and contrite over his sin.

It is one thing to sin and go on sinning, without tenderly dealing with the sin to gain God's deliverance. It is another to sin but to have a heart that sensitively acknowledges it and seeks cleansing and an insistence to go on in God's will. David is in the latter class here. He is so sincere in repudiating of the wrong that he takes all the blame and is willing for discipline to come only on himself and his house (17).

David's Results in Numbering the People (11–25)

God sent His prophet Gad to deal with David.

God's choices for discipline (11–15). God sets before the king three choices: famine for seven years on Israel, flight for three months from enemies, as he fled from Saul, or pestilence (plague) on Israel for three days.

David reasons out his choice. He would prefer to fall into God's hands in a pestilence, for God is merciful (probably in not being as severe as He might be), so the three-day distress. For he fears to be at men's mercy as in securing food during a famine or being a fugitive chased by foes. He no doubt is mindful of how a famine feels (cf. 2 Sam. 21), and he remembers with a shudder the days of evading Saul's searchers.

God's compassion in discipline (16). God's angel carrying out the pestilence had just gotten underway when God proved compassionate as David had perceived beforehand. He commanded the angel to cease, for "It is enough."

A truth related to prayer is this. The praying believer is opposed by Satan (as 1 Chr. 21:1) and his demons (Eph. 6:12), and on God's side good angels minister to him (Heb. 1:14). Good angels can carry out aspects of His will, even if humans do not see them (Isa. 37; Ezek. 9). In this case David seems to see the angel.

David's conviction of sin (17). As in verse 10, David is smitten with a sense of his sin, only now he is deeply concerned over the effect on others. His prayer pleads that God deal only with him, the guilty one who misused his authority. He sees the people as "sheep," as in Psalm 23, the ones not directly responsible as he has been. He wants

God to put the pressure on himself and his house, and spare others. Two things are clear in his prayer: the wickedness of his sin and the willingness for personal loss.

David's consecration at an altar (18–25). Gad returns to David, this time to direct that he erect an altar to the Lord. David purchases land for this on the threshing floor of Araunah in the Jerusalem area. He insists on paying for the site and for sacrificial oxen. His conviction is against offering sacrifices to the Lord that cost him nothing. This is not contradicting grace, as if to buy his way to deserving God's favor. It is a spirit of devoting himself to God. He is like a missionary who "pays the price" that service takes in sacrifices. He does it, not to merit God's reward, but to manifest the servanthood of which his grateful heart feels God is worthy.

The site for the altar is itself significant. It is on Mount Moriah, where Abraham offered Isaac (Gen. 22) and the location of Solomon's temple (2 Chr. 3:1).

David offered, possibly via priests, two kinds of sacrifices. *Burnt* offerings were entirely consumed, a picture of the offerer's complete dedication to God's will. It is hard to imagine this being true without prayer that gives it the accompaniment of heart and lips. *Peace* offerings expressed the offerer's thanksgiving, hence one presented these with prayer, celebrating peace with God in the covenant bond and in particular situations (cf. Lev. 7:12–13). Here, David had sinned, and Israel also was not without sin in some way (2 Sam. 24: l). So the sacrifices were a token of renewed commitment, also gratitude in receiving the way of peace and not ongoing judgment.

God responds to the prayer and the sacrifices, taking away the plague that had resulted in 70,000 dying (1 Chr. 21:14).

What of prayer standards here? One for any leader or believer is to keep such close accounts with the Lord that He will guard the person from foolish sin affecting others. A second is that when one is convicted of sin, it is right to clear the matter forthrightly with God, rather than deny it and try to save face. A third is to be ready in the prayer life to render costly devotion to God. Samuel's counsel is apt here, counsel that David may have heard the prophet speak, since their lives overlapped: "Only fear the Lord and serve Him in truth with all your heart; for consider what great things He has done for you" (1 Sam. 12:24).

This is a fitting meditation to climax the prayers of 2 Samuel.

Prayer in 1 Kings

Introduction

David the king endorses his son Solomon as the succeeding king, and the Israelite kingdom theme in the books of Samuel continues. It is evident that the writer traces a selective spiritual history of the Solomonic Kingdom, then after Solomon the two separated kingdoms of the south (Judah) and north (Israel), and later the surviving kingdom, Judah, in the south. This panoramic sweep reaches from David (1 Kgs. 1) to the ruin of both kingdoms as God judges His people for sin. Two words crystallize the aspects of the kingdom theme—*disruption* (1 Kgs.) and *dispersion* (2 Kgs.).

The two books carry on the historical narrative describing the kingdom from the end of 2 Samuel. First, a focus is on key movements in Solomon's reign. Then attention transitions to trends in the two divided kingdoms from 1 Kings 12 on until the fall of the northern kingdom in 2 Kings 17 in 722/21 B.C. After that, 2 Kings extends through the southern kingdom (Judah) to its final fall in 586 B.C. and to the thirty-seventh year of King Jehoiachin's captivity in Babylon ca. 560 B.C. The span is from about 972 to 560 B.C.

The Title

To ancient Hebrews, what we know as 1 and 2 Kings were originally one book, entitled "Kings." This is based on the way 1 Kings 1:1 opens, "Now King David. . . ." The title is fitting, since the history mentions forty-two kings of Israel and Judah from David to Zedekiah in 2 Kings 24–25. During the age between the Old and New Testaments, the Septuagint (LXX) Greek translation divided the work into two volumes, "1 Kings" and "2 Kings." Later in the Christian era the Latin Vulgate followed the LXX lead, and much later so did the English translations. In later Hebrew Bibles, the two parts are "Kings A" and "Kings B."

The Author

Some Jewish tradition named Jeremiah the prophet as the writer, as in the Talmud in Baba Bathra 14b. For a good part of 1 and 2 Kings, this is not impossible, yet problems face this view. These embrace such matters as some differences in vocabulary between the Book of Jeremiah and this history, and a question of whether Jeremiah lived to the time of Jehoiachin, whose exile to Babylon is right at the end of 2 Kings (25:27–30), ca. 561 B.C. Scripture's last glimpse of Jeremiah is when he was with the Jews who left Judah to live in Egypt, ca. 585–582 B.C. (Jer. 43–45). Church fathers say that Jews stoned Jeremiah to death at Daphne (Tahpahnes), Egypt (cf. Jerome, Adv. Jovin ii.37; Tertullian, Contra Gnost., viii). But Rabbinic tradition claims that Nebuchadnezzar, invading ca. 569–568 B.C., took Jeremiah and Baruch from Egypt to Babylon, where Jeremiah died (cf. Seder Olam, Rabba 26). This is uncertain evidence, yet if it is true, Jeremiah could have survived until the end of Jehoiachin's days.

One conclusion seems probable. The Kings writings are by the hand of a person God chose to use in His inspired scripture (cf. 2 Tim. 3:16–17; 2 Pet. 1:19–21), who secured a keen grasp on this span of God's drama with His people. It is reasonable that some prophet in the exile to the end of Jehoiachin's days (2 Kgs. 25:30) was the author. God providentially furnished help for him, as He would later give support to Luke to write his gospel product (Luke 1:1–4), using trustworthy accounts. For references keep popping up in 1 and 2 Kings to Israelite accounts. These are "the book of the acts of Solomon" (1 Kgs. 11:41), "the chronicles of the kings of Israel" (1 Kgs. 14:19 and eighteen other times); and "the chronicles of the kings of Judah" (1 Kgs. 14:29 and fourteen more instances).

It is impossible for us now to say for certain who authored the books. Of course God could use any writer, or contributors who aided a final writer, keeping these faithful to give His Word as He wanted it to be. Some claim Jeremiah (cf. the Talmud, Baba Bathra 14b), or a prophet who outlived him, for 2 Kings ends at a time to which Jeremiah's life may or may not have lasted.

Date

Again, 2 Kings concludes after the death of Judah's King Jehoiachin, ca. 561 B.C. A second factor in dating is that the books do not carry on to the return from exile to Jerusalem ca. 537–536 B.C. (cf. 2 Chr. 36:22–23; Ezra 1:1–4, etc.). So the writing seems to be after 561 but before 536.

The Theme and Outline

The concern of the writer seems to have been to trace the selective spiritual history of the Solomonic Kingdom (to ca. 941 B.C.), the Separated Kingdoms (to 721), and the Surviving Kingdom (to 586) and to the end of Jehoiachin's life in captivity (561). He gives a panoramic sweep from David's last days to the woeful end of the kingdom because God judged sin, as it was clear that He would. David had warned Solomon of this (1 Kgs. 2:1–4). Review at the outset of this 1 Kings introduction the two words that characterize this book: *disruption* and *dispersion.*

A broad outline of the two books is as follows.

- I. The United Kingdom—Solomon to Rehoboam (1 Kgs. 1–11)
    - A. Solomon's Coronation (1:1–2:46)
    - B. Solomon's Wedding, Wisdom, and Wealth (3:1–4:34)
    - C. Solomon's Building of the Temple (5:1–9:28)
    - D. Solomon's Reign of Splendor (10:1–29)
    - E. Solomon's Unfaithfulness and Death (11:1–43)
- II. The Divided Kingdoms—Judah and Israel (12:1–2 Kgs. 17)
    - A. The Beginning of Division under Rehoboam and Jeroboam (12:1–14:31)
    - B. The Continuation of Division to the Reign of Ahab (15:1–16:27)
    - C. The Continuation of Division to the Reign of Jehu (16:28–2 Kgs. 9:10)
    - D. The Reign of Jehu to the Destruction of Israel (2 Kgs. 9:11–17:41)

III. The Surviving Kingdom—Judah until its Fall (2 Kgs. 18–25)
   A. The Reform in Judah under Hezekiah (18:1–20:21)
   B. The Relapse under Manasseh and Amon (21:1–26)
   C. The Rebound under Josiah (22:1–23:30)
   D. The Ruin under the Final Kings (23:31–25:30)

The Relation to Prayer

Only 1 Kings is in view at this point. The 2 Kings introduction will review prayer in that book.

The frequency of prayer. 1 Kings has about thirty references to prayer. These occur in twelve of the twenty-two chapters.

The aspects of prayer. Six of the Bible's normal parts of prayer are obvious, as follows.

Oaths are not infrequent (cf. 1:17, 29; 2:8, 23–24; 17:1; 18:15; 22:14, 16). These are prayer appeals to the Lord to witness and monitor the integrity of strong claims about a follow-through on what is said.

A second aspect is plain *petition*. Elijah invites followers of false prophets to petition these, and he will call on the Lord (18:24), in either case to ask for fire that consumes a sacrifice. Shortly after this, a discouraged Elijah petitions the Lord that he might die (19:4).

Third, *praise* flows on the lips. It comes from pagans who do not appear to know the Lord, as they courteously exalt Solomon's God. Examples are Hiram, the king of Tyre (7:1) and the visiting Queen of Sheba (10:9). And David, definitely a believer, praises the Lord (1:48).

Fourth, *questions* appear late in the book. Elijah asks God if He has brought calamity to a kind widow who gave him lodging, since God has allowed this woman's son to die (17:20). Later, evil King Ahab of the northern kingdom asks the faithful prophet Micaiah whether his army should go into battle or hold back. He is insincere, for he wants the man of God to give the go-ahead to attack, to rubber-stamp what he already is determined to do (22:15).

The *intercessory* focus in prayer is fairly frequent. Bathsheba, in respect and love, prays "May my Lord King David live forever" (1:31). Benaiah who is to be Solomon's executioner (cf. 2:25, 29–34, 46) and later his army commander (2:35), asks that God will bless the reign of Solomon (1:37). Other royal servants pray this for Solomon as well (1:47).

Solomon himself prays for blessing to his people (8:15, 23–53). King Jeroboam of Israel, the northern kingdom, defies and tries to destroy a prophet who speaks against his sin. Then God withers the king's arm, and, humbled for the moment, he requests of the prophet that he intercede to God to restore the arm. God does (13:1–6). Along with Solomon's concern in Chapter 8, Elijah pleads in intercessory vigils that are highlights in the book. He stands before the Lord in prayer that it will not rain, and even makes an oath in prayer (17:1). Later, he beseeches God to restore the life of a widow's son, and God does this (17:21–22). Soon one reads of the prophet's sevenfold pleading to the Lord to bring rain (18:42–43), and in the New Testament the Book of James uses Elijah as an example of effective prayer (5:16b-18).

The intercessory emphasis rises to a peak in 18:36–37. For the sake of those given to false gods and worship as well as for his own vindication, he cries out to God on Mount Carmel, "today let it be known that You are God in Israel, and that I am Your servant, and that I have done all these things at Your word." When bogus gods failed to respond to the errant prophets, Elijah pleads to the Lord twice, "answer me" (37). And what he longs for is "that this people may know that You, O Lord, are God, and You have turned their heart back again."

The sixth aspect of prayer in 1 Kings is in simply *reciting* things to God that are true. For example, Solomon rehearses what God said in His covenant pledge to David about his line not lacking a king on the throne (8:25). He agrees with the Lord that "heaven and earth cannot contain You" and mingles affirmation with questions (v. 27). He also declares other things said in God's words (26, 29, 39), and other truths, one of which is that foreigners "will hear of Your great name and Your mighty hand, and Your outstretched arm" (42). One vital point he affirms is that God will render to each person according to his ways, "whose heart You know, for You alone know the hearts of all the sons of men" (39; cf. 1 Sam. 2:3; Ps. 62:12; Prov. 24:12).

When Elijah had fled to escape Ahab and Jezebel, the Lord asks why he is in a cave far out in the desert (19:9). God already knows but wants the prophet to reflect on his reason and evaluate it properly. The prophet's reply in verse 10 consists of affirmations about his zeal for God, his people forsaking God's covenant, he himself alone being left (which God later tells him is not true, v. 18), and his enemies seeking to put him to death. He is entrapped in his fixation on the human perspective only, and is not dwelling on what God is able to do as He did in Mount Carmel. God even repeats His question, and Elijah cannot get past the snag of his own limited perspectives (13–14).

Not only do we see the frequency of prayer in 1 Kings, and the aspects of it, but some extraordinary acts closely related to prayer.

The acts related to prayer. It is helpful to review a few of these.

God answers one prayer of Solomon by giving him incredible wisdom (3:12). The account testifies to the king displaying such wisdom (3:16–28; 4:29–34; 5:12). The visiting Queen of Sheba bears witness to being overwhelmed with this host king's wisdom (10:3–8), and she recognizes that God is the reason (v. 9). His perception likewise impressed visitors from other nations (23–24).

Another unusual part of the book is Solomon's long prayer in dedicating the newly built temple (8:15–16, 22–61). It is the Bible's longest prayer recorded for an individual, outside the psalms.

A further standout prayer is Elijah's pleading that the Lord allow him to die when he is so discouraged and overcome with fatigue (19:4). Such a cry occurs only a few times in the Bible.

Prayers of praise to God are not normal when they rise on the lips of people who may not know the Lord personally. Hiram of

Tyre (7:1) and the Queen of Sheba (10:9) utter such tributes to the Lord.

Elijah's prayer when pitting God against false gods (Chap. 18) is one of the most dramatic highlights in all of Scripture. One can see the prophet's bold cry (36–37), God's answer (38), and the result in witnesses recognizing "The Lord, He is God; the Lord, He is God (39).

Building the temple is an extraordinary thing (Chap. 9). It becomes, in the history of Israel, a "house of prayer" (Isa. 56:7; Matt. 21:13; Mark 11:17; Luke 19:46). It is a place of God's special presence, and to it people come and pray. Solomon himself prayed that they would, whether in battle (1 Kgs. 8:44), or repentant in exile (46–50), or other situations. Daniel would pray in Babylon toward the site of the temple before Babylonians laid it in rubble (Dan. 6:10).

The temple is related to prayer in other ways. Priests ministering there would pray often, whether in vital purity before the Lord or in nominal ritual. Worshipers would keep an "hour of prayer" there at various times (Ps. 55:17; Dan. 6:10; Acts 3:1; 10:30).

Once Solomon has prayed to dedicate the temple to Him (1 Kgs. 8), the Lord responds with His dedication to the temple: "I have consecrated this house . . . by putting My name there forever, and My eyes and My heart will be there perpetually" (9:3; 2 Chr. 7:15). True, Israel's sin would lead to God's judgment in allowing enemies to destroy the temple (cf. Jer. 39, 52), but it would be rebuilt in the days of Ezra, later beautified by Herod (cf. John 2), destroyed again in A.D. 70 (cf. Matt. 24:2), and will be built even again in a future day (cf. Matt. 24:15; 2 Thess. 2:1–9; Rev. 11:1–2).

Still a further highlight linked with prayer in 1 Kings comes in Chapter 22. In this case, a good king, Jehoshaphat of Judah, wants to ask God for guidance when evil King Ahab of Israel seeks direction via his false gods. The effort to inquire of God (in effect prayer) is through His mouthpiece, the true prophet Micaiah. This man, committed utterly to be true to God's word and not be a "yes-man" who falls into line with the false prophets (v. 14), hears and relays the king's inquiry to the Lord (15–28). In his ministry, he says from his time in prayer, "I saw the Lord sitting on His throne, and all the host of heaven standing by Him . . ." (19). And the answer to prayer he gains from the Lord is in effect the disastrous results of going into battle. If the kings do go, they will be doing what evil spirits persuade them to do; but the Lord's answer is that if they insist on the battle, Israel's people will be scattered (17), Ahab will fall (20), and other ruinous results (28).

What is extraordinary here is that the passage is one of but a few in Scripture that refer to evil spirits (demons) moving men to battle. God is sovereign over all, yet can permit evil beings to play out their will where they insist on this. Angelic powers are behind nations in Daniel 10, good or bad, and the same is true in some other Scripture (Ezek. 9; Rev. 16:12–14)

Yet another notable thing related to prayer is pertinent in 1 Kings. It involves cases of mighty miracles God is able to accomplish. One instance is His ability to answer prayer wherever His people are and whenever they live as time goes on, as in Solomon's prayer (Chap. 8). A second example is in His restoring the king's withered arm (13:1–6) or, in that same passage, His power splitting an altar and spilling the ashes (v. 5). God also displays His power by enabling the prophet Ahijah to discern evil King Jeroboam's wife though she comes in a disguise to inquire for healing of the king's sick son (14:1–16).

Still other cases appear. God causes ravens to do His will, bringing bread and meat morning and evening to a weary Elijah (17:1–6). He replenishes a widow's vessel of flour and pot of oil (17:14–15), and brings a boy who died back to life in answer to prayer (17–24). Later, the Lord sends fire down to consume Elijah's sacrifice to show the Israelites that He is God (18:36–39). In another context of Elijah saying words of prayer, God sends a fierce wind, an earthquake, fire, and a gentle blowing, and gives new direction to His servant (19:9–21).

One final matter related to prayer is this. An unusual gesture joins with prayer when Elijah helps a widow and her dead son. He stretches his body upon the son three times, and God raises up the boy (17:21).

Now the study can transition to specific instances of prayer, one by one, as these appear in 1 Kings.

1 Kings 1

Prayers Relating to David's Successor

Prayer begins in verse 13, but the background preparing for it is in the preceding verses. Other prayers of the opening chapter are sequences in an overall unit.

The Plot of an Upstart (1–10)

David, at age seventy, suffers chills and is given constant care. One of his sons, Adonijah, puts events in motion to attract a following and snatch the throne. Some top men in the kingdom join his conspiracy—Joab the military commander and Abiathar the priest. But notable men who remain loyal to David are Zadok the priest, Benaiah of the mighty men (cf. 2 Sam. 23), and Nathan the prophet.

The Prayers for Solomon (11–48)

David's people had lived in a rich tradition of prayers. Here, four prayers reflect a sensitivity to call on the Lord.

The prayer of David (13). When Nathan warns David's wife Bathsheba of Adonijah's mounting plot to snatch the kingdom and counsels her to act quickly with David, she does. Another son, Solomon, had been named "beloved of the Lord" (2 Sam. 12:25). In another place, David tells Solomon that he was God's choice to be king before he was born (1 Chr. 22:9–11; 28:5–7; 29:1). David, at a point Scripture does not record, had based on his prayer pledge to Bathsheba that Solomon would be king. So the wife briefs David on Adonijah's plan and urges the king to make good on his promise. Nathan follows her into the king's chamber to verify her words. The prayer about which Bathsheba reminds her husband was of the vow variety. He had sworn (promised), summoning God as his attesting witness (vv. 17, 30) and seeking His help to carry out His will. Now it was urgent to act swiftly, seize his opportunity and fulfill his part in the pledge. David calls Bathsheba back in, reaffirms his vow, and guarantees he will keep it.

The prayer of Bathsheba (31). The wife bows and prostrates herself in respect before the king, and as befits a worshipful respect for God (v. 47; cf. Gen. 47:31). Her response to her husband's renewed promise is a form of intercessory prayer, invoking God's blessing on the king to live forever. Since David's declining condition shows expectation of his death, and Bathsheba realizes Solomon is to be the next king, her meaning seems to reach into the afterlife. Only there could David live forever.

Such a prayer is possibly informed by what her husband himself had written of his hope in Psalm 16:10f. Bathsheba could also know of Samuel's life after death when he appeared, by God's almighty power, to King Saul. Others of that time also had hope that after the present life God would receive believers. Their hope was in contrast to unbelievers who went to another destiny (Ps. 49:15; cf. 73:24). And she could know of Enoch who walked with God, and God "took him" (Gen. 5:24),

The queen's prayer, then, appears to be in advocacy that God will do for David what she has reason to believe He has willed for others. Such a hope would become more defined in detail as God's revelation continued (cf. Isa. 26:19f.; Dan. 12:2; John 5:28, 29). Bathsheba's will for David is, she hopes, God's will as her yearning aligns with His.

David acts with expedition. He directs Zadok the priest, Nathan the prophet, and Benaiah a mighty man in the army to lead in installing Solomon on the throne.

The prayer of Benaiah (36, 37). His response to his king in prayer is in two phases.

First, his faith gives an "Amen" to David's plan and calls on the Lord, David's Lord (and no doubt his) to say or approve this. He believes it is His will. Second, he invokes the Lord who had faithfully been with David to be with Solomon. The reference to His being with David is an *affirmation* suggesting a spirit of thanksgiving for God's help. Benaiah's prayer for Solomon is an *intercession* pleading the will of God. The military hero calls on God to prosper David's throne even beyond what has yet been done in David's own career. That is not a slight to David, and the king would not take it that way in envy. Rather it is in line with God's pledge to bless David's house, kingdom, and throne (2 Sam. 7:16). David in thinking back to God's glorious guarantee to him would be encouraged by his mighty man's appeal for the kingdom's success after him.

King David's leaders carry out his bidding. They have Solomon ride on David's mule, and Zadok anoints him, no doubt with a prayer calling on God to bless him (cf. Num. 6:22–27). At a trumpet blast, the people that the leaders had summoned cried, "Long live King Solomon!"

Very quickly the priest Abiathar's son Jonathan broke from the crowd to burst in on Adonijah's meeting. His news struck like a thunderclap. "Our lord King David has made Solomon king." He added details about leading men conducting this induction on the king's authority, Solomon riding on the king's mule, and his occupying the throne! He finished his stunning news with references to prayers for God's blessing by Benaiah (cf. above), and David himself (below).

The prayer of David (48). Jonathan reports this prayer, which apparently occurred when David's leaders visited him before the crowning. This is the first readers see of its recording. News of the prayer has gotten out, too. David bowed in worship, agreeing with Benaiah's intercession. He concluded the meeting with prayer before the leaders rushed to make Solomon king.

Praise to God is the aspect permeating David's prayer. It is adoration to Him as the Lord, the covenant Lord (cf. Ex. 6:3), and the God of Israel, giving His authority for the entire nation. David acclaimed this Lord, this God of this people, as giving His strength to this crowning. *He* has granted a man to sit on the throne, *His* choice, while David is still alive to witness it. Certainly praise/thanksgiving filled the heart of the king as he passed the baton on to the new king.

Such news from Jonathan crushed the assembled supporters of the would-be king. Gripped with terror at being identified with a loser which might spell their own downfall, they hastened from the pretender's presence.

The Prevailing of Solomon (49–53)

The consternation of Adonijah. All the man's bravado was seized in the grip of panic. He fled to the tabernacle to grasp the horns of the altar. He was desperate for mercy from the real king.

The compassion of Solomon. A swift report of Adonijah's latest act came to the king, possibly from a priest. The news even included the pretender's plea that Solomon promise him in an oath to spare his life. Such a sworn guarantee would involve calling on the Lord to attest the king's promise and assist him see it through.

No detail clarifies if Solomon spoke in the form of a prayer oath. But he did affirm safety to Adonijah if he proved worthy and punishment if he opposed the new authority. Adonijah was brought, and fell before the king seeking clemency. Solomon sent him home in peace.

Standards for prayer are rich in Chapter 1. One lesson is to commit to a line of action true to God's will, then hold to one's word promised on the honor of God's name. David did this (cf. vv. 13, 17), later Bathsheba (31) and Benaiah (36, 37). Today prayerful sensitivity to know and do what God's word approves in direct statement or principle correspond. A second guideline is to remember to give praise/thanks to God when He answers prayer. David does this when God has answered his prayer oath according to His will (48).

1 Kings 2:8

Prayer in a Final Charge

David charges Solomon (v. 1) in his son's early reign, while David's life still lingers. He does this in regard to two things.

Concerning Devotion (1–4)

In strength. The passing king is zealous that the new king be strong, strong in God. That would be in walking with the Lord in a true communion, drawing sufficiency to live after His heart. David himself, for the most part, had done this (cf. 1 Sam. 30:6; 2 Sam. 5:10). It came from expressly seeking Him in His word and prayer (Ps. 138:2–4), delighting in Him (37:3–7).

David was passionate that his son prove himself a real man. To be God's kind of man, a man as God intended a man could be, Solomon would need to cultivate His presence as above.

In steadfastness. The old man's wisdom is to obey God's will in His word, which counsels taking one's steps in His ways. Such steps must be established by the Lord, ordered by Him (Ps. 37:23). Again this is according to His guide manual, His value system as in His word through Moses (v. 3).

In securing of the blessing. A walk in the ways David has just highlighted is a life open to receive God's blessing. God will validate and honor a life sensitive to His priorities, and fulfill promised blessing (4). Solomon needs to focus on a careful walk, in truth, real in the heart, as Paul would say to the Ephesian believers (5:9, 15; cf. 3:16–21; 5:18).

This kind of life would prove to be the way of success. In it, kings in the line of David would be blessed with maintenance on the throne. The other way would be disobedience, drawing God's judgment, even loss of the throne (Deut. 28:36). However, eventual continuation of the throne was secure in God's promise (2 Sam. 7:16).

Concerning Decisions (5–9)

David feels it urgent to brief his successor about men he needs to deal with early in his reign. In two cases these are troublemakers Solomon must be aware of, the other is a true friend worthy of honor.

Joab. Solomon has been around long enough to hear the stories of this military commander who took justice into his own hands, defying David's authority. Two examples of murders Joab committed are apropos. He carried bloodshed to the extreme, heedless and severe, and at times had the smear of blood on his body even for betraying peace (cf. 2 Sam. 3, etc.). David does not even mention Joab's intense savagery against Absalom when the latter hung helplessly at his mercy and was shown none (2 Sam. 18).

Now David advises that Joab be executed. He sees this as a step of wisdom for a man who has invited it time and time again. It may be that David perceived that a man with such a bloody habit would persist in a way that would demand a showdown, firm even if difficult action. More will be said about this below.

Barzillai. David has sweet memories of this man's special kindness showing mercy when David was fleeing during Absalom's revolt (2 Sam. 17:27–29). Barzillai and others displayed great thoughtfulness. They brought David and his party beds, basins, pottery, and foods, quelling hunger and providing even so that they could rest more comfortably. It is fitting to treat the man's sons kindly in return for compassion. To be kind to the kind does not mean that David treated only these well; he often was kind to the unkind, as when he twice spared Saul.

Shimei. This evil man had cursed and hurled stones at David and his people when the king evacuated Jerusalem to prevent violence from the revolting Absalom (2 Sam. 16:5–8). Shimei had heaped insults on David, bad-mouthing him as a man of bloodshed, a low-down scoundrel. He called the king a man from whom the Lord had wrenched the kingdom to present it to Absalom. This treason was worthy of death (Ex. 22:28; 1 Kgs. 21:10).

A strong officer of David, incensed, wanted to whack off the offender's head. In amazing control and mercy, David protected Shimei. Humility prompted him to say that if the Lord had a lesson for him to learn he was sensitive to yield to it. But he hoped the Lord would render good in his hardship in place of the cursing.

Now David explains. His response to Shimei actually had been one of pardon with *prayer*. He pledged, appealing to God as his witness and help, that he would not execute the man.

Now near death, the king's thoughts are in different currents, however. Solomon, he feels, should take care of the unpleasant but necessary task of punishing Shimei. This, rather than breaking David's promise that preserved Shemei's life at that earlier time, is the wise course as he discerns the situation years later. Shimei had cursed the Lord's anointed, this indicting himself under the spirit of God's covenant with Abram to curse those who cursed him or his people (Gen. 12:1–3). David himself had been kind to King Saul as the Lord's anointed. David also considers action against Shimei as what Solomon, in wisdom, ought to pursue. Solomon's early acts as king were in the wisdom that God gave (1 Kgs. 3:9, 12, 28), suggesting that more than we may now realize was involved. David also has on his heart the peace of Solomon's rule against threats.

One problem is David going back on his earlier, solemn pledge before God and this in not finally being truthful to his word. It is possible to regard his promise as for his lifetime only so that He honored what he had prayed. This may be with the perception that Solomon can also show mercy, if Shemei will abide by it, and Shemei later violates his own agreement to bring a death sentence he could have been spared (2:39–46). Or one can view David as failing to keep truth with his prayer, and acknowledge this as one failure added to others as a sinner—adultery, plotting a deception against Uriah, murder, lying, tolerance of Amnon's raping of Tamar, shutting Absalom out from loving contact, arrogance in the census, and so forth. All believers are sinners, and fall short of God's glory even if their lives to a great degree are godly. What God confirms with His oath (cf. Gen. 15; Heb. 6), He keeps in total integrity; man in various cases does not attain to this, yet God saves by grace and not by merit of works that earn this (Eph. 2:8–9).

A part of the integrity, too, is this. Solomon in wisdom extended to Shimei a fair and kind probation. It was Shimei's choice to live in peace, if he would. This was attended with a candid warning (2:36–38). Shimei proved his insincerity and invited Solomon to keep his word against him for treating with contempt his king's word. So the king only acted after Shimei's death warrant on himself (39–46).

Now let us consult the principles. First, always live, in prayer and other ways, to point others to be at their best for the Lord. Second, even after failures before God it is important to finish well in His grace. Third, the godly can encourage others to be godly, yet whether they live this way and remain in it is up to them. Fourth, tough decisions on how to deal with evil people may confront a praying man as life is not a bed of roses. Fifth, the godly can show kindness to the kind and the unkind, as Jesus would do and teach (cf. Matt. 7:12). Sixth, one who gives a treacherous person plenty of rope to walk in freedom may see him use the rope to get himself hanged.

1 Kings 2:13–46

Prayer Related to Punishments

Three illustrations entail prayer oaths that draw the Lord's attestation and action into matters.

Related to Adonijah (13–25)

The leader in plotting the revolt had received Solomon's peace gesture and could have enjoyed that the rest of his days (1:50–53). Now he asks his mother Bathsheba to be his advocate, using her leverage to induce Solomon's approval of Adonijah's marrying Abishag, a palace woman. Solomon interprets the bid as tantamount to designs still to possess the throne.

Prayer enters at this point (23–24). The new king voices a prayer by oath, appealing to God to attest his decision and discipline him if he is lax to fulfill it. On the surety of the Lord's own life and will, as attestor whose will set Solomon on the throne (cf. 1 Chr. 22:9–11; 28:6), any ambitions to contest his kingship will be defeated. God's own promise had been to establish Solomon a house (throne right) in David's line (2 Sam. 7:12–16). So, Adonijah's revived plot, as the king sees it, must be doomed with his death.

At Solomon's directive, his military chief, Benaiah, executes Adonijah. The latter had been given opportunity to enjoy peace as Shimei had, and like Shimei threw this mercy away.

Related to Joab (28–35)

Solomon showed kindness to the priest, Abiathar, giving him his life though removing him from his ministry. The rejection fulfills God's will, a curse on Eli's line (26–27; cf. 1 Sam. 2:27–33; 3:12–14). Then Joab hears of Adonijah's execution and Abiathar's dismissal, and, having plotted with them, is stung by his guilt. News reaches the king that Joab is at the bronze altar before the tabernacle with the Ark, seeking mercy. Solomon then sends Benaiah to execute this troublemaker, too. This done, the king accords the former military head an honorable burial (34).

Joab had done some good things, such as advising David not to take the sinful census (2 Sam. 24). But he committed very brutal things too, sins which catch up and find him out. Joab had deceived and slain men contrary to David's will, acting in high-handed defiance (1 Kgs. 2:32).

Now Solomon brings prayer into his words in two ways (33). First, he appeals for David's prayer oath, drawing judgment on Joab's house to be answered (2 Sam. 3:29). Second, he intercedes by calling on God to give the Davidic house peace forever. Of course God will answer that affirmatively in accord with his covenant with David, fulfilling His own word (2 Sam. 7:12–16). But it will leave room for discipline necessary at times on Solomon (14), just as David had faced (2 Sam. 12, 24, etc.). And loss of the kingdom in Israelite exile, though drastic, would not nullify restoration and ultimately its peace (Ezek. 34:15, 25; 36:16–38).

Relating to Shimei (36–46)

Prayer here is in 42–43, mentioned above.

Principles for prayer are instructive in the chapter. One lesson is, as often in oath prayers, to let appeals to the Lord flow wisely out of a saturation with His own word. This is by invoking His attentiveness to things one can confidently say are true to His will, not trotting out one's own selfish will and asking Him to write His signature endorsing it. A second, vital thing is to let a life in some real degree sincere in godliness be behind the prayer. Here, David and Solomon pray in ways that fit their life context. David keeps his word throughout his life to Shimei (8), yet is firm to counsel wisdom in his case (9) and righteous dealing in Joab's (5). Solomon is willing to make firm decisions to do God's will (27, 31–32), shows mercy in peace for Shimei, and yet holds him to a test of truth when it calls for decisive action. A third principle is to insist on prayer's relevance in all the issues of life.

1 Kings 3:5–15

Solomon's Prayer for Wisdom

God invites the new king to ask for things his heart counts important for his rule. Solomon asks for wisdom, God gives this and more, and man gifted with wisdom displays the answer. The wisdom a believer shows can be the fruit of prayer, as countless details of life are in the Proverbs.

The Occasion of the Prayer (1–5)

Solomon's dependence. Early in his reign, the king forms an inept dependence on the leader of Egypt for military security or trade advantages. He seals this union by marrying the pharaoh's daughter, beginning a long pattern of taking foreign women. These were wrong for lustful motives, and also for enticing his heart to worship false gods (cf. 11:1–8). The latter passage plainly says that it is sin to marry the women with that taint of idols, as was a failure of Israel in Judges 1.

Solomon's devotion. His walk did display considerable devotion to the Lord and His word, at least in the early years. The devotion became flawed by the false trust above. The idolatry found expressions in offerings on high places rather than at God's special tent before the Ark, which David had provided (2 Sam. 6). Of course the tabernacle of Moses was then still at Gibeon (1 Chr. 1:3, 5–6, 13). Even before the temple was built, David or Solomon could have had the tabernacle brought to Jerusalem. True, Solomon could offer to God at Gibeon (1 Kgs. 3:4), but shortly after shows that he can offer at Jerusalem (15).

Offerings on the many high places away from Jerusalem would soon be linked with a drift to false gods.

Solomon's dream. At Gibeon, after presenting offerings to the Lord, the king is visited by his Lord in a dream.

A prayer soon comes into the picture. How can it be real in a dream? God's power can enable Solomon to pray it genuinely. This word from *man*, under God's leading, can be just as real as *His own* word to man often in dreams—to Jacob at Bethel, Joseph (Gen. 37), to the butler, baker and pharaoh in Egypt (Gen. 40–41), to Daniel (Chap. 7, etc.), Joseph (Matt. 1–2), and others. Such a prayer is unusual, but God is unusual. He is able to impress a person by unusual means when it fulfills His will. That God chose to use dreams He memorialized in inspired Scripture puts no stamp of approval on people who fancy that their dreams outside this guardianship are moved by God.

The occasion for the prayer, then, is set.

God's Offer in the Prayer (5b)

The Lord *encourages* Solomon to ask what he desires. It should be kept in mind that He also *enables* Solomon to have unselfish motives by the rich scriptural heritage through David and men such as Nathan and Zadok. A generous saturation in His word, which is so much in evidence in prayers of Chapters 1–2, can prepare a heart to let godly purposes dominate. True, Solomon's devotion is partially tainted in verses 1–5. But he has just been engaged in worship, apparently to the Lord (4). Besides, now the Lord Himself is confronting the king, a very pointed encounter that can stimulate a person to weigh his response in this case.

The principle even today is apropos. At times when God, through His word, is very real and powerfully stimulating the thoughts, a devoted believer finds grace to choose wise values. It is all the more crucial, then, to be sharpened in a sense of God's presence by a steeping in His word.

Solomon's Object in the Prayer (6–9)

This is evident in two phases.

His remembrance of mercies to David. His prayer is affirmation at first, of a sort suggesting reason to praise God. The Lord has shown covenant love to David in the overall picture, and the kindness in promoting David's son to the throne is a special instance. Solomon is aware that God's goodness was manifest in consistency with David's receptivity in aspects sensitive to God's will—truth, righteousness, and so forth. This is in grace, and not because David's life merited favor, which it could not.

It is always a God-honoring practice in prayer to put much stock in mercies gratefully offered up as sweet incense. This meets readers often in the Psalms (136, etc.). Solomon's prayer has a second phase.

His request of mercy for himself. The request will not come until verse 9. First, the young king presses three arguments that underscore his need for what he asks. These, too, are of the affirmation aspect in prayer as he pleads his case.

(1) His *rule* itself is of the will and bounty of the Lord.

(2) His *restriction* is a factor that impresses him keenly. Exalted to such a capacity as king, still young, he is smitten with a sense of inadequacy, ineptness, inability to carry the task out successfully. He

is, in his own estimation, but a little child in knowing how to be a king, a king in David's line. He does not know where to start and where to end, how to go out or come in. His need of guidance is overwhelming.

Now there is a good principle. Proverbs 3:5, 6 captures it in a nutshell. Trust in God with all the heart, and do not fall back on personal ability to figure things out. Rather, humbly acknowledge Him in every aspect of life, and He guarantees He will guide the life (cf. Ps. 32:8). Paul would capsule it in these words: "not that we are sufficient of ourselves, but our sufficiency is of God who has made us able ministers. . . ." (2 Cor. 3:5).

(3) Solomon's *relationship* with people gets to him with its own particular urgency of need. They are *God's* people, people in the special bond of His choice and covenant. They need to be dealt with in the manner that God is able to reveal—His way. They also are a *great* people in number, though their line had started with one man, Abram. Since they are both God's and great, Solomon's need for what he will ask is all the more desperate.

(4) The *request itself.* All that the new leader has argued for flows out now. Since his insufficiency is so utterly great, he cries out for an utterly great ability that only an utterly great God can supply. "So give Thy servant an understanding heart to judge Thy people to discern between good and evil."

The principle is pointed here. Cast it in the form of a prayer today. "If I ask one thing of God, it is this. . . ." Careful! Think it through! Whatever the master passion of life is, it should come, as here, out of a heart recognizing servanthood to God and accountability to Him and others ("Thy servant . . . Thy people"). It also, as here, should pertain to the essence of spiritual value—discernment between good and evil, and commitment to the good.

All our days, and in a thousand ways, we are ever coming again to this issue—this crux that can draw all our details of need and vision into one consuming choice. It is the God who is our life, or just ourselves, our little selfish desires, disoriented from Him. Paul drew the focus well: "Christ, who is our life" or "to me to live is

Christ," or "not I, but Christ," or "this one thing I do," or "that I may know Him." So much hangs on the decision; it is worth thinking about, worth coming to the right prayer about, worth the right stand.

What Solomon longs for is wisdom to serve God's people. It is understanding by a wisdom that is fed by God as the source of wisdom, His word, His will, His way. A believer can study the Scriptures through on prayer. And this is the key that keeps coming back to unlock the right door—prayer at its essence as God desires it is submission to do His will.

One more detail, and Solomon's prayer is done. The prayer's aspects switch from affirmation and petition to a question. This aspect says the same thing, the bottom line, by seizing attention to putting God first. He is first in the doing of His will, in submission to Him. It is the case in all the facets of Solomon's prayer.

Who is able? True submission to do the will of God asks about ability, and concludes with the answer that the ability comes in servanthood drawing from His ability. Who becomes able but the person who comes to Him in prayer in this spirit?

Who is able to serve? In Solomon's case, as the king who must render decisions, the issue is submission to God to *judge*. A believer can put there his own role, whatever it is, applying the same principle.

Who is able to judge this great people? Any submission to God, mustered as it is by Him for His interests, will sooner or later involve His people. It may be many, it may be few, it may be one person at the moment. But they, believers, are His, and true submission to Him puts a premium on living out that submission in serving others who are His. No man or woman is an island. We dare not be like the island Eloise, who was surrounded on all sides by Eloise. We are to live not to ourselves, but to God in helping God's people, and helping others not His people become His people (cf. Luke 19:10; John 17:20).

Humility in submission to God by God's wisdom permeates the prayer. It exalts God and sees oneself as one's own size but as a channel for God to be His size working through His servant.

God says, in response, "That is talking my language. I can use a person who will think like that."

His Obtaining By Prayer (10–14)

The spotlight shines on four things here.

What he did ask. God draws it into focus, "this thing," and later defines it, "discernment to understand justice."

What he did not ask. A vital principle in prayer is to count as crucial even what one does not ask, and his value system that leads him not to fix his heart there. Of course believers will always think about what they do *ask*.

Here, God lists as on a billboard even things Solomon might have pled for. He was not at this point smitten with the disease of some, the "gimmes.""Lord, gimme, gimme, gimme." The emphasis would be on the "me," and the gratification of desires that can be selfish.

Principles are plentiful here. The things one sets his or her passion on in prayer can be a revelation of where his heart really is on the spectrum of doing God's will, or off of it entirely.

Solomon did not plead for a long life (longevity), or riches (power to be in charge dictating what one could have, or control over others), or removal of enemies (ease by people cooperating). What else could be added today—facial or bodily beauty, supremacy in athletics, renown as an author, artistic mastery, oratorical skill, leisure to pursue hobbies or be a world traveler? The list goes on, each person filling it in to suit his or her values. What a person asks of God, especially at a crossroad, is a measure of how big he really is in the estimate that counts most. It is a frightening thought to consider what some would do if they could push buttons and summon whatever they wanted. It is a true test to ask, "What button would I push?"

And it could be a turning point, if the true answer points along the road of repentance, to a prayer life as it can be before God.

What he got that he asked for. Solomon received from God a wise, discerning heart. This was in a degree greater than any of his day (4:30, 31) or later, except for Jesus Christ. The principle is simple. When a person asks in line with God's will, his batting average in "yes" answers can go up (1 John 5:14, 15). It is a fruitfully fulfilling way to live (John 15:7, 8).

What he got that he did not ask for. God at this point could entrust to Solomon even the things he had not asked. His bounties included long life, riches, and freedom for the most part from enemies during his reign. In wealth his holdings would become astounding (10:14–29).

Today, a person may see the principle work out differently. He asks for wisdom to know God's word and teach it as a servant, and God gives this plus riches in relationships of spiritual ministry (cf. Mark 10:29, 30), perhaps the impact changes lives in many parts of the world. Even the person in a relatively obscure role of service can have "much fruit" in terms by which spiritual riches are counted (cf. John 15:7, 8).

His Offerings in Worship (15)

Prayer contact with the Lord prompts two immediate responses in Solomon.

His realization. Once awake, the king felt deeply stirred. He knew "it was a dream," not meaning that he was merely aware but that he was amazed. It was a dream, yes, but how great a dream, so momentous in his life. He was impressed and captivated, for this dream was a deep interchange with God!

His rejoicing. After his return the seven miles to Jerusalem, Judah's leader still felt so gripped by God meeting him in prayer that he could not contain himself. He had to express his thanksgiving to the Lord of prayer. So he went before the Ark that David's priests had set in the special tent (2 Sam. 6). There, apparently at an altar similar to that at the tabernacle of Moses still at Gibeon (2 Chr. 1:3, etc.), Solomon presented offerings. Those of the *burnt* variety were fully consumed, picturing his own desire to be fully devoted to the Lord who had appeared (cf. Rom. 12:1). The *peace* variety were in gratitude to God for peace and its blessing in the covenant bond. Today believers can know a fuller significance in Christ who is the most perfect burnt offering (cf. Heb. 10:5–10). He also is the ultimate peace offering, for He is peace, He *made* peace, and He *preached* peace (Eph. 2:14–17).

True, prayer in thanksgiving is not explicitly mentioned. But it reasonably is implicit, accompanying the expressions of devotion. Since "all" of Solomon's servants are said to be present, the prayerful celebration might be, with Levitical music, of the essence of that on a similar occasion (2 Chr. 7:3, 5–6).

His Opportunity to Show God's Answer (16–28)

God's answer in giving the wisdom Solomon had requested is soon put on display. This, in his people's minds, shows both his own glory and that of God who supplied the wisdom (v. 28).

Two prostitutes who were roommates in the same house each give birth to a baby. One child dies in the night, then mother switches the dead infant to the other sleeping woman and steals her live child. The wronged woman detects the swap and appeals that Solomon arbitrate. He shrewdly calls for a sword and issues the command that the live child be halved, a part given to each claimant. This evokes the truth as the real mother is passionately willing to sacrifice possession if the infant can but live. On the other hand, the child-stealer puts up a calloused front. A wry smile no doubt steals across the king's face, and he orders that the woman showing the mother's love claim her baby. Word spreads to "all Israel" of the king's dramatic wisdom—actually, of God's answer to prayer!

Still other principles can join those mentioned along the way. First, seek to ask in prayer for things that God's Word clearly favors in a godly life, or things in line with these. Second, since God gives wisdom by His Word and in answer to prayer (cf. Proverbs; James 1:5), He answers the kind of person who values such wisdom in a concrete situation (cf. Prov. 3:5–6).

1 Kings 8

Prayer in Dedicating the Temple

Prayer is pervasive at this high point of Israel's experience as they move from the tabernacle of Moses and special tent of David to their first temple. In fact, prayer is the main stream of thought.

Two supplementary accounts help weave together all the details on prayer in the celebration (1 Kgs. 8–9; 2 Chr. 5–7).

The Preparation for the Prayer (2 Chr. 5:1–14)

Once the temple was completed, Solomon started the phases to use it and to celebrate. His moves were steeped in prayer.

The completion of the temple (1). At last the structure was ready for use. Solomon directed that items David had dedicated for the house be set in place, such as objects of silver and gold and utensils for priestly services.

The conveying of the Ark (2–9). David's priests had carried the Ark into Jerusalem and placed it inside a special tent David had prepared. This was distinct from the tabernacle (tent) of wilderness wanderings, still at Gibeon (2 Chr. 1:3). Now Solomon has Levites, the ones God had prescribed for this role, convey the Ark, tent, and utensils from David's site to a nearby part of Jerusalem where the temple is situated.

Sacrifices coordinate with the transfer, no doubt accompanied by much prayer by the assembled thousands visiting from all Israel (cf. vv. 3, 6).

The content of the Ark (10). Only the two tablets of the law (cf. Ex. 34) are still in the box. The pot of manna (Ex. 16) and Aaron's rod that blossomed to authenticate his priesthood (Num. 17; Heb. 9:4) are no longer there. The law is a reminder of God's singular right to receive worship and the doing of His will, the foundation for all of life, such as prayer.

The celebration of a prepared Temple (11–14). Levitical singers and musicians on instruments praise God for a Temple now ready to be a house of worship. Their prayer, not mentioned in the 1 Kings account, exalts the Lord. Two elements stand out in the praise. The essence of God's character is one emphasis. Worshippers laud His goodness in covenant love. As they do this, they recognize the eternality of His covenant expression. Many Psalms develop in detail such musical tributes to God (135, 136, 138, 145–150, etc.).

The confirmation by God (14; cf. 6:1). The covenant Lord of Israel (cf. Ex. 6:3) confirms the appropriateness of the worship. He expresses His endorsement by filling the temple with His glory cloud, as He had done for the completed tabernacle (Ex. 40:34). The sense of His presence must have gripped the priests with compelling power, for they could not stand to minister, or even to be seen, because of the cloud. They had to move away some distance, overwhelmed at the glory of their great God.

A principle of prayer is clear in all of this. As prayer can fill the life, prayer as here even prepares for other prayer! The Levitical leaders pray in praise even before the later prayer of Solomon and the prayer of those who respond to that. Prayer is heaped upon prayer. Believers can never pray too much if their prayer is along right lines!

The Posture of the Prayer (1 Kgs. 8)

Actually three prayers occur, or three phases in prayer. First, Solomon stands and blesses the people, then the Lord (14–21). Second, he kneels, spreads out his hands to God (22, 54), and leads in a longer prayer (23–53). Finally, the king stands and prays God's blessing on the people (55–61).

Kneeling follows a posture of submissive reverence for God in bending low for worship. Lifting hands, Moses' gesture atop a hill praying during a battle (Ex. 17:8–13), symbolizes contact with the Lord who is sought. Solomon stands after the long prayer (55), a frequent posture in talking with God. In this case, Solomon may do it to transition into the closing prayer devoted heavily to God's blessing on the people (cf. 55). But it is finally difficult to say why the posture of prayer changes; at least it shows the beauty of variety.

The Particulars of the Prayer

All three phases of prayer above are in view here. Leading aspects of prayer throughout Scripture appear here—affirmations of truth, praises, intercessions, and petitions.

Affirmations. These occur often, as in recounting what God has done or other statements rehearsing facts, for example, "who spoke with His mouth to my father David" (15). Solomon also reviews that David's heart had been warm with passion to build a temple (17), God had responded to David by commending the motivation (18), and His aim was for Solomon to be the builder instead (19). These are but a few examples. They point up a principle. It can be vital just to talk with God about truth important to Him and to the one praying, or His people in general.

Praises. It is on this note that Solomon begins (14–21). He blesses or praises the covenant Lord, the God of Israel, who made a promise to David and has kept His pledge. That God is worthy of praise the king shows by God's choice of David to be king, His commending David's aspiration to build a house of God, His raising Solomon to reign, and His fulfilling His promise that David's son would build the temple.

Praise is prominent also at other points. The Lord is God incomparable in heaven or earth (23). What He is relates very closely with what He does that expresses it, for example in His fidelity to His covenant with loving-kindness. He honors His word (24). "Blessed be the Lord," the leader exults again (56), and ties this in anew with God's keeping His promises through Moses to bless Israel (Lev. 26; Deut. 28).

Intercessions. Prayer in this aspect has the most examples, at least seven.

(1) Solomon intercedes for God's future blessing in honoring His promise to David to keep a man of his house on the throne if his sons obey (25). This is prayer for what God's word clarifies is His own will. It reflects submission to His will and a heart set on what glorifies Him.

(2) He pleads for answers to people of Israel who will pray toward this temple, not simply as a structure but as a symbol of God's presence that they seek (29, 30). Four centuries later Daniel would pray in Babylon toward the temple hundreds of miles away (Dan. 6:10). Of course God is not confined to the site of the temple. He is present everywhere in the universe, even right with Daniel (1 Kgs. 8:27).

Solomon makes advocacy for prayer answers in various scenarios his people will come to be in (28–40, 44–53). One is a need of forgiveness (30). Another is in wisely helping those fulfilling prayer vows (31, 32). Still a further one is in pardoning in a specific case of sin, when Israelites are removed from their land as God's act of judgment, but confess the sin. The king prays for God to restore the people to their land (33, 34).

(3) Solomon seeks blessing on foreigners who visit Jerusalem and approach God in prayer. This he defines as seeking God after these are moved by truth impressing them of His great name and power. It relates to God helping them know and fear Him (41–43).

(4) He intercedes for God's continuing presence with His people (57). This, as so many other details, is prayer for what otherwise the Lord assures in His own word to His people whom He will enable to walk with Him. In the most ultimate sense He promised to guarantee

that Israel will be blessed in its land, never to be disturbed again (2 Sam. 7:10). He would often reaffirm that objective (Jer. 31:31ff.; 32:36–42).

(5) The king prays for God to incline hearts to Him to walk in obedience to His word (58). This, too, is often what God pledges to do in His word (Jer. 24:6; 31:18), a work our faith expects Him to carry out (Lam. 5:21; Phil. 2:13). The psalmist would often echo this expectancy in his prayer (119:25, 28, 32, 35–36, etc.).

(6) Solomon yearns for the Lord even to keep up the vigil of having this prayer in remembrance (let Him make it count through all the sweep of years!). This is so that God will support what is best for His royal servant (Solomon, then later kings in David's line) and for Israel His people. He specifies that this pertains to whatever needs a day may bring forth (1 Kgs. 8:59). Of course God would work this out in covenant loving-kindness (cf. 23) by His inclining grace (58) and in equitable consistency with trust and obedience that He enables (cf. (4) above).

(7) The king summons God's blessing to assure that by His people's being blessed, all the peoples of the earth might know that He is God and that no other is God (60). Other Scripture shows that God will answer this, even with spiritual salvation, not to every individual absolutely but to people of all nations, those who trust Him (cf. Rev. 5:9; 7:9). In the ultimate regathering of Solomon's people to their land after dispersion God will cause those of other nations to know He is the Lord, whether in real salvation or in respect at what He has done (Ezek. 36:22, 23). The peoples will realize that God has blessed Israelites by regathering them to their land and giving spiritual benefits, and honoring them (Isa. 61:5–9). This will entail even the desire of Gentiles to seek God (Zech. 8:20–23).

Petitions. Many of the details that are intercessory (for others) are at the same time petitionary for Solomon himself as he is one with these in need. For example He prays that the Lord will be with "us" (57) and "incline our hearts to Himself" (58). And he presses to have God's perpetual recall of "these words of mine" (59).

After such simple yet magnificent prayer, one can wonder what would be the reaction of the people and God. These responses are clear.

The Pleasure in the Prayer (1 Kgs. 8:62–9:8)

Israel's. The king and others alike offered sacrifices as a response to the prayer and the dedication of God's house. The jubilation was great, attested by the astounding numbers of sacrifices, 22,000 oxen and 120,000 sheep (63). Offerings were so abundant that a special altar was brought into service, added to the bronze altar before the temple (64). The offerings were many because completing the temple was a remarkable advance, giving Israel a central sanctuary (16). Another reason was that God's name was memorialized there (16, 20). A final cause was the great host from all Israel wishing to offer sacrifices.

The people's prayer, though not mentioned in the 1 Kings account, is said elsewhere to be a part of it (2 Chr. 7:3). It was not only a response to the temple completion, Solomon's prayer, and presenting offerings, but God's glory filling His house. The people threw themselves to the ground in awe and praised God crying out, "Truly He is good, truly His loving-kindness is everlasting." Their words repeated much that was the essence of Solomon's (1 Kgs. 8:23).

God's (9:1–9). The details of 1 Kings are supplemented by 2 Chronicles. Only (1) below is drawn from the latter.

(1) His approval (2 Chr. 7:1–3). God displays this in a grand way by letting His presence be seen, a reflection of it at least. He fills the temple with His glory; 1 Kings 8:10 also gives that observation. The glory appeared visibly in a cloud, as the Lord had displayed in a pillar of cloud in Israel's exodus and wanderings (Ex. 13, etc.). It also filled His dwelling place within the temple as glory had filled the tabernacle, then His dwelling place (Ex. 25:8), upon its completion (40:34). It was His stamp of approval, accepting the house as His own.

Another evidence to the people of His approval was His fire flaming from heaven and consuming sacrifices. This was probably in sudden bolts of fire (cf. Lev. 10:2; Judg. 6:21; 9:20), somewhat like lightning flashes.

(2) His appearance (1 Kgs. 9:2–9). Sometime after the dedicatory service, God appeared to Solomon in Jerusalem (cf. 3:5). This was "at night" (2 Chr. 7:12) and presumably in a second dream, "as He had appeared to him at Gibeon" (1 Kgs. 9:2). He showed His response to the temple in several details.

First, He assures that He has heard Solomon's prayer. Second, He has consecrated this house by putting His name there forever. Despite destruction of the temple in Babylonian conquest, He would see that a restored house would be built, having continuity in His covenant faithfulness (cf. Ezek. 40–48; Hag. 2:7–9). Third, His eyes (awareness) and heart (commitment) would be there always. Again, even during the later exile when this particular temple had been destroyed, God heard Daniel's prayers uttered toward this site, for truly His awareness and commitment in answering prayer were sure (cf. Dan. 6:10; 9:4–19). Daniel's prayer, for example, would be fulfilled in restoration for His people (9:24–27; cf. 7:22–27).

Fourth, if Solomon obeyed God's word, God would establish His kingdom of that time. Solomon later would stray from God, and God would tear away part of the kingdom (11:9–13). If Solomon's sons (other Davidic kings) continued in disobedience, God would remove Israel from its land and bring the temple to rubble. This, too, would happen three and a half centuries later (Jer. 39–40, 52; Ezek. 33). The Lord does not mention in 1 Kings 11 but does earlier that He will restore Israel finally, never to be uprooted again (2 Sam. 7:10), and put a king on the Davidic throne forever (16). That king is, as God later defines, Jesus Christ (cf. Jer. 23:5, 6; Ezek. 21:26, 27; Acts 2:30).

The Prayer of Solomon after This (1 Kgs.)

Never after the temple dedication does the biblical record state a prayer of Solomon. He had so far walked with God, though not as closely as David (1 Kgs. 3:3). He already was tolerating sins that would be reasons for his spiritual decline (cf. 3:1). After the temple prayer, Solomon would drift from loyalty to God (11:1–8), and God would be angry (9). Though the king's salvation was secure in God's gift, his honoring of God was smudged greatly, and the degree of his special reward in eternity reduced from what it might have been (cf. 1 Cor. 3:8, 15; 2 Cor. 5:10).

While Scripture gives no explicit words of Solomon's prayers after 1 Kings 8, he probably did pray, though with decreasing effectiveness. The reference later in 9:25 to his offerings would entail accompanying prayers, yet the end of the verse shows the summary pertains only to the time up to his finishing the temple.

Principles are abundant. First, a prayer-saturated life can have a ministry reaching out to seek God's blessing for many others. Second, a prayer-permeated life now is no necessary guarantee that one will always cling to this. Third, God's "house" began as one of prayer (here), and was what God desired later to be "a house of prayer" even when sin largely dimmed this ideal (Isa. 56:7; Matt. 21:13; Mark 11:17; Luke 19:46). Likewise, God's spiritual dwelling place that is the church is to be in consistent touch with Him (Eph. 2:18, 21–22; 3:12). And the same is true of each believer's body as God's "temple" (1 Cor. 6:19–20), as God's people are to pray in "everything" (Phil. 4:6) and each is to offer up spiritual sacrifices (1 Pet. 2:5) in a priestly service (v. 9).

A fourth guideline is obvious. We may approach God with hearts that adore Him, whatever our bodily posture is. Fifth, cultivate prayer that in mind-boggling potential can reach to answers in far-flung places and touch people long after one's own life. Sixth, a leader's prayer for those in a group can stir and elicit their prayer as well to the One who is their God, too. Seventh, God does hear and honor prayer of the person who trusts in Him. Eighth, a prayer in the Word (as here) can evoke prayer in another at the time or much later for certain of its same, essential concerns (cf. Dan. 9:4–19).

1 Kings 13:6

Prayer with Obedience—Up to a Point

This drama fits with the strange episodes of Scripture. A young prophet of Judah resolutely carries out God's word in proclaiming judgment on the northern kingdom. He even works miracles, prays, and gets God's answer. But then he lets another prophet entice him to disobey what God told him to do.

An Obedient Consistency to God's Word (1–10)

The young prophet is, for a time, a model in setting his face like flint to do God's will.

His speaking (1, 2). He makes the trek north to Bethel, one of the new King Jeroboam's two centers of calf worship. He obeys the prompting of God's word to go.

God has the timing figured out right, so in His guidance His spokesman reaches the false worship altar right when Jeroboam is preparing to offer incense, which is defiance against God's will that the people go to the new house of God in Jerusalem. Jeroboam is making his resistance to God's will an issue (12:27). He deliberately seeks to lure worshipers here, or to his calf altar in Dan, instead of them going farther to the temple.

The prophet, unnamed here, cannot be Ahijah who is faithful to deliver God's word before and after this (11:29–39; 14:5–16). The present servant is faithful at first. He boldly proclaims judgment on the bogus altar. God will fulfill what he predicts 300 years later by using a Davidic king, Josiah, who will burn bones of false priests here. Mention of the fulfillment is in 2 Kings 23:15–20. The prophet's forecast is a miracle of God, and of course comes true.

His signs (3–5). In addition to the miracle just proclaimed, the prophet works three others. He predicts a splitting apart of the altar, and bang, it splits. The king, on hearing criticism against his enterprise, lifts his hand and commands officers to arrest the troublemaker. God withers the hand and arm so that the king is not able to pull it back. A third miracle is to be added as the prophet prays.

His supplication (6). Two things happen quickly.

(1) An imploring by the king. His attitude changes in an instant. Now he begs the prophet to entreat "the Lord your God." That may acknowledge that He is not genuinely Jeroboam's God (cf. v. 33; 14:9). He pleads, "pray for me, that my hand may be restored to me." An attitude of repentance, or confession of sin, is not mentioned, and is denied in verse 33, showing it was not in the king.

(2) An interceding by the prophet. The visitor did beseech the Lord. He is called "a man of God," a minister in God's service and so far living in His honor. His entreaty is answered with a miracle, God healed Jeraboam's hand. The prophet's prayer life was very effective, fitting with his sensitivity to God's will (cf. John 15:7, 8).

His steadfastness (7–10). This is clear in a pair of acts. Up to now the prophet is displaying fine-tempered discipline to carry out what God told him.

(1) His denial. He sidesteps a subtle strategy of the king to "butter him up" and win over his reward by a bribe. What favor did the northern leader design to give him—poison, or pleasure in lavish eating, or women, or comfort to lure him into his service? The subsequent bent of Jeroboam reflects consistent evil, and a dark scheme is probable here too.

The prophet's avowal makes clear that he means business for God. If the king gave him half his house he would not go with him or eat or drink in Bethel. His mission grips him. He is under command of the Lord, and he will carry it out to the full, not eat, drink, or go back by the way he came. Possibly the wisdom of his unpredictable route home was part of God's way of keeping him safe. The king's crowd, noting his approach, might know where to lurk in ambush along his trail.

God has no safer place for His servant than to be in His will.

So far the obedience has been sterling, and now the boast is big.

(2) His departure. Persisting in obedience, God's man struck out for home by a different way. So far, to his credit, he has obeyed four times—going (1), speaking judgment (2), giving the sign God planned (3), and following other specific directions (8–10).

The vignette of his life suddenly changes. Obedience gives way to disobedience. It can for any servant of God, hence the imperative of vigilant watchfulness in prayer and fidelity to His word.

The Disobedient Change from God's Word (11–32)

God and an old prophet living in Bethel put the visitor to a test. God knows how to test His people to see if they will obey, really obey, all the way (Deut. 8:2). Standing true to the test for a while can *encourage* further faithfulness if handled properly, but it does not *guarantee* staying true.

Consistency for a time (11–17). The old prophet hears from his sons about the incoming prophet's astounding ministry and his standing for something right. The miracles and the message ring true. But a bit of rascality teases the man's mind. What if he pushes the test of fidelity a few rungs higher, really makes it subtle? What stuff will the departing prophet be made out of then?

The homeward bound messenger is walking the crest of success. He is, in modern vernacular, "on a roll." Why, he had done it all. Now, taking a break to rest under an oak, he feels elated, mission accomplished. Just a matter of time and he will be home. The danger has all been left behind now. He can let down his guard.

Suddenly a man on a donkey swings into sight. The young prophet sits and eyes him, friendly-like. The words of the rider came almost a compliment; they could make a man feel good. "Are you the man of God who came from Judah?" That he is, and he had stuck right to the directions.

"Come home with me and eat," the man on the donkey proposed.

Well, that was an easy one. "No, thanks. I can't do that. Why that would be disobeying what the Lord made so clear to me. No room for misunderstanding, you see. He said don't eat or drink or return the way you went in."

Step five in obedience!

Then the old prophet puts things on the rung his mind had figured. Let us see now. "Why, that's okay. No problem. I'm a prophet like you." The young prophet probably relaxes a bit at this, and lets his guard drop even lower. "Why, I know how important it is to go by the word of the Lord. Sure . . . but an angel told me by the word of the Lord it's all right now. He says to me, 'Go bring him back so he can eat and drink.' "

By the word of the Lord . . . well, that sounds quite okay. The young prophet relaxes his vigilance even more. After all, this is a *prophet* like he is, a man after his heart, and this was *the word of the Lord*. The man says so. In a moment great folly can steal into the camp. That is why it is necessary to keep up sentry watch over the mind. The man under the oak rather fancied this modification, this change of directions. For a moment he does not think straight, and that is all it takes.

The tempting prophet also fails. He lies (18). His word runs counter to that of God, and this is his own dark design, possibly in envy against the young man's success. God can entrust a person with a test, permitting Satan to incite the heart to evil (1 Chr. 21:1; 2 Sam. 24:1). God can bring outward trial (James 1:3–12) and in it permit fleshly lust to respond in sin that a person wants to commit (James 1:13–15). He is able, however, to provide a way of escape if the person will in trust take it (1 Cor. 10:13), and grow through obeying.

The young prophet fails by compromising the word of God. It is not true all the way to him.

Compromise in a temptation (19–32). He does three things wrong, goes back, eats, and drinks. Every one of these was against what the Lord clearly told him to do. It would be grand if the account could speak of obeying. He might have said, "That you are a prophet is fine, so fulfill it well. It makes no difference to me what you say. The word I have from the Lord is clear, and I am trusting Him not to change it." Or at least he could reply, "Since this drastically changes what the Lord told me plainly, I must pray and insist on His unmistakable guidance before I could ever accept a different word."

The messenger's heart is open like a book as the old prophet feeds him. God now speaks through the sly host, this time His word and not the man's baiting lie. "You have disobeyed the command of the Lord, and not kept it, so you will not get home safely." God assumes His word was clear enough; His servant blundered in being lulled into supposing a definite command could be modified, with God's blessing.

How often believers do the same. "Yes, God says for a believer not to marry an unsaved person, but it's different in my case; it will be all right. After all, this is true love, God wants this person to be saved, and I will bring His will about." The principle can apply in another matter. "I know God gives many reasons why this is His word, but I now see reasons to take a different view on that, and really this is the way God wants me to see it." Or, "I know God's word is plain that He will never let a saved person be lost, but these other considerations show it must be His word that this can happen." Or, "you say God's word calls you to worship in this kind of church, but God has shown me you and I can marry and worship in this church you do not now accept. God can make it work." On and on it can go. God said . . . but!

The disobedient prophet must have been shaken by the word that he would never be able to reach home safely now. He took a trail back, and the crisis happened suddenly. A lion pounced on him, and he knew it was the end of his trail, short of his Judean home.

A decent burial was the old prophet's follow-up. Then he asked his sons eventually to inter his own body in the same grave. This was because it was *his* grave, because he wanted to lie by a man who had obeyed in much, or because he was smitten with his own misuse of God's word and saw that both of them were cut of the same cloth. One final reason is in verse 32. He wished to be beside the man whose prophecy (God's word) against the God-defying worship surely would be fulfilled. At least he would pay tribute that God's word stands true.

Why does God act so drastically against the young prophet? After all, he obeyed in five steps, only failed in one. It is probably because the day is one of high danger and widespread disobedience. Jeroboam and many others were dishonoring God's word. It was all the more crucial, then, that a man standing for truth should stand for it all the way. To build such a record of obedience, then discredit the effect of it by a scandal of compromise, was to make it appear that loyalty to God's word was just a facade. If someone could entice the person to yield for a price, the word of God need not be taken seriously after all.

God can keep a servant's eternal salvation safe, but bring drastic temporal discipline on him. This is for his own greater benefit, for others' sakes, and to uphold God's honor. So it was with Samson (cf. Heb. 11:32) whose life came to an end. So it was with David in losing his child (2 Sam. 12) and in discipline on his people over the census (2 Sam. 24). And so it was with the prophet who was obedient only up to a point.

A great principle of prayer looms here. God wants the person of prayer to maintain steadfast fidelity to His word. Some muster a certain measure of obedience, and some prayer that works. Yet they are susceptible to voices that lure them to compromise what God has truly said. It is best to get the whole act together, persist in obeying His guidelines, and go the distance.

1 Kings 17:1–7

Standing Before the Lord in Prayer

Time moves on from the compromising prophet to the great prophet Elijah of the Gilead region east of the Jordan. He will pray for rain later and get it (18:41–45). Here he prays for withholding rain and gets it (v. 1). James in later times would sum up both phases in using Elijah as an extraordinary example of effective praying (5:17, 18).

The Declaration of No Rain (1)

The relevance for prayer. Admittedly the verse does not mention prayer. But Elijah's claim, will soon indicate it. He focuses on what God is—alive and able—to authorize and verify that there will be no rain for some years. Only He, the creator of heaven and earth (Gen. 1:1), controlled the powers of the skies. Other gods as Baal, depended on for rain, were not living as God is; they were but dead idols fashioned by men, fabricated as objects of trust. They were powerless, in truth. That God lives shows that He can give His guarantee to Elijah.

That no rain will fall for a period God's spokesman proclaims becomes a proof to point Israelites to a trust in Him alone.

The reference to prayer. Prayer is assumed in the claim, "before whom I stand." The bold declaration carries with it the inference of a live contact, an interview, a communion in face to face encounter. To stand in God's presence is to assume familiar approval, allegiance, ambassadorship, and appeal or advocacy rights. Elijah stands welcomed there, loyal to God, a messenger of God, an intercessor for God's will to His people.

And so in 17:20–22 the prophet goes to God in another specific prayer and God gives what he asks. He certainly has access to God's presence and power there. Likewise James, led by the Lord, views 17:1 here as involving prayer.

The Direction for God's Supply (2–5)

God could control not only the rain on which Israel depended to teach them to trust Him. He could control the resources His prophet needed to tutor him to depend on Him. Here He pledges two supplies.

Drinking at the brook. At the brook Cherith that spills into the Jordan from the east, God would assuage his thirst. Eventually, as God answered Elijah's prayer relating to no rain, the wadi dried, and God guided His servant to other quarters.

Dining with the birds. God caused ravens to carry bread (perhaps grain he could pound and cook in patties) and meat to the rocks nearby. Possibly this was a ravens' roost where, in God's providence, the birds came in abundance with catches of prey in their claws. Elijah was a guest at their table! But his food was not for the birds. He could wash, cut or pound and cook it to suit his taste.

God who made the waters and birds and all their prey (Gen. 1) can richly provide for the person who trusts Him in prayer, loyal to His word (cf. Phil. 4:19).

The Drying of the Rain Supply (7)

God's own will was being realized for the land (1), and He was prompting His man to go to another place where He would use him. His trek would take him across Israel's territories to Zarephath of Sidon along the Mediterranean. Careful in guidance, the Lord not only led from Elijah's end by sending him, but from the other end by preparing a widow to feed him. That He "commanded" her no doubt means He works in her to will and do (Phil. 2:13), and commands a supply for her to sustain her family and the prophet (14–16)

When God has used one supply (the rain), He is able to provide another, and abundantly. It is good to serve a God who "lives" (1), is able and faithful.

Principles emerge. First, prayer of a usable channel can go from talking with God to an audience with people. Elijah moves from prayer before God to proclamation before King Ahab of the northern kingdom. Then he shifts from the ravens to a room above the widow and her son (19). He is where God wants him to be. A sensitive prayer life, trusting the Lord, has the benefit of moving in step with His leading (Prov. 3:5, 6).

Second, cultivate being available before God as in prayer, and make a ministry count to the full for Him. Third, a person who appears before the heavenly magnet can discover that the same God appears to him with what he needs (cf. Matt. 6:5–13, 33; 7:7–11). Fourth, when God is blessing, a person abandoned to going forth for Him can find that He can place on people's hearts to be there for him or her. The God who provides takes care of all the aspects.

1 Kings 17:20–22

Prayer for a Dead Son to Live

One miracle already had displayed God's power through Elijah to the widow. God had increased a handful of flour and a little oil in a jar to a continuing supply. His Son would similarly increase a few loaves and fishes to a banquet to feed 5,000 and 4,000, besides women and children.

It is helpful to meditate on the Godhood of God. He created the heavens and earth out of nothing. To furnish more flour in a bowl and oil in a jar would be easy by comparison. When His power as God is one's perception, questioning how He could do it is out of the question.

Now a second miracle blesses the widow and her son.

The Crisis of the Boy's Death (17)

Sickness so extreme overtook the lad that in a short time the mother and Elijah were aware that he had expired. Elijah understood that he had died (20) and prayed for a return of life (21).

The Concern of the Boy's Mother (18)

Grievance swept over her heart. She was smitten with a sense of two things that crushed her. One was the thought that calamity from God, whose man of God had recently come, was her portion in return for her sin. The nature of the sin is not defined, and she is not described as a woman of bad repute. No doubt she is just overwhelmed with remembrances of sins such as any mother might remember in human failure. She assumed she was to blame. The other disturbance was, of course, the most heart-rending. She had lost her son.

She was not necessarily to blame. God was using the occasion to teach His sufficiency again, to authenticate His prophet further, and to encourage those who heard to trust Him, not idols. That idol worship was rampant is clear in Elijah's "battle of God verses the gods" on Mount Carmel (Chap. 18).

The Calling on the Lord (19–21)

The supplication to the Lord. Elijah is gentle with the distraught mother. "Give me your son." She let him take the boy from her grasp and watched as he carried him upstairs to his quarters. Her concern naturally could have pushed her up those stairs also, to watch what the man of God did. But verse 23 shows she remained downstairs, probably wringing her hands and crying out to God.

Elijah's prayer is in two aspects frequent in Scripture.

(1) The asking of a question. Laying the boy on the bed, he cried out his query to the Lord. He sought to know if God had done this as a judgment on the mother, as He was putting pressure on the land by holding back rain. Possibly he thought of David losing a son due to sin (2 Sam. 12), or not as far back, Jeroboam and his wife (1 Kgs. 14:12). An honest question asked in sincere travail is no offence to God (cf. Hab. 1, 2). Today most questions find resolution in the principles of God's word, others later become irrelevant, or must await further light.

(2) The asking for a healing. As he said before, Elijah again called his hearer "O Lord my God." He is the covenant Lord of Israel (Ex. 6:3) and is the God of infinite ability who is, for the trusting servant, "my God." Those who really can call Him this are in a role of accountability to come before Him as their's and show Him to or seek Him on behalf of others.

Here, Elijah was quite direct, definite, and brief. A lot of faith can be invested in the prayer of a moment; and for those whose God is the Lord, a lot of power is available without delay, if He wills. No need exists, in a sudden crisis, to pray around the world or to pray lofty prayers for hours saying the same thing over and over. "Let this child's life return to him." Few were the words, but they were heard on high.

The stretching on the boy. Elijah hovered over the boy's body, either crossway or along his frame, careful not to crush him. This is not for identification with him, or three times to signify Christ's resurrection on the third day, or three for faith, hope and love or Father, Son, and Spirit, or other meanings forced on this. Elijah was simply seeking to give the child all the bodily warmth he was able, and did it three times as a natural number of completeness often seen in biblical times, a series he could do in a short time.

Elijah was not trying to work in place of God. He just was faithfully doing all he humanly could as he interceded for a divine restoration of the life so recently expired.

The Comfort in Healing (22, 23)

God's answer was as definite as the prayer. He heard, the life returned, and with vitality now back the boy soon showed signs of reviving. The concise narrative makes no mention of a prayer of gratitude, but it was eminently natural and probably on the prophet's lips as well as the mother's later.

Taking the boy by the hand, probably, the visiting servant of God led him downstairs to his mother. As the two stepped into the room, the boy likely leaped into waiting arms and some sobbing or ecstatic cries ensued.

The Confirming of God's Man (24)

Finally tearing herself away from her son, the woman looked at the prophet quietly standing by. Two things, she testified, were very clear to her, almost words of praise to God whom she knew worked through this tenant.

His relation to God. "I know that you are a man of God." This speaks of more than spirituality in a good testimony of modeling

God's graces, though it does not omit that. She had seen on display the man's trust ("do not fear," 13) and his compassion (19). She saw Elijah as a channel of God's power, a man close to Him and reflecting His will, a prophet she could highly respect.

His reflection of the word. She also recognized that the word he spoke was from the Lord, His truth that she could count on. Earlier, Elijah's guarantee from God that the food supply would be replenished had come true. And in these present moments, his prayer to God had secured a life snatched back from the dead. His tender invitation, "Give me your son," suggesting reason to entertain hope, had resulted in his truthfully getting the remedy.

Soon, Elijah would leave this family at God's new leading to confront Ahab the troubler of Israel (18:1, 18).

Guidelines are easy to discern. First, if we have questions in or out of prayer, God almost always has the answers in His Word. Second, as mere humans we have no power to effect miracles, but it is grand to serve God who can answer prayer by mighty things (Jer. 33:3). Third, longer vigils of servant-like commitment in prayer can prepare for other prayers that find God's incredible answers in a brief span, when needed. Fourth, what we who pray can do in a sensible human way can cooperate with the work God alone can do in His way. Fifth, as the praying Elijah was God's channel for a great answer, we too can do amazing things as we pray and God does what He is able to do (cf. John 14:12–14).

1 Kings 18

Prayer to Idols and to God

As the three years without rain were drawing to a close (1), God did two things to prepare for the next episode in the prophet's ministry. He *guided* His spokesman to go and confront King Ahab of the northern kingdom, and more than him, his false prophets and the spurious gods they trusted. He also *guaranteed*, near the end of the three years without rain that Elijah had prayed for (17:1), that He will send rain.

God's authority over the heaven—to withhold rain or to give it—was the overall backdrop of the confrontation. He will prove that *He* alone is God, and that Elijah speaks for Him, and do this in a "battle with the gods." He will send from heaven both fire and rain, obviously in His control, and after the fire bring an assembled crowd to acknowledge that *He is God* (39).

Elijah's Proclamation of the Challenge (17–25)

Moving as God led, Elijah sent Ahab's God-fearing palace servant Obadiah to summon the king to a rendezvous (7–16). Now the prophet and the king met.

Ahab and Obadiah had scouted the land to find any last grass to keep their horses and mules alive. The severity of the famine (2) had the king riled. Elijah was to him the human troublemaker who had pronounced no rain. Now the king's anger vented itself in a denunciatory blast. Is this prophet the "troubler of Israel"? Elijah's ready reply was that he was not the culprit; the king and his forebears were the cause. God's man reminds Ahab about two aspects of sin that the Lord's fair warning had said would bring judgment in no rain (cf. Deut. 28:23, 24). They were two sides of one sin really. One was Israel's *forsaking* God by disobeying His word; the other was their *following* of false gods, the Baals honored in various places (18).

The true prophet hurls out a challenge to the king. Let him require a gathering of three groups which represent the idol-infested worship. Summon people of all Israel, 450 prophets of Baal, and 400 prophets of the Asherah, female deities. Call these to Mount Carmel for a reckoning.

A few days later when these came together, Elijah shouted his challenge. How long would they divide their loyalties between God and gods? If the Lord of Israel is God, go all out in worship of Him, but if Baal was worthy of allegiance, give all devotion to him.

Stolid silence answered him. Then he went on. He stood, he said, one man against all of Baal's prophets. Let a demonstration here and now show who was God. Here was his plan. Let two oxen be readied for sacrifice, one for each side, laid on the altar. Then let each side pray to its god, and whichever answered by fire consuming the sacrifice would be acclaimed God (24).

He gave Baal's devotees their opportunity first. Once they had laid the sacrifice on the wood, the issue was *prayer*, and who answers it (25).

Prayer to the False God (26–29)

Their cries to Baal. The 450 false spiritual leaders set up an onslaught of prayers to coax their god to prove himself. They kept up the cries for hours, morning to midday. Still, they got no action out of Baal.

They performed various dramatics leaping about the altar to provoke their lord to verify himself by a devouring flame.

Elijah's coaxings to stir greater effort. When noon was apparent and Baal showed no action, the true prophet began to mock those who led in falsehood. His sarcasm belittled the bogus god and underscored the futility of prayer to an improper object of trust.

Perhaps if the leaders of Baalite religion prayed more loudly, Baal might be able to hear. Elijah added a dig, "for he is a god," that is he surely must be able to hear since he is an object of confidence to his devotees! Jesus later would teach that straining in prayer was not necessary with the true God; those who prayed need not suppose He was willing to respond just because they came with special noise or exercised their vocal chords in special effort, as in much speaking (Matt. 6:2, 5, 7).

Elijah added some other challenges, each a prick on the conscience of the hearers. Let them consider what kind of god they vested their trust in. Perhaps Baal is busy, and able to give his attention only to one thing at a time! Keep praying and he may finally be free to handle your case. Or, maybe Baal is taking a break (to rest, or relieve himself?). After all, he might be weak at times, and need special allowances.

It may be, Elijah shouts again, that Baal is away at the moment, beyond the reach of your voices. Give him a break. Give him time to get back in range to hear when you need him. Then comes the consummate suggestion to stir reflection on Baal's limitations. Perhaps your god is "out of it" just now, taking a snooze, so he cannot hear. After all, be fair, a god cannot be expected to act if he is not awake. It could be that if you just pray more loudly, it will stir him out of the nap.

The continued cries. Stung by Elijah's challenges, the prophets set up quite a din of appeals to rouse their lord. Can one imagine how loud the racket really must have been? For 450 men, now quite embarrassed, cut loose in a tremendous effort to evoke an answer and save the day for their god!

That was not all. These men Israelites looked up to went to extreme pains to show their god a devotion that would earn his reward. They mutilated their bodies to provoke his appreciation. But the utmost effort went even farther. They broke into ravings of ecstatic prophesying to stimulate Baal into action.

The time of the evening offering drew on, 3 p.m. Still the 450 men of false prayer looked up at a heaven of bronze. No voice brought them to a hush. No act responded to their waiting sacrifice. Nothing showed Baal heard their prayers at all.

Elijah's Preparing of the Altar (30–35)

In the face of such idol failure, the prophet shouted to the people to press near. Possibly as the hours had dragged on, stunned disappointment had shattered confidences, devotees swallowed hard, and fell back trying to puzzle this out. Or they were just worn out trying to urge their leaders on.

Elijah repaired the Lord's altar which some had torn down, and set up a stone to represent each tribe of Israel. The altar represented the Lord, the Lord of Israel. To make things more impressive, he dug a trench about the altar, then placed his ox on the wood. Then, in drama causing the people's suspense to mount and to make it all the harder for God to answer, he commanded that water be poured on the offering and wood, even spilling over. He did not stop until twelve pitchers were emptied, and the trench itself was filled.

Baal had not shown up. And now, it seemed, it was ever so much harder for God to act against all the added handicap.

His Prayer to God (36, 37)

Prayer to Baal had proven pointless. Now Elijah calls on his Lord. His prayer reflects zeal that God's answer show two things.

Demonstration that He is God. First, prayer is affirmation. This God who hears is the Lord, covenant Lord of His people (Ex. 6:3), faithful to His own covenant plan. He is the God of Abraham, Isaac and Israel. How often He had answered prayers of each, showing His Godhood in various ways.

Elijah did not say "Jacob," but "Israel," possibly for two reasons. One is that God had answered Jacob in a crisis, changing his name to Israel, the one who struggles with God. Now a great battle is going on too, and Elijah is fighting his own fight, not willing to let God go until He blesses. Another reason is that "Israel" was the more common name of the whole people who needed this demonstration of who is God. Ahab and Elijah both had used it in the passage (17, 18).

It is good, when praying, to affirm once again who God really is, and meditate on Him being this. If He is everything He claims to be and has proven to be, He is the God to whom to pray and the God who answers.

The second aspect of Elijah's prayer as it seeks a demonstration is intercession. He appealed, for Israel's sake, that God display Himself as God in their midst.

Authentication of His servant and word. Let them see this for their good, for to worship Him alone is their highest good. As God demonstrates this to Israel, let Him prove that Elijah is His servant and has done all these things on the authority of His word. If it is shown that he is God's servant and His word is true, then *He* is Elijah's Lord and should be theirs. *His word* ought to be honored, not that of the 450.

Who God is filled Elijah's concern and was the bottom line (37). He interceded that the people watching the drama will know this by God answering with fire.

The Proof from God (38, 39)

Three steps follow in rapid order.

The coming of fire. This answer was exactly what Elijah made his challenge (24) and asked God to do (37). It was an outright miracle. And it came from the God whom Elijah had seen do other things only God could do, withheld rain, replenish flour and oil, and bring a boy back to life. That fire should fall was for others' benefit as God met the challenge.

The consuming of all. Everything at the altar of the Lord (32) vanished as fire licked at the area. Not even a stone or a drop of extra water was left.

The convincing of the people. At first the people ("all," it says) gasped in wide-eyed astonishment. Right before their eyes was evidence. God had won the battle of the gods. Then, smitten by the proof, they fell prostrate in the presence of the Victor. Baal had done nothing even in hours; God had done it all, and done it in quick answer. After hitting the ground in reverence, they cried out what must have been as loud or louder than the cries of the 450. "The Lord, He is God; the Lord, He is God."

God often shows people He is God as He gives compelling answers to prayer. This ought to cause His servants all the more to trust Him, call on Him, see big answers, and show those who need Him too that He alone is worthy of their worship.

The Punishment of the False (40)

Two things happened swiftly after the winners has been declared. Both were obvious steps. The 450 prophets have had opportunity to know the true God, and falsified their message against great light. In doing that, they have misled those who listened to them in sin as great a disservice as a person can commit against others. They have turned them away from the only One who can ultimately help them, and enticed them to trust in a god that cannot help.

The two steps are these. First, Elijah whose authority was from God and was now recognized, commanded that the false leaders be *seized.* This must be thorough, the crowd closing in to cut them all off from escape. As far as the record suggests, not one got away. Second, Elijah *slew* the 450. This drastic judgment followed their drastic wrong to God and the other people. It also prevented later acts of hatred and returning to misleading ways when Israel desperately needed to follow the Lord.

Jesus, greatest teacher of love, was even more severe in his forecast about the future of false leaders. It would be better for each to have a millstone bound to his neck and he be cast into the watery depths (Matt. 18:6). The worse destiny was suffering in hell (23:33). The best thing they can do, in light of this and in view of who God is, is repent and trust Him in the right way.

What principles of prayer stand out here? One is not to pray trusting a false god as Baal's devotees did. Another is to affirm who God is as the object of proper trust, and let it move the heart in real worship (36). A further one is to intercede that others may know God aright, and listen to one who is true to His word (36).

1 Kings 18:41–46

Prayer for God's Will—Rain

The Connection of God's Will and Prayer (18:1)

God has made clear here that His will for Elijah to meet Ahab is closely linked with His will to provide rain. Elijah has met Ahab, called him and his people to a showdown, and secured God's great display of power. Now, the prophet pleads that the God who showed

His will so far will show it in producing rain. He is praying in submission to God's will.

The Counsel to Ahab (41)

It is late afternoon by now (cf. 29, 39). Elijah counsels the king to go to his evening meal. He already hears the sound of a strong rain. Since not even a cloud is in sight until later (44), he hears as a prophet sensitive to an impression from the Lord. He desires that the king finish his meal and depart in his chariot before rain changes the road home to a quagmire (44).

Of course after God's authoritative events through Elijah that day, Ahab would be sharply impressed to do as counseled.

The Calling on God for Rain (42–44)

After going down to the brook Kishon to deal with the 450 deceivers, Elijah climbed to the summit of Carmel. A bit below the top, he crouched and put his face between his knees, probably kneeling and bending down in reverence and submission before his Lord.

That he was seeking God in prayer is obvious in his *posture*. It also fits his *pattern* of being in prayer, at least at strategic times (17:1; 20–21; 18:36–37). And it agrees with the *proclamation* of God's Word (James 5:18).

The prayer was intermittent, a series of prayers. For the prophet took time out between each stage to tell his servant to clamber higher and gaze out at the sky over the Mediterranean. When the servant reported, Elijah sent him back again each time and kept on praying until God's answer was evident.

No words are supplied of the prayers. The case is similar to that of Moses praying on a hill but the passage not furnishing his words. What did Elijah say? It would be nice to have a cassette from a recording kept in a Carmel library! In the absence of words in the text, or such an audio, one can well imagine things Elijah might have prayed.

One aspect could be *praise* for God's action only a short time before, and His worthiness of worship demonstrated for all to see. Another would be his *gratitude* as the events vindicated his own servant role and encouraged him in being used of God. Still a further aspect would be *intercession* for the rain which now was the issue, and in it fulfillment of his prophetic word of no rain until he said (17:1). Israelites needed water desperately, as the scouting trip of Ahab and Obadiah had illustrated earlier in the chapter. Rain now would show the people God's provision and encourage growing trust in Him.

Might the praying man also have *petitioned*, as he thought ahead? He needed strength to run ahead of Ahab's royal chariot to Jezreel (46). As David had appealed for strength (1 Sam. 30:6), so might Elijah, and so would the psalmist (cf. 138:3).

The Coming of the Rain

The servant returned from his seventh vigil at the crest. This time he descended with a quickened step and excitement in his words. In today's phrasing, he reported: "Hey, would you look at that! It's coming—a cloud away out there, so far about the size of a man's hand. But it's getting closer!"

Elijah may have breathed a quick word of further *thanks*. Then he said, still in a crouch, or having risen: "Get to Ahab: fast. No time to lose. Urge him to have his chariot made ready and get out of here ahead of the downpour, or he'll bog down."

Perhaps he continued to pray, and gazed out at the coming storm. It was growing darker from oncoming night and the overcast, and he could feel wind tugging at his robe. Then the rain came, and it laced the land in sheets. Elijah reached the road, saw the king's chariot streaking toward him, and raced ahead. As his strides lengthened, he felt the surge God gave him, knew the strength was coming from on high. The hand of the Lord was on him as his legs pumped tirelessly on, in a marathon of about twenty-five miles to Jezreel.

As he ran, his thoughts may have been as active as his legs. God had shown him great answers to prayer this day!

Final principles of prayer beckon meditation. Ask in harmony with God's word and in cooperation with what He is seeking to do in the world. Second, it is all right at times to pray in surges, pause between efforts, and reflect on what God is doing. It is okay to talk with God and quickly talk with a man, if this is necessary or advisable. Often it will not be, and one can pray for a long time, beholding only the face of God. One just needs to exercise his heart not to lose a sense about the wonder of God's presence and will. Finally, as one trusts in God for an answer as for rain here, he also can trust for other things as in this case for strength to run. God is sensitive to all the needs that confront the person of prayer.

1 Kings 19:4, 10, 14

Prayer after a Mountain Top Experience

God has a rendezvous with His servant by a desert tree and at a cave. It is far away from the crowd and the glory of mountain top victories. He is still the God who hears prayers.

Elijah's Retreat from Jezebel (1–4b)

A trio of things happen here.

The telling of the prophet's actions. Ahab moves from his chariot into his palace to report to his wife how Elijah's God had defeated his and her prophets. When he describes Elijah's slaying of the 450 spiritual leaders, Jezebel convulses with raving anger. She summons a messenger right away to deliver a message to this pest Elijah.

The threat of the queen. Jezebel's courier finds the prophet. The news shows how personally she has been stung by the blow to her pride. She is a poor loser. Her threat is to have Elijah killed within twenty-four hours.

The terror in the prophet. This man had gone bravely before Ahab to proclaim a drought, and sought him out boldly to confront his whole enterprise. Now he felt shivers run through his frame, a pounding come to his heart, and a weakness strike him about the knees. Perhaps he thanked God even for the gift of time now—he had up to twenty-four hours—and found himself running. This time it was not in confidence God put in his body, but in terror that reduced him to cowardice before a strong-willed woman.

The Request to Die (4c)

Pushing far to the south, he left his servant at Beersheba and pressed on alone. A day's flight into the desert, he sank beneath a juniper tree, all done in. His prayer was one of self-pity, a petition that God would just allow him to die right here. His forebears had died, and he was no better than they; he was ready to call it quits.

Others would pray along the same line, men such as Jonah. Foolish prayers come up before a gracious God. He does not always grant us what we carelessly ask, throwing away all possibilities due to a crisis that blinds at the moment. When we sink to our worst, God soars at His consistent best.

His Renewing by an Angel (5–8)

Twice one of God's angels feeds Elijah at the juniper. Both are miraculous provisions. The celestial visitor also speaks with tender compassion, wanting to strengthen the prophet, not slay him as he asked. How often has a servant of God whimpered to die over some defeat or a shattered love relationship, and so many other things. God has instead restored hope and made a finer vessel still. How great is His desire to use His servants.

His Reviving for Ministry (9–18)

Elijah was so refreshed by God's renewing acts of grace that he went in God-given strength on a forty-day trek to Horeb where God had given Moses the ten commandments. Here God confronts him in two counseling sessions. His word revives the servant's outlook for being used again. In each, a question provokes Elijah's prayer.

God's session about might (9–13b). In a cave, God asks, "What are you doing here, Elijah?" The prophet really has no good reason to be here, for God was sufficient to protect him just as He had before all Israel and the false prophets. Now God patiently illustrates His strength again, by a *wind* so mighty that it shatters rocks in pieces, by an *earthquake*, and by a *fire*.

In each case Elijah in some way is aware that the Lord is not in the demonstration of power, though it is from Him. It is not clear what the drama means. Possibly God is showing Elijah that even when God works the mightiest trials that could hurt him, as Jezebel's threat, if God is not allowing these to work this purpose, He would keep him safe. He would be as safe before the trial back in Israel as here in the remote cave, in each case in the keeping care of God.

Some have proposed that God's examples suggest a switch in God's type of ministry for Elijah. He used him in acts of momentous power, as in the fire on Carmel and the storm raging over Carmel's brow bringing a rain long awaited. Later he would use the prophet in tamer ways, as in anointing two kings and summoning Elisha to a prophet's work. But this change does not appear to find support. Elijah had some rather gentle ministries before as in the supply of the widow's oil and supplication for her son's life. And after this his ministry, though at times gentler as in calling Elisha, was violent in calling fire down on two companies King Ahaziah sent to arrest him (2 Kgs. 1).

In the final analysis, further light will explain the wind, quake and fire. Possibly they do have the significance first offered above.

God's session about ministry (13c–18). A sound of a gentle blowing after the three examples of power drew Elijah to the lip of the cave. The Lord asks the same question, and Elijah prays with the same answer as before. What does he pray?

(1) God's challenge. This came in the question asking why he is here. God wanted to use him with people back in Israel; he did not belong skulking in a hide-out away from people.

(2) Elijah's concept. As he prays, his focus is on what he has accomplished in the past, not on what God has the power yet to accomplish. He also betrays a negative, untrusting spirit, as if the God of power is not sufficient to take care of things, and him.

He trots out his zeal for the Lord, and the affirmation is true. Yet the prophet is putting too much focus on this and not the focus he ought to on God's zeal to perform His will in Israel through an available servant. He prays in gloom, citing the abandonment of God's covenant and persecution of His servants. It would be better to throw the emphasis on possibilities of changing forsakers into followers. Elijah had seen some success in the recognition of God on Carmel, now he was letting the positive be blocked by pessimism. He says he only is left, an exercise in short-sightedness and self-pampering. God will soon show him that 7,000 others have not yielded the knee to Baal (18).

How different the dismal mood of prayer from Elijah's positive, trusting prayer optimistic about God's greatness and his own servant success (18:36). How the contrast instructs believers like Elijah today on how to pray and how not to pray.

(3) God's commission for new ministry (15–18). Even when the servant is weak in his prayer, God can be patiently tender. God knows His people, knows how to deal with them according to fluctuating need, and knows how to renew them for a thrust back into service.

Go back, God says. He wants His man to anoint Hazael as king of Syria and Jehu as Ahab's successor in Israel. In addition, He asks him to anoint Elisha to carry on as his successor. This is not necessarily a discipline in gradually phasing Elijah out as God phased Moses out and brought Joshua on. Elijah would carry out much ministry yet, be immensely usable (cf. 2 Kgs. 1), and go out on the high road, so to speak (2 Kgs. 2).

Elijah has let his discouragement cloud his thinking. God still does not chide him, but reminds him of the truth. The Lord yet has the 7,000 in Israel as a remnant to worship Him (18), and His program goes on.

Principles are frequent. First, after a great victory we can go on to other victories by trust in the same Lord. We need not go from the peak to the pit, from confidence to collapse, from glory to gloom. Second, let us thank God when He spares us from things we foolishly wail when our eyes are only on ourselves or our difficulties. Third, God can use His phenomena for destruction when He wills, and also keep a servant secure from threat to go on being used for great things. Fourth, lack of faith can cause us to look only within for hope, and wonder what is the use. But faith can prompt us to look to God as able to do what seems impossible, and go on with work for Him.

1 Kings 22 (2 Chronicles 18)

Praying Through a Prophet

Indirect prayer occurs here, as often in Scripture when men ask for God's help through God's prophet who has His word. Jeremiah responded to such contacts (21:1, 2; 37:3; 42:1–3). King Jeroboam had entreated a young prophet to pray for him in 1 Kings 13:6.

It may or may not be amiss to ask for another's prayer. It may be an assist to one's own prayer in a real effort to obey God (Eph. 6:18–20). Hezekiah did this with Isaiah (Isa. 37:1–7). A bid for prayer may be a candid admission that one has no part with God, as Pharaoh in asking Moses to intercede for him. It may be a grudging concession, as Ahab goes along with Jehoshaphat's desire in 1 Kings 22. Here, Jehoshaphat's quest for a true prophet's prayer (v. 7) is in the class of Hezekiah's. It is the appeal of a good man who prays to God (2 Chr. 17–20) but casts God's wisdom aside at times as in this unholy alliance.

Here the flow of 1 Kings 22 has Jehoshaphat's desire for prayer, Micaiah's prayer, and later Jehoshaphat's cry in battle (32).

Ahab's Invitation to Jehoshaphat (1–4)

Jehoshaphat, though basically a godly king (2 Chr. 17–20), entered into two alliances with Israel, here and in 2 Kings 3. In both, he was in union with very evil kings (cf. 2 Cor. 6:14–18).

Here, wicked Ahab of Israel gains the Judean leader as an ally in attacking Syria to possess Ramoth-Gilead east of the Jordan.

The Inquiry of Prophets False and True (5–38)

Jehoshaphat's wish in prayer (5). The Judean head proposes prayer before the two kings invade. To his credit he desires "the word of the Lord." Having respect for God's will, he seeks to be sure about attacking. The problem is that even when Micaiah warns of great defeat, Jehoshaphat weakly permits Ahab's will to override wise judgment. He contrasts with David, who inquired of God whether men of Keilah would turn on him, learned they would, and acted on God's word to gain safety (1 Sam. 23:9–13).

The false prophets' prayer counsel (6). Ahab, despite losing 450 prophets of Baal to Elijah (Chap. 18), has around 400 again. Sin appeals, and the false gravitate to positions of security with a king; a king not close to God gathers around him those who stroke his ego. When Ahab asks if their prayer contact shows the Lord says attack, the 400 say it does.

It has long been popular, and is today, to make all kinds of claims supposedly based on the Lord's word gained in prayer. "The Lord spoke to me,""the Lord said," or "I felt the Lord moving me to. . . ." are examples. To separate between God's word and human whims that misguide, the person of prayer needs to be vigilant to stand on the true word. Today it is in Scripture, the real spiritual bureau of standards by which all claims can be measured. In 1 Kings 22, it was God's word written so far, and what one of His true prophets said when moved by Him.

The true prophet Micaiah (7–28). (1) The desire for a prophet of God (7). Jehoshaphat knew the difference, a very distinct one, just as Elijah had demonstrated it in Chapter 18. This kind want to channel their prayer desires through a source genuinely in contact with God.

(2) The dispatch to bring Micaiah (8, 9). Ahab admits Micaiah meets this profile, but is sour toward him. At least he is candid about his hate. It smolders because Micaiah, like Elijah, is not a "yes" man speaking encouraging things about Ahab's course in evil, but judgmental things.

Why was Elijah not mentioned? He had been negative to Ahab in killing his prophets (18:40) and announcing judgment on the king and his house (21:20–24, 29). He was, as a standout prophet, "Public Enemy Number 1" in Ahab's eyes. Jehoshaphat asks if a prophet of the Lord was present "here," in this area, handy (22:7). Even when he gets the admission that Micaiah is near, he has to insist to overcome Ahab's opposition even to this less-known prophet. Ahab reluctantly orders an officer to bring Micaiah.

(3) The demonstration of the false prophets (10–12). Led by Zedekiah, these 400 "rubber stamps" who made bogus claims to be in touch with the Lord were prophesying victory. Zedekiah even dramatized this with a visual aid, iron horns to picture goring the Syrians in an utter rout.

(4) The determination of Micaiah to speak the truth (13, 14). "Everybody agrees on what the word of the Lord is," the summoning officer informs the prophet. "Don't rock the boat; just be positive, play along, if you know what's good for you. The king will nail you if you don't. So, play wise." Micaiah replies that he will not fall into line but line up with the Lord. Not compromise before men but concord with God is his marching order.

Express inquiry for a word from God carries with it the idea that Micaiah would *pray* to secure that message. Somewhere in the time with the officer, or en route to the royal meeting, God's man sought His answer. As Jesus would say later, a person who abides in the Lord, and His word in him can ask what he wills and gain God's will (John 15:7).

(5) The declaration of Micaiah before the kings (15–28).

a. After the officer's "tip off" that minds were made up, Micaiah at first gives a *facetious* answer. Sarcasm is his dramatic device for attention-getting. He knows the message that the king is bent on following, yet also what Ahab expects him to say. So he employs a shock effect. "It is a foregone conclusion," he says in effect. "Go right on, and the Lord will fit right in with your plans."

Ahab gets the point in an instant. The truth is the very opposite, in Micaiah's opinion.

b. Having snatched the king's attention, the prophet delivers, second, a *faithful* answer—what God actually says in reply to his prayer. Israel's army will be scattered in defeat, their king cut off.

c. Ahab is *fault-finding*, rejecting Micaiah's message in the presence of Jehoshaphat. He would have been wise to back off and get serious about God's word. Once he had done this, even if lightly, when Elijah told it to him straight (21:27–29).

d. Micaiah counters with a *faithful* vision of a *false* spirit (19–23). This is a difficult passage as it may appear that the prophet is making God guilty of condoning a lie. Such is not the case. Micaiah forthrightly shows what God's truth is. God is not deceiving; if Ahab attacks he will fall (20). Ahab had that warning, and should be in no doubt where God stood. Second, those before the Lord can include good angels and evil ones (cf. "His right . . . left"). The scene is similar to angels meeting before Him in Job 1.

An evil spirit is bent on evil (21, 22), eliciting Ahab's decision to go against God's clarified will (cf. James 1:13–15). God permits this. It is as He allows Satan who desires to do so to disturb Job and as He permits Satan or demons to do other evils. Evil angels do their will, yet even with this or in spite of it, God, being in authority over all, accomplishes His will (Dan. 10:13, 20). Satan works evil in Judas who chooses evil (John 13:2), or Satan and demons incline armies at Armageddon, and so forth (Rev. 16:12–14).

God who ultimately is in charge sends the deceiving spirit (23) in the sense that He lets a demon motivate men who insist on welcoming a lie. Though God is honestly up front about His standard, He does not force the evil to perform as puppets, but allows evil to elicit reception in wicked hearts. Even this will finally have its role amid factors by which He shows the governing forces in angels and men.

e. The false prophet Zedekiah levels a *falsifying* attack on Micaiah (24). He cuffs God's man in the face, and claims that *he* has the Spirit of God, not Micaiah. The Lord's servant certifies that this deceiver will be faced with the truth when his word has been shown up as a lie and he scurries to hide from public shame. (26–28).

f. Prayer for and giving of God's counsel buys God's faithful spokesman Ahab's *fury*. The king has Micaiah slapped into confinement for contesting his will. He even makes this more severe by restricting him to bread and water, and reducing the rations to a minimum. Expecting to come back safely by overturning God's word, he seems to plan further indignity for God's servant to sharpen the pain.

Micaiah seizes a last advantage in two ways. To Ahab he proclaims that if the king gets back safely the Lord has not spoken by him. The obvious import is that Ahab will not be coming back that way, for Micaiah is confident that God will answer prayer, and His truth will stand. Then to all in the royal meeting, his words before an officer whisks him away are, "Listen, all of you people." He is challenging them to ponder well the Lord's word that he spoke before and has just said in a nutshell. As Elijah had shown on Carmel, they would see the difference between listening to messengers of a lie and a mouthpiece of the Lord.

The outcome that Micaiah predicted (29–38). This is actually an answer to Micaiah's prayer inquiry. Ahab took God's word with some fearfulness. He disguised himself, a fleshly scheme to throw Syrian fighters off, beat God's prediction, and uphold the false prophets' word that he believed. But God's word is true. An enemy arrow split a seam in Ahab's armor and pierced him fatally. He died at sunset and was wheeled to his capital, Samaria, a slumped corpse. His troops were in disarray and fled in a desperate bid to reach home alive.

Jehoshaphat had played a hypocrite. He had said that he wanted a word from the Lord to confirm or to counter invading, and had heard it. Then he sat by (cf. 10) weakly going along with majority impulse against God's man rather than showing backbone. He could have backed out resolutely and returned to Jerusalem, refusing any part in Ahab's scheme.

But here he was, going against God's will in battle. Even then, when Syrians mistook him for the king of Israel and picked him out as a special target, he cried to God (32). That this was a cry in *prayer* for safety is confirmed by the parallel (2 Chr. 18:31; cf. 13:14). It is stated in 18:31 that God helped him, suggesting that his cry was a plea for protection. God in mercy spared him, as He often does for foolish believers. Later God had plans to use him to glorify Himself in many, though not all details (2 Chr. 19, 20).

The 1 Kings 21 context shows that God's word is to be fulfilled in Ahab's demise (38). Not only did Micaiah predict it, but a bit earlier Elijah had told the king that God will "utterly sweep you away" (21:21). Elijah defined the reason, Ahab's *sin*. The king sells himself to do evil in Chapter 22, as earlier (21:20, 25). He *hates* God's man (8), *rejects* God's word (18), *mistreats* God's messenger (27), and *disguises* himself in a fool's deceit that he can defeat God (30).

Principles of prayer abound here. First, the object in prayer is to be sensitive to God's word, as Jehoshaphat at first saw (5, 7). He inconsistently failed to take a stand on the word later! Second, if one really "means business with God," he will need to keep his prayer from the delusions in prayer some tolerate. They snatch at fallacies of their own minds in place of God's word, and as the false prophets guide themselves away from God. Third, any commitment to God in prayer that truthfully honors Him is one that staunchly insists on loyalty to His word. Micaiah was valiant in this fidelity in seeking of God's mind in prayer (14).

Fourth, God hears prayer in desperate crises as he was merciful to Jehoshaphat. But rather than just drift, courting sinful works and crying for God to bale us out of danger, how much better to seek God early with a heart tender to obey. How many needless perils God could keep His people from even entering (cf. Matt. 6:13)! Fifth, while we ourselves pray, we sometimes gain lifts by asking others who trust God to pray with or for us.

Sixth, some want to know God's direction so that they can critique it, others so that they can commit to it. Seventh, false spiritual leaders easily become "yes people" for their own acceptance; true leaders of God prize His Word, seeing that they do His will and glorify Him. Eighth, people who insist on hearing from a genuine person God has taught open the door to getting the truth. Ninth, God is not a god to rubber stamp men's ideas, but the true God to give them His sure message, take it or leave it. Tenth, God permits evil spirits to do what titillates the taste of evil people, but does not support them and will hold them accountable in judgment.

Two further principles are vital. So, eleventh, it is better to speak God's truth and suffer than speak words convenient before men and go against God. Finally, God can protect a believer when he cries for help even after he has failed Him. This often gains a merciful safety and further free way to do His will. Or God can permit a foolish believer to face chastisement or even to die (cf. Samson, Judg. 16; 1 Cor. 11:30–31). For those who really are His own through grace, eternal safety is certain after this life, its failings and triumphs.

Prayer in 2 Kings

Introduction

The Title, Author, Date, Theme, and Outline

What is given on 1 Kings fits this continuation of the kings account as well.

The Relation to Prayer

The accent on it. Around thirty-four references occur in thirteen of the twenty-five chapters.

The aspects of it. Utterances of words to the Lord branch out into at lcast six aspects of prayer most common in the Bible. These include intercessory entreaty for blessing or judging (ten times), oaths (nine times), petitions (seven times), praise (two times), confession (one time), and affirmation (one time).

Examples display this.

Quickly in the book, Elijah uses *intercessory* pleadings to summon judgment on enemies an evil king orders to arrest him (1:10, 12). Later Elisha takes up the prophetic ministry as Elijah's successor, and invokes God's curse on hardened gang members who fling disrespect at him and his Lord (2:24). This same Elisha pleads for God to bring a boy to life (4:33). Much later, he asks God to open his servant's eyes to heavenly protection (6:17), to blind Syrian invaders (v. 18), and then to give these soldiers sight again (20).

Strategic intercession occurs as Judah's King Hezekiah sends to ask the prophet Isaiah to plead for safety from besieging Assyrians (19:4), then also beseeches the Lord in his own prayer (vv. 14–19). A bit later, Isaiah appeals for God's miracle to bring back the shadow on a sun dial as a sign to Hezekiah that the Lord will heal him of illness (20:5–11).

A final example of intercession is when King Josiah of Judah sends a committee of five to request special advocacy to gain the sparing of Judah from judgment (22:13).

Oaths keep springing to lips. Elijah expresses three in a row (2:2, 4, 6) when he reassures his understudy, Elisha, who faces heartache at the thought that God will take Elijah away. The temporary relief is in the prayer that invokes the Lord, by His very life, to attest that he will not leave the other prophet quite yet. When it is time, however, God does take him up into heaven (vv. 11–12). Other oaths are rather frequent (3:14; 4:30; 5:16, 20; 6:31; 11:4, 17).

Petitions come directly to the Lord or to Him through the prophet who represents His heartbeat. The leader of a third detachment of soldiers coming to imprison Elijah is wise after God destroyed the two detachments before him. He goes to his knees before the prophet, and to God who works through him, and begs that he and his men will be safe (1:13–14). Elisha requests of Elijah, and God who alone can bestow this, a double portion of his spirit (2:9).

A widow woman who provided a "motel" for Elisha came to ask him, and God with whom he was so closely in touch, to raise her son who had died (4:28). Elisha took the matter to God (33), and God gave the blessing (35). In 5:8ff., Elisha invites Naaman the leper to visit and ask him (and God who was his resource) for healing from the leprosy. Even Naaman expects the prophet to call on God (11), and it would be Elisha's way to intercede before the Lord, even if behind the scenes.

An interesting combination of prayer aspects crops up in 5:18. Naaman, after God has healed him, *petitions* Elisha (and God) for pardon in regard to a desire he has, and his words are at the same time a *confession*. One cry that may be simply to Elisha, or meant also as casting a burden on the Lord via him, is the troubled utterance about losing an ax head in the Jordan (6:5). The one issuing the cry says the object was borrowed, and he especially needs to retrieve and return it. In this light, his words may in effect amount to an appeal for help by the God known to work wonders through Elisha.

One passage reflects a God-defying king, Jehoahaz when he asks for God's grace. The evil king faces ominous war threat from Syria and appeals to the Lord to give victory (13:4). It is an interesting case that shows that God can give a positive answer to prayer, not expressly to bless an individual or people who cling to sin (vv. 2, 6), but show long-suffering mercy to His hard-pressed people, or move in on a pagan enemy (4–5). For normally God blesses those who walk in His will (1 Sam. 2:30; Ps. 14:5; 3:18–19; Ps. 84:9–11; 2 Tim. 2:22; 1 Pet. 3:12; 1 John 5:14–15)).

Another instructive passage is 1 Kings 22:13. A godly king, Josiah, inquires of God in a yearning of prayer to gain Judah's safety, as Hezekiah did in 19:4. God's answer at that point in 22:14–20 is His judgment on Judah that will go into the Babylonian captivity, yet His respite to Josiah personally. For He will hold back the calamity that much sin invites until after this obedient king has died.

Prayer's aspect of *praise* is strangely infrequent in 2 Kings. We see it briefly during the drama of Assyria's threat to conquer Jerusalem. King Hezekiah spreads out before God the Assyrian challenge that Judah's God will fall as gods of other nations have gone down before these mighty hordes. God is set to take up the challenge. Hezekiah spreads the Assyrian threat before the Lord in His temple with words to Him such as "enthroned above the cherubim" and "You are the God [far above all the gods that bit the dust]," and "You have made heaven and earth" (19:15). Later in the same session of prayer he wants all nations to see a demonstration "that You alone, O Lord, are God" (19).

Other aspects of prayer also are present, but do not occur often. Examples are *questions* to God (2:14; 8:89) and *affirmations*, several of these in 19:14–19 (cf. 20:3).

The accompaniments of prayer. In 2 Kings, prayer occurs with certain things that seem peculiar, unique, or extraordinary. God works His wonders in many ways to perform. For instance, one passage has prayer in a context of seven dips in the Jordan and God cleansing Naaman of leprosy (Chap. 5). Other exhibits are Elijah and Elisha smiting a river with a cloak (Chap. 2), God whisking Elijah away into heaven (2), heavenly armies appearing to protect a prophet and his servant and stop the Syrian invaders (6), a shadow going back on a sun dial as a miracle to attest a king's healing (20), and that king receiving fifteen more years of life than his illness seemed to allow (20). The phenomena are varied and special, for nothing is too hard for God.

At this point the exposition of prayer passages can unfold in detail.

2 Kings 1:10, 12–14

Elijah's Prayerful Pronouncements

Israel's King Ahaziah (853–852 B.C.) provokes the Lord and Elijah by resorting to a Philistine god Baal-zebub instead of to God for help in his illness.

Ahaziah Seeks Counsel by a False God (1, 2)

The king plunged through lattice work from his palace upper room and was laid up badly injured. It was an opportunity to trust the Lord in prayer. But he dispatched men to inquire of the god at Ekron whether he would recover. This was a vain trust, and in contrast to Jehoshaphat's inquiring of God through His prophets (1 Kgs. 22; 2 Kgs. 3).

Such a slap in the face of God became an issue.

God Sends a Challenge by Elijah (3–18)

First the angel of the Lord leads in rebuking recourse to an idol. Then Elijah speaks out in obedience to the angel and God.

The first challenge to the king's men (3–8). (1) The statement of the challenge (3). The angel delivers God's verdict on Ahaziah's spurning act. He *sends* Elijah to intercept the ambassadors and *supplies* him with a stunning challenge about repudiating God. It hits the nail on the head. Is it because no God is in Israel that the king would consult a heathen god? The challenge draws attention to the bottom line, what Ahaziah is really saying: God is not present and He is not powerful.

(2) The prediction of the king's death (4). Failing to acknowledge God and appeal to Him, Ahaziah will get what his own trusted resource supplies—no help. So, he will die leaning on a support that will hold him up no better than his lattice work did. James of a later day would say, "You do not have because you do not ask [in this case, of *God*]. You ask and do not receive, because you ask with wrong motives . . ." (James 4:2, 3).

(3) The report to the king (5–8). Ahaziah's delegation is back early, to his surprise. Their briefing around the bed on being inter-

cepted and sent home tingles the king's ears. A thought ticks in his brain that resistance to his will would probably be from a certain man. So he asks for a description of the challenger.

(4) The recognition of Elijah (8c). In a flash the king is sure. Elijah is the culprit who defies him. He is aroused to show that prophet how the big boys play the game!

The second challenge to the king's men (9, 10). Ahaziah in a show of power sent a captain and fifty men to demand that Elijah submit to him for a reckoning. Elijah discerned that the king's power was a defiance of *his* prophetic credentials, and above all the *God* who spoke through him. The captain had called him a "man of God," but Ahaziah and probably this underling did not really respect him as this.

Then came the show of real power. Elijah said that if he indeed was a man of God as this military head dubbed him, let God show this, causing fire to consume the fifty-one men. Fire came, as God sent it on Mount Carmel.

The call for judgment is actually prayer. It is an invoking of God's power, a summoning of Him to show His own authority against that of the king contesting Him. It is another among a great host of biblical cases where prayer is brief, to the point, issuing from faith and a person walking with God.

The third challenge to the king's men (11, 12). Ahaziah got the stunning report, but was stubbornly tenacious to save face. He would show Elijah who had the power to last. Another fifty-one men challenged the prophet and died by fire. Elijah prayed as he had when the first detachment came.

The fourth challenge to the king's men (13–18). Apparently stiff-necked, Ahaziah commanded a third force to get the job done. It was, no doubt, in a livid tone. The captain of these fifty men went as his king demanded, but he was not dense as his leader. He was a thinking man, a careful strategist. He came not in military bravado but in respectful humility. His words to Elijah are in reality a prayer, humbled to his authority and that of the God he served.

His prayer is in three aspects that appear in other scriptural prayers. One is petition for his life, for he perceives that the real power is not in his fighting men but in the God of Elijah. Twice he pleads for his safety. A second aspect is *intercession* to protect the men he leads. This aspect reflects his care for the men's welfare, an honorable sensitivity; it also shows a tender submission, for he sees the men under his charge as under Elijah's protective charge, "servants of yours." A third aspect is his *affirmation*. He declares the simple fact he knows, that men of both previous detachments have died before this prophet and his God, 102 precious lives.

How different is this third captain from the other two. They relied on human power. He depends on prayer, or the man of God (finally the God of the man) who hears prayer.

This time the angel gives counsel different to Elijah. Go with the captain. He honors a man of this prayerful attitude, and expects him to follow through sincerely.

Elijah goes from his two prayer sessions and the captain's prayer to confront the king. Once in the leader's chamber, he repeats God's first challenge. It includes the king's slap at God's person and power by courting a false god, and the sentence of his death ending this illness. Shortly after, the king does die, confirming the prophet's word.

Which principles are relevant? First, even an unbeliever can be convinced by evidence of God's power and pray for his own and others' safety. Yet this is no sure evidence in itself that the person has been spiritually saved (cf. pagan sailors in Jon. 1). Second, the passage is another of many testimonies that God is able to answer prayer in His will whether immediately or after a long time.

2 Kings 2:2, 4, 6, 9, 14

Tenacity of Prayer in a Crisis

The Difficulty (1a)

Men in the school of prophets received advance consciousness that God would soon take Elijah away into heaven. These students at two locations even ask the prophet's apprentice, Elisha, if he realizes this too, and he does (vv. 3, 5). It is a difficult burden for which Elisha needs comfort, for he has been the understudy of the great prophet since 1 Kgs. 19:19–21), and it would be painful to think of being without his awesome, respected mentor. He probably had the perception that God would take Elijah up by a whirlwind, a highly unusual phenomenon (v. 1). This could cause uncertainty as to exactly when, and also what, such a sudden parting would be like.

The Direction (1b–8)

Elijah knows the time is short, and God can take him soon. As the two men travel, Elijah seeks to commit Elisha to stay behind at some stage of the journey and permit him to go on alone to face privately the rendezvous when God will choose to take him.

They leave Gilgal. Elijah bids his friend to "Stay here please, for the Lord has sent me as far as Bethel." These words may be due to Elijah's humility in not wanting glory in another's eyes. But Elisha will not part with him. He prays, in an oath form, appealing to the realities that the Lord lives as witness and monitor of his resolution. His appeal also is that Elijah still lives in this world so that Elisha still has him. On this strong confirmation, "I will not leave you." He cannot bear to face losing his honored leader, but will stay with Elijah as long as he can. Loyalty, commitment, and love mingle.

Later, when they reach Bethel, men in a band that engages in prophetic ministry show that God has given them perception, too, that He intends to take Elijah (v. 3). They ask Elisha if he is aware that the Lord will take Elijah away (lit., "over you [your head]") today, apparently up into the heavens. Elisha replies that he as well has this realization, so they can "be still," that is, "do not press the matter, be quiet," for they need not rehearse what he already knows. His quieting them may also be a considerate act toward Elijah, for he has enough to think about without this being rehearsed.

Prophets show up at the three stages of Elijah's final earthly journey here. Scripture has borne witness to a prophetic ability as early as Abraham (Gen. 20:7) and Moses' day (Ex. 7:1; cf. Num. 12:6; Deut.

13:1, a false prophet; 34:10; and Judg. 6:8). A prophet quite early was called a "seer," as Samuel was (1 Sam. 9:6, 9, 11ff.). Samuel while still youthful was established to be a prophet (1 Sam. 3:20). A group of prophets existed in King Saul's day (10:5–6, 10–13), earlier in Elijah's career (1 Kgs. 18:13; 20:41), and in Elisha's ministry (6:1; 9:1–10).

Elijah again directs his companion, this time to remain behind at Bethel, for he himself has the Lord's guidance to go on to Jericho. It is sometime and somewhere later that God will take him; it is a departure he can experience by himself. Elisha repeats his prayerful appeal, invoking for his intent the confirming reality that the Lord lives and guarantees his inegrity. So, "I will not leave you" (4). One can be reminded of Ruth respectfully refusing to leave Naomi.

Farther on the trek, at Jericho, local men devoted to prophetic service ask Elisha the same question about awareness that those at Bethel had put to him (5). Elisha's reply again is also the same. He admits that this conviction seizes him, and they need not give him details that even now press him. Elijah directs him to stay at Jericho, for the Lord is leading the older prophet even farther, to Jordan. For the third time, the more recent prophet utters his prayer commitment (6). This being settled, the two travel on, and fifty in the prophetic ministry stay close as well, probably driven by curiosity, respect, and the ache of losing a great leader.

Elijah removes his robe, folds it, and strikes the Jordan waters. God causes the waters to part and a path dry-shod to open up in the river for the two prophets to cross. He had done this kind of miracle earlier for Israel when they crossed the Red Sea (Ex. 14), and when they invaded the promised land (Josh. 3). At the Red Sea, Moses had stretched above the waters the sin of his own leadership, not a mantle but his rod (Ex. 14:21).

The Desire (9, 10)

Once they two climb the far bank, another prayer passage occurs. Elijah prods Elisha to "Ask what I shall do for you before I am taken from you" (9). Then Elisha, out of awesome respect and value he sees spiritually in Elijah's ministry, replies with his request. It is to Elijah, but beyond him a petition to God who alone is able to fulfill it, and who works through Elijah. "Please," he appeals, "let a double portion of your spirit be upon me." He is like the youthful Solomon who did not ask for things of this world to gratify himself, but for spiritual good to guide God's people (1 Kgs. 3). He desires to be used of God.

The Demonstration (11–15)

That verse 9 seems ultimately to be a prayer through Elijah to *God* appears in the verses that follow. And still a further prayer occurs in verse 14. After God has taken Elijah up (11–12), Elisha picks up the departed prophet's mantle that had dropped from his rising body, ready to strike the river waters as Elijah had exemplified (8), and cried out in prayer. "Where is the Lord, the God of Elijah?" He is available for this *God* to give him the answer in his petition of verse 9. His prayer is one example of praying to God in the aspect of a respectful and honorable question. Demonstration that God answers is dramatic in the next statement. "And when he had struck the waters, they were divided here and there [into two walls]; and Elisha crossed over. The watching prophets, taking in these miracles involving one prophet, then the other, are sure when they exclaim, "The spirit of Elijah rests on Elisha" (15). This is further evidence that the one who answers the prayer of verse 9 is God, the source of Elijah's confidence.

The various prophets, those spiritually receptive, would have something of the spirit of Elijah, and work for the Lord, in His power. Elisha would have not just the portion they had, but even a doubling, and be in a special, great capacity of ministry. The way God would use this man of the prayer here (vv. 2, 4, 6, 9, 14) in subsequent ministries from 2:16 to 13:21 would exhibit the answer to prayer.

Principles for prayer leap readily from the verses. First, whether in an oath or not, a believer can appeal to what the Lord is as his confidence and surety, then follow through on what he pledges. Integrity counts, and God can back it up (1 Sam. 2:30). Second, a mind honed by God can rightly ask God for great things and expect great things from Him, as in verse 9. Third, we can pray in faith laying hold of the same One, "the God of Elijah," then find His presence and power. This is not necessarily in the same form as given to Elisha, but whatever is the will of God in His plan for our lives.

Fourth, when God takes away one of His servants, He can help others to go on with His work.

2 Kings 2:24

Prayer in a Curse of Judgment

The Circumstance

Since his prayer judgments on the king's soldiers in Chapter 1, Elijah has prepared Elisha his successor. God has snatched Elijah up into heaven in a chariot of fire by a whirlwind (2:11). The astonished Elisha has picked up his tutor's fallen mantle, and smitten the Jordan's waters crying "Where is . . . the God of Elijah?" He has seen the waters divide for his crossing, and rejoined other prophets. He has even worked a second miracle in making bad water drinkable at Jericho.

Now Elisha is approaching Bethel.

His Climb to Bethel

He is ascending by the road to the town when he hears voices and sees a gang of young men mocking him.

The Chiding of the Hoodlums (23)

Tough youths are showing deep disrespect for him as a prophet of God by chanting a slogan. "Go up, you baldhead; go up, you baldhead!" they repeat in razzing tones.

The gang is a large, apparently more than forty-two (24). Their scorn for a prophet who is worthy of high respect, and by association the God he represents, reveals what today would be called a hoodlum mentality. They are utterly without a sense of honor for what is right, and emboldened by gang bravado.

The "baldhead" jeer may be in contempt for literal baldness, though this is not certain. Some believe that it refers to a marking associated with being a prophet, and the slogan meant as a slam. The chant, "go up" could just refer to Elisha's ascent to Bethel, aimed at deriding his work as a prophet there. Students of Scripture sometimes link it with the news of Elijah's having "gone up" (cf. 2:11). If so, the gang is prodding Elisha to show them he can "go up" too, mouthed as a jibe in disbelief that what he had reported could really have happened. It is, then, a swipe belittling God's ability.

The young men (not children), in any event, are not to be defended as unfairly treated. They poked fun at God in high contempt as Ahaziah had degraded Him. They reflect the saturation of sin in an Israel ripe for judgment.

The Curse from the Lord (24)

Elisha's response is to pray. Four phases relate to the prayer.

The aspect. It is prayer in a curse. Elisha invokes God's judgment on the gang members. It is a quick calling of God to act, right to the point.

The attitude. It is in anger, apparently—not sinful anger, but anger at sin against God and His word. It is no more unloving than God's bolts of fire against 102 men who defied Him, or letting Ahaziah die, or slaying false prophets in 1 Kings 18. If one sees the respect due to God and how He and His man are maligned here, the wonder would be if Elisha or God did nothing. Whether immediately or later, God will deal severe judgment to all who make light of Him (cf. Rev. 20:11–15).

The authority. Elisha does not say this in his own authority. Like Elijah and other true prophets, he was in proper contact with the Lord and sensitive to pray according to His will. God has as much right to deal firmly here as in Chapter 1 or any number of other times.

The answer. When God answers prayer by judgment here, He is not as severe as on Ahaziah's men. They died, never to defy Him again; these gang members are lashed and chewed up but are alive to learn from the lesson. God sends two she bears to do this. He made animals and can control them. He drew some to the ark, multiplied Jacob's herd, spoke through Balaam's donkey, and inclined cows to pull the cart with the Ark from Philistia.

Elisha went on from this occasion of prayer to visit Mount Carmel and Samaria. He would be near at hand to be used by God in 3:11.

A guideline is natural here. When people who show sneering contempt for God and His godly servant invite His morally just dealing with their sin, this will surely come sooner or later (cf. Jesus in Luke 13:1–5).

2 Kings 3:11, 14

Prayer Sought from Elisha, and His Oath

This is one of many instances in the Bible where men seek to pray second-hand. They ask someone they know is close to God to pray on their behalf. Jehoshaphat did this through Micaiah in 1 Kings 22 and does it by Elisha here. Jeremiah's prayers were often sought in this way (37:3; 42:1–3).

The Pact Between Judah and Israel (1–9)

Ahab's son Jehoram, succeeding him, planned to attack Moab for not continuing tribute gifts (cf. 4, 5). He summoned Jehoshaphat of Judah as an ally to bolster his forces, and the latter agreed. No seeking of God's will in prayer is mentioned.

The Problem the Army Faces (9b, 10)

Together with the army of Edom, Israel and Judah penetrate into Moabite territory. They are in distress over a problem of no water either for the soldiers or the cattle herded along for food.

No word has indicated God's leading to invade, or any prayer to discern His will. However, Jehoram thinks of the Lord now, yet in a spirit of criticizing Him for the predicament. His suspicion is that God positioned the three kings to desert them into the hands of Moabites.

The Prayer that Elisha Offers (11–15)

Jehoshaphat, as he did in an earlier alliance with Israel (1 Kings 22), asks for a prophet of the Lord they can call on. A soldier of Israel advises the kings that Elisha is present. His slant on things honors the prophet: Elisha had poured water on Elijah's hands. The point is his closeness and service as a trainee to the revered prophet, and by implication, his potential to carry on such work.

Judah's king is sure, right away, that the Lord's word is with Elisha to be their man. So the kings travel to meet with Elisha.

The man of God greets them with distrust of Israel's king. He had God's word on that. Elijah had predicted divine judgment on Ahab and his house (1 Kgs. 21:19–26). Elisha also recalls that Ahab and Jezebel, this king's parents, had favored their false prophets. Waving this distrust aside without any word of repentance over its cause, Israel's leader voices again the dark design he suspects God has drawn to oppose the three kings' chances.

The past pattern of Ahab and this son's slam at God incite Elisha's further disdain (14). Recoiling at Jehoram, an evil king before him, he utters a prayer oath. His appeal summons or invokes the fact that the Lord lives before whom he stands in prayer and all ministry. He swears by His life in a very strong statement that if it were not for his respect toward Jehoshaphat, he would not look at Jehoram or give him the time of day. He would dismiss the visitors and not be at their beck and call.

An unusual thing occurs. Elisha, willing to seek the Lord for the kings, asks for a minstrel to play. The music possibly soothes him from his mood of distrust toward Jehoram; at any rate God uses it to prepare him to be sensitive to counsel that will aid this contingent. Prayer is not further mentioned, but Elisha surely prays, expressly asking to receive the Lord's message to suit the occasion. Then he feels the hand of the Lord on him and hears Him speak.

The Provision for The Victory (16–27)

Three steps indicate God's goodness in helping the alliance.

The appearance of water (16–23). God asks the armies to dig many trenches in the valley. He promises to fill these with water without using wind or rain. Provision to quench their thirst by a miracle is easy for Him to do. Surely it is for a God who created the heavens and the earth and all the water to start with. But satisfaction with water is only the beginning of His kindness to the kings now; he will also effect a surrender by the Moabites.

The next morning an abundant supply of water flowed from Edom to fill the trenches. God alone was the explanation. Moab's soldiers advanced to fight, saw the hue of blood in the water, decided the invaders had slain one another, and boldly surged on.

The ascendance of the invaders (24–26). Fighters of Israel leaped to the attack, routed Moab, and spoiled their cities, lands, springs, and trees. A desperate Moabite bid for 700 soldiers to drive a wedge through to the Edomites failed.

The act that stopped the war (27). Moab's King Mesha made the most desperate move. He offered his son, heir to his throne, in sacrifice hoping to win help from his god, Chemosh, for his culture put stock in child sacrifice.

Why did wrath come on Israel, then? Some propose that Judeans were so angry at the child sacrifice God hated (Deut. 12:31) that they withdrew from Israel. Israel had drawn them to an invasion that led to this horror, and they left the battle that was already decided. Or it may mean that Judah in fury abandoned the effort before Israel could conquer even Mesha and force vassalage as fully as it desired.

How does prayer fit in? A man respected as in touch with the Lord secured an answer that gave victory. God used the answer to demonstrate by a miracle His almighty power to do the impossible. This should have challenged men of all the alliance armies to trust Him alone, as God, by a miracle, changed Naaman's loyalty (5:15, 17). Prayer gained not only a supply (water) that only God could explain, but a great success in battle. The God who answers had won again over a false god who could do nothing, as He had won by giving fire when the false prophets' god was not able.

Reflect on a principle. Keep in mind that God is able to do great things even thought impossible. But also recall, from examples in His Word, that it can be His purpose in one given case to work a miracle and in another to work via some natural means. He has the right to meet each case in His own wisdom, and it is our servant place to trust Him in any event.

2 Kings 4:28, 30, 33–34

Prayer for God to Raise a Dead Son

God uses a praying Elisha to restore a boy to life much as He had used a praying Elijah to gain a child's life (1 Kgs. 19).

The Crisis of a Son's Death (8–32)

A stop in the prophet's itinerary is at Shunem, about seven miles east of Megiddo in the hills above the Valley of Jezreel in Israel. Some focus is placed on a woman's prominence, then her provision and her problem.

The woman's prominence. She is called a "great" or "prominent" woman, and her husband is with her.

She is "great" in several possible details: in *hospitality*, supplying food and a special room for Elisha and his servant Gehazi to lodge; in *hardiness*, being a woman of action and risk in a time of danger (22–24); in *devotion*, motivated to serve the Lord by serving the visitors (9–10); and *gratitude* to God (37).

The woman's provision. Elisha is impressed by her graciousness, and in return, prays God will supply the one prize that will mean the most to her humanly, a son. The intercession itself is not mentioned, but once the prophet is aware of her longing, he seeks God's provision for her. He can then promise her a son, and this word from the Lord comes true.

The woman's problem. After the son grows for a few years and is able to visit his father during harvest, a terrible headache smites him. He dies, and the mother carries him up to Elisha's guest room, then asks a servant to take her by donkey to locate Elisha. She is daring, compelling the man to run the donkey furiously to gain help from God via His man of prayer.

Prayer is probably the intent in 4:28. What the woman says in her heartbreak voiced in questions is no doubt beginning to broach her longing for the main thing—that God will restore her son. She comes to Elisha, yet as in many passages where people come to a person close to God, the spirit is to reach via the person to the God who is able.

Verse 30, as well, is prayer in the form of an oath. The woman makes a pledge, a strong one, appealing to the reality of God's life and Elisha's life. She intends with determination to stay right with this prophet as he goes to help her son.

Elisha's Calling on the God of Life (33–37)

Shutting himself in with the boy upstairs, Elisha prayed.

His supplication to God. Only three were inside the closed door. The son lay cold and lifeless on the prophet's guest bed. Elisha exercised himself in an agony of prayer. And the hearing God was present.

Much was at stake. The woman's greatness in the many ways might have pushed at Elisha's thoughts, may have been a part of the prayer. "Lord, you know how she . . ." could well have been an *affirmation* as he cried out. It is so human, so natural, so frequent in Scripture. Also tugging at his heart could be the thought that it was *his* promise from God that gave her this boy; and the mother honored him as a "man of God." When she had reached him with her heartbreak to summon him here now, she had reminded him. Hope for a son was *his* initiative; she had urged that he not build up her hopes to let her down (28). He had not; God had not.

Now the room was filled with the soft—or loudly passionate?—pleading of a man who knew what it was to call on the God of the impossible. Elisha had asked for judgment on troublemakers defying God, and God had brought it. He had asked for water where there was no water, and streams had flowed. He had asked for a son when the woman's husband was old and could give no son, and God had given a son against the odds. Now Elisha interceded for the impossible again—life from the dead.

His stretching on the boy. As Elijah had done, Elisha presses his warm body to the cold, pallid body. God can even use means when He chooses—He can work without means or in cooperation with them—and the prophet now did all he could to participate with the Lord. The boy's body grew warm.

His success in restoring the life. Elisha went downstairs, walked in the house a single time, pacing back and forth, possibly praying even in this. He kept at his vigil. Again he climbed to the boy and stretched his body upon him to bring warmth.

A sneeze . . . ahhh, praise the Lord! Another sneeze . . . a third . . . seven of them! Elisha bent over the boy, his heart pounding, his eyes moist, his mind racing with gratitude. The boy's eyelids flickered, he opened his eyes, alive from the dead, and stared up at the man of God.

Praise God! Elisha felt like leaping for joy. He may have. Spinning, he reached the stairs, shouted down to Gehazi. "Call this Shunammite." The woman seemed catapulted up to her son. Something wonderful had happened, it must be. She burst into the room, and her eyes fell on her beloved. Elisha, eyes still glistening, spoke in quiet but confident invitation. "Take up your son."

She gasped, felt the rush of emotion, and was filled with gratitude. She fell at the feet of God's man, man of prayer, and bent to the floor in worship of the Lord. Her heart was lost in wonderment at God and respect for such a man as this.

Principles of prayer are evident. One is to pray believing God, as Elisha surely did for the son to be born. As a prophet he was even a special instrument to receive God's word. Today, the one who would pray in step with God needs to fill the life with proper meditations on His word. God wants the prayer warrior to believe that nothing is too hard for Him, but He works according to His will. He aims for the asking to be in submission to the plan He desires. Second, be flexible since not every situation is the same. In some cases God has brought the dead back to life. In many, He does not. Third, realize that a time out can be all right, and then a new surge in prayer as when Elisha left the boy and soon came back to pray again.

2 Kings 5:11, 16, 18, 20

Prayer in a Leper's Cleansing

This is the famous account of Naaman, drawn to Israel by a girl's testimony that God was able and leaving Israel with a transformed life. Prayer plays a strategic role in this.

His Problem—Leprosy (1)

A decorated man of war is front and center here. Naaman was captain of the Syrian army under King Ben-hadad and the man the king depended on most highly (18; cf. 7:2, 17). He had carved out a career winning towering respect from the king and all-around admiration. For as a field general he had led the military in victory for his nation. Besides, he was a fighting man par excellence, a man's man. He had reached the top, and one might think he did not have a need in the world.

All this, "but . . . ," the verse says. Sometimes the world swings on that awesome word. It does for Naaman here. He had it all, "but he was a leper." No cure had been found. His form of leprosy was not one that kept him from contact with others. That was well, but still he was a leper.

His Prospect for Healing (2–8)

Humanly speaking he knew no cure and was locked in to this as his future. Then a prospect for healing came. It began with the testimony of an Israelite girl the Syrians captured in war, now a servant to Naaman's wife and a girl who cared for this master.

One day the girl expressed trustful words that beamed a ray of hope in that household. She sighed before her mistress, "Oh, how I wish my master were with the prophet in Samaria! If he were, he would cure him." It was a testimony, and it would be worth more than life to Naaman. In it were care, hope, respect for a man of God, and faith. She had been old enough to hear the stories while in Israel of the man Elisha . . . water where no water could be . . . life where only death reigned. "Oh," she almost sobbed, "I wish my master. . . ."

The wife snatched at that. It had a ring of truth. She could hardly wait to tell her husband, see what he thought. He heard, fondled the idea, took it before his king and friend. Ben-hadad smiled. Stories had drifted back to him too. Why not? Yes, why not? He cared for this captain. "Get yourself ready, go there," he approved. "You'll have my letter of courtesy to the king of Israel."

His Preconceptions Hindering Blessing (9–13)

Naaman finally stood before Elisha's house. The prophet, who knew he was coming, had time to pray (cf. 8) though this detail is not recorded. He must have prayed, wanting Naaman to see God's power, and sent a messenger out, probably Gehazi (10, 20). Possibly Elisha held back to heighten the captain's sense of submitting to God's power. Even if His man were not present, God was able to heal. The power was in Him, not in the servant.

The counsel was astounding to Naaman. It was a great letdown, and he felt put off, given a ridiculous way of healing. His mind felt rebuffed by the absurdity: "Go and wash in the Jordan seven times, and your flesh shall be restored to you and you shall be clean." And he had come all this long, tiring way to hear only this! This—and his very welfare depended on a way that would work! It met none of his preconceptions of a high-powered method of working a wonder. The prophet could not be taking seriously his position or his need.

The way Naaman had expected is in verse 11. Prayer leaps into the picture here. The Syrian had felt that this great prophet would "stand and call on the name of the Lord his God, and wave his hand over the place [his body], and cure the leprosy." A prayer, a set of motions, and presto, all was done. But he had not seen that.

Naaman fumed at his driver. "We've wasted our time. Let's go back home. Why, who does he think I am? I'm a thinking man. I can read through things that don't add up. A man would expect some fanfare that is fitting, like, he'd come out and meet me, stand, and say an impressive prayer calling on the Lord, his God. Then, he'd wave his hand over the place where I was, cover me, and the leprosy would vanish. Instead, we get this nonsense.

"Can you imagine the absurdity? It's too simple. Go dip in the Jordan. Humpf! As if we don't have rivers back home, without this journey, the Abanah and Pharpar. The Jordan! Why, if I could be cleansed of this leprosy in a river, our rivers have all the waters of Israel beat. Oh, what a dance! We might as well be on our way."

Perhaps Naaman started to climb into his chariot. Some in his caravan came over as he settled down. They spoke respectfully in quiet, caring tones. "My father, suppose the prophet told you to do a great thing. You'd have tried it, wouldn't you? Why can't it make sense, then, when he says 'Wash, and be clean'?"

Naaman sat and pondered this for a moment. He was grateful for friends who took his well-being to heart. He had cooled off a bit. "Well, he had come all this way. Why not? Why not just do it the way the prophet of the Lord said? Give it a chance."

He looked from the counselors to the driver. "Sure. Take the way to the Jordan, and let's make good time."

His Pursuit of the Solution (14–17)

The compliance (14). The captain stepped from his chariot, walked down to the Jordan, and did just what God's man said. He dipped seven times. Number five . . . six . . . well, he was almost there, nothing yet. The prophet had said seven. One more . . . seven. He came up, wiped the water out of his eyes, blinked, and stared at his flesh.

The cleansing (14). His own heart erupted with a chorus of voices of his companions on the bank. It was true! He stared again, gasped his astonishment, and felt friends grabbing him. They danced on the bank for sheer joy.

He felt like a young boy again . . . new, cleansed, a spring in his step, an elation within.

The conversion (15–17). Possibly all Naaman could say as he went back to the chariot was, over and over, "The Lord, He is God, the Lord, He is God" (cf. 15). His caravan made its way back to Elisha's house. The captain was bursting to tell the prophet, and more. Elisha himself came out to meet him this time.

(1) The transformation. The Syrian now was broken, submissive. His mind no longer was filled with his own preconceptions on how it had to be. He had trusted the Lord to do it His way, and He had done it. His face was radiant as he spoke to Elisha. "Behold now, I know that there is no God in all the earth, but in Israel." Elisha smiled too. The visitor had come a long way, found healing, found God—after God had found him in Syria.

(2) The thanksgiving. Naaman is so grateful that he wants to present a gift. Elisha stands firm; he is not in this for money, and what Naaman had discovered is entirely of grace, free from God. He must not tarnish the gift aspect in any way. His answer is itself a kind of oath prayer, an affirmation of God's very life as a guarantee of his pledge. "As the Lord lives, before whom I stand [in prayer and availability to speak His word], I will take nothing."

Of course Naaman is thankful to the Lord, as his statement in verse 14 makes clear. He only wishes to give to Elisha in gratitude to him also for his agency in the blessing from God.

(3) The testimony (17). It is a clear-cut one, consistent with the transformation in verse 14. Would Elisha permit him to haul back two mules' load of earth? Naaman does not worship the earth, rather the Lord of the earth (14). But he wants to build an altar using soil from this area where God changed his life so dramatically. On that altar he will present burnt offering to the Lord, to Him alone, never to other gods. He now knows who is worthy.

His Prayer for Pardon for Duties at Home (18)

His appeal for pardon. Naaman poses this scenario to the prophet. Back at home, King Ben-hadad counts on him to show respect for his king and carry out his duty graciously. This will entail even bowing in courtesy to the Rimmon worship, yet no longer recognizing Rimmon as God in his heart.

Elisha's answer of peace. Elisha realizes that the Lord looks on the heart (1 Sam. 16:7), and by Him actions are weighed (2:3). God will discern Naaman's genuine motives. In worshiping God in truth, the Syrian convert is assured of peace (cf. Isa. 26:3).

Which principles of prayer are pertinent here? As suggested, Elisha surely was in contact with the Lord as he knew Naaman was en route to his home (8). A servant of God need not invariably pray publicly just because certain others may think, as Naaman, that it has to be this way. One may choose to pray only in secret, as is most likely here, in some situations. That God is pleased is the approval His servant prizes, even if people take exception (11). Others do not finally have authority to dictate how and when one prays. God's leading is the issue, and variety is possible.

Prayer occurs again in verse 18, for confession is the essence. In Naaman's purity of motive to worship only the Lord, it is not really necessary. But tenderness seeking to please God, and not offend Him, is vital in effective prayer and all spiritual living. Third, Naaman resolves to honor God alone with burnt offerings (17). Genuine prayer with consuming the whole offering each new time would involve devoting the sacrificing life itself anew entirely to the Lord, Naaman could, without hypocrisy, respect Syrian religious forms in courtesy to others. But he would worship only God in his *heart* in public and in private. An example of God's servant honoring Him even amid duties to others opposing Him is Obadiah (1 Kgs. 18:3, 4, 13). This principle is also true of Daniel (6:10), Nehemiah for a time (2:1–4) and Esther.

Verse 20 has prayer once again. Elisha's servant, Gehazi, has no doubt heard his master's refusal to take a present (15–16). Now, driven by greed, he pursues a plan to slip away, catch up with Naaman's caravan, and get the treasure for himself. He puts this plot into words that in essence are a form of prayer; if not a prayer to God, God still knows the deceit and avarice.

Gehazi appeals to the very reality that God lives as a voucher that he will get his hands on riches.

He misuses the Lord in this.

Principles can even be added to those mingled above. First, if God has given clear directions for a person to follow, relevant to his day, he should follow these and insist on his own preference. Second, God can answer prayer by the ordinary or the extraordinary, for His infinite capacity affords Him this liberty.

2 Kings 6:17

Prayer When Surrounded by the Enemy

The Plot of Syrians to Capture Elisha (8–14)

God's amazing help to His people through this man filled with His word and prayer has one of its finest examples here. Elisha moves from being surrounded by the enemy to seeing *them* surrounded by God's army and later surrounded by Israelites. The passage is a vivid illustration of almighty resources that prayer can call upon.

The detection of Syrian strategy (8–10). King Ben-hadad of the enemy cannot make a move against Israel without some informer alerting those in Samaria of his exact strategy. God gives the word to Elisha of enemy strategy, and he tips off Israel so that it is ready to avoid Syrian maneuvers.

The demand of the Syrian sovereign (11–14). Suspecting a traitor, Ben-hadad is enraged to find and execute him. An advisor briefs the king that the intelligence leak is not in Syria but in Israel. Elisha gets the information from his God and tells Israel's king what Ben-hadad secretly devises in his bedroom! The Syrian commander in chief is still livid. He slaps Elisha on his "hit list," rather his "get list." Get the prophet, bring him to headquarters, and he will not be in Israel to inform his king. A massive army is on the move to Dothan to make Elisha its prisoner.

The Panic of Elisha's Servant (15, 16)

The cause of his fear—the enemy's presence. Rising early, the prophet's servant, possibly the Gehazi of 2 Kings 5, is smitten with panic at seeing a band of enemy horses and chariots locking in the city. He scrambles inside, or shouts the alarm to Elisha, wringing his hands and at his wits' end. This time, he swam, his master had not gotten an alert ahead of time. This time there was no hope.

"Alas, my master," he wailed out his desperation, "What now?"

The confidence of Elisha—the Lord's presence. Reaction on the prophet's part is not one of going to pieces but a study in peace. He possesses a believer's calm composure banking on resources in God that are sufficient (cf. Isa. 26:3). He has the cool poise to counsel two things. This is especially remarkable in what is probably to him and his servant the most terrifying trial they have yet faced.

(1) Cancel the alarm. "Do not fear." He says to cancel the alarm that elicits the most frequent exhortation in all of the Bible. "Do not fear" begins with Genesis 15:1 and occurs more often than any other counsel, for trials do besiege the heart, and their solutions are urgent. Is it fool's advice not to fear here, or in Genesis?

The answer is that it is wise counsel if said in balance with Elisha's second word, but makes no sense if dependent only on human factors.

(2) Count on the Adequate. This explains Elisha's calm, puts a new face on everything, transforms a trial into a triumph. The explanation why the servant can cancel the alarm begins with the word "for." For those on our side are more than those with the enemy. Here, as is soon to be seen, the resource that upholds Elisha and his servant is from God. The same essence is true in Genesis 15:1 and in countless other situations. To Abraham, God said, "for I am your shield and your exceeding great reward."

Count on the Adequate, then. The old song phrases it this way, "Be not dismayed whate'er betide, God will take care of you."

Three Prayers of Elisha (17–23)

Significantly, the man who is perceptive of the resources that assure safety is the person steeped in prayer. Three prayers follow fairly soon. Elisha must have already been prayerfully in touch with the Adequate, as the previous context suggests. He knew of Syria's movements even when the king first concocted them (12). He also had his eyes on God when the forces were approaching and encircling the city. The servant's word was not a wild alarm to shock him (16; cf. 1 Pet. 4:12).

Prayer ahead of time as well as prayer in the midst of trial is God's way. God's servant who lives in prayer, an all-the-time reality (Eph. 6:18; Phil. 4:6), is a person living in resources when the enemy closes in. As Elisha was in God's word and God's word was in him; believers today must be in His word to be sensitive to the stratagems of the enemy and prepared when they are launched. When one is ready like this with the word as his habit he can take the sword of the Spirit—God's word wielded relevantly in a given situation—and pray in the Spirit. He can lay hold of victory over the devil, his demons, their devices, their darts, and the day that is evil (Eph. 6:10–20).

Elisha who is ready in prayer ahead of the crisis is also ready in prayer in the midst of the crisis. To three exhibits of this the attention now turns.

Prayer for sight of spiritual defenses (17). It is a simple prayer, to the great Lord, direct, concise, and in faith that itself already sees Him who is invisible. "Open his eyes that he may see." Before, the servant in frantic alarm had seen only the enemy, how big this was, and how impossible safety appeared. A grand old song in prayer looks rather to God, and cries, "Fill all my vision."

God answers Elisha's prayer. The man lived in His presence, lived with answered prayers. This was part of a whole lifestyle. He was "on praying ground." And here "the Lord opened the servant's eyes, and he saw." Before, his vision had been overwhelmed by the size of the enemy; now he was able to see the size of God's hosts watching over the two. Incredible, for "the mountain was full of horses and chariots of fire all around Elisha," and all around the servant! God's resource to one can be as good as His resource to another. Some know astounding resources; others can know them too. The seeing *can* open up to the one who is looking.

Greater is He who is for us than he who is against us, the servant now saw long before the Apostle John wrote that truth (1 John 4:4; cf. 5:4, 5). Truly Elisha's attendant could cancel his alarm and count on the Adequate! He could feel as the psalmist would express it, "The angel of the Lord encamps around those who fear Him, And rescues them" (Ps. 34:7).

Let the thought not be lost that the reason the servant saw was because the Lord opened his eyes to see. And in the way the Lord had given to Elisha, the reason why He opened the servant's eyes was because He was answering another's prayer! Any who read this, and take it to heart, can also have a ministry praying and seeing the Lord open eyes.

The second prayer becomes relevant with a new phase of the trial. Syrian soldiers were coming down to the two men, not seeing the resources Elisha and his servant saw. The enemy was getting closer when Elisha prayed.

Prayer for smiting them with blindness (18, 19). Again the petition is short, not padded; it is definite, and to the Lord. Is Elisha cruel for asking blindness on the enemy? Of course not.

It was a temporary thing. They would be kept utterly safe, and God would give their sight back (20). The ones who were cruel were the Syrians bent on snatching Elisha away to a king enraged at him, and Elisha would advise kind treatment of these (21–23).

God's answer, temporary blindness, came in a flash before the army could even lay a hand on the prophet.

Elisha tells the Syrians that this is not the way nor the city, but he can lead them to the man they seek. Is he resorting to a lie after being such a man of God's truth? Is it okay to pray successfully, then speak falsehood? This *was* the way to Elisha. Elisha may have meant that this is not the way or place in *God's* plan for the invaders *to see* their prey. They had *their* plans, but God had *His* that would win out. Elisha's intent fits the emphasis of the verse before and the verse after about their *seeing*. The enemy indeed would not see Elisha here, but would in Samaria. There they would find the man they had come to seek. The explanation also fits the fact that, in the whole account, what *God* does or wills is the greater point. He knows Syrian strategy, helps His people, protects His two servants, and answers prayer. The way and city of *His* choosing is the focus of the man committed to His word.

Prayer for sight in captivity (20–23). Elisha led the enemy army right into Samaria. There, with Israelites surrounding them and set for defense, he prayed in his regular direct way. The intercession for removal of the blindness gained God's answer, arguably the greatest shock of the soldiers' lives.

The enemy received protection and pleasure, captivity, or death. A great feast replaced their travel hunger before the Israelites released them to go home safely.

Now peruse principles that are pertinent. First, God and His host of celestial servants are really present, even if not physically visible for believers (cf. Matt. 28:20; John 14:21–23; 2 Tim. 4:17; Heb. 1:14). Second, God's heavenly hosts can appear to believers if and when God chooses to make this happen, for with God nothing good is impossible. Third, when a believer has real power in prayer as a steadfast pattern of life, he will be ready for prayer during a sudden crisis.

Fourth, by faith one can see God as greater than all the enemy. Fifth, if we ourselves walk in a real life of prayer in which we see God in faith, we can help others see Him.

2 Kings 6:31

An Evil Oath by an Evil King

The kind of prayer a person prays in a crisis may be a mirror of what his whole life is. Such is the case with King Joram.

The Peril of a Siege (24–29)

A new Syrian invasion results in a siege of Samaria that reduces the entrapped people to utter desperation. A factor in the crisis is a famine that has caused a drastic shortage of food. The extremity was so intense that outrageous prices were slapped on anything that might drive back starvation, a donkey's head or even a dove's dung!

King Joram toured his city's pathetic pain. He did not realize how grievous conditions really were. A woman spotted him walking on the wall, his vantage point for seeing, and screeched out her anguish for help. He replied that if *God* did not help her, where would *he* find food? At least he had that right, and it should have turned him to repentance (cf. 2 Chr. 7:14). Then he paused to ask what her problem was.

A heart-wrenching story poured from her lips. Conditions had grown beyond belief. She had agreed to cook her son as food one day and had gone through with the terrible affair. A neighbor woman had promised her son the next day but had gone back on her word and hidden him.

Joram probably felt a strange sensation clutching at his stomach, a shudder raking his body, and a foul taste in his mouth. He felt like retching. The passage shows his feelings. He ripped his royal robe in consternation and people below caught a glimpse of sackcloth underneath covering him. He was angry, intensely angry, and he took his frustration out on Elisha.

Why the prophet? The king probably traces the siege torments on Israel's capital to Elisha's act that caused the Syrians to lose face when he led them into Israelite custody. The Syrians were vehement to exact revenge. Not only that, but the Syrians had been in Joram's grasp to kill them all, and Elisha had advised to let them off with kindness. Joram now construed that as a treacherous cruelty that brought on his people the Syrian boomerang. Disturbed by his people's agonies and their idea that he did nothing, he sees one act as his most shining gesture for Israel. Kill the prophet who helped the enemy, hurt the king's subjects, and put the king in a bad light. A further reason for wanting Elisha's head appears under "self-will" following.

Passion can manifest as goodness honoring God or evil serving selfish interests. Joram's is evil, a misuse of prayer by craving his own will, not God's. He prays in an oath, invoking God's death sentence on himself if he fails to have Elisha's head whacked off that very day. God could not approve his prayer spawned from sin, according to a principle Psalm 66:18 crystallizes. His blessing would come rather from the very man the king wanted to execute.

The Proclamation of Elisha (6:32–7:2)

The spirit in which it comes (32). This is an atmosphere of consultation. Elders meet with the prophet, reasonably seeking hope from God to resolve Israel's crisis. The spirit is one featuring the word of the Lord and prayer depending on Him for His will, as fits the situation.

The sight that accompanies it (32). Elisha not only knew the plans the Syrian king made in his bedroom privacy (6:12) but also knew the Israelite king's scheme to snatch him away and bring him to his death. His prophetic sight (like an inward TV screen) gives him a newsreel as the arresting officer is hastening to his door. The elders ought to have been impressed by the sight he tells them ahead of time, evidence that indeed the Lord alone was their hope.

The safety that fits with it (32). Elisha advises keeping the door braced to prevent the officer's entrance.

The self-will that resists it (33). Joram's officer, facing the door's barrier, yells the king's message to be heard inside. Joram wants the prophet for a reckoning. He perceives that Samaria's calamity resulted from the Lord's heavy hand, and Elisha should have produced a solution. Possibly the prophet had given some unrecorded prediction that God would protect the city. Since his word was not coming true, Joram could wait no longer and would try some other method (cf. 1:2). In the meantime, Elisha deserves punishment for traitorous and false ministry.

The substance that comprises it (7:1, 2). Two parts make up this prophecy of God's action during the emergency.

(1) Prosperity for the city (1). The word of the Lord guarantees abundant provisions by tomorrow at this hour. In some way God will reverse Samaria's situation so fully that instead of drastic shortage (6:25) delightful surplus will prevail. Finely ground flour and barley will be so plentiful that their price will plummet. In turning

around such a grave situation, fulfillment of such a promise would be a great miracle and authenticate God and His prophet.

(2) Perishing of a doubter. The visiting officer protests in distrust that such a thing could occur. He notes that even if God could make windows in heaven to drop down provisions, abundance like this could not meet the need. And such a remedy just cannot happen in twenty-four hours.

God's servant gives two replies to the disbelieving aide. First, he assures him that the official's eyes will see it. Second, he exempts him from enjoying the miracle. Discrediting what God's power can do is a great insult, belittling Him, reducing His honor of Godhood and truthfulness. Unbelief is not a slight sin, it is a serious one, and it can infect others with its poison. God is firmly against it. So He did to ten scouts and their followers, barring them from the promised land (Num. 13, 14). Disbelief in God's Son and His salvation can cost an eternity of enjoyment with God (John 3:36).

The Protection by the Lord (7:3–20)

Elisha's ministry of prayer and proclamation issues, as he guaranteed, in God's miracle. Four leprous men have been first to detect it. Venturing out to the enemy camp knowing they can die in Samaria but live if shown mercy out there, they find a deserted campsite. Food, clothes, and treasures have been abandoned by a fleeing host.

The lepers may not have known about Elisha's prediction, and certainly did not act by faith on it. But, once they come upon great abundance, they are commendable for sharing the good news to attract others to enjoy the supply.

God's explanation for the Syrian flight appears in verse 6. He works deliverance by doing what in man's eyes is against all natural law. Of course, He made the universe and its laws, and is able to manage these to serve His will. He caused the besieging soldiers to hear an awesome sound as if a vast army was approaching as Israel's ally to wipe out the Syrians. Such panic seized them that they left all that might slow retreat and cost them their lives—tents, horses, gold, clothes, food, and so forth.

The rich plunder brought into Samaria results in Elisha's illustrations being fulfilled. Flour and barley are so easy to obtain that what is sold goes at a low price (1, 20). Joram's disbelieving officer, stationed at the gate to oversee handling of spoils, dies as people trample him. He *sees* results of the miracle but does not live to *enjoy* them, just as God's prophet predicted.

The man King Joram wanted to behead for failing Israel is Israel's greatest human benefactor. As mentioned, the scenario includes Joram's sinful prayer that God could not honor (6:31). It contrasts this with Elisha's faithful prayer/proclamation (6:32–7:2) that God could endorse. The passage underscores the principle that God answers prayer in harmony with His faithful will.

Principles, again, abound. First, God distinguishes prayer in a vow out of an evil heart, and can deal with this in His sure way. Second, evil people can see evidence that a praying servant of God shows power from God and still shut this out in willful unbelief. Third, those who come upon great abundance that God allows should pass on blessing by sharing with others in need. Today we can share God's riches through praying, giving His good news of a greater deliverance in eternal salvation and life that is transformed now. We also can share temporal provisions.

Fourth, a person of prayer can minister help in normal times or situations of special pressure. In either venue they can make a difference, as Elisha did.

2 Kings 8:8

A Sick King's Prayer Through a Man of Prayer

King Ben-hadad, who had tried to capture Elisha (6:13), now seeks his prayer help when he is desperately ill.

The Request of a Sick King (7–9)

Elisha was visiting the Syrian capital, Damascus, and the ailing leader heard the news and enlisted his prayer. He respected the prophet's proven ability to tell the truth about information that required God's help.

Hazael, second in command, brought Elisha a gift—forty camels' loads—to win his favor. A man of integrity did not require this, he would not be bought off, but he gave his help for his own proper motives. The reason why the king did not invite Elisha to his chamber was probably his extreme weakness, possibly also uncertainty as to how Elisha would react when he recalled Ben-hadad's aim to bring him by force earlier.

The issue Elisha was to inquire about before God was whether Ben-hadad would recover.

The Response of the Prophet (10–13)

Prayer obviously occurs, though the text does not specifically mention it. Hazael's visit requires it, and Elisha was often engaged in prayer. A pair of phases are united here.

The death of Ben-hadad. Elisha is a truthful man. On some matters it takes two sides to state the whole. One side of the picture is, yes, the king will recover if the natural course of events occurs, without interference. The other side is, Hazael's death plot will assure that the king dies so that he himself can take the throne.

Putting it this way, Elisha then fixes Hazael in a steady gaze, waiting for the words to register. He has not spelled things out in exact detail, but has been so clear that the Syrian understudy should realize that Elisha knows. As he feels himself being read, Hazael is aware that his face stings with shame. Then Elisha begins to sob.

Hazael plays it as if he is lily white. Why is the prophet weeping? Elisha wipes tears away and, again, those eyes are gazing into the visitor's soul. It is, he explains what they both know, because of the evil Hazael (as the new king) will perpetrate on Israel (cf. 8:28, 29; 9:15; 10:32, 33; 13:3, 7, 22). Hazael denies that he would ever sink to that. Such is his word, worth nothing. For Elisha immediately counters it with a word that is true—God's word that Hazael will act like this.

The deceit of Hazael (14, 15). Reporting back to the king, Hazael was primed for Ben-hadad's lead question, "What did Elisha say to you?" The man's life was at stake. Hazael smoothly gave him only the part about his recovery—assuming nobody committed treachery. He wanted to make the old king feel good; keep his own plot hidden from him.

It happened quickly. Hazael got the king's cover wet and heavy where it laid over his face. As he slept, the cover would dry, and when no evidence of deceit remained, Hazael could call others in to witness that natural death had taken its course. As he designed it, Ben-hadad died when his breath was blocked, and the murderer was king.

Principles of prayer appear even in such an episode. One is that a God-exalting intercessory service to others needs to be joined with other elements faithful to Him. Here, prayer unites with fidelity, the truth (10), even when Elisha delicately has to state two parts of the picture. Second, a prayer warrior passionate for God's honor and His people's welfare will weep as the prophet does (11). Jeremiah often sobbed as he prayed (13:17, etc.) and saw the need to (9:1). Jesus wept over a sinful people (Luke 19:41). and Paul prayed with weeping about enemies of the cross (Phil. 3:18). Third, even when a person who does not know the Lord seeks a true believer's help from God, some kind of truthful ministry can be interwoven with the prayer part. Some even come to know the Lord during this caring contact, although Ben-hadad and Hazael are not in this class.

2 Kings 11:4, 17

Prayer in a Covenant and an Oath

A priest, Jehoiada, exercised a faithful ministry of God in a time of bloodshed and spiritual distancing from the Lord. The contextual flow begins earlier, and soon Jehoiada carries out key services involving prayer.

The Prophecy Designating Jehu (9:1–10)

Elisha in his older years sends a man from the school of the prophets across the Jordan to anoint as Israel's king Jehu, son of Jehoshaphat. The prophet located Jehu, an army captain, in Ramoth-gilead. He anointed him and gave him God's commission as a king to carry out heavy judgment due on Ahab and Jezebel's corrupt throne line.

A part of the private session included God's will for Jehu to execute all in Ahab's kingly line (7). This, the prophet clarifies, is to avenge the blood of prophets and other servants of God under the authority of these wicked leaders.

The Purge by Jehu (9:11–10:36)

Jehu gains a following under God's prospering. Driving swiftly to Jezreel he found King Joram wounded by Hazael's Syrians (9:15). But Joram came out in a chariot to inquire of his visit, and Jehu sent an arrow through Joram's heart shot from his bow by powerful arms (24). The new king's orders to shoot the visiting King Ahaziah of Judah are fulfilled, too, as he flees (27).

At Jericho, Jehu demands that Jezebel's men throw her from a window, then tramples her under chariot horses. God's prophecy (9:10) is fulfilled in her body being so torn apart that no corpse remained to bury, and dogs licked up her blood (33–37).

Next, Jehu demanded execution of Ahab's seventy sons and got this plus others (10:1–17). His purge even included a summoning of all prophets and priests of Baal under the guise of fostering Baal worship at one of Baal's temples. His own strong men, stationed in readiness, slayed them in mass execution at his signal (10:18–27). He blotted Baal worship out of Israel at that time (28), though it would rebound later.

God called on Jehu to lead in judgment on those sold out to idolatry and various forms of rampant sin. This does not mean that God condoned Jehu's method, a lie in enticing the Baal devotees to assemble. He also did not approve of Jehu's own continuation in sins Jeroboam had fostered, such as worshiping golden calves at Bethel and Dan (29). The part of his work that was *right* God validated and promised to uphold his throne through four generations (30). The sin still tolerated brought God's judgment in another way, in defeats to Syria that forfeited lands of Israel (32, 33).

The Preservation of Joash to be the King (11:1–3)

A purge in Judah occurred also, involving Ahaziah's mother Athaliah destroying all the royal seed and seizing the throne. One possible king was spared. Jehosheba, daughter of King Joram, hid a one-year-old baby boy, Joash, in her bedroom and kept him for six years, making sure Athaliah was unaware of it. Jehoiada the priest proclaimed Joash king after gaining a following. His trusted men put Athaliah to death (11:4–16).

The Prayer to the Lord (11:4, 17)

On two occasions, closely-related, Jehoiada led others to join him in a covenant of faithfulness to God. First, in verse 4, this involved a pact to cooperate in backing Joash so that his kingship could be recognized. In this was a prayer oath invoking the Lord's name attesting to their intent and seeking His support.

The second instance (17) featured a covenant between the Lord and King Joash, now seven (21) as well as the people. The prayer was in two parts, one in devotion to be the Lord's people and the other in a pledge of king and people to work together for God's cause.

Though details are not recorded, the prayer reasonably would entail *affirmation* of God's word being true and allegiance to Him in obedience. It also could involve *petition* for His prospering of the effort. And third, it conceivably might embrace *confession* of sin that had been tolerated, as in idol-worship and laxness to honor God's word (cf. 2 Chr. 7:14).

At any rate, those giving themselves to this agreement mean business to some degree. They tear down Baal's house and smash articles of idol worship. Their firmness embraces an execution of Mattan the priest of Baal, who had escaped the earlier purge in the house of Baal (18). Jehoiada, a true priest, designated priests to lead in the house of the Lord.

Guidelines are in lavish supply. First, those honor the Lord in prayer who show a true heartbeat to live unto Him (cf. Phil. 1:19–21). Second, God always knows perfectly which devotion is genuine and which is not. The right way is to give Him an allegiance with the whole heart, holding nothing back.

2 Kings 13:1–7

Prayer of an Evil King for Help

King Jehoahaz of Israel wallowed in evil, perceived God's hand was against his domain in bringing Israel under Syrian conquest, and prayed for God's help.

His Pathetic Drift (1–3)

The Israelite head in Samaria plunged on in sin.

The duration of his sin. Jehoahaz ruled for seventeen years, a time giving ample opportunity to make his life and his kingdom count for the glory of the Lord.

The depth of his sin. This is obvious in two descriptions.

(1) The assessment in general shows depth. He did evil in the Lord's sight, the writer records. Such a terse profile indicates that this is the flavor that permeates his tenure. No qualification blurs the unsavory nature.

(2) The association with Jeroboam is revealing. Jehoahaz "followed" this evil model. The northern kingdom's first king had thrown his efforts against the valid worship of God at the temple (1 Kgs. 12:27). He had set up golden calves at Bethel and Dan to pry Israelites' worship from the true to the false (28, 29). He built houses of false worship on high places and imposed bogus priests not of Levi (31), plus other evils.

God believed that this king did more evil than those before him (14:9), provoking Him to carry out a clean sweep of judgment on him and those of his house (14:10). God announced His raising up a king who would fulfill this purge (v. 14). This God effects through Baasha, who kills all in Jeroboam's household (15:27–29). Baasha himself is also judged for following in the sin of Jeroboam (16:1–4, 8–1). So are later kings such as Zimri (16:15–20), Omri (23–26), Ahab (20–33; 21:17–26; 2 Kgs. 9–10), Ahaziah (1 Kgs. 22:51–53; 2 Kgs. 1:15–17), and others.

Many of the passages emphasize the Lord's anger at the sin and the kings who gave impetus to it. So the course Jehoahaz *follows* is marked by God's anger.

The determination of his sin. Verse 2 in 2 Kings 13 says that the king "did not turn" from the sins.

The distress due to his sin (3). This is clear in two details.

(1) God's anger that brings judgment.

(2) God's arousal of an instrument of judgment. He raises up the kings of Syria, Hazael and Ben-hadad over the years, in waves of pressure. This has its analogy in God having used surrounding nations in cycles of judgment on Israel during the judges period. He also does it in His later using of Assyria (Isa. 8:7, 8) and Babylon (Ezek. 21:3, 19). Today, outward trials that God arranges can do His people the service of pricking them to their spiritual senses to repent and draw close to Him.

Jehoahaz does this in some degree here, although in his case it appears to be only "skin deep" to get out of trouble at the moment (6).

His Prayer Desire (4a)

The king "entreated the favor of the Lord." No detail defines how he did this, whether on his own or by inquiring of the Lord through a spiritual leader. He probably did it the latter way. He is ungodly, and even godly Josiah would inquire of God through a delegation visiting a prophetess (22:13, 14), though he sought God in personal attitudes and acts, too (19; 23:3, 25).

God's Patient Deliverance (4b, 5)

Three steps reveal this.

His reaction. He "listened" to or "heard" Jehoahaz in a favorable sense. Even when God gives blessing in response to an individual's prayer, it is not valid inevitably to draw from this that the blessing is in accord with faith, or obedience (as John 15:7; 1 John 5:14, 15). God has the right to answer due to other factors also, even when the norms attached to His blessings are not present. The one who prays always needs to assess his walk with God or in sin by a true sensitivity to the various factors in His Word, and "get his act together."

His reason. God's answer to the king's prayer, whatever his spiritual temperature at the moment, was to relieve *others* and not just him! Two factors are facets compromising His reason in the context.

(1) His *sensitivity* to the hurt of His people. He saw, as He often did with cries to Him in the judges era, the bondage the oppressing cruelty of the enemy dealt (4). He was aware of *hurt* in his people, also the *hatefulness* (sin) the enemy had in their hearts and acts. The unlimited God is an all-the-way God. He looks at the entire picture and not just fragments as humans in their myopic limitations do. More factors can come within His dealings.

Consideration of all that is involved, and compassion appears here. God is patiently kind to the unthankful and the evil, and Israelites in Jehoahaz's day as in Paul's should have let this kindness point them to repentance (Rom. 2:3). The principle is the same today.

(2) His *steadfastness* in His covenant (23). The compassion is consistent with God's covenant with Israel's fathers, and them. Abraham, Isaac, and Jacob receive mention. The Lord who initiated the covenant with Abraham (Gen. 12:1–3, 7) had also ratified it. He conducted a ceremony pledging by Himself, by His very life to bless his descendants in grace, unconditionally (Gen. 15:9–17). And later He was consistent in His covenant with David. He promised that even when He disciplined David's people by the rod and strokes of men He would maintain loving-kindness (2 Sam. 7:14, 15).

His resource. God answered the prayer by giving Israel a "deliverer" who helped free them from the Syrian pressure. This sounds like the

Lord's provisions of judges to lead in deliverance. But the deliverer is not identified.

Some propose that reference is to Assyria's King Adad-nirari III (811–783 B.C.). He pulled Syrian attention away from Israel to concern for their own problems when he defeated Syria at Damascus in 803. His invasion also hit Tyre, Sidon, Edom, and Egypt. Relieved of Syria's pressure, Israelites were free to return to their homes. This might explain a method God uses to answer the prayer, as the earth is His (Ps. 24:1), and He uses other nations in relation to Israel.

Another explanation is that the deliverer is Elisha ministering to a king and people as often before. He presumably is still able, for the illness that brings his death is later (2 Kgs. 13:14, 20). Also, the more normal pattern God uses to deliver His people from afflictions is by a man from their own ranks. The period of the judges has many examples where the Lord answers prayer cries for help. In addition, Elisha often fulfills deliverances for few or many in Chapters 2–13. And God's key man in deliverance against *Syria*, involved here, has been Elisha (Chaps. 6–7).

This second view seems to fit best with the flow of context. The question why Elisha is not named, if he is strategic here, is just as much a problem for the Assyrian view or any other. One often is unable to explain why Scripture does not go into detail after a given point.

Elisha could be a deliverer by meeting with Jehoahaz for advocacy in prayer. Or Jehoahaz could have sent visitors to inquire as some other kings did. Otherwise, a prophet's God-given awareness of events elsewhere could prompt Elisha to intercede and gain merciful relief (6:12, 32; 8:10, 15).

His Persistent Disobedience (6, 7)

Again it appears that Jehoahaz's spiritual tenderness was shallow. It is probable that the king as well as his people continued in sin. But even if he was sincere he had by now so misled his people that his change did not have clout to inspire a real turn by the masses.

Two details are here. One is the *refusal* to repent of sin and walk following the Lord (6). The other is the *reduction* in Israel's defenses now evident after Syrian victories. Sin has a high price tag. Only fifty horsemen, ten chariots and 10,000 foot soldiers are left. Those lost in defeats due to sin are like the dust at threshing, gone with the wind (cf. Isa. 64:6).

Before leaving the prayer careers marking Elijah and Elisha, it is revealing to observe the way effective prayer coordinates with godliness in the whole lifestyle. At least ten traits reflect this.

(1) Righteous zeal to see God receive the glory, as Elijah praying on Mount Carmel (1 Kgs. 18) and Elisha's prayer curse near Bethel (2 Kgs. 2).

(2) Compassion when interceding for others. Elijah showed this toward the widow and her son (1 Kgs. 19), and Elisha toward the couple and their son (2 Kgs. 4).

(3) Selfless freedom from covetousness. Elisha exhibited this in declining Naaman's gifts, in contrast to his servant Gehazi's energetic greed (2 Kgs. 5).

(4) Faith in God's presence and power. Elijah modeled this in trusting his God to outshine the false gods and their devotees on the mount (1 Kgs. 18). And faith was Elisha's response to trial when surrounded by Syrians at Dothan. As ten of Moses' scouts saw God as greater than Canaan's giants and high-walled towns, Elisha saw God's resources as overwhelming against the enemy's encirclement.

(5) Truth. Elijah gave the truth to wicked Ahab without watering it down (1 Kgs. 18:18; 21:17–24). Elisha told Syria's Hazael plainly enough that this villain would murder his king and be cruel to Israelites (2 Kgs. 8:10–12).

(6) Vision. Elisha manifested this in asking for a double portion of the power on Elijah (2 Kgs. 2).

(7) Promptness to help in need. Elijah was alert to advise Ahab to travel before rain made a road bog (1 Kgs. 18). Elisha was ready with God's solution when prophets became violently ill from stew (2 Kgs. 4).

(8) Integrity versus compromise. Elijah was steadfast for the Lord against the unfaithfulness of 850 false prophets (1 Kgs. 18). Elisha did

not play favorites in dealing with his close associate Gehazi's greed and lying, but spoke God's judgment to the servant (2 Kgs. 5).

(9) Purity with women. Elijah demonstrated this toward the widow (1 Kgs. 19), Elisha to the woman of Shunnem (2 Kgs. 4).

(10) Persevering in prayer. Elijah is a pattern of this in his seven stages (1 Kgs. 18:41–44), and Elisha in keeping to his steadfast vigil with the boy (2 Kgs. 4:33–35).

Such qualities of praying can be trumpet calls to others who pray to take care of their *whole life*. The life overall is strategic in effective prayer (cf. John 15:7; 1 John 5:14, 15).

Other principles combine with these. First, God may show favor to the ungodly when they pray, not to honor them but for other reasons. One is to encourage repentance (cf. Rom. 2:3); others are to lighten pressures on others, or test others by His action, or show glorious depths of His mercies. But Scripture does not promise the unsaved an answer to their prayers. Second, God is pleased to use a person sold out to Him to bless others, as Elisha was a channel for His acts.

2 Kings 16:15

Prayer in a Wicked Life

King Ahaz of Judah is one example among several of following a God-defying life, then wanting help from the Lord through prayer. Here the case is simple.

The Insistence on Evil (1–9)

This king takes the throne at age twenty and rules for sixteen years (v. 2). His walk away from God is plain, and the writer has cited atrocious acts (3–4). Armies from Syria and Israel besiege Jerusalem (5–6), and Ahaz contacted Assyria's potentate, Tiglath-pileser, offering his servanthood and seeking his military aid against the coalition. Assyria gives this help, conquering Damascus, chief city of Syria.

The Inquiry to God (10–18)

When Ahaz visited Damascus for a parley with the Assyrian king, an altar there so caught his eye that he had a priest build one back home after its pattern. Ahaz presented various offerings on his new altar. His intent was to use the bronze altar there to "inquire" in prayer for God's blessing (15). His worship was out of an evil heart, even the brazenness of various details that departed from God's instructions about His place of worship and copied another nation's features.

It was a case of drift from God (2) and deceit in praying while skewing God's directions to please his own will.

Principles are clear enough. First, one cannot expect God's blessing if he substitutes his way in the face of God (cf. Ps. 66:18). Second, when one commits to disobedience, his feet can find it easy to go more and more along the path that offends heaven and does not open it for his success, in prayer or any other seeming spiritual thing.

2 Kings 19:4, 14–28; 20:2, 3, 11

Prayers of Hezekiah and Isaiah

Comment on these cases of prayer is reserved for 2 Chronicles 29–32. The present passages and Isaiah 36–39 are in large part parallels, and all can be incorporated at *one* time with the more detailed passage rather than dealt with *three* times. At the moment, one can just sum up the instances of prayer here.

In 19:4, Hezekiah sent men to ask for the prophet Isaiah's prayer when Assyria threatened (cf. also Josiah in 22:13). The king's own prayer appears in verses 14–19, and Isaiah's encouragement that God has heard Hezekiah (20–28). Later, this king when ill pleads for God to heal him (20:2–3), and in verses 5–11 Isaiah again reassures him that God is favorable to his prayer., even cries to the Lord and sees God work a miracle as a sign (11).

2 Kings 22–23

A King's Seeking God in Prayer

Judah's King Josiah (640–603 B.C.) is of great importance in prayer among all the kings of Judah and Israel. David often is held up as the pattern of obedience other kings are compared with (2 Chr. 29:2; cf. 28:1). But after David, of two kings it is said that no king before or after equaled them in godliness, Hezekiah (2 Kgs. 18:5; 19:10) and Josiah (23:25; cf. 2 Chr. 31:21; 34:26–28). Hezekiah's career came first, Josiah's later, so one can wonder in what distinctive sense both accolades are true and in harmony.

Hezekiah is assessed as having "trusted" the Lord above others (2 Kgs. 18:5). His great faith in God's deliverance during the trying Assyrian siege stands out. Verse 6 explains the tribute; he clung to the Lord, to His word (positive devotion) and did not forsake Him (negative departure). Yet Josiah is noted for turning to the Lord more fully than others, doing this with "all" his devotion, insisting on being true to the word (23:25). God is able to discern what distinguishes each servant, and how His words about them coordinate (cf. 1 Sam. 2:3; 16:7). Readers of His word do not perceive all the factors He appraises, or the value to ascribe to each.

The prayer-saturated career of Josiah in 2 Kings 22:1–23:30 has its parallel in some details in 2 Chronicles 34–35.

The Recovery of God's Word (2 Kgs. 22:1–10)

Josiah's holiness of life (1–2). He began his thirty-one-year reign at age eight, and at twenty-six in 622 B.C. would assert the loyalty to God recorded here (3). The overall *profile* of Josiah's godliness is that he did right in the sight of the Lord. His *pattern* was in the model true of David, so consistent that he did not deviate into disobedience to the right or the left. In other words, he kept to the true paths of righteousness of which David had written (Ps. 23:3).

Josiah's hearing of the book (3–10). The young king sent his scribe Shaphan to counsel the priest Hilkiah on distributing temple contributions. The mission resulted in far more than he knew the day would bring forth (Prov. 27:1). Hilkiah put in Shaphan's hands a copy of God's book of the law found in the temple. Josiah listened as the scribe read from it.

This would stir prayerful response to God. Today, public reading of Scripture can stimulate obedience or be resisted in disobedience. A greater impact than even this public exposure comes from private meditation in the word, asking God to open the eyes and the heart (Ps. 119:18).

The Request for Light on the Word (11–13; cf. 19)

Verse 19 makes it clear that Josiah's response to the word burns like a flame out of a spirit of prayerful sensitivity. God says that.

Josiah is strongly moved by the word. It is so rousing to him that he sends five men to inquire of the Lord for him and his people. His prayer quest of verse 13 is ignited by the bugle appeal the word issues to incite obedience, and its warning about judgment for disobedience. He is stung with conviction about his people's drift in sin, and his own, and the consequences God warned would follow this.

A principle here is to take God's word seriously in one's response of prayer.

The Reply with Light from God's Word (14–20)

The consultation of God's prophetess (14). As Miriam long before had been a prophetess, so now is Huldah. Living nearby in Jerusalem, she is in touch with God and watchful to give His answer to Josiah's prayer.

The content of her answer (15–20). Huldah clarifies two parts of God's reply to the king (1). Desolation for the kingdom (15–17; cf. 23:26, 27). True to what His word says, God will bring *retribution* dealing with long-continued sin (Lev. 26; Deut. 28). It is to be on Jerusalem and Judah's people, and complete judgment ("all the words"). Though not defined here, such retribution will involve God using Babylon to bring three destructions and deportations (605, 597, and 586 B.C.). These would begin in just seventeen years, though Josiah himself did not know that exact timing as we do after the fact.

The twofold *reason* for this judgment is the forsaking of the Lord and the worship of gods (17; cf. Jer. 2:13).

(2) Consolation to the king (18–20). Now God specifies His answer to the praying Josiah as to His personal dealing with him. This answer is clear in two phases.

First is *the privilege God shares.* He will give Josiah hope after death, gathered to his fathers. If this meant no more than his corpse joining their bones, it would be empty of any consolation at all. God assures the king he will have peace to the end of his life, being spared the sorrows shortly after that calamity on the city and people will bring (cf. 21:12–15).

Second is *the profile God sees* in Josiah. He discerns in four things the king's seriousness about godliness (19). These are tender sensitivity to God's word; humble submission to God; tearing his garments, in a gesture of contrite concern; and weeping "before Me" during prayer, as Hezekiah (20:3, 5).

A principle that stands out here is the value God places on genuine devotion in prayer. Only purity pleases Him, never phoniness in merely pacing oneself through a set of motions. For what is real in the mouth and the heart counts (Ps. 19:14; 139:23, 24).

The Revival under the King (23:1–27)

Josiah's sincere spirituality that relates to his prayer is manifest in his aggressiveness to honor God's interests.

His conference with his people (1, 2). Josiah requested Judah's leaders and others to attend a "spiritual life conference" at Jerusalem. He read from the copy of God's word what He said about the covenant. Due to the time that reading would require, this was probably not the whole Pentateuch. It was the Lord's guarantee of blessing for obeying but judgment for disobeying (Deut. 27:9–28:68).

His covenant to walk with God (3). Prayer is surely essential in this covenant the king promotes between his people and God. The agreement (pledge) is to walk following the Lord, and probably the next words define the essence of this—to do it by obeying His word with a whole heart ("all" the heart, etc.). The commitment the leader makes is one that those led make as they follow the example.

Prayer, though not spelled out, could be natural: in *affirmation* of their aim, *confession* of sin now repented of (cf. 2 Chr. 7:14), *petition* for God's help, and *praise* for His great Person and standards. We at least are told that Josiah made a covenant "before the Lord." That even could involve prayer in the aspect of an oath confirming a strong intent. On the one side of the covenant was God with His Word, and on the other is Josiah and those joining with him, speaking their hearts and words that agree with God.

His clearing away idolatry (4–20, 24). Josiah, like many a faithful preacher for God since his day, calls vigorously for a purge of sin, and gets it. His followers burn vessels devoted to idols, and idols; they remove priests who offer incense to the gods; and tear down temple chambers housing male cult prostitutes. They destroy idol shrines and objects; demolish the Bethel altar of Jeroboam in fulfilling what a young prophet had predicted 300 years before (1 Kgs. 13), and honor the young prophet by protecting his grave; they even execute many false priests, and see to other things.

Principles are evident. Suppose God's people today were this decisive in putting away sin and objects that promote it in their individual and collective lives. Then they would not require God to judge them (1 Cor. 11:31), and it could herald a day of impact for godly values. Also, such zeal can begin with taking God's word seriously and responding in prayerful tenderness fervent to obey it (22:13).

His celebration of Passover (23:21–23). Josiah's leadership impacted his people not only for the negative but the positive. Observing Passover occurs here in the most thorough manner in centuries, since the days of Samuel (2 Chr. 35:18), about 450 years.

To remember this earliest feast of Israel from Exodus 12 was to dwell on the covenant Lord (Ex. 6:3) redeeming His people from bondage. He did this by the blood of the lamb (Ex. 12) and by His power in the plagues and parting of the sea (Ex. 5–15).

More details of the Passover appear in 2 Chronicles 35. Josiah did this right by reinstituting priests and Levites to temple service, correcting a long era often darkened by leaders whose worship was a denial and a sham before the Lord. He also had Levites put the Ark back into the temple, for false leadership had sinfully removed it (35:3). Furnishing the people with animals in his own good will and sponsorship of certain officers, Josiah directed the priests and Levites to offer lambs and bulls for Passover.

God-pleasing prayer would be involved whenever a sacrifice was in true worship to God. The offerings were substitutes given in place of the people, accompanied by *affirmation* of their own entire devotion to the Lord and *gratitude* for God's deliverance, past and present.

Josiah fostered prayer in yet another expression. He revived the singers from the sons of Asaph as David had designated them.

A part of the Passover worship was the observance of unleavened bread (17). This, as well, entailed prayer in *affirmation* and *praise* for God's redemption.

His completeness in godliness (2 Kgs. 23:25). The king's vigor in the things of God is seen in three ways in this capsule summary of him. He was complete in these ways:

(1) His distinction to other kings. The only exceptions are David, often mentioned as a pattern to compare by, and Hezekiah (18:5). How Josiah and Hezekiah are to be distinguished will have to be left with the Lord, as stated earlier. For both of them, the plaudits are great, for a life that glorifies God is the highest honor for a person.

(2) His devotion of "all." Four times in verse 25 the word "all" characterizes Josiah's completeness in commitment. He was a yielded man, giving no place to being half-hearted in doing God's will. His

all-out seeking of God is commemorated in another passage as well (2 Chr. 31:21).

(3) His direction in God's word. It is one thing to be fully given to things in outright opposition to God. It is another to be sold out to the religion related to God, but merely in an empty form of godliness, not true to His word. It is an entirely distinct thing to be set wholly, as Josiah, in a direction guided by God's word. Verse 25 clarifies that this was the path the king pursued. Like Caleb he wholly followed the way God pointed, and like Ezra (7:10), the word became incarnate in his life. Like the Christian Paul calls for, he let the word dwell richly in him (Col. 3:16).

Even the finest godly person, excepting Jesus Christ, is still sinful (cf. Eccl. 7:20). Josiah at the very end intruded himself where he should not have, intercepting the Pharaoh of Egypt who led his army across Palestine toward the Euphrates. Advised to step out of the way, since the pharaoh had no quarrel with him, Josiah insisted and was shot to death (2 Kgs. 23:29, 30). He died due to his error in judgment, but in the world to come the banner over his life will still be that of 23:25.

The calamity that sin brings to the kingdom (26, 27; cf. 22:15–17). God's answer to prayer in the promise of blessing for Josiah but judgment on Judah and Jerusalem (22:15–20) remains steadfast. At the end of the account on the revival the king led, the writer repeats the Lord's judgment, in two emphases.

(1) The steadfastness in judging (2 Kgs. 23:26). His persistence in judging Judah, as He had judged Israel (the north) is firm. The provocations to go ahead with the calamity were in King Manasseh's notoriously evil reign. Manasseh repented in sincere prayer after the Assyrians took him to their land in captivity (2 Chr. 33:11–20). God moved the Assyrians to restore him to Jerusalem and he fostered service to God, yet died leaving a kingdom invested with the idol worship he had earlier supported. The need for judgment was far developed.

(2) The subjects of judging (27). God intends to remove the people of Judah to Babylon, Egypt, and so forth (Chap. 24; Jer. 39–44,

etc.). This is as He had removed Israel to Assyria in 722–721 B.C. (2 Kgs. 17). Second, He will cast off (reject) Jerusalem, the greatest description of which is in Lamentations (and Jer. 39, 52). Third, He will reject the temple. He had said "My name shall be there" (1 Kgs. 8:29; 9:3). This house of God, place of prayer to Him (Isa. 56:7), temple where everything was meant to express glory (Ps. 29:9), became devoted to idols (cf. Ezek. 8). God disowned it and departed (Ezek. 8–11). He would return in a future day of restoration (Ezek. 43:7).

Failure to pray to God, and to pray rightly was a key in Israel's and Judah's decline to the precipice of judgment and the plunge over the brink.

Principles here to join others at various points above are apropos. First, being like the Lord and prizing His Word can strategically fashion the life for effective prayer. Second, women can have a ministry awesome in prayer—for example Hannah, Huldah, and Anna. Third, ambitious works for the Lord can be close accompaniments of aggressive prayers before an answering God.

Prayer in 1 Chronicles

Introduction

Prayer in the two books of Chronicles is actually prayer in the one book, Chronicles. The ancient Hebrew product did not become divided into the two parts until the Septuagint, the Greek translation around 200 B.C. English translations have followed the two-part idea, which shortens what would be sixty-five chapters to twenty-nine and thirty-six. The message remains the same either way, but for the convenience of greater brevity, in each part the prayer focus will now be seen in two divisions.

The Title

Hebrews gave the one product the name "Chronicles (or Events) of the Days," a name captured in a word for happenings and a word for days. When Jews translated their Old Testament Hebrew into the Greek Septuagint, they chose the title ***paraleipomena***. It considered the contents as giving accounts (often, at least) "alongside" or in addition to things in the books of Samuel and Kings, things passed over there. Luther favored the name "Chronicles," which English Bibles have used.

Either name is fitting. These are chronicles, highlighting the Davidic and Levitical priestly lines and place in God's plan (cf. "Purpose" below). In pursuing this emphasis, they often give material not in Samuel or Kings (though they often do not) and survey directly only the Judean line of kings (southern kingdom), not the Israelite (northern).

The Author

The evidence does not furnish certainty, but the most convincing possibility is Ezra. Early Jewish tradition in the Talmud (Baba Bathra 15a) named Ezra for Chronicles and Ezra/Nehemiah. Second, Ezra was eminently qualified as a skilled and unusually recognized scribal servant and man of God (Ezra 7:6, 10). Third, Ezra came from Babylon to Jerusalem in 457 B.C. (7:8) and his life could have extended until the latest person mentioned in Chronicles, Anani (1 Chr. 3:24) in the eighth generation from Jehoiachin (from ca. 597), perhaps 425–400 B.C. Or Ezra could have written the high majority and another writer extended the genealogy, just as another could have added Moses' death to his writing (Deut. 34).

The possibility of Ezra, prominent in the Book of Ezra, is enhanced by the tie in giving the decree of Cyrus (538) twice (2 Chr. 36:22, 23; Ezra 1:1–4). Further, Ezra could have used Nehemiah's good library mentioned in the Jewish writing called 2 Maccabees 2:13–15. The Chronicles writer refers to nearly twenty sources that were a help in his work (1 Chr. 16:11; 27:24; 29:29, etc.). This suggests scribal diligence and exacting consultation of documents, as the writer of the Gospel of Luke did (Luke 1:1–4). A zealous writer is reflected in the kind of detail (genealogical lists, 1 Chr. 1–9, etc.), the focus on temple interests, and vigor for the law of Moses.

The Date

Ezra, or whoever wrote the books, did so by around 425–400, as mentioned above.

The Purpose

The close relation to prayer is apparent in several aims that emphases in the Chronicles reflect.

To stir zeal for the law and worship. Ezra loved the law (Ezra 7:10) and worked to inspire temple worship (7:19–23, 27; 8:33, 34). He led in overcoming marriages with pagans whose loyalty to gods worked against praying to the Lord (Ezra 9–10). The Chronicles emphasize fidelity to God's law, temple ministry to His praise (1 Chr. 13, 15, 16; 22), and priests that lead in praise (6, 22–29; 2 Chr. 3–7, 29–31; 34:8–35:19).

To stress God's power in victory by faith/obedience. This is evident often, steeped in prayer (2 Chr. 13–14, 20, 25, 29–32, etc.).

To survey the Davidic Kingdom line God elected to bless. The Lord promised this (2 Sam. 7:12–16). The contents of the Chronicles develop a genealogy from Adam to David (1 Chr. 1–9), reigns of Saul (10) and David (11–29), then Solomon (2 Chr. 1–9) and other Judean or southern kings (10–36). Kings of Israel (the north) are not included except now and then and only in special relation to Judean kings. The focus is clearly on the Davidic house, and, of course, the books of Samuel and Kings survey *both* Judah and Israel.

To show positively what kings and others can do. The emphasis is often on David's positive steps, with no mention of sinning with Bathsheba or a stress on his several or Solomon's many wives. This is not to mismanage, manipulate, or recast things in a false light to cover up sin. Rather, it is a positive focus, even while some foolish steps gain faithful mention (1 Chr. 13:9–14; 14:3–7; 22:8; 28:3). Besides, the books of Samuel and Kings had shown the other side too, and these leave out some things Chronicles mention, as none of the accounts aim to be exhaustive.

What *is* given in Chronicles fits with the theme (below).

The Theme

It is God's purpose in grace to keep His elective and covenant will with David and his kingdom and through the priesthood. Prayer interlaces vitally with these aspects in trust giving its obedient response to God's will and power to bless (cf. 2 Chr. 15:2, 4; 16:7–9). The impact of this fits with earlier and later Scripture that expects or sees the ultimate fulfillment of the ideals in the Messiah. He is the ultimate of the kings God predicted (Gen. 17:6; 49:10), the greatest King in David's house (2 Sam. 7:12–16; Acts 2:30) and greatest Priest (Ps. 110:4; Heb. 7:17).

The Relationship of Prayer

The way prayer is a permeating flavor within the theme is clear in episodes of David, to choose the most notable example. God turns the kingdom from Saul to David on the issue of Saul's disobedience to the Lord, to His word, and prayer in trusting Him (1 Chr. 10:13, 14). David begins his kingdom with a prayer covenant "before the Lord" (11:3), pleads for guidance in battle (14:10, 14), and has Levitical singers and musicians appointed to praise God (15:16–24; 16:4–6) and to offer thanks (16:39, 40). He writes a song of thanks and prompts his people to thank God 16:7–36).

That is not all. David prays in response to God's will that Solomon should build the temple (17:16–27). He intercedes that the Lord will help Solomon in building the house (22:11, 12; 29:19), and in many other things. Prayer keeps recurring, saturating the attitudes and acts of people.

The Outline

The sixty-five chapters fit in a simple sequence developing the emphasis on kings in the Davidic lineage (all except Saul of Benjamin, 1 Chr. 10):

I. Genealogy from Adam to David (1 Chr. 1–9)
II. Saul (10)
III. David (11–29)
IV. Solomon (2 Chr. 1–9)
V. Other Kings of Judah (10–36)

1 Chronicles 4:9, 10

A Prayer that Gained its Blessing

Tucked away in a long section of genealogies (Chaps. 1–9) is a sudden, shining scenario of a man who asked in prayer and received (cf. Matt. 7:7). The man Jabez is unknown in Scripture except for these two verses, but they profile much about a life that counted on prayer.

His Distinction (9)

Jabez was, says the chronicler, distinguished in three relationships.

In the circle of his family. He had brothers, but he stood out among them as more honorable. This is probably, as befits the emphases of the Chronicles, in godliness that honors God's law and His power. Verse 10 shows what the writer means to highlight of this man, and its focus is effective prayer. In this, for sure, Jabez was notable as a living force among his family members. Or his distinction might be in his spiritual walk as a whole, of which prayer is a strategic expression.

In the conviction of his mother. The one who gave birth to Jabez was impressed with the special pain he brought her in coming into the world. She named him for this, for Jabez means grief or sorrow. His mother thought of him early as linked with ill fortune, for a name was sometimes given for what an early act seemed to portend (cf. Gen. 35:18, "son of my sorrow"). God can overcome human apprehension and transform things into distinction in success instead of sorrow. Jabez would seize that possibility, depending on what God could do to shape his life in place of any natural drift of events.

In the context of Israel's family lines. The writer did not, in verse 9, do his normal thing in Chapters 1–9. He gave no family names (genealogy), but thrust in comments about a remarkable prayer and a remarkable answer from God. When one reads all of the genealogical section, he often finds not merely names but instructive notes on the bad and the good that marked people.

Jabez is distinguished even in his overall context. Cush carved out a fame for worldly achievement (1:10), Er a niche for selfishness (2:3), Achan a tag for covetousness (2:7). Reuben was marked by sexual sin (5:1; cf. Gen. 35:22), Judah for leadership (5:2), Levites for music in God's house (6:31, 32). The sons of Tola and Benjamin stood out as mighty warriors (7:1, 2; 8:40). But the sons of Reuben and also Jabez himself had names towering over the centuries for people of prayer that counted (5:18–22).

A principle for this, framed in a question, can be life-changing to a tender heart. "If a single distinction could sum up the life I lived on the earth, what would I want it to be?" As Jabez acted in a way that drew an honored memorial, so can others who will make their move while time still permits.

His Desire (10)

Four details in verse 10 expound this.

The principle he acted on. Jabez was cast under a dark shadow hovering over his background, the grief remembered about him. But he was gripped by a principle that could make all the difference—the principle of prayer. This shows that he believed, as Job expressed it, in prayer as a key and God as a God of power. Eliphaz in the Book of Job (5:7–9) also knew that the dark shadow of trouble lengthened over every man (v. 7). It was sinister. This counselor has said in one of his speeches to Job, "But as for me, I would seek God, and I would place my cause before God; Who does great and unsearchable things, Wonders without number." Prayer for both men, prayer to God, was the key that they wielded to be victors, not victims.

Prayer is only as good as the object it depends upon. Jabez called on the God of Israel. This God had shown in a long relation to His people His covenant compassion, commitment to what was good, and power. He was the right one to approach by this principle of prayer. Jabez probably remembered accounts of God's answers to

Abraham, Isaac, Jacob, Joshua, Moses, and others. Many testimonies of effectual prayer were a treasury available to inspire his spiritual stride, and even more exist to cheer those on today.

The progress he aspired to. Jabez pleaded before God his desire to have His blessing and enlargement. Like Caleb who set his heart on a territory God was able to give, this man desired an increase in his land. In that, he is presented in a favorable light here; he evidently desired with proper motives that honored God and not selfish ends God would turn down (cf. Ps. 66:18). He came as one who delighted in the Lord, a man whose desires God could meet (Ps. 37:4). The principle of his request for progress could also apply to spiritual growth, increase in usefulness for God in serving others, and so forth.

The presence he valued. Jabez had passion to experience the presence of God. His cry was that "Thy hand might be with me." This is a witness to his sense of values. Many speak as if the really important thing is to have power in their own human strength, abilities, plans, and the like. Jabez wisely put his trust in what God was able to do. He was convinced, as David in Psalm 62, that "power belongs to God" (11). In that context, David waits for God only, his hope is from God, God is David's rock and deliverance, his stronghold who keeps him from being shaken. Jabez, too, made his quest the Presence that wins.

The protection he sought. Jabez longed to be kept from harm, that it might not bring pain on him. The word "pain" (10) is the verbal form of the same word for "pain," a noun, in verse 9. Jabez in verse 10 may well have the idea that the word means in other passages: God's deep grief at the sin of men bringing on the flood (Gen. 6:5); the hurt of remorse, or else fear in Joseph's brothers convicted of the wrong they did to him (Gen. 45:5); the agony of spirit a deserted wife can feel (Isa. 54:6); the grief God's Spirit knew at Israel's sin (Isa. 63:10; cf. Eph. 4:30).

It is one thing to be committed to face pain if it is God's faithful trial to craft one's good (James 1:2–12). It is another to shun pain when the pain can be to one's detriment and to trust God for protection from falling victim to it. Jesus Christ mentioned deliverance from being in temptation in the model prayer He gave His disciples (Matt. 6:13). The writer of Psalm 91 knew God as a deliverer from a snare, deadly pestilence in His judgment that befell others (3, 8, 10), the arrow that flies by day, the lion, the snake, and shortened life (16).

Pain from others or from his own sin could lay treacherous hurt on Jabez. He prayed that God would guard his life. As early as with Abraham, God had promised to be a shield (Gen. 15:1), and knowing Him as a shield is a theme often repeated as vital in His word.

His Deposit

When Jabez prayed, he gained God's answer, a deposit of what he had requested. He had pled in God's will and not with sinful motives (James 4:3), and as Jesus would later assure, what he asked he received (Matt. 7:7).

What did he receive, then? He secured progress, because that was what he asked. He gained a sense of God's presence, for that was what he specified. He got guardianship from what would hurt him, because that was what he desired.

Principles are like a beacon flashing to the person of prayer here. One is that the potential for a life of pain due to sin is with each believer, yet God's presence to help is available if he (she) will take it. Another is that it is never amiss to plead for blessing that is in God's will. In giving the blessing, God Himself is glorified, even as the one petitioning is made glad. Third, to ask for an increase, as in land or money, can please God when the asker lives in sacred trust to use it for His sake. God can entrust much to the person who uses His deposit well, as George Mueller showed in asking supplies for his orphans in Bristol, England.

1 Chronicles 5:18–22

Men Who Pray and Win

Another vignette like that of Jabez takes the reader by surprise in the midst of genealogies. Soldiers of three tribes that chose their Israelite land east of the Jordan in Joshua's day show their prayerful trust in God for victory.

Their Skill for Battle (18)

Sons of Reuben, Gad and half the tribe of Manasseh numbering 44,760 have ability in three particulars. They use shield and sword, shoot with bows, and display prowess in fighting.

This all sounds impressive, but as the description continues it is soon clear that victory is not a foregone conclusion just because of these assets. Even the enemy is no doubt adept in the use of human means to win. And so are enemies of believers today—Satan, demons, other people, the world system, the flesh with its lusts (cf. 1 John 2:15–17), and so forth. For *any* battle, the believer needs the Lord's power, and not just the most supreme battles.

Their Success in Battle (19, 20b, 21, 22)

The enemies attacking. A coalition from east of the Jordan mounts against Israelite fighters. Hagrites, otherwise unidentified in Scripture, may be an Arab people near Moab, Edom and the Ishmaelites because they unite with them in Psalm 83:6, 7. Also, two names in 1 Chronicles 5:19 (Jetur and Naphish) are Ishmaelites in Genesis 25:15. The enemies against those who trust in God are usually many, as above—Satan, demons (cf. "lying spirit," 1 Kgs. 22), the world, the lusts that war against the soul (1 Pet. 2:11), and humans who serve in Satan's ranks (1 Thess. 2:14–16). This points up how crucial it is to rely on God.

The end achieved. Victory is evident in that the Israelite soldiers were "helped" and the enemies "given into their hand." It is also apparent in the conquests of animals and men, and the falling of the enemy (21, 22).

Their Secret in Battle (20, 22)

Three details expound this.

Their appeal. The transjordania soldiers "cried out to God in the battle." Prayer was the weapon for success rather than all their ability with shield, sword and bow. It is possible that priests and people back home also prayed, though not mentioned in the brief account.

Their answer. God "was entreated for them," answering prayer.

Their attitude. God answered with victory "because they trusted in Him." They did not finally vest their confidence in their own prowess, but in the Person who had all power. He lifted them above an army more than twice their size (21).

When God answers trust, He is being true to His word of promise. He had pledged overwhelming victory when Israelites depended on Him. One would chase a hundred, a hundred win over ten thousand (Lev. 26:8), one even pursue a thousand and two rout ten thousand (Deut. 32:30). David would state the principle in Psalm 20:7: some trust in horses, some in chariots, but believers like him remember the name of the Lord.

These who trusted had a rich heritage to stimulate their reliance. Abraham won over a great Mesopotamian invader (Gen. 14), Joshua beat back Amalek (Ex. 17), Gideon routed a vast Midianite army (Judg. 7). Later Israelites would know of further overwhelming triumphs through prayer, as in the days of Samuel (1 Sam. 7, 12), David (1 Sam. 30, etc.), Jehoshaphat (2 Chr. 20), and Hezekiah (2 Chr. 29–32). Solomon, dedicating the temple, even interceded for future victories of his people (2 Chr. 6:34, 35).

The believer's prayer secrets for battle today are clear not only in such a passage as 1 Chronicles 5. Other key summaries are among the well-known: 2 Corinthians 6:7; 10:4, 5; Ephesians 6:10–20; 2 Timothy 2:1, 3–4.

Which principles attend prayer in the transjordania triumph? First, prayer should be remembered as a great key of life even in the midst of details that occupy the mind, as the long section of genealogy here. Second, "the battle is the Lord's" who will fight for the believer (Ex. 14:13, 14), so he ought to trust Him. God gives people abilities, but wants them to remember always that success is not in the abilities on their own right but in His power (Prov. 3:5, 6; 2 Cor. 3:5). Third, prayer can be before, in, or after the battle (here, *in* it), and God can honor it. David often prayed before (2 Chr. 14:10, 14, etc.), and that is a good principle. Better yet is the discipline of praying without ceasing (1 Thess. 5:17). Fourth, prayer should always be with trust as here, for God sets a high importance on faith (Heb. 11:1, 6). He also makes it clear that prayer is always to be with thanksgiving (Phil. 4:6, 7; 1 Thess. 5:18). A final principle is that no matter what odds are pitted against those who pray in faith, as two to one here, God is able to win. He won with Gideon's three hundred, and He won in Hezekiah's day by one angel who defeated 185,000 Assyrians (Isa. 37:36). In the testing of Elisha and his servant, the Lord won without a human soldier (2 Kgs. 6). And at Samaria He put the Syrians to flight just by a sound He produced in the enemy camp (2 Kgs. 7). God is rich with a variety of ways to win, and with each His power avails.

1 Chronicles 10:12–14

Prayer a Matter of Life or Death

Now the chronicler sketches a capsule summary of Saul, looking only at his final demise and reasons that brought him down. He omits details of the king's life that 1 Samuel 9–31 had already surveyed, and presses right to the crux of Saul's failure.

The Death of Saul (1–6)

Pursuit by Philistines in Saul's last battle results in archers' fatal wounds to the king (1–3). The pursuit is followed by Saul's plea that his armor bearer finish him with a sword before Philistines heap on indignities while he lingers, suffering. This request is refused, so Saul plunges on his own sword and dies as three of his sons die (4–6; 1 Sam. 31:4, 5).

The Dishonoring of Saul (7–10)
People of Israel evacuate their cities in the battle region. Philistines display Saul's head in the temple of their god Dagon and display his armor before their gods, heaping credit to them for victory.

The Decency toward Saul (11, 12)
Israelite men of Jabesh-gilead, east of the Jordan, took the bodies of Saul and his sons and gave them an honored burial in the city of Jabesh. David's later transfer of Saul's and Jonathan's bones to their Benjamite family plot is not mentioned here, but is in 2 Samuel 21:12–14 (cf. comments on that passage).

The Destroyers of Saul (13, 14)
Who really killed Saul? Besides the Philistines and Saul's own collapse on his sword, other answers emerge. Saul inflicted death strokes to himself before archers wounded him; he did this by his evil choices and actions. And the Lord brought about his death as a judgment that was sin's overdue paycheck. Though several terrible deeds ushered the king to a sad end, the chronicler offers a two-point summary here.

His antagonism toward God's word. Saul's life for years had consisted of one long descent in sin toward the precipice of personal ruin. He trespassed against the Lord in not obeying His word, which was a great denial, defamation, and defiance flung in the face of God. It denied God's rights to have a life offered in personal and kingly obedience to His majesty; it defamed His character as unworthy to be honored; and it defied His power, which could have brought blessing instead of blight.

His asking of a witch. The bottom line of Saul's tragedy is a failure in prayer! How different his life and death might have been had he prayed as Jabez and men of the transjordania army did, or later examples in Chronicles illustrate.

A person's triumph or tragedy often turns on the same two pivots relating to prayer that define Saul's case here.

(1) What he should not have done (13). Saul never should have resorted to a medium, the witch of Endor (1 Sam. 28). He sought light on the future from a source of darkness, and put his trust in what gave no true light. He was like many who, choosing their own varying channels, vest their confidence in some source opposed to God—some false god, a fallacious philosophy, a bogus book in place of God's word, a fortune teller, and so on. The god of this age who blinds men's minds lest they come to the true source and find hope thinks of endless schemes to misguide (2 Cor. 4:4).

(2) What he should have done (14a). Saul ought to have prayed, esteeming proper light from the Lord. How many examples of this proper object of prayer appear in the word! God blesses in the humble inquiries of David for guidance at Keilah (1 Sam. 23) and in meeting the Philistines (2 Sam. 5). Prayer in these cases has already been put under the spotlight.

Saul, too, should have prayed. The way lay open to him to show trust as Jabez did, and show humility in repentance, thanksgiving, and other qualities that move God. Instead, he verily destroyed himself in stiff-necked devotion to self-will and other confidences that betrayed him.

To others, also, comes the call to the word and to prayer, the secrets Saul spurned. The way of blessing is here, and here alone.

1 Chronicles 14:10, 14

David's Prayers for Guidance

See 2 Samuel 5:17–25 where these two inquiries for the right steps in battle are already dealt with.

1 Chronicles 15, 16

Prayer in Bringing the Ark

Attention to 2 Samuel 6 has brought this under review. One added point is instructive. When David and his priests disobeyed God's word by moving the Ark on a cart rather than by priests carrying it with poles and not touching it, God took the life of Uzza (2 Sam. 6:3–7). David repented, getting in sync with God. He reminded the priests (1 Chr. 15:2, 13–15) of the method God's word said was His will (Num. 4:15). They, too, consecrated themselves to obey, followed the word, and all went well. Prayer that is not coordinated with honoring God's word has no guarantee of God's blessing.

1 Chronicles 17:16–27

Prayer in the Davidic Covenant

This duplicates the record of God giving David His covenant to bless his house, kingdom, and throne forever (cf. 2 Sam. 7, already seen in focus).

1 Chronicles 21

Prayer in the Sin of the Census

Discussion of 2 Samuel 24 has previously considered prayer here.

1 Chronicles 22–26, 28–29

Preparations for a House and Ministry of Prayer

David, in old age, prepares for future prayer by careful designs, appointments, challenges, and his own prayer. He gets various details set for Solomon to build a temple and Levitical ministers to carry out different phases of service saturated with prayer.

Prayer is usually made prominent and is always crucially related in all the steps of the exposition in these chapters.

Devotion in the Temple (22:1)

That prayer is strategic in the temple becomes evident at the very outset here, and also from other considerations.

Concepts of verse 1. Two details of 22:1 point immediately to a focus on prayer. The occasion is David's reflection on the need for a temple after his sin of the census, God's discipline, and his offering sacrifice at the threshing floor (cf. 2 Sam. 24).

The two concepts are plainly in view. David conceived of the sacrifice site as a place to build "the house of God." The phrase "house of God" permeates Chapters 22–29, appearing thirty-nine times. God's house would be the formal place of meeting with Him in sacrifice and prayer.

The second reference in verse 1 is that this is the altar of burnt offering. Here, with a house to be built, will be an altar for sacrifice in place of the temporary altar David used for sacrifice at the threshing floor. As in Leviticus 1, the burnt offering would be entirely consumed, a substitute representing the offerer giving himself up wholly to God. The outward gesture was attended by inward and vocal prayer *affirming* yieldedness for service pleasing to the Lord (cf. Rom. 12:1). Other aspects of prayer were natural with this as well—*thanking* God for who and what He is and the privilege of serving Him, and *petition* for help. In twice daily priestly burnt offerings for Israel (Ex. 29), the aspects of prayer would broaden to embrace all the people, and become *intercessory.*

The two details in the opening verse set the prayer tone for the entire context. Yet much more besides this shows the dedication in prayer related to the "house of God."

Concepts in addition. Relating the temple to prayer is clear in a number of ways.

First, God had told David ahead of time in the Davidic Covenant that his son would "build for Me a house" (1 Chr. 17:12). David had bathed this expectation in prayer, petitioning that God's word of promise for the house would be realized (23). This is one of countless examples in Scripture where *prayer* is submissive to God's *plan*, the *will* of man in accord with the *will* of God.

Second, David made the house a matter of prayer in declaring God's will to Solomon when charging him to build the temple

(29:10–20). Third, Solomon when completing the temple dedicated it in prayer (2 Chr. 6; cf. exposition of 1 Kgs. 8).

Fourth, the centering of the temple in prayer is evident in David's appointments of ministers to lead in phases of prayer and other temple service (1 Chr. 23–26, etc.). Fifth, God dwelt in the house manifesting His glory at the outset (1 Kgs. 6:10, 11) as He had filled the tabernacle (Ex. 40:34). He responded to Solomon's dedicatory prayer by saying He put His name there and His eyes and heart would be there perpetually (1 Kgs. 9:3). In light of that, the temple was, in a special sense, a place to appear before His eyes and heart in prayer. The psalmist later could say that in the temple, rightly used, everything says or expresses His glory (Ps. 29:9).

A sixth indication that the temple was centered in prayer is that David had received the details for the house in a meditative time with God's hand on him moving his writing (1 Chr. 28:19). Similarly, Moses received God's pattern for the tabernacle while before Him in communion (Ex. 28:9). Seventh, God would call the temple "my house of prayer" (Isa. 56:7). Jesus insisted that it be that place of prayer, in contrast to the place to make profits that some had distorted it to be (Matt. 21:13).

That is not all. An eighth factor is that Solomon prayed that God would make the temple a center where He would receive prayer (2 Chr. 6:20–42). Daniel faced toward the temple from far away Babylon (Dan. 6:10). And ninth, the temple and the rebuilt temple continued to be a central place of prayer in later centuries (Joel 1:14; Matt. 21:13; Luke 19:46; Acts 3:1).

Devotion of the temple to prayer in 1 Chronicles 22:1 is a theme readily carried on by other parts of the context.

Directions for the Temple (22:2–19)

David issued a mandate to prepare for building the temple. He could at least do this, though God did not permit him to be the builder, as he explains. His guiding ambition shows care to prepare for several necessities.

Supplying for the construction (2–4, 14–16). David was the human authority zealous to assure that what was needed for the project would be available. Among the materials were hewn stones, iron for nails and clamps, bronze, cedar timber, gold, and silver. David also arranged for stonecutters, masons, carpenters, and other skilled workers.

Prayer is strategic in this, as in all proper work for the Lord. David challenges workers to devote themselves to the task, and intercedes for them (16). He invokes, or calls on them, the Lord's presence and ability to carry out His will.

Specifying the splendor of the building (5). The old king is forthright to those preparing in advance for the temple. He tells them of his successor's inability due to his youth and inexperience. This explains his own key role. He also emphasizes the glorious magnificence the house is to reach, giving them a high standard to prompt the utmost effort and skill. More than four centuries later, the prophet Haggai (2:3) would mention the extraordinary glory that those who had seen that temple could remember.

Singling out the son to build (6–16). There is some overlap in verses here. David challenges his son Solomon in a private session here to build the house. Later, he charges him in a public assembly (Chaps. 28, 29). In both meetings, David reviews his desire to build the house and God's plan that Solomon fulfill this. In both he also prays.

David says that God revealed ahead of time the birth of Solomon and even supplied his name (22:9). He was to lead in the actual construction. He would also be a "son" in kingly relationship with God in His covenant promise to David of a continuing house, kingdom, and throne (10; cf. 2 Sam. 7:12–16).

Stressing support that would sustain (11, 12). The prayer in David's private conference with Solomon was to the point. David interceded that the Lord would give His presence, prospering, perception, and prerogative in royal leadership. In His power, Solomon would find sufficiency to obey His law. The new king would have success as he exercised vigilance to follow the Lord's word (13).

Due to God's adequacy, David then could exhort his son in two ways: *positively,* to be strong and courageous as God supplied him, and *negatively,* not to fear or be rattled by any obstacle.

The outgoing king, as stated above, also challenged the workers (in another setting) to rest in God's presence. He appealed to them to set their heart and soul to seek the Lord, a crucial part of which would be vital prayer. His challenge was to get the temple built so that they could put the Ark of God's presence and other articles there (19).

Divisions of Levites for Temple Service (23)

God had appointed Aaronic priests to minister in sacrifices, and other Levites to assist in attendant services (Ex. 28, 29, 39; Lev. 8–10, etc.). David, for the temple ministry, followed God's will in His word for His dwelling place, which at first was the tabernacle.

All things are done in a fitting way and in order (cf. 1 Cor. 14:40). First, David takes a census of the tribe of Levites; later, the services of these can be specified.

The summons for a Levitical census (1, 2). In his latter years, David twice designated Solomon as king—first to nip Adonijah's bid to seize the throne (1 Kgs. 1:33), and the second time, later (1 Chr. 23:1; 29:22). David, still king, however, was carrying out steps preparing for the future.

He called Israel's leaders together with priests and Levites to take a Levite census so as to utilize these wisely in coming temple service.

The sum of the census (3–5). Learning of a total of 38,000 who were ages thirty or older, David organized them for overseeing the work of the temple (the largest number), and for being officers and judges, gate keepers, and those praising God with instruments.

The specifics by families (6–23). Sons of Aaron were newly commissioned to burn incense before the Lord's presence (cf. Ps. 141:2), to carry out holy services in sacrifices for themselves and the people, and to bless in His name (13).

Each ministry was intertwined with prayer and was to be saturated with it. The occupation in incense was in fragrance fitting to communing with Him (cf. Ex. 30). Offering sacrifices and representing people before God could involve any aspect of prayer—confession, praise/thanks, petition (even in oaths), intercessions, affirmations, and so on. As shown in Numbers 6:22–27, blessing in the Lord's name was in various details of prayer.

Levites not of the sons of Aaron were strategic in fulfilling various roles necessary to assist in temple service. Whatever their tribal branch and role, as in the examples in verses 4, 5, 28–32, all men in the whole tribe of Levi did some service, some at age thirty and older (3), some between the ages of twenty and twenty-nine (27).

A distinction is drawn between the *realm* of their service (24–26) and the *roles* they fulfilled (27–32). The realm, formerly the moveable tabernacle, was soon to be the stationary temple (26), so those who carried the tabernacle would not to have to do so, as the Levites used to do. In the new realm, the roles were the priestly services for the sons of Aaron, and then the many supportive details fulfilled by the other Levites.

All Levites, however, were vitally related to all the functions. All had to be careful that every vessel and act was purified to maintain a standard honoring God as truly set apart (28). Even those not engaging in sacrifices saw that vessels met high qualifications. All cooperated in presenting offerings (29), some doing the offering, and others assisting to keep things clean, making sure the flour was ground and properly prepared for shewbread and grain offerings, and so forth. All were inter-related in praying, going about their roles in communion with God (30), or so they did if they worshipped God according to the ideal.

More about Divisions for Levite Service (24)

David recognized a census and distinct services for Levites to attend to (23). Now, closely related to this, he puts the men of the tribe into twenty-four specific groups to fulfill temple service in successive courses. Those of a particular course would serve for a period of time, then those of the next course would relieve them, and so on.

The wise orderliness could contribute to fresh, efficient service. With this, aspects of prayer, just as other facets in the procedure, could be enhanced. Such an order of courses was kept up even into New Testament times. Zacharias, in Luke 1:8–10, fulfilled his ministration on duty when his course was due, and a part of it was a ministry in prayer.

Courses for sons of Aaron in priestly service are listed in 1 Chronicles 24:1–19, along with courses for other Levites (20–31). The division to carry out all phases and lines of service prepared for unity in completing the entire ministry. It also aided cooperation to see that all functions were conducted well.

Designations for Prayer in Temple Songs (25)

David, who had written, by now, many of the psalms for the "Hymn Book of Israel," sets apart twenty-four courses of Levites to sing and prophesy in accompaniment to musical instruments. This temple service is devoted to thanksgiving/praise to the Lord (2, 3). The ministers of music were chosen from three families, sons of Asaph, Jeduthun, and Heman.

The choosing of the ministers (1–7). An introduction relates that David and a committee designated the musicians. It also mentions some of the instruments to furnish music for songs.

After the introduction are lists of singers/players in the three families: four of Asaph (2), six of Jeduthun (3), and fourteen of Heman (4, 5). Each man was answerable to his father and to the king. A splendid ministry in prayerful singing is suggested by the large pool of trained vocalists and skilled instrumentalists to call upon, a total of 288!

The courses for the music (8–31). Teachers and talented trainees took part in this (8). The list of the twenty-four courses follows, totaling 288 musicians. Casting lots was the method of choosing, a means of looking to the Lord to point out His will by the way stones showed

(Prov. 16:33; cf. 18:18). We have no mention of the method after Acts 1, as the emphasis turns to the Holy Spirit who fills and gives guidance.

Deployment of Other Servants (26)

Temple service would need other dedicated personnel, now named: guards for the gates (1–19), treasury attendants to supervise monies given to God's service (20–28), and officials and judges to arbitrate in many questions (29–32).

The Levite guards (gate attendants) of Korah's and Merari's lines (1, 19) included those blessed in spiritual service (5), men of strong ability (6). This was an important niche of service, and Psalm 84 from the sons of Korah exemplifies a writer exulting in prayer at his privilege—being a gate keeper in the house of his Lord. This service to God's glory is so much better than dwelling in the tents of wickedness, for it is to the Lord who is a sun and shield, who gives grace and glory and holds nothing good back from those who walk trusting Him (10–12).

These servants, like others in 1 Chronicles 22ff., are selected with a desire to live by God's leading, shown by lots (26:13).

Appointees to temple treasury service dealt with such matters as assuring that gifts dedicated to certain phases of God's work were used that way. For example, spoil won in battles could be devoted to God to finance repair of God's house (27). To lead giving the Lord what was His would require sensitivity to His word and to Him in prayer. Servants seeking His will in prayer would need wisdom, purity of motive free from greed, and vision to see His cause advanced.

Magistrates in various capacities in the work of the Lord and of the king (30) would likewise only pursue the service rightly if they did it by the word and by prayer. The passage here does not specifically mention these, but the Chronicles' focus on tenderness to God's will shows how they pertain (2 Chr. 16:9). For *any* role of service to God, trustful prayer as in Jabez (1 Chr. 4:9, 10) and the transjordania soldiers (5:18–22) would be relevant.

This applies, then, even for David's civil leaders (Chap. 27). Verse 24 there is a reminder of God's judgment for sin even in a civil census, and the value put on doing God's will. David had not sought God's will about a census, but when God rebuked his project, he sought the Lord in humble prayer (cf. 2 Sam. 24; 1 Chr. 21). The principle of acting in submission to Him in His word and prayer is as important for any servant as it was for Saul (1 Chr. 10:13, 14) and for David!

Declaration to Solomon of God's Temple Plans (28, 29)

David had charged Solomon in private (22). Now he declares to him in public his clarification and charge for the temple (28). After this he testifies to the assembly (29:1) his commitment in giving to the project. His example rouses others, too, to a fervor to share in giving (29:6–9). Finally, David expresses the content of prayer befitting the great God of the temple (29:10–20).

The outgoing king's declarations are in three steps.

In clarifying (28:1–7). David addresses all Israel (vv. 2, 8, 21), reviewing his earlier desire to build a house for God but God's choice for his son to fulfill this. God's authority had been for David to be king, now that authority is shifting to Solomon (5), and so is the project (6). If Solomon steadfastly obeys the Lord's word (and those in his line continue to, 8), the Lord will establish the Solomonic kingdom forever (7). Later, Solomon's drift in disobedience, and that of some kings after him leads to a temporary loss of the kingdom (cf. 2 Chr. 36:1–21). God will resume it with the greater David as king (Ezek. 21:26–27).

In charging Solomon and Israel (28:8–29:9). After his clarification sets things in perspective, David challenges his son before "all Israel" and "our God" (8). If he obeys, and kings in his line obey, God will bless; if not God will reject them. Obedience involves seeking Him (9), and prayer is at the heart of this (2 Chr. 7:14).

David charges his successor to show courage and lead in building, keeping in step with God (10). He gives Solomon the temple blueprint, a guide manual for divisions of priests and Levites in service there, and other details (11–18). God gave all the detail to David, moving him as he recorded His will (19). This assures Solomon and his people that the charge is truly God's, not a brainchild of David.

The charge goes on in verses 20, 21. David gives two sides of it. The *positive* side is for Solomon to be strong and courageous. Of course, God will be His wisdom, strength, and everything else (22:12; 28:9). On the *negative* side, Solomon is not to let fear cripple his effort, for the Lord of the covenant, the God of all power, "my God" provides His presence to assure success. God, on His side, will not fail or forsake the new king who fulfills His will.

This is a great reassurance to show God is able to help Solomon rise to the challenge.

Not only does David encourage his son with *God's* enablement, but he bolsters him with *men's* help (21). The divisions of priests and Levites is arranged for (Chaps. 22–26), and every man of any skill needed will be there to assist. All Solomon needs do is speak, and needs will be met.

David's charge widens to all Israel (29:1–9). He emphasizes who the temple is for, God, as an incentive to cooperation. Then he reviews his all-out commitment in providing for what is needed in the temple. Inspired by this example, others also devoted various treasures to be used in God's house. The immediate result was a shared rejoicing by David and all the people.

David's declaration about the house, finally, is one of prayer (29:10–20). It reflects a content of David's own exemplary concept in God, and calls on others to pray, blessing the Lord the temple is to honor.

In content. David prays with a content of four aspects important in talking with the Lord.

(1) Praise (10–13). He blesses (ascribes praise to) God as Israel's God, lauds the greatness of His Person and His power, glory, vic-

tory, majesty, and possession of all that is in heaven and earth (cf. Ps. 24:1). The last detail agrees with Melchizedek's and Abram's recognition of the possessor of heaven and earth (Gen. 14).

David praises God as the source of riches and honor, as Solomon will discover in answer to his own prayer later (cf. on 1 Kgs. 3). God is able to make people great and strengthen them to do His will (12).

(2) Affirmation and questioning in humility (14–17). David feels that he and his people are unworthy even in their offerings for the house. Even what they contributed was first a gift from God's generosity. They are only sojourners in a land He gave them, short in their lives, without hope apart from Him. He also affirms his joy in seeing the people offer so willingly.

Much prayer in Scripture, as here, is affirmation. It expresses a worshipful humility, recognition of Him and His blessing, the fulfillment He gives, and so many other things.

(3) Intercession (18, 19). David is an advocate pleading for God to continue the commitment in the people, drawing their hearts to Him. He also intercedes for a sound heart in Solomon to obey God's word and lead in realizing the temple.

(4) Concern that calls others to praise God, too (20). When their long-time king stirred them to "bless the Lord your God," the people did this, bowing low in worship to God and in honor to David.

This prayer was followed the next day by Israel's sacrifices. Among these were burnt offerings, consumed entirely on the bronze altar as a reflection of the people's whole-hearted submission to the Lord (21).

Principles for prayer are bountiful in 1 Chronicles 22–26, 28–29. Here are only a few:

(1) David who calls others to do God's will in building a house of prayer models obedience himself in his praying. When a leader's prayer challenges others, how different it is from the leaders who plead for prayer in others but practice little themselves.

(2) David credits God's word as determinative in coordination with prayer. He cites that word in the covenant as sufficient to sponsor the steps he is taking. He knows, as he himself wrote, that "The steps of a man are established by the Lord . . ." (Ps. 37:23). He realizes what Psalm 119 expresses in such a variety of ways, for example,

verse 38: "Establish Thy word to Thy servant, As that which produces reverence for Thee."

(3) Lots are a legitimate method, at the time, of seeking God's will, as Proverbs 16:33 confirms. The last mention of their biblical use is in Acts 1. After that, and especially as believers had a message completed in Christ and apostolic writings, they would seek His will in the Word, still by prayer, guided by the Holy Spirit, as Acts often emphasizes.

(4) David's prayer is governed by the conviction that God's sufficiency is able to supply every need (1 Chr. 22:11, 12; 29:10–16).

(5) Songs on the heart and lips as vehicles of prayer can have a transforming effect expressing worship that glorifies the Lord. Prayer songs can be at His house, a building; or they can be in His greater house, the temple that is the believer's body that He indwells today (1 Cor. 6:19, 20). In Old Testament times, as now, a believer might speak to God wherever he or she might be. Many are the examples: Abram at an altar (Gen. 21:33), Jacob with a pillow of stone (Gen. 28), Moses on the mount, Samson in a Philistine arena, Paul on a river bank (Acts 16), departed saints in heaven (Rev. 6:9–11), and soon. God is present wherever one cries to him (cf. Ps. 139).

(6) The impact of a godly life, as David's, sometimes is a help to another, as Solomon in his early reign having a longing for godly wisdom (1 Kgs. 3). Reading the accounts of differing kings shows, however, that this is no guarantee. Even Solomon drifted later, good kings such as Asa and Jehoshaphat failed badly at times, and some successors to godly kings were very evil. It is important to leave a godly legacy to those who follow; it is also realistic to admit that everyone must personally insist on the decisions that pursue true godliness. A borrowed walk with God wears off fast.

Prayer in 2 Chronicles

2 Chronicles 1:6–12

Pertinent points on the possible authorship, date, theme and outline were a part of the 1 Chronicles introduction.

Several passages are near enough reduplications of parts in Samuel and/or Kings to make further comments unnecessary. One such prayer scenario is Solomon's petition for wisdom to guide His people (cf. 1 Kgs. 3).

2 Chronicles 2:12

Hiram's Praise to God

King Hiram (Huram in Heb.) of the city-state Tyre on the Mediterranean sea coast prays after Solomon contacts him for supplies to build the temple.

The Proposal of Solomon (1–10)

Judah's new king follows up on his father David's passion and preparation for a temple. Now he himself will see that it is built. He also plans a royal palace.

All of this sets the context for Hiram's prayer.

Solomon assigns men to transport materials, workers to secure quarry stones, and supervisors (2). He also contacts Hiram, worshipper of a Phoenician god. The other king's friendship with David encouraged Judah's leader to request cedars and other trees for lumber, also a man skilled in craftsmanship to help Judah's men of expertise. Solomon in return pledges wheat, barley, wine, and oil.

His letter sets before Hiram his enterprise to build a temple befitting the God he worships. He acknowledges his God in forthright testimony to the Phoenician. God is, he bears witness, two things that make a splendid temple reasonable. He is *over* all gods in greatness, and He is *omnipresent*, everywhere present in the heavens, highest heavens, and beyond. As for himself, Solomon expresses *unworthiness* to construct a house for the God so great, but a passion to have a place to offer incense to Him.

Incense, as mentioned in Exodus 30, seems vitally related to prayer rising as it does in fragrance well-pleasing to the Lord (cf. Ps. 141:2).

The Praise of Hiram (11–16)

Only verse 12 relates Hiram's prayer sentiment as a part of his letter answering Solomon. The prayer and attendant remarks involve three points.

His awareness (11). Hiram states his awareness that God's love for Israel had prompted Him to raise up Solomon as king. This shows some knowledge of truth, probably gained from David. For the Lord's covenant love was behind His many blessings to Abraham, Isaac, Jacob, and their descendants (Gen. 12:1–3). Hiram's statement is probably at the same time a good will compliment to Solomon as in verse 12, expressing confidence that he will be a good leader.

His acknowledgment (12). The Tyrian potentate says two things here. One is a high tribute acknowledging God. He invokes blessing on God, or else affirms the worthiness in Him as Solomon's source of blessing. In either case Hiram's gesture has the words if not the spiritual reality of praise. The One he extols to please Solomon is the powerful God of Israel and before and beyond that the creator of heaven and earth. He also as the author of life is the One who has given David a wise son.

The second focus in the verse is a high compliment to Solomon. He is, writes the head over Tyre, a wise son endowed (he probably means by God) with skill in decision-making and grasp of situations. A report of special wisdom that Solomon had shown (1 Kgs. 3; 2 Chr. 1) may have spread even to the leader of Tyre (cf. 1 Kgs. 3:28).

His acceptance (13–16). Hiram promised the services of a skilled craftsman, Hiram-abi, whose name in honor of Hiram meant "Hiram my father." The king also agreed to float logs on rafts from the forest of Lebanon by the Mediterranean to Joppa. Solomon's haulers would then transport them overland to Jerusalem.

Reflect on principles before moving on. First, a life of prayer to God can also be a life of speaking outright testimony in honor of God to an unbeliever. Second, even a pagan in whatever gesture of prayer to God he makes, can have some idea, second-hand, of how God has worked among those professing to know the Lord. With this can be at least a dulled sense of God's worthiness to receive praise (cf. Hiram). How much of it is genuine and how much tact in saying the "right thing" in good social relations, God knows. Third, a believer who prays sincerely to God may get His answer by His inclining even a pagan to provide his favors. God is never limited in the ways He can work.

2 Chronicles 5:13, 14

David's appointed Levitical singers and players of instruments (cf. 1 Chr. 22–26, 28–29) provide music when the Ark of the Covenant is placed in the temple's most holy place. This was in view earlier (cf. 1 Kgs. 6–7).

2 Chronicles 6:1, 2; 6:3–42; 7:3; 7:12–22

Prayers in dedicating the completed temple and God's response to Solomon accepting the house were the discussion in 1 Kings 6–7. Here the details are a part of the Chronicles as well.

2 Chronicles 9:7, 8

Praise from a Visiting Queen

The visiting queen of the Arabian Desert area, Sheba, praises the Lord after listening to Solomon's wise answers to her questions.

Her Experience of His Wisdom (1–6)

The queen makes the camel trip just to test the Judean king's wisdom of which she had heard. She asks Solomon every question that occurs to her, and in each case the Judean king's answer impresses her favorably. Her quest of answers is one example of several national leaders who came to hear this man's wisdom (9:23). Seen in its right connection, the wisdom is a credit to the Lord who had given it in answer to prayer (cf. 1 Kgs. 3; 2 Chr. 1).

Of course the queen also feels deeply awed in seeing the splendid temple, the food served at Solomon's meals, the seating of his royal servants, the roles of his counselors, their dress, and other details. But the one paramount subject that drew her respect was his wisdom (5, 6). She could not believe a man could be so wise until she has heard him herself; now she feels that the half had not been told her of this remarkable leader.

Her Expression of Her Worship (7, 8)

Sheba's leader is persuaded of two things.

The privilege of those who hear such wisdom. Any servants of Solomon are in a blessed sphere. She is so right. The same is true of any who hear and follow the light of such wisdom, for it is from Him and is His gift. Such wisdom would come to be expressed in the myriad details of biblical books such as Proverbs and Ecclesiastes. It also would be in all writings of God's servants which would become parts of His word. In essence, Proverbs 3:5, 6 would crystallize its relation to prayer: when a person would *trust* the Lord with his whole being, *refuse dependence* on his own wisdom, and in all the currents of life *submit to God* letting Him guide, *God would smooth his way.* That is, He would clear obstacles out of his path, and open the way for himself.

The praise-worthiness of God who is in control. Here, now, is the queen's praise to the One who is the source of all the good. She invokes or calls a blessing on Him; she wishes Him praise. He is, she acknowledges "your God," a very high privilege for Solomon. She may or may not have responded to Him to be "my God" during the visit or reflecting on it later. Some in high places have, such as Melchizedek, king of Salem (Gen. 14), Naaman the Syrian commander (2 Kgs. 5), and so on.

A part of the queen's praise, as well, is the tribute to God for His favor in giving Solomon the throne, and His aim that the rule be His. A broader recognition of God giving all kings their privilege to rule appears in Psalm 75. The visitor even recognizes that God's raising of her host to the kingship was an expression of His love to Israel. Hiram of Tyre had perceived that, too (2 Chr. 2:11). Finally, the royal lady of Sheba discerns the tone Solomon's leadership must take to fulfill God's will. The role is his "to do justice and righteousness."

In all probability, Solomon's answers from God to all the questions had instructed the queen so that she would have these clear perceptions. God's word, in written or oral communication, is a lamp to a person's feet, a light on his path (Ps. 119:105).

Their Expressions of Worthiness (9–12)

Both the visitor and the host conferred lavish gifts on one another. Bounties of the queen included about 144,000 ounces of gold, abundant spices, and many precious stones. Judah's king bestowed on his guest in turn rich gifts that he deemed appropriate, though neither 1 Kings 10 nor the account here identify what they were.

Principles in prayer are evident here. First, praise is fitting on the lips of a pagan person. His or her transaction with God may or not enter into salvation, but God is worthy of praise from everything that has breath (Ps. 150:6). This is true of God whether the tribute comes from this queen, Nebuchadnezzar, Cyrus, Darius, or whoever. That it is appropriate for all to bow before God, which finally will occur (Isa. 45:23–25; Phil. 2:10, 11), is not to say that any without salvation have His special promises of answers. And it does not say that they have an effective prayer life.

Second, the register of divine wisdom on human thinking is the best stimulant for suitable prayer. The true wisdom comes to be written as part of "God's Word" in the long process of progressive revelation. This wisdom reflecting God's will is the very source for guiding prayers to be aligned with His will (cf. John 15:7, 8; 1 John 5:14, 15).

Third, it is always suitable to give God the credit in praise. Here the queen traces Solomon's reign to his God, discerns something of His love for those of Israel, and sees the wise course that wisdom should take—in justice and righteousness. Even when the one praying cannot think of other things to pray, he or she always can be apt in exalting the Lord. Many prayers in the Bible furnish ideas for praise, as here and in Psalms 145–150, for example.

2 Chronicles 12:6, 12

Humility in Prayer Touches God

It is relevant to show, at least briefly, the possible relation to prayer though prayer is not mentioned.

Succeeding Solomon his father, Rehoboam the king and his people following his lead abandoned the Lord (1). As in the cycles of sin in Judges, God brought pressure in the form of Egypt's King Shishak conquering several Judean cities. Jerusalem was next on his target list.

God's prophet Shemaiah was frank with Rehoboam and his officials at a strategic defense conference. God had forsaken them to the mercy of Shishak due to their forsaking Him. The king and his princes humbled themselves, with prayer no doubt on their hearts and lips (6, 12). The acknowledgment "The Lord is righteous" (6) is their confession, the heart of their prayer.

An attitude such as Proverbs 3:5, 6 articulates would be the essence of the prayer affirmation here. The governmental leaders trusted the Lord, did not fall back on their own wisdom, and acknowledged Him (here His righteousness and probably their own unrighteousness, cf. 1 John 1:9). He made their paths smooth, or smoother than they might have been. Though Egypt's king took many treasures away in a treaty, God did not permit him to take over Jerusalem. He withdrew, so that Rehoboam and his people breathed easier in basically good conditions for a while (12).

The principle of humility as strategic in prayer, and blessing God can give, has already been a part of 2 Chronicles (7:14).

2 Chronicles 13:14

Prayer in a Desperate War Trap

King Abijah succeeded Rehoboam on the throne of David and Solomon. He found himself in battle against King Jeroboam and his soldiers of Israel (the north). This arena became one of prayer and victory.

The Conflict of Israel and Judah (1–3)

According to the chronicler Judah went to battle with Israel outnumbered two to one (3).

The Contrasts in Their Trust (4–12)

An introduction (4, 5). Abijah of Judah stood on the slope of Mount Zemaraim in Ephraim's tribal territory and challenged the warriors of the opposing Israelite army. His first emphasis was on God giving kingship over His people to David and his sons (cf. 2 Sam. 7:12–16). The point is that Israel, which had rebelled against Judah and broken away, ought to humble themselves and come back into unity.

The trust of Israel (6–9). Abijah yells out that Jeroboam has led a rebellion, gaining momentum for his northern kingdom while Rehoboam had not had great military strength. He reminds Jeroboam that if he goes ahead in attack now it is even further resistance to the Lord's true royal line based on human military advantage. He points out Jeroboam's reliance on two golden calves he set up as gods (cf. 1 Kgs. 12), also his rejecting God's designated Levite ministers and installing false priests from any of his tribes.

The trust of Judah (10–12). By contrast, Abijah shouts, his southern people look to the Lord as their God and honor His legitimate priestly servants. He warns that God is going ahead of Judah, that His priests will sound the trumpets signaling attack. Israel will be fighting against "the Lord God of your fathers," and "you will not succeed."

Unlike some situations before this in Scripture, Abijah did not secure this confidence through inquiring of a true prophet. Or he apparently had not consulted the high priest and the Urim and Thummim in the pouch of his breastplate. Without prior preparation of this sort, he was on the spot in the crisis before the clash.

The Cry in Prayer (13, 14)

Two things occur rapidly. One is the *peril* Judah sees when they become aware that Israel has caught them between two large forces, in a death trap. The other is the *prayer* itself, a call for help from God. There is no way out but up. A simple, desperate petitionary appeal, probably on the lips of Abijah, his soldiers, and his priests, is the strategy to meet the crisis.

The Conquest by the Lord (15–20)

God caused Judah's warriors to prevail and put the northern troops on the run. Twice the verses say that *God* accomplished the victory, He "routed Jeroboam" and "gave them into their (Judah's) hand." More than 60 percent, or 500,000 of Israel's soldiers lost their lives fighting against the Lord, as Abijah had warned in advance (12).

The secret of victory is plain in verse 18. Judah's men conquered "because they trusted in the Lord, the God of their fathers." God had given a firm lesson to the northern ranks; He had demonstrated that He was faithfully in line with His will that David's sons be recognized as kings, and the men of Levi as His priests and attendants.

Defiance against His will cost the Israelites dearly; a strong lesson was needed to try to bring them to their spiritual senses.

One other note is significant. The leader of resistance to God, Jeroboam, could not regain military strength with God holding him down. The end came when the Lord "struck him, and he died." The 1 Kings 13 record shows that Jeroboam never turned from his evil (v. 33). As Scripture often illustrates, the way of the treacherous is hard (Prov. 13:15). If what is hard does not come in the present life, it will in the next (cf. Ps. 73:4, 17–20), in contrast to the blessing of the saved (23–25).

Foremost among principles of prayer here is the role of trust in calling on God (14, 18). Those praying can have misgivings about the feebleness of trust in itself; it is God, the object of trust, that makes all the difference. They "trusted in the Lord, the God of their fathers." As is so often repeated in the roll call of faith in Hebrews 11, "by faith" in God a victory was gained. The Lord had pledged His help in covenant love to Abraham's people who would look to Him (Ex. 6:3, etc.). His many mighty works had given triumph to Abraham, Isaac, Jacob, Joseph, Moses, Joshua, Samuel, Jabez, David, Elijah, Elisha and others. The way of victory had always been the way of prayer with trust in the right Object.

2 Chronicles 14:11–15

Prayer Against Great Odds

Asa began to reign over Judah with a spiritual zest, and his trust was put to a special test facing an awesome army. But first the context.

His Expressive Allegiance to the Lord's Way (1–8)

The chronicler paints the background for the prayer first. Asa filled his initial ten years modeling a godly impetus for his people. His zeal for the good and the right is summed up in verse 2. Examples appear. He got rid of altars and high places devoted to other false gods. He issued a staunch call to his people to seek the true God and obedience to His word (4), and to some extent saw them rally to this (7).

God's response was as James frames His principle centuries later: draw near to God and He will draw near to you (James 4:8). Asa's expressive allegiance to the Lord's will brought His rest from enemies, a blessing mentioned three times after Asa began (5, 6, 7).

His Exclusive Acknowledgment Of God's Strength (9–11)

An Ethiopian invasion by a million soldiers and three hundred chariots threatens. Asa's army is outnumbered nearly two to one.

Asa goes to God in prayer. The first aspect he emphasizes is *affirmation* of the Lord's singular sufficiency. No one besides the Lord can help in the battle between the powerful (here the invaders) and the weak (Asa's forces). His own fighters, he affirms, have no strength—none that is adequate to contend with an army so vast and so well-supported by chariot warfare.

That candid admission is not a denial of truth. Asa's warriors did have some strength as men adept in battle and as valiant soldiers. Asa means that they have no strength that can match what they are up against in the situation. The principle is like that of John 15:5. "Without Me," says Jesus, "you are not able to do anything." Of course, believers can do many things in self-sufficiency, not relying on Him, and can be as busy as a cat in a dog kennel. The idea is that the believer is not able to do what the John 15:15 context calls for, bear fruit of abiding, apart from Jesus living through His "branch."

Asa showed honesty, humility, and a gaze fixed on God. When a person comes to the end of his resources, or preferably before, God has the resources guaranteed to be enough. He is the great El Shaddai of Genesis 17:1, the God all-powerful, the God who is Enough. Human weakness, acknowledged, is the background for the display of incredible divine strength.

His Explicit Asking For God's Deliverance (11)

Asa turns into the *petition* aspect of prayer. His reasoning is in three phases.

The request. "So help us." Prayer in a tight spot need not be long and drawn out. Simplicity is a keynote when one cries to God in faith. God hears the sincere but brief appeal as well as the sincere lengthy one.

The relationship. "O Lord our God" defines it. Later, Asa says "Thou art our God." It makes all the difference that He is "our God." Naaman the leper had discovered that when he turned from reliance on Syrian gods to the God of Elisha, and had come up out of the Jordan a healed and saved man. Asa had known the Lord for several years, and would see His greatness afresh.

The reliance. "For we trust in Thee." Asa returns to *affirmation* in prayer, "and in Thy name have come against this multitude." The Lord's name had been important to people from Seth who called on Him, and would continue to be in the teaching of Jesus (John 14–16) and the apostles (Eph. 5:20). True believers of all times run to it and are safe.

What does Asa rely on God for? "Let not man prevail against Thee." If God failed, when His people met His principles of prayer, He would lose more than men. He would lose His honor, His integrity. But that is impossible. God can always win over men. His servants can be confident when their cause is His cause, their aim is His glory. For then the battle is the Lord's, and He is the greatest warrior (Ex. 15:2, 3).

The Exciting Accomplishment of God's Victory (12–15)

Descriptions of the conquest are vivid: "So the Lord routed the Ethiopians"; "they were shattered before the Lord"; "they (Asa's men) carried away much plunder"; "the dread of the Lord had fallen on them." Not only did the invaders flee toward Gerar in Philistine territory. So many fell to the Judeans that they could never regroup, but were at an utter loss.

The victory God gave to the praying Asa included even a conquest of several cities around Gerar, and taking plunder home.

When the mighty triumph came to Judah, the people in the cities felt a dread at what God could help His own do.

Prayer principles spring from this. First, prayer need not shrink back in asking humanly impossible things. God is able to do great exploits against any odds. He cannot fail. This encourages prayer. Second, rather than turning to God as a last resort after relying on other avenues of help, it is wise to come before the Lord before the battle as Asa did. Third, be sure that the heart's trust is in God, and not simply the mouth in action. And with this be certain that the prayer is presented in His name, His ability, His honor, and His will.

2 Chronicles 15:8–16

A Prayer Oath of Obedience

The key verses are 14 and 15 which mention the oath. It is part of a larger context. As prayer always should do, it begins with the input of God's word which inclines men to His will (1–7).

The Conviction of God's Word (1–7)

One of the faithful prophets, Azariah, was moved by the Holy Spirit to minister the word to his King Asa. He focuses on one principle God can honor, the past, then the present which Asa faces.

The principle declared by God (2). This is the prophet's bottom line, and he puts it up front for the king and all of God's people. God's blessing or His blight is before them; they must choose. He is with them when they are with Him, for integrity blends with integrity and He honors in harmony with men honoring His ways. Blessing will be theirs if they seek Him (which includes prayer), for He will show His presence and help. The reverse is blight, in that forsaking Him meets with His forsaking them.

The past drift from God (3–6). God's spokesman reminds his countrymen of Israel's past generations abandoning God. They have turned from His spiritual leaders (priests) and His word. As in the days of Judges and often since then, the drift resulted in distress of every kind as God let them have what their own devices invited. They did not experience His presence or peace, for He sent special trials of other peoples conquering and pressuring them. He was seeking to turn them back to Himself.

In such trials, when Israelites did turn to God (including prayer as in the Judges cycles), He answered by His presence and support. The import of all this is already as clear as noonday, but the prophet spells it out as he did in verse 2.

The present devotion to God (7). Rather than grovel in distress, Asa and his people can enjoy the blessing. Azariah names two facets in such devotion.

(1) They must grasp their resource in God. The way to do this is to "be strong and do not lose courage." They can be strong by looking to God to be their strength as David had done in prayer (1 Sam. 30:6; Ps. 138:3). Asa had done this not long before (2 Chr. 14:11). Courage would come with His resource. God can rout discouragement that clouds a life shut up to its own inadequate supply.

(2) God will reward them for their work. Their work of trust and its obedience, in His grace, will bring the dividends of reward. The aspects of this that fit the context would be blessings such as a confidence of God's presence (3, 4), the benefits of proper priestly teaching and example (3), the enrichment of the word (3), and peace (5). Beyond these can even be blessings forever (cf. Ps. 23:6; 49:15; 73:23–25).

God's prophet has issued quite a challenge to provoke choice. What is the result?

The Covenant in Their Worship (8–19)

Asa took the challenge to heart and acted promptly to gain blessing rather than blight. Four steps sum up a spiritual revival.

The removal of sin (8, 16). Asa saw that the people got rid of idols in all the territory under his control. A prime example was the king's destroying of the image his own mother, Maacah, had made and his deposing her from queenship. This is quite an example of following integrity for the Lord over favoritism even to one's own family.

The restoration of the temple (8, 18). Asa led in restoring the bronze altar in the courtyard before the temple, to use it in worship of God. With this impetus, sacrifices to the Lord became common there (11).

The recovery of the people (9, 10). Asa summoned people of his kingdom to Jerusalem to seek the Lord. That the revival he led was registering its impact is evident in its attracting even people of Israel (the north) to join the worship. The aspect that was a magnet to them was seeing that "God was with him" (9), true to His word that the prophet had pledged (2).

The resolve in prayer (12–15). Those who assembled for the "spiritual life conference" meant business with the Lord. They joined in a covenant to seek Him "with all their heart and soul." This featured joining their decisions in a prayerful oath invoking (calling) the Lord to bless them as they clung closely to Him. Their gusto for this appears in their loud voices, shouting, and priestly trumpet blasts as well as rams' horn peals. These were probably in *affirmation* of their intent to God, *acclamation* to Him in praise, and *appeal* that prized Him for His leadership.

The quality of the resolve to do God's will was so stout that their covenant pledged to put to death any who held out against seeking God (13). When one realizes that every sinner is worthy of death that his sin deserves apart from grace, then refusal of grace is a choice for death. Here it is immediate; spurning God will inevitably lead to death for *all* who reject Him (Rom. 3:23; 6:23; Rev. 20:11–15).

God read sincerity in the approach to Him, letting the seekers find Him. A big way in which He manifested His presence where it was felt was in effecting rest from distress for those who prayed (15).

Human dedication may be legitimate even if lacking in absolute perfection. Asa the revivalist fell short. He did not remove the high places that were such a lure to his people (17). Still, the verse says, Asa's heart was blameless all his days. In view of his turning to an evil course later in Chapter 16, the meaning possibly is that he was blameless all his days of this era in his life.

Which principles stand out here? First, proper prayer lays hold of God's presence and peace (cf. Isa. 26:3; Phil. 4:6, 7). Second, the way of prayer as God designs it to be is the way to be (7; 1 Sam. 30:6; Ps. 138:3). Third, valuable reward results from prayer that is pure and earnest before God. For God is strong to the one whose heart is His completely (2 Chr. 16:9). Fourth, those who pray need to be whole-hearted in meaning business with God, pledging their hearts as He pledges His. Fifth, God-honoring prayer can result in firm steps of loyalty to honor His worthiness.

Sixth, prayer of a willing heart draws God's acceptance even when the one praying, as Asa, is imperfect. For such are we all. Seventh, a victory in prayer today is no guarantee of a victory tomorrow; tomorrow's victory is bonded to tomorrow's trust (cf. Asa's turning from God in Chapter 16).

2 Chronicles 18:6

This is a reduplication of details 1 Kings already gave about Jehoshaphat's league with Israel's wicked Ahab and inquiry of the Lord through Micaiah.

2 Chronicles 20:1–30

Victory in Praise

As other men, Jehoshaphat had his ups and downs. He was spiritually up most of his career as king (Chaps. 17, 19–20), though, to some degree, a compromiser in his alliance with Ahab (20).

Chapter 20, well along in his reign, relates a case of great triumph saturated with prayer. Jehoshaphat is here a shining example.

His Dependence on the Lord (1–13)

First, his peril is clear, as a coalition of invaders is marching to attack; then he utters his prayer.

The peril he undergoes (1, 2). A scout reaches Jehoshaphat with a report of a coalition on the move to strike him. Joined together against Judah are Moabites, Ammonites, and Edomites. The invaders had already gotten to Engedi, south of Jerusalem and not far west of the Dead Sea.

The prayer he utters (3–13). (1) The fear he feels. Naturally the king was disturbed, smitten by fear for his people, his city, the temple, and all that was dear. It is not a sin to feel fear; it is a sin when we feel fear and do not look to the Lord. God is understanding. The most frequent exhortation in the Bible is "fear not," first given by God in Genesis 17:1 and mentioned, as someone has counted it, 365 times in Scripture. That would be enough for every day of the year, and most days bring things to fear.

(2) The faith he fosters. Quickly the king devoted himself to seek God's remedy. He called his people to fast, and summoned them to Jerusalem to seek God in unison. Standing before the assembly in front of the temple, he himself led in prayer.

Aspects of prayer frequent in biblical prayers fill Jehoshaphat's pleading before God (6–12). The first is *praise* (6–8). He acknowledges, in question form, that God is God in the heavens, in control over all kingdoms (cf. Ps. 75), and has power so great none can stand against Him in battle. He affirms that one example of God's ability was His driving out the nations from Canaan and giving it to His people in covenant loyalty. Still on a praise note, he affirms that His people built a temple there for His name, recognizing His worthiness to be praised.

The second prayer aspect is *intercession* (9–12a). As Solomon also had prayed, Jehoshaphat tells God that whatever peril threatens His people, they will come before His face at this house, cry to Him for safety, and gain His deliverance (9). At this moment an alliance is en route to Jerusalem, aiming to drive God's people out from "Thy possession which Thou hast given us as an inheritance." His intercession asks if God will not judge the enemy, admits Judah's inability to cope with an army so large, and acclaims Him as the One their eyes are on (10–12).

The three verses just cited underscore reasons, actually, for expecting God's intervention. Prayer needs to be voiced in faith, expecting God to do His will. He ought to act because the enemy is challenging *His* land and people, because *He* alone is able (12; cf. 6) and Judah unable, and because *He* is the hope of His people who fix their gaze on Him (Prov. 3:5, 6).

Much of verse 12 is not only a request for help, but an *affirmation* of truth and a *confession* of where their trust is placed.

God's Defense of the People (14–30)

Four steps follow quickly in relation to victory.

The anticipation of it (14–17). Jahaziel is moved by God's Spirit to anticipate triumph. He, like Jeremiah and Ezekiel, is both a prophet and a priest. His words, "thus says the Lord," go right to the issue. He reminds them that "the battle is not yours but God's." He directs them in the way of approach to the enemy, and about the place where the Judeans will see the invaders coming. God will leave no need for Judah to fight this time. He alone worked deliverance at the Red Sea and at Samaria (2 Kgs. 7) and would in Hezekiah's day (2 Chr. 32:21), and at the cross of Christ. He would work alone in this as well. Jehoshaphat's people would merely be onlookers to testify that God answered prayer.

The awe over it (18, 19). Jehoshaphat and his people were in worshipful awe upon hearing this reassurance of deliverance. Some bowed, some fell down, all giving thanks/praise to the Lord. What God does, or what His word assures He is yet to do, ought to stimulate believing hearts to magnify His name. Why is there so little fervent prayer when we have such a great God worthy of abundant praise?

The appropriation of it (20, 21). A model of leadership here, Jehoshaphat did three things that helped his people. First, he did not stay behind but was right out there with them in the way to the enemy. Second, he encouraged them with words modeling a spirit of faith. Trust in the Lord and in the words of His true prophets, and they would be established and succeed. Third, he appointed qualified Levites to sing and praise the Lord in front of Judah's army. The essence of their message, drifting back along the ranks to inspire others, was "Give thanks to the Lord, for His loving-kindness is everlasting."

To act in such faith, and to sing that way, is certainly an appropriation of victory before it comes. Or, better, it is victory before victory, victory in expectation before victory confronting the enemy.

The accomplishing of it (22–30). God does it, but is able to use means He chooses. While the Judeans made the trek to the area, God removed the threat. As verse 23 explains, soldiers of two nations (Moab and Ammon) joined in attacking Edomite soldiers and cut them all down. Then those of the two nations left struck down one another. The Judeans gazed at the corpses left from the explosion that hatred ignited.

No explanation is offered for any human reasoning that may have been the Lord's means in this. Did the soldiers so expect to overwhelm Judah that greed over how the spoils would be dealt out led to killing others who could lessen their own shares? Remembrances of longstanding enmity could have had a part. God Himself is often said to work what He uses means to do, as bringing Babylon as His instrument to deal with Judah's sin, yet Babylon acting to gratify its own ambitions (cf. Hab. 1, 2).

After gathering spoils the alliance left, the Judeans gravitated to a great praise meeting. They then gave the site where they met the name "The Valley of Beracah," meaning "blessing." They blessed the Lord with praises for His deliverance. Returning to Jerusalem, they brought their instruments of praise to the temple. There they would continue to worship.

The God who heard and answered prayer gained fame even among other kingdoms. For in due time they heard the news of His victory. And Judah, now free of the threat the alliance posed, had rest in safety.

Principles for prayer are rich in this episode. First, it is wise to pray rather than faint (Luke 18:1). Jehoshaphat led in acting on that. Second, it is a help to faith to remember in prayer who God really is—God in the heavens, over all peoples and able to influence them. This is a great encouragement for intercessors who plead for conversions to His glory in other lands, or at home. Third, prayer mentioning God's temple (8) rightly focuses on this being the place of God's name, with all it stands for. Whether in prayer today for His church as the universal temple (dwelling place), or the local church of believers (not the wood, stone, pews, etc.), or the believer's body/temple, the temple is the place of His name. Taking that to heart can arouse more fervent prayer.

Fourth, make prayer specific; name the details clearly and without vague generality, as Jehoshaphat specified the enemy (10). Fifth, pray realizing that attacks on God's people are attacks against God, and He reacts to these as His challenges. Sixth, reflect in prayer that God can win a victory in whatever valid way He prefers at the time. He can do it through His people or without their lifting a finger. Seventh, steep prayer in praise ahead of meeting a crisis, while meeting it, and after the answer distills sweetly in the heart.

2 Chronicles 26:5; 27:6

Prayer and Seeking the Lord

Neither passage mentions prayer. Yet both speak of men at the time sold out to God, for whom prayer undoubtedly was a mainspring of life.

In 26:4, 5, King Uzziah is honored with one of the finest tributes in God's word. He "did right in the sight of the Lord" whose eyes move to and fro throughout all the earth to furnish strong support to those whose hearts are perfect (soundly devoted) toward Him (16:9). This is joined with the summary that Uzziah "continued to seek God" and "as long as he sought the Lord, God prospered him."

Former governor Mark Hatfield of Oregon, a Christian, liked to keep an inscription on his desk with those last words.

In 27:6, Uzziah's son Jotham as king "became mighty because he ordered his ways before the Lord his God." While he followed in the obedient path of his father, he did not turn aside to a shameful failure as Uzziah did. Uzziah insisted on offering incense, intruding into the ministry of a priest, and God covered him with leprosy (27:2), though his salvation remained sure.

To have a favorable summary written over one's life such as Jotham's, or to a large degree Uzziah's, is a very great blessing. Those who read of it should take to heart the challenge it issues to walk in God's way all the way. The doing of right and the seeking of God will be flavored much in the incense of prayer.

2 Chronicles 29–32

Prayer in Hezekiah's Reign

Prayer permeates the kingdom under Hezekiah, one of the truly good kings of Judah (715–687 B.C.). His prayerful leadership sets the tone for his people; they are revived in prayer, and even the great prophet Isaiah is a prayer example sought out.

Two other biblical passages offer parallels or details adding to the chronicler's record (2 Kgs. 18–20; Isa. 36–39), so these will be drawn into the one summary here.

The Righteousness Of Hezekiah's Reign (29–31)

This saturating focus is clear in at least five emphases in the three chapters. Prayer plays a large role an these as they, in turn, prepare Hezekiah and his people for prayer facing the fearful Assyrian challenge in Chapter 32.

Here are the ways righteousness appears.

The character in capsule (29:1, 2). Hezekiah took the throne at twenty-five, and reigned twenty-nine years until he was fifty-four.

Verse 2 sets the overall tone of his emphasis. He did right in the sight of the Lord, right as God appraises values (cf. 1 Sam. 2:3). This represented following the good parts of the example David had patterned for those taking the throne after him.

Later, 31:20, 21 adds further summary. Hezekiah kept to what was "good, right, and true before the Lord his God." The three areas of godliness are later a summary of a life with the fruit of light, or of the Spirit (Eph. 5:9; cf. Gal. 5:22, 23). Verse 21 of 2 Chronicles 31 comments that every work Hezekiah began in the service of God's house sensitive to His word and in seeking Him, he did with all his heart. His devotion was fervently full, and he prospered, just as 26:5 so aptly expresses the principle.

The commands to be true (29:3–11). Hezekiah lost no time when he assumed the throne and did not drag his feet. Right away he was in action, zealous to do the will of God, "in the first month."

Prayer, though not mentioned at this point, will exercise a pervasive influence. This will be explicit in verses 10, 35, 36, as it is certainly assumed in the capsule (2) and corrections Hezekiah fosters for God's glory (6, 7, 11).

What does he command of his subjects? He is zealous to repair in God's house so that it might serve God's purpose. He calls priests and Levitical attendants in ministry to consecrate themselves and the temple for God-exalting worship. He has them think in a way opposite to former Israelites in verse 6, to do good (not evil), follow God and not forsake Him, and approach His presence rather than turn away from Him.

His impetus also entails removing uncleanness from the temple, having doors open for holy service, keeping lamps lighted, offering incense (cf. Ex. 30 and its prayer relation), and presenting offerings acknowledging the Lord.

Hezekiah is forthright in telling the spiritual leaders that former Israelites suffered distresses due to sin. His passion is to follow a covenant pledge to God in seeking His friendship toward this people in place of His anger. He charges the Levitical servants to fulfill the holy ministry God chose them to carry out (cf. Deut. 33:9). This will involve services in the paragraph immediately above. Here Hezekiah phrases it as "to minister to Him (in prayerful worship), and to be His ministers (to lead others in worship) and burn incense (in seeking His face with fragrance, cf. Ps. 141:2)."

The righteous fervor is already quite evident.

The cleansing (12–19). Responding obediently, the priests and Levites consecrated themselves and the temple. They threw out anything unclean. Within about two weeks they had completed the purge, making the temple a fit place for worship.

The celebrations (29:20–30:27). (1) First Hezekiah leads in a celebration by people in Jerusalem. These initially and officially consecrate the temple afresh to be set apart to the Lord (29:20–36). Prayer is a large part of this. It accompanies sin, burnt offerings, and peace offerings: three of the five main ones (Lev. 1–7). With the sin offerings it was natural to *confess* sins that God would remove from the sinners and relate to the sacrifices He accepted, in substitutionary atonement. These sacrificial animals represented, in God's provision, Christ's offering, which alone could take away sin (Heb. 10:4). Yet God was pleased to give the worshipers in the Old Testament days His forgiveness, as He validated the offerings by that of Christ which He reckoned in advance to their account.

Burnt offerings, totally consumed on the altar, pictured the complete sacrifice of the person to Him. Prayer was apt in this whether in the form of *affirming* God's worthiness of full devotion, or one's (or the nation's) wishes to be yielded to Him, or in *thanksgiving/praise* for the privilege, or *petition* for being led in full surrender. Christ finally was the truest burnt offering (Eph. 5:2), and He consecrated believers to God (cf. Heb. 10:10, 14). Believers' offering themselves in that same devoted spirit follows as a fitting response (cf. Rom. 12:1; 6:13).

Peace offerings celebrated the peace of God and peace with God which His grace and mercy provide in covenant bounty. An appropriate response is one of *affirming* the reality in which one exults, also in *thanking/praising* God for such compassionate care.

But prayer is not just involved in the offerings. It is a permeating content and flavor in the music of God's celebrating people, led by Levites here (29:25–28, 30). It was an inspiration stimulating rejoicing in *worship* and in *praise* (29, 30, 36).

That was just the preliminary worship service. Hezekiah led in another, broader one.

(2) The Passover for all of the kingdom (30:1–27).

First comes the king's summons to meet in Jerusalem (1–12). He sends messengers to call all in his kingdom there for the celebration.

Second are the specifics of the Passover (13–17). An assembly, a very large one, answered the call and made the trek to the temple (13). The respondents were fired up, following the tone of their leader. Their *action* follows in ridding altars devoted to idols from the city (14). This done, they give their *acknowledgment* of God by sacrifices and songs. As mentioned in Chapter 29, aspects of prayer were integral to these.

Another expression of prayer was in *advocacy*. Hezekiah exercised it when interceding to God to pardon those among his people who had not yet consecrated themselves (18). When he pled for His mercy, He gave it, presumably working a spirit of worship He could approve in the people's hearts. A second example of *advocacy* was that of the priests in blessing the people (27). As Numbers 6:22–27 has already reviewed, their intercessory ministry was expressed in several details seeking blessing on the people they led. What they invoked from God was "heard," reaching God and gaining His answers (2 Chr. 30:27).

Other changes in a godly trend (31:1–21). Hezekiah's passionate example for the Lord draws the chronicler's further descriptions.

(1) Destruction of idol objects throughout the kingdom (1). Before, God's people took care of this in the temple and Jerusalem. Now, their spiritual courage impelled them out to other cities to

conduct a similar, thorough purge. Fervency for God's glory leads to fervency against what stands opposed to it. By the same principle, believers of God's church are urged to put on the Lord Jesus Christ (the positive) and make not provision (the negative) for the flesh to fulfill its lusts (Rom. 13:14).

(2) Designation of Levites (2). Hezekiah designated men of Levi to minister in offerings and lead in thanksgiving/praise. Prayer is strategic in each phase as shown on Chapter 29.

(3) Distribution to temple service (3–19). The king led his people by giving to support the temple ministry and called on others to contribute as they were able. Numbers 18:8 and other passages in God's word had called for such giving. The people gave abundantly in grain, new wine, oil, honey, and other produce, offering tithes of all. The treasure of contributions was more than enough to meet the needs of the priests and other Levites.

Prayer in praise was on the lips of Hezekiah and his leaders when they saw the amount given (8). Hezekiah directed that store rooms be allocated to hold the gifts, and Levites be named to distribute them to the proper uses.

(4) The devotion in summary (20, 21; cf. 29:2).

Reliance on the Lord Against Assyria (32)

Assyria's mighty army is invading the land in a strike that Assyria's annals report brought forty-six cities under their conquest. While occupied in Lachish, southwest of Jerusalem, the Assyrian leader Sennacherib sent an envoy to demand Hezekiah's surrender before the Assyrians inevitably would conquer Jerusalem.

The threat occurs in a context the chronicler is careful not to let the reader miss. Then the drama mounts swiftly. Passages parallel or adding details are 2 Kings 18–20 and Isaiah 36–39.

The context (1). Sennacherib issues his challenge "After these acts of faithfulness" by Hezekiah and his people (2 Chr. 29–31). This is important, for God's principle is that His eyes move through all the earth that He might show Himself strong in behalf of any whose hearts are perfect before Him (2 Chr. 16:9). This is of the same essence as Abraham walking with Him, then "after these things" (Gen. 22:1), God put him to the most difficult test, asking that he offer his son.

The capitulation at first (2 Kgs. 18:13–16). In Hezekiah's fourteenth year (701 B.C.) Sennacherib began his conquests nearby. Jerusalem's king initially agreed to pay tribute if Assyria would back off. This he did in all the silver in the temple and the royal treasury, plus gold stripped from the doors of God's house.

This rich plum was not enough to gratify the lust for gain working in the greedy enemy. An envoy returned to demand total surrender (2 Kgs. 18:17–37; cf. "The Challenge" following).

The counsels to withstand Assyria (2 Chr. 32:2–8). Hezekiah's counsels included steps of natural preparation for siege (2–6) and *strengthening* in spiritual resources (7, 8). It is right for believers to do what they responsibly can do, yet trust in God to do what lies beyond their ability to perform. This is like a preacher praying for God's almighty help, and working diligently with God to get his message prepared.

Natural *steps* here include plugging springs outside Jerusalem to conceal water that could aid besiegers, fortifying the city walls, making further weapons and shields, appointing leaders to have charge during battle, and other tactics.

Strengthening spiritually involved Hezekiah's counsel to his assembled people. This coordinates two emphases.

(1) Exhortation to be strong (7). He challenges his people to be strong and exercise courage expecting to win. The issue will not be decided on the basis of the Assyrian king's formidable nature or the great army he commands. The defenders have a resource to allay their fear.

(2) Encouragement from their Source (7, 8). Hezekiah says two things to reassure his hearers. They can take heart in having a *greater* strength defending them than the power of the Assyrian god, "for

the one with us is greater than the one with him." John the Apostle reminded believers of the same essential truth: "You are from God, little children, and have overcome them (false prophets peddling error); because greater is He who is in you than he who is in the world" (1 John 4:4). Similarly, Hezekiah says that Assyria has only an arm of flesh (human means), "but with us is the Lord our *God* to help us and to fight our battles" (cf. 2 Cor. 3:5).

In the present age, believers have counsel for facing a greater foe, not Sennacherib, but Satan (Eph. 6:10–20). In this, they, too, have a battle resource: they need to be "strong in the Lord" and to be "praying always."

The challenge by the Assyrians (2 Chr. 32:9–19; 2 Kgs.18:17–37). Sennacherib sent ambassadors back to deliver his threats and terrify the Judeans into surrender. These really are one long series of insults that belittle God. They make vividly clear who the invaders are ultimately challenging. The challenge defames God in at least four ways.

(1) *Death* is what trusting God will get the Judeans. For rather than deliverance, they will die by hunger and thirst, their God powerless to defend them (2 Chr. 32:9–11).

(2) *Defeat* of God already is apparent in His inability to stop Hezekiah from taking away His high places and altars (12). This argument is based on ignorance of the real explanation for the removal—false worship devoted to other gods. The enemy loves to distort truth, and often dupes the unwary by clever mind games.

(3) *Destiny* sure for God. Other gods of attacked nations were unable to defeat the lethal Assyria. God will have to get in line and fall when His time comes (15). This huge error degrades God to the level of idols (17–19).

(4) *Deceit* in claiming God's backing (2 Kgs. 18:25). The Assyrian commander purports to have God's directive to destroy in Judah. God does sometimes use other nations in judgment on His people, as often in Judges and later with the Assyrians against the northern kingdom and Babylonians versus Judah. But in the context of a righteous focus in Judah this is probably a twist of the truth to incline

Judeans to yield as if even God is capitulating, realizing that defeat is inevitable.

What will be Hezekiah's response to such a challenge?

The calling on the Lord. The chronicler in verse 20 says that Hezekiah and Isaiah prayed. But 2 Kings 19 provides detail in four phases.

(1) The *assurance* from Isaiah (1–7). Hezekiah did three things in deep distress. He tore his royal clothes and covered himself with sackcloth, gestures of mourning before God. He also went into the temple to seek the Lord in prayer.

Soon the king dispatched Eliakim, governor over the palace, Shebna the scribe and elders of the priests to visit Isaiah with a request for prayer. *Assurance* is the keynote of Isaiah's reply, though his prayer is not mentioned, only assumed. He gives them a bright, upbeat word from God.

First, Isaiah's pronouncement from the Lord is *calming* (6). Hezekiah need not entertain fear. There is no panic with God, and He would have the king and his people know His peace. Second, Isaiah's word is *clear* (6). He perfectly understands that Assyria is hurling its challenge in God's face. He conceives of it as blasphemy, defaming the Lord's reputation. Third, the prophet's counsel is *certain* (7). He promises to put a spirit in Sennacherib so that he returns to Assyria and dies by the sword.

The appeal of Hezekah (2 Kgs. 19:14–19). Isaiah's counsel came back. Then the Assyrian commander sent a threat letter to Judah's king. It again defames God as tottering on the verge of collapse as other nations' gods have bitten the dust (8–13). Hezekiah's prayer in the temple is a response to the defiance.

(1) His spreading the problem before the Lord (14). He unrolls the scroll of ultimatum before he prays. In any age it is a good idea to do this. Today, by the same essential principle, one can lay out a missionary report telling of need, open a prayer journal list, or spread out a letter expressing some matter that provokes concerned prayer. The writing here is the enemy's letter that boldly demands surrender, but believers today can bring their own challenges to God.

(2) His supplication over the problem (15–19). Several key aspects of prayer appear as Hezekiah talks with the Lord.

First, he *praises* God. He extols Him as enthroned above the cherubim in the most holy place, the all-powerful God, God alone, creator of heaven and earth (15). Second, he *petitions* for God's ear to hear, His eyes to see, and His mind to take this as a challenge against Him, for it reproaches Him, the living God (16). Then he *affirms* the Assyrians' wreckage of nations and false gods, and the truth that the gods were helpless gods, merely the work of men's hands, of wood and stone. They were unworthy of trust, and so they have been destroyed (17, 18).

Finally, Hezekiah *petitions* again (19). His request is that God will deliver His people from Sennacherib, and his reason is a God-glorifying one. His vision is that people of the kingdoms will be brought to see that God alone is God.

The answer through Isaiah (2 Kgs. 19:20–34). Word reaches the king from the prophet. At the outset Isaiah says from God, because you prayed, I heard. Then he details God's answer in two steps.

(1) The despisal He sees (21–27). God sees Assyria's despisal of Zion, His people and place (21), and in despising Zion's God (22–27). He is closely identified with His people. The Assyrians' challenge is ultimately a reproach against Him. The invaders' ego has seduced them to boast of military conquests, but they actually do so only because God has permitted them the opportunity. He is provoked by their haughty raging that drags His glory in the dust.

(2) The devastation He plans (28–34). God will turn the invaders back to the trail to Assyria. Isaiah pictures this answer to prayer as the Lord's putting His hook in the enemy's nose and bridle in their lips, as a land or sea creature or a horse is turned, mastered, and brought to submit.

This answer to prayer will mean, for Judah, abundance of food in a land cleared of the enemy (29). They will be rooted securely in their land, not taken off as captives. The Assyrian army would not be able to besiege Jerusalem, throw up a shield or a mound, or even shoot an arrow there (32).

God's reason for such an answer to prayer then appears (34). "For I will defend this city to save it for My own sake and for My servant David's sake." This no doubt means for the display of His own honor in compassion that upholds His covenants with Abraham and David (Gen. 12:1–3, 7; 2 Sam. 7:12–16). It also includes His honoring of His own reputation as God against estimates that rated him no better than the gods. For David's sake refers to validating the comfort David took in God keeping His promise to him, and His faithfulness to carry it out.

The commitment of God to His people (2 Kgs. 19:35–37). True to His word and in answer to prayer, God sent an angel who took the lives of 185,000 Assyrian warriors in one night. This seems to have cut down the top brass and most honored soldiers (2 Chr. 32:21).

The next morning, enemy survivors must have been seized in the cold grip of panic. Such a massive loss portended even further widespread death if they lingered at their encampment. Sennacherib ordered his forces to beat a hasty retreat out of that region and back to Assyria. The armies slunk away like whipped dogs that have their tails between their legs. Twenty years later, in 681 B.C., Sennacherib himself was slain by his older sons, probably in an attempted coup. For he had bypassed them to give the throne to a younger son, Esarhaddon. His death by sword fulfilled Isaiah's prediction in 2 Kings 19:7.

That God defended His people here is His faithful answer to prayers in the context. At the same time it also answers Solomon's earlier prayers for those who look to God in His house and trust Him (2 Chr. 6:28–31). And it keeps His promise in another famous passage (2 Chr. 7:13, 14).

The celebration of victory (2 Chr. 32:22, 23). These verses follow up the deliverance in two ways. The first is in summarizing the victory just given by the Lord. He has done what He said He would do when conditions were met (2 Chr. 7:14). The second is in a scenario of celebration. God's display of His Godhood prompted joy in many to bestow gifts to honor Him, and also Hezekiah. These probably came both from people of Judah and those of other nations that wanted to be in good favor with a people that such an awesome God helped. The principle, for other people, would be like Nebuchadnezzar's conferring gifts on God through His man, Daniel (Dan. 2:46–48).

The Request For Healing (2 Chr. 32:24–26)

Hezekiah faced the towering threat of the Assyrians and saw God deliver; now the Bible gives more on his life of prayer during the crisis (2 Kgs. 20:6).

Two other passages providing additional detail are 2 Kings 20 and Isaiah 38.

The sickness threatening death. The king was bedridden with a sickness that appealed for his life (24). At this point it is good to turn to Isaiah 38:1–8, and follow its greater detail.

Isaiah visited the king with a two-part message from God.

(1) His appeal for Hezekiah to get everything ready while he had the time (Isa. 38:1).

(2) His announcement that he would soon die. Hezekiah was only thirty-nine at the time, fourteen years into his total of twenty-nine (2 Chr. 29:1). He did not know of the total yet, and this news from God through His spokesman brought him to deep distress. Sometimes man's extremity is God's opportunity to show His grace.

The supplication pleading for life (Isa. 38:2, 3). Hezekiah's fervent prayer has three facets.

(1) His asking. He is obviously asking, in the plea "Remember now, O Lord," for healing now that shows God's remembrance of his past faithful life (cf. 2 Chr. 29–32). The petition is never stated

explicitly in 2 Chronicles, but is in Isa. 38:10–20. How does he voice it?

First, he *affirms grief over dying* (Isa. 38:10–14c). In the middle of his life, he reasons that he is to die, losing years he still could have. This would remove his privilege of seeing the Lord in the land of the living. It also would end his seeing men in the present life. He thinks of two scenes picturing what such departure will be like. Death is like a shepherd's tent pulled up for the move to the new site (cf. 2 Cor. 5:1), and similar to the weaver rolling up his unused cloth that he has cut from the loom.

The Judean king *affirms* his grief that God is bringing his life to an end at any time, day or night. He mourns as the swallow, crane, or dove voice their chirps or moans. His eyes gaze wistfully to the heavens, waiting as a desperate man for God's help.

The second portion of his supplication is an *appeal* for grace that can give life (14d-16). Urgent in his distress, he asks God to be his security, restore him, and give him longer life. He is very specific.

Third comes his *acknowledgment* that life is from the Lord (17–20). In this the king stresses God's care up to now (17), his losing the privilege of thanksgiving in the sense that people on earth know it before they die (18, 19), and his confidence that God's answer will be in extending his life (20). Due to this bounty, he expects to praise God in songs accompanied by music of instruments throughout his life in God's house.

(2) His argument. The king does not argue in animosity, opposing God. But he does do what the preacher Charles Spurgeon counseled as a God-glorifying thing. He sets forth before God his case, his argument, his reasoning behind the desire (2 Kgs. 20:3; Is. 38:3, 10–19).

Hezekiah longs that God would remember his walk in faithfulness that reflected a heart of soundness or integrity spiritually (2 Chr. 29:2; 30:20, 21). Both in the *character* of his way and in the *conduct* of his works ("done what is good") he could plead a good testimony for God's glory.

(3) His accompaniment. He "wept bitterly," not bitter at God in distrust due to his predicament, but distressed over death requiring him in his prime. Sobbing can be all surface show, staged for effect to manipulate, "crying over spilled milk" or just emotional self-pity. Even unbelievers shed many tears. But tears can also be a sincere expression of being moved deeply for what will honor the Lord. God says later that not only has he heard Hezekiah's prayer, but he has seen his tears. So He must have viewed them with approval.

The sign marking the answer (Isa. 38:4–8). Isaiah himself probably prayed, and received God's answer relating to Hezekiah. It can be related in three phases.

(1) God's accord with the request. God grants His accord as the God of Hezekiah's father, that is, his ancestor David. This is probably to remind the king that the latest mercies to him also relate to God's faithfulness to keep the covenant with David (2 Sam. 7:12–16). It is a sobering thought that when God answers one's prayer, He can also be considering others in the larger picture, not just him.

So the Lord assures the king by Isaiah, "I have heard your prayer."

(2) God's addition of years. He gives the king fifteen more years, from age thirty-nine to fifty-four. God originally had his life planned certainly, and was not now correcting that plan. Man did not know the set plan, unchanging from God's standpoint. So, in the king's own grasp of things fifteen more years were added from the time of his sense that death hovered near, and his prayer. God spoke of these from Hezekiah's standpoint.

Hezekiah would fail the Lord in those years, to some extent. He no doubt did in foolishly showing Babylonian diplomats His enticing treasures (Isa. 39:1–8). Hezekiah misused his extension of life by pride in his resources (2 Chr. 32:25). But every believer is imperfect before God in the last analysis, even David and Daniel (cf. Dan. 9:4–19). As verses frequently review other imperfect leaders as examples of godliness overall, Hezekiah fit this to a large degree.

(3) God's attestation. To confirm his answer, God pledges a miracle. It features a stairway near Hezekiah's palace, upon which

possibly an arm cast the declining sun's shadow, so indicating the time. In the miracle, the shadow went the opposite way ten steps or degrees.

If God were not able to work a mighty miracle, the first verse of the Bible could not be true. But He can, and it is. Whether by some local miracle (as Egypt's plagues) or by a broader one, He caused the shadow to return against its normal course. Upon reflection, this miracle is no harder for Him than His predicting the demise of the seemingly invincible Assyria in Judah, then taking away 185,000 soldiers in a single night.

Which principles of prayer greet the mind from the entire record of Hezekiah in the three passages?

First, a godly life overall is a great secret to effective prayer. So it was for Hezekiah. Second, spiritually uplifting music can be a genuine stimulant to prayer, as in praise or any aspect. Praise can freshen the life, clear the vision to glorify the Lord, and be a catalyst for thinking in harmony with what honors God in any aspect of prayer. So the person praising Him can often think of matters about which to affirm, confess, petition, or intercede. Third, the prayer life must be stationed on and seasoned by God's word. Hezekiah's was set in the law and commandments that expressed the Lord's way.

Fourth, one's prayer life can be directed on a path of impacting others for the Lord. Hezekiah was concerned for God's priests and other Levites, then for all of his kingdom. Fifth, the fervor people gain from a true model in prayer can ignite them to go out and change their world. Hezekiah's people went out to all the kingdom in zeal to foster worship to Him. Sixth, victories in prayer today can prepare the heart for victories in the future, though they do not guarantee them (cf. 2 Chr. 32:1). Seventh, stand unequivocally for the Lord and He will stand as a strong one for you (2 Chr. 32; 16:9; Ps. 84:9–11).

Eighth, if one is to blaze a trail exalting God, he will need to get tough in throwing out the idols. Ninth, spiritual leaders, in a special sense, are chosen by God to lead the way in godliness as Hezekiah does and as he challenges the priests and Levites to do.

2 Chronicles 33:12

Praying Before It Is Too Late to Pray

King Manasseh succeeded his father Hezekiah and reigned fifty-five years, the first eleven as a co-regent (697–642). He was very wicked but repented to live righteously in his twilight years.

His Pursuit of Sin (33:1–11)

Manasseh went all out in a pattern of evil so intense that verse 9 (cf. also 2 Kgs. 19:9) rates his misleading of his people as worse than that of heathen kings Israel had conquered. He rebuilt high places to devote to idolatry, and set up altars honoring Baal even in God's house where His name was to be revered. These altars fostered worship of all the starry host. Contrary to God's detesting child sacrifice (Deut. 12:31; Jer. 7:31), he offered his sons in fire ovens to the god Molech near Jerusalem.

The rampant sin even sponsored witchcraft, catering to divination, sorcery, and traffic consulting mediums and spiritists like the one King Saul sought out (1 Sam. 28). That insult to God, in place of respectful prayer to Him, had caused God to take Saul's life (1 Chr. 10:13, 14). Also a slap in God's face was Manasseh's intruding of an idol he made into the house God endorsed for His own name.

Angered at such misuse of life and opportunity, God judged Manasseh and Judah by letting Assyria's Ashur-banipal (648) conquer. The victors took Manasseh as a captive to Babylon. Their gestures of humiliation and pain to him were a hook in his nose as a ring is used on a bull, and fetters further reduced the king to helpless anguish.

His Prayer in Submission (12, 13)

God used this pressure as "a wake up call" to stir the king to repentance. The change can be traced in four facets.

The anguish (12a). Manasseh, in distress, took a serious and proper look at values. How often when a person is brought to the end of himself, he is ready to do business with the Lord. How good of God to work that which leads to such a benefit.

It would be deeply deflating to the king to be led by the nose, subject to scorn and seeming to have no hope.

The asking (12b, 18, 19a). A person may harden himself and get even more adamant against God in difficulty. He might put forth a stoic stiff lip and last out the ordeal without turning. However, Manasseh does a third thing. He submits to God in tender prayer, pleading to receive His mercy as the tax collector would in Luke 18.

The attitude (12c). Along with prayer, Manasseh humbled himself in an intense earnestness. When brought to a reckoning, he saw where true values were found and prized God's pardon and a righteous walk His grace can help one accomplish. This is so different from many of the kings of the north and south who persisted all the way in sin.

The answer (13, 19). God was inclined by the king's heartfelt prayer and heard it with a positive response. The Lord forgave Manasseh, as Isaiah had promised from Him (cf. Isa. 1:18). God was also following His promise that when the people humbled themselves, prayed, and sought His face, He would hear and heal them (2 Chr. 7:13, 14).

His Pattern of Sensitivity (14–17)

Many seem to repent, but immediately or later drift on in sin without convincing indication that the change was really serious. It was not so with this man, whom God allowed to be reinstated at Jerusalem. Along with his military reinforcements for Jerusalem, he was spiritually zealous for righteousness. Fruit reflecting this was his *removal* of idols from God's house and altars devoted to false gods. His sensitivity for the right also showed in his positive recognition of God's altar before the temple, where he sacrificed peace and thank offerings. As has been noted, peace offerings as outward acts should be joined with prayer of inward faith sensitive to the peace God gave. Prayer also accompanied thank offerings when a worshiper expressed gratitude for God's kind provisions (cf. Lev. 7:12–13).

A third way Manasseh showed a continuing godly sensitivity was his *requesting* his people to serve the Lord. That could have some good response, but righteousness cannot be forced and people make up their own minds, as Manasseh had. Sin, long entrenched in hearts, would persist. Though God pardoned Manasseh individually, He announced that He would carry out judgment on the southern kingdom (2 Kgs. 21:12–15). This is for the sin of many, "because they have done evil" (15).

Principles of prayer stand in bold relief. First, prayer, even in a dramatic turnabout, cannot undo sin's damages left in one's work and in human lives. Forgiveness is true, yet reaping what we sow is also true. A person who ruined his health by sin can repent and be gloriously pardoned forever, but his body still reaps results of sin's toll. Second, a situation of anguish may be the backdrop for God bringing a person to prayerful repentance when he comes in brokenness, tender to deal with God in humble need. Third, no matter how deep one's sin, God is able to forgive if the person is truly open to draw near. Even the ability to draw near is of God's gracious inclining (John 6:44).

Fourth, God does not require a guarantee of a changed lifestyle as a condition for His gracious forgiveness. He does not give it in merit for works. At the same time when prayerful response to Him is genuine, the spiritual change of heart does lead on to works God's grace sponsors in the life. The works can never earn any acceptance, but carry out another purpose, manifesting allegiance that is real.

These are stimulating reminders as prayer passages in Chronicles come to an end (cf. Josiah earlier).